P9-CQO-270

A
WORSE PLACE
THAN HELL

ALSO BY JOHN MATTESON

Eden's Outcasts:
The Story of Louisa May Alcott and Her Father

The Lives of Margaret Fuller:
A Biography

A

WORSE PLACE
THAN HELL

How the Civil War Battle of
Fredericksburg Changed a Nation

JOHN MATTESON

W. W. NORTON & COMPANY
Independent Publishers Since 1923

Copyright © 2021 by John Matteson

All rights reserved
Printed in the United States of America
First Edition

For information about permission to reproduce selections from this book, write to
Permissions, W. W. Norton & Company, Inc., 500 Fifth Avenue, New York, NY 10110

For information about special discounts for bulk purchases, please contact
W. W. Norton Special Sales at specialsales@wwnorton.com or 800-233-4830

Manufacturing by LSC Communications, Harrisonburg
Production manager: Beth Steidle

Library of Congress Cataloging-in-Publication Data

Names: Matteson, John, author.
Title: A worse place than hell : how the Civil War Battle of Fredericksburg
changed a nation / John Matteson.
Description: First edition. | New York : W. W. Norton & Company, 2021. |
Includes bibliographical references and index.
Identifiers: LCCN 2020041510 | ISBN 9780393247077 (hardcover) |
ISBN 9780393247084 (epub)
Subjects: LCSH: Holmes, Oliver Wendell, Jr., 1841–1935. | Whitman, Walt,
1819–1892. | Alcott, Louisa May, 1832–1888. | Pelham, John, 1838–1863. |
Fuller, Arthur B. (Arthur Buckminster), 1822–1862. | Fredericksburg,
Battle of, Fredericksburg, Va., 1862—Social aspects. | United
States—History—Civil War, 1861–1865—Influence.
Classification: LCC E474.85 .M38 2021 | DDC 973.7/33—dc23
LC record available at https://lccn.loc.gov/2020041510

W. W. Norton & Company, Inc., 500 Fifth Avenue, New York, N. Y. 10110
www.wwnorton.com

W. W. Norton & Company Ltd., 15 Carlisle Street, London W1D 3BS

To a grand trio of friends, Stephen M. North, Scott Halvorson, and Paweł Jędrzejko, this book is respectfully inscribed.

Let me not then die ingloriously and without a struggle,
but let me first do some great thing
that shall be told among men hereafter.
—HOMER, *THE ILIAD*,
TRANSLATED BY SAMUEL BUTLER

Contents

A

WORSE PLACE

THAN HELL

Prologue

A Brahmin's Baptism

Strange to say, Captain Holmes was laughing. There was little apparent humor in the moment, however, for on this overcast morning of September 17, 1862, in a bramble-strewn woodlot near Sharpsburg, Maryland, the young infantry officer was running for his life. He recollected later that he had laughed only to himself. Yet in the chaos sweeping through the grove, to be known forever as the West Woods, Holmes could have laughed out loud and still have attracted little notice. As his regiment retreated, they tried hard to preserve order. Here and there, however, men were succumbing to panic, melting, as one of them put it, "like frost in the sunshine."[1]

The joke that Holmes had in mind was a bitter one, and it had been played both upon him and on whoever relied on the newspapers of New England for truth about the ongoing civil war. Holmes had gotten his first taste of combat eleven months earlier at Ball's Bluff, a battle that was already legendary as one of the Union Army's bleakest disasters. Driven backwards toward a steep embankment above the Potomac River, the ineptly led Federal forces had had no place to go but over the side. Countless men had fallen ingloriously down the slope. Many of those who survived the Rebel gunfire tried to escape by swimming away from their attackers. A shocking number, including two of the officers in Holmes's regiment, were carried away by the current and drowned.[2] Holmes had been seriously wounded, pierced through the chest by a Confederate ball.[3] An enterprising columnist, writing for

Harper's Weekly under the peculiar name "The Lounger," had singled out Holmes for some words of praise. To be candid, Holmes had done little more at Ball's Bluff than stop a bullet, and many bodies had stopped bullets at Ball's Bluff. But he was Oliver Wendell Holmes Jr., and his father was one of the nation's most famous men, respected both as a poet and as a professor of anatomy at Harvard's medical school. Eager to make a hero of the great man's son, the *Harper's Weekly* pundit had triumphantly observed that Holmes had been shot "in the breast, not in the back; no, not in the back. In the breast is Massachusetts wounded, if she is struck. Forward she falls, if she fall dead." In raptures, the columnist concluded, "The men of New England never run."[4]

But now, in the West Woods, Holmes, a stalwart son of New England, was running as though his life depended on it—as, in simple truth, it did. The absurdity was too rich for Holmes. As the Lounger's praise reverberated in his mind, he felt laughter welling up inside him. What if another Rebel bullet were to strike him now? Getting shot in the back, he later remembered thinking, "was not so good for the newspapers."[5]

In the next instant, the laughing stopped. A bullet slammed into Holmes's neck, tearing the flesh perilously close to his trachea, jugular, and spine. By the time he hit the ground, Captain Holmes was unconscious. At Ball's Bluff, he had been conscious throughout his ordeal, and as he was being carried to an improvised field hospital, he had been lucid enough to meditate on the nature of military honor. This time, there was not an instant to reflect or wonder or regret—not even a moment to tell himself, this is how it feels to die.

✶

HOLMES DID NOT, HOWEVER, DIE OF his wound. Astonishingly, the bullet that struck him in the woods at Antietam managed to miss every vital piece of him. He recovered and fought on until July 1864. Yet throughout his service in the army, another Oliver Wendell Holmes Jr. was dying all along: the Holmes who had cherished an unexamined faith in the sanctity of duty; the Holmes who strove eagerly to please his father and thereby win his love; and, above all, the Holmes who believed that the universe made sense. In the place of that young man, another was slowly being born—one who viewed skeptically the very nature of authority and who could no longer regard the cosmos as either orderly or just.

This book is part of the much larger story of a country that, diseased by slavery and sectional anger, broke apart and was then refigured and reborn. However, it is more concerned with the personal than the political. It tells the stories of five Americans and the paths they followed during the latter months of 1862. This book follows each of the five from the Battle of Antietam in September of that year until—and in most cases well beyond—President Lincoln's signing of the Emancipation Proclamation on January 1, 1863. It speaks of the different ways in which each of them came face to face with the pain and slaughter of war and how each was transformed by the ordeal. The destinies of all five were brought together by the Battle of Fredericksburg in the second week of December 1862. The first of the five we have already met. For the second, a slender, graceful young artillery officer from Alabama with a preternatural eye for terrain, the fall of 1862 would be a season of exhilaration, culminating in a day of audacity and glory that would durably link his name with the adjective "gallant." During these months, a third man, a poet whom the early months of war had depressed into sullen silence, would spend many evenings in a Manhattan cellar, gazing at the follies of beer-soaked bohemians. Then he would read in the newspaper accounts of Fredericksburg that his brother had been wounded. Seeking him there, the poet would also recover his own voice and would use the sights and sounds of war to rephrase the meaning of America. Still another figure, a man of God from an illustrious family, would wrestle with mortality, as his passions for abolition and personal vindication pushed his frail body toward its limit. The transformation that Fredericksburg and its aftermath would work upon the final member of the five, a self-described literary spinster from Concord, Massachusetts, was to be perhaps the most powerful of all. Rejecting the life of passivity to which her sex and social station might normally have consigned her, she would fling herself into the fight to save the Union and, in so doing, would nearly die. But, in coming close to losing everything, she would find a courage and a creative gift that would change the face of American literature and its perceptions of womanhood.

Oliver Wendell Holmes Jr., John Pelham, Walt Whitman, Arthur

B. Fuller, Louisa May Alcott: some of the names still resonate; others have fallen partly or wholly into obscurity. But if these five had not lived, or if the calamity of Fredericksburg had never touched their lives, we would now inhabit a different nation. Beyond argument, other battles bore more heavily on the outcome of the Civil War. Viewed militarily, Fredericksburg was merely one in a series of Union blunders that tested the will of the Northern states before the tide eventually turned and the nation was preserved. As a matter of cultural significance, however, no battle of the war surpasses Fredericksburg. Through its impact on the thinking of Holmes, it modified the theory of American jurisprudence. Had Alcott never tended the wounded of Fredericksburg, it is unlikely that *Little Women* would ever have been written. Whitman, America's most indispensable poet, later claimed the war was the fact of his life that shaped him more than any other, and it was Fredericksburg that drew him into the war. Though less well known, the gallant Pelham became a unique icon in the Confederate mythos. More than any other figure in the war, he came to epitomize the hyacinthine Southern hero, blooming early and dying young. More obscure than any of the others, Arthur Fuller offers not so much a cultural legacy as an enduring parable: a story of a man whose skills suited him best for peace and piety but whose destiny instead awaited him in war, and whose response to that destiny effaced the line between sublime courage and pitiable folly.

In the background of these five stories, there is a sixth. Whereas this book narrates five stories of individual change, it also concerns a man who, at a moment of crisis, chose not to change. Almost three months before Fredericksburg, Abraham Lincoln had declared his intention to issue the Emancipation Proclamation. The measure was set to take effect less than three weeks after the battle, and the Union's defeat there gave the president every reason to leave the document unsigned. Placed in a position that he called "a worse place than hell," Lincoln stood firm. That firmness, if it did not lead the nation to heaven, set it finally on the road toward hope.

For what they did during and after the battle, four of the five Americans featured here became the subjects of poetry. The fifth, Whitman, wrote a collection of poems (as well as a great deal of other work) about those who passed through the ordeal of war beside him. Their fine and fearful stories are offered here in prose; the only poetry that is needed emerges from the struggles they undertook, the thoughts and feelings they expressed, and the lives they lived.

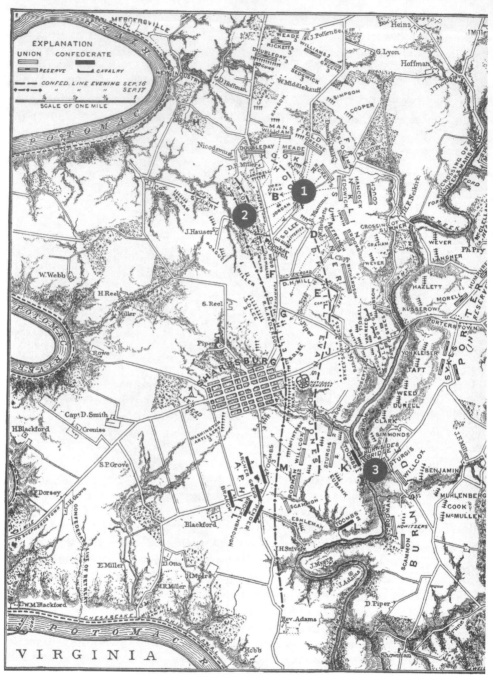

THE FIELD OF ANTIETAM.

The Battlefield at Antietam, September 17, 1862

1. The East Woods. Here Oliver Wendell Holmes and the Twentieth Massachusetts were organized into the formation that marched across an open field toward the West Woods.
2. The West Woods. Here, surprised and outflanked by Confederate infantry, the Twentieth Massachusetts retreated northward, melting "like frost in the sunshine."
3. Burnside's Bridge. Here, George Whitman led a company from the Fifty-First New York across Antietam Creek, driving the Confederate forces from the heights on the western side. From *Battles and Leaders of the Civil War*

Book 1

ANTIETAM

Chapter One

The Poet's Son

"The Governor," as his elder son was pleased to call him, worked cheerfully among corpses. The work that fed his family occurred inside the old Harvard Medical School on North Grove Street in Boston. There, as the early afternoon light shone through a single tall window and filtered through clouds of tobacco smoke, a small team of assistants would look on as the diminutive doctor strode into the demonstrators' room and walked smilingly toward the day's cadaver. Then, Dr. Oliver Wendell Holmes Sr., Professor of Anatomy, would pause to catch his breath. Plagued by asthma, he typically called upon a janitor to help him climb the long flight of stairs from the street below, and the noxious haze that filled the place did his lungs no great service.

After taking a few moments to compose himself, the doctor would prepare the cadaver and make the other final preparations for his lecture. Meanwhile some three hundred boisterous students tumbled into the steep aisles of the adjoining amphitheater. As the students settled in, Holmes's orderlies would bring in the body on a board and lay it on a revolving table, veiled in a clean, white sheet. The professor then would appear, greeted by shouts and applause of a kind that might, in a different place, have heralded the entrance of a famous actor.

Dr. Holmes delighted in teaching. His lectures, patient and precise, were enlivened with puns and anecdotes, "cloth[ing] the dry bones with poetic imagery."[1] An assistant, Thomas Dwight, recalled that the professor "let no opportunity for a jest escape him."[2] Yet the humor somehow did not seem to disrespect the poor, dissected corpse that had so recently enveloped a soul. Respect for the patient and love for the subject—these were the feelings that Dr. Holmes brought to his craft. Standing at the nexus of two worlds—explaining death to life, introducing the living to the dead—he daily imparted these values to his students, for them to carry through their careers. What Dr. Holmes wanted for his eldest child and namesake was a more complicated matter.

When the doctor wrote about raising one's sons up to manhood, his metaphors turned toward the training of horses. Commencement Day at Harvard, he wrote, always reminded him of "the start of the 'Derby,' when the beautiful high-bred three-year-olds . . . are brought up for trial."[3] In his mind, two qualities in a human thoroughbred mattered more than any others: aristocratic bloodlines and superior scholarship. He believed the two were related. Holmes believed in chosen families, blessed with hereditary gifts for learning, and he never doubted that he and his offspring belonged to one.[4] But, he insisted, the inheritance must be environmental as well as genetic.[5] A proper gentleman ought to have eaten with monogrammed silverware, taken his leisure among claw-footed chairs and mahogany tables, and grown up among portraits of illustrious ancestors. But, above all else, "a child . . . should have tumbled about in a library" and handled books from infancy.[6] It was for the life of a Brahmin scholar-gentleman that the doctor intended his son.

Born March 8, 1841, Oliver Wendell Holmes Jr. was the eldest of the family's three children. When his son was a day old, Dr. Holmes announced to his sister the birth of "a little individual who may hereafter be addressed as——Holmes, Esq. or the Hon.——Holmes, M.C. or His Excellency——Holmes, President."[7] The father's puffery was only partly in jest. Little Wendell, as his family called him, had emerged into a family laden with expectations.

When Wendell was in his late teens, the doctor wrote a novel, *Elsie Venner*, in which he gave his impressions of the typical prominent young Bostonian. The features of that image correspond closely to Wendell's. The young aristocrat as the doctor depicted him was slender. His smooth cheeks were slightly pale. His eyes were bright and quick, and his lips "play[ed] over the thought he utter[ed] as a pianist's fingers dance over their music." Timid and awkward in a drawing room, he was the soul of confidence when the conversation turned academic. He took to his books like "a pointer or a setter to his field-work."[8]

To an extent, the elder Holmes fostered his son's love of verbal jousting; when, as a boy, Wendell made clever ripostes and observations at the family table, the Governor would reward him with extra spoonfuls of marmalade. Younger brother Edward noticed Wendell's desire to regale and impress the rest of the family; he later recalled that during dinner conversations, Wendell would always append a "but" to his sentences, in order to hold the floor.[9]

As the clever boy became a furtively rebellious adolescent, however, Dr. Holmes came to regard his son's bolder flights of rhetoric as an attempt to dethrone paternal authority. Tensions between them grew. A young domestic revolutionary, sitting across the table and eating his father's bread while simultaneously plotting his overthrow, can be an interesting adversary. In later years, the future psychologist and philosopher William James was to state, "No love was lost between W. *père* and W. *fils*."[10] Dr. Holmes wondered aloud to James's father, the elder Henry James, whether it was a universal trait among sons to despise their fathers. The doctor knew firsthand that the battles between generations could acquire a cannibalistic fierceness that the presence of tablecloths and fine china did little to soften:

> Each generation strangles and devours its predecessor. The young Feejeean carries a cord in his girdle for his father's neck; the young American, a string of propositions or syllogisms in his brain to finish the same relative. The old man says, "Son, I have swallowed and digested the wisdom of the past." The young man says, "Sire, I proceed to swallow and digest thee with all thou knowest."[11]

Few fathers would have been harder for Wendell to outdo. Dr. Holmes's renown went far beyond his reputation as an anatomist. As a medical researcher, he had an extraordinary breakthrough to his credit. Studying puerperal fever—a postpartum disease that killed thousands of women each year—he had concluded that doctors and nurses were spreading the contagion by failing to wash their hands and change clothes between patients. In an age where bacteriology was unknown, many prominent doctors took Holmes's findings as an insult. But those who heeded them saved lives.

The polymathic doctor also ranked among the most respected writers in America. A number of his poems still surface in literary anthologies: "Old Ironsides"; "The Last Leaf"; "The Chambered Nautilus." In 1857, Holmes Sr. became suddenly famous; his new book of genial wit and fireside philosophy *The Autocrat of the Breakfast Table* won an eager audience among Boston cosmopolites, Pennsylvania farmers, and Georgia planters alike. In London, William Makepeace Thackeray, the author of *Vanity Fair*, proclaimed that no one in England could have written a wittier, more imaginative book than *The Autocrat*.[12]

It was not merely his father's extraordinary achievements that made it hard for Wendell to escape his shadow. He also had to contend with the doctor's unforgiving and unpleasantly insightful criticisms. The elder Holmes belonged to a generation of writers, typified by Emerson, Thoreau, and Margaret Fuller, who searched continually for the ideal. Dr. Holmes did not. His medical training made him always conscious of the frail and the finite. He observed, "Ministers talk about the human will as if it stood on a high look-out, with plenty of light, and elbowroom reaching to the horizon. Doctors are constantly noticing how it is tied up and darkened by inferior organization, by disease, and all sorts of crowding interferences." As a scientist, Dr. Holmes looked upon his fellows, including his son, "as . . . self-conscious blood-clocks with very limited power of self-determination."[13]

While many parents looked at their children with an exuberant sense of possibility, the elder Holmes saw limitations—specifically, the curbs and barriers imposed by heredity. "Outside observers," he wrote, "see results; parents see processes."[14] An astute relative, he added, could size up pretty nearly the possibilities and limitations of a family's children.[15] The doctor coolly scrutinized his son for the traits of his ancestors. Did the boy cross his legs in the fashion of an uncle he had never known? Did a movement of his eyebrows recall a grandfather, long since dead? All the critical observation made Wendell wonder "whether my father, who certainly taught me a great deal and did me a great deal of good, didn't also do me some harm by drooling over [my] physical shortcomings . . . and by some other sardonic criticisms."[16] It seemed to the elder Holmes a lucky thing that children were unconscious of the deterministic oracles of Nature that were written in their every gesture. However, to be a parent and to see such things was "almost to be a fatalist."[17] Oliver Wendell Holmes Jr. would wrestle with fate, both practically and philosophically, for most of his life.

For an intelligent male Bostonian of Wendell's pedigree, the path to adulthood led inevitably through Harvard College, where Wendell enrolled in 1857. Harvard, across the Charles River in Cambridge, was only a horse-trolley ride from his parents' front door, and of course, Wendell's father was on the faculty. Thus Wendell's sense of independence as he walked the famous Yard was muted at best. Moreover, Harvard in the 1850s was perhaps less a place for acquiring manhood than one for prolonging boyhood. Wendell's near-contemporary Henry Adams, in an early phase of his lifelong quest for education, found little of it there. "As far as it educated at all," Adams grumbled, Harvard was "a mild and liberal school, which sent young men into the world with all they needed to make respectable citizens. . . . Leaders of men it never tried to make."[18] The school was also insular to the point of being inbred. The young men were uniformly white and almost exclusively Protestant. Of the ninety-five who made up Holmes's class, all but twelve hailed from New England, and sixty percent had grown up in Boston or its environs. Wendell's experience of Harvard was ever more exclusive; like his father before him, he belonged to the most elect of the college's societies, the Porcellian Club. Socially, at least, Harvard kept Wendell's little world little.

As was not unusual at the time, Holmes came to Harvard at sixteen. And, amid their Latin, Greek, and rhetoric, he and his classmates behaved like sixteen-year-olds. The dining commons was the scene of epic food fights. One student avenged himself on a mathematics tutor by screwing the latter's door shut, trapping him inside. Another did his part in the war against decorum by breaking at least seventeen windows. Residing in a boardinghouse a few blocks off campus, Holmes held himself aloof from the worst of the mischief. Still, he whispered in class and was routinely late for recitations. In his first year, he was fined twice for defacing the rooms of faculty members. More respectably, he hosted regular discussions of religion and philosophy in his rooms on Linden Street. Members of the group read essays and debated questions with adult solemnity. Sooner or later, though, as Holmes remembered, the serious portion of the evening yielded to "the business of the bottle."[19] In his senior year, temptation grew harder to resist; he broke a few windows of his own—an offense punishable by expulsion—but got off with a public reprimand. The college's president, Cornelius Felton, discussed the matter with the elder Holmes: Wendell, he said, was an excellent young man. But of late the doctor's son had started yielding to bad influences, acquiring habits that only a precocious boy might mistake for gentlemanly.[20]

The college itself was not growing up very quickly, either; it was notably slow to acknowledge the new ideas that would both transform and trouble mature minds for the rest of the century. The ideas of Marx and Engels, already convulsing Europe, made no impression on Harvard. During Holmes's junior year, Francis Bowen, the college's endowed professor of natural religion, advised the prestigious *North American Review* not to bother with reviewing Darwin's *On the Origin of Species*, predicting that the interest stirred by the naturalist's theories would subside before July.[21] Believing that "all restraint upon speculation in science, philosophy, politics, and social economy" had been cast aside in France and Germany, Bowen feared for the future of Christianity. On the other hand, he saw Harvard as an embattled refuge of true belief, and he meant to do all he could protect his citadel against licentious and infidel speculations.[22] Harvard struggled to reconcile fact and faith; wherever the balancing act proved too difficult, it opted for religion.

The college's pious orthodoxies were too much for Wendell to stand. During his final term, as he suffered through Bowen's course on political economy, he was publicly reprimanded for "repeated and gross indecorum" in the professor's class.[23] Despising the college's emphasis on rote learning, he found his real education far from the dusty classrooms. Off campus, he raided the stately private library known as the Boston Athenaeum, carting home Vasari's *Lives of the Painters*, Northcote's *Life of Titian*, and Ruskin's masterpiece, *The Stones of Venice*. As a sophomore, he joined the college's Christian Union, a nonsectarian society that was devoted to free religious inquiry and liberal principles.

Flashing like quicksilver through Wendell's undergraduate life, influencing his mind and sentiments more than anyone other than his father, was the essayist and poet Ralph Waldo Emerson. Wendell never had much use for Emerson's transcendental philosophy, but he was drawn powerfully toward the great man's message of self-reliance—his exhortation to think and act in radically original ways. Published less than a month after Wendell was born, Emerson's "Self-Reliance" had declared, "To believe your own thought, to believe that what is true for you in your private heart, is true for all men,—that is genius."[24] At the same time that Emerson praised independent thought, he insisted on eclecticism. He admired Chinese philosophy and Persian theology as much as he cherished the ancient Greeks, and he strove through his reading to give himself the most complete mind imaginable.

Both this independence and this breadth of influence sank into Wendell, who displayed his love of Emerson in an anonymous article for *Harvard Magazine*, titled "Books." The style of the piece is unmistakably Emersonian, as is Wendell's argument. In it, he proclaims his belief that his generation, almost the first ever to be brought up in a spirit of free inquiry, had been given a mission to seek out the new, the dissonant, the unsettling. "We *must*," he wrote, "have every train of thought brought before us while we are young, and may as well at once prepare for it." The Western tradition, for all its majesty, was not enough; the rising American scholar must also master, and risk being mastered by, the works of Confucius, of Buddha, and Zoroaster—sacred books that the typical American condemned without ever bothering to look into them.[25] Through his culturally omnivorous reading of ancient classics, Wendell was not submitting to a dead past; he was actively rebelling, defying a Harvard establishment that acknowledged little beyond the Greeks and Romans and the Bible. Wendell's essay on books appeared in the same volume of the *Harvard Magazine* that included a brief commentary on his father "as a wit and poet."[26] Here, as at the Governor's dinner table, the generations lightly jostled for position.

Emerson frequently saw Wendell's father at meetings of the Saturday Club, an exclusive cadre of intellectuals who gathered monthly for dinner and conversation at the Parker House, a hotel in Boston. He paid Wendell the compliment of advising him on his early writing. As Wendell was tackling an essay on Plato for another campus literary journal, Emerson counseled him, "You must say, 'Plato, you have pleased the world for two thousand years; let's see if you can please me.'" Emerson perused the printed essay. He saw promise in it, but did not consider it bold enough. He told Wendell, "I have read your piece. When you strike at a king, you must kill him." Though the criticism stung, Wendell always fondly remembered Emerson's mentorship. He recalled telling him, "If I ever do anything, I shall owe a great deal of it to you."[27]

Wendell also wrestled with the country's most inflammatory political issue. Along with the rest of the country, he had read *Uncle Tom's Cabin*. At some point—the time is unclear—he went to a blackface minstrel show and came away aghast at the "belittling of a suffering race." By his last term at Harvard, he had announced himself a convinced abolitionist.[28] He sent some money to William Lloyd Garrison's antislavery paper, *The Liberator*, and, when proslavery hooligans threatened trouble at an oration by leading abolitionist Wendell Phillips, he joined the ranks of the speaker's bodyguard.

These gestures barely hinted at the ferment in his mind. The struggle against slavery was, for Wendell, only his most vivid reaction to a dangerous American ethic—one that prized hierarchy and order over liberty and decency; one that praised God not only for setting white over black, but also for elevating the complacently prosperous above the aspiring dispossessed. Against this state of affairs, Wendell sided with the heresies of humanism. Skeptic though he was, Wendell felt that the impending war on slavery would be a holy war for democracy and liberal culture, driven by the kind of sacred duty that had inspired the crusaders centuries before.[29]

Holmes Sr. acknowledged the patriotic zeal of the moment, but he thought the war fever of 1861 had even more to do with the hot blood of youth. In his view, it fed on a variety of fuels: "the love of adventure, the contagion of example . . . the desire of personal distinction."[30] These motives, the doctor said, turned the most peaceable young men into the most ardent soldiers. His son's excitement was not exceptional; hundreds of thousands of young men south of the Mason-Dixon Line had been bred to believe in the sanctity of Southern soil. Even greater numbers to the north of the line had learned to venerate the holiness of the Union. The two regions had poured into their young men two irreconcilable ideas of what it meant to be an American. There was another lesson that both regions had learned in common, one that Wendell's father observed in a lecture he gave eleven months before the war began:

> How could a people . . . which has contrived the Bowie-knife and
> the revolver, which has chewed the juice out of all the superlatives in
> the language in Fourth of July orations . . . which insists [on] send-

ing out yachts and horses and boys to out-sail, out-run [and] out-
fight . . . all the rest of creation; how could such a people be content
with any but "heroic" practice?[31]

Deeply excited both by violence and by victory, America had insinuated
to its young white men that they could and naturally ought to be heroes.
It was a recipe for brutal, passionate conflict.

From this passion, the doctor remained aloof. Contented and com-
placent amid the Harvard intelligentsia, floating pleasantly between his
poetry and his sparkling evenings with the Saturday Club, Holmes Sr.
could imagine no existence sweeter than his own life, and he wanted
none of it to change. He had coined a term for the kind of gentleman-
thinker into which he had shaped himself, the "Boston Brahmin." His
epithet for the Boston State House, "the hub of the solar system," reveals
the extent to which he placed himself at the center of a benign and eru-
dite cosmos.[32] His opinions on armed conflict were blithe. As men were
dying in the Mexican War, he had written to James Russell Lowell, "War
is one of the most powerful stimulants in bringing out the power of the
human intellect." Yes, he admitted, war was revolting. Yet he confessed,
"I cannot shut my eyes to the beauty of heroism and self-devotion which
the battlefield has witnessed."[33]

Dr. Holmes considered slavery a tragic, ghastly business. Nonetheless, he saw no cause to raise his voice against it. After all, he reasoned,
"the people about me are not slaveholders and hate it pretty thoroughly
already."[34] Many of them, he felt, could denounce the institution more
effectively than he could. The elder Holmes prized the Union more
than the freedom of the enslaved millions, and he valued peace and
quiet most of all. Preferring compromise to violence, he wrote, "The
catastrophe of disunion we can prevent, and thus avert a future of
war and bloodshed which is equally frightful."[35] But at the core of his
position was a preference for the aesthetic over the actual. He wanted
his writing to please, not provoke. He desired "rather to show what is
beautiful in life around me than to be pitching into giant vices, against
which the acrid pulpit and the corrosive newspaper will always anticipate the gentle poet."[36]

In early 1861, as Wendell's final Harvard spring approached, the
mood on campus was anything but gentle. As their states abandoned the

Union, the handful of Southern students packed their bags. Wendell was two months from graduating when, on April 12, the South's bombardment of Fort Sumter made it impossible to think normally about one's future. In his study, Wendell's father set aside the historical novel he had been reading. "The romance of the past," he wrote, had abruptly faded "before the red light of the terrible present."[37] He had once lamented that young men of old New England families were never tested for their gallantry or coolness under fire. Shielded by wealth and tradition, the son of a Brahmin was never expected to put on a uniform. Consequently, the doctor thought, the army lost an element of refinement, and the moneyed class had forgotten what it meant to count heroism among one's virtues. Never doubting that the young Brahmins had pluck and courage, Dr. Holmes hoped that they might amply demonstrate these qualities "when the time comes, if it ever does come."[38] Now the time had come. For Wendell, the course was obvious: he must join the army, not only to aid in the extermination of slavery, but also to prove his completeness as a man.

On April 15, President Lincoln called for 75,000 volunteers to help quell the Confederate rebellion. Eight days later, Holmes ceased his studies and, without bothering to notify the college, reported to Fort Independence for training in the Fourth Massachusetts Battalion of Infantry. His father later wrote, "The prologue of life is finished . . . at twenty."[39] Wendell was seven weeks past his twentieth birthday.

It proved to be a false start. A month after Holmes enrolled, the battalion abruptly disbanded. Holmes the soldier was again Holmes the student. He returned to the Yard to discover that his absence had resulted in a staggering number of demerits, jeopardizing his graduation. He resolved to muddle through, but his once-respectable class rank was in ruins. Wendell accepted his descent without complaint. The doctor, however, took his son's fall from grace as a crying injustice. That summer, the elder Holmes begged President Felton to reinstate Wendell's rank. True, he had left the college without permission. Yet, "if he did not stop to kiss his Alma Mater, neither did many of the other volunteers stop to kiss their mothers and wives and sweethearts."[40]

Felton stood firm. Wendell was allowed to take his final examinations and earn his degree, but the demerits stuck. There were at least some compensations: Wendell shared the prize for scholarship in ancient Greek and, like his father before him, was elected Class Poet. In his graduation poem, which survives only in fragments, Holmes likened the Class of '61 to a warship, outfitted by the college's chandlers for a perilous voyage. "Be brave," he urged his classmates, "for now the thunders roll."[41]

✶

THE THUNDERS DID NOT ROLL IMMEDIATELY for Holmes, but they came soon enough. In July, Holmes was walking past the Massachusetts State House with a copy of Hobbes's *Leviathan*, which he had just borrowed from the Boston Athenaeum. An acquaintance stopped him with portentous news: Holmes was now a lieutenant in the just-formed Twentieth Massachusetts Volunteer Infantry. Sensibly, Holmes retraced his steps to the Athenaeum and handed back the book. Hobbes's classic treatise on "the war of all against all" would have to wait until a more specific conflict had been settled.

Holmes's commission was for three years—a seemingly meaningless length of time in a war that almost everyone thought would end before Christmas. Unlike most Massachusetts regiments, which filled their ranks with the men of a single town or county, the Twentieth took in soldiers from across the commonwealth, from the Berkshires to Nantucket Island. The regiment's officers, however, were predominantly sons of the Crimson, so noticeably so that the unit acquired the nickname "the Harvard regiment."

The regiment's commander, however, was a West Pointer. A professional soldier, Colonel William Lee had studied alongside Robert E. Lee and Jefferson Davis. Both pious and tolerant, the colonel ordered that a regimental prayer meeting be held each Sunday but made attendance optional. He was less flexible in other aspects of discipline. Holmes surely felt the slight when Lee, addressing his assembled officers, observed, "Of course all you capt[ain]s are all right. It is these young lieut[enant]s . . . that . . . are very heedless & need a great deal of looking after."[42] Nevertheless, Holmes mostly agreed with a fellow lieutenant, who wrote, "The colonel is a regular old brick & I think we could all bear being snubbed every day for the sake of being commanded by such a bully old fighter."[43]

It seemed bad form to credit the rumors that the colonel enjoyed a glass of whiskey more than was strictly prudent.

One promising junior officer was Holmes's blond-haired cousin. Willy Putnam, who had withdrawn from Harvard Law School to join the Twentieth, drew attention with his boyish good looks and his fierce pronouncements against slavery. For him, a century of fratricidal war was preferable to a single day of slavery, and he prayed to heaven "that every river in this land of ours may run with blood," as the army shot and slashed its way toward "the utter destruction of every vestige of this curse so monstrous."[44]

Of the men who made up the Twentieth, two mattered more to Holmes than any of the others. The first was the grandly named and luxuriantly bearded Norwood Penrose Hallowell. "Philadelphia Quakers," Nathaniel Hawthorne's son Julian once noted, "know how to live."[45] A scion of that city's Quaker elite, the sophisticated Pen Hallowell lived up to the statement. Opposed to slavery but committed to pacifism, young men of Pen's faith faced a moral crossroads in 1861. Pen elected to fight. An indifferent student, Hallowell could speak with passion when the occasion arose; on the day Holmes declaimed his class poem, Pen sat beside him as the Class Orator. Probably, Hallowell's staunch and aggressive abolitionism helped to nudge Holmes's views in the same direction. But he seems to have served Holmes best as an affable and somewhat mischievous companion, prized more for his joie de vivre than for his influence on Holmes's mind or character.

Such could not be said of Henry Livermore Abbott, who eventually commanded Holmes's admiration more than any of his other regimental companions. The son and grandson of congressmen, one on each side of his family, Abbott worried about his fitness as a soldier. His two brothers were in a hurry to go and save the Union. Comparing himself with them, Henry could only sigh. "I know myself to be constitutionally timid," he confessed. "My tastes are not warlike like Ned & Fletcher's, but literary & domestic. I can think of nothing more odious than the thought of leaving home & profession for a camp."[46]

Yet Abbott did know of at least one act more odious, and that was to stay home while his friends and brothers risked their lives. "I should be ashamed of myself forever," he wrote his father, "if I didn't do something now." Personal honor mattered immensely, but so, too, did another elemental need. Abbott reflected, "I felt that I had never done anything or amounted to anything in the whole course of my existence; & that there was no better prospect in view for a long time. . . . I . . . got so disgusted with being nothing & doing nothing; & resolved if I couldn't do much, to do what other young men were doing."[47]

Whatever Abbott's doubts about his gifts for soldiering, Colonel Lee was quick to detect promise in him. In mid-August, he set down a ranking of his junior officers, according to his estimate of their promise as officers. Abbott placed first among the second lieutenants. Holmes, a step higher than Abbott at first lieutenant, placed a lackluster eighth in a group of ten.

The regiment left Boston for Washington by rail on September 4. That evening in New York, Holmes had time and money enough to dine with some of his regimental chums at the famous Delmonico's, which had famously prepared a banquet for the Prince of Wales the previous year. Holmes's first adverse encounter with the fortunes of war came in Washington, where a wagon wheel rolled over his trunk, smashing it and the brandy flask inside it.[48] Within days, he had immersed himself in a regular soldier's life, an existence made more pleasant when he found a baker who sold peach and apple pies for the irresistible price of 12½ cents each. If military duties still did not come easily to him, he was at least able to report to his mother, "I think I am learning, as I certainly am trying."[49]

In his first days of service, Holmes slowly grew accustomed to the fleas, spiders, and boredom of life in the field.[50] Along with the rest of the army, he endured his first touches of the diarrhea that, in more virulent forms, was to prove as deadly in this war as enemy gunfire. He carried a small bottle of laudanum, the addictive opiate that doctors of the time threw at everything from yellow fever to insomnia. While Holmes may have taken small doses of the drug to combat his diarrhea, he also kept it handy for a darker purpose: if he were to receive a crippling or mortal wound, he would use the drug to commit suicide.

The army was adjusting to a new commander. In July, the Union had been routed at First Bull Run, the battle known to the Southerners as First Manassas.* Five days later, President Lincoln had summoned

---

* Northern commentators on the war tended to name battles for bodies of water, e.g., Bull Run and Antietam. Southerners preferred nearby towns, like Manassas and

thirty-four-year-old Major General George B. McClellan to Washington and entrusted him to reorganize and train the Army of the Potomac. McClellan was vain, ambitious, and intemperately critical of his superiors in the government. When speaking in private, he denounced Secretary of State William H. Seward as "a meddling, officious, incompetent little puppy" and likened the president to "a well-meaning baboon."[51] But he also possessed a genius for winning the devotion of the men who served under him, and he seemed to have just the right confidence for the mammoth job ahead of him. After a first visit to the United States Senate, McClellan told his wife, "All tell me that I am held responsible for the fate of the Nation & that all its resources shall be placed at my disposal. It is an immense task that I have on my hands, but I believe I can accomplish it." With the earnest vow "We shall have no more *Bull Run* affairs," he turned resolutely to his work.[52]

On September 12, the Twentieth moved northwest along the Potomac, marching for three days before coming to the town of Poolesville, Maryland. Nearby, the regiment established an outpost, Camp Benton, that would be their home for the next six months. Federal law provided that officers could employ servants, whose pay was to be deducted from the officer's salary.[53] An Irish attendant, John O'Sullivan, saw to Holmes's personal needs, but there was no keeping off the overnight chills, which Holmes thought were as cold as the pit of Dante's *Inferno*.[54] From the camp, Confederate troops could be seen through binoculars. It felt strange to Holmes "to see an encampment & twig men . . . and think they are our enemies."[55] On the Virginia side, a few miles west of the river, lay Leesburg, a town McClellan was determined to capture. His plan called for the Twentieth Massachusetts to cross the Potomac partway to Harrison's Island and then to complete the crossing at Ball's Bluff. Somewhere between that point and Leesburg, the regiment would have its first battle.

The night before the crossing, Colonel Lee was in great spirits. He told jokes, quoted Shakespeare, and bubbled with excitement at the idea of getting his regiment into action. Impressed with Lee's carefree outlook, Henry Abbott was no less inspired by Lee's thoroughness of preparation. The colonel's planning touched on a thousand points. In Abbott's judg-

---

Sharpsburg. This text will use the Northern designations.

ment, he had not omitted a single circumstance that would help to make the regiment safe. Nevertheless, Lee offered an ominous prophecy. In the case of defeat, he said, no retreat would be possible. The Twentieth "must either conquer or die."[56]

Lee's all-or-nothing prediction was prompted by the inconvenient topography that lay ahead. Ball's Bluff was a hundred-foot-high cliff, strewn with shrubbery and boulders and rising almost straight up from the riverbank. At the top of the cliff was a stand of trees about thirty yards deep. Beyond the trees lay an open field, flanked by dense woods; an opposing force could use this cover to devastating effect, raking the field with musket fire. Furthermore, the river beneath the bluff was swollen with recent rains and impossible to ford. The few available boats, while adequate to accomplish a slow crossing, would soon be overloaded if the Federals were forced to withdraw under fire. Finally, only a single road—a narrow, tortuous switchback—led to the top of the bluff. If forced to pull back, the bluecoats would have just one place to go: over the side, through rocks and brambles to the riverbank below. The edge of the heights was unpatrolled, but only because the Rebels thought that no force would be so foolhardy as to attempt a landing there. Abbott had considered Lee's preparations meticulous, but Abbott, like the other young Harvard officers, was more green and trusting than he would ever be again.

Because a portion of the regiment was on picket duty or performing other work, Colonel Lee led only seven companies, or about 280 men, into the fight.[57] One of these was Company A, whose ranking lieutenant was Wendell Holmes. It was Monday, October 21.

The field command belonged to Colonel Edward Baker, a senator from Oregon and former Illinois lawyer, so beloved by President Lincoln that he had named his second son Eddie in Baker's honor. The name had brought no luck to Lincoln's child, who had died at the age of three in 1850. At Ball's Bluff, at the first sounds of Confederate fire, Baker looked jaunty. Riding up to the line formed by the Twentieth, he congratulated Colonel Lee "on having a chance to meet these fellows [the Rebels] at last." He called out to the men, "Boys, how are you? Are you ready for work?"[58]

The "work" quickly turned grim. The woods around the field, thought to be unoccupied, were teeming with Confederate infantry. Their bullets "flew like hail," and the Union men began to fall.[59] His confidence in Lee's battle plan abruptly stripped away, Lieutenant Abbott now realized the truth: the field at the top of the bluff was "one of the most complete slaughter pens ever devised."[60] Baker also saw that the bluff could not be held. So recently convinced that he was marching toward glory, he was now seeking merely to avoid disaster. Standing tall as his men lay down to protect themselves, he resisted every call to protect himself. He was heard to say it was "of no use, it is all over with us."[61] Moments later, struck almost simultaneously by eight bullets, Baker fell dead.

The hopelessness of the struggle dawned as well on Colonel Lee. He urged the Twentieth to hold its position, buying time so that the mounting number of wounded could be evacuated. Untested but well drilled, the regiment worked with admirable calm. They were making a good show until an ill-considered order came from Colonel Milton Cogswell, now the ranking officer on the field. Hoping to break through the Confederate line on his left flank, Cogswell commanded the Massachusetts men to strike in that direction, little realizing the strength of the Mississippi riflemen awaiting them in the woods. Under horrific fire, Cogswell's attack collapsed and, with it, much of the order in the Union line.

Around this time, something in Colonel Lee gave way. A captain of the regiment found him sitting behind a tree. Though Lee seemed perfectly composed, the captain soon realized that his commander's apparent calm was, instead, shock. When Lee spoke, it was to announce that the best and only recourse was to surrender and "save the men from being murdered."[62] He was too disoriented to move on his own and required the captain's help to trudge down the switchback to the shoreline.

There Lee found a chaotic scene. Having walked, run, or tumbled down the bluff, a frantic knot of men had discovered to their disbelief that there were not enough boats to carry them to safety. Some were making a swim for it; a number of these were caught in the current and drowned. Others, ignoring the threats of officers to shoot them if they did not calm themselves, piled into one of the few serviceable boats. Already loaded with wounded, the boat could not bear the additional passengers and sank. When it was all over, the Twentieth counted eighty-eight killed or wounded. One hundred thirteen more were taken prisoner, including Lee, who had gallantly refused to take the place of another man in one of the boats, and Major Paul Revere, the grandson and namesake of the revolutionary hero. Of the men from the regiment who had crossed the river, a startling seventy percent had been killed, wounded, or captured. All in all, more than a third of the Federal force at Ball's Bluff had been taken prisoner.

By the time the Union effort had melted into confusion, Holmes's part in the battle had long been over. About an hour into the fight, he was shouting encouragement to Company A on the left side of the regiment's line when he felt the wind knocked out of him and found himself on the ground. A spent bullet had struck him, bruising his belly. He crawled a few paces to the rear, where a sergeant and Colonel Lee helped him to his feet. Satisfied that the young lieutenant had seen enough action for a while, Lee ordered him to the rear. Holmes disobeyed. Reasoning that his little bruise had given him no excuse for quitting, he rushed forward and took a place next to the colonel, waving his sword and exclaiming, "Will no one follow me?"[63]

An instant later, he was down again, felled by a force that, as he later put it, "felt as if a horse had kicked me." This time the harm was more serious. A bullet had passed through his chest from left to right, precisely over Holmes's heart.[64] Feeling faint and unable to speak, Holmes saw that he had fallen next to one of the company's sergeants, a man he had personally recruited for the regiment. The man had been shot through the head. Sickened, Holmes closed his eyes. A moment later, he discovered that he himself was spitting blood—a sure sign that the bullet had pierced a lung.

Holmes then fell into a state of awareness that was both confusion and clarity. As he tasted his own blood, his first thought was literary; he remembered a character from Frederick Marryat's *The Children of the New Forest* who is shot through the lungs and dies "with terrible hæmorrhages and great agony."[65] He felt around in his waistcoat pocket for his bottle of poison. Yes, it was there. But he was in no great pain yet, and perhaps his condition was not as serious as he feared. The time for using his fail-safe had not yet come.

Because he was wounded so early in the action, Holmes was probably brought down to the riverbank before the evacuation effort started to fall apart. As he hovered on the edge of consciousness, he saw a small boat filling up with wounded and heard the groans of another injured man. Another thought, again of a courtly, literary turn, occurred to him:

"Now, wouldn't Sir Philip Sydney [*sic*] have that other fellow put into the boat first?"[66] It interested Holmes that the question came to him in just this way: to him it showed the workings of "a *mind* still bent on a becoming and consistent carrying out of its ideals of conduct—not . . . the unhesitating instinct of a still predominant & heroic *will*."[67]

The distinction, for Holmes, bore directly on his evolving notions of where good behavior comes from. In asking himself what one of Queen Elizabeth's knights—and a poet at that—would have done, Holmes showed that he regarded ethics as a system of imitation and of aristocratic formality. Instead of trying to do good for its own sake, he was striving to imagine and reproduce the choices of an idealized man of honor. That Holmes used the adverb "still" to cast light on his ethical condition suggests that his own moral development was as yet unfinished. It seemed possible to him that his ethics, thus far rooted in culture and correct upbringing, might eventually yield to a sense of right that was both transcendent and absolute. But in the moment on the riverbank, all this theorizing was quickly swept aside; while still debating the likely conduct of Sir Philip Sidney, Holmes let himself be loaded into the boat.[68]

The craft carried Holmes back to Harrison's Island, about a hundred yards offshore. There, in a makeshift hospital, he listened as his cousin Willy Putnam refused treatment; Putnam knew that his abdomen, torn open by a Confederate ball, was beyond repair, and he wanted no attentions that might give another man a better chance to survive. A surgeon told Holmes that the odds were against him, too, and again Holmes fingered his bottle of laudanum. He begged one of the doctors ("or meant or tried to," he wrote) "to write home & tell 'em I'd done my duty—I was very anxious they should know that."[69] Holmes also confided to the surgeon his contingency plan to kill himself with his laudanum. In response, the doctor gave him a safer dose of the same substance. Soon after, as Holmes's mind wandered, the surgeon wisely "prigged" his patient's bottle.[70]

Though now quite lightheaded, Holmes still felt capable of reasoning, "even if through a cloud." He began to wonder whether he was going to Hell. Holmes considered himself a very poor Christian; he had little doubt that "the majority vote of the civilized world" would send him directly to Hell.[71] The thought shook him. Nonetheless, he dismissed the idea of a deathbed conversion. He and the "Governor" had debated this tactic in a more detached moment and had agreed that it was the recourse of a coward. Furthermore, the threat of death had not altered Holmes's religious convictions, and he had no wish to die as a hypocrite. If he had to go, he would go honestly, even if it meant having "to take a leap in the dark."[72]

And yet, if he was not reconciled with the Christian God, he still felt *something* that, though indistinct, seemed undeniable. As his thoughts and the opium freely intermingled, Holmes found himself afloat in cosmic immensities. Drifting in the dreamy current, he all at once regarded dying as "the most natural thing in the world." It seemed as if life and death and all creation had been calculated for the best, for all seemed "in accordance with a general law—and *good & universal* . . . [were] synonymous terms."[73] Indeed, it felt vain for the intellect to argue questions of good and evil, for these were truths that only the heart and will could rightly grasp. And as Holmes thought this, the future of his being became a subject of serene indifference:

> Would the complex forces which made a still more complex unit in *Me* resolve themselves back into simpler form, or would my angel be still winging his way onward when eternities had passed? I could not tell. But all was doubtless well—and so with a "God forgive me if I'm wrong," I slept.[74]

When he came to, Holmes was eager to share his newfound theories of the Infinite. However, when he tried to lecture a lieutenant on the subject, he could not express himself without profanity. Evidently his most printable utterance was, "Well, Harry, I'm dying but I'll be God-damned if I know where I'm going." Holmes swore frightfully enough to convince his horrified servant that he "was booking [him]self for Hell" rapidly. As O'Sullivan attempted to quiet his employer, the lieutenant tried to drag his thoughts back toward orthodoxy. "Why, Homey, you believe in Christ, don't you?" he pleaded.[75] But Holmes was still blaspheming lustily as he was being ferried the rest of the way across the river and back to Maryland.

Fanciful dreams gave way to flesh-and-blood nightmares. Before his evacuation to Maryland, Holmes overheard the regimental surgeon say,

"It is a beautiful face." Without asking, Holmes knew the face belonged to Willy Putnam and that his cousin was dead. After the horse-drawn ambulance had jolted him along the road to a care station in Maryland, Holmes gazed on a ghastly antithesis of beauty. Insensible and breathing heavily, Ferdinand Dreher, a German-born captain in the Twentieth, lay near him with a portion of his face shot away. Dreher looked like a modern Oedipus: "Two black cavities seemed all that there was left for eyes—his whiskers & beard matted with blood which still poured black from his mouth—and a most horrible stench."[76]

Just two days after Ball's Bluff, Holmes was well enough to be sent to Philadelphia, where he stayed a week with Pen Hallowell's parents. Holmes Sr. then came to bring him home to Boston.[77] By the end of November, Wendell was thriving and able to walk, despite having, as his father described it, "a considerable open wound, which, if the bone has to exfoliate, will keep him from camp for many weeks at the least."[78] Dr. Holmes marveled at his son's narrow escape.

Recuperating at home, Wendell greeted a stream of well-wishers. The procession included the anthropologist Louis Agassiz, Senator Charles Sumner, and the novelist Anthony Trollope, who had come from England to observe "the manners and institutions" of the American people.[79] Perhaps the most welcome visitor was Wendell's childhood friend Fanny Dixwell, whom he was to marry eleven years later. As gifts from friends piled up around him—flowers, grapes, pears, even ice cream—he became quite practiced at telling the tale of his trial by fire. His father, though proud of Wendell's courage, grew somewhat miffed at not being the center of attention. Recalling the great warrior-storyteller from Shakespeare, he told his friend John Lothrop Motley, "Wendell is a great pet in his character of young hero with wounds in the heart, and receives visits *en grand seigneur*. I envy my white Othello, with a semi-circle of young Desdemonas about him, listening to the often told story which they will have over again."[80]

Arthur Fuller, chaplain of the Sixteenth Massachusetts, observed that after Ball's Bluff, Massachusetts was "bleeding at every pore."[81] Despite the catastrophe, Dr. Holmes praised the valor of the soldiers of the Twentieth, who, he averred, "did all that men could be expected to do."[82] Such private praise surely pleased Wendell. He wisely said little, however, about the more public rhapsodies of *Harper's Weekly*'s "Lounger," the writer who had boldly proclaimed, "In the breast is Massachusetts wounded, if she is struck. Forward she falls, if she fall dead." The purple propagandist had gone further. In his view, the men of New England, typified by Holmes, "are not machine-soldiers; they are men-soldiers," with every rifle "loaded and rammed down with an idea." These men were "of stuff so tried and true that the sea might as hopelessly clash against Gibraltar as rebellion against their ranks."[83] Wendell thought the Lounger's rhapsodies were nonsense. As far as they concerned him personally, they were more than a nod to a military novice who happened to have a famous father. They brought him no honor—only the ruefulness of knowing that he had stood alongside other men who deserved as much or more notice and had not gotten it.

Holmes did not rejoin the Twentieth until he was fully well the following March. Throughout his absence, the regiment had been essentially idle. Colonel Lee, freed from his Confederate prison as part of a prisoner exchange, also came back to the regiment. It was a different unit now. Of its thirty-seven original officers, twenty-two had either resigned or been killed, wounded, or captured at Ball's Bluff. The army to which Holmes returned had also transformed: it was a more confident, efficient force than the one he had left behind. With incessant drill, meticulous reviews of endless regiments, and a strict imposition of order, enforced at gunpoint when necessary, General McClellan was imparting discipline to the Army of the Potomac, as well as raising morale. When he appeared astride his favorite horse, Kentuck, to perform personal inspections, enthusiastic shouts went up along the ranks. McClellan returned their affection. Two months into his mission, he proudly declared, "I think that . . . our Army is composed of the best men who ever formed an army."[84]

Shortly after assuming his command, McClellan had told Lincoln that he hoped to smash the rebellion with a single blow. Targeting the Confederate capital at Richmond, he proposed to march his army up the peninsula bounded by the York and James Rivers, crushing the Confederate forces under General Joseph E. Johnston in the process. While the campaign was in its early phases, McClellan confidently predicted, "One more battle here will finish the work."[85]

The Peninsular Campaign of March–July 1862 was a miserable slog through swamps and along bad roads, worsened by squadrons of flies and mosquitoes. Heavy rains slowed operations and depressed spirits. Cottonmouth snakes occasionally surprised the unwary, and numberless soldiers fell prey to dysentery, measles, and malaria. McClellan complained that the roads and fields were literally impassable for artillery.[86] The Twentieth Massachusetts performed well during the campaign, seeing heavy action first at Fair Oaks and then during the famous Seven Days Battles at the Battle of Glendale. The fighting differed greatly from what Holmes had seen the previous autumn; the daily exposure to combat wore heavily upon his mind and nerves. It was strange, too, to be fighting in a populated area. At Fair Oaks, he listened as the shingles of a roof "rattled with the hail of Reb. Bullets," making a lasting impression.[87] At the same battle, under orders to move forward on the double quick, Holmes tossed aside his haversack so that he might go faster. In so doing, he threw away "all my food, my dressing case, my only change of stockings, my pipe and tobacco," all grievous losses for a soldier on the move.[88]

Holmes was becoming a fighting man, learning now how to keep his men from breaking under fire. He told his parents of the smart use he was making of his "file closers"—men entrusted to keep formations in order as they pressed toward the enemy—ordering them to shoot any man who ran. The file closers eagerly obeyed, "lustily buffet[ing] every hesitating brother." Holmes also meted out discipline: "I gave one (who was cowering) a smart rap over the backsides with the edge of my sword—and . . . swore I'd shoot the first who ran or fired against orders." But one could easily understand why a man should feel unnerved under fire. Holmes wrote, "A bullet has a most villainous greasy slide through the air."[89]

Wind and rain buffeted and soaked the army day and night. Holmes stumbled constantly as he picked his way through the woods. After dark, every step might bring his foot down on a "swollen bod[y], already fly-blown and decaying." Yet he got used to it. He noted with surprise, "It is singular with what indifference one gets to look on the dead bodies in gray."[90] If your company had time, you buried the dead as fast as you could. If not, you tried not to look too much at the wounds that had made a mess of "head, back or bowels," and moved on.[91] Without so much as a blanket to lay upon the ground, Holmes became infested with body lice. He had no time to wash, and the absence of fresh food disordered his intestines. Still, he proudly observed, "I stand this experience . . . better than many a stout fellow who looks more enduring than I."[92]

Failing to take Richmond after a week of hard fighting, McClellan's army slunk back to Harrison's Landing, some twenty miles from Richmond, where it spent July before finally being ordered back toward Washington. Holmes fell silent until September 5, when he sent a letter to his mother. He told her that, while on leave in the capital city, he had taken a room at the National Hotel. He indulged himself heartily, laying in about eighty dollars' worth of clothes and other supplies and eating himself "into a plethora."[93]

In the early morning twelve days later, Holmes's days of pleasure were already a fleeting memory. At three in the morning, as his regiment lay encamped near Sharpsburg, Maryland, Holmes stared by candlelight at a blank sheet of paper, trying to decide what words to send his parents in what might be his final letter.

Since Holmes's brief sojourn in Washington, events had unfolded quickly. Emboldened by his crushing defeat of the Federals at Second Bull Run at the end of August, Robert E. Lee had taken his army to Union soil for the first time. Even as Holmes was writing his parents on September 5, the Army of Northern Virginia was crossing the Potomac into Maryland. Despite being heavily outnumbered, Lee divided his army, sending roughly half his men under Major General Stonewall Jackson to take the Union garrison at Harpers Ferry and ordering the remainder, led by Major General James Longstreet, to Boonsboro, Maryland, to guard against a possible assault from the east. Lee was taking a chance, but he seems to have taken the risk without deep concern; he had never been punished for relying on McClellan's slowness and excesses of caution.

But now an extraordinary happenstance turned the odds sharply against him. On September 13, the Twenty-Seventh Indiana, seeking a place to camp, had happened onto a site that had lately been vacated by Major General Daniel Harvey Hill's division of Confederate infantry. A corporal of the Twenty-Seventh, Barton Mitchell, looked down and saw a piece of paper wrapped around a trio of cigars. To Mitchell's astonishment, it bore the heading "Special Order No. 191." "Special" only began to describe it. The order directed the troop movements of Lee's entire army and disclosed a priceless piece of information: the two halves of the rebel force were over fifteen miles apart and were, thanks to the separation, ripe for destruction. Within hours, General McClellan was exulting over the discovery. His task was clear, and he had the means and opportunity to achieve it. "My general idea," he wrote, "is to cut the enemy in two & to beat him in detail."[94]

But his army failed to carry out this idea, partly because McClellan failed to urge his corps commanders to act quickly. They fell short, too, because McClellan could not work free from his habitual caution. Unaccountably, he believed that Lee was commanding 120,000 men or more. McClellan insisted that he was vastly outmanned, little realizing that the entire Confederate force numbered slightly fewer than 40,000. McClellan's force was at least twice that size.[95]

Jackson's wing of Lee's army seized Harpers Ferry on September 15. The day before, about fifteen miles north, a division led by Daniel Harvey Hill had hastened to plug the gaps in a long, curved ridge called South Mountain, through which McClellan's forces were attempting to surge. By their fingernails, the outnumbered Rebels held the gaps long enough to keep the Federals from smashing Lee's still-divided army. The Confederates fell back. The greater part of them regrouped near Sharpsburg, a sleepy town just barely on the Maryland side of the Potomac. East of Sharpsburg meanders a placid waterway, known as Antietam Creek.

Holmes's regiment missed the fight at South Mountain. They had spent that day marching west from Frederick toward Middletown—close enough to hear the ominous music of distant cannon, but well out of danger. Two days later, in the midst of a late-summer heat wave, the Twentieth arrived at a sloping hillside to the east of Antietam Creek, looking west across gently undulating farming country toward another set of camps, where Jackson's men, having left a division under Major General A. P. Hill at Harpers Ferry, were just then rejoining the other half of the Confederate army.

Far from any large town, the fields and country lanes near Sharpsburg seem to have been made for the peaceful contemplation of nature. Their beauty is not spectacular. It is humble and abiding. It is a place of few striking features: a farmhouse here, a woodlot there. Gazing at the rude rail fences constructed by the local farmers, one could easily smile at the simple joys of life at its quietest. Yet the day when Holmes first saw these fences was to be the last when one could look at them and not be reminded of twisted limbs and stark, bleached bones.

The troops on both sides "slept upon their arms," knowing they would have hot work in the morning. In the hours before sunrise, it was a rare man who slept soundly. The heat of the day now broken, a light rain fell upon the fields. The enemy was so close that any sound or action might invite fire from the opposing batteries. Thus, under orders of silence, the camps were ominously still. In whispers, some read to each other from the Bible. From time to time, the quiet was broken as scattered bursts of picket fire crackled up and down the line. Frederick Hitchcock, a volunteer infantryman from Pennsylvania, recalled these hours well:

> Letters were written home—many of them "last words"—and quiet talks were had, and promises were made between comrades—Promises providing against the dread possibilities of the morrow: "If the worst happens, Jack . . ." "Yes, Ned?" "Send word to mother and to ___, and these; she will prize them," and so directions were interchanged that meant so much.[96]

As the army passed the night, neither stirring nor still, Holmes gazed at his sheet of paper, contemplating what, he, too, thought might be a farewell. He did not feel like himself; his digestion had not felt right since the Battle of Fair Oaks, three and a half months earlier. He insisted that he could still comfortably consume anything from hardtack biscuits to shingle nails. Nevertheless, he admitted, "one damp night recalling those dreary times plays the deuce with me." Such complaints aside, Holmes felt eager for a fight. He liked the army's chances in the coming battle and, though he was well aware of the dangers that awaited him, he was determined not to turn sentimental. He refused to play upon his parents' emotions, though his words must surely have had that effect in any case:

> I don't talk seriously for you know all my last words if I come to grief—You know my devoted love for you—those I care for know it—Why should I say more—It's rank folly pulling a long mug every time one may fight or be killed—Very probably we shall in a few days and if we do why I shall go into it not trying to shirk the responsibility of my past life by a sort of death bed abjuration—I have lived on the track on which I expect to continue traveling if I get through—hoping always that, though it may wind, it will bring me up the hill once more with the deepest love.[97]

Holmes's regiment belonged to the Second Army Corps, under the command of Major General Edwin Vose Sumner, a sixty-five-year-old veteran who had been an army officer since 1819. Sumner ordered his men awakened at 2 a.m. so they could eat breakfast and prepare to move as early as possible. At 7:20, Sumner received orders to march two of his three divisions west, cross Antietam Creek, and support the assault on the Confederate left flank—an action that was already being pressed by the First and Twelfth Corps. To Sumner's front lay a large expanse of woods, then an open stretch of pastureland that extended to the Hagerstown Pike, the principal road leading north from Sharpsburg. Beyond that road lay another densely forested tract. The two wooded areas served the local families as sources of fuel and building material. From this day forward, they would be enduringly, if unimaginatively, known as the East and West Woods. Just to the south of the West Woods stands the battlefield's most distinctive building, a one-room church maintained by a congregation of Dunkers, so called because they favored total immersion as their means of baptism. The Dunker Church occupies slightly elevated ground, which made it an attractive place for Stonewall Jackson to place some artillery batteries. Painted white, it was visible from a distance to the Union corps commanders and thus became a natural focal point for the advancing bluecoats.

In the East Woods, some minutes before nine o'clock, Sumner saw much to disconcert him. Not only was the woodlot strewn with wounded from the earlier attacks, but an inordinate number of unwounded comrades had also slipped back into the woods to help them. Sumner knew from long experience that good Samaritans multiplied rapidly when the fire up ahead was especially terrible. Emerging from the western fringe of the East Woods, the general scanned the field. It seemed wisest to press forward and pour his men into the West Woods, a position from which he thought he might be able to turn Lee's flank and drive the Rebels back toward Sharpsburg. Sumner ordered the division led by Major General John Sedgwick, which included the Twentieth Massachusetts, to cross the pasture and seize control of the West Woods. Sedgwick organized his force into three long lines, each led by a brigadier general. In the lead came four regiments under Willis Gorman: the First Minnesota, the Thirty-Fourth and Eighty-Second New York, and the Fifteenth Massachusetts. Bringing up the rear were four Pennsylvania units under the command of Oliver O. Howard. In the middle line, Napoleon J. T. Dana led five regiments: the Seventh Michigan, the Forty-Second and Fifty-

Ninth New York, and the Nineteenth and Twentieth Massachusetts—and, among the latter, Captain Oliver Wendell Holmes Jr.[98]

The march was flawed from the start. The three lines began their advance too closely bunched on one another's heels, as they discovered when a hail of Confederate artillery fire descended from beyond the woods. The gray-clad cannoneers could hardly miss: a missile that sailed over the heads of Gorman's line was sure to strike Dana's or Howard's men. But the Rebel gunners seemed to require no such margin for error. The barrage was not only the most intense that Holmes's regiment had ever seen, but it was preternaturally accurate, so much so that one private in the Twentieth stood convinced that the artillerists had measured the ground. The shells and shot careened right into the advancing line, he recalled, and "they would take out 8 and 10 men at a time."[99]

Gorman's line entered the West Woods a little after nine, encountering, for the moment, little resistance there. Holmes and the rest of Dana's command entered the woodlot moments later. Apart from the gentle paths maintained by the National Park Service, the West Woods of today are not a pleasant place to walk. In 1862, they were a difficult place to maintain an orderly line of men. Thick, thorny ground cover catches ceaselessly at one's pant legs, and it is even possible to blunder onto a poisonous snake. The trees grow densely, too, and one might imagine that a host of men could conceal themselves quite close by without one's being the wiser. Into this dark wood, barely embarked on life's journey, walked Captain Holmes.

Gorman's brigade pushed through the woods and was emerging on the western side. They had just made their way over a fence into a farmer's pasture when a Rebel force, previously undetected, poured a furious fire into their front. At the same time, the Rebel cannon, now moved to a different position, let loose a barrage of canister and solid shot. Less than twenty feet behind Gorman's line, the situation of the Twentieth Massachusetts was edging toward catastrophe. The troops behind them were crowding them forward, but the Twentieth had no place to go. Moreover, they could not return the Rebel infantry fire without endangering the friendly line in front of them. They were, for the moment, helpless. Holmes recalled that he and his company had been "shoved . . . up so close to the front line that we could have touched them with our bayonets, and we got hit about as much as they did, but of course could do nothing."[100]

In short order, the anxiety of the moment turned to shock. The woods to the left of the Twentieth, in the same general direction as the Dunker Church, erupted with gunfire and the shrieks of men, some in bloody exhilaration and others in pain or fear. A shout went up in Holmes's vicinity: "The enemy are behind us!" It was true. Two divisions under Stonewall Jackson, approaching the West Woods from the south, had slammed into the left and rear of Sedgwick's force. They first hit Howard's back line, and the stunned Pennsylvanians scattered. Just to Holmes's rear, one of the regimental surgeons was kneeling over a wounded man, trying to save him. A moment later, the surgeon fell dead.[101] There Sumner stood, shouting, "My God, Howard, you must get out of here!"[102] But the din was too overpowering for Howard to hear him. Even if he had, the direction that constituted "out" was hard to determine; the Confederate fire seemed to be coming from all sides. The back rank having been shattered, Dana's brigade was the next to feel the onslaught. Almost before the men of the Twentieth could react, the Rebels were within a hundred paces, their guns blazing forth with some of the deadliest fire of the war.

Holmes spotted one of his regiment's men firing toward the rear. Thinking that the soldier was firing into his own men, Holmes burst into a fury. "You damn fool," he cried, bringing the flat of his sword down upon the hapless private.[103] But the man was not a fool at all; Confederate infantry were hitting the Twentieth from behind. The men of the Fifty-Ninth New York, the last regiment standing between the Twentieth and the assault from the left, were now fleeing every which way. Pen Hallowell recoiled in pain, his left arm shattered above the elbow by a Rebel bullet. One moment, the Massachusetts men were holding. Then, an instant later, they were "at the mercy of their enemy."[104] Sumner ordered a retreat. In that moment came the break, the rise of fear, and Holmes's desperate, deliriously laughing run through the trees and brambles with which this book began.

✳

AFTER THE TWENTIETH HAD, AS HE later described it, "run away like rabbits" and the bullet had torn through his neck, Holmes lay helpless in the undergrowth of the West Woods. He hovered between knowing and not knowing, his perceptions out of joint.[105] Incredibly, the bullet had missed his spine, his esophagus, his veins: everything essential to life and function was intact. And yet, to all appearances, he was done for. As he fluttered on the edge of consciousness, a man sauntered up to him and spoke: "You're a Christian, aren't you?" Holmes's eyelids flickered. "Well, then, that's all right," the man said with satisfaction, and wandered off.[106] There followed a span of time whose length Holmes had no way to measure. At the end of it came a second man, who fortunately cared more about Holmes's prospects in this life than in the next. William Le Duc, a regimental quartermaster, saw the prostrate captain and called for a surgeon. The doctor looked at Holmes with annoyance. "I've no time to waste on dead men," he snapped. But Le Duc did not give up. The next thing Holmes felt was the liquid burn of brandy pouring down his throat and jolting him back to awareness.

Le Duc and another man helped Holmes to his feet. Could he walk? He discovered that, with assistance, he could. The two men helped him to shelter at the home of the Nicodemus family, some distance north of the woods. Pen Hallowell was also there. Though surgeons were expending every effort to save Pen's mangled arm, Holmes felt certain that the damage was beyond repair. Still unable to speak, he did the best thing he could think of to raise his own chances of survival. He found a scrap of paper and haltingly scribbled on it, "I am Captain O. W. Holmes, 20th Mass. Son of Oliver Wendell Holmes, M.D. Boston."[107] Perhaps someone would recognize the name and give him better care. Surely Holmes was never more grateful to have a famous father.

Le Duc, who had possibly saved the captain's life, did him one further service. He sent a telegram to Boston, advising the Holmes family that their son had been wounded in the neck but assuring them that the wound was "not thought fatal." The message, intended to allay the family's fears, was to have a different effect.

Chapter Two

The Blond Artillerist

On the same field with Captain Holmes at Antietam, but on the other side of the line, there stood another doctor's son, and as Holmes marched toward the West Woods, that second doctor's son was trying to kill him.

The shelling that bedeviled the Twentieth Massachusetts—the cannonade so accurate that its targets felt as if the gunners had measured the ground—came through the courtesy of Captain John Pelham of Major General Jeb Stuart's Horse Artillery. The officers in General Lee's army who garnered the most favor tended to be sons of Virginia. Pelham, however, was well on his way to becoming the most celebrated Southern soldier to emerge from Alabama. He defeated expectations in more immediately visible ways. The great heroes of the Army of Northern Virginia were, for the most part, in their thirties and forties. They were men of impressive, hirsute countenance and still more impressive military experience. Many of them—Stonewall Jackson, James Longstreet, and A. P. Hill, to name only a few—had service records dating from the 1840s. Many had proven themselves in the desperate struggles of the Mexican War. That war had begun when John Pelham was seven years old. It was over before he turned ten. At Antietam, Pelham was only ten days past his twenty-fourth birthday. In emulation of his superiors, he had once stopped shaving in hopes of raising a beard. Knowing that the appearance of maturity sometimes counted more than the quality itself, he had been heard to remark, "If I had a beard, it would be worth a brigadier's commission to me."[1] But his razor had been set aside in vain; his cheeks remained frustratingly smooth.

The young man's father, Atkinson Pelham, came to Alabama only a year before John was born. After graduating from Philadelphia's Jefferson College Medical School in 1826, he had practiced as a doctor in North Carolina for the next decade or so. He then sought greater fortunes in the thriving cotton economy of the Deep South.

The hamlet of Alexandria, Alabama, was then part of Benton County. Retaining much of its agricultural character to this day, it sits in high country, near the southern end of the Appalachian Mountains. The area's thick belts of oak and pine trees give way to broad swaths of open pasture. Cotton once grew here. Now a cornfield is the more common sight. The place savors of stability and stasis. To Atkinson Pelham, arriving in 1837 to clear the land and build a life, it smelled of opportunity. Keeping up his medical practice, Dr. Pelham also acquired property, gradually increasing his holdings until they exceeded a thousand acres. On this land, on September 7, 1838, John Pelham was born. He joined a growing family, already populated by his older brothers Charles and William. Martha Pelham gave birth to three more sons—Peter, Samuel, and Thomas—as well as a daughter, formally christened Eliza but known as Betty. All six brothers eventually fought for the Confederacy.

Atkinson owned about thirty men, women, and children. A man who can feed, clothe, and house thirty other people, in addition to a large family of his own, is a person of considerable means, even if those means are built on unpaid labor. Scarcely one Southern slaveholder in ten owned as many men, women, and children as Atkinson Pelham. Yet, as he surely knew, his holdings in land and human flesh did not place him among the highest echelons of Southern privilege; about ten thousand families in the South could claim fifty or more of the enslaved millions. But in Benton County, far removed from the concentrated wealth of cities like Charleston and New Orleans, an estate the size of Atkinson's commanded respect.

Whereas most rural Alabamians espoused states' rights and decentralization, Atkinson, a Southern Whig, voted with an eye on his pocketbook. Believing that the young nation would be made rich only by government spending in support of industry, he supported Henry Clay's American System, which called for a strong federal bank and aggressive public investment in roads and canals. If Atkinson ever considered freeing his slaves, there is nothing to prove it. But he also opposed secession, once again on economic grounds: Alabama and her sister states would prosper more from cooperation than by conflagration.

John grew up knowing how to swim, fish, and shoot. He hunted with the family hounds and, in so doing, became a splendid horseman. He and his brothers also grew up assuming that they would often be deferred to, not only by their father's slaves, but in the white community as well. The Pelham brothers began and ended each day with a reading from scripture. In between, they tended to forget the gentle counsels of the Savior. With the insouciance that often goes with entitlement, they were, for a time, almost ungovernable children, and all kinds of mischief followed in the wake of "those wild Pelham boys."[2]

Some of their mischief was mere thoughtless (and to some observers, mildly comic) amusement, as when they secretly took turns riding a neighbor's cow and temporarily ruined her as a milk producer. The irate farmer ordered John to stop worrying his cows and recommended that he ride a bull instead. The boy agreed, and, it was said, eventually tamed the animal so thoroughly that his sister could ride it.[3] But the fun could also turn cruel. After their schoolmaster physically punished John and his brother Charles for some infraction, the boys swore vengeance. They broke into a storage area and spirited away some school benches and desks. They smeared ink on the instructor's clothes and threw some of his books down a well. One day they loosened the joints of his chair so that it gave way under him. In the wake of these assaults, a committee of concerned parents convened. It says something unflattering about the community's social order that the committee solved the problem not by suspending the boys but by dismissing the teacher.

Another incident is still harder to forgive. After an Independence Day picnic, Charles, John, and William played a trick on their father by concocting a fake medical emergency. They accosted a young black boy, most likely a family slave, and drenched him in the blood of a slaughtered hog. Then they dragged the boy to Atkinson's medical office, claiming that he had suffered some horrible accident. The child was, of course, powerless to resist. As the Pelham boys pulled him along, he could do nothing but shriek and cry. Undeceived, Atkinson punished his sons, though whether more for trying to lie to him than for the fear and humiliation they had caused the boy the records do not show.[4]

Probably very few boys perfectly respect the feelings and dignity of others. Yet John Pelham's circumstances were especially unsuited to teaching him this lesson. In his *Notes on the State of Virginia*, Jefferson railed against the slow, sure poison with which slave ownership destroyed the moral sensitivity of the class that called itself master. The corruption, he said, was invariably passed from father to son:

> The whole commerce between master and slave is a perpetual exercise
> of the most boisterous passions, the most unremitting despotism on
> the one part, and degrading submissions on the other. . . . The parent
> storms, the child looks on, catches the lineaments of wrath, puts on
> the same airs . . . and thus nursed, educated, and daily exercised in
> tyranny, cannot but be stamped by it with odious peculiarities.[5]

The callous mistreatment of the blood-soaked slave boy shows the outlines of this hereditary defect. The Pelham boys surely did not consider themselves cruel or cowardly. However, where a black slave (or a poor schoolmaster) was concerned, it seemingly did not occur to them that such values were at issue. Decency was rigorously observed only within one's caste and color.

Accounts of John's boyhood reduce his mother to a hazy, idealized image of warmth and piety. One gets a more textured sense of Dr. Pelham's ideas of parenthood. He knew that his boys needed reining in, and he enforced order in the fashion of a man unaccustomed to contradiction. Wendell Holmes's father invented a whimsical "autocrat" in his fiction. Atkinson imposed a real domestic autocracy, expecting his sons not merely to follow his will, but to anticipate it. His son Charles recollected, "He . . . tried to rear his sons so that they would do just what he wanted done without an order." He added, "John [was] an obedient, affectionate son & . . . never disobeyed him."[6] But John was not so submissive as all that, and, as has been seen, the Pelham boys' affectionate obedience waned when their father left the room. Boys with stern fathers tend to learn not only the rigors of discipline, but also the pleasure of throwing it off when the iron hand is absent. Atkinson Pelham may eventually have succeeded in teaching his sons to respect his principles. But it was on authority, not reason or empathy, that he founded his instruction.

At seventeen, John sought admission to the United States Military

Academy at West Point. The hope of becoming a cadet transformed him as a student. Although he worked long hours on his father's farm, setting aside Saturdays for fishing and Sundays for church, he made time for the necessary studies and approached them with extraordinary will, tackling the books with a "cheerful, happy disposition."[7] Then, as now, one applied to West Point by obtaining a recommendation from a representative in Congress.[8] Although Atkinson was well connected with Alabama's political establishment, John's admission was no foregone conclusion. He struggled to achieve proficiency in some of the required subjects, and the family enlisted a local pastor to tutor him twice a week.

In March 1856, a letter from Secretary of War Jefferson Davis brought happy news: John Pelham had been appointed to the Academy. The circular that accompanied the appointment, however, was less than congratulatory in tone. Davis warned the entering cadets that only a third of them were likely to graduate, and that if they lacked aptitude in certain areas of study—mathematics in particular—they ought not to accept the appointment to begin with. Undaunted, Pelham submitted to the required physical examination, performed by his father, and pledged his next eight years to the United States Army.

As John prepared to depart, his father gave him a book that tells much about the virtues he wanted his son to practice at the Academy. Written for aspiring collegians, *The Student's Manual* by the Reverend John Todd was dedicated to "forming and strengthening the intellectual and moral character" of young men. Above all else, Todd insisted, success at college called for discipline. A boy would never achieve the needed focus if he were in the habit of yielding to his appetites and passions.[9] Todd conceded that it was hard for a young man, fresh from "the brooks, the groves, or the hills and ponds near his home" and still thinking of "his skates, his gun, or his fishing-tackle," to sit in a bare dormitory room and study his lessons. Yet, said Todd, the mental discipline that the student acquired would one day raise him high in the esteem of his fellows.[10]

Atkinson left handwritten notes in the book's margins for John to find. The passage that sparked his most extensive commentary was one that Todd had written in Latin, deeming it too scandalous to be printed in English. Todd's warning concerned "the crime of Onan," which, he said, not only impaired the memory and led to imbecility but also aroused God's anger and set the self-abuser on the fastest way toward an early grave. Dr. Pelham wrote to John, "My experience in the practice of medicine confirms this paragraph—read this Latin carefully." He added ominously, "I have been consulted frequently [in] incipient cases of lunacy & physical diseases brought on by this unfortunate practice, fraught with much peril to life and mar[ring] all happiness common to our mundane career."[11] Precisely why, among all of Todd's admonitions, Dr. Pelham underscored this more emphatically than any other, is a delicate question.

John diligently marked Todd's cautions against drinking, losing one's temper, speaking severely about an acquaintance in his absence, and "indulg[ing] in levity upon what is sacred."[12] Pelham's copious annotations reflect a zeal for self-improvement and an awareness that his years at the Academy should also mark a conscious transformation in character. He would put the arrogant, ungovernable child to rest. He would deliberately re-create himself in the image of his own romantic ideal.

A series of trains and a steamboat up the Hudson brought Pelham to West Point, a thousand miles from the Alabama hills that had, until now, defined his world. Entering the Academy on July 1, 1856, he underwent a change in circumstance so swift that few young men could pass through it without a tremor. Instantly the life of soft beds and superiority gave way to two months of "encampment," a grueling period passed in simple tents in the summer heat. The discipline was unbending; the hazings by older cadets were merciless. With September came better times as the new cadets, or "plebes," settled into the barracks, but the rise in comfort was slight. Pelham spent his seven hours of sleep on a thin mattress and an iron bedstead. He studied at a small table, while sitting in a straight-backed chair that refused to acknowledge the actual contours of a human form. The food was nearly inedible.

Holmes's Harvard, as has been noted, was consciously homogeneous, an institution of and for Bostonians. The Point, by contrast, attracted cadets from across the country, such that no section's manners or opinions could be deemed ascendant. Furthermore, cadets were encouraged to overlook class distinctions. A graduate of the class behind Pelham's recalled, "There were no unapproachable lords of wealth and birth, no flaunting vulgarity . . . but everywhere genial good manners, cordiality, and the grace that comes from assured position."[13]

The Point sought to reshape almost every feature of its cadets' behavior. The same contemporary fondly recalled the pleasure of mastering "one's motions in walking, marching, or entering the presence of a superior, with the constant regard for neatness and the habit of scrupulous truth-telling."[14] One walked amid monuments and flags and captured cannons. Cadets were meant to realize that their mission was not only to master tactics and weaponry, but also to preserve and add to a legacy of honor.

To this atmosphere, Pelham readily warmed, though he did not set aside his frivolities overnight. Records of his first year reveal demerits for "laughing in the ranks," "boyish conduct" in class, and performing his sentry duties in an overly "relaxed" manner. Nor did he excel as a scholar. He found a close friend in Henry Algernon du Pont, whose grandfather had founded E. I. du Pont de Nemours and Company. Du Pont, who was to graduate first in Pelham's class, respected Pelham's natural abilities, but he added that the Alabama cadet "could not have been called clever and did not stand very high in his class, my recollection being that he did not apply himself particularly in his studies."[15] But Pelham did not regard self-culture chiefly as a question of academic performance. In a letter to his younger brother Samuel, he urged a simple precept: "Fear God, and know no other fear." He added with earnest simplicity, "I do not think a man can be strictly honorable unless he is brave. If he fears and cringes to other men, he cannot fill the full definition of a man." Filling that definition certainly called for courage, but it encompassed other skills and virtues, too.

A year after Pelham arrived at West Point, a new British novel encapsulated the ethic that he was seeking to embody. *Tom Brown's School Days*, Thomas Hughes's tribute to Rugby School under the eminent Victorian Thomas Arnold, proposed that the true bulwarks of a student body were not its budding poets or mathematicians but rather the ones with broad backs, generous smiles, and love of a good, fair fight. Strong in faith as well as in body, the model young man set himself against whatever seemed mean or unmanly in his world. Hughes and others gave a name to this ethic: "muscular Christianity." Whether Pelham read Hughes matters less than that he caught the scent of its doctrine and, knowingly or not, made himself its exemplar.

Pelham placed piety near the center of his moral being. A cadet could incur demerits for almost any conceivable cause. Surely, however, Pelham was one of the few who received a "slug" for reading the Bible instead of studying his book of military tactics. As an athlete, John was unsurpassed. A surgical fencer, he was said to be able to flick the buttons off another man's coat without damaging the fabric. He became an artful boxer, of whom his friend and roommate Tom Rosser recalled, "It was beautiful to watch his quickness and his dodging of blows. You could see it was always fun for him, even when he got hurt."[16] As a horseman, he built upon his early training to become an Academy legend; tales of his skill "went down from class to class as a sort of tradition, and long years after . . . the cadets would relate to gaping plebes how Pelham rode."[17] A fellow cadet also recalled him as a beautiful dancer and added, "it may well be asserted that Nature was in a fine mood when she moulded his clay."[18]

Were all these efforts at improvement compensating for something? If Pelham was trying to atone for some perceived defect, it may have been a quality that some might consider no defect at all: his appearance of extreme youth and a softness of feature that made him look almost feminine. At the Academy, where female companionship was scarce and the cadets were typically obliged to pair off with each other at dances, a young man of girlish appearance could both experience and trigger some discomfort. Physically drawn to Pelham but also possibly bewildered by what the attraction might mean, his classmates reacted with awkward humor. E. Porter Alexander, who instructed Pelham in fencing and who, like Pelham, later won fame as a Confederate artillerist, observed:

> [Pelham] was a very young looking, handsome, & attractive fellow, slender, blue eyes, light hair, smooth, red & white complexion, & with such a modest & refined expression that his classmates & friends never spoke of him but as "Sallie," and there never was a Sallie whom a man could love more![19]

Pelham's peers used such epithets both to build bonds and to gain subtle ascendancy over one another. If Pelham disliked the teasing nickname aimed at his masculinity, he seems to have accepted the ribbing. His calm good nature and warmth of manner made him, as his classmate Adelbert Ames recalled, the most popular man in the Corps.[20] His popularity and his growing capacity for tact served him well as the country's political landscape began to buckle beneath him.

Cadets with Union loyalties—the Northerners and Westerners—outnumbered Southerners in Pelham's class by about two to one. However, when Pelham arrived at the Point in 1856, antislavery feeling there was only lukewarm. As Kansas bled and Preston Brooks caned abolitionist Charles Sumner nearly to death on the floor of the United States Senate, a surprisingly tranquil mood persisted at the Academy. The school's administration worked hard to retain its identity as a national academy, exempt from regional prejudice.[21] One alumnus recalled that cadets never talked politics. As he remembered it, the Stars and Stripes received equal reverence from every cadet and flew above the grounds "with a spirit light as our own."[22]

Or so it seemed on the surface. Beneath it, the egalitarian spirit to which the Academy aspired was less than perfect. Despite their larger numbers, the cadets from free states turned restive when some of their Southern classmates flaunted their aristocratic roots. One of the Yankee students voiced the opinion that even in colonial times, New Englanders had deferred to their Southern countrymen, and that the South had come to accept its social superiority as a matter of course. He added:

> The descendants of those planters carried into the life at West Point their fathers' notions of precedence. . . . After slavery had become a national issue, [the Southern cadets] did not hesitate, when angered, to show their inherited contempt for the North; and . . . the cadets from the North, and those especially from the West, would not and did not stand it.[23]

Disdainful entitlement on the one hand slowly stoked resentment on the other. Still, this unrest stayed latent until October 1859. Then, in Pelham's fourth year as a cadet, John Brown's raid on Harpers Ferry sent the same jolt through the Academy that shook the rest of America. Fistfights erupted between Northern and Southern partisans, and at least one duel was fought when Northern abolitionism clashed with Southern honor.[24]

Alabama's anticipated departure from the Union agonized Pelham, though the principles that prompted its secession troubled him less than its timing. Some of the cadets from South Carolina caught the separatist fever almost immediately after Lincoln's election in November 1860; they were gone from the Academy even before their state began the parade of secessions on December 20. Pelham, however, prayed that Alabama might somehow hold on for just a few more months. He had worked assiduously toward earning his diploma, and the idea of leaving without it felt profoundly unjust. On December 11, 1860, he wrote to his father, "I had hoped, fondly hoped, to graduate here. It would be exceedingly gratifying to me and I know to the family also for me to receive a Diploma from this Institution, but Fate seems to have willed it otherwise. I don't see any honorable course other than tendering my resignation when Ala. leaves the Union, and offering my services to her."[25]

Yet the question of honor was more ambiguous than Pelham cared to admit. Upon entering the Academy, he had sworn an oath "to bear true faith and allegiance to the United States of America" and to defend the nation "against all enemies and opposers whatsoever." If honor means keeping one's word, the greater claim upon his honor lay with the government whose Academy he had chosen to attend. Strip away the rhetoric, and Pelham's intention to abandon the Union was founded on a loyalty to home and family, as well as to that special theory of states' rights that walked arm in arm with slavery. Honor potentially cut both ways.

On January 11, 1861, a state convention in Montgomery published its ordinance of secession. Pelham did not resign. On February 1, Dr. Pelham sent a letter to his son: if John wished to leave the Academy, he would not oppose him. Still the young man did not resign. Instead, he took his concerns directly to the newly inaugurated president of the Confederacy, Jefferson Davis. Though still legally committed to the Academy, he declared himself ready to side with the Confederacy. He advised the president, "Being still a member of the Mily. Acad'y, I don't think it would be exactly proper for me to offer my services to the new government, but I am anxious to serve it to the best of my ability. If you think it would be better for me to resign now than to wait and graduate . . . a single word from you will cause me to resign."[26] But that word did not come, and Pelham's wait continued.

The crisis imparted strange contours to the young man's loyalties. In a letter to his sister-in-law, Pelham declared himself "a most ultra Secessionist." Nevertheless, he retained a reverence for the country's symbols. Punctuating his thoughts with a quotation from Daniel Webster, he wrote, "I am still proud of the American flag. It does not belong to the North any more than to us, and has never had anything to do with our wrongs. I think that both sides ought . . . to . . . lay it aside as a memento of our past greatness and of our Revolutionary renown. . . . It should be stored away with our other household goods, cherished and preserved spotless and unstained 'not a single stripe erased or polluted, not a single star obscured.' " But if Lincoln's government persisted in flying the flag as a symbol of Union and antislavery, Pelham declared, "I would fight harder and longer to tear the 'Stars and Stripes' from every Northern battlement than for any other cause." [27]

Graduation drew tantalizingly closer. As it did, the voices in Pelham's ears became more strident. Atkinson, still hoping to claim a West Point graduate for his family and despite having given his permission for John to leave, urged his son "to remain as long as it was prudent to stay." Pelham's brothers agreed. But his friends, in a chorus, counseled him to resign. The pressure only intensified toward the end of March when Pelham opened a newspaper and read that, without his knowledge or consent, the Confederate Congress had commissioned him a first lieutenant in its newly established army. Pelham chafed at the legislators' presumption. His position was delicate enough without a band of hotheaded politicians jumping the gun. He distracted himself by rereading a book from the Academy's library that had captured his attention at least once before: *Cavalry: Its History and Tactics* by Louis Nolan, a British horseman who had died in the Charge of the Light Brigade. Nolan's book featured a section on a subject typically neglected by military analysts: the use of highly mobile horse-drawn artillery.[28]

Week by week, the Southern cadets melted away. By the beginning of April, only one other man from a seceded state remained in Pelham's class. This lone exception was an important one: Tom Rosser, the dark-haired Texan who had been both Pelham's roommate and his regular dance partner at the Academy's all-male cotillions. The two men had grown so close that Pelham deemed them "inseperable [sic]—like his presence is necessary to my happiness."[29] If fate or the Confederate government decreed that Pelham and Rosser must leave the Academy, they resolved to do so together.

On the morning of April 12, Confederate shells burst over Fort Sumter, and all doubts and postponements ended. In that same moment Pelham's last hope of graduating exploded as well. Five days later, Pelham and Rosser tendered their resignations. The next day brought the final mention of Pelham in the Academy's records: he was marked absent for breakfast and assessed the customary demerits. Wendell Holmes had been in a fever to leave Harvard for the army when the war began, yet he had been allowed to graduate. Pelham had hung on at West Point as long as honor would permit, desperate for a diploma that he was never to receive. His disappointment was immeasurable. And his trepidation rose. Before his departure on April 22, he took a walk with his friend and classmate Adelbert Buffington. Almost fifty years later, Buffington recalled Pelham's melancholy farewell: "Buff, I am going home. I shall be in two or three fights and then be killed."[30]

Subject to arrest for desertion during their southbound trek, Pelham and Rosser passed first through New York and brazenly stopped at a photographer's studio to pose for portraits. After a visit to one of Pelham's cousins in Philadelphia, they grew more furtive in their movements as they rode west through Pennsylvania and Ohio. On the way they encountered local denizens who had been "worked up to the last degree of frenzy and madness by their abolition leaders" and who talked of nothing but shooting or hanging the Southern traitors.[31] Arriving in Indiana, Pelham and Rosser proposed to cross the Ohio River into the still nominally Union but slaveholding commonwealth of Kentucky. At New Albany, they slipped past a patrol by posing as couriers bearing dispatches from General Winfield Scott. Upon reaching the river and finding the crossings guarded, they prevailed upon a woman to take them across in her rowboat.

On May 2 the two former cadets arrived at the Pelham homestead to a grand welcome. A pig roasted on an outdoor spit as friends and neighbors gathered to wish Pelham and Rosser well. The two rested from their travels for just over a week before answering the call of duty. During that interval, the captain of the newly formed Tenth Alabama Infantry called upon Pelham to assist in training a company of men, and a fair percentage of the town turned out to watch their proud West Point alumnus display his gifts for command. It went miserably. The new soldiers, loutish and uncouth, saw a chance to take out a morning's worth of vengeance on an aristocratic Pelham. They chewed tobacco while standing in ranks, thrust their hands into their pockets, and shifted out of line. Pelham's voice rose. Before long, he was on the verge of swearing, but the more strident his commands became, the more the men defied him. Pelham's face reddened with anger and embarrassment, and the neighbors began to whisper that the money spent on him at the Academy had been as good as thrown away. Offered a second chance to drill the company that afternoon, Pelham sullenly declined. Stung by the insult of their behavior, he would not further drill these mounds of insolence "to have saved their lives."[32]

Pelham bade farewell to his family on May 10, taking with him two enslaved brothers named Willis and Newton who had been his playmates in their youth. Pelham's mother fought back tears. "God bless you, John," she told him. "Bring you back safe to us." He urged her to modify her prayer: "If we win, Mama, your boy wants to come back. But if we lose, pray God to take [me] from the battlefield."[33]

By mid-June, Pelham was in Winchester, Virginia, charged with training an artillery battery whose regular commander, Ephraim Alburtis, was too ill to instruct them. During his last days at the Academy, Pelham had observed, "The army suits me better than anything else—and I feel a confidence that I can succeed in it."[34] He was now in a hurry to test his prediction. His failure with the Tenth Alabama was not repeated. Unlike the more scholarly and diffident Holmes, Pelham took his new command readily in hand and impressed onlookers with his firmness and love of precision. He trained his gunners seven hours a day, molding the recruits into a model of efficiency.

Among the many Virginia-born officers at Winchester, two were of particular note. The first was Thomas Jonathan Jackson. Equally fascinated by the Bible and by infantry tactics, Jackson had taught without much distinction at the Virginia Military Institute. Quiet and thin-lipped, he wore an ill-fitting uniform and sat awkwardly on his horse. At VMI, his careless appearance and a variety of petty eccentricities had earned him an uncomplimentary nickname: "Tom-Fool" Jackson. A better one awaited him on a hill near Manassas, Virginia. The second man took an early interest in Pelham's abilities. He was a lieutenant colonel of the cavalry, as showy and dramatic as Jackson was taciturn. Energetic and inclined toward reckless displays of daring, he had been among the marines under Robert E. Lee who foiled John Brown's raid on Harpers Ferry. He, too, had received a sarcastic nickname: "Beauty." His parents had christened him James Ewell Brown Stuart. His friends found it easier to call him "Jeb."

A lesser-known officer, Charles L. Scott, was perhaps the first to write an extensive description of Pelham at his guns:

> I recollect one morning . . . hearing a voice with a long and peculiar drawl drilling a squad of men. The difference in sound and pronunciation . . . were so marked that my curiosity was excited to know who this drill instructor was. . . . I saw a youth who was apparently not over 18 years of age with a fair complexion, blue eyes, smooth face . . . lightly built . . . and remarkably sinewy. . . . His boyish appearance, manly looks, handsome face, and soldierly bearing riveted my attention . . . I became drawn to him at first sight.[35]

Scott chose terms that would become commonplaces of Pelham hagiography—the focus on his physical beauty, the flood of laudatory adjectives, and above all the emphasis on his extreme youth. Pelham was a few months shy of his twenty-third birthday when Scott observed him—still not young enough to fit the mythos that Scott and others were eager to construct around him. His story was forever to be the romantic legend of a boy.

On Sunday, July 21, 1861, Confederate general P. G. T. Beauregard clashed with a large Union force outside the Virginia railway junction of Manassas, not far from a torpid, muddy stream called Bull Run. Later, far away in Brooklyn, New York, Walt Whitman pieced together a secondhand account of the scene. That summer weekend, he wrote, was "parch'd and hot to an extreme—the dust, the grime and smoke, in layers, sweated in, follow'd by other layers again sweated in, absorb'd by those excited souls—their clothes all saturated with the clay-powder filling the air—stirr'd up everywhere on the dry roads and trodden fields by the regiments, swarming wagons, artillery, &c."[36] But despite all the heat and perspiration, the fields around Manassas were a lovely sight. Edmund Clarence Stedman, the correspondent for the *New York World*, recalled, "the scenery was too beautiful and full of nature's own peace, for one to believe in the possibility of the tumult and carnage just at hand, or that among those green oak forests lurked every engine of destruction which human contrivance has produced."[37]

With Alburtis still too weak to take command, Pelham led the gunners into battle. On this day, victory depended on the control of a rolling eminence called Henry House Hill. In the confused early fighting before

Pelham's battery was engaged, the Confederate troops took a beating. At a critical moment, however, Confederate brigadier general Barnard E. Bee rallied his men by gesturing toward "Tom-Fool" Jackson, who was managing to hold a section of the hill while the other Rebels were falling back. "There is Jackson standing like a stone wall," Bee shouted. "Let us determine to die here, and we will conquer!" Having instantly and forever transformed "Tom-Fool" into "Stonewall," Bee took a shell fragment in the gut from which he died the next day. As his men made their stand, Jackson called for support from his artillery, and Pelham's men rolled their pieces forward. They were outnumbered and outgunned. In the roaring chaos, many units on both sides were seized with panic. But Pelham's gunners had learned their tasks so well that they were virtually automatic. Coolly and methodically, they repaid the Federals with determined fire.

On this day, Pelham had no need for tactical brilliance. What he most required he already had: a stubborn refusal to yield his ground. War was, in that moment, all he could have imagined—defending an embattled position with a small but dogged force, holding a line in the most ferocious battle the nation had ever seen. The thrill of it spurred him to recklessness. He ordered his guns beyond the point that Beauregard and Jackson had specified, seeking better scope for his shot and shells but also placing himself in a dangerously vulnerable spot. It was too much for one of his officers, who ran for cover. "If Pelham's fool enough to stay there," he was heard to exclaim, "I'm not!"

A bullet struck Pelham's horse but did not do enough damage to bring the animal down. As his guns blazed, two Union batteries also pushed too far forward for safety. Pelham's luck held; a regiment of Jackson's Virginians rushed forward and set upon the Union gunners, driving them back. Capturing the abandoned cannons, the Virginians turned them against the Yankee lines. At roughly the same time, Jackson ordered the Confederate artillery to fall back. Pelham, however, saw something Jackson did not: a Union brigade under William Tecumseh Sherman advancing on his right flank. Shouting "I'll be dogged if I'm going any further back," he moved his guns forward and began pelting Sherman's men with canister. In his enthusiasm, Pelham dismounted and directed the guns himself. On a dare from one of his gunners, he leveled a cannon at a Union flag and shot it down. "You ought to have heard the cheers [my gunners] gave me," he later wrote. Sherman soon abandoned the attack, and Jackson's line was saved.

In the midafternoon, after Pelham's stand, fresh Confederates arrived, sending the Federals back in stark confusion. On a bridge essential to their retreat, a wagon overturned, adding to the disorder. The pathways of the Union army's escape looked like a garbage dump, strewn with pots, kettles, muskets, flags, and other items that the soldiers, desperate to save themselves, had flung down and left behind.[38] They had taken little more trouble to carry off their casualties, and the field was dotted with the wounded and the dying. Profoundly distressed by accounts of the calamity, Whitman wrote, "The sun rises, but shines not."

After the battle, Pelham walked the blighted ground in dismay. By one account, coming across a pool of congealed blood where a Union battery had been overwhelmed by Jackson's men, he sank to his knees and vomited.[39] Two days later, recounting the battle to his father, he composed a letter that was at once a cry of victory and a stunned lament. He had been under heavy fire from muskets and cannon for more than seven hours. "How I escaped or why I was spared," he wrote, "a just God only knows." He wrote of how shells had burst and scattered their fragments around him, of the wounding of his horse, and how, amid it all, his men had been "cool and brave and made terrible havoc on the enemy." Pelham had also felt calm and deliberate—"as if I had been at home by our fire-side—I did not feel fear at any moment." His pride rose as he told Atkinson, "I was complimented several times . . . by general officers."[40] Still more excitement had come when President Davis himself arrived to survey the victory.

But even as he was writing, other feelings crowded into Pelham's mind, and his tone grew dark:

> I have seen what Romancers call glorious war. I have seen it in all its phases. I have heard it all nearby and have been under its destructive showers. I have seen men and horses fall thick and flat around me. I have seen our own men, bloody and frightened, flying before the enemy. I have seen them bravely charge the enemy's lines and heard the shout of triumph as they carried the position. I have heard the agonizing shrieks of the wounded and dying—I have passed over the battle field and seen the mangled forms of men and horses in frightful abundance. Men without heads, without arms, and others without legs. All this I have witnessed and more, till my heart sickens; and war is not glorious as novelists would have us believe.[41]

Pelham seldom wrote with greater poetic sensibility. The slow accumulation of overpowering sense impressions—"I have seen . . . I have heard . . . I have heard . . . I have seen" is the testimony of a mind upon which a new and shocking awareness has cataclysmically burst.

He was astounded as well at the difference between the thrill of battle and the woe of its aftermath. The mayhem that had been so enthralling to inflict was now piteous to observe:

> It is only when we are in the heat and flush of battle that it is fascinating and interesting. It is only then that we enjoy it, when we forget ourselves and revel in the destruction. . . . I am now ashamed of the feelings I had in those hours of danger. The whistling bullets and shells were music to me, I gloried in it—it delighted and fascinated me—I feared not death in any forms; but when the battle was won and I visited the field a change came over me. I see the horrors of war, but it was necessary. We are battling for our rights and our homes. Ours is a just war, a holy cause. The invader must meet the fate he deserves and we must meet him as becomes us, as becomes men.[42]

Thus Pelham rejected the supposed glory of battle. But into the void that glory had left behind, necessity, manliness, and even holiness were quick to rush. Battle had disillusioned, but it had not discouraged.

Was he blessed, or was he cursed? His skills were supremely suited to his time and task: his daredevil courage under fire, his genius in maneuvering a cannon, his ability to translate the idea of honor into deed. To sate his passion for adventure, to find the only possible proving ground for the strengths he felt inside himself, John Pelham needed a war. And that war had come. Few young men had ever fit their historical moment more exquisitely than John Pelham.

But Pelham's blessing—if war can ever be called a blessing—was born out of horror. On the field of First Bull Run, he discovered that he truly excelled at his chosen occupation. He had a gift: an aptitude for turning other young men into ruined heaps of blood and bone. Upright and modest, he had the looks and magnetism of what would, in a later time, be called a matinee idol. But he was to perform his wonders in a theater of pain.

In his report of the battle, Stonewall Jackson briefly praised Pelham and his men, noting how "nobly did the artillery maintain its position for hours against the enemy's advancing thousands."[43] Jeb Stuart had a richer reward to offer. An imaginative tactician, the cavalryman wondered: what might he achieve if he could unite his horsemen with a rapidly mobile unit of artillery, able to keep pace with the cavalry but armed with devastating firepower? Horse artillery had received careful study in Europe. However, although the United States Army had used mobile cannon effectively in the war with Mexico, its usefulness had never been fully explored in the Western Hemisphere. Eager to try the experiment, Stuart petitioned the War Department to create just such a mobile fighting force, and, on November 11, Secretary of War Judah P. Benjamin signed into existence the Stuart Horse Artillery.

Benjamin's order named no commander for the unit. Stuart knew that the Horse Artillery could succeed only if assigned to an officer of superior abilities. That its leader must be an excellent rider went without saying, but he must also keenly judge his horses: how much weight a particular animal could pull and how fast. He would have to be able to assess terrain and distance, and he would have to make these judgments while rapidly on the move. Louis Nolan had written that the task of artillery was "to deal with the most dangerous foe" at a given moment, and, indeed, Stuart's new force would routinely come under fearsome enemy fire.[44] Its captain would need both the courage to hold difficult ground and enough sense to abandon it when necessary. It was a combination of qualities that few soldiers came close to possessing.

By a turn of events that was not quite coincidence, two chief candidates for the post immediately emerged: Pelham and his friend Rosser. Stuart wrote to his wife, "Pelham wants it and he may get it, and next to Rosser probably no graduate would do better."[45] On November 29, Pelham received orders to report to Stuart. Although he still had not been officially named as the unit's commander, Pelham took assertive control of his de facto position.

After Bull Run, the war in Virginia slowed. Occasionally a relatively small clash took place, like the catastrophe at Ball's Bluff. But Bull Run had made both sides painfully aware that their armies lacked training, and the autumn and winter of 1861–62 were seasons of incessant drill. Pelham took advantage of the lull by returning on furlough to Alabama, where he recruited men for the Horse Artillery. When finally assembled, the unit comprised 153 men, culled from seven of the eleven seceded states, as well as Maryland. Among the most flamboyant contingents in

Pelham's command was an assortment of French Creoles from Louisiana, given to singing lusty choruses of "La Marseillaise" as they serviced their guns. The gunners had another favorite song. Contrasting sharply in mood with the work the singers performed, its buoyant lyrics went: "Ain't you—ain't you—happy? / Anchor by-and-by! / Stand the storm, it won't be long / Anchor by-and-by!"[46]

The horse artillerists were, for the most part, a band of roughs. A future memoirist rode with them: a Prussian-born soldier of fortune named Heros von Borcke had traveled to America to join the Confederate cause. An imposing six feet, four inches tall, the barrel-chested von Borcke became one of Stuart's closest confidants and served as his chief of staff. He was probably putting the matter gently when he wrote, "Many of these men [in the horse artillery] had not brought to the standard under which they served an immaculate reputation."[47] Winning their respect, to say nothing of the greater task of turning them into crack artillerists, called for more than mere resourcefulness.

When Pelham returned to camp in March 1862, the relentless drill began again, sometimes extending from dawn to sunset. It was no longer enough for Pelham's men to be efficient gunners; he also needed to mold them into exceptional horsemen, for in agility would lie the special power of the Horse Artillery. Pelham the West Point boxer knew that the ability to dodge a blow was as essential as the capacity to land one, and Pelham the dancer knew the value of grace and precision, even when applied to the ponderous machinery of war. He and Stuart wanted a corps of gunners who could position and reposition their weapons with utmost speed, both offering an all but unhittable target and convincing the enemy that the force attacking them was larger than it was.

As they honed their skills, Pelham's men learned not to challenge or anger him. They discovered that his gentle appearance masked a surprising firmness. Two men under Pelham's command slipped away to Richmond without leave. When they returned, the young lieutenant told them what he thought of them, and called to a subaltern, "Sergeant! Have these men walk up and down over there with their arms folded—keep 'em at it for a week." A color-bearer for the band of cannoneers recalled:

He didn't say much. He didn't need to. He would look at you and you felt his eyes going through you and all of a sudden you felt pretty mean [low or ignoble]. I saw the fellows stammer and blush before him; the biggest and the strongest just wilted when he called them into account.[48]

Firm discipline was only part of what solidified the Horse Artillery. Few adhesives bind more powerfully than the satisfaction of well-executed teamwork. As the gunnery crews grew in confidence and expertise, von Borcke marveled at their transformation: "They . . . established such an enviable character for daring and good conduct that the body was soon regarded as a corps d'elite by the whole army."[49]

In the Horse Artillery's first engagement, at the Battle of Williamsburg in early May, Pelham dashed from one cannon to the next, maintaining a rhythmic, coordinated fire that stunned and pummeled his antagonists. Several weeks later, at Gaines Mill, the third of the Seven Days Battles, he used a single cannon to battle two Union batteries to a draw. Although his crew was loading and firing almost as fast as men could do, Pelham was not content; as at Bull Run, he dismounted and helped to work the gun himself. His work at Gaines Mill earned him a meeting with Jackson, who, although he had relied on Pelham at Bull Run, had evidently never met him. Robert E. Lee had only recently taken command of the army, and Jackson was at the time the most idolized officer in Virginia. Pelham was ill prepared for the interview. His face and hands smeared with sweat, dirt, and grease, he looked more like a uniformed urchin than an officer. The warmth of Stuart's introduction, however, eased some of his embarrassment. "This is Captain Pelham, General," said the horseman. "He has fought with one gun that whole battalion on the hill, at point-blank range, for nearly an hour."[50] Jackson was known throughout the army as a man of few words. Now he used none at all. Silently, he extended his hand and grasped Pelham's soiled one. Pelham bowed, the crimson on his cheeks glowing faintly through the soot.

As the Seven Days Battles raged and the Horse Artillery saw continual action, Stuart's reports on their exploits waxed ever more rhapsodic. At Williamsburg, Stuart wrote, the Horse Artillery "was speaking to the enemy in thunder tones of defiance, its maiden effort on the field, thus filling its function of unexpected arrival with instantaneous execution and sustaining in gallant style the fortunes of the day."[51] At Gaines Mill, Pelham's conduct was "one of the most gallant and heroic feats of the war . . . the noble captain directing the fire himself with a coolness and intrepidity only equaled by his previous brilliant career."[52] His duel with a gunboat, the U.S.S. *Marblehead*, was equally "gallant" and unfaltering in its determination. When the week of fury was over, Stuart was again effusive: Pelham had displayed "such signal ability as an artillerist, such heroic example and devotion in danger, and indomitable energy under difficulties . . . that, reluctant as I am at the chance of losing such a valuable limb from the brigade, I feel bound to ask for his promotion, with the remark that . . . no field grade is too high for his merit and capacity."[53] Official military records are typically a good deal drier reading than this. But when the subject turned to Pelham, Stuart could not help himself.

After the Seven Days, Pelham again distinguished himself in a small but nasty engagement at Groveton, and again in the much larger one at Second Bull Run where, at the end of August, General Lee's forces outflanked and crushed the Federals. Refusing to let his momentum dissipate, Lee pressed into Maryland. On September 5, Stuart's cavalry forded the Potomac.

Two days later, Pelham marked his twenty-fourth birthday. To add some cheer to the celebration, one of his gunners filched an enormous pig from a nearby farm, which he proposed to roast in the captain's honor. Reminded that Lee had given strict orders not to steal from Maryland citizens, whose goodwill the army desperately needed to maintain, the hog thief shrugged. The pig had attacked him, he insisted, and he had dispatched the animal in self-defense.[54]

Although Southern sympathies ran strong in many Marylanders, the state government had remained loyal to the Union. Whereas Confederate armies had previously been active in Kentucky and Missouri—two other slaveholding states that had not seceded—Lee's army was now encroaching on enemy territory for the first time. Whether the Marylanders were friend or foe, Jeb Stuart was intent upon making himself very much at home. If much of Lee's army was ragged and barefoot, Stuart was determined that the mud and fleas and ugliness of war would not cling to him or his staff. Where Stuart went, music and romance must follow. On Pelham's birthday, as the cavalry made its quarters in the town of Urbana, Stuart and von Borcke happened upon a young ladies' academy that had lain vacant since the outbreak of the war. Von Borcke heard Stuart exclaim, "What a capital place for us to give a ball in honor of our arrival in Maryland."[55]

The next day, Stuart's staff transformed the neglected building into an impromptu ballroom, decorating the walls with roses and regimental flags, and procuring tallow candles to light the room. Seemingly from nowhere, Pelham produced a pair of tinted lanterns and suspended them over the entryway. Von Borcke advertised the fete throughout the area, while Stuart hired the regimental band of the Eighteenth Mississippi. Laughter and conversation hung lightly in the late-summer air as the guests arrived for Stuart's ball. Democratically, Stuart had invited the ordinary as well as the august, and they came by whatever means their pocketbooks allowed: on foot, in light rockaways, or in stately carriages, driven by enslaved coachmen. Inside the academy, those who wandered upstairs after sunset looked out on the handsome countryside, tinted blue by the moonlight. Von Borcke compared it with some elaborate stage extravaganza, and only the campfires dotting the fields and the neighing of horses kept him from thinking he had been transported to the world of the Arabian Nights. The band marched into the hall playing "Dixie." Taking their place in the ballroom, they struck up a polka, followed by a lively quadrille.

It was the kind of scene that a Southern cavalier might consider an earthly paradise. A kind of fairy-tale grace suffused the evening, and no one seemed to mind that its beauty was inseparable from class distinction—the necessity that all should go by "social rank and fortune"—or that it all was painted in a style of racial chiaroscuro—the fair white maidens being both borne to the soirée and visually offset by their African coachmen to whom the unconsciously ironic von Borcke ascribed "great dignity."[56] It seemed not to matter that it took place as hungry Confederate infantrymen, some of them wearing shoes they had been obliged to steal from Yankee corpses at Second Bull Run, foraged for apples and corn. It was a celebration of courtliness and aristocracy, of the gentle fineness of alabaster hands and faces neither scarred nor sullied by the inconveniences of labor. And in it, Stuart and his men, intent on pleasure only, saw not a trace of wrong.

Around eleven, an orderly, covered with dust, burst into the hall with a breathless message: some enemy troops had struck against the Rebel picket line. Even now they were bearing down on Stuart's camp. The sound of not-so-distant musket shots confirmed the bulletin. The music crashed to a halt. As parents collected their daughters, the officers rushed to their weapons and called for their horses. Minutes later, Pelham and Stuart were riding toward the action. The First North Carolina had already checked the Federal advance but were still hard at it. Despite the darkness, Pelham found a strong position for his guns and was soon firing rapidly into the enemy's ranks. Stuart ordered a general attack, and his men obeyed with rage and fury.[57] The Union force broke and fled, with the Tar Heels in pursuit. A little past midnight, all was again quiet, and Stuart and Pelham rode back to the ball. The band resumed, the more intrepid young ladies returned, and the dancing went on till morning. At dawn, a host of ambulances arrived, carrying wounded from the skirmish. The academy was the only suitable building in town to which to bring them, and the ballroom was repurposed again, this time as a hospital. The hall that had rung with music and gossip just an hour earlier now bore witness to the cries and groans of soldiers who had no further thought of dancing.

Stuart's ball came five days before Barton Mitchell's discovery of Lee's Lost Order, and just six days before McClellan attempted to smash through the Confederate forces that plugged the gaps at South Mountain. Lee had entrusted the defense of these gaps to five brigades under Major General Daniel Harvey Hill. He also sent Stuart's cavalry, including Pelham's artillery, to support Hill's infantry. Soon after dawn on September 14, as Hill rode the mountain's crest, he was dismayed to hear the rumbling of wheels and the shouts of Federal officers. Union troops were on the move and making their way toward the lightly defended gaps. Heavily outnumbered, his only possible reinforcements more than eight hours away, Hill cobbled together a defense as best he could and braced himself for disaster. Soon came the news from Fox's Gap that one of his brigades had been routed and its commander killed. "I do not remember," he later wrote, "ever to have experienced a feeling of greater loneliness. It seemed as though we were deserted by all the world."[58]

Pelham, also situated at Fox's Gap, responded less abjectly. His men opened with solid shot and aimed low, unleashing a fire that temporarily stymied the advancing Federals. They then fell back and switched their ammunition to canister shot. Judging by the fierceness of the cannonade and what little they could observe through the trees, the Federals falsely concluded that they had stumbled upon a large nest of Rebel firepower. The Confederates could not win this battle; all they could hope to gain was time. And time was what Pelham gave them. Rather than storm his position, which they could have carried with ease, the Federals chose to wait for reinforcements. For the ensuing two hours, his infantry seriously depleted, Hill was almost helpless. For those two hours, however, the Union force did not advance. During the lull, more Confederates arrived, not to turn the tide, but at least to prevent the wholesale breakthrough that might have crushed Lee's army. Weary from the ordeal, Pelham and the rest of Hill's tattered command fell back in good order. The next day, under irresistible pressure from Jackson, the Union troops at Harpers Ferry surrendered. Nevertheless, with the Federals now in control of South Mountain and moving freely through its gaps, Lee was forced to fall back and reunite his force. They would do so at the town of Sharpsburg, about a half hour's brisk walk from Antietam Creek.

The field at Antietam was not well suited to cavalry, and in this battle, the bloodiest single day of the war, Stuart's horsemen were to be essentially idle. But there was little idleness for Pelham. The previous day, he had arranged his cannons near the crest of Nicodemus Heights, about a mile and a half north of Sharpsburg and several hundred yards to the north and west of the West Woods. It was good ground, as both he and Stuart recognized, giving the Horse Artillery a sweeping command of the approaches to the woods. As the sun sank on the 16th of September, Pelham tested the range of his guns, beating back a tentative advance by men of the Pennsylvania Reserves. Satisfied with his preparations, but choosing to leave the final positioning of his force until later, the captain sought out a haystack behind the line and drifted off to sleep, only to be roused by a vigilant Stuart. "My dear fellow," the general warned, "don't you know that the cornfield at the foot of the hill is full of Yankees? And that you ought to have your guns in position now, for if you wait until daylight the hill will be swarming with bluecoats?"[59] Thus chastised, Pelham roused himself and ordered his men to roll his guns into place on the highest points of the ridge.

The opening scenes of the Battle of Antietam belonged to John Pelham. At five-thirty, a few minutes before daybreak, his guns opened fire on the still-sleeping or barely stirring men of the First Corps under Major General Joseph Hooker. Beneath the hail of canister and solid shot, Union gunners scrambled to return fire. The magnificent positioning of the Horse Artillery grew increasingly apparent as the sun rose higher. The Union advance against the Confederate left came in three waves, each represented by a different corps. The first to be engaged was, coincidentally, the First Corps, which marched from the north. From Nicodemus Heights, to the right of Hooker's force, came "an appalling confusion of shattering sound" as the air seemed filled with missiles.[60] Marching through the tumult and the roar, Hooker's men felt as if "an hundred cannon" had been trained upon them.[61] The sound was the least of it. In the blasts of shrapnel, men fell fast. Striking the very center of the Sixth Wisconsin—a regiment of the famed black-hatted Iron Brigade—a percussion shell from one of Pelham's guns killed two men and wounded eleven with a single blow.[62] As in the past, Pelham's tactics not only threatened the Federals' bodies but also played upon their minds. The heights from which he had been firing lay far to the leftward extremity of the Confederate position, creating the illusion that the line was longer and more densely manned than it actually was. Shaken by the Horse Artillery's fire, Hooker's corps had still worse times ahead: they soon collided head on with Jackson's men in the fields of a farm, fighting and dying by the hundreds on a patch of ground known ever since as "the Cornfield." A detachment of Hooker's men attacked the heights from which Pelham was firing, but all but a few of them were forced back. At least one, a mounted officer, reached Pelham's gun crew. Seconds later, however, the horseman was on the ground. One of Pelham's youngest gunners, a teenaged Creole named Jean Bacigalupo, had knocked him from his mount with a long wooden-handled sponge.[63]

Next into battle was the Union's Twelfth Corps. Led by Major General Joseph Mansfield, the corps hurried from the vicinity of the East Woods to support Hooker's corps. Mansfield fell mortally wounded early in the advance, and his men, mostly green recruits, marched without him into a barrage of lead and iron. The intensity of the fire convinced them, too, that they were facing a much larger force than was actually there. Even as the Twelfth Corps was being taken in by this deception, Pelham threw another maneuver into the mix. He shifted his ground southward, moving from Nicodemus Heights to the slightly lower but equally well-protected Hauser's Ridge. When the terrain there proved too much of a challenge for his gunners' horses, Pelham dismounted and labored alongside his men to wheel the heavy cannons into place. As at Bull Run and Gaines Mill, his enthusiasm would not permit him merely to give orders;

soon, he was working one of the guns himself. The move came at just the right moment; Mansfield's men had succeeded in linking up with the remnants of Hooker's corps, and after finally pushing the Confederates from the Cornfield, they were driving southward with little resistance toward the heart of the Confederate position. Pelham's guns, however, held fast. His move to Hauser's Ridge enabled him to sweep the entire terrain over which Mansfield's corps was required to cross. The forward press of the Federals slowed to a crawl. It was, as a recent analysis has concluded, "one of the most skillful and effective" maneuvers of the battle.[64] An early historian of the battle wrote that no single movement on either side more greatly influenced the battle than Pelham's deployment of his cannon. He compared the Horse Artillery's work as "a move on the chess board, though perhaps by a pawn, which baffled the most powerful pieces of the enemy."[65]

From this same position, less than two hours later, Pelham made Holmes and the Twentieth Massachusetts feel the sting of his artistry, and it was Pelham's gunners who were so accurate that the Massachusetts men thought they had measured the ground. The Twentieth had never seen such precise and heavy cannon fire.[66] Its effect on Holmes's regiment is best summarized by a single statement of the obvious. Appalled by the intensity of Pelham's fire, a recent recruit to the Twentieth exclaimed, "I declare. . . . I believe they know we are here and are doing it on purpose!"[67]

✫

IN PELHAM'S AND HOLMES'S PART OF the field, the battle was essentially over by midmorning; the two sides had fought to exhaustion. As the wounded Holmes was escorted to safety, Pelham and his batteries were at rest, with every reason to presume that their fighting was over for the day. Yet, as the afternoon lengthened, General Lee had one more hand to play. Still hoping for a breakthrough at Stuart's end of the line, he ordered the Horse Artillery to move forward from the heights and test the strength of the Federal force.

Thus far, Pelham had exquisitely balanced prudence with audacity. He now lurched toward recklessness. After moving obliquely forward and to his left, he ordered his men to ready their guns in a stand of trees within five hundred yards of the Pennsylvania Reserves under the ill-tempered and exacting George Gordon Meade, who would later lead the Union army at Gettysburg. Though the woods offered some protection, Pelham's gunners realized that they would need all the cover they could find. Attached to Meade's force were thirty rifled cannon, situated on high ground and ready to return fire at the slightest provocation. At Pelham's side was Captain William Poague, a Confederate battery commander whose guns Jackson had given to Pelham for the day. Poague felt anxious. No one had bothered to tell him the purpose of sending Pelham forward. Whatever the initial objective, Poague thought, Pelham was not treating his sortie as a mere reconnaissance mission. Instead, he had the air of a man looking for a scrap.

Poague leaped to a conclusion: Pelham had gone to his superiors and asked for the opportunity "to look up a fight." Poague was no coward, but he had rather firm convictions regarding suicide. He pleaded with Pelham to withdraw, only to be rebuffed by an unwelcome burst of laughter. "Oh, we must stir them up a little and then slip away," came the reply.[68] Moments later, Pelham gave the order to fire. Before his gunners could even get off a shot, however, the Federal cannons opened on them, spewing ordnance of almost every description into the woods. The Rebels answered back, but they could do little to resist the onslaught that their presence had invited. "Almost every second," a Confederate gunner recalled, "a bomb would burst over our heads and among us."[69] They held the position for less than fifteen minutes, long enough for Poague's battery to sustain a half-dozen casualties and lose more than a dozen horses. Pelham then maneuvered his guns out of range with a skill that even Poague, still bristling at the pointless bloodshed, felt compelled to admire. Though Poague later forgave Pelham for his evident rashness, Pelham's love of combat for its own sake had been disquieting.

Across the field from Pelham's guns had stood a thirteen-year-old boy. Charley King, the eldest son of a tailor from West Chester, Pennsylvania, had learned to play the drums before the war began. Though he was only twelve in April 1861, he had pleaded with his parents to let him join the army as a drummer boy, a request that they prudently denied. But as Company F of the Forty-Ninth Pennsylvania Infantry was forming, Charley became a regular visitor to the recruiting station. The officer in charge, Captain Benjamin Sweeney, observed Charley's zeal for the army and his unusual command of rhythm. At Charley's insistence, Sweeney paid a visit to the Kings. Drummer boys, he told Charley's mother and father, were kept to the rear during combat, and the threat to their safety was usually slight. Moreover, Sweeney promised to see personally to Charley's welfare. The Kings relented, and Charley proudly took his place in the Forty-Ninth Pennsylvania.

The regiment, part of Winfield Scott Hancock's brigade, saw only light action at Antietam. By the early afternoon, after the Forty-Ninth had been ordered to the northern end of the Union line, that sector of the field was mostly quiet. It was then, however, that Pelham, from his grove of trees, saw fit to "stir up" the enemy lines. One of the shells from Pelham's guns exploded in the ranks of the Forty-Ninth, sending a metal shard through the body of Charley King. As he fell, a soldier from a Maine regiment caught him, but the damage was done. Three days later, Charley died of his wound. Of the hundreds of thousands killed in combat during the war, he is thought to be the youngest.[70]

Pelham's cannonade at daybreak had begun the battle of Antietam. His ineffectual advance at day's end brought it to a close. His failure in the waning minutes of the day, though memorable to those who lived through it, was soon forgotten by the chain of command above him. Jackson, who had shaken Pelham's hand without comment less than three months before, was silent no longer: "He is a very remarkable young man. . . . I have never seen more skilful handling of guns. It is really extraordinary to find such nerve and genius in a mere boy. With a Pelham on each flank, I believe I could whip the world."[71] Stuart was again rhapsodic: "The gallant Pelham displayed all those noble qualities that have made him immortal."[72] The praise lavished on Pelham might have struck some as tempting fate. But in the fall of 1862, fate seemed firmly on John Pelham's side.

Chapter Three

———⌣⌣———

Burnside's Bridge and
a Broadway Bar

As John Pelham was raining iron on the Union right and Wendell Holmes was marching toward a catastrophe in the West Woods, a Brooklyn-born second lieutenant, assigned to Samuel Sturgis's division of Ambrose Burnside's IX Corps, was having an anxious morning. Gathered on the eastern bank of Antietam Creek, near the southern end of the Union line, the divisions on McClellan's left had been commanded to fall in around six o'clock and await further orders.[1] Further orders had not come. In the distance, these soldiers could hear the fight unfolding to the north of them. It seemed to be very heavy. Beyond that, they knew nothing. Among these uncomfortably idle units was the Fifty-First New York Volunteer Infantry. Three days earlier, the Fifty-First had lost its beloved division commander, Jesse Reno, killed by friendly fire at South Mountain. Now more anguish seemed imminent. Company D of the Fifty-First was under the command of the second lieutenant, who had nothing to do as the hours ticked by.

The lieutenant was a carpenter, a spare, compactly built man with a brow line straight as the level he used in his trade. The mustache he wore in his best-known photograph did little to relieve the impatient glare that he directed at the camera. Blunt and indelicate, he was just the sort of officer that the Harvard men of the Twentieth Massachusetts found hard to tolerate. At the same time, though, he was the kind of man a brigadier general could grow to love. The lieutenant had neither social standing nor pretense. He could write better than the average Civil War soldier, but his letters were peppered with basic errors in spelling. Simple words like "field," "strict," and "city" all rose up to trip him. He had become a lieutenant and would later be promoted to captain without taking the trouble to reliably spell either word.[2]

Though his parents came from the working class, they ambitiously named this son after George Washington. For all his lack of education, the lieutenant was a faithful correspondent. During his four years of service, he sent his mother and siblings at least sixty letters, which he typically signed "G. W." When these letters describe the Fifty-First in battle, they crackle with rich detail. But at almost no point do they disclose a trace of humor, a hint of philosophy, or any interest in language except as a tool for blunt narration. George's military superiors, however, were not concerned about his literary gifts. They cared whether the wiry carpenter could fight. And that he could assuredly do.

George was, to begin with, admirably eager; he had enlisted on April 19, 1861—only a week after the first shell exploded over Fort Sumter. He also thrived on harsh conditions in the field. While still a private, he proudly wrote home to his mother, "I am Just as well and hearty as can be. I have slept out in the rain and on the ground but have not felt a bit worse for it so I think I can go through like a book."[3]

He had proved equally resilient in battle. In the amphibious assault on Roanoke Island, North Carolina, in February 1862, he had slogged through a thick swamp where the mud and water came over the tops of his boots and the shrubbery had been all but impassable. As Confederate bullets knocked the bark off the trees around them, the Fifty-First advanced through an almost impenetrable thicket. Then they charged, seizing a Rebel battery and sending up "some tall shouting" to celebrate their conquest.[4] The following month, at New Bern, the regiment clashed with an entrenched detachment of Confederate infantry. George's part in that battle won him an officer's commission, over which he crowed to his mother, "I like the position first rate and am getting along very well indeed, and as the pay is *good*, I am glad both on my own acount and yours, *Mamy*."[5]

Amid the mud and marching, George found a host of simple pleasures. He befriended a munificent captain, a man from Buffalo named Morris Hazard, who treated his friends to "lots of eggs, fish Oysters, milk and everything else he can see. We have three . . . boys to cook and wait on us, but Cap can afford it so I dont care."[6] Several weeks after his promotion, as George was preparing for a dress parade, some of his men sent for him. Upon reaching their quarters, he found his entire company formed in a line and grinning broadly. One of them vanished into a tent and emerged with a splendid sword and sash, sword belt, and shoulder knots—all gifts from his admiring men.[7]

At Second Bull Run, at the end of August 1862, George's division fought desperately to prevent the capture of a supply train. Claiming to be Yankees, a Confederate unit lured his company into the open and fired a volley into them at close range. After a moment of shock and confusion, George rallied his command. Snatching a rifle from one of the wounded, he fired a few shots into the Rebels "on my own hook."[8]

By September 1862, battles and diseases had decimated the Fifty-First New York. George contracted a rash that broke out in blotches nearly as large as his hand. He also developed jaundice. Yet he remained for the most part imperturbable. Early in his service, he had been sickened by the sight of a troop of wounded men stumbling along a road, but, as with Wendell Holmes, the shock of such scenes faded. George wrote, "I expected sutch things so that it did not effect me mutch and after a while we would pass them lying in the bushes and think nothing of it."[9] He shrugged off his illnesses in like fashion and, not long before Antietam, wrote proudly that he "never was heartier or ruggeder in my life."[10] "Sogering," as he spelled it, suited George just fine.[11]

His letters to his mother spoke tersely of what he had done and said little about what he felt. It was of just such a man that Melville had written in *Moby-Dick*, "In him courage was not a sentiment; but a thing simply useful to him, and always at hand upon all mortally practical occasions."[12] To judge from his letters, the lieutenant was a hard, thick shell of a man who wrote with the intuition that the less he brought to the surface, the less there would be to hurt.

In that regard, George could not have differed more from one of his older brothers, a man who brought so much of his spirit to the outside and fused so much of it with the world that the difference between inside and outside seemed no longer to exist. That brother, whom George didn't much understand and seldom mentioned in his letters, had thus far taken no part in the war. When he did, however, George would be the reason. The lieutenant's full name was George Washington Whitman. His brother Walt wrote poetry.

In a conflict that famously pitted brother against brother, not all differences between siblings were political. George Whitman was far more at home amid the physical and the practical than in the realms of art and imagination. He could respond to Walt's literary inclinations only with head-scratching perplexity. In 1855, George examined the freshly published result of his brother's labors. The first edition of *Leaves of Grass* is a thin, green volume with gilt lettering. The title page does not include the author's name. On the facing page, however, Whitman is there, wearing a broad-brimmed hat, his head slightly atilt, and his shirt open at the neck. If Walt expected George to praise him, he was disappointed. George remembered, "I saw the book—didn't read it all—didn't think it worth reading—fingered it a little. Mother thought as I did—did not know what to make of it."[13] The same year, a more conventional book of verses came into George's hands: Longfellow's *Hiawatha*. George and his mother turned the pages of that book, too, and saw no particular difference, finding each no more nor less a muddle than the other. The closest thing to a compliment Mrs. Whitman could manage was, "If *Hiawatha* was poetry, perhaps Walt's [book] was."[14]

If George thought about Walt on the morning of September 17, 1862, it may have been to wonder whether they would ever see each other again. Around ten, the long-awaited orders finally came: Burnside's corps was to take a bridge that ran across Antietam Creek.[15]

Burnside had a love of aggressive tactics and a reputation for extreme bravery. Six months earlier, Whitman had fought under him at New Bern. Ever since, his admiration for the luxuriantly whiskered general had been fervent. After New Bern, George firmly believed that Burnside "was just about ready to walk through North Carolina," and would have done it if orders had not held him back.[16] George had not yet learned that Burnside's courage was his chief merit—an asset that made for an outstanding line officer. Sadly, the attributes required for a higher level of command—like a knack for organizing large troop movements, an eye for sizing up terrain, and simple prudence—thoroughly escaped him. Burnside's stolid, plodding bravery, unsupported by any other gifts, was a dubious asset.

The bridge Burnside had been ordered to take is an arched structure, made of pale stones. It broadens at either end but is, for nearly all of its length, less than five paces wide. A regiment trying to cross it would find it impossible to crowd more than four soldiers abreast. In such a formation, the troops would be exposed to merciless slaughter; any bullet fired at them would surely collide with human flesh. Worse still for the Federals, the Confederates who defended the bridge on its western side could not have asked for better ground. After a few yards of relatively flat space next to the creek, the ground rises abruptly to a height of about 110 feet. On the hill stands a stone fence, running parallel to the stream and lining a roadway. Looking across the stream, Brigadier General Cox, Burnside's second in command, saw that the turns in the roadway were studded with rifle pits and breastworks made of rails and stone. All these defenses, as well as the woods that covered the slope, were filled with the enemy's infantry and sharpshooters. In addition, the Rebels also had batteries of cannon, ready to enfilade the bridge and all its approaches.

The Confederate infantry that Cox observed, under the command of Georgian Robert Toombs, was literally within pistol range of their targets. In Cox's view, a direct assault across the span could produce only one outcome: a narrow file of men dashing into "a fire plowing through its length, the head of the column melting away as it advanced."[17] The remaining troops might be unable to move forward at all, because of the dead and dying choking the path. And that was if they even reached the bridge. The most natural approach to it was a road that followed the creek from the south for about three hundred paces. Any unit traveling that road would be exposed to withering fire from the same Confederates waiting to shower the bridge with bullets. The only factor weighing in favor of Burnside's corps was that the Confederate line beyond the bridge was thin. General Lee had been shunting troops from the right side of his line to support efforts farther north. If the Bluecoats could make it across the bridge, Toombs's Georgians would be no match for them. But Burnside had no way of knowing this.

According to respected historian Bruce Catton, there may have been a solution to Burnside's problem, if only he had had the eyes to see it. A slow, placid rivulet at any time, Antietam Creek in that fading summer was running so shallow that, as Catton argues, a soldier could have forded it without moistening his belt buckle.[18] Shelby Foote concurs: the shortest man in the corps could have crossed without wetting his armpits.[19] But Burnside, having been told specifically to take the bridge, had fixated upon it. Whereas the objective was securing the far side of the creek, Burnside read his orders literally: the attack must come across the bridge itself. The general also failed to grasp the need to move without delay.

McClellan was desperate to relieve the pressure on other parts of his formation. But Burnside's movements were glacial. The first force entrusted with the mission got lost, ended up about 350 yards above the bridge, and bogged down in irremediable confusion. The second group to go in, the Eleventh Connecticut, were cut to pieces by artillery and rifle fire; short of the bridge, they fell back, leaving more than a third of their number dead or wounded on the field.

It was now time for Sturgis's division to try its luck, though George Whitman's moment still had not yet come. Assigned to the division's second brigade, the Fifty-First was held in reserve in a protected valley while a trio of regiments from the first brigade—the Second Maryland and the Sixth and Ninth New Hampshire—were hustled forward. George later told his mother that these units lacked the will to go in and fight.[20] The casualty lists, however, tell a different story. The Marylanders went forward as commanded, but under the same intensity of fire that had beaten back the Eleventh Connecticut, they, too, lost a third of their force, advancing only to within 250 yards of the bridge. The Sixth New Hampshire was also badly shattered, and the Ninth managed scarcely better.

At last, the call came for two regiments that coincidentally shared a number: the Fifty-First Pennsylvania and Whitman's Fifty-First New York. As General Cox drily put it, the officers and men of these units "were made to feel the necessity of success."[21] The leader of the two regiments' brigade, Edward Ferrero, called out to the men: "It is General Burnside's especial request that the two 51st's take that bridge. Will you do it?"[22]

Ferrero's phrasing his command as a request was excessive courtesy: the men were in no position to decline. They were not in a place to impose conditions, either, but that didn't stop one cheeky Pennsylvania corporal. In response to some excessive merrymaking in the ranks, the Pennsylvanians' colonel had recently suspended his regiment's whiskey ration. Remembering this indignity, the corporal shouted, "Will you give us our whiskey, colonel, if we make it?" "Yes, by God!" replied Ferrero, to the delighted whoops of both regiments.[23] Whitman and his brothers in arms piled their knapsacks in the field where they were standing, filled their canteens from a nearby spring, and marched over the hill that had shielded them from enemy fire.

The officers of the two Fifty-Firsts were no fools. They readily saw that following the north-south road as their predecessors had done was a doomed gamble. Instead, they led their men west, charging down the hill and directly toward the bridge. Then, seeing that it made no sense for so many men to try the bridge at once, the two regiments made for the ground on either side of the base of the bridge. The Pennsylvanians sheltered themselves behind a stone wall to the north side while the New Yorkers huddled to the south of the span, taking some limited cover behind a rail fence. With evident relish and his usual respect for spelling, George Whitman gave his mother his version of the assault:

> As soon as we were ordered to forward we started on a double quick and gained the position [south of the bridge], although we lost quite a number of men in doing it. We were then ordered to halt and commence fireing, and the way we showered the lead across that creek was noboddys business. . . . [A]s soon as the men got steadily settled down to their work I took a rifle from one of the wounded men and went in, loading and fireing as fast as any one. After about half an hour the enemys fire began to slacken a little, and soon the order was given for our Brigade to charge.[24]

The Pennsylvanians were supposed to go first. But the blood of the New Yorkers was up, and they couldn't wait. With a hearty cry of "Remember Reno!" they rushed onto the bridge, the first New York men arriving an instant ahead of the Pennsylvanians.

From the east bank of the stream to the west is a distance of about forty-five paces. At a moderate run, a person can cross the bridge in fifteen seconds. The span rises at its center, so that the first half of the run across it is uphill. If terrain affects emotion, the brief climb surely sowed doubt in some of the minds of Whitman's company. But those doubts vanished in an instant. Seeing that they were outnumbered, Toombs's Confederates pulled back at once, fleeing through the woods and over the top of the hill. The pathway under the feet of Whitman's company leveled out and then started sloping downward. Amid the thundering noise and chaos, the entire prospect had changed. Every part of the Union line from which the bridge could be seen erupted into cheers. By heaven, they had made it.

It was about one o'clock. The effort to take the bridge had cost

McClellan three hours and 500 Union soldiers their lives.[25] The Fifty-First New York had more work to do before its day was over. After passing some more time in reserve, they were again ordered to the front and again engaged with the Rebels. After using up their own ammunition and all that they could snatch from the dead and wounded around them, they lay down and let the Confederates blaze away over their heads until other units came to relieve them. George and his men were ordered back to the bridge, where they sank to the ground exhausted and were given food and fresh ammunition. The latter served no immediate purpose; the end had come to their part in the Battle of Antietam.

Whitman's regiment had begun the day with about 335 able-bodied men. That evening, not counting "the sick and teamsters, Stragglers, and cowards," George guessed that the force was down to about 180 men.[26] The soldiers got their promised whiskey the next day, but George seemed more grateful just to "have a chance to go in camp and rest awhile."[27] Lieutenant Whitman put little stock in words like "hero." He saw up close the vanity of such designations, and he let them be. Nevertheless, he had done something remarkable that day, a deed that did not make him personally famous, but which, in its larger significance, would never be forgotten. Oddly, George was finding warfare more comfortable than his brother Walt, back home in Brooklyn, was finding the peace.

★

IN THE SAME SEASON WHEN GEORGE was taking delight in his new epaulets, sash, and sword, Walt had adopted a less honorific uniform. As he walked the bustling avenues of lower Manhattan in the fall of 1862, he seemed always to be dressed in a blue flannel coat and gray, baggy trousers. To these he added a broad felt hat and a woolen shirt "with a Byronic collar, low in the neck without a cravat."[28] Despite the simplicity of his clothing, he had the air of a man who thought a good deal about his appearance. Though he was only in his early forties, his hair, mustache, and luxuriant beard had already turned a shade of iron gray.[29] His small blue eyes beamed with good nature.[30] His large frame and richly tanned face and neck gave an impression of physical vigor, though the hand he extended in greeting was soft to the touch.[31] The previous seven years, during which he had published three editions of his poetry collection *Leaves of Grass*, each more ambitious and artistically daring than the last, had brought him some degree of notoriety. Still, when he made a new acquaintance, his name often struck no spark of recognition.

In the mammoth poem that he eventually christened "Song of Myself," Whitman calls himself "of Manhattan the son." But the filial bond was more one of affection than of actual geography. He had done most of his city living in Brooklyn—not yet a part of New York City—and his life had begun in the tiny hamlet of West Hills, Long Island, on May 31, 1819. With an author's love of multiple meanings, Whitman recorded in his memoir *Specimen Days* that "True Love" had brought his family to America; a ship by that name carried the brothers John and Zechariah Whitman to New England in the 1640s. Zechariah had a son, Joseph, who traveled south and raised a family in Huntington, Long Island.

In old age, Whitman fondly recalled the landmarks of his childhood: the sloping kitchen garden; the stately grove of black walnuts; the twenty-plus acres of apple orchard. Near that orchard, the Whitman family had kept a farmhouse of heavy timbers, where they roasted pigs and fowls in their great smoke-canopied kitchen. [32] Whitman's father, Walter Sr., had been born there in 1789, on the same day that Parisian revolutionaries stormed the Bastille. Nearby, in a long, rambling house with dark gray shingles, had lived a Dutch family, the Van Velsors. Their daughter Louisa, born in 1795, spent more time on horseback riding than schooling. She was to be the poet's mother. The union of Walter Sr. and Louisa produced three daughters and six sons who lived to adulthood.

Whitman's recollections of youth evince a boundless quality, a feeling beyond mere optimism or ordinary joy. Notably absent, especially from the poetry that recalls his early years, is a clear separation between himself and the world around him. He does not merely see sights and have adventures; he merges into them. A poem from 1855 alludes to this fluid relation with life:

> There was a child went forth every day,
> And the first object he looked upon and received with wonder or
>   pity or love or dread, that object he became,
> And that object became part of him for the day or a certain part of
>   the day.[33]

Not all the things that became a part of the youthful Whitman were benign. By the time Walt's father was born, the family's lands had diminished and its fortunes had dwindled. By the time Walt entered the world, they were in steep decline. When Walt was four, his father, incapable of halting the slide, moved the family to more affordable lodgings in working-class Brooklyn.

Walter Sr. excelled in carpentry and little else. Given to fits of depression and outbursts of fury, he inspired more fear than affection. Walt found it impossible to love him. So expansive in its early lines, the mood of "There Was a Child Went Forth" turns dark when the poem describes the subject's father:

The father, strong, self-sufficient, manly, mean, angered, unjust,
The blow, the quick loud word, the tight bargain, the crafty lure.[34]

The elder Whitman's flaws were only worsened by an addiction that, during Walt's childhood, amounted to an American epidemic. Its price driven down by a glut of corn production, whiskey sold for about twenty-five cents a gallon.[35] Masses of Americans in the 1820s were drinking almost as much as their bodies could metabolize.[36] The typical adult man was downing a half pint of liquor every day.[37] Walter Whitman, it seems, did his part to keep the average up. The vice took root in the Whitman family; Walt's older brother Jesse and younger brother Andrew both grew up to be alcoholics as well. In his only novel, *Franklin Evans, or, The Inebriate*, Whitman wrote bitterly of life with an alcoholic father: "[H]abits of drunkenness in the head of a family are like an evil influence—a great dark cloud, overhanging all, and spreading its gloom around every [aspect] of that family, and poisoning their peace."[38]

Whitman's feelings toward his mother were utterly different. Late in life, he scribbled on a scrap of paper, "No tenderer and more invariable tie was ever between mother and son than the love between her and W.W."[39] He said that he inherited many of her traits precisely—the shape of her face, her emotional makeup, her "full-bloodedness," even her voice.[40] He favored her in both senses of the word; he resembled her and took her side in family quarrels, which, one may presume, were sometimes fierce. Walt noticed early on the friction and distrust between his parents. When, in his fifties, he complained of America at large, "The men believe not in the women, nor the women in the men," he had his own experiences to draw upon.[41]

Though his mother could read and write a little, Walt considered her "illiterate in the formal sense."[42] Nevertheless, more than any other woman, Louisa Whitman was her son's muse, both by her moral example and by her strong skills as a storyteller and mimic. "The reality, the simplicity, the transparency" of her life, Whitman maintained, underlay "the main things in *Leaves of Grass*."[43] His poetry, he asserted, was "the flower of her temperament active in me."[44] Yet Louisa Whitman, as has already been noted, could not understand the poetry she helped inspire— a failure of comprehension that, despite their closeness, created a crucial gap between them. Whitman wrote with regret, "She and I—oh! we have been great chums: always next to each other: always: yet my dear mother never took [the creative] part of me in: she . . . felt sure I would accomplish wonderful things: but *Leaves of Grass*? Who could ever consider *Leaves of Grass* a wonderful thing: who? She would shake her head. God bless her! She never did."[45]

The Whitman children were, for the most part, shot through with congenital frailties. Jesse's alcoholism intertwined with some independent form of madness. His violent outbursts compelled Walt to have him committed to an asylum in 1864.[46] Scholars think Walt's younger sister Hannah may have been psychotic, her frantic, self-condemning letters suggesting irrational feelings of persecution.[47] Whitman's youngest brother, Eddy, suffered from a mental disability, one symptom of which was that at meal times, he would not stop eating until forcibly restrained. In the mid-1850s, Eddy and Walt shared an attic room—an arrangement whose effect on the poet's tranquility can only be guessed. Walt and George Whitman, along with their sister Mary and brother Jeff, escaped the family maladies and lived normal lives. On the whole, however, the Whitman home was a place of disquiet and sometimes horrifying disturbance. For Walt, it was also a place of isolation. In old age, he asked, "Who of my family has gone along with me? Who? Do you know? Not one of them. . . . [T]hey have not known me: they always missed my intentions. . . . [T]hey say that blood is thicker than water: but what does blood mean in a case like this?"[48]

At the same time, Whitman made few efforts to fit in with his parents or siblings, evading even the family's basic daily routines. George recollected, "If we had dinner at one, like as not he would come at three. . . . If he wished to go out he would go—go where he was of a mind to—and come back in his own time."[49] Working a little, loafing a little, writing a lot, Whitman showed an indifference to the worldly side of life that mystified George and the rest of the family. "He got offers of literary work," George reminisced, "good offers: and we thought he had chances to make money. Yet he would refuse to do anything except at his own notion."[50] The family tried awhile to point him in more practical directions, but eventually, they "gave him up."[51] Walt shrugged off the lack of support. "I have no more right," he said, "to expect things of my family than my family has to expect things of me . . . we are not alike: that's the part and the whole of it."[52] In the early 1850s, Whitman wrote occasional pieces for New York and Brooklyn newspapers but spent more time doing carpentry and building houses like his father. As he shaped boards and hammered nails, he was shaping his thought as well. In spare moments, he worked quietly on the dozen poems that would fill the first edition of *Leaves of Grass*.

Meanwhile, he opened himself to every kind of influence. He made friends with artists who frequented the studio of his sculptor friend Henry Kirke Brown, and their idealism impressed him. He wrote, "I think of few heroic actions which cannot be traced to the artistical impulse. He who does great deeds, does them from his sensitiveness to moral beauty."[53] He also found pleasure in riding the omnibuses of Broadway. Typically, he sat on top, next to the drivers, whom he considered "a strange, natural, quick-eyed and wondrous race."[54] When, as often happened, his driver friends were injured or fell ill, Whitman got into the habit of visiting them in the hospital.[55] The strength and confidence of the drivers raised his spirits, giving more inspiration than roomfuls of scholars could provide. He later wrote, "I suppose the critics will laugh heartily, but the influence of those Broadway omnibus jaunts and drivers . . . undoubtedly enter'd into the gestation of Leaves of Grass."[56] Whitman felt that booklearning alone, without fresh air and honest work to give it sinew, stood in the way of true artistic expression. "[The] poets of the earth," he observed, "never come from the depths of the schools."[57] A man, he thought, should also learn to run, leap, swim, wrestle, fight, and take good aim.[58]

Nevertheless, he devoured books and journals in abundance. He read British literary magazines and marked passages that helped to refine his worldview. In the *Edinburgh Review*, he underscored the line "a first-rate poem . . . is the off-spring and exponent of the poet's total being."[59] In one article, he found a line that might have served as personal manifesto: "As a thousand rivulets are blended in one broad river, so the countless instincts, energies, and faculties, as well as associations, traditions, and other social influences which constitute national life, are reconciled in him whom future ages are to recognize as the poet of the nation."[60]

Essential to Whitman's thinking was Lucretius's poem *On the Nature of Things*, a work that, for him, cast essential light on the problem of mortality. Writing in the first century B.C.E., Lucretius advanced a new idea that modern science takes for granted: that the physical world is composed of atoms. Furthermore, he dared to suggest that the mind itself was only a mortal substance, and consciousness a purely physical process. Our thoughts and feelings, the very essence of what we call spirit, result merely from the intricate motions of "exquisitely small seminal-atoms."[61] At death, the atomic dance comes to an end, "substance of the mind and soul . . . depart[s]," and consciousness vanishes, "dissolved, as smoke, into the sublime air of heaven."[62] Yet, Lucretius insisted, this mortality was no cause for sadness. Since death meant a complete end to consciousness, no self would remain to feel regret: no pain, no grieving. Moreover, the atoms were indestructible; only their combinations were transient and mortal. Thus people live eternally after death—just not in a self-aware, integrated state. Indeed, Lucretius neatly reversed the religious belief that matter perishes and the soul survives. Matter, instead, was the deathless thing, its components combining and recombining into new wonders until the end of time.

The inspiration of a more contemporary mind also helped drive *Leaves of Grass* toward its realization. "My ideas were simmering and simmering," Whitman remembered, "and Emerson brought them to a boil."[63] Emerson had also kindled the thought of Wendell Holmes at Harvard, but his influence on Whitman started sooner and left deeper traces. Whitman first heard Emerson lecture in 1842, three days before Wendell's first birthday. Emerson's subject was "Nature and the Powers of the Poet." Whitman reviewed the event for the *New York Aurora*, calling it "one of the richest and most beautiful compositions, both for manner and style, we have ever heard anywhere, at any time."[64]

While Emerson's remarks from that evening do not survive, it stands to

reason that at least some of his arguments resurfaced in "The Poet," published two years later. In that essay, Emerson called human beings "children of the fire," a species of "divinity transmuted."[65] Poets stood among
them as "liberating gods," giving words to the beauties and ecstasies that
all men and women could see and feel but could not express, and drawing
us on with both love and terror.[66] Yet, Emerson confessed, "I look in vain
for the poet whom I describe. . . . We have yet had no genius in America,
with tyrannous eye, which knew the value of our incomparable materials,
and saw, in the barbarism and materialism of the times [a] carnival of
the . . . gods." In its boisterous, teeming diversity, America was already an
inchoate poem, the writing of which "will not wait long for metres."[67] For
Whitman, seeking the literary means to move a nation, Emerson's words
offered a clear challenge. The youthful Wendell Holmes used Emerson as
a model for his prose and critical approach. Whitman went further; as he
crafted his new and unprecedented verse, he daily responded to Emerson's
admonition, "The only sin is limitation." With "the wildest and most exuberant joy," Whitman set forth to write a poem "incarnating the mind."[68]

By coincidence, or perhaps more than coincidence, Whitman composed the first *Leaves of Grass*, published in 1855, as his father, his health
precarious since the late 1840s, entered his final decline. The book of
poems appeared in the first week of July; Walter Sr. passed away on July
11. The death of the father coincided almost perfectly with the birth of
his son's second self.

Extravagant though it may sound, to speak of *Leaves of Grass* as the poet's
second incarnation accurately captures the author's intentions. Whitman,
to use his own words, desired "to articulate and faithfully express in literary or poetic form, and uncompromisingly, my own physical, emotional,
moral, intellectual, and æsthetic Personality."[69] Had his ambition stopped
there, his work might be dismissed as a mere flight of egotism. Yet, paradoxically, his book evades the trap of narcissism because his understanding of
self extended beyond the limits of ordinary identity. He conceived himself
as a "kosmos," containing multitudes, a representative man who, through
sympathy and imagination, extended his consciousness to embrace the life
of his nation. In more than one sense, *Leaves of Grass* was Whitman's effort
to comprehend America: not merely to understand it, but in an almost geo-
metric sense to circumscribe and to hold it within himself—to comprise and
contain the soul of the teeming country within his own multifaceted spirit.

He aimed, as he would eventually put it, "Not to exclude or demarcate, or pick out evils from their formidable masses . . . but to add, fuse, complete, extend—and celebrate the immortal and the good."[70]

Whitman's urge to embrace and comprehend was both political and spiritual, both patriotic and pantheistic. He had no interest in reprising "the stock ornamentation . . . of Old-World songs." He wanted instead to sing and to celebrate "the broadest average of humanity and its identities . . . especially in each of their countless examples and practical occupations in the United States today."[71] A single section of his most ambitious poem, "Song of Myself," offers verbal snapshots of a presidential cabinet meeting; a harpooner in a whale-boat; an assemblage of dancers in a ballroom; a factory girl at her sewing machine; a gang of slaves on a sugar plantation; a "pure contralto"; a shoemaker; a madman; a prostitute; a peddler; a boy lying awake, listening to the rain—and more than four dozen other sketches besides. But Whitman is not content to delineate his countrymen and women; he wants to become them. After seeming to list as many Americans and their daily activities as he can bring to mind, he wrote regarding every person he had mentioned:

> And these tend inward to me, And I tend outward to them,
> And such as it is to be of these more or less I am,
> And of these one and all I weave the song of myself.[72]

Whitman took his poetics of inclusiveness further still. His reading of Lucretius had guided him toward the conclusion that the whole of creation shared not only the same atoms, but an identical spirit. "The soul," he observed in his notebook, " . . . transmutes itself into all matter—into rocks, and can live the life of a rock—into the sea, and can feel itself in the sea . . . into an animal, and feel itself a horse, a fish, or a bird." The vocation of the poet, Whitman insisted, was to create and encourage these cosmic sympathies: to translate inscrutable mysteries to the person whom they surround, but who knows them not. These secrets, Whitman knew, were both large and small; he meant not only to give his readers the rumble and crash of thunder, but also the modest crawl of an ant and the whistle of a quail. He must, he wrote, "bring all the art and science of the world, and baffle and humble it with one spear of grass."[73]

In "Song of Myself," Whitman speculates that a blade of grass may be "the beautiful uncut hair of graves."[74] But even though the grass is the sign of decaying corpses, it is an emblem, not of death, but of the renewal and universality of life; the Lucretian atoms have already recombined to form a new and vital force: "And what do you think has become of the women and children? / They are alive and well somewhere; / The smallest sprout shows there is really no death."[75] Whitman knows that this meek resurrection waits for him as well; near the end of the poem, he antici-pates a tender reunion with the grass, and through it, a rendezvous with the reader: "I bequeath myself to the dirt to grow from the grass I love, / If you want me again look for me under your bootsoles."[76]

Yet, despite the eagerness with which Whitman's poetry embraced the world, a reader can sense a curious absence of deep human connec-tion. While the poet proclaimed his love of humankind, his poems rarely entered into the thoughts or feelings of another person. It was all Walt, all the time. Rich and exuberant in their declarations of Whitman's own spirit, his verses addressed others chiefly as externalities. The fellow men and women whom the poet professed to adore, he seldom took the steps to understand. His adorations were more sensuous than sensitive.

From 1855 to 1860, Whitman pursued his hoped-for identity as America's poet with unbridled zeal. The second edition of *Leaves of Grass*, published in 1856, added twenty poems to the original dozen. In 1860, a third edition ran to 456 pages and featured 146 new poems—the largest single expansion of the volume that the poet ever undertook. With this new collection, Whitman appeared to reach a turning point. Whereas he had been obliged to self-publish the 1855 and 1856 editions, the third finally found a publisher: the Boston house of Thayer and Eldridge.

But, in his creative exuberance, Whitman was edging toward trouble. Even in the first edition, the frankness with which he had written about sexual matters had raised eyebrows. When Thoreau read the 1856 copy that the poet had given him in person, the sensuality of the verses had shaken him. "It is as if the beasts spoke," the Concord naturalist wrote, and he feared that few "men & women were so pure that they could read [these poems] without harm."[77] When Whitman came to Boston to consult with his publishers, Emerson was forced to withdraw an invitation to dine with the Saturday Club; three of the most prominent members—Longfellow, James Russell Lowell, and, notably, Oliver Wendell Holmes Sr.—had advised him that they had no wish to meet the Brooklyn ruffian.[78]

In the 1860 volume, Whitman's daring reached new heights. The book included two new clusters of poems, "Enfans d'Adam" and "Calamus," whose eroticism pushed hard against the limits of propriety. Fearing the worst, Emerson pleaded with Whitman not to publish the "Enfans" cycle. The poet, however, was not dissuaded, and his readers soon found themselves reading what seemed to some of them like pornography:

> From my own voice resonant, singing the phallus,
> Singing the song of procreation
> Singing the need of superb children and therein superb grown
> people,
> Singing the muscular urge and the blending . . .
> The female form approaching, I pensive, love-flesh tremulous
> aching[79]

At first, the 1860 *Leaves* enjoyed a brisk sale, but a fierce backlash was soon in coming. A Georgia critic called the collection "disgusting and abominable" and recommended the use of disinfectants.[80] In Massachusetts, the *Springfield Daily Republican* wrote that no man could read it aloud "to a decent assembly."[81] A letter to New York's *Saturday Press*, a paper whose editor was one of Whitman's strongest supporters, concluded by suggesting that the author commit suicide.[82]

Whitman the poet fell virtually silent, and he remained so for more than two and a half years. Only a scattering of letters exists from this period. Whitman's withdrawal from view from the spring of 1860 to December 1862 was so complete that this period has long been referred to as his lost years—a curiously timed interlude for a man seemingly near the height of his creative powers.[83] But the reception of the 1860 *Leaves* had stung Whitman badly, as did the realization that his beloved America was coming apart.

Only months after the 1860 *Leaves of Grass* appeared, South Carolina seceded. On the thirteenth of April 1861, toward midnight, Whitman was strolling down Broadway from Fourteenth Street after attending a performance of Verdi's *Un ballo in maschera*, which had had its New World premiere in New York two months earlier. A crowd of newsboys came shouting up the street, rushing from side to side with stacks of extras. Whitman bought one and crossed over to a hotel where a crowd was gathering. The news had struck everyone speechless: Rebel batteries had fired on Fort Sumter in Charleston Harbor, and the country was at war with itself. Whitman was devastated. Five years earlier, he had proclaimed, "The United States themselves are essentially the greatest poem." That poem, his beloved "teeming nation of nations," was ripped to shreds.[84] Forty-one years old and ill suited for a fight, he could think of nothing he could do to restore what had been lost. In the ensuing months, as his brother George was leading charges, Walt retreated. One particular retreat awaited him time and time again.

❉

WHITMAN'S SECOND HOME IN THE LATE 1850s and early '60s lay a ferry ride and a long walk away from his Brooklyn home. It was Pfaff's, a restaurant and drinking establishment just north of Bleecker Street on Broadway, owned and operated by the Swiss-German immigrant Charles Ignatius Pfaff, a connoisseur of beers and a brewer of superior coffee. Whitman thought it "a pleasant place to go in the evening after taking a bath and finishing the work of the day," and he wound up there almost every night.[85] By 1860 Pfaff's had acquired a unique reputation as a gathering place for artists, writers, and radicals of all descriptions. Pfaff's was situated underground, in the cellar below the much tonier and more respectable Coleman House Hotel. Pfaff's patrons did not enter the cellar through the hotel lobby; instead, they ingloriously went down a steep, narrow flight of stairs, through a hatchway in the sidewalk.[86]

Well before reaching the bottom, one encountered clouds of tobacco smoke, as the aromas of the pipes and cigars freely mingled with the smells of stale beer and frying sausages. Cellars like Pfaff's were common on Broadway at the time. Typically they featured white-painted walls, a bar, an oyster stand, and a number of booths. Pfaff's was not so tidy of a venue. The walls were dingier than elsewhere on the avenue, and there were tables instead of stalls.[87] The long, narrow restaurant extended far out below the sidewalk of Broadway. Through thick pieces of bull's-eye glass, embedded in the pavement, a tiny amount of natural light filtered into the tavern. An inadequate number of gas lamps only partly dispelled the darkness, giving a slightly weird, spectral quality to the faces that thronged the tables. The ceiling was low and vaulted. Sawdust covered the floor. Richard Henry Stoddard, a minor poet, seemed to feel somewhat tarred even by a casual association with the restaurant; despite being able to describe it minutely thirty years later, he insisted that he "never went inside the place."[88] Evidently, not everyone came to Pfaff's for the atmosphere.

Still, for a certain kind of person, the human attractions were irresistible. On a typical night, one might first observe the scintillating Ada Clare, the black-sheep daughter of a Charleston cotton magnate. Spontaneous and daring, Clare was said to be raising a love child fathered by the composer Louis Moreau Gottschalk—a rumor she chose not to discourage. Nearby, one might notice the pale form of Fitz Hugh Ludlow, scapegrace son of a Hudson Valley preacher. A seeker of chemically induced thrills, Ludlow had scored a succès de scandale by publishing *The Hasheesh Eater*, his memoir of encounters with an interesting array of intoxicants. The comic writer Artemus Ward often stopped in for a glass and seldom stopped at one. Heads turned when Adah Isaacs Menken slunk down the stairs. A sultry beauty who incessantly embroidered her life story, Menken was, depending on her mood, a scion of Spanish royalty, the adopted daughter of Sam Houston, or a linguistic prodigy who had translated *The Iliad* into French at age twelve. Deficient in talent but long on nerve, she was crafting a notorious stage career by performing in revealing costumes and flesh-colored body stockings. These and others came to Pfaff's to drink, trade bons mots, and laugh their cares away.

The acknowledged lord of Pfaff's bohemians was Henry Clapp Jr., the founding editor of the *Saturday Press*: a jaunty, often satirical literary sheet that tried to make up in cleverness and bravado what it perpetually lacked in subscribers. In the '40s, Clapp had gone to Paris to translate the writings of the famous socialist Charles Fourier. There he had fallen in love with the city's carefree, artistic café culture. The nightly salon at Pfaff's was Clapp's attempt to transplant that lifestyle to New York. Of all the Pfaffians, none mattered more to Whitman. He later said, "It is essential . . . to know about Henry Clapp if you want to know about me: . . . he gave me more than one lift: contended for me against odds."[89] Clapp embraced Whitman as a worthy cause, publishing almost a dozen of his poems in the *Saturday Press*, as well as several generous reviews of *Leaves of Grass*. Clapp was a beer-soaked version of Dr. Holmes's Autocrat, routinely occupying the head of the long table at Pfaff's, sharpening his wit on every subject from Wall Street, which he rechristened "Caterwaul Street" and shamed for its "lie-abilities," to sexism in the press: he later opined that the *Nation*, which excluded female contributors from its pages, would be better known as the "Stag-Nation."[90]

Whitman sought out no place of honor at Pfaff's. A friend remembered him at a table near the privy, "eat[ing] sweetbreads and drink[ing] coffee, and listen[ing] to the intolerable wit of the crack-brains."[91] It would have been remarkable if, during these long, smoky evenings, Whitman always managed to keep his mind on the conversation. A man who has written an unsuccessful book has much to ponder. As he thought about the nation of nations he had so extravagantly lauded in *Leaves of Grass*, he knew that its actual inner life did not live up to his rich imaginings. Sunk in vain appearances and moneygrubbing, the country was not yet dead to higher impulses. But it was, Whitman thought, "threatened with a certain ossification of the spirit" and was being increasing borne away from its founding ideals by a "current . . . broadly materialistic and infidel." Worse, this faithlessness was of a kind that one could practice almost unconsciously, even as one preserved the outer forms of a good and pious life. This porcine self-satisfaction, he wrote, "proceeds complacently onward and abounds in churches." But all the gluttonous consuming had bred no happiness; in fact, the republic had grown sad and numb. The poet lamented, "I do not believe the people of these days are happy. The public countenance lacks its bloom of love and its freshness of faith—For want of these, it is cadaverous as a corpse."[92]

Whitman was scarcely more optimistic when he turned his gaze back upon himself. In his poems, Whitman claimed to be the cosmos whose soul subsumed a nation. More privately, though, he confessed, "Every thing I have done seems to me blank and suspicious.—I doubt whether my greatest thoughts, as I had supposed them, are not shallow—and people will most likely laugh at me.—My pride is impotent, my love gets no response. . . . I am filled with restlessness.—I am incomplete."[93] Even more than that of most poets, Whitman's poetic project demanded deep sincerity and confidence; his claims were so extravagant that one could make them only from a standpoint of purest belief. That belief was now shaken.

Ruminating thus, the graying man in the blue flannel coat sat apart. As much as he loved the other frequenters of the cellar, he was never completely like them. Whitman was the only one of Pfaff's regulars whom no one could ever recall getting drunk. On those nights when he washed down his beefsteak or sweetbreads with lager instead of coffee, a single pint sufficed him. Whoever expected him to join heartily in the deft satires and verbal joustings of the place came away disappointed. Whitman's mental habits were slow, deliberate, and in no way adapted for clever repartee. One evening, on Clapp's birthday, the Pfaffians raised their glasses to their chief and called on Whitman to offer the toast. In a moment, anticipation gave way to awkwardness, as the poet could muster only a wan, if well-intentioned, "That's the feller." Whitman told his literary executor Horace Traubel decades later, "My own greatest pleasure at Pfaff's was to look on— to see, talk little, absorb. I never was a great discusser, anyway,—never. I was much better satisfied to listen to a fight than take part in it."[94]

Whitman felt the downward tug of Pfaff's, and he sensed the hollowness behind its festive air. The patrons of Pfaff's came not to do, but to drink and to dream, and Whitman's childhood reminded him that the glasses they raised to one another's health contained a slow, destructive poison. Clapp, their leader, was to undergo several stints in asylums before dying, bankrupt and forgotten, in 1875. Whitman mourned him, saying, "Drink—drink—took him down, down."[95] In 1862, Whitman wrote two poems about the trap into which he was daily descending. The first, which he neither completed nor published, contained lines that rendered the bar as a metaphoric tomb:

> —The vault at Pfaffs where the drinkers and laughers meet to
> eat and drink and carouse,
> While on the walk immediately overhead pass the myriad feet of
> Broadway
> As the dead in their graves are underfoot hidden
> And the living pass over them, recking not of them,
> Laugh on laughers! Drink on drinkers! . . .
> Oft I doubt your reality[96]

Whitman broke off the poem in mid-sentence. He somehow could not bring himself to fully admit that his beloved saloon so strongly resembled a black and lifeless charnel house. He was in the company of phantoms— the drinkers and laughers whose carefree descent into Pfaff's was only a prelude to a farther fall.

The second poem appeared in the 1865 edition of *Leaves of Grass*, the first to be published since 1860. Though less explicitly about his nights in the saloon, it also voiced the poet's fear of losing his bearings and being swallowed up by inertia. It begins: "Quicksand years that whirl me I know not whither, / Your schemes, politics, fail, lines give way, substances mock and elude me." The lyric concludes with a pair of questions: "Out of politics, triumphs, battles, life, what at last finally remains? / When shows break up what but One's-Self is sure?"[97] In the bleary half-light of Pfaff's, where shows were always breaking up, oneself was not so very sure at all. The line between mere decadence and utter decay could feel distressingly thin.

Whatever its faults, Pfaff's offered Whitman the reassurance of friends. But even there, political tensions could sour the mood. Seeing no more active role for himself in the fight to preserve the country, Whitman wrote fervid patriotic poems, including "Beat! Beat! Drums!" The poem ran in *Harper's Weekly* on September 28, 1861—just ten days after George Whitman enlisted with the Fifty-First New York. One evening, Whitman brought to Pfaff's a draft of "Beat! Beat! Drums!" to entertain his friends. They listened as he read the following lines:

Beat! beat! drums! Blow! bugles! blow!
Make no parley—stop for no expostulation;
Mind not the timid—mind not the weeper or prayer;
Mind not the old man beseeching the young man;
Let not the child's voice be heard, nor the mother's entreaties.
    Recruit! recruit![98]

Not everyone in the bar was impressed by Whitman's call to arms. The war was almost half a year old, and, with no significant victories to point to, many in the North had begun to wonder whether the war was worth fighting. After Whitman's voice had died away, the Pfaffians took up this argument, and a squabble ensued until one of them, a minor poet named George Arnold, quieted them. Standing and raising his wine glass, he looked defiantly at Whitman and exclaimed, "Success to the Southern Arms!" Goaded, Whitman spat out a hotly worded retort.

Accounts differ as to what happened next. According to a Boston newspaper editor who happened to be on hand, Arnold "reached across the table . . . and seized Whitman by the hair," but that was as far as the violence went. Another witness, Jay Goldsmith, however, recalled a wilder scene. He remembered that after Whitman warned Arnold "to be more guarded in his sentiments," Arnold "fired up more and more." Exasperated, Whitman aimed a fist at Arnold's ear. The secessionist reached about for the nearest weapon, a bottle of red wine, and swung it into Whitman's forehead. At the same moment, Pfaff was on his feet, blustering in broken English, "Oh! mine gots, mens, what's you do for dis?" As the two men scuffled, coffee, rum, and wine flowed together from spilled cups and glasses, dousing the knees of several patrons. Clapp grabbed at Arnold's coattail and had his pipe broken for his pains. Another man, Ned Wilkins, had his wind knocked out while trying to restrain the brawny Whitman by the arm. Then, almost as quickly as it had begun, the row subsided. Both a bit embarrassed, the two men shook hands "and wondered much that they were so foolish."[99]

Whitman had his own recollection of the unpleasantness. He dismissed Goldsmith's tale as the "silliest compound of nonsense" he had ever heard and swore that all that happened was this: when Arnold stood up and proposed his toast, Whitman reacted by breaking out "into a fierce and indignant speech, and left the place, never to return, going on shortly afterwards to the seat of war."[100]

Certainly this was how Whitman preferred to remember the aftermath of his set-to with Arnold. He found it pleasant to convince himself that, with his patriotism brought to a boil by Arnold's jibes, he had instantly shed his passivity and set forth to take a manly, respectable part in the national struggle. But the facts were very much otherwise. Far from never paying another visit to Pfaff's, Whitman retraced his steps back to the cave countless times for the next year or more. He was still taking meals at Pfaff's in September 1862, when he is known to have dined there with Fred Gray, a close friend who had been at Antietam. Another friend, John Burroughs, wrote that in the fall of 1862, Whitman was at Pfaff's "almost every night."[101]

After the clash with Arnold, the stream of stories regarding Whitman again runs virtually dry. He was still writing very little, doing nothing of consequence for months on end. Near the beginning of December 1862, he sent a letter to his brother George. The letter is lost, though it delighted George so much that he read it over three or four times.[102] But there were few delights for Walt. He wandered through Brooklyn and rode the omnibuses up and down Broadway, inevitably returning for more doses of witty but unproductive gab at Pfaff's, always Pfaff's. To all appearances, the poet's "quicksand years" still had a long course to run.

Chapter Four

〜

An Army in Crisis

As the battle of Antietam drew toward its close, a lone Union officer was observed wandering the battlefield. He had with him, impaled upon his sword, an immense quantity of salt pork, a burden that had him in a dreadful quandary. He explained to another man that the pork had been dispensed as the ration for his company. He did not know what to do with it because all the other men in his company had been killed.[1] It is not known what answer the soldier received. He was, presumably, left to consume what he could of the salt pork, the only recompense he had received for his loss of comrades and innocence.

Two nights later, General Lee, realizing that his battered army could likely not withstand another clash, took advantage of the darkness and pulled his army back across the Potomac. Instead of sending his divisions in pursuit of Lee, McClellan busied his army with the grim task of burying the dead from both sides. He estimated that his men laid twenty-seven hundred Confederates in the long trenches they had hastily dug for the purpose, though that number seems inflated.[2] McClellan overestimated the strength of the Rebels even when they were dead.

For some, the losses were simply too great for their minds to withstand. As the soldiers on burial detail began their work, Colonel Lee of Holmes's regiment was distraught. The pressures of command had played a vicious game with his nerves, and he had been drinking more than an occasional glass of whiskey to ease the burden. Until Antietam, he had managed to hang on. As he watched his command being cut to pieces in the West Woods, however, his grip shook loose. It was Ball's Bluff all over again, but worse. After the sun went down on the bloodiest day of the war, Colonel Lee issued no orders. To the alarm of a fellow officer, "He wouldn't do anything." Lee decided that a drink would help. After that drink came others. The next morning, he mounted his horse and simply rode away. He didn't bother to request a formal leave, and he left no word as to his destination. He had none.

Four weeks passed without a word. Then, Captain George Macy, another officer of the regiment, caught sight of the colonel about ten miles from camp. He had not a penny in his pockets and had kept alive by eating God knows what. He had had no change of clothes, and, for much of the time, he had been racked by "this horrible diarrhea," with which his uniform pants were now encrusted. He was making his way toward a stable, where he meant to spend the night. To Macy he looked like "a little child wandering away from home." Macy gave the colonel a drink and found a house that would take him in. He saw to the cleaning of the mess from Lee's underclothes and put him to bed naked. Once the colonel's mind was somewhat settled, Macy brought him back to the regiment. Lee still looked shaken, his face an unnatural shade of red. The men presumed "he had been on an awful spree."[3] Soon after Lee's return, a rumor reached him that an aide to Willis Gorman, a general whose men had fought alongside the Twentieth Massachusetts in the West Woods, had accused Lee's men of cowardice. Enraged, Lee buckled on his sword and rode off to challenge Gorman to a fight. Gorman talked him down, but Lee's outburst fueled the rising suspicion that he was no longer fit for command.[4] As quietly as possible, Colonel Lee was sent back to Massachusetts on medical leave. A future for him in the army was hard to imagine.

*

ON THE DAY FOLLOWING THE BATTLE, after nightfall, the first news of Wendell Holmes's wounding found its way to his parents. Dr. and Mrs. Holmes were in bed when they were awakened; a boy was at the front door, holding a telegram:

Hagerstown 17th
To Oliver Wendell Holmes:
Capt. Holmes wounded shot through the neck thought not
mortal at Keedysville
William G. LeDuc[5]

At once, the elder Holmes started thinking like a doctor. Through his mind flowed a litany of the vital tissues that the bullet might have hit, but apparently had missed: "Wind-pipe, food-pipe, carotid, jugular, half a dozen smaller, but still formidable vessels, a great braid of nerves, each as big as a lamp-wick, spinal cord."[6] Significant damage to any of these would have brought more or less immediate death. If the bullet had not killed at once, Holmes knew, it would very likely not kill at all. At the same time, the poet in him started playing word games: which phrasing would have been more dire, "thought not mortal" or "not thought mortal"?[7] For a moment, his son's life seemed to teeter on a nicety of syntax. Then a mundane concern snatched him back into the moment: the telegraph boy wanted his dollar and thirteen cents. The Holmeses fumbled about for change, found it, and sent him on his way. Then, there was nothing to do till daylight.

The next morning, Dr. Holmes called on the Central Telegraph Office in hopes of further news. He discovered there that another father had received a telegram in the night: William Dwight, an attorney whose son Wilder, a lieutenant colonel in the Second Massachusetts Infantry, had been wounded during Mansfield's advance toward the Dunker Church. Holmes went directly to Dwight's house and found him preparing to leave on a midafternoon train, bringing a skilled surgeon with him. They were going to look for Wilder; would Holmes come with them and try to find his own son, too? Holmes knew the Dwights, who were among the most distinguished Boston families and counted among their ancestors Yale president Timothy Dwight, the theologian Jonathan Edwards, and the novelist Catharine Maria Sedgwick. Holmes also knew and liked young Wilder, who had traveled to Switzerland with a nephew of the doctor's in the mid-1850s.[8] Dr. Holmes had observed in Wilder an abounding vitality and "a still fire . . . which . . . would blaze up to melt all difficulties and recast obstacles into implements."[9] He gladly accepted Dwight's invitation.

The three men were thankful for one another's company. Nevertheless, they passed much of the train ride to Philadelphia in silence. Holmes liked it that way. The vibrations of a speeding railroad car were just right for stirring his thoughts into new and pleasing patterns. As he gazed out the window and watched the fences and the distant hills go by, Holmes had plenty of time to let his musings wander. Yet they came back time and again to his wounded son.

Dr. Holmes knew that if anyone had news of Wendell, it would be Pen Hallowell's family. When the train arrived, he hurried alone to their home on Walnut Street. There, he found their gracious surroundings transformed into a small hospital. Pen lay on one bed, his shattered arm miraculously saved by a surgeon but still needing careful attention. Pen's brother Edward, also of the Twentieth Massachusetts, lay in another, prostrated by fever. A third bed contained still another officer from the regiment; Paul Revere had been shot in the wrist. The Hallowells had readied a fourth bed for Captain Holmes, but it lay empty. Pen himself had heard nothing of his friend since Holmes had ridden off in the ambulance for Keedysville. Dr. Holmes's fellow searchers were pressing on to Baltimore. He said a quick farewell to the Hallowells, rejoined his traveling companions, and climbed aboard the noonday train.

Crossing into Maryland, the elder Holmes caught his first glimpse of land transformed by war. The first view was more ominous than shocking; otherwise peaceful-looking bridges were guarded by sentries. Most of all, he was struck by the fact that this war had no boundaries—any part of the countryside might become embroiled in conflict at almost any time. He reflected, "Belgium, for instance, has long been the bowling-alley where kings roll cannon-balls at each other's armies; but here we are playing the game of live ninepins without any alley."[10] As Holmes and his two friends stood on the Baltimore platform waiting for a train to Frederick, a messenger handed Dwight a telegram: Shot in the left hip, Wilder had died on the 19th of September. The body was already on its way to Baltimore. Mr. Dwight said farewell to Holmes and waited there for the sad cargo to arrive.

Nearing Frederick, Holmes saw signs that he was closer to a battleground. The train rolled by a troop of Confederate prisoners—"a most forlorn-looking crowd of scarecrows"—and soon thereafter came to a halt: the bridge leading to the town had been blown up by Lee's army.[11]

Frederick showed few signs of the recent strife, apart from an unusual profusion of Union flags, hanging, it seemed, from almost every building. Holmes procured a wagon into town, where he searched the buildings for bullet-marks and the temporary hospitals for Wendell. He found neither. Now and then, he would glimpse a familiar shade of hair or the outline of a half-turned face that caused his heart to quicken, only to have the face turn toward him and the illusion fade away.[12]

By slow degrees, however, the trail was warming. Upstairs at a hotel, he found his son's friend and regiment mate Henry Abbott. Abbott was struggling with what looked like typhoid but, despite his weakened condition, was "soldier-like and uncomplaining." Another junior officer from the Twentieth yanked the doctor's heartstrings in two directions at once: he had heard that Captain Holmes's wound was less grave than first thought, but had also recently been told that Wendell was dead. The soldier hastened to add that the second rumor was "a fiction, doubtless . . . a palpable absurdity,—not to be remembered or made any account of."[13] Nevertheless, Dr. Holmes felt a dull ache rising in his chest.

On the far side of the town, signs of the recent disaster were everywhere. The road the doctor traveled was choked with straggling and wounded soldiers. It made him think of the aftermath of a tornado. The wounded who could walk, did. Those too gravely hurt to move were cared for on the spot or shunted off to neighboring villages. The sheer mass of suffering made it impossible to individualize. The doctor's capacity to sympathize quickly neared its limit, though here and there he was affected by the sight of a boy, flushed with fever or pale with exhaustion, dragging himself toward some place of rest. The blunt truth of the war was pressing in upon the doctor. He compared it to the outward pulsation of some malignant vortex, which, having sucked everything toward its bloody center a few days before, was now "driv[ing] everything off in long, diverging rays." He saw that, even in death, the man of social consequence fared differently from the simply born: "the slain of higher condition, 'embalmed' and iron-cased, were sliding off on the railways to their far homes; the dead of the rank and file being gathered up and committed hastily to the earth."[14]

On Saturday, the 20th of September, the doctor combed the improvised hospitals in Middletown, Maryland. Along the way, he was meeting Rebel prisoners as well. When he happened on an educated Southerner, he felt a bond that transcended region and social ideology. He was delighted to converse with a North Carolina lieutenant who hailed from a good family and was an exemplar of humanistic education and Christian culture. "One moment's intercourse with such an enemy," he wrote, "takes away all personal bitterness towards those with whom we or our children have been but a few hours before in deadly strife."[15] Confederate foot soldiers, on the other hand, seemed like an exotic, atavistic species. Some days later Dr. Holmes accosted "a wild-haired, unsoaped" seventeen-year-old Georgia private:

"Where do you go to church when you are at home?"

"Never went inside 'f a church b't once in m' life."

"What did you do before you became a soldier?"

"Nothin'."

What do you mean to do when you get back?"

"Nothin.' "[16]

The only connection Holmes could feel with such a boy, a "poor human weed . . . [a] dwarfed and etiolated soul," was one of pity. When he asked a few other captives what they were fighting for, a surprising number claimed not to know, and "manifested great indifference" to the entire business.[17]

He was still no nearer to finding Wendell. The following day he went by wagon to Keedysville and had a near miss: his son, riding in a milk cart, had left that town for Hagerstown the previous morning. Learning that Antietam was only three miles away, the doctor could not suppress his curiosity: he would have to see the battlefield. As he strode the field, with no guide to tell him what units had fought where, he felt lost and disoriented. In every direction were dark red patches of earth where pools of blood had curdled and caked. More or less by chance, he came to the spot now known as the Bloody Lane. The sunken road had witnessed one of the great clashes of the battle: the one near the center of the lines that unfolded after Captain Holmes's wounding in the West Woods and before George Whitman's dash over Burnside's Bridge. The doctor came upon a long ridge of fresh gravel, beneath which, he was told, eighty nameless Confederates lay recently buried. Everywhere and in profusion, Holmes found the trash of war: half-eaten rations, fragments of clothing, haversacks, canteens, cap-boxes, bullets, cartridge-boxes, and scraps of paper.[18] Holmes picked up a few stained relics—a pair of canteens, one from each army; a bullet or two, a belt buckle—but he was in no great mood for souvenir hunting. His child had fought and bled here. The field repelled him. It looked like a table left uncleared after some sick orgy.

Certain that his son must by now have moved on from Hagerstown to Philadelphia, the doctor journeyed back to Walnut Street, fully expecting to stand at his son's bedside. But again the sight was dismal; the three wounded officers were all now in serious condition, and the captain's bed still lay empty.

More anxious time and travel lay ahead. The captain might be any-where between Philadelphia and Hagerstown. With no new clues to guide him, the elder Holmes was obliged to scour the intervening dis-tance "as one would sweep a chamber where a precious pearl had been dropped."[19] He headed back westward, stopping in Harrisburg. There, he ran into a well-intentioned lieutenant who swore that he had seen a man answering Wendell's description on his way toward Philadelphia with a party of other wounded officers. An exchange of telegrams with the Hallowells, however, disproved the report. Dr. Holmes sent wires in every direction. Still, nothing.

Fresh out of ideas, the doctor made ready for yet another trek to Philadelphia. However, only two hours or so before he was to board a midnight train for that city, a telegram arrived from Hagerstown: Cap-tain Holmes was doing well and would be on his way to Harrisburg in the morning.

✳

AT THE SAME TIME COLONEL LEE was straying off into the Maryland countryside, the younger Holmes had been returning to health. For sev-eral weeks, his neck wound impaired the function of a nerve, making it impossible for him to move his left arm away from his body.[20] On the day after the battle, however, he was already feeling well enough to send a letter home. Given what he had been through, both his physical condi-tion and his outlook were excellent. He wrote:

Usual luck—ball entered at the rear, passing straight through the center seam of the coat & waistcoat, coming out toward the front on the left hand side—yet it didn't seem to have smashed my spine or I suppose I should be dead or paralyzed or something. It's more than 24 hours & I have remained pretty cocky, only of course feverish at times—and some sharp, burning pain in left shoulder.[21]

Wendell's letter had reached Boston long after Holmes Sr. had departed on his quest, and the news that his son was alive and recovering had failed to catch up with him.

That Wendell ascribed his condition to mere luck says much about his agnostic frame of mind. Twice given up for dead at Antietam, first in the West Woods and later in the field hospital, Holmes had experienced what many soldiers would have considered a resurrection. A bullet had come within an inch of ending his life. But the tilt of his head had been just right, and the bullet had come at just such an angle that he had been spared. Yet his deliverance, which looked so miraculous, spurred him to no religious awakening. As far as can be known, Holmes regarded his survival as mere happenstance—confirming, not disrupting, his sense of the universe as a place of inscrutable, mindless forces. If it had any effect on his thinking at all, the wounding at Antietam more stoutly convinced Holmes, already a religious doubter, that the world had neither plan nor reason. The power that drove the world could be neither understood nor appeased. Randomness had become God.

The great work of Holmes's life was to comprehend the nature of justice—to determine what phenomena were governed by laws and the precise principles by which those laws were seen to operate. To such a mind as his, the very notion of miracles was suspect, for what was a miracle, if not the suspension of ordinary, predictable rules? And even assuming such a suspension of rules, why should he have been its special beneficiary? The logic of it, if any, was beyond poor Wendell's power to discern.

✳

ON SEPTEMBER 25, 1862, THE MORNING train to Harrisburg from Hagerstown, due to arrive at 11:15, was late, at first delayed long enough to cause irritation, then long enough to trigger worry. Fifteen minutes. Half an hour. Dr. Holmes began to fear that the train had been wrecked.

At last it rolled into the station, so quietly that Holmes was almost startled to see it on the track. He boarded the train and looked around.

Holmes the poet would never have forgiven himself if he had not imbued the scene that followed with just the right tincture of deep but restrained manly emotion:

> In the first car, on the fourth seat to the right, I saw my Captain; there I saw him, even my first-born, whom I had sought through many cities.
> "How are you, Boy?"
> "How are you, Dad?"[22]

The elder Holmes described the reunion as he would ideally have wanted it. Whether the exchange of stoically suppressed affection took place just that way is a matter for debate. Holmes Jr. knew all too well his father's tendency to poeticize. Five days after his wounding, he had written home, pleading, "May I remark I neither wish to meet any affectionate parent halfway nor any shiny demonstrations when I reach the desired haven."[23] The account of Alexander Woollcott confirms that the captain was less than thrilled, not only to see his father, but also to receive the patronizing pat on the head that his father's greeting implied. Woollcott very credibly asserts that Wendell replied not with a sweetly filial "How are you, Dad?" but with an indignant "Boy, nothing!"[24]

✭

AFTER ANTIETAM, IN A STREAM of letters to his wife, George McClellan heaped glory on himself. The morning after the battle, his words strutted across the page: "The spectacle yesterday was the grandest I could conceive of—nothing could be more sublime. Those in whose judgment I rely tell me that I fought the battle splendidly & that it was a masterpiece of art."[25] McClellan may be the only person who ever mistook Antietam for a great military victory. Although his army had succeeded in thwarting Lee's invasion and leaving him no choice but to retreat to Virginia, it had done so at a staggering cost. More than 2100 Union soldiers died at Antietam. More than 9500 had been wounded. Yet by an odd twist,

Antietam, a battle fought by a Union commander who was sympathetic to slavery, gave Abraham Lincoln just enough political capital to take the first decisive step toward ending slavery: the issuance of the Emancipation Proclamation.

It was the existence of the war that gave the president the legal loophole he needed. Although a peacetime administration had no authority to end slavery, it was generally conceded that a president enjoyed a broader grant of emergency powers in time of war. The courts had never ruled on just how wide that extension might be. However, as early as the 1830s, former president John Quincy Adams had argued that a national emergency might authorize Congress "to interfere with the institution of slavery."[26] Almost as soon as the first shell exploded over Fort Sumter, Senator Charles Sumner had appealed to Lincoln on the basis of Adams's logic, insisting that the war powers of the executive empowered the president to emancipate the slaves.[27]

There was a certain irony to it all. The Southern states had made war on the Union in order to perpetuate slavery, yet, in so doing, they had handed the Lincoln administration perhaps the only legal justification for freeing their human property. In declaring themselves no longer subject to the laws of the United States, the Confederate states had given up the protection of the Constitution that had preserved their slaveholding rights for almost 75 years.

The firsthand accounts of how Lincoln broached the subject of the Proclamation to his cabinet confirm the private, personal nature of his inner journey. Somewhat strangely, he first confided his intention to members of the cabinet on the way to a child's funeral. James Hutchinson Stanton, the son of Lincoln's secretary of war Edwin M. Stanton, had been born the previous October. On July 10, the infant died, the victim of a botched smallpox vaccination.[28] Three days later, most of Lincoln's secretaries gathered at the Stantons' summer home two or three miles northwest of Georgetown to pay their respects.[29] The president invited two of his advisors to ride with him in his carriage: Secretary of State William Seward, who brought along his daughter-in-law, and Navy Secretary Gideon Welles. In his diary, Welles recorded that, as the four rolled toward their melancholy destination, Lincoln turned the conversation to a topic of "gravity, importance, and delicacy," regarding which he desired the two secretaries' frank opinions. He saw no evidence that the South was likely to abandon its war against the government. It had become clear to him that the Union would need increased leverage to bring the rebellion to its end. That being the case, he had concluded, "it was a military necessity absolutely essential for the salvation of the Union, that we must free the slaves or be ourselves subdued, etc., etc."[30]

Years later, Welles filled in the meanings shrouded by that tantalizing pair of etceteras. Lincoln explained that his reluctance to interfere with slavery, which had been sheltered for generations by a cluster of constitutional safeguards, was great. He had hoped to persuade leaders in the slaveholding border states, still loyal to the Union, to accept "some plan of prospective and compensated emancipation," but such plans had been greeted with hostility.[31] Congressmen from those states had argued, with some logic, that it would be unfair to deprive loyal citizens of their long-established system of labor, while allowing slavery in the rebel states to go, as yet, undisturbed. Lincoln believed that slavery was doomed. However, the border states could not be induced to suffer the first assault on the status quo. That blow must, instead, fall upon the states of the Confederacy. Those who had sought a war must bear its consequences.[32]

Welles found the change in the president's attitude remarkably sudden. Until that moment, whenever the topic of emancipation had arisen, the president "had been prompt and emphatic in denouncing any interference" with existing institutions.[33] Lincoln's previous reluctance to move toward emancipation had little to do with his feelings about slavery, which he regarded as a stain on the nation's soul, and everything to do with two other matters: his slowness to accept that he would have to adopt more radical means of waging the war, and his understanding of the Constitution.

The Constitution never used the word "slavery." Still, it plainly presumed that slavery was within the power of the states to impose, if they so chose; both the provision authorizing the enactment of laws compelling the return of fugitives and the infamous three-fifths rule made sense only in relation to slavery. Moreover, in an era far less accustomed than our own to broad exercises of presidential power, Lincoln well knew that the Constitution gave him no grant of authority to intervene in what had always been considered, as Welles called it, "a local, domestic question." When Lincoln took office, not one member of his cabinet believed that the federal government could legally act against slavery.[34] Lincoln had confirmed this position in his First Inaugural Address:

> I have no purpose, directly or indirectly, to interfere with the institution of slavery in the States where it exists. I believe I have no lawful right to do so, and I have no inclination to do so.[35]

So, then, what had changed? How could the president now dare to consider ending slavery in the South, when he had been powerless to do so before?

For Lincoln, the necessity of interfering with slavery lay in the nature of the rebellion itself. Even though the Confederacy was not arming black men, its armies were benefiting daily from the thousands of the enslaved whom they had forced into service as noncombatants, in every job from waiters and teamsters to builders of fortifications. In early July, a few days before the death of Stanton's son, and soon after the failure of McClellan's Peninsular Campaign, Lincoln had traveled to Harrison's Landing, Virginia, to review the army. Until then, he had hoped that the rebellion could be quelled without an all-out effort. At Harrison's Landing, he saw an army in remarkably high spirits. However, McClellan's forces had been thinned by combat and disease, their battle flags pathetically tattered by Rebel gunfire. The general's half-measures had been clearly insufficient. What Lincoln saw during his review persuaded him not only that the war would have to be pursued more vigorously, but that its outcome might hinge on whether the enslaved could be incited to resist their masters. By declaring the Confederacy's enslaved population free, Lincoln hoped to deprive Jefferson Davis of his captive workforce. He hoped that white Southerners, working alone, would lack the manpower necessary to sustain the war effort.

As the Stantons welcomed Seward and Welles into their parlor, the two men were likely wondering why their chief had chosen an infant's funeral as the occasion for raising such portentous ideas. But perhaps it wasn't so strange. The president's recent visit to Harrison's Landing was fresh in his mind, and it is possible that he simply couldn't help himself; like a chick pecking at its shell, the idea of emancipation had reached its time to be born, and the president could not hold it back a second longer. But beyond this, the funeral of little James Stanton had stung Lincoln with memories of another recent farewell.

Mary Lincoln had given birth to four sons. The eldest, Robert, was studying at Harvard when his family moved to Washington and was never much of a presence in the White House. Second son Eddie had died at three, eleven years before his father became president. But the two youngest boys, William Wallace, known to family and friends as "Willie," and Thomas or "Tad," were ten and seven, respectively, when the Lincolns came to the capital. Willie disliked the public attention that naturally fastened onto a president's offspring; he complained, "I wish they wouldn't stare at us so. Wasn't there ever a President who had children?"[36]

There had been, but not since John Tyler's son Tazewell in the early 1840s. But even if their existence had not been quite such a novelty, the Lincoln boys would have attracted a good deal of notice. People disagreed as to whether the two merely enlivened the White House or, with the help of their young playmates "Bud" and "Holly" Taft, threatened to tear it down. In 1861, the halls of the Executive Mansion rang with childish laughter, war-whoops, and, more than once, the sound of shattering glass or china. Inspired by the military fever that surrounded them, Willie and Tad built a fort atop the White House, armed with a small log that they declared to be a cannon, as well as a few old condemned rifles. At times their imaginations transformed the fort into the deck of a man-of-war, but in either guise the little redoubt stood ready to defend the capital against all enemies. For good measure, they dug a "rifle pit" in one of the White House gardens, much to the annoyance of the groundskeeper. They also commandeered a vacant room in the attic that became the "Old Capital Prison," where they shut up a black cat and a neighborhood dog as prisoners of war.

Alike in their capacity for mischief, Willie and Tad were otherwise vastly different. Tad suffered both from a lisp and from a learning disability that rendered him barely literate. Hot-tempered and recklessly impulsive, he seemed constrained only by the possibility that "Pa might mind"—though in fact the president almost never did. While people typically despaired over what might become of Tad, they usually predicted a grand future for Willie. He was, said Mrs. Lincoln's cousin Elizabeth, "a noble, beautiful boy . . . of great mental activity, unusual intelligence [and] wonderful memory."[37] Frank and loving, Willie was "a counterpart to his father, save that he was handsome." Julia Taft thought him the most lovable boy she had ever known, "bright, sensible, sweet-tempered and gentle-mannered."[38] Willie was, Attorney General Edward Bates grumbled, "too much idolized by his parents."[39] The president's heart was large enough for all three of his living sons, yet those who knew them agreed that Willie was his father's favorite.[40]

The Lincoln boys' defense of the White House from their rooftop fort was the stuff of comedy. They had no defense at all against an enemy worse than Jeff Davis's legions. Sanitation near the White House had been a scandal before the war had begun. Flowing just to the south of the Executive Mansion was a noxious canal. Conceived by George Washington and Pierre L'Enfant at the city's founding as a majestic manmade waterway that would extend all the way to the Ohio River and would rival the Erie Canal in commercial importance, the Washington Canal became largely irrelevant with the rise of the railroads. By 1861, it had become little more than an open sewer and a stagnant breeding ground for mosquitoes. Contaminated by dead animals and every other kind of refuse, it was, to quote one revolted commentator, "a stink-trap, man-trap and mud-hole."[41]

Now making conditions still worse were the countless Union soldiers encamped in and near the city, with no sewage system capable of handling their waste. The entire city was routinely exposed to foul air and contaminated water, and Lincoln's sons stood constantly in the path of contagion. In early February 1862, the two boys fell ill with typhoid. Tad got better. Willie's case grew more serious. For almost three weeks, he grew steadily weaker, racked by vomiting, dehydration, and delirium. Around 5 p.m. on February 20, Lincoln's secretary John Nicolay was sitting drowsily on his office sofa when the president entered, worn, exhausted, and choked with emotion. He managed a few words: "Well, Nicolay, my boy is gone—he is actually gone." In tears, the president staggered away.[42] He was to call Willie's death "the hardest trial of my life."[43]

Now, five months later, James Stanton was about to be buried in the same cemetery that held Willie's remains. Historians have discussed exhaustively the president's political motives for emancipating the enslaved millions in the South. Much less has been said about his reasons for first declaring his intentions as he rode to an infant's funeral. It seems impossible that, on that Sunday morning, no thoughts of Willie pressed upon Lincoln's mind. It was not in his nature to believe that events occurred at random; he felt continually driven by some transcendent force or will. As his great speech at Gettysburg reveals, he recoiled at the notion that good people die in vain. He sought meaning in tragedy, and, if the meaning was in doubt, he highly resolved to create it. Lincoln could never have been content to believe that Willie's death lacked a larger purpose. Almost inescapably, one concludes that Lincoln saw in Willie's death a moral imperative: his private loss demanded to be redeemed by a higher objective for his presidency: an aim more sacred than preserving the Union. If Lincoln needed some final impetus to announce his intention to emancipate when he did, where he did, that inspiration was waiting to be found in his loving memory of Willie.

On Tuesday July 22, nine days after James's funeral, Lincoln met with his cabinet in the second-floor library of the White House. He read aloud his first draft of the Proclamation and asked for a "free discussion" of what he had written.[44] But the discussion was not to be entirely free; the president explained that he was not presenting the idea of emancipation for their debate or approval. That question was already settled in his mind. He was going to issue a proclamation, and he would take responsibility for it. He wanted advice only regarding the strategy of how it should be done.

Though the cabinet did not hesitate to express their views, only one member, Secretary Seward, raised a point that Lincoln had evidently not considered beforehand. Seward's concern was as to timing. The army had suffered serious reversals, and "the depression of the public mind [was] great." Whatever Lincoln's desires might be with regard to the future of slavery, it had not yet been proven that he had the power necessary to enforce his will. Above all, the Proclamation must not look like "the last measure of an exhausted government, a cry for help."[45] Announce it too soon, before the Union had shown it was likely to win the war, and the Proclamation "would be received and considered as a despairing cry—an anguished shriek from and for the Administration, rather than a manifesto of freedom."[46] Instantly, Lincoln felt the correctness of Seward's warning. Like, as he later said, an artist laying aside the sketch for a contemplated painting, the president put the Proclamation aside; it would have to wait for a victory.

*

LINCOLN DID NOT BOTHER TO CONSULT his commanding general regarding emancipation; there would have been no point. McClellan was convinced that if the administration even gestured toward emancipation, his army would pay a bitter price. The fighting resolve of the Rebels would redouble, lengthening the war and intensifying its fury. At the same time, talk of emancipation would flatten the morale of McClellan's own troops, for most of whom the freeing of enslaved blacks was hardly an inspiring goal. Wendell Holmes's friend Henry Abbott exaggerated when he described the Proclamation as an object of "universal disgust."[47] Nevertheless, McClellan had spoken for a majority of his soldiers when he warned the president in early July that no "forcible abolition of slavery should be contemplated for a moment."[48] He thought a war to restore the Union could be won. A war for freedom could not.

But, almost in spite of himself, McClellan at Antietam gave Lincoln just enough daylight to do the very thing that the general saw as the greatest imaginable blunder: on September 22, five days after the bloody stalemate in Maryland, Lincoln convened his cabinet to announce the issuance of the preliminary Emancipation Proclamation. As he prepared to present the Proclamation to the cabinet, Lincoln prefaced his reading with a statement that Secretary of the Treasury Salmon P. Chase recorded in his journal:

> When the rebel army was at Frederick, I determined, as soon as it should be driven out of Maryland, to issue a Proclamation of Emancipation such as I thought most likely to be useful. I said nothing to anyone; but I made the promise to myself and (hesitating a little)—to my Maker. The rebel army is now driven out, and I am going to fulfil that promise.[49]

In July, Lincoln had presented his advocacy of the Proclamation as a pragmatic political judgment. By September, it was, in his mind, a holy covenant.

The day after Lincoln announced the finished Proclamation to his cabinet, the document was in the newspapers. Secretary Stanton's brother-in-law declared the Proclamation "the greatest act of justice, statesmanship, and civilization, of the last four thousand years."[50] But relatives of the president's inner circle were not a key constituency. As the story broke,

Lincoln privately worried that his move had been premature. "I did not think," he admitted, "the people had been quite educated up to it."[51] Predictably lauded in abolitionist circles, the Proclamation found few friends among conservatives and moderates. Pundits across the country "rose in anger to remind Lincoln that this is a war for the Union only" and that he had no authority to transform the cause into a fight for abolition. In so doing, they clamored, the president had marked himself as "a more unconstitutional tyrant and a more odious dictator than he ever was before."[52] In the ranks, soldiers hinted darkly that they would leave the service sooner than fight a war against slavery. The president looked on fretfully as stock prices declined. He told a group of well-wishers who had formed a parade in support of his action, "I can only trust in God I have made no mistake."[53]

As expected, McClellan railed at Lincoln's lack of judgment. The Proclamation, he fumed, had made it "almost impossible for me to retain my commission & self-respect at the same time. I cannot make up my mind to fight for such an accursed doctrine as that of a servile insurrection—it is too infamous."[54] More infamous in Lincoln's view was McClellan's inaction. It was not merely that he had failed to renew the fight on September 18th, allowing Lee to slip back across the Potomac; weeks had then passed, and McClellan still did nothing to follow up on the Confederate retreat. Now that the Proclamation had been announced, McClellan's refusal to move was looking less like mere aversion to risk and more like a political statement. On the same day that Lincoln read the revised Proclamation to his cabinet, McClellan complained to Lincoln's logistics specialist Henry Halleck that the army had been greatly exhausted by overwork, fatiguing marches, hunger, and loss of sleep. Under the circumstances, McClellan had not felt "authorized" to cross the Potomac in pursuit of Lee.[55]

In one respect, McClellan's caution was understandable. He heartily believed that the Army of the Potomac was his own creation, fashioned lovingly with his own hands. When he had taken command of these men, they had been a ragtag force, given to every blunder of amateurism and every failure of self-restraint. Day by day, he had molded a corps of capable officers and then, through them, had taught his men order and discipline, and with these values had come a sense of pride and honor. Overwhelmingly, too, McClellan had instilled in this army an almost mystical personal devotion to himself. He was not without his detractors; Arthur Fuller, for instance, thought him "a good engineer but no general." Alluding to McClellan's preference for defensive tactics, the minister maintained that Little Mac's weapon of choice was "the spade, not the sword" and that his penchant for caution "ha[d] been fatal to thousands."[56] But the more typical soldier's response was adulation. When word arrived after Second Bull Run that Little Mac was again in command of the army, men had howled, danced, and wept with joy. As one of them wrote, "The effect of this man's presence upon the Army of the Potomac . . . in victory or defeat—was electrical, and too wonderful to make it worth attempting to give the reason for it."[57]

Having done so much to shape this fighting force, and having received such affection from it in return, McClellan was ironically reluctant to use it for the very purpose for which it was created. When he resolved to send the army into battle, having brought it so near to his idea of perfection, he forever wanted to make it more perfect before ordering it forward. Always, a few thousand more men were needed, or his men were too tired or ill equipped. But too often he found it hard to order it forward at all. Having made this thing of beauty, he could hardly bear to see it mauled and broken, to see these men who loved him and whom he loved suffer the agonies of combat.

On the first of October, Lincoln traveled to Sharpsburg, where McClellan's forces had remained encamped. He intended to review the army—to "slip off . . . and see my soldiers," he said—but also to ask McClellan in person why he did not move. For Lincoln's benefit McClellan showed off his divisions to fine effect. The review, one observer reported, was a splendid affair throughout, with the troops presenting a fine appearance.[58] But McClellan's effort to impress the president backfired; he meant to argue that he had declined to pursue Lee across the Potomac because his battle-weary men were not yet ready for another fight. It was hard to persuade Lincoln that an army that looked so handsome on the parade ground was unfit to perform on the battlefield.

On October 3, photographer Alexander Gardner made a series of images of the president and the general together. In one of the best known of these pictures, much can be inferred from the dress and postures of the two men. McClellan, his uniform coat casually unbuttoned and his weight shifted onto one foot, looks defiant and unimpressed by the presence of his commander in chief. Lincoln, a head taller than his antagonist, has donned a stovepipe hat, as if intent on dwarfing McClellan all the more. With his left hand, he grips the back of a chair, as if to signal his refusal to retreat a step if McClellan should press him. Lincoln tried to keep the observable physical tension from carrying over into their conversations. He assured McClellan that he considered him the best general in the country. The president was, McClellan told his wife, "very affable, and I really think he does feel very kindly towards me personally."[59] But beneath the flattery and good cheer, Lincoln brought an imperative message: McClellan must pursue the Confederates without further delay. On October 6, after returning to Washington, already concerned that his instructions would be ignored, Lincoln sent the general a wire via Henry Halleck that put the matter with utmost clarity: "The President directs that you cross the Potomac and give battle to the enemy or drive him south. Your army must move now while the roads are good."[60]

McClellan liked the idea of the president's dictating military strategy to him no better than Lincoln enjoyed getting political advice from the general. He interposed pretext after pretext for failing to move: the army lacked the proper tents; it needed shoes and uniforms; his cavalry's horses were fatigued.[61] Lincoln witheringly responded, "Will you pardon me for asking what the horses of your army have done since the battle of Antietam that fatigues anything?"[62]

On November 7, a heavy snow fell on the Army of the Potomac. Trees groaned beneath the weight on their branches, and men shivered as they built great fires that blazed through the night.[63] That evening, at about eleven thirty, as his army slept, General McClellan was writing a letter to his wife. He was interrupted by a knock at his tent pole and looked up to see "the shape of dear good old Burnside" and, at his elbow, a staff officer: a brigadier general with the high-sounding name of Catharinus P. Buckingham. The two visitors looked solemn. After some abortive attempts at small talk, Buckingham handed McClellan an order. As he read it, McClellan steadied himself stoically. Immediately after the two men left, McClellan would write to his wife, "As I read the order in the presence of General Buckingham, I am sure that not a muscle quivered, nor was the slightest expression of feeling visible on my face. . . . They shall not have that triumph."[64] Lincoln had fired McClellan and replaced him with Burnside.

It is hard to pinpoint the moment when Lincoln decided that McClellan must go. For a while, a practical consideration stayed the president's hand. Near the start of November 1862 came a delicate round of midterm elections. With the public mood restive and divided after the announcement of the Emancipation Proclamation, Lincoln did not dare to further alienate the country's voters by dismissing the highly popular commander. It turned out that it was wise to wait: the elections left Lincoln's Republicans comfortably in control of the Senate and, despite losing more than twenty seats, clinging to a plurality in the House. With the elections over, Lincoln's last reason for keeping McClellan disappeared. Lincoln wrote the order dismissing him the following day.[65]

If McClellan saw his dismissal as a "triumph" for his enemies, that word was far from Ambrose Burnside's mind. Only a short while earlier, when Buckingham had awakened him with news of his appointment, he had responded with worry. He had protested to Buckingham that he owed great personal obligations to McClellan and that he did not feel competent to assume command. His humility was sincere, but Buckingham was ready for it. He explained that if Burnside refused, the offer of command would pass to the scheming, politically minded Joseph Hooker. Burnside had seen at once that keeping the army out of Hooker's hands mattered more than his concerns about his own unfitness; he had accepted the command on the spot. Now, as McClellan said, "Well, Burnside, I turn the command over to you," he saw that his successor was plunged in misery.[66] "Poor Burn feels dreadfully, almost crazy—I am sorry for him," McClellan told his wife. Then pity yielded to self-righteousness. "They have made a great mistake," he railed. "Alas for my poor country—I know in my innermost heart she never had a truer servant."[67]

"The army is in tears," wrote a Pennsylvania captain the following day.[68] Burnside began the huge task of learning his new responsibilities: piecing together his staff; making sense of the pending orders and strategic plans he had inherited. He worked at it a couple of days and then stopped awhile: historian Bruce Catton has suggested that it was all just too much for him.[69] In fairness, Burnside may have found it a touch unseemly to tackle his work at full speed while his predecessor was still in camp. As a courtesy, he arranged for the departing general to make a farewell review of the army on November 10. On the eve of that final gathering, McClellan attended a reception, held by his former officers in his honor. It was a cheerless occasion. Some were threatening to resign their commissions in protest. There were even whispers of support for a mutiny against the government. "Lead us to Washington," one general is said to have told his former commander. "We will follow you there." McClellan told one of the assembled officers, "I feel as if the Army of the Potomac belonged to me. It is mine. I feel that its officers are my brothers, its soldiers my children. This separation is like a forcible divorce of husband and wife."[70]

McClellan did not contest the divorce. What felt important now was to ride through the camps, attend the review, and hear the cheers of the men one more time.

Book 2

———

TO THE
RAPPAHANNOCK

Chapter Five

A Man of God

On the last Sunday of October 1862, the Reverend Arthur B. Fuller, on his way south from Watertown, Massachusetts, was waiting out an endless train delay that had stranded him in Philadelphia. If he was conforming to army regulations, he was wearing the uniform of a chaplain: "plain black frock coat with standing collar, and one row of nine black buttons, plain black pantaloons, black felt hat or army forage cap, without ornament."[1] Like many Union chaplains, however, Reverend Fuller tended to prefer the uniform of a cavalry captain, the rank whose salary was equal to that of his own position. He dressed this way as a gesture of solidarity, reminding the men whose souls he cared for that he and they were all in this together. Fuller was not sure whether he had been wise to have traveled this far already. Though he was doing everything he could to deny the fact, Arthur Fuller, in what should have been the prime of his life, was a physical wreck.

He had left home the previous year, going to Virginia as the chaplain of the Sixteenth Massachusetts Volunteer Regiment. During the Peninsular Campaign in the early summer of 1862, he had suffered from blinding headaches and dysentery. Eventually, he had contracted malaria, and the mounting conspiracy of ailments had forced him to request an extended medical leave. Since midsummer, he had been at home in Watertown under the care of his wife Lucilla. His mind had required almost as much repair as his body. It was said that the horrors he had witnessed in the swamps and hospitals near Richmond had cast a long shadow over the minister's sensitive spirit. For a time, it seemed that he would not recover. Fuller heightened the distress in his sickroom by offering suggestions regarding his funeral. When he rallied from his sickbed to undertake this trip to rejoin his regiment, Chaplain Fuller was no more confident in the likelihood of the Union's winning the war than he was of his own physical recovery. But the perilous state of the nation was part of what was driving him forward.

Only forty, Fuller might have been mistaken for several years older. Blind in one eye since childhood and never robust, he struck most people as better suited to a pulpit and a writing desk than to the rigors of army life. The previous afternoon, in New York, he had endured a fearful headache and wondered whether he should attempt the trip to Philadelphia. Against his better judgment, he had proceeded. Thin and haggard, Fuller was making others wonder whether they should offer him assistance. The chaplain was a tired, needy man.

A young woman named Emily Wilkinson noticed the minister's distress, and, in Arthur's words, she "took compassion on" him.[2] She found a basin of water and bathed his head in hopes of bringing down his fever. When that effort failed, she insisted on fetching him some medicine. By the time she came back, Fuller's condition had grown more alarming—so much so that Wilkinson would not hear of his boarding any train. He must, at the very least, spend the night in Philadelphia. Fuller agreed; he would look for a room. Wilkinson stopped him; he needed a hospital, not a hotel. Fortunately, a government hospital lay opposite the depot. Wilkinson escorted him there and then walked off into obscurity, still knowing only a handful of facts about the man she had rescued. Had she stayed to hear his story in full, she would have found it extraordinary.

Arthur B. Fuller had been born in Cambridgeport, Massachusetts, on August 10, 1822, to a family that already included two sons and two surviving daughters. The Federal-style house on Cherry Street where he was born still stands. Arthur's father Timothy, like three of his four brothers, had earned a degree at Harvard. All five brothers had become lawyers, and they were known in Boston as men of great energy, ambition, and self-esteem.[3] Their collective swagger had inspired as much resentment as admiration. In 1850, Arthur was to write, "We have in our family all the elements required for great happiness & great usefulness, yet our very talents & strong originality, together with not a little will, bring us into collision . . . which make[s] great forbearance needful."[4]

By the time Arthur was born, Timothy had risen to become one of the most powerful politicians in Massachusetts. He was serving his third term in the United States Congress and would soon be elected to a fourth. He was on such familiar terms with future president John Quincy Adams that the two men shared a pew at the church they attended in Washington. Although Virginia slaveholders dominated the Democratic-Republican party to which he belonged, Timothy stood staunchly against slavery. Arguably his finest moment in Congress came when the Missouri Compromise was being debated in 1820. The legislation proposed to admit Missouri to the Union as a slave state. Timothy, who believed that "not an inch of territory should be left to the blighting influence of slavery," found the measure unconscionable.[5] The bill became law, but not before Fuller had addressed these words to the House chamber:

> If . . . all men have equal rights, it can no more comport with the principle of a free Government to exclude men of a certain color from the enjoyment of "liberty and the pursuit of happiness" than to exclude those who have not attained a certain portion of wealth, or a certain stature of body, or to found the exclusion on any other capricious or accidental circumstance. . . . Election and representation . . . would exist only in name—a shadow without a substance, a body without a soul.[6]

Timothy's eldest daughter also drew her share of attention. At a very early age, Sarah Margaret had shown precocious gifts for language. Her extreme cleverness caused Timothy to wonder: under carefully monitored conditions, might a gifted girl be brought up to be the academic equal, even the superior, of an intelligent boy? Yielding both to curiosity and to a temperament that led him to press every opportunity for its fullest advantage, Timothy subjected Sarah Margaret to a rigorous—some would say brutal—course of study. At six, the little girl was tasked with learning Latin grammar. The basics of ancient Greek soon followed. When his schedule allowed, Timothy supervised the lessons personally. Long after dark, with frayed nerves and short tempers, the two pored over their weighty tomes. Line by line, declension by declension, Timothy achieved his goal: Sarah Margaret became a celebrated prodigy, boasting the best education of any girl in New England. In adolescence, she discarded her first name. By the late 1840s, everyone in America with an interest in transcendental philosophy or in women's rights knew the name of Margaret Fuller.

Within his family, Arthur felt closest to his handsome younger brother Richard. A lawyer and sometime poet, Richard was his sister Margaret's favorite sibling and a companion of the writer and naturalist Henry David Thoreau, who, Richard said, "abounded in paradox."[7] Richard regarded Arthur highly. After the latter's death, he published a biography of his brother that remains the most comprehensive record of Arthur's life.[8] In it, Richard tells of the mischievous but mostly happy childhood that he and Arthur passed together. They worked in their father's hayfields, took fishing trips along the Nashua River, and spent dream-filled afternoons of boating on Martin's Pond in North Reading. In his early years, Arthur was a child of buoyant spirits who kept his sister Margaret "full of joy and eagerness."[9]

In addition to his biography of Arthur, Richard also wrote his own memoir. In neither work could he bring himself to confront the aspects of his family that savored of serious imperfection. One glaring source of his discomfort was the family's youngest son, James Lloyd Fuller, who suffered from a mental disorder that made it impossible to care for himself. To Arthur, Lloyd's condition was "a source of bitter, great sorrow."[10] However, Richard's books never mention Lloyd, even excluding him from his list of still-living Fuller children. Richard also chose to omit a devastating accident that befell Arthur when he was ten. It is a striking omission, for this event, which Richard sought to erase from his brother's life story, drastically altered Arthur's perception of himself, and powerfully shaped the man he was to become.

It occurred in mid-April 1833. Timothy, weary of Boston and eager to sample the life of a country gentleman, had just moved the family to a spacious farmhouse in Groton, Massachusetts. Margaret, who had spent unhappy times in Groton at a finishing school, took a dim view of the move, but she consoled herself with the thought that Arthur, at least, would be happy there. That happiness was almost immediately blighted. Timothy had hired some workmen to improve the property, and one day Arthur evidently paused to watch them. Among the workmen was

a man named John. He was, to use Richard's euphemism, "an inveter-
ate follower of Bacchus, in his cheaper and grosser cups," a man whose
only merit was his good-natured temperament.[11] Carelessly, John flung
a large piece of wood in Arthur's direction. Arthur recoiled in pain. The
projectile had struck him hard on the right side of his face. The blow had
severely damaged his eye.

Margaret, who had not yet joined the family in their new home, was
promptly summoned. She arrived to find her brother "in a dark room,
burning with fever and both his eyes closed to the light."[12] It was feared
that Arthur might be permanently blinded in both eyes. To Margaret,
it seemed that all had been ruined. She had thought "much more highly
of [Arthur's] talents" than of any of her other brothers and believed that,
with her influence, he might truly distinguish himself. "And now," she
wrote despondently, "he may be possibly quite blind, certainly greatly
injured for all this world's glory."[13]

Arthur feared that he would "never be happy again."[14] He could imagine no brighter future for himself than working as some man's private
secretary. Nevertheless, he bore his pain patiently, and his mother wrote,
"His gratitude & tenderness for me & his affection and delicacy toward
[Margaret] are most affecting."[15] Arthur completely lost the use of his
right eye. Enough vision returned to his other eye that, with glasses, he
could lead a normal life. But in an era less accepting of handicaps of any
kind, his partial disability hung over him.

For the next two and a half years, Timothy Fuller tried as hard
as he could to counteract any feelings of weakness or invalidism that
might have taken root in Arthur's mind. An aficionado of cold-water
baths and bracing barefoot runs in the New England snow, Timothy
tried to instill both Richard and Arthur with "Spartan endurance."[16]
As for domestic discipline, Timothy gave Arthur at least one "calm
and deliberate" whipping.[17] Arthur resisted his father's efforts to guide
him toward a strenuous life; he was most content in a world of reverie.
Richard remembered, "His very active fancy could not be bound down
to the slow round of manual labor, and [he] was perpetually star-gazing,
or sky-gazing."[18] More influential than his father's admonitions were
the simple beauties of the family's estate. Richard commented, "The
overcasting cloud, the returning triumph of sunshine, the rainbow . . .
the sun, moon, stars, day and night, spring summer, autumn, winter,—

These were his alphabet or vocabulary, learned by heart in his childhood's intimacy with nature."[19]

Yet at the same time Arthur was learning the glories of nature, he was learning—and resenting—his own limitations. It was not simply a question of his impaired vision. As a boy, he lived with a father who had done much and who demanded more. Across the dinner table sat a sister whose brilliance would one day become the stuff of legend. Arthur was imperfect in a family that prized perfection.

Remembered mostly as the man who all but smothered his famous daughter with Virgil and Cicero, Timothy Fuller was also a man of simple joys and gentle kindnesses. He had a religious love of nature, and hand-fed small morsels of his lunch to a mouse that had set up residence in his law office. When riding with his sons, he would give them coins to pay the toll-keeper, and the boys would pocket the money when the man refused payment. The children learned only years later that their father had prepaid the toll, and that this little ruse was his way of slipping them some extra spending money.[20] The fond memories stopped accumulating far too early. On September 30, 1835, when Arthur was thirteen, Timothy was seized by a violent illness. He fell to the floor, vomiting. His blood pressure plunged, and he went into shock. The next evening, Timothy Fuller, only fifty-seven, was dead of cholera.

His father's death left an aching void in Arthur's heart. The economic impact was just as daunting. Timothy had left behind much less property than he had allowed the family to believe he owned, and his investments had not proved fortunate. The late congressman, as his son Richard recalled, had always shielded the family from worry. Now that "the strong pillar of . . . our security" had vanished, Mrs. Fuller found she had neither the practical knowledge nor the courage to face the troubles that instantly arose.[21] Although Margaret had "always hated the din" of financial affairs, she rallied herself and took charge of the family's business matters.[22] She called a family meeting and gloomily announced that they would have to slash their expenses. The Harvard educations that Richard and Arthur had taken for granted might be out of reach. As the boys listened, Richard recalled, "Helplessness and fear sat there with us."[23]

The double shock of his partial blinding and his father's death drained much of the joy from Arthur's adolescence. On his twenty-sixth birthday, he wrote, "I think myself happy, much more happy than as a child. Then

I had very much to endure & not the inward strength to bear the petty griefs that assail." He also saw that his father's passing had disrupted his progress toward physical and emotional manhood. He lamented, "Were I to live over my childhood I would do everything to gain a sound, strong constitution, for lack of strength has hindered my best efforts from full success. I would gain, too, accomplishments which should beguile sick hours & would be taught methodical habits. Father's death & the consequent griefs & anxieties probably prevented these."[24]

After Timothy's death, Margaret took on the task of educating Arthur and Richard. She regarded both boys as underachievers. Her disappointment regarding Arthur was especially keen. He remained a dreamer, reluctant to engage in "the solid structures of history, mathematics, etymology and grammar" when airier pursuits were available.[25] Margaret measured her brothers' progress "principally by her own achievements"— a high standard that unnerved the two boys.[26] Richard remembered that he and Arthur would tremble for fear of giving a bad performance. When reciting a lesson for his sister, Arthur began to manifest a nervous twitch, making matters still worse. Exasperated, Margaret made no effort to conceal her displeasure. While Arthur learned a great deal under his sister's supervision, her tutelage also reinforced his view of himself as feckless and inadequate. Nevertheless, his and Richard's efforts were rewarded: both brothers were accepted by Harvard, and the family's frugality made it possible for them to attend.

Into Arthur's mid-twenties, surgeons tried unsuccessfully to restore his vision; Margaret wrote of her brother's "repeated operations, [which] must shake his nervous system terribly."[27] At the time, modern anesthesia was in its infancy. It is unclear whether Arthur's doctors had access to either of the two most trusted anesthetics, ether and chloroform, without which the surgeries would have been excruciating. Margaret realized that Arthur had never emerged from the shadow of his disability. In another 1848 letter, Margaret added that she had hoped Arthur might rise to "outward prosperity," but that "his calamity hangs on him like a cloud."[28]

Although Margaret had bluntly criticized his lack of academic progress, Arthur also suspected that, during his formative years, his physical condition had led others to subtly coddle him, protecting him even from an objective knowledge of his shortcomings. As a young man, he wrote to

Richard of the importance of having someone to "tell you of your faults [with] a single view to your improvement." He added, "I lament often enough that no one ever wisely did this for me, & now none gives me wise counsel."[29] Despite his doubts and disability, Arthur worked steadily to build a career that would give strength and comfort to others: he had decided to become a Unitarian minister. At Harvard, he stood among the top scholars in his class until ill health interfered with his work and dragged his ranking downward. In 1843, newly emerged from college, he went west, taking over the directorship of a Christian school in Belvidere on the Illinois prairie. The work satisfied him greatly, but further concerns for his health sent him back to Boston two years later. He then enrolled in Harvard's Divinity School, earning his degree in 1847. For three months, he stood in for the Reverend Edward Taylor, the famous whalemen's minister who supplied the model for Father Mapple in *Moby-Dick*. Although his substitute preaching produced nothing as memorable as Mapple's sermon in Melville's novel, Fuller evidently did his best to emulate Taylor's vivid use of nautical metaphor, "ma[king] the billows roll" and commanding the attention of his seafaring parishioners.[30]

Yet Arthur's frailty became a motif of his early career. Always eager to serve the common good, he was equally fearful that his next effort would throw him into a sickbed. An incident from 1849 was typical. His mother wrote enthusiastically that Arthur had delivered "a powerful sermon on election." However, she added, "the exertion always gives him headache, and he has gone out for air."[31] When her son was only twenty-five, Mrs. Fuller was already of the opinion "that he must be [careful if he is] to live long on the earth."[32] For his own part, Arthur began predicting his early death in his mid-twenties, when his birthdays began to "talk to me of time & yet more loudly of eternity."[33] He was becoming a diligent servant of the Lord, but not an especially cheerful one. "Life," he explained, "has been a serious, thoughtful business & has shown me too much suffering in the world . . . to allow much mirth."[34]

✦

IN THE EARLY AUTUMN OF 1847, Frederick Douglass gave a series of four antislavery lectures to a respectful audience at the State Street Baptist Church in Albany, New York. His lectures won a convert. Fuller, who happened to be preaching a few Sabbaths in the city, attended Douglass's lectures, and was fascinated by what he heard.[35]

No transcripts of Douglass's remarks in Albany are known to exist. However, a fairly complete account can be given of what Douglass said only a few days earlier in Syracuse, where he spoke at the invitation of Samuel J. May, a prominent abolitionist minister and an uncle of Louisa May Alcott. If Douglass's oratorical agenda in Albany resembled what it had been in Syracuse, it is easy to see why Fuller listened so attentively. While Douglass's principal targets were the slaveholders of the South, he saved some of his harshest words for another group of men who were unwittingly helping to keep slavery in place: the clergymen of the North. More than a president, more than any wealthy merchant, the minister possessed the ability to change the character of the nation "from the spirit of hatred to that of love to mankind." That being true, Douglass argued, "The power that holds the keys to the dungeon in which the bondsman is confined, is the pulpit." As it was, however, the Northern churches were a breeding ground for slave owners and overseers. "The men who wield the blood-clotted cow-skin," he averred, "come from our Sabbath schools in the Northern States." If the clergy of the free states were simply to preach the gospel in its true spirit, "a man would as soon think of going into downright piracy as to offer himself as a slave driver," and a Christian would as soon speak of having "a brothel keeper" as an uncle or a brother as he would confess to sharing kinship with a slaveholder.[36]

Douglass's opinions on the clergy hardly made for pleasant listening. Still, as Fuller knew, the heat of Douglass's rhetoric was justified by the rightness of his cause. A few months later, Douglass launched his abolitionist newspaper *The North Star*. Arthur Fuller was an early and highly interested subscriber. In only the sixth issue of the paper, a letter appeared bearing the reverend's name. Though he declined to specify the points on which he dissented, Fuller did not agree with all the editor's sentiments. Nevertheless, he earnestly embraced Douglass's goal: what Fuller termed "the elevation of the colored man to his just rights and respectful consideration." The unjust degradation of one class of people, Fuller insisted, lowered every other class as well. It was, he wrote, a self-evident law of justice that "the wrong-doer is always injured to the full extent of his victim's suffering."[37]

In the 1840s, while Arthur patiently tended to the Lord's work, his sister Margaret struck America and Western Europe like a force of nature. She changed the course of American culture at least three times: by editing Emerson's groundbreaking transcendental magazine, *The Dial*; by authoring the first great American plea for female equality, *Woman in the Nineteenth Century*; and by writing artistic and social criticism for a national audience in Horace Greeley's *New-York Tribune*. Finding America too small an arena for the exercise of her powers, Margaret then went to Europe, where she met Wordsworth, Carlyle, George Sand, Mazzini, and the national bard of Poland, Adam Mickiewicz. Continuing her work for the *Tribune*, she chronicled the rise and collapse of the Roman Revolution of 1848–49. As the democratic insurgents fought for freedom in the streets of the city, she directed a hospital that cared for the wounded.

Margaret Fuller's comet burned out prematurely. In July 1850, returning to America with her husband, the Marchese Giovanni Ossoli, and their infant son, Angelino, she had the horrendous luck to book passage on the freighter *Elizabeth*. As Arthur and the rest of the family prepared to welcome her, the ship, guided by a novice captain, missed New York by fifty miles, ran aground on a sandbar, and broke up in a hurricane off Fire Island. The wreck took place within sight of land, and more than two thirds of the passengers and crew were able to swim to shore. However, all three of the Ossolis drowned.

At Margaret's death, intellectual New England convulsed. Emerson declared that he had lost his audience. Thoreau, with Emerson's prompting, traveled to the spot of the wreck in hopes of retrieving whatever remained of the lost genius. Hawthorne's wife, Sophia, exclaimed, "Oh was there ever any thing . . . so unspeakably agonizing as the image of Margaret upon that wreck, alone?"[38] Arthur and Eugene Fuller sped off to Fire Island on the same errand that had brought Thoreau. Margaret's body, like her husband's, was never recovered. Thieves had pillaged the couple's luggage, and beachcombers brazenly sported buttons and tassels plucked from Margaret's wardrobe. The ocean had, however, yielded up one bit of flotsam for which the scavengers had no use: the body of Fuller's infant son. Arthur and Eugene claimed the little boy and carried him back to be buried alongside his maternal grandfather in Cambridge.

Arthur withstood the shock with dignity. Months later, he wrote, "There are sad memories which at times oppress me, and the sense of the loss we have met only grows deeper as time passes. But I know it is not right to be absorbed by these griefs. . . . I seek only to remember what Margaret has been, is still, and *shall be* to us."[39] The knowledge that her body had not been entombed—that there was no physical place devoted to her remembrance—struck him as profoundly melancholy. After visiting a cemetery the year after his sister's death, he wrote, "I thought most constantly of Margaret—& almost wished among the many beautiful monuments to commemorate the dead, scarce known beyond their family circles, there could be one monument to the memory of her who was & is so truly illustrious."[40]

Throughout the 1850s, tragedy seemed to pursue the fragile preacher. On January 6, 1853, he boarded a Boston train for Concord, New Hampshire. Pulling out of the station at Andover, he was surprised to find himself in the same car with the president-elect of the United States. Franklin Pierce, his wife, Jane, and eleven-year-old son Benny took seats toward the front of the car, near where the minister was sitting. Arthur, who was fond of children, glanced over at Benny. "Interesting little boy," he thought. As the train surged up to speed, Benny kneeled on his seat, studying the passing scenery. Arthur, too, stared out the window, idly laying plans for the future. A mile or two out of Andover, the passengers felt a severe shock. The car dragged forward a few seconds, and then the coupling that held it to the locomotive gave way. Fuller and the Pierces were thrown out of their seats. The car, traveling at forty miles an hour, had broken an axle and derailed. After spinning around, it swung over a rocky ledge and rolled down a fifteen-foot embankment. Pierce instinctively restrained his wife with one arm and reached for Benny with the other, but he grasped at empty air. As the car jolted and heaved, Benny was thrown the length of the car. Eerily, horribly, as the train car fell, the passengers were utterly silent; the astonishment of the moment, it seems, had literally taken their breath away.

The car turned over twice as it fell. Then it "was arrested with a violent concussion, parted in the middle, and then broke into many thousand fragments."[41] Amid the shattered glass and splintered wood came groans and calls for help. One passenger, his ribs smashed, seemed beyond recovery. His daughter's foot was so badly crushed that it could not be saved. After a moment of shock, Fuller became aware of a woman's voice, speaking "such affecting words as I can never forget." It was Jane Pierce.

Beside her "in that ruin of shivered wood and iron lay a more terrible ruin—her only son, one minute before so beautiful, so full of life and hope."[42] Except for a bruise above his right eye, Benny's face, though streaked with blood, was unmarred. His features, however, were etched with a mute expression of pain. The boy's head had slammed against some hard, unyielding thing. The impact had sheared off the top of his skull.

Arthur Fuller, bruised and shaken but otherwise unhurt, gave what comfort he could offer to the Pierces.[43] He accompanied Benny's body to the nearest house. Even as the child's limbs were beginning to stiffen, Fuller read in his countenance "something resigned and tender, impressed even by the awful hand of death."[44] The scene he had witnessed, he told Richard, had been written on his memory "with a pen of iron." He had expected to die but had accepted the prospect calmly. He was astounded that he was still alive. "Surely," he wrote, thinking of his father and of Margaret, "one family . . . ought to need no more repetitions of that great lesson, that in the midst of life we are in death."[45]

Benny Pierce's tragic passing splintered his parents' marriage. Jane, who had never approved of her husband's presidential ambitions, saw Benny's death as God's judgment against Franklin's pride. Two months after the wreck, when Franklin took the oath of office, Jane refused to attend the ceremony. She spent much of the next two years cloistered in the upstairs living quarters of the White House, writing letters to her dead boy. Benny's death also haunted his father's presidency. Already an indecisive man, Pierce began his term drained of vitality and emotionally alone. Rumors of his dependency on alcohol, which had already circulated during the campaign, intensified. One of the few women in Washington to whom Jane turned for comfort was Varina Davis, the wife of Pierce's secretary of war, Jefferson Davis. Historians have suggested Secretary Davis exploited the connection between the two wives to augment his influence on the president, which he used to sway the administration toward proslavery policies. One such measure, the Kansas-Nebraska Act, touched off a storm of violence in the middle of the continent that is now regarded as a dress rehearsal for the Civil War.

Now in his early thirties, Arthur Fuller was beginning to accept that his own life would add little to his family's fame. Instead, he undertook a different contribution to the family legacy. In the mid-1850s, working under the auspices of Margaret's former employer, Horace Greeley,

Arthur edited and reissued several volumes of his sister's work. He tackled the task with a sense of high purpose, saying, "If I only live to send forth Margaret's works from the press, as they should appear, I shall not have lived wholly in vain."[46] He also worked with a pecuniary purpose in mind. Choosing to serve her muse instead of Mammon, Margaret had left behind a fearsome amount of debt. Although many of her lenders were friends who had never expected her to repay them, Arthur applied the profits from the new edited collections to his sister's obligations, eventually paying all of them in full.

Arthur had few talents as an editor. He deleted long passages and changed wordings without notation. Shaping the texts to suit his own aesthetic sense, he sometimes missed his sister's intentions and robbed her work of layers of meaning. Although his editions sold respectably, they succeeded only modestly in preserving his sister's fame. The prevailing judgment was acknowledged by Oliver Wendell Holmes Sr., who had been Margaret's schoolmate at the age of nine. In his 1861 novel, *Elsie Venner*, Holmes described a character as follows: "She narrowed her lids slightly, as one often sees a sleepy cat narrow hers,—somewhat as you may remember our famous Margaret used to, if you remember her at all."[47]

✦

THE 1850S WERE A FOREBODING DECADE for America. The slow steps toward civil war, now so familiar to students of the era, resounded like a dreadful tolling of bells for those who lived through them. The Fugitive Slave Law . . . the Kansas-Nebraska Act . . . the caning of Charles Sumner on the Senate floor . . . the *Dred Scott* decision. Reverend Fuller denounced the assault on Sumner from the pulpit and quietly formulated his own theory of politics—one deeply tinted by his religious convictions. He was, to begin with, highly impatient with the separation of church and state. The idea of a public official who was not guided and restrained by scripture was, to him, a frightful prospect. "It is an unholy and dangerous divorce," he wrote, "a sundering of things joined by God."[48]

To the same degree that Fuller regarded Christ as the savior of the spirit, he saw America as the place of deliverance for all those who yearned for freedom. In a published speech, he looked forward to the day when

any person, "no matter in what language his doom may have been pronounced, no matter what complexion an Indian or African sun may have
burned upon him, no matter in what disastrous battle his liberties may
have been cloven down," might come to America's shores and, from that
moment, stand redeemed by the breath of freedom.[49] Fuller welcomed
immigrants even when his professional self-interest might have argued
otherwise. When he wrote his speech in praise of immigration, he was
leading a parish at the New North Church in Boston's North End. Once
a stronghold of well-heeled Protestantism, the neighborhood was now
increasingly populated by foreign-born Catholics. Fuller's daily bread
depended on maintaining a thriving congregation; his gracious acceptance of these new arrivals who would never attend his church reveals
the firmness of his belief that America should offer a home for all who
embraced its values.

The minister's memories of his sister were more than enough to make
him, for his time, a strong supporter of women's rights. His ideal, he said,
"demand[ed] for woman the right to do all she can do well, [to live] neither as man's handmaid and servant, nor idol and superior, but his helper
and equal." Fuller presumed that the home would always be the principal
sphere of action for most women. Yet, when women chose to do more and
did it capably, he urged his fellow men to appreciate "that these women
have not forgotten their sex, have not departed from its duties, but have
nobly fulfilled them all, and are truly womanly women."[50]

As the 1850s tested the strength of the nation, they also battered the
Fuller family. Arthur married in 1850. His wife Elizabeth, known in the
family as Lissie, worked alongside him, visiting the sick, helping in his
Sabbath school, and winning "both love & respect . . . for her goodness
& warmth."[51] In July 1851, after a harrowing labor of fifty hours, she
delivered a dead child.[52] The effort and the ensuing complications nearly
killed her as well. Her struggle to regain her health pained Arthur deeply,
making her "tenfold more dear for what she has suffered for my sake."[53]
Joy returned to the couple in 1854 when Lissie safely delivered a daughter,
Edith. In 1856, however, the Fullers suffered a year of numbing losses,
during which almost an entire generation of the family's women passed
away. Richard's wife Sarah, only twenty-six, was the first to perish. Weakened by the birth of her daughter Gracie, she went to her rest on January

10. On March 4, only two and a half weeks after delivering a healthy son, Arthur Ossoli Fuller, Lissie also died. She was twenty-four. As the minister grieved, he was tasked with finding care for two children under the age of two. In September, Arthur's surviving sister, Ellen Fuller Channing, succumbed to tuberculosis at age thirty-six, leaving five children.

Two more deaths came three years later. While working as a journalist in New Orleans, Arthur's oldest brother, Eugene, suffered a fever that disordered his mind, leaving him in "a shattered condition."[54] As Eugene was traveling by ship to New York for medical treatment, his attendant became distracted. Wandering away, Eugene either was swept or leaped overboard, becoming the second Fuller sibling to be lost at sea. Later that year, Arthur's mother also passed away. Of the thriving family that had seen seven children reach adulthood, only four brothers remained. The eldest survivor, William Henry, had distanced himself from the family and surfaces only rarely in its archives. The youngest, the mentally compromised Lloyd, was barely considered a member of the family. Of Arthur's generation, only he and Richard were left to carry the family's legacy forward.

Amid the losses came signs of regeneration. In September 1859, Arthur remarried. His bride was Emma Lucilla Reeves. Although he swore to Lucilla that he loved her as much as he could ever love again, he saw the liaison in a coolly practical light. Sadly, the minister's regard for the dignity of woman appears to have diminished where his own relationships were concerned. He told Lucilla, "What I have sought in this marriage is a companion and helpmeet; to be such you will need study & effort in the future & I will try to be very gentle & considerate & not expect too much at once." He seemed unable to explain the purity of his motives without disparaging her. He protested, "I believe I have been wholly disinterested in choosing you, looking neither for wealth, nor family position nor personal beauty but for a true, loving heart & a sound, capable & improving mind." He stiffly cautioned her, "Do not let me be disappointed in these reasonable expectations."[55]

It was less clear what Arthur Fuller expected of himself. He found much meaning in his relationship with God, and he took some satisfaction in his many tributes to his family's great but fast-receding past. Furthermore, his career in the pulpit did not lack achievements. In 1854, he was elected chaplain of the Massachusetts House of Representatives.

Four years later, he was chosen for the same position in the State Senate. During his time there, he impressed the legislators with his genial manners, his patriotism, and the fervor of his prayers. But, as he confronted middle age, these accomplishments felt paltry. To Richard he confessed his feelings of futility: "I . . . have lived half the term of years allotted to man," he wrote. "I ask myself whether half life's work is done, & if so cannot but feel how little will be the entire sum."[56] When he prayed before the legislature, he called upon the Lord to "help us really to live,—not merely to exist and to while away our passing hours, but to live in deeds more than years."[57] As the 1860s began, Reverend Fuller was still searching for that real life.

✳

RICHARD RECALLED THAT ARTHUR ANTICIPATED the war "with the anxious regard of a patriot, a Christian, and a minister of the Gospel."[58] In Arthur's view, these three roles were synonymous. The Fuller brothers agreed that there was a unique strain of thought and feeling in American patriotism, from the Puritans on down, that made it impossible to separate love of country from religious devotion. Because New England's first settlers had come there seeking religious freedom, the New Englander's "love of liberty and of country is, therefore, always a love of the open Bible. . . . Therefore, patriotism in America, more than anywhere else in the world, is an intensely religious sentiment." America's best soldiers, Richard ventured to suggest, perceived "in the loved stars and stripes of the Union the standard of the cross."[59] Richard Fuller described this melding of spiritual faith and republican fidelity as forming "the almost theocracy of American liberty," in obedience to which "our Gospel ministers . . . are like the Elijahs, Ezekiels, and Isaiahs, who guarded the integrity of the nation as a part of their spiritual charges."[60]

Richard conceded that the religious quality of Americans' love of country would be puzzling to anyone who regarded patriotism as a purely secular impulse. Still, he insisted, the Puritan idea of country "as a province of God's domain" furnished the key to understanding why, when war erupted, so many embraced the struggle as a literally holy cause.[61] The crusade was for America, but it was for more than America. As the

Fuller brothers knew, the country's founding manifesto "does not say, we [Americans] are free and equal; but all men are born free and equal." To keep true to its animating vision, the nation could never rest easy while people anywhere struggled against oppression. It was America's task to pursue a global mission of freedom and deliverance, which would not cease "while the sighs of a downtrodden brother-man are wafted to it by the farthest wind."[62]

As war threatened, the minister became a father for the third time. On February 13, 1861, Lucilla safely delivered a son, whom the couple named Richard in honor of Arthur's brother. Arthur was now chiefly concerned with public affairs, and his preaching became ever more political. The texts he now chose for his sermons came from the more martial portions of the Hebrew Bible. This passage from Numbers 32 is an example: "But we ourselves will go ready armed before the children of Israel, until we have brought them into their place. . . . We will not return into our houses until the children of Israel have inherited every man his inheritance." Fuller's typology was clear: the Union armies were the new children of Israel, as specially chosen to defend the cause of freedom as their ancient predecessors had been chosen for sanctity. Addressing a gathering in his home city of Watertown, Arthur exclaimed, "Nothing is ever settled, that is not settled right. Let us stand right ourselves, and then we can demand right from others."[63] He went also to the camps where new recruits were training, preaching gospel and glory under the open sky.

The minister seemed to forget all the old worries about his frailty. As his cause possessed him, he found inside himself an energy and a fire that he had never displayed before. Sunday after Sunday, meeting after meeting, he added poetry and piety to the Union cause. A company of young volunteer soldiers in Boston proudly christened themselves "The Fuller Rifles" in his honor. But Fuller knew that talk went only so far. Still missing from his life was an episode of great and virtuous struggle, in which he might finally throw off his former doubts and weakness, and prove himself worthy. On the first day of August 1861, less than two weeks after the Union defeat at First Bull Run, Arthur B. Fuller accepted a commission as chaplain of the Sixteenth Massachusetts Volunteer Infantry. Resigning his pastorate, Fuller used his farewell letter to outline his mission:

*If God requires [the ultimate] sacrifice of me, it shall be offered on
the altar of freedom, and in defence of all that is good in American
institutions.*[64]

Before he left, his friends gathered at his home on a Wednesday evening
to bid him farewell. They brought gifts, including a handsome portable
writing desk. A local dignitary handed him a purse, stuffed with 250
dollars. The money had come from believers from every church in town.
Special note was taken that Father Flood, the town's Catholic priest, had
reached across the doctrinal divide to add a contribution.

On August 17, Chaplain Fuller and the Sixteenth Massachusetts left
Boston on their way toward Virginia. Despite the setback at First Bull
Run, morale in the North was brimming. As the regiment rolled southward through the free states, Fuller described their journey as "one continued ovation, city and country vying in patriotic demonstrations and
exhibitions of good-will."[65] Bonfires blazed, and well-wishers pressed little gifts into the hands of the grateful foot soldiers. The unit was under
orders to move south as quickly as possible, and, to Fuller's distaste, it was
obliged to travel on Sunday. As they passed through New Jersey on that
Sabbath, the tracks were lined with men and women in their best attire,
cheering the Bay Staters toward glory.

In secessionist Baltimore, where the regiment was told to remain for
almost two weeks, the reception was different. Just after the war had
begun, the presence of the Sixth Massachusetts in Baltimore had incited
a riot in which soldiers and civilians had both been killed. Four months
later, the city remained less than hospitable to Federal troops. The chaplain considered the city "beautiful," but as he walked the streets, silent
and unarmed, he was bedeviled by Southern sympathizers who thrust
Confederate flags in his face and by women and children shouting hurrahs for Jefferson Davis.[66] One woman even fired on a soldier of the Sixteenth in broad daylight. Fuller had been in Baltimore only a day when
he felt compelled to assure Lucilla that he was safe. "A fight may come,"
he admitted, "but while I will not be a coward I will be prudent."[67]

Civil War chaplains had a mixed reputation. The majority saw to their
duties with energy and good conscience. They tended to the sick and
sometimes braved hostile fire to bring water to the wounded or to carry
them to safety. They undertook, as one man put it, "to make a business of

kindliness."[68] But it was not the efforts of the brave and the virtuous that made the best stories. The chaplain of the Second Connecticut Heavy Artillery happened on some soldiers playing stud poker in camp. Instead of reprimanding them, he joined in the game and, before the night was out, had cleaned out the whole company.[69] Some chaplains were no more than uneducated impostors, whose habits of profanity and drunkenness ate away at the moral fabric of their units.[70] Relations between soldiers and the camp clergy were not improved by the evident contradiction between the ministers' heavenly calling and the ungodly business of warfare. As one historian observes, "Soldiers were moving away from chaplains as rapidly as they charged that chaplains were drifting away from them. Combat could no longer be fitted easily within Christian precepts, and in men compelled to resolve that tension, religious ordinances could be suppressed as the daily experience of war could not."[71]

Chaplain Fuller did not lower himself to the debased expectations. Realizing the importance of habit in pious observances, he instituted a schedule for worship: Sunday School every Sabbath at nine; a formal service every Sunday at five; prayers and conference meetings every evening between six and seven. It pleased him to note that the men formed nightly circles for prayer and praise. He liked the conference meetings best, when soldiers would appear at his cabin and ask advice on everything from curbing their profanity to how to send money to relatives. They also came for news. Papers were scarce in camp, and the minister made it part of his duty to keep abreast of goings-on back home and to share whatever information came to him.[72] The regiment's observances took place outside, and inclement weather became a frequent enemy of the camp's religiosity. Rainy days were uncomfortable in the extreme, and the reverend regretted having to suspend services on the dreary days when "the men so much need[ed] the cheering and reviving influences of . . . prayer."[73]

The minister found that one potent way to raise spirits was through song. One of the Sixteenth's assets was an excellent brass band—the best that Fuller had seen in any regiment. To complement the instrumentalists, Fuller oversaw the creation of a regimental choir. Before long, a person on an evening stroll through the unit's camp could hear patriotic and religious songs emanating from more than half the tents. Fuller believed that music, depending on its nature, could either raise the soul toward heaven or hasten its decline. "Ribald songs," he noticed, were "sadly common in the army and on shipboard." He hastened to supply his men and others with more redemptive fare.

Joining forces with another minister, John William Dadmun, Reverend Fuller published a 64-page, pocket-sized volume called *Army and Navy Melodies*. Appearing in 1862, the book was a kind of patriotic hymnal, designed to answer "the social and religious needs of those who are striving in the national defence."[74] Some selections were predictable: "The Star-Spangled Banner"; "America (My Country 'Tis of Thee)"; "The Battle Hymn of the Republic." But the editors' preface called special attention to other titles whose fame was destined to fade with time: "The Alarm"; "Sailing on Life's Stormy Sea"; "Song of the Negro Boatman."

A glance at some of the lesser-known selections shows that *Army and Navy Melodies* was very much a family project. Richard Fuller penned the words to four of the songs. Fuller's wife Lucilla contributed the lyrics for four more pieces. In one of them, "Freedom's Era," she gently prophesied that America's war for freedom might lead to a loosening of chains across the globe:

> Russia's already freeing
> Her long down-trodden sons;
> A voice from fair Italia
> Of hope and gladness comes,
> That ne'er shall cease its shouting
> Till answering echoes sound
> From every cliff or valley
> Where tyrant's foot is found.[75]

The volume offered further evidence that a certain New England poet had overcome his political reticence; it contains both an "Army Hymn" and a new verse for "The Star-Spangled Banner" by Oliver Wendell Holmes Sr.[76]

At the start of September, the regiment was sent to Fortress Monroe, Virginia, an imposing, star-shaped installation encircled by a moat, standing at the very tip of the peninsula formed by the James and York Rivers. The largest stone fort ever constructed on United States soil, Fortress Monroe was to be Fuller's home for the next eight months. Fuller wrote of his new home as if it were paradise. "Lucilla," he exclaimed in a letter, "it is beautiful here!" He marveled at finding fig trees full of fruit and wondered what his daughter would think of them.[77] Throughout his time at the fort, the reverend restored himself by admiring the rich profusion of flowers and trees that he seemed to find at every turn. He wanted to know their names, but the locals he encountered seemed to think everything that bloomed was a lily. While it pleased the preacher to think that he was nestled amid the flowers of Judea, his botanical curiosity went unsatisfied.[78] In the winter, he built a modest log cabin, which the soldiers dubbed "the Parsonage." He used an American flag as a window curtain and decorated the structure's walls with pictures from *Harper's Weekly* and *Frank Leslie's Illustrated Newspaper*.[79]

When spring came, he wrote with delight of the stately cypress trees he could see from his door, of plum and apple blossoms, and of the luxuriantly blooming tea roses that someone had planted outside each window. Reminded of his garden at home, he told Lucilla, "Cherish my flowers, dear wife, in my absence & when I am gone even to a country farther than this, if it should be God's will, & in the spirit-land we will rejoice over those flowers, unfading there."[80] Almost five hundred miles from Boston, Fuller had never felt more at home in his life.

His sense of having found his true place was not merely geographical. In his work as well, he discovered a new depth of contentment: "I have found my sphere, one in which I am useful & respected and wherein I believe God is permitting me to do much spiritual good."[81] He meant to perform that good by bringing as much decency and moral rectitude to the war as any single man could deliver. Simply to win a war against slavery, however immense that task might be, seemed morally insufficient; other battles were waiting to be waged. He created within the regiment a chapter of the Sons of Temperance, declaring his intention to promote "wholesome recreation and intellectual and moral stimul[i]" as alternatives to the bottle.[82] After some difficulty, he persuaded the colonel to ban cursing in the ranks. He also established a regimental school, deputizing five of the best-educated soldiers as teachers. With satisfaction, Fuller observed, "All, or nearly all of the scholars are of foreign parentage, and have not had early advantages, through no fault of their own." On these earnest strivers, "who, though uncultured, desire strongly improvement," the reverend called down the special blessings of the Almighty.[83]

With his campaign to perfect the morals of the Sixteenth Massachusetts, Fuller acquired a singular reputation in camp. There were those who, like the unit's colonel, grew to respect the minister's strict consistency in principles. Yet one could also, with equal reason, complain of his priggishness. With his choir, his temperance speeches, and his war on profanity, Fuller seemed bent on turning a band of fighting men into a Sunday school. Fuller might have responded—and in fact he did—by echoing his brother's judgment that the most moral men and the best Christians were also the best and bravest soldiers. He also suspected that men who have to do the barbarous work of warfare required a strong system of constraints to preserve some sense of themselves as moral beings. He therefore meant to do everything in his power to "prevent their becoming weary in well-doing, or being tempted to desert the ranks of the army of the living God, and enlisting in the service of sin. . . . Away from . . . home influence, that man is arrogant indeed who believes he stands so firm that he is in no danger of falling if he neglect to seek loving, fraternal watch-care, and Christian sympathy."[84]

Beyond the walls of Fortress Monroe, the war was beginning to intensify. Before Fuller arrived, Confederate Major General John Magruder had ordered the nearby town of Hampton burned to keep its resources out of Federal hands. As Fuller walked amid the charred ruins of the once-thriving town, the mournfulness of the scene shook him: the churches, schoolhouses, and stately dwellings all reduced to blackened ruins. But amid the seemingly barren waste, he found a message of hope. A rosebush that the flames had not destroyed, its soil enriched by the ashes, was in radiant bloom.

But there was less and less time to think of flowers. He was discovering just how much of an army chaplain's time was consumed in patching up the human wreckage around him. His cabin was half a mile from a former religious seminary that was now a hospital. Although none of the facility's 700 or so patients belonged to the Sixteenth, Fuller went there each day to pray with the dying, to soothe the sick, and to bury the dead. He was, to his astonishment, the only chaplain who came to see them. Coming and going, he passed an impromptu cemetery that was adding an average of three new graves each day. The only memorials accorded to the dead men were pine headboards, on which a name had been scribbled in pencil.

Fuller had also taken on another voluntary duty: writing news dispatches for the *Boston Journal*, the *Boston Traveler*, the *Christian Inquirer*, and, most impressively, Horace Greeley's *New-York Tribune*—the same newspaper that had published his sister Margaret's dispatches when she covered the Roman Revolution. At the same time that she was sending columns to Greeley, Margaret had become the matron of a hospital, caring for insurgents wounded in the fight against the French army. Now Arthur, too, had embroiled himself in a war of liberation, caring for its wounded, and sending stories to the press. It was strange to see how much his life had come to resemble hers.

At Fortress Monroe, Fuller's abolitionism ceased to be a philosophical abstraction. Whereas he had known few black people back home, he now looked on daily as a stream of fugitives from slavery came seeking refuge in the fort. At one point, he reported no fewer than 2200 refugees within its walls. He wrote, "They impress me as a remarkably intelligent class of Africans." Instead of concluding that Africans on the whole might be more intelligent than he had been led to believe, Fuller credited self-selection: he presumed that he was seeing only those who had been shrewd and energetic enough to escape their masters. Despite his unconscious bias, Fuller set out to learn more about the fugitives' lives. He attended their religious meetings, which he found overly demonstrative for his taste, but which also impressed him with "a . . . simple eloquence that is most affecting."[85] He performed about a dozen marriages for couples who had never been accorded the right to wed. He went to the funeral of one who had escaped from bondage just in time to die as a free man. Over the body, the mourners chanted "their plantation religious songs . . . so mournful, so despairing . . . in their view of this life," yet so ecstatic when they sang of the eternal world to come.[86]

He discovered that the African reputation for laziness was a baseless slander; they would gladly do any work for reasonable pay. Fuller hired a black youth to care for his house and found him "skillful, truthful, and energetic."[87] Everything he witnessed confirmed what he already believed, "that the normal condition of every race and individual is freedom." It was a condition that he hoped to see made universal. "Today," he wrote, "these are not slaves, they are men."[88]

One Sunday, a steamer arrived under a flag of truce, carrying a cargo of released prisoners who had been taken at Ball's Bluff. The party included Colonel Lee and Major Revere from the Twentieth Massachusetts. As the men's feet touched Union soil, a few hurrahs went up, but the shouts were outnumbered by softly spoken prayers of thanks. Fuller grieved over the state of released prisoners of war from Confederate prisons—"poor mangled, wounded, *half-starved* sufferers"—the harbingers of worse atrocities to come at Libby Prison and Andersonville.[89] Viewing these sad scenes, he told himself, "Let our national enemies forget humanity if they will. We cannot, we will not, except first we forget the precepts of that blessed Book which, while it sternly declares the necessity of war and bloodshed in sin's remission . . . yet also demands, as the highest of duties, visiting the sick and imprisoned, feeding our hungry enemy, and the forgiveness of every repentant man."[90] Surely, few men have ever tried harder than Arthur Fuller to Christianize a war.

Efforts to make the war holy inevitably cut in two directions. Hymns, temperance, and mercy might soften the war in some respects, but they also reminded one that this struggle was not mere combat, but a crusade, and crusades are fierce undertakings. At the same time that Fuller was trying to mitigate the war's brutality, the war was adding a hard edge to the chaplain's Christianity. Two of the regiment's enlisted men fell asleep while on sentinel duty. Although Fuller sympathized with the men and prayed that they might be pardoned, he wrote inflexibly, "This endangers the whole army, and the sacred cause for which we are contending. . . . Death is the awful yet righteous penalty."[91] The mercy of God might be infinite. That of General McClellan's army could not afford to be.

On the sunny afternoon of March 8, 1862, Fuller watched in amazement as "a mysterious monster—half ship, half house—came slowly steaming from Norfolk." It was the Confederate ironclad *Virginia*, the first armored, steam-powered vessel ever seen in those waters, on her way to her tumultuous debut. The ship moved "with terrible and resistless force," firing her heavy guns at the USS *Cumberland* while piercing the Union ship's side "with her immense iron beak."[92] The monster then turned her attention to the USS *Congress*, setting her ablaze and compelling her to surrender. Two other Union ships ran aground and lay helpless. Fuller felt a personal humiliation as the *Congress* raised her white flag. He wrote soon after:

A Man of God + 131

I am afraid I felt hardly like a Christian for the moment, if indeed a longing for vengeance upon my country's enemies be unchristian. I would have given all I possessed to see that accursed tyrant of the seas, with the rebel pennant defiantly flying, sunk beside her victim[s].[93]

Her bow and smokestack damaged and her captain wounded, the *Virginia* withdrew, but no one doubted she would return to finish her work. The ensuing evening was filled with bleak anxiety. Undefended by sea, the denizens of the fort braced themselves for a Confederate attack by land—though thankfully no gray-clad soldiers appeared. Refugees from Newport News arrived in droves. "Contrabands"—the unfeeling name given to escapees from bondage—entered Fuller's cabin seeking food and rest. Others tramped by in a long, sad procession as the flames from the still-burning *Congress* lit their way. Everyone wondered what mayhem the *Virginia* might inflict elsewhere. With no similar vessel to oppose her, she could sweep southward and destroy the Union's coastal blockade. Or she might steam north, raining shells on Washington, Boston, or New York. Fuller saw no panic during those troubled hours, but he heard urgent prayers that God might somehow intercede.

On the dark waters to the ocean side of the fort, a speck of light gleamed above a distant wave. It moved nearer, and by 10 p.m. had been identified: The USS *Monitor*, the Union's own ironclad ship. Still not quite finished, she had been rushed to the scene from the navy yard in Brooklyn. Her low, cylindrical gun turret looked unimpressive, "a cheesebox on a raft," some people said, and Fuller thought the comparison was apt. In contrast to the *Virginia*, which rose much higher above the waterline, the *Monitor* looked contemptibly puny, "nothing but that little round tub appearing above the water," as Fuller noted. But the slim hope she offered was better than none.[94]

The next morning, the *Virginia* reappeared, unleashing a fearsome cannonade upon the *Monitor*. From the shore, Fuller tried to see through the smoke, fearing the worst. When it cleared, the *Monitor* was still there "with white wreaths of smoke crowning her tower, as if a coronet of glory." For five hours, the two ironclads exchanged fire, with "shaking earth and sea, [as] was never heard before."[95] The *Monitor* finally drove the *Virginia* back. The harbor had been saved, and the *Virginia*'s advantage had been neutralized. Fuller exulted. Days later, he visited the *Mon-*

itor, and some crew members proudly revolved the "cheese-box" for his inspection. The iron deck seemed almost sacred as he walked across it. He thought it possible that he owed his life to the homely little vessel, a mechanical David that had conquered a fire-breathing Goliath.

The duel of the ironclads was an exception to the monotony of camp life. Fuller's emotions oscillated between the boredom of his routine and the emotional stress of tending the wounded. The combination made him peevish, and the letters he wrote home in his darker moods were not the work of a gentleman. The kindliness that Fuller showed his regiment changed to pettiness and pedantry when he turned toward the woman he had sworn to love. In early April, he criticized Lucilla's spelling, penmanship, and lack of literary culture. Though she spoke of making him happy when he returned home, he wondered aloud how they could be truly close companions so long as she failed to improve herself. In a tone that was hardly endearing, he added, "'Tis because I love you truly and fondly that I say all this. It has been in my mind long to say it, but knowing you were sensitive I have forborne."[96]

Unsurprisingly, his words did not inspire Lucilla to reform herself, nor did his protestations of love impress her. He had hurt her, but when she wrote back to protest, he made no apology. Tone deaf to her feelings, he wrote defensively: "I felt disappointed in the way you received my criticism. . . . It was kindly meant, much needed, & I thought kindly done. . . . I have tried to be your helper as well as husband, God knows."[97]

Finally, on June 18, 1862, the men of the Sixteenth were tested under fire. General McClellan ordered them to execute a reconnaissance in force against the right flank of Lee's army. At 3:30 p.m., the regiment moved forward into a dense wood. Fuller had been excited by the coming danger. "Terrible as is the ordeal of battle," he wrote, "I would not shrink from that fearful sight. . . . I know no holier place . . . than this battle-field shall be. Let any deem the feeling wrong who will, on that ground I would rather stand than in any pulpit in America."[98] Yet now, at the moment of crisis, came one of his violent headaches, and he thought it best to stay back at his tent. His rest lasted only a few minutes. As he lay prostrated by his migraine, he heard some of the regiment's men as they hurried past. One of them remarked, loud enough for the pastor to hear, that he wished *he* had a headache.[99] There was only one answer to this insult. The reverend gathered himself, rose, and marched into battle with the men.

The woods were teeming with Rebels, ensconced in rifle pits and substantially outnumbering the Federals. Driven back, though not in disarray, Fuller's regiment carried with them five dying soldiers whom the chaplain would soon bury. Two days later, the regiment again came under fire, and Fuller again went with them to the field. Thereafter, the attacks came more or less daily, and Fuller grew accustomed to the screaming noise of shot and shell. In the week of their first brush with the enemy, the Sixteenth sustained approximately ninety casualties. In the midst of it, Fuller wrote home of the continual discomforts that were almost as demoralizing as enemy fire. For nine days, he had had no change of clothing and no food but hard crackers and coffee. And yet, he told Lucilla, "God blesses my labors, particularly among the sick & wounded. . . . *Of all places in the world I am glad I am here now.*"[100] He felt no fear. Still, the end could come at any time, and it felt like the right time for an apology. He had often been, he confessed, "petulant and nervous," and for this he was sorry. And yet, he insisted, "My true love has been & is yours & never have I for a moment been faithless to you or failed to seek your highest good and truest happiness."[101] The letter was sent, but its sender was spared from harm.

As McClellan's attempt to take Richmond fell apart, Fuller saw up close the meaning of military defeat. After their two skirmishes, the Sixteenth was sent to help protect an immense Union supply depot at White House Landing. When Jeb Stuart's cavalry cut off the depot from McClellan's chief force, its guards had but one option to avoid capture: they would have to destroy a vast quantity of their own army's supplies, retreat down the York River to Fortress Monroe, and then steam back up the James River to reunite with the larger portion of McClellan's command. Literally millions of army rations and hundreds of tons of ammunition—and nothing to do with them but destroy them.[102] Fuller described the scene as the army's provisions were set ablaze:

Horses careered wildly about, terrified contrabands brought over boats, while the incendiaries . . . applied the torch on every side. . . . The very clouds caught the lurid glow, and reflected in radiant hues the sad, fearful splendor below. Bursting bombs made noise like the shock of thunder-clouds and scattered fragments about till earth and sky seemed mingled in one awful conflagration.[103]

Every now and then, an explosion tore through the night, sending fragments into the air and producing towering columns of smoke and flames. It seemed to Fuller as if all the prophecies and pictures of Judgment Day had come to life.

When, a few days later, he was brought to Harrison's Landing, he witnessed a grotesque juxtaposition of heaven and hell. Outside the military hospital, the James River flowed by, its gleaming waters whitened with the sails of countless schooners bringing stores to the sick and wounded. Sturdy elms lined the avenue toward the infirmary, and tremendous cottonwoods commingled with stately oaks. Inside, however, patients writhed from ghastly wounds. Men nearly dead from fevers moaned weakly, as other men, brought low by hunger, exhaustion, and four days of hard fighting, pleaded for a slice of bread. The dying sought a word of counsel or prayer and dictated final messages to their families. Fuller was busy at the hospital from morning till night, administering medicine and words of comfort. An army correspondent wrote, "I know but little of the theological notions of Chaplain Fuller, but I can tell you that he has got the name . . . 'of a man going about doing good.' It matters not how poor or how degraded a man is who comes in contact with Mr. Fuller, he withdraws from that contact a better man. None know him but to love him."[104]

Fuller did not "think it manly" to discuss the details of his own suffering. Nevertheless, he admitted to enduring "much privation in the way of food, clothing, and exposure."[105] After the Seven Days Battles, his health started to fail. By July 13, he was a patient in the hospital at Fortress Monroe that he had known so well as a visitor. Four days passed before he was able to sit up, take a short walk downstairs, and write to Lucilla. The scandalously poor army diet had given him a painful case of dysentery. He was also prostrated by the heat and humidity of the Virginia summer. The climate, he told his wife, " is terrible & affects my bowels so much as to threaten life."[106] Fuller also had, or was about to have, another complaint he did not mention in the letter. The hordes of mosquitoes that besieged the Army of the Potomac during the Peninsular Campaign bore malaria, a disease that eventually infected more than a million Union men during the war. Reverend Fuller was now one of them.

The minister wanted to be brave. But, as had happened so often in the past, his body was weaker than his will. "You know how sensitive I have always been," he told Lucilla. "I may have to resign before the time I set, but I hate to leave the army now."[107] To travel, work, and pray with this army, Arthur Fuller had overcome his sense of frailty. He had found a place where his spirit felt utterly at home. But that place, so congenial to his heart, was wickedly hostile to his body. The physicians agreed: he could not stay in camp and hope to live. They told the chaplain to go home.

Fuller concluded his letter to Lucilla with a series of political reflections. Some of his predictions missed the mark. He thought the war would soon end; if the Union failed to win quickly, foreign powers would step in and negotiate a permanent separation of North and South. But he saw correctly that the Union could never be restored while slavery remained. Either "the black must be freed, or Secession will triumph by the decree of a righteous God [who has] taken vengeance on guilty nations." He thought President Lincoln "thoroughly honest," though perhaps "too slow for the times." Fuller could think of only five Union men whom he considered "real generals."[108] The first name he wrote down was Ambrose Burnside.

Chapter Six

"The Most Beautiful Girl Runner"

The Mill Dam in Boston was picturesque in name only. The byproduct of a failed development project, its waters were choked with every form of refuse, and city inspectors warned that the buildup of decaying matter, if allowed to continue, would expose the city to a lethal epidemic. The dam stood above an enormous cesspool, coated with greenish scum. The water bubbled frothily like a cauldron as noxious gases rose up from below the surface.[1] It was no place for anyone to go walking alone. But as the shadows lengthened one evening in the autumn of 1858, a tall, modestly dressed woman of twenty-five walked to the dam, stood above the fetid water, and stared into it, wondering whether it was the place where she belonged.

She knew she should not have come there. Still, the waters held her with a "perilous fascination." Her temples throbbed and "a troop of wild fancies" ran riot in her mind. Years later, her recollections of that moment inspired the following description:

> Leaning on the railing, [she] let her thoughts wander where they would. . . . [T]he heavy air seemed to clog her breath and wrap her in its chilly arms. She felt as if the springs of life were running down, and presently would stop. . . . She tried to shake off the strange mood that was stealing over her, but spent body and spent brain were not strong enough to obey her will. . . . [T]he impulse that had seized her grew more intent each moment.[2]

The young woman did not act on her thoughts of suicide. The description just cited, though it recalls an actual incident in its author's life, appears not in a memoir but in a novel called *Work: A Story of Experience*. The despairing young woman who gazed long into the waters below the Mill Dam in 1858 was a struggling, and as yet unknown, writer named Louisa May Alcott.

Habitually frank and forthright, Alcott wrote of the incident to her family in Concord, Massachusetts, a week later. Her courage, she told them, had almost failed her. Unemployed, feeling forgotten by the world, she had decided that no one greatly cared whether she jumped in the river. But her fighting spirit had stopped her. She wrote, "It seemed so mean to turn & run away before the battle was over that I went home, set my teeth & vowed I'd make things work in spite of the world, the flesh & the devil."[3] The determination was more characteristic than the despair, but both were real, and one needed to understand both the will and the woe to comprehend Miss Alcott.

Though born in Germantown, Pennsylvania, Louisa spent most of her upbringing near the heart of literary New England. Her childhood was steeped not only in marvelous books, but also in the physical presence of the extraordinary men and women who wrote them. Her father, Bronson, knew the anthropologist Louis Agassiz, and the poets Longfellow, Lowell, and, of course, the elder Oliver Wendell Holmes.[4] Emerson, her father's closest friend, shared the riches of his library with Louisa, and she repaid him by leaving wildflowers on his doorstep and singing songs beneath his window "in very bad German."[5] Thoreau took Louisa and her sisters for nature walks in the woods of Concord. Nathaniel Hawthorne and his family lived next door to the Alcotts for a time, though the novelist was known to take circuitous paths so as not to be roped into conversation with the garrulous Bronson.

The Alcotts also associated with the country's most influential social visionaries. William Lloyd Garrison, the famous abolitionist, broke bread at the Alcotts' table. Bronson conversed and quarreled with the eminent Unitarian theologian William Ellery Channing. Of the notorious "Secret Six" who quietly funded John Brown's raid on Harpers Ferry, three—Thomas Wentworth Higginson, Theodore Parker, and Franklin Sanborn—were close friends of the Alcott family. It has been observed, with some exaggeration, that "the young Louisa never knew anyone who was less than a general in the armies of reform."[6] Taking courage from such influences, Louisa never doubted the correctness of her radical politics. She was less sure of how to fit in with society.

When people tried dressing her in pretty Victorian frills or lacing her up in any other kind of propriety, the results pleased no one; she was never more awkward or restive than when she was trying to fit someone else's standards of deportment. But take her outdoors in comfortable clothes, let her run, cavort, and get into mischief, and she transformed into a child of grace. "I always thought I must have been a deer or a horse in some former state," she recollected, "because it was such a joy to run. No boy could be my friend till I had beaten him in a race, and no girl if she refused to climb trees, leap fences and be a tomboy."[7] Fred Willis, a friend from those times, remembered, "She was full of spirit and life; impulsive and moody. . . . She could run like a gazelle. She was the most beautiful girl runner I ever saw."[8] Two of the best portraits of her came from Louisa herself: one for her alter ego Jo March in *Little Women* and the other for Sylvia Yule, the heroine of her early, somewhat autobiographical novel *Moods*. Jo, said Alcott, "reminded one of a colt; for she never seemed to know what to do with her long limbs, which were very much in her way. She had a decided mouth, a comical nose, and sharp gray eyes, which appeared to see everything, and were by turns fierce, funny, or thoughtful."[9] Sylvia confronted the world with "a face full of contradictions,—youthful, maidenly, and intelligent, yet touched with the unconscious melancholy that is born of disappointment and desire."[10] Her desires, both artistic and political, were fervent. The disappointments, of every description, had been many.

From an early age, Louisa dreamed of becoming a successful author, though fame was never her strongest motive. She spoke often to Annie Brown, John Brown's daughter, of her wish "to make money and supply her mother's wants."[11] It was not that Mrs. Alcott's wants should have been so hard to satisfy, as she was a woman well accustomed to self-sacrifice. But even her modest needs went unfulfilled, for, almost throughout Louisa's upbringing, the Alcotts were nearly penniless. Though many have said so, Louisa's father was not a feckless, lazy man; no one acquainted with his teaching career, nor anyone who saw the energy with which he plowed his neighbors' fields for a pittance after his teaching career had been taken from him, ever accused him of a want of zeal or effort. Bronson Alcott fell victim, not to a lack of ambition but, in a curious sense, to an extraordinary excess of it. If people failed to recognize his determination to succeed, it was because he was trying to succeed in pursuits that they could not have imagined. He aspired, not toward wealth, but toward a new knowledge of the human condition. He enthusiastically imagined new ideals of education and social organization. In attaining these, he hoped to nudge the world toward perfection.

Bronson began working as a schoolmaster in his mid-twenties. He believed in the power of childhood education with almost religious fervor. At the bottom of his teaching philosophy was an experiment in child development that tried to mix science with theology. He believed in a heaven where perfect truth presided, and he stood convinced that young children, recently arrived from that transcendent realm, were the unheeded messengers of a sacred revelation. He deemed it the work of the teacher to preserve and call forth this natural divinity of the child. If the world's teachers could find the right way to awaken and invigorate their pupils' minds and morals, he believed, they could transform humankind within a generation. With that goal in mind, Bronson treated his classroom as a laboratory, trying to establish the atmosphere that would most effectively prepare his pupils for wise and ethical lives.

When Louisa was three, Bronson presided over a school in Boston whose every feature was calculated to draw out the highest intellectual and moral faculties of his pupils. The Temple School, so named because it was housed in the city's grand Masonic Temple, was, by design, a place of grace and beauty. Sunlight streamed through a large gothic window. The four corners of the room were adorned with busts of Socrates, Shakespeare, Milton, and Scott. Bookcases stood in all directions. "Every part of [the room]," his assistant Elizabeth Peabody wrote, "speaks the thoughts of Genius."[12]

To supply training in Latin and other advanced subjects, Alcott hired, in succession, Elizabeth Palmer Peabody, who later organized influential women's-rights discussion groups in Boston and established America's first kindergarten; and Arthur Fuller's sister, the extraordinary Margaret. It mattered that Bronson chose female helpers. He believed in the ennobling, saving character of the family, and he consciously organized his most inspired efforts at reform around familial structures. Nevertheless, Bronson felt largely thwarted in his efforts to elevate the hearts and minds of the children; they had already undergone too many years of imperfect influence at home by the time they came to him. To further his experiments, he turned to the purest subjects available: his own children.

Louisa's elder sister Anna was born in 1831. Louisa joined the family on November 29, 1832, her father's thirty-third birthday. From the moment each girl was born, Bronson kept journals that recorded every aspect of their development; he wanted to create two comprehensive records of how an infant grows into awareness and character. He intended to continue these narratives until Anna and Louisa were old enough to assume the work themselves, charting their inner lives until they died. Bronson hoped thereby to create "a treasure of inconceivably more value to the world than all the systems which philosophers have built concerning the mind up to this day."[13] Bronson kept his records of the girls going for a few years before putting them aside. The experiment made him only somewhat the wiser regarding the mysteries of the infant mind, but it had gone on long enough to set the tone for the early lives of the eldest Alcott girls; few people have ever undergone such scrutinized childhoods.

Two more daughters followed: Elizabeth, or "Lizzie," in 1835; and Abby, who preferred to be called "May," in 1840. While all four girls endured their father's pressure to strive for moral perfection, Bronson's gaze fell hardest on Louisa. Whereas her sisters more or less shared their father's placid nature, Louisa took after her fiery mother, Abigail. Temperamental and impetuous, Louisa was the despair of her father, for she was the walking refutation of all his theories for raising the perfect child.

Bronson's efforts to tame her were incessant but unavailing. Under her father's supervision, Louisa compiled inventories of her vices, which included "idleness, wilfulness, vanity [and] impatience." Sadly, she also wrote down "activity," and, most pathetically of all, "love of cats."[14] It did not help that so many of Louisa's early influences regarded her father as an almost messianic genius. Emerson called Bronson "a God-made priest."[15] One of the Temple School's young pupils told the schoolmaster, "I think you are a little like Jesus Christ."[16] Bronson did not bother to correct the child. For Louisa to defy her father meant inviting all the guilt and self-condemnation that might trouble a religious heretic. No matter how deeply in error her father might be, the blame always seemed to double back onto her.

Louisa had one staunch defender. The moody, headstrong nature that perplexed her father appealed powerfully to her mother, Abba, who shared Louisa's energy and eagerness to fight in a righteous cause. Abba wrote, "I believe there are some natures too noble to curb, too lofty to bend. Of such is my Lu."[17] She also noted that Louisa had "the most decided views of life and duty. . . . Nothing can exceed the strength of her attachments."[18] None of Louisa's attachments was stronger than the one that bound her to Abba. "People think I'm wild and queer," she wrote at thirteen, "but Mother understands and helps me."[19] In later years, Abba made Louisa a green silk cap for her to wear for inspiration and brought her tea as she wrote her stories. Continually she invited her daughters to come to her whenever they were in need. Louisa promised that she would, for she considered her mother "the best woman in the world."[20]

But the family's fortunes were bound to Bronson's, and Bronson, forever misjudging the openness of his society to radical ideas, was highly fallible. The bubble of his success at the Temple School burst catastrophically, largely because he failed to realize that people who find revolution fashionable in small doses can find it terrifying in larger ones. Emboldened by the school's early success, he published a volume of his colloquies with his pupils on the doctrines and mysteries of the New Testament. The concept now sounds harmless, even innocently charming. To its initial readers, however, Alcott's *Conversations with Children on the Gospels*, in its presumption that children might be consulted on the meaning of the holy scriptures, looked like a blasphemous assault on the social order.

The real scandal of *Conversations* was a lesson about Jesus's birth that blundered into a discussion of how babies were made. Bronson handled the topic with respect, and the closest he came to talking about sex was to suggest "that the body is made out of the naughtiness of other people."[21] No one's innocence was greatly threatened. But these were delicate topics. The newspapers howled their condemnation; scandalized parents fled his academy en masse. Tuition revenues plunged, and Bronson, unable to pay the rent, was driven from the Temple. With his remaining band of pupils, he kept on awhile at a smaller location. A second crisis arose when the schoolmaster agreed to enroll a black student, Susan Robinson. It was more than the remaining parents could withstand. They sent an ultimatum: either the black girl must go, or they would. Bronson's reply was immediate: Susan would stay.

Bronson's moment of courage effectively ended his teaching career. The scandal at the Temple and its aftermath threw the Alcotts into poverty. The family tried to make a new start in Concord, under the partial protection of Emerson. Though Bronson earned some money plowing fields and doing odd jobs, the Alcotts became dependent on gifts from friends and family and the grudging patience of their creditors.

Rebuffed in his efforts to reform the world through education, Bronson resolved to redeem a small portion of it through primitive agriculture. In June 1843, in concert with a British social reformer named Charles Lane, Alcott moved his family to a farm thirty-five miles west of Boston. There, with a ragtag band of eccentric followers, he proclaimed the founding of a vegan community called Fruitlands. Determined to exploit no sentient creature, the Fruitlanders declared that they would do away not only with animal products but also with animal labor. They also eschewed the products of the Southern slave economy. Thus depriving themselves of wool and cotton, they became heavily dependent on linen—a fabric well suited for the Massachusetts summer, though much less so for the winter. It was one of the many choices that prompted Emerson to observe, "They look well in July. We will see them in December."[22]

Bronson's commune also sought to revolutionize family relations; all its members were expected to cease acknowledging any particular affections based on blood or marriage, and to treat all fellow Fruitlanders with equal dignity and affection. Alcott and Lane referred to this system of universal harmony as "the Consociate Family."

It didn't last. The crops failed. As the autumn winds turned cold, the fellow visionaries departed. Before Christmas, the tiny colony was reduced to Lane, his adolescent son, and the six Alcotts. In desperation, Lane made a rash proposal. He had visited a thriving nearby community of Shakers. Theorizing that the secret of the Shakers' success lay in their strict segregation of the sexes, Lane argued that Fruitlands must divide into male and female communities. Since the only female members remaining were the Alcott women, Lane was proposing de facto that Bronson leave his family. On December 10, 1843, Louisa, recently turned eleven, told her journal of a cheerless meeting, where Bronson suggested to Abba and his two oldest daughters that the family should separate. Louisa wrote, "I was very unhappy, and we all cried. Anna and I cried in bed, and I prayed to God to keep us all together."[23]

GALLANT CHARGE OF HUMPHREY'S DIVISION AT THE BATTLE OF FREDERICKSBURG.—Sketched by Mr. A. R. Waud.—[See Page 17.]

John Suhre, Louisa May Alcott's "prince of patients," received his mortal wound in the hopeless assault on Marye's Heights at Fredericksburg, depicted here. In the middle distance, Suhre's division commander, A. A. Humphreys, appears on horseback.

Library of Congress, LC-DIG-ppmsca-22479

Newly commissioned officer Oliver Wendell Holmes Jr., of the Twentieth Massachusetts, wore a determined expression for this 1861 portrait. *Library of Congress, LC-DIG-ppmsca-49594*

Oliver Wendell Holmes Sr. wondered aloud whether sons always despised their fathers. *Old Paper Studios, Alamy Stock Photo*

Colonel William Lee, the commander of Holmes's regiment, drank intemperately and, after Antietam, suffered a pitiable breakdown. Even so, Holmes never ceased to admire him. *Collection of Massachusetts Historical Society*

staunch abolitionist, Willy Putnam thought a
century of civil war would be better than slavery.
His personal war lasted only a few months.
Library of Congress, LC-DIG-ppmsca-59844

Henry Livermore Abbott of the Twentieth
Massachusetts. Holmes regarded him as
the epitome of courage. *Civil War Photograph
Collection, United States Army Heritage and Education Center, Carlisle, PA*

After the war, Holmes shed his chivalric ideals and
cast himself as a "bettabilitarian." *Harvard Law
School Library*

The grand old man of the Supreme Court, Holmes
never parted with the uniform jacket whose collar
was torn by a bullet at Antietam. *Library of Congress,
LC-USZ62-47817*

Unkempt and unruly in this faded photograph, John Pelham had a rough-and-tumble Alabama boyhood. *Heritage Auctions, HA.com*

While still at West Point, Pelham posed for this striking portrait at the New York studio of Mathew Brady. *National Portrait Gallery, Smithsonian Institution*

The Academy in the 1850s. As other Southern cadets resigned and departed, Pelham remained as long as possible, hoping to be granted the diploma that he would never receive. *North Wind Picture Archive / Alamy Stock Photo*

Bold and flamboyant,
J. E. B. Stuart wrote that
Pelham had "won a name
immortal on earth."
*Library of Congress,
LC-DIG-ppmsca-38003*

Kelly's Ford, Virginia, March 17, 1863. With the light of battle in his eyes,
shouting "Forward!," Pelham fell from his horse, never to rise again. *The New York Public Library*

Walt Whitman before the war. His friends recalled "the gentle and refined cast of his features, which were rather rude, but noble."
Library of Congress, LC-USZ62-79942

Walt's younger brother George was known by his comrades-in-arms as the luck-iest man in the Union army.
David M. Rubenstein Rare Book & Manuscript Library, Duke University

Whitman and Peter Doyle. Toward the end of the war, the two men met and fell in love. They lived happily, if not quite ever after. *Library of Congress, LC-DIG-ppmsca-07387*

The Good Gray Poet. Already a man of deep sensitivity, Whitman found that the Civil War led him to discover "undream'd of depths of emotion." If the war had never happened, he maintained, *Leaves of Grass* "would not now be existing." *Library of Congress, LC-USZ62-89947*

Pfaff's beer hall in Manhattan, the scene of the poet's "Quicksand Years."
The Vault at Pfaff's, Lehigh University

At Burnside's Bridge at Antietam, George Whitman became a hero.
Library of Congress, LC-DIG-cwpb-00664

Bronson eventually thought better of the plan; rather than continue in his reckless pursuit of earthly perfection, he chose the humbler consolations of an intact family. Just days into 1844, Fruitlands failed, and so too, for a while, did Bronson's nerves. For days, he refused food and seemed resolved to starve himself to death. His family's love restored the hope that he needed to live, but an emotional breakdown ensued. Fifteen years would pass before Bronson held a steady job. As eleven-year-old Louisa watched his downfall, the ground shifted beneath her. The father whom she had been led to revere as a grand and knowing saint now seemed given to horrendous failures and capable of any betrayal. Fruitlands had made Louisa realize that a family could consist of any group of people bound together by love and duty. At the same time, however, she had seen how readily such structures could collapse. She had also sampled the fear and isolation that can ensue when family can no longer be relied upon.

The Alcotts eventually returned to Concord. In the ensuing years, Bronson held public conversations that brought in a few dollars. He periodically made speaking tours of the Middle West, with no more than moderate success. By necessity, the Alcott sisters became expert at fashioning their own entertainments. They lightened the housework by telling stories, by reading to one another, and by sharing all the dreams and secrets that sisters share. They sang together as Lizzie accompanied them on piano. Anna and Louisa wrote melodramas, which they staged at home with the help of improvised costumes and large doses of imagination. "Nothing," a friend of Louisa's recalled, "gave her more pleasure than plays and tableaux."[24] Yet, despite all the family's efforts to make do, they were, in Louisa's words, "poor as rats & apparently quite forgotten by every one but the Lord." A family friend observed that, as she passed into adulthood, Louisa routinely suffered "the mortifications that poverty brings to a girl of high spirits."[25] The marks left by deprivation ran deep; in her mid-thirties, Alcott still wrote of having learned to "dread debt more than the devil."[26]

Financial pressures drove the family to one of the poorest neighborhoods in Boston. The burdens fell hard upon the Alcott women. To make ends meet, Abba, Anna, and Louisa performed almost every kind of work in which a respectable woman might engage. Louisa took in sewing, taught school, and worked as a governess. She even hired herself out as a maid of all work, a month's misadventure that left her "starved & frozen" and only four dollars richer.[27]

Nevertheless, the family resisted most of the temptations of self-pity. Through it all, a deep bond of love united them. Louisa had just cause to resent her father's moralizing inertia. Yet in her journal she called him a "dear man," and if his speaking tours lost money, she faulted the public for failing to "listen to and pay for his wisdom."[28] The ties among the four sisters were even more powerful. Smiling at the joy and loyalty they shared, Bronson called them "the golden band."[29] The family directed its goodwill outward as well. Abba held to a simple creed that she passed on to her children: "No one [is] so poor he can't do a little for someone poorer yet."[30] Abba found work as a city missionary in Boston and eventually opened an employment office, which she used "to find places for good girls." The little Alcott home became a temporary shelter for the less fortunate, taking in "lost girls, abused wives, friendless children, and weak or wicked men," until they could make a go of things on their own.[31]

All the Alcotts vehemently hated slavery and segregation, and they were willing to stake their fortunes and their freedom in their fight against them. Bronson's defense of Susan Robinson was just one example of the family's commitment to racial equality. In the late 1840s, Bronson and Abba risked prison when they harbored fugitive slaves in their house. Louisa, then in her teens, took on the task of teaching one of them, "a very black George Washington," how to write. Finding that his lack of practice made pen and pencil too awkward to use, she handed him a lump of charcoal and looked on as he formed letters on the family hearthstone.[32] Louisa's sympathy for African Americans had begun with one of her earliest memories. As she ran after her hoop on the Boston Common one day, she fell into the Frog Pond. Unable to swim, she was rescued when a black boy pulled her out of the water and then ran off into anonymity. Mrs. Alcott always declared that her second daughter had been an abolitionist from the age of three.[33]

The mood of the country darkened in 1850 with the passage of the new Fugitive Slave Law. Tensions in Boston escalated the following year when the Supreme Judicial Court of Massachusetts, led by Lemuel Shaw, Herman Melville's father-in-law, declared the law constitutional. Louisa and her father attended a large antislavery gathering at the city's Tremont Temple, where educator Horace Mann, reformist orator Wendell Phillips, and others assailed Shaw's decision. Louisa, then eighteen, fantasized about freeing Thomas Sims, the subject of the case, from his shackles. To save the man from being sent back to his Georgia master, she felt that she would do anything—"fight or work, hoot or cry."[34] Louisa cried in vain: under military guard, Sims was returned to Georgia, where he was publicly whipped and sold to a new master.

In the years before the war, the sacrifices the Alcott family undertook did not always feel noble. They were hard and grinding and, it seemed, unrewarded. Understandably, the sisters grew fond of escapes into fantasy. Anna imagined herself as a famous actress. May dreamed of going to Paris and becoming a famous painter. Louisa also sometimes envisioned a career on the stage, but most often she saw herself as a weaver of tales. In her early twenties, she found that she had a gift for writing stories in a lurid style, which she could sell for the going rate of ten dollars a piece. At twenty-four, as the holidays drew near, she bucked up her spirits by attending a lecture on "Courage" and turned out stories with Christmas and New Year's themes. The trickle of income was gratifying, though at times she felt like a spider, "spinning my brains out for money."[35]

The quietest of the four sisters, Lizzie seemed to have almost no ambitions at all. She wanted only to stay comfortably at home, caring for her parents as they grew old. The family grew used to referring to her as "Little Tranquility" and the "Angel of the House." Lizzie's modest expectations seem to have troubled no one. It was hardly unusual in those times for one daughter in a family to be chosen as her parents' caretaker, and Lizzie's lack of interest in broader horizons was quietly accepted by all as a rather convenient feature.

As they neared adulthood, the Alcott sisters had cause to doubt whether even their humblest hopes would come to fruition. For two of the four, the most daunting impediments were physical. Anna became prematurely hard of hearing, and her deafness made it hard for her to pick up cues onstage. Lizzie's troubles were more menacing. In 1855, the Alcotts had given up on Boston and moved to Walpole, New Hampshire. There, in the following spring, Abba found a new object for her endless campaign of good works: she brought food and clothing to the Halls, an indigent family who lived in a squalid space above a cellar where pigs had been recently kept. Though two of the Halls' children had contracted scarlet fever, Mrs. Alcott was not deterred from bringing along Lizzie and May on her charitable visits. Both sisters caught the disease. May recovered. Lizzie nearly died from it, and the ordeal left her with rheumatic heart disease. Though she seemed to regain strength for a while, the year 1857 saw her grow gradually thinner and paler. By September, Bronson fretted that Lizzie had "neither flesh nor strength to spare."[36] In addition to the physical causes for her sister's slow decline, Louisa thought she saw a psychological one. "I fear she may slip away," she wrote, "for she never seemed to care much for this world beyond home."[37]

In October 1857, the Alcotts moved back to Concord after an absence of nine years. The following year, they would move into Orchard House, the seventeenth-century home on Lexington Road where they were to spend the next twenty years. In their temporary lodgings on Bedford Street, Louisa fitted up a pleasant room for Lizzie. In the ensuing months, Louisa lived two contrasting lives. In the more cheerful one, she acted in plays and had jolly times with friends. The other she spent mostly in Lizzie's room because, as she wrote, "Betty loves to have me with her."[38] At first taking the nighttime shifts so her mother could sleep, Louisa watched over her sister more and more as the winter of 1858 settled over Concord. No more time for friends and acting now; Louisa wrote of "sad quiet days in [Betty's room], and strange nights keeping up the fire and watching the dear little shadow try to wile away the long sleepless hours without troubling me."[39]

Louisa marveled at Lizzie's "gentleness and patient strength."[40] At the same time, she discovered similar qualities in herself. "Dear little saint!" she wrote in her diary. "I shall be better all my life for these sad hours with you."[41] Despite the pain of watching Lizzie fade away, Louisa gained a sense of worth and self-assurance from easing her sister's suffering. Nursing became, for her, a beautiful vocation. In early March, Lizzie put aside her sewing needle because she found it "too heavy."[42] A week later, as Louisa, Abba, and a doctor sat by, she took her final breath. Moments later, Abba and Louisa saw a light mist float up from the body and vanish in the air. The doctor affirmed that they had beheld "the life departing visibly."[43] Lizzie went to her rest with Emerson and Thoreau for pallbearers. Louisa seems to have absorbed it all with surprising calm. She wrote, "Death never seemed terrible, and now it is beautiful, so I cannot fear it, but find it friendly and wonderful."[44]

Nevertheless, the first break in "the golden band" shook Louisa more deeply than she immediately professed. The shock did not fully strike her for a month. Then, however, news that should have been happy flung her into confusion: her sister Anna announced that she was engaged. Her intended, John Pratt, was "a true man—full of fine possibilities," as Louisa admitted. But the betrothal stung her. Lizzie had had no choice in leaving the family; Anna's intentional departure felt almost treacherous. "So another sister is gone," Louisa lamented. "I moaned in private over my great loss."[45]

For Louisa, Lizzie's death was potentially calamitous in another way. It had always been assumed that Lizzie would care for Abba and Bronson in their old age. Now that she was gone, another sister was needed for the task. Anna was about to start a family of her own. Evidently no one ever dreamed that May, the youngest sister, would fill the role. It was starting to look as if Louisa, who desperately needed time and tranquility to focus on her writing, had drawn the short straw. The family that had supplied structure now threatened to impose stricture.

Albeit a building of considerable charm, Orchard House was so weather-beaten and neglected that Louisa called it "Apple Slump."[46] As her parents renovated the sagging homestead, Alcott kept away the blues with writing and domestic chores. She swept, dusted, and washed dishes, scratching out a few pages whenever a free hour arose. A magazine story went for twenty-five dollars, enough to spruce up the Alcott women's dresses and bonnets. "The inside of my head can at least cover the outside," Alcott quipped.[47] As she simmered soups and vegetables in the family kitchen, she was simmering novels and plans as well. The hard truths of her existence had taught her to dream modestly now; she hoped above all to bring in enough money to care for herself, her parents, and May. But her writing income fell far short of the task. In October, she looked for work in Boston. She found none, and the despair and anxiety that had been building since Lizzie's death reached up to throttle her. She walked to the Mill Dam and looked down into the churning waters.

But, as we know, she pulled back from the edge. She told herself, "There is work for me, and I'll have it." She went back to her room "resolved to take Fate by the throat and shake a living out of her."[48] A few days later, she heard a sermon by the noted abolitionist minister Theodore Parker on "Laborious Young Women." Parker seemed to be speaking directly to her. "Trust your fellow-beings," he urged, "and let them help you. Don't be too proud to ask, and accept the humblest work till you can find the task you want."[49] Taking his words as a personal directive, Alcott summoned her courage, went to Parker's house, and asked his wife if they had work for her. She appeared at their door muddy and shabby, looking more like "a reckless highway woman" than an applicant for a position.[50] With the minister's help, she found a job. Parker said, "The girl has got true grit . . . Louisa will succeed."[51]

As she turned twenty-six that November, Alcott reflected on the vast changes that a year had effected. A bit braver now, she made up her mind to "grub away with a good heart." Though physically departed, Lizzie still helped her spiritually; the memory of her meek example showed Louisa how to moderate her moods. Grief, she said, had taught her more than any sermon. "Work of head and heart, " she now knew, would be her "salvation when disappointment or weariness burden and darken my soul."[52]

A larger darkness was sweeping the land, and its influence in both Concord and Boston was impossible to ignore. On May 8, 1859, Concord's town hall welcomed a remarkable guest. Tall and square-jawed, with a peculiar wildness in his gaze, Captain John Brown made no secret of his work during the recent upheaval known as "Bleeding Kansas." Driven to fury by the criminal acts of proslavery men in the territory, Brown had led an armed posse to Pottawatomie Creek, abducted five proslavery men from their homes, and murdered them with broadswords. Bronson excused the massacre in the name of liberty, calling Brown "about the manliest man I have ever seen . . . superior to legal traditions."[53] Though Louisa missed Brown's speech, she found the antislavery fervor irresistible. In September, Concord hosted a large encampment of military units, whose grand marches and exercises enchanted the town for three days. It thrilled Louisa to walk amid a "Town full of soldiers, with military fuss and feathers." She continued, "I like a camp, and long for a war, to see how it all seems. I can't fight, but I can nurse."[54]

In the late 1850s, Alcott gained confidence, both in herself and in the beneficence of God. But her external life had failed to transform. She was seeking, above all, a field of action commensurate with her capacity to feel and to dream. Throughout August 1860, she took up an absorbing task: the draft of her first novel, which she called *Moods*. Even more than *Little Women*, *Moods* was the book into which Alcott flung her "love, labor, and enthusiasm."[55] Arguably more even than Jo March, Sylvia Yule, the heroine, embodies the spirit of her creator. Like Alcott, Sylvia has inherited "pride, intellect, and will" from her father. Her mother has given her "passion, imagination, and the fateful melancholy of a woman defrauded of her dearest hope."[56] By her own admission, Sylvia is "always in extremes." Another character comments that she is "either overflowing with unnatural spirits or melancholy enough to break one's heart."[57] Sylvia protests in her own defense, "I don't try to be odd; I long to be quiet and satisfied, but I cannot; and when I do . . . wild things, it is not because I am thoughtless or idle, but because I am trying to be good and happy."[58] For Louisa, it was an apt self-portrait.

Alcott had come a long way in managing the ungovernable temper that had plagued her in her youth, but her fighting spirit was far from being subdued. Like many young Americans, she wanted the war to happen. Her book about the war, *Hospital Sketches*, begins with her alter ego Trib Periwinkle exclaiming, "I want something to do!"[59] Alcott, too, wanted something to do, but it was more than this. Oppressed by small-town life and frustrated with the glacially slow progress of her writing career, Alcott felt a brewing anger every bit as strong as her hatred of slavery. She needed an object that she could strike against, one that would turn her feelings into action. In April 1861, as the first bombs exploded over Fort Sumter, that object became clear: it was Jeff Davis's Confederacy.

That spring, as little boys made a tiny uproar with fifes and drums, the young men of Concord marched and drilled in preparation for battle. Louisa could not suppress a smile as she watched them "poke each other's eyes out, bang their heads & blow themselves up with gunpowder."[60] Older citizens studied the papers and made predictions, as patriotic hats and handkerchiefs abounded. Before long, Alcott mused, the rainbow would be condensed to red, white, and blue, and the old Yankee greeting of "How are yer?" would entirely give way to "Hail, Columbia!"[61] The Concord Artillery, already formed before the war, departed on April 19, 1861— the anniversary, as everyone knew, of the Battle of Concord in the Revolutionary War. Seeing them off at the train station, the town felt the sadness as if it were a single family.

In the sphere that was permitted them, Concord's women were also active. Alcott's mother took in two of John Brown's daughters as boarders. In the parlor one afternoon, Mrs. Alcott nodded off to sleep. Annie Brown heard her benefactress draw a deep sigh and announce in drowsy earnestness, "I've enlisted!"[62] May Alcott picked lint for bandages, though she was happier going for horseback rides and boating excursions with Hawthorne's son, Julian. Louisa joined in the war effort, though the role that was open to her felt frustratingly small. During the first months of the war, she sewed "violently on patriotic blue shirts" for the men to wear into battle. She was glad to do her part, but when she could put aside her needle and reach for her pen, she did so gratefully. She told a friend, "The first article [is] my abomination & the last my delight."[63]

As she watched the town's young men depart for scenes of imagined glory she would never witness, Alcott turned wistful. "I've often longed to see a war," she told her journal, "and now I have my wish. I long to be a man, but as I can't fight, I will content myself with working for those who can."[64] She yearned "to fly at somebody," she told a friend, "but there is no opening for me at present so I study Dr. [William] Home on 'gun-shot wounds' & get my highly connected self ready to go as a nurse."[65] But there was to be no nursing for many months. Dorothea Dix, who led the Union's nursing corps, worried that dewy-eyed maidens would invade the hospitals in search of slightly damaged husbands. She there-fore decreed that no woman under the age of thirty need apply. Louisa could do nothing until November 29, 1862.

✳

FIVE HUNDRED MILES FROM CONCORD, a far less documented life than Louisa's had been unfolding. John F. Suhre was born in Somerset County, Pennsylvania, on October 29, 1841, in a handsome valley in the Allegheny Mountains where the fog lay thick on cold autumn mornings. Though inhospitable to corn, the land was good for raising wheat, rye, potatoes, and oats. During Suhre's boyhood, a plank road had connected the town of Somerset with the rail terminal at Cumberland, Maryland, and commerce with other regions had begun to flow more freely. How-ever, the road could not support the transportation of heavy freight, and thus the old-growth forests were still largely untouched by loggers. John grew up accustomed to gigantic chestnuts, oaks, and hemlocks, which grew so thick that hardly any underbrush could flourish beneath them.

John was the first child of his mother Sarah's second family. With her first husband, Michael Lowry, she had had five children: Maria, Sam-uel, Anna, Emanuel, and Michael Conrad. Her second marriage, to the

German-born Joseph Suhre, took place in Maryland the same year John was born.[66] Two younger siblings joined the family: Johanna in 1845 and George in 1848. Only one specific event in John's childhood has been preserved. On March 27, 1847, when he was five, he and his family were asleep on the first floor of their house in Elk Lick Township when they were awakened by the terrifying sound of falling embers. They rushed out of their burning home, which the fire then destroyed. The loss to Mr. Suhre, a local newspaper reported, "is a serious one."[67]

One suspects that circumstances were seldom easy for the Suhre family, and the loss of their home was a grievous setback. The newspaper reported the conflagration; the family's recovery took place without notice. Joseph died the year John turned fifteen, and the young man was obliged at once to learn a trade. He had embarked upon a career as a blacksmith when, less than three months before his twenty-first birthday, he answered the call of his country. He was reluctant to leave home; George, at fourteen, would have his hands full assisting his fifty-five-year-old mother as the man of the house. But Sarah pressed a ring into his hand, a talisman for safekeeping, and said, "Go."[68] And then he was gone—to Camp Curtin in Harrisburg, where, in exchange for the promise of a twenty-five-dollar bounty, he was inducted into the 133rd Pennsylvania Volunteer Infantry on August 14, 1862.

The 133rd was a nine-month regiment, set to be disbanded the following May. As a bounty regiment, it was subject to scorn and suspicion from the soldiers of "the old 1861 regiments"—men who, like Pen Hallowell and George Whitman, had enlisted out of loyalty to the Union, hatred of slavery, or perhaps just the love of a good fight. What, by contrast, could be said of a man who came to his country's aid only in response to a bribe? The bounty soldier was an unpleasant reminder that the war was becoming a business. Sometimes deserting while still in training camp, frequently sneaking off from one regiment to claim a second bounty by joining another, the worst of these men stained the others with a bad reputation.[69] Yet there were some bounty men who, knowing the prejudices against them, wanted all the more to prove their detractors wrong. To judge from all we know, John Suhre was one of these.

The regiment's original muskets were Austrian, cheaply made, and practically useless. Traveling to Washington, the unit was brigaded with the 123rd, 131st, and 134th Pennsylvania under the command of a Mexican War veteran, Colonel Peter Allabach. Toward the end of August, they were encamped in Alexandria, Virginia, as the Battle of Second Bull Run raged thirty-five miles to the west. Suhre and his mates spent two weeks performing picket duty and digging entrenchments before being sent back across the river to Washington. There, they gratefully exchanged their inferior guns for Springfield muskets, traded their company tents for lighter shelter tents, and received sixty rounds of ammunition each.

Suhre was not present for the carnage at Antietam; his regiment had been held back to guard the city of Frederick, Maryland. The night after the battle, expecting the fighting to resume the following day, Suhre's division commander, A. A. Humphreys, drove his men on a twenty-three-mile march to Sharpsburg. On the 18th of September, Suhre arrived at a silent, stricken battlefield. Quite possibly, the first tool he used on a battleground was not a gun, but a shovel: he may well have been assigned to a burial detail, digging graves marked with headboards made from hardtack boxes and ammunition cases.

The 133rd settled into camp a mile outside Sharpsburg, where they passed a dreary month. In his only surviving letter, Suhre reported receiving his bounty, along with a two-dollar premium. He talked about the weather. He noted that the regiment had been forced to leave its warm woolen blankets in Washington and hoped that his mother might send him a quilt. He misspelled the names of both his brigade commander and his regimental commander and sent the letter home.[70]

In the camp, disease was rampant. By the 22nd, the newly arrived regimental chaplain, Andrew Jackson Hartsock, counted 200 men on the sick roll, some of them seriously ill.[71] Hartsock saw no sense in keeping so many men exposed to the elements, doing nothing, just so they could sicken and die. "Why keep these men here to suffer . . . ?" he demanded. "What good to our country? Why not send them home?"[72] Rumors that a great battle was coming filtered through the camp and then died out. Though the men did not relish fording the chilly Potomac, they were eager to move. "Better die on the bloody field," Hartsock opined, "[than] in the miasmic influence of this place."[73]

On October 31, the regiment crossed the river at Harpers Ferry. Despite their fatigue, some new energy passed through them as they stepped onto Rebel soil. Chaplain Hartsock observed, "They look upon rebel poultry, rebel hogs, and think they have a right to . . . the plunder. It was amusing to hear the pigs squeal and the boys after them with a vengeance. . . . Pork was plenty."[74] After taking part in a march through the Loudoun Valley in vain pursuit of Stonewall Jackson, the regiment was sent to Warrenton, where they were present for McClellan's last review of the troops. Some, at least, were disappointed by the outgoing commander's appearance, thinking him "not half the man the artists represent him."[75]

In the third week of November, Suhre and his fellows were ordered on to Falmouth. They passed through country that, after months of foraging, looked as if it had been destroyed by locusts. Raw, soaking weather went with them. Tent pegs would not hold in the mud; rivulets of rainwater ran through the camp, soaking blankets and dragging down spirits. Fires started with damp wood guttered and died out. Another soldier in the 133rd wrote that he would have given five dollars for the grand improvement of sleeping in his father's hog pen.[76] They reached Falmouth on the weekend of November 22. Once they had arrived, there was little to do but wait; General Burnside would not move into Fredericksburg until he had the materials to build pontoon bridges across the Rappahannock. Marking time as the snow fell, sometimes three inches deep, the men of the 133rd awaited pontoons that, it seemed, would never come.

✶

As the 133rd settled in at Falmouth, Louisa May Alcott was safe at home. But she had never relished safety. She yearned for battle "like a warhorse when he smells powder." She had nearly had her fill of sewing bees and lint picks. "The blood of the Mays," she declared, "is up!"[77] On November 29, she turned thirty, and the ban on her entering the nursing service lifted. In her journal, she listed the arguments for enlisting: help was needed, she loved nursing, and she "must let out [her] pent-up energy in some new way." Winter at home would be hard and dull. By leaving she would give the family "one less to feed and warm and worry over." Really, she needed no convincing. She sent in her name and, as she awaited word, she scribbled some tales for the magazines "to leave all snug behind me," and mended her old clothes in anticipation of her hoped-for departure. She wrote, "Nurses don't need nice things, thank Heaven!"[78]

Chapter Seven

"Beauty" and "Sallie"

H e blushed continually.
Virtually every Confederate veteran who wrote about John Pelham recollected how quickly and brightly the color rose to his cheeks—his natural and irrepressible response whenever anyone teasingly mentioned his skill as a charmer of women or praised his mastery of artillery warfare. And the praise was growing now. After observing Pelham's command of the guns on the Confederate left at Antietam, John Esten Cooke, a staff officer with Stuart, admired more than ever the young man's preternatural abilities. He wrote, "There is a genius for every thing—Pelham's was to fight artillery."[1]

The Horse Artillery seemed to grow more agile and efficient with every battle. The expert training in limbering and unlimbering that Pelham had given his men, coupled with the strength and speed of their mounts, enabled the unit "to dash . . . ahead of all infantry support, to pursue as if he led cavalry, and to withdraw . . . swiftly."[2] Surprising, unpredictable, and uncannily accurate, the fire from his guns was uniquely effective in sowing confusion among the Union forces. The highest levels of the Confederate command were taking notice.

Louis Nolan, whose work Pelham had read and reread at West Point, had commented, "Horse-Artillery with Cavalry is not only a powerful auxiliary in the attack, but a friend in need in the hour of danger and defeat."[3] In Stuart's command, the professional "friendship" between artillery and cavalry was reflected in the strengthening attachment between the two men who led them. As his list of successes lengthened, Pelham's performance bound Stuart ever closer to him. Pelham's feelings toward Stuart were also appreciative. Combining his firmness with human warmth and an insatiable love of fun, the general exuded a style of authority that contrasted favorably with that of the rigid, domineering Atkinson Pelham. A figurative older brother suited Pelham better than a second father. Stuart's adjutant H. B. McClellan (not related to the Union general) expressed a widely shared opinion when he wrote that two spirits more congenial than Stuart and Pelham never met on the field of battle:

> Stuart's fondness for artillery was almost excessive; Pelham's skill in its management amounted to genius. Stuart and Pelham imparted to the horse artillery an independency of action and a celerity of movement which . . . was nowhere equaled or imitated.[4]

This independence of action was a key aspect of the partnership. Nolan had also observed the horse-artilleryman functioned best when given free rein: he must be allowed to choose his own ground and the proper moment for opening fire—judgments that officers not used to handling cannons were almost sure to bungle.[5] Mindful of this advice, Stuart placed a level of trust in Pelham that was remarkable given Pelham's youth. That trust was continually rewarded.

Stuart, like Pelham, was drawn to daring. During the Union's Peninsular Campaign of early summer 1862, Stuart was assigned to scout George McClellan's position. He took a select detachment of 1200 men and, risking annihilation, led them on a ride all the way around the Union army. In the process, Stuart destroyed a quantity of Yankee supplies, took more than 160 prisoners, and routed a Federal force under the command of Philip St. George Cooke, who happened to be Stuart's father-in-law. Though the raid had little effect on the campaign's outcome, it deeply embarrassed the Northerners and buoyed the spirits of the South.

Stuart's penchant for attention-getting feats did not always serve him well. A second raid later in the same campaign put him out of contact with the rest of the army. Deprived of cavalry support at a moment when he sorely needed it, Lee suffered a painful defeat at Malvern Hill. Some also felt that, by impetuously firing on the enemy the following day,

Stuart had spooked the Federals into taking a strong defensive position on a long ridge known as Evelington Heights. Had the Rebels been able to seize the high ground first, Stuart's detractors claimed, Lee's infantry might have dealt McClellan a crippling blow. Unimpressed by Stuart's shows of bravado throughout the campaign, the eminent Confederate artillerist E. Porter Alexander considered Stuart a prime instance of the "dangers [that] lurk in excess of enterprise as well as in its deficiency."[6] But for most observers, Stuart's value both as a scout and a cavalry tactician, to say nothing of the lift he continually gave to the army's morale, more than atoned for his lapses. General Joseph E. Johnston, who preceded Lee in command of the army, likened Stuart to "a yellow jacket . . . no sooner brushed off than it lit back."[7]

As much attention as Stuart attracted for the bold maneuvering of his cavalry, he garnered just as much with his personal appearance and habits—and he liked it that way. He wore a cape lined with scarlet and accentuated his brown felt hat with a black ostrich plume. He fondly wore a red rose in his jacket when roses could be had, and replaced it with a love-knot of red ribbon when the season for flowers had died away.[8] Esten Cooke wrote that Stuart "was as fond of colours as a boy or a girl." He noted the general's fine buff gauntlets, the silk sash he wore around his waist and, the crowning touch, a set of spurs that shone with the luster of pure gold.[9]

The spurs were especially important to Stuart. He took for himself a nickname that was striking in its vainglory: "Knight of the Golden Spurs." Lee's army contained a peerage of officers known for their eccentricities: in addition to sucking lemons during battles, Jackson was convinced that his arms were of different weights and acquired the habit of holding one aloft hoping to balance the circulation of his blood; A. P. Hill was loath to go into combat without his red battle shirt. But it was Stuart who, in the words of an admiring biographer, uniquely "filled the eye."[10]

One of Stonewall Jackson's staff officers told of a night when Stuart and Pelham arrived late at night on a visit to Jackson's camp. While Pelham bedded down in the officer's tent, Stuart, bothering to remove only his sword, climbed in alongside the famous general. The next morning, rubbing the sore spots on his legs, Jackson greeted the cavalryman with a request. "General Stuart," he said, "I'm always glad to see you here. . . . But, General, you must not get into my bed with your boots and spurs on and ride me around like a cavalry horse all night!"[11]

Stuart was a member of the Presbyterian Church and was known to be "a consistent, conscientious Christian."[12] Honoring an oath that he had made to his mother when he was a boy, he refused to touch alcohol. Most of those who were close to Stuart insisted that, although the general was noticeably fond of female companionship, he remained faithful to his wife Flora, with whom he had three children. Pelham's friend Tom Rosser believed otherwise. Irked by Stuart's failure to reward him with a promised promotion, Rosser wrote to his own wife in fury, "[Stuart] has been as false to *me* as [he] has ever been to his country and his *wife*."[13] Stuart was also drawn powerfully to young male beauty. Captain William Blackford, Stuart's adjutant, noticed that Stuart perpetually surrounded himself with attractive men: "He liked his staff to present a handsome, soldierly appearance, and he liked a handsome man as much almost as he did a handsome woman. The members of his staff, the ladies all said, were remarkable for their personal appearance."[14] It seems no coincidence that, immediately after this observation, Blackford devoted a paragraph of his memoirs to John Pelham.

Between battles, Stuart insisted that Pelham remain at headquarters, whether or not Pelham wished to be there.[15] "The General," Blackford explained, "would not agree for him to do otherwise, for he loved him dearly."[16] The young man's presence in or around Stuart's quarters became so compulsory that Blackford mistakenly listed him as a member of the general's staff.[17] The two men regularly pitched their tents next to each other.[18] If Pelham were absent, Stuart demanded to know why. Esten Cooke recalled, "Once associated with the command of Stuart, [Pelham] secured the warm regard and unlimited confidence of that General, who employed his services upon every occasion. Thenceforth their fortunes seemed united, like their hearts."[19] Stonewall Jackson's aide Henry Kyd Douglas put the matter succinctly: Pelham was Stuart's "artillery pet."[20]

Before leaving West Point, Pelham had predicted that he would fight in a few battles and then die. His subsequent good fortune, however, had changed his mind. He now told Cooke that he had never felt that destiny would lead him to be killed in the war.[21] Similarly, Stuart struck one of his aides as "unconscious of the feeling of fear."[22] Both men had the kind of trust in God that can make death seem impossible, or at least irrelevant. Yet they, like every other man in both armies, lived with the continual possibility of death. Such an awareness can intensify friendships and deepen attachments. The possessiveness Stuart exerted and the affection he evinced regarding his "artillery pet" were more than might be expected from a commanding officer. Many strands were woven in the ambiguous tie that he felt with Pelham: a worshipful regard for his skill and courage under fire; an ever-lengthening catalog of shared adventures; the knowledge that a single moment of catastrophe could divide them forever; and, certainly, the fact that Pelham was charming, handsome, and young. All these elements combined to forge a connection of surpassing strength.

The life of the ordinary soldier in Lee's army in the months that followed Antietam was far from pleasant. It was a season of lice, ragged clothing, short rations, and worn-out shoes—if a man was lucky enough to have shoes at all. But Stuart believed that even war need not be grim at every moment, and there were music and dancing in his camp that early autumn. At the invitation of Adam Dandridge, the property's owner and a descendant of Martha Washington's family, the general set up quarters near the banks of Opequon Creek, on the grounds of a federal-style mansion built in 1806. "The Bower," as it is still known, is an elegant brick house of fourteen rooms, graced by a spacious front porch, its overhang supported by Ionian columns. To Heros von Borcke, the site of Stuart's new camp seemed no less than "the elysian fields."[23]

The first-person accounts of those weeks at the Bower that come down from Stuart's men are anything but objective. They are roseate, idealized, and sentimental, and there is nothing like them in the stories of Holmes, George Whitman, or Fuller. It is easy to understand why Stuart's veterans wrote so romantically. They set down their recollections at the end of the war, when the sting of defeat was fresh and painful. To comfort themselves, they looked back upon the autumn of 1862 as the last moment when the courtly grace of their lives felt durable and real. More than a century and a half later, the pictures they painted are too attractive for many of us to believe.

We tell ourselves and one another that war cannot be romantic. And, indeed, any idyll founded on slavery is inwardly warped by elements of cruelty and decay. The memories of men like Esten Cooke and von Borcke strike us as illusions. In many ways they certainly were. But to them the memories were true—or, at least, they had to make them true in order to feel that their lives had not become mere masses of destruction and failure. The story of the Bower is essential to the story of John Pelham, and it was told by people who wanted to make that story beautiful, according to their flawed ideas of beauty. Because theirs are the only accounts of the interlude, the languid days at the Bower can be seen through the gauze of their idealizations, or not seen at all. Perhaps their memories are best read not as a neutral representation of truth, but as reflections of a state of mind, the same feeling that leads one to keep and treasure a dried corsage long after the dance is over. How Stuart's men told these stories is likely the chief significance of the stories themselves.

Von Borcke remembered the trees and the water. Stuart's headquarters were, he recalled, situated on a hill under the shade of enormous oaks of primitive growth. One could follow the trees up to the Dandridge mansion, whose brick walls stood behind a well-tended garden. At the foot of the hill ran the creek, whose waters tumbled over cliffs and rocks, forming a cascade. Von Borcke wrote fondly of the rainbows emerging from the spray "as the sun changed every falling drop into a ruby or a diamond."[24] In the camp itself, under its fluttering battle flag, officers and men strolled about in the morning air and cleaned their guns as their enslaved servants stood over campfires to cook their breakfasts. For the soldiers, a scene of peace; for the men they held in servitude, another time of toil. All in all, von Borcke recalled, the Bower gave "a feeling of thankful happiness to the soldier, weary of the excitement . . . the hardships, and the anguish of war."[25] H. B. McClellan primly remembered the Bower for its "pleasant and ennobling social intercourse."[26] One may assume, however, that some in the camp cared only secondarily about being ennobled. To be sure, Dandridge's home was one of grace and culture, but it also happened to be filled with eligible daughters and nieces, who peered out through the curtains of their upstairs rooms to gaze out on "heroes of romance fresh from fields of glory."[27]

Stuart had a fondness for sentimental popular tunes. To indulge his musical cravings he kept with him a small band of amateur musicians. They were led by a banjoist named Sam Sweeney, a mere private, whom Stuart added to his staff—a position typically reserved for officers—on the strength of his musical talents alone.[28] Two of Stuart's couriers struggled to sound tuneful on violins, though the rhythms were ably supplied by an enslaved man, Mulatto Bob. Bob's special gift was for playing the bones, a simple hand-held instrument carved from a pair of animal ribs.

He clicked them together between his fingers, creating dazzling rhythms. As he played, both his head and feet stayed constantly in motion, and his body twisted so rapidly "that one could not help fearing that he would dislocate his limbs and fly to pieces in the midst of the break-down."[29] At daybreak, Stuart's band awakened the staff with military tunes. Out of respect for their hosts, the officers put on their best uniforms. Their official duties tended to consume only the morning hours. Thereafter, they formed parties for riding, walking, or fishing. Afternoon tea formed part of the almost daily ritual, and as the sun sank low, tea gave way to further bucolic enjoyments. Blackford recalled "music, singing, dancing and games of every description, mingled with midnight strolls along the banks of the beautiful Opequon or boating upon its crystal surface."[30]

Pelham, for his part, added to his reputation for being "as grand a flirt as ever lived."[31] He focused his attentions on one of his host's daughters, whose name was the same as Pelham's old, teasing nickname, Sallie. When a singing circle assembled around the Dandridge fireplace, Pelham held her hand. They promenaded through her father's rose garden and rowed at night on the river. Stuart observed it all and wondered aloud whether the romance might spoil Pelham's love for fighting. In this beautiful country, Pelham spent what seemed to be some of his happiest hours.[32]

Those hours were enlivened by the entertainments that Stuart always insisted on having near at hand. To supplement the concerts of the camp musicians, the staff engaged in broadly farcical theatricals, in which von Borcke often played a starring role. At his soldiers' antics, Stuart would guffaw until the tears came.[33] His heart was light during these days, and he showed himself to be "as conspicuous a leader in a ballroom as he was on a field of battle."[34] At the Bower, his presumed faithfulness to Flora did not prevent him from kissing several pretty young women, though his adjutant would later insist that none of his little dalliances led to grander improprieties.[35] Yet the merrymaking at the Bower had a melancholy edge, for no one could revel wholeheartedly when so many of their fellows, who had so recently ridden beside them, lay dead at Antietam. At times, Stuart had to strain to keep up the jollity. If one of his officers tried to slip away from a party to take some extra rest, Stuart would indignantly rouse him from his bed and return him to the frolic. Amid his revelers, Stuart's voice was always the loudest, as if to force his friends to abandon any thoughts or recollections that might dampen the mood.

At these soirées, Pelham was present, too. Though his reactions to them are unrecorded, it is reasonable to suppose that he was grateful for the diversions. The beauty of the Bower, the attentions of Sallie Dandridge, and Stuart's insistence on maintaining the highest of spirits all helped to keep the foul muck of war at a distance. And indeed, somehow, the stain and the chaos of the fighting seemed not yet to have fastened themselves to Stuart's command. For these weeks of grace, Pelham and his comrades could imagine themselves exempt from the consuming tragedy. Miles away, in the darkness, the Army of the Potomac waited. But for now these soldiers were happy, as Sam Sweeney plucked his banjo and they sang songs under the stars.

On October 8 an order from General Lee interrupted the idyll: Stuart was to form a detachment of 1200 to 1500 men, cross the Potomac, and mount a raid on southern Pennsylvania. Stuart's troopers were to ride to Chambersburg with three objectives: destroy a railroad bridge on nearby Conococheague Creek, over which large quantities of Yankee supplies were known to pass; kidnap government officials to be exchanged for Southern prisoners; and inflict such other damage as Stuart saw fit. Somewhat exceeding his authority, Stuart assembled 1800 of his best horsemen. He told Pelham to bring sixty artillerymen and four cannons. As they departed, Stuart and Pelham rode side by side. By 7 a.m. on the 10th, the last of Pelham's guns had crossed the river, and Stuart's column was pressing toward the Pennsylvania border. By late morning, the expedition reached the town of Mercersburg. In a gesture of intimidation, Pelham rolled two of his cannons into the town square, while some of his comrades patronized local merchants and jokingly paid in Confederate currency.

That night, William Heyser, a sixty-seven-year-old businessman living in Chambersburg, wrote that Stuart's men had arrived, demanding the town's surrender: "They immediately took possession of the bank and telegraph office. . . . They will be busy stripping our stores and gathering up horses."[36] The demand of surrender had come with a threat. If the town chose to resist, Pelham's guns would open on it in three minutes. Chambersburg capitulated at once. The telegraph wires were cut. A detachment of Stuart's men, led by William E. "Grumble" Jones, rode north of town to burn the targeted rail bridge. They were disappointed; the bridge turned out to be made of iron. Stuart had ordered his men not to steal or destroy the private property of Chambersburg's citizens, and these orders were more or less obeyed. However, the prohibition did not extend to United States Government property, and the undefended Union army depot near the railroad station was pronounced fair game. Enthusiastically, Stuart's troopers liberated overcoats, underwear, socks, hats, and trousers, as well as an untold quantity of rifles and sidearms. What they could not carry, they burned, along with the storehouse that contained them.

Another depredation of Stuart's forces was evidently recorded only in a single document, but it is an agonizingly poignant one. Heyser, who had carefully hidden his important documents at the approach of Stuart's legion, lamented that people were not so easy to conceal as papers. He told his diary that Stuart's men "did take eight [free] young colored men and boys along with them, in spite of their parents' pleading. I fear we will never see them again, unless they can escape."[37] The actions observed by Heyser set a shameful precedent, soon to be followed on a larger scale. In late June 1863, Lee's army moved into Pennsylvania in full force. Confederate cavalry again rode into Chambersburg and rounded up approximately 250 free black residents to be taken to the South and enslaved. Powerless citizens looked on as the crowd of captives, mostly women and children, were "driven . . . just like we would drive cattle" through the streets of the town.[38]

Stuart's raiders were already in jeopardy. By the evening of the 10th, at the War Department, General-in-Chief Henry Halleck had ordered General McClellan to cut off Stuart's retreat. "Not a man should be permitted to return to Virginia," Halleck stipulated. "Use any troops in Maryland or Pennsylvania against them."[39] Stuart's horsemen had no hope of going back the way they had come; that route was now teeming with Union forces. The Confederates were behind enemy lines in unfamiliar country. It seemed at last that the Army of the Potomac would bag the wily Stuart. The gray commander himself doubted that he would survive. As he plotted the path back to safety, Stuart rode with his adjutant out of earshot from his other officers with his adjutant. "Blackford," he said, "if I should fall before reaching Virginia, I want you to vindicate my memory."[40] As the general set forth his plan to Blackford, the captain's eyes grew wet. Stuart also shed tears.

The escape called for spectacular daring. Stuart's regiments would ride east through open country. They might easily be discovered, but by the same token the openness of the fields around them would keep them from losing their way or being ambushed. They would loop around McClellan's main force and try to cross the Potomac far downstream. Undoubtedly, Federal units would be awaiting them at the best-known fords. However, if Stuart succeeded in attacking them in the rear, he might dislodge them long enough to effect a crossing.[41] Leaving Chambersburg on the morning of October 11, Stuart's men rode that whole day and for almost the entire following night, stopping only a half hour to feed and rest their famished, nearly exhausted horses. As it was, they managed to keep up their pace only by switching from their own horses to ones they had captured during the raid, letting their original mounts trot along riderless.

A soaking rain had watered the roads that they traveled—a stroke of luck. The column of riders, which stretched out over five miles, would normally have raised a great cloud of dust, giving away its whereabouts. Pelham divided his guns, keeping two apace with the advance guard of the expedition and leaving the other two to bring up the rear. His horses, having to pull their load of cannons and caissons, were prone to fatigue and needed to be substituted frequently. Stuart's riders had started off in the direction of Gettysburg, a place whose name as yet had no special meaning for them. Before reaching the town they veered south, crossing back into Maryland near Emmitsburg, where they took their thirty-minute rest. The townspeople, surprised but sympathetic to the rebellion, brought out baskets of food. However, the blue coats that many of Stuart's men had taken to wearing after seizing them at Chambersburg alarmed one young woman. Mistaking the men for Federals, she leaped onto a horse and dashed away. Presuming that she meant to alert McClellan's army, Pelham spurred his horse after her. Only after a desperate chase of a mile or so did he catch her, and both were able to laugh at their respective errors.

Time was ticking by, and Stuart knew that every mile that could be gained before sunup on the 12th might prove crucial. Promptly, he ordered his command out of Emmitsburg. There was no sleep that night. In the darkness, Stuart rode alongside Pelham, buoyed by his companionship. The long gray column's officers had their orders: "Keep this pace. Slow the gait for nothing, and ride over anything that gets in the way."[42]

By daybreak, just twelve miles lay between Stuart and the safety of Virginia. But they were dangerous miles. Ahead were rolling hills, steep ravines, and thick woodlands—hardly ideal terrain across which to drive Pelham's artillery pieces. An anxious moment arose when Pelham's gunners reached the steep banks of a creek. Was it passable? Pelham rode into the murky water. Seconds later, he shouted the go-ahead: "The Lord's been good to us! It'll hold well! It's all right. Come ahead."[43]

Worse obstacles awaited. Advance scouts brought word that between four and five thousand Union cavalry were guarding the lower fords of the Potomac. McClellan, instead of pursuing Stuart with all the force at his disposal, had laid a trap into which he was sure his adversary would blunder. "I did not think it possible for Stuart to re-cross," he wrote in his official report. "I believed that the capture or destruction of his entire force was perfectly certain."[44]

Stuart had four potential crossing points in mind. Heeding the advice of his chief guide, he opted for White's Ford, a little-used passage only a mile or so upstream from Ball's Bluff. There was now no way that his men could slip across the river without a fight. The first clash took place at the forefront of the column, with Stuart directly involved. His party of horsemen had just emerged from some woods and onto a road when a troop of Federal cavalry came into view. Throughout the chill of the previous night, many of Stuart's men had worn the blue overcoats that had startled the young woman in Emmitsburg. Confused, the Federals held their fire. Sensing their uncertainty, Stuart and his vanguard rode calmly toward them. Then, when the distance had been sufficiently shortened, they spurred their horses directly at the Northerners. The stunned Yankees fired off a wild volley, hitting almost nothing, and raced away. Their cover destroyed, Stuart's men had to act fast. Their escape would depend on whether their artillery could cover their approach to the ford. It was Pelham's moment. Looking about, he observed a long ridge, from which his cannons could command both the road of the Federal advance and the approaches to White's Ford. The maneuver he had in mind placed him and his gunners at extreme risk; they could execute it only by being the last of Stuart's force to cross the river. He gave the command.

Groggy from their long ride and sleepless night, Pelham's men unlimbered their guns along the ridge. Below them, under orders not to let their parched horses stop to drink, lest the entire column be halted, the Southern troopers splashed into the ford. Pelham, with his unerring sense of distance and position, turned his firepower on the Federals.[45] He was again the nimble boxer, moving his guns to a spot, halting, firing, and retiring again—all the while moving his artillerymen gradually closer to the ford. The work was hotter than he had expected, for, as Stuart's men crossed at the ford, Pelham discovered that he was in peril from two directions. A force under George Stoneman, a Union general who had been Stonewall Jackson's roommate at West Point, was pressing south from Hauling Ford. At the same time, additional Federal cavalry were moving upriver from Edward's Ferry. Pelham gamely accepted his double duty, pounding away with two guns, first to one side and then the other, with great spirit.[46]

All looked well until Stuart made an alarming discovery. His rear-guard cavalry unit, a regiment of some three or four hundred South Carolinians under Colonel Calbraith Butler, had become detached from the main force and were nowhere to be seen. After several couriers reported no sign of them, Stuart sent Blackford to find the missing men. Beginning his search, he passed Pelham, who was rapidly firing up and down the river at enemy troops who were at most a quarter of a mile away. The two men waved their hats to each other, and Blackford rode on. Three miles went by before Blackford found the missing detachment. Urgently he conveyed Stuart's order: the Carolinians must come at a gallop or be cut off. As the regiment rushed to the ford, Pelham's cannons continued to rumble. It was a welcome sound, for as long as Pelham kept up his barrage, the ford must still be open. As Blackford and Butler approached the river, they found Pelham just as Blackford had left him, his cannons still keeping the Federals at bay. Moments later, the rear guard was at the ford. The horses sped into the water with Pelham's gunners and their weapons just behind. They were not yet halfway across when Federal bullets began splashing around them "like a shower of rain," as Blackford incongruously put it.[47] But the other guns from Pelham's command, already secure on the Virginia side, opened fire, largely silencing the Federal riflemen. Soon the last of Pelham's men stood on Virginia soil.[48]

Stuart, Pelham, and the rest of the general's staff returned to the Bower amid great demonstrations of joy. On the 15th of October, a grand ball celebrated their return. However, Stuart's band was forced to play without their percussionist: during the expedition, Bob, the master of the bones, had fallen asleep drunk on applejack by the side of the road and, along with two of Stuart's personal horses, had been captured.[49] Pelham put on his full-dress uniform for the party, which he spent in the company of Sallie Dandridge, both on the dance floor and on a long stroll beside the Opequon.

✶

THE AUTUMN HELD ONE MORE CAMPAIGN for the Horse Artillery: a series of small but fierce cavalry skirmishes known as the Ten Days Battles. The fighting ranged for miles up and down the eastern slopes of the Blue Ridge Mountains. Producing few lasting results, the battles elicited peculiar angers and frustrations on both sides. On the 2nd of November, the Horse Artillery came under fire from a company of Federal sharpshooters. Firing from a wooded area, the marksmen killed several of Pelham's artillery horses. Simultaneously, Union cannon opened on Pelham's position, mortally wounding two men, Christian Costigan and John Phillips. Another shell struck one of Pelham's caissons, killing two more of his soldiers. Normally calm under fire, Pelham became infuriated. Taking a single howitzer and a crew, he moved forward, beyond the area where Stuart's horsemen could offer him any cover. Maneuvering onto a hilltop position concealed by trees, he loaded the gun with double canister. When the Yankee sharpshooters came into the open, Pelham opened fire. The hail of iron swept through the Union ranks, killing eight soldiers and wounding several more. The remaining men ran off in disarray. His wrath not yet sated, Pelham shouted, "Come on, men, let's charge them."[50] The gunners descended on the remaining sharpshooters, taking prisoners and capturing arms and equipment. Astoundingly, Pelham's assault did not cost him a single man. Later that day, he took more vengeance. Seeing an exposed detail of Indiana infantry, Pelham took charge of one of the cannons. Sighting the gun, he said grimly, "Here goes one for Costigan and Phillips!"[51] With perfect accuracy the shot screamed through the air, killing the regiment's color-sergeant and his corporal and wounding almost twenty others.

Historian Douglas Southall Freeman describes Pelham's action on November 2 as "develop[ing] new tactics for horse artillery."[52] There was nothing scientific or clinical, though, in Pelham's efforts that day. They were simply the reflex of a young man who had seen his comrades mowed down in agony and had responded with rage. Shrugging off praise for the work he had done that morning and afternoon, he said simply, "Well, it was a pretty good day."[53] In the shadow of the Blue Ridge, fair was foul, and the goodness of the day was measured in its carnage.

In his official reports, Stuart strained for the words to enshrine Pelham's performance. He described his major's choice of ground as "military genius" and saw in him a "skill and courage which I have never seen surpassed."[54] After the fight on November 2, Stuart encapsulated the artillerist in a single word: "incomparable."[55] He sent dispatches to Richmond, lobbying energetically to have Pelham promoted to lieutenant colonel, dating retroactively from his daredevil actions at Antietam. John G. White of the Second Maryland Infantry outdid even Stuart in his appreciation. To him, Pelham was nothing less than "some god of battle."[56] But in an instant, a battle can turn a god to dust.

Chapter Eight

"Believe Me, We Shall Never Lick 'Em"

As Dr. Holmes scoured two states in search of him, Wendell Holmes had been in far less danger than his parents had dared to hope. The evening after the battle, William LeDuc, who had sent the telegram to the Holmeses, dressed Wendell's neck wound. In a joking mood, Wendell gave thanks that the injury was not a case for amputation. On September 22, 1862, three days before his father found him and unaware that anyone considered him missing, he was still in buoyant spirits, feeling "disgracefully well" and "doing all that an unprincipled son could do to shock the prejudices of parents . . .—smoking pipes, partaking of the flesh pots of Egypt [and] swelling round as if nothing had happened to me."[1] If anything, Wendell experienced his reunion with his father as a letdown.

Oliver Wendell Holmes Sr., spinning his romantic tale of a father-son reunion, missed capturing the deeper story. When Wendell flung the chummy "How are you, Boy?" back into his father's face, he was tacitly asking a question for which the poet had no good answer: Just who, in that train car, was the actual boy? The old governor, who prided himself upon a certain clever knowledge of the world, would have had to confess that the son now knew things that the father had seen only from an insulating distance. In his knowledge of pain, duty, and struggle, Holmes Sr. was Wendell's junior.

Holmes Jr. had gone to Ball's Bluff with chivalric ideals he had acquired in his father's library, and his reward had been a bullet in the chest. One autumn later, the ideals were less firmly in place, but at Antietam he had still been eager for a fight, marching into the West Woods as to a field of honor. But one's feelings about honor can be shaken when one has been shot while fleeing for one's life. The old library moralities no longer felt quite credible. After the war was over, novelist-turned-poet Herman Melville would ask, "What like a bullet can undeceive?"[2] Wendell Holmes's romantic self-deceptions were fading now. In the flashing impatience of his "Boy, nothing!" he voiced the frustrations of a young man who still felt bound by duty to risk his life for his nation's cause, but who could no longer act out the sentimental melodrama that his father insisted on attaching to it.

At the same time that Wendell was beginning to feel the strain of duty, patriotic fever irresistibly enticed his father. Even before Ball's Bluff, the elder Holmes had assailed the North's young men who, unlike his son, had ignored the call to arms. The doctor could see only one motive that an able-bodied young man might have for avoiding the fray: cowardice, which, in the doctor's mind, equaled effeminacy. He lashed out against the shirkers in his September 1861 poem "The Sweet Little Man," acerbically dedicated to "The Stay-at-Home Rangers" and calculated to shame them into enlisting. The stanzas dripped with contempt:

Bring him the buttonless garment of woman!
Cover his face lest it freckle and tan;
Muster the Apron-String Guards on the Common
That is the corps for the sweet little man!

. . .

All the fair maidens about him shall cluster
Pluck the white feathers from bonnet and fan,
Make him a plume like a turkey-wing duster,—
That is the crest for the sweet little man![3]

The formerly apolitical author had transformed almost overnight into an outspoken patriot, more vociferous in his declarations than any of the other New England poets.[4]

As Wendell recovered from his neck wound, Doctor Holmes turned the search for his son into a lengthy travelogue titled "My Hunt after the Captain." The piece appeared in the *Atlantic* in December 1862, just as the Army of the Potomac was girding for its clash with Lee at Fredericksburg. It ends with the image of Wendell at home again, sleeping off his aches and weariness in his own room, where the bookshelves were lined with the works of poets and philosophers who taught "that life is noble only when it is held cheap by the side of honor and of duty." For the Governor, peaceful rest and grateful thoughts had returned to the family home, "For this our son and brother was dead and is alive again, and was lost and is found."[5]

As he had fled through the woods at Antietam, Wendell had laughingly wondered how the Northern press could possibly give a heroic twist to his retreat. The Governor's article supplied the answer. Historians have long presumed that the article displeased Wendell. There had been no gallantry in his sprint for safety at Antietam, yet the press had again managed to make him an object of the nation's admiring sympathy. And this time, his father was leading the cheers. In his expression of paternal pride, the Governor could hardly have chosen a more certain means of embarrassing his son.

Wendell convalesced for six weeks at home at 21 Charles Street, barely a stone's throw from Boston Common. His father perceived Wendell's overall mood as "nervous" but did not speculate about the cause.[6] As his strength returned, Holmes left the city for a quiet refuge in the Berkshires. He settled in with some friends of his father, the Kelloggs, who maintained a handsome Greek Revival home in Pittsfield, its Ionic columns richly entwined by Virginia creeper. Under the elms, an especially eager young hostess awaited his arrival. The previous autumn, while he was in the area seeking recruits for his regiment, Wendell had captured the admiration of the Kelloggs' nine-year-old daughter Carolyn, who thought that the young officer's voice alone ought to charm the village's men into enlisting.

Wendell had treated Carrie's crush with smiling indulgence and friendship. He had nicknamed her "Buster" and had gently humored her juvenile idolatry. Thereafter he had sent her letters and poems from the front, playfully addressing her as "Carrie, carissima" and "Belovedest of Busters." Carrie's heart thrilled at having her gallant soldier back again. On crisp autumn days, he drove her in her phaeton through the turning foliage of tree-lined streets. He went to her school to watch her perform a tableau. And, of course, by his very presence he enhanced her girlish notions of military glory. It was, one imagines, a sweet moment for Holmes as well. Seeing the war through Buster's innocent eyes, it was possible to pretend, for a moment, that the fighting was as pure and noble as she supposed.[7]

During his recovery, Wendell happily returned to the life of a scholar. He read John Stuart Mill's *Considerations on Representative Government*, published the previous year, and John Austin's *The Province of Jurisprudence, Determined*, which, though published in the 1830s, had only recently won popularity among legal thinkers. For Wendell, the questions taken up by Mill and Austin could not have been more pertinent: Mill discussed the basis on which a free government might function; Austin wished to explain the nature and limits of duty. By choosing these works, Holmes showed an interest in two questions that must be answered by any theory of social relations. First, given that nations are governed by authority and force, what are the acceptable grounds upon which the state may exert its power? And second, at what point does authority become illegitimate, and when does a person presumed to be under that authority have the right to say no?

Mill's *Considerations* warmly praised the federal system that Holmes was fighting to preserve. Mill argued that governments are legitimated by their abilities to preserve order and to foster progress and that, but for slavery, the American government had demonstrated its fitness in these regards. Austin's book cared more about force than freedom. Reading Austin's preface, Holmes was confronted with a firm proposition: "Laws proper, or properly so called, are commands."[8] Austin, himself a military veteran, knew something about the nature of commands. He gave this definition: "A command . . . is a signification of desire . . . distinguished from other significations of desire by this peculiarity: that the party to whom it is directed is liable to evil from the other, in case he comply not with the desire."[9] What transforms a wish into a command is "the power and the purpose of a party commanding to inflict an evil or a pain in case the desire be disregarded. If you cannot or will not harm me . . . your wish is not a command."[10]

Holmes, who had lately come from a place where human actions were visibly governed by the infliction of evil and pain, was intrigued. Austin's theory was founded on a great and necessary contradiction. Law obviously existed because of a desire to lessen the quantum of suffering in a society.

And yet law could only be said to exist where its enforcers had the power and will to inflict harm. Law, then, was not the setting of good against evil; it merely authorized the use of some kinds of evil to combat others. Moreover, Austin's theory located the law's authority in the power of the command-giver; law was law not because it was morally right, but because a person or institution had the ability to impose its will. And, conversely, one's duty to obey the law did not emerge principally from any code of honor—an idea that Austin classified among ideas that were "merely opinions or sentiments"—but from fear of the threat of punishment.[11] In Austin's book, Holmes found a sterner idea of his military mission than he had found in the pages of Sir Philip Sidney. Seen through Austin's theory, the war was not about chivalry or honor or even the right or wrong of slavery, but only a clash between two claims to sovereignty, Union and Confederate, to be decided exclusively by which side proved to be the stronger.

In mid-November, well enough to resume his service, Holmes headed back to Virginia. He made the journey with a welcome traveling companion, his friend Captain Henry Abbott. Stricken with typhoid just four days before Antietam, Abbott had been sent home on sick leave and had missed the battle. Holmes wrote home to say that his departure had made him "more or less blue," but that having Abbott along for the ride had "made the journey easier & pleasanter."[12]

Holmes could hardly have asked for a more interesting listener on whom to try out his evolving ideas on democracy and duty. Abbott, like Holmes, conceived of himself as a thinker first, and a soldier second. Nevertheless, he had become a first-rate military man, taking to army life as Holmes was never able to do. Winfield Scott Hancock, whose corps was later to hold the Union line against Pickett's Charge, thought that Abbott was better known in the army than any other man of his rank, and expected him to become "one of our most distinguished commanders."[13] John Sedgwick, another of the army's most respected corps commanders, called Abbott "a wonderfully good soldier" and considered him "a bright, particular star."[14] At Ball's Bluff, Holmes had been impressed by the "splendid coolness" with which Abbott had led his company into danger and then managed an orderly retreat from the ensuing debacle. Holmes's later assessments were still more admiring. "In action," he later said, Abbott "was sublime."[15]

But despite his staunchness under fire, Abbott was at best a skeptical supporter of the cause for which he was fighting. He believed reverently in the Union and had no great love for slavery. But abolition seemed to him an overreaching of the government's power; even after the Emancipation Proclamation took effect, Abbott was to view the enactment with "disgust, particularly the part which enjoins officers to see that it is carried out." He vowed that he would not "see to any thing of the kind, having decidedly too much reverence for the Constitution."[16]

For Abbott, the war had never felt like a moral crusade. If he had ever cherished some ideas of glory, those notions had dissolved less than three months earlier, when Abbott's older brother Ned, a captain of the Second Massachusetts, had been killed at Cedar Mountain. Henry was still reeling. "To think of the subject," he wrote, "unmans me."[17] Helpless regrets besieged him: he should have been at his brother's side; he should at least have gotten to see the body before it was buried. Love for Ned mingled with self-condemnation when Henry told his father, "He was the best son you had."[18] Henry's only solution had been to clench himself tightly around the idea of duty. Two weeks before Antietam, fearing that the morale of the regiment was already near collapse, Abbott had found it essential to put on a cheerful face for his men. Anyone who did less, he believed, was a mere coward, betraying the trust of those who had commissioned him. For a brief time, he confessed, he had failed to keep up appearances. But he had vowed not to let his feelings interfere with his sworn and sacred tasks.[19]

In Abbott, Holmes had a companion who quietly defied Austin's assumptions about law and duty. Abbott obeyed without fear of punishment; indeed, he seemed to fear nothing. The code of honor that Austin dismissed as mere sentiment was, for Abbott, the trellis that gave structure to his existence. As pure a man of integrity as one might hope to meet, Abbott fought more for the principle of democracy than for the people whom the democracy governed. Except for slavery, it seemed to Holmes and Abbott, the American system of laws was beautiful and majestic. Yet the people for whom those laws existed often seemed little better than cattle. By the time they reached Virginia, Holmes and Abbott had staunchly confirmed each other in their sense of Harvard-bred superiority. Holmes wrote to his sister Amelia:

While I'm living en aristocrat I'm an out-and-outer of a democrat in theory; but for contact, except at the polls, I loathe the thick-fingered clowns we call the people—especially as the beasts are represented at political centres—vulgar, selfish & base.[20]

Echoing his father's Beacon Hill chauvinism, he added that only two places in America deserved to be called civilized: "Boston, known for its Statehouse and some cultivation, and Philad[elphia], celebrated for . . . cold slaw [*sic*] & large-grained hominy."[21] Elsewhere, almost everything that met his eyes seemed "shiftless, nasty, ill-conditioned, mean & beastly." The nation's capital, where hogs foraged in the mud a few yards from government buildings, aroused particular scorn. "Wash[ington] stinks of meanness," he declared. "It's absolutely loathsome."[22] Enamored of the ideal, revolted by the real, he slowly made his way toward the regiment.

Finding it was no easy task. Arriving in Warrenton, Abbott and Holmes found the Twentieth had moved out. Trying to determine where the unit had gone, they received no reliable advice—though people did tell them they were a nuisance for not knowing a good thing when they saw it and staying home in Boston. Holmes felt inclined to agree.[23] On November 17, someone told them the best they might do would be to store their valises and go off on foot toward Fredericksburg. Holmes and Abbott prepared for their long march by handing over their suitcases, by coincidence, to the Reverend Arthur Fuller.

Their meeting with the minister did not go well. Holmes and Abbott, who had not eaten that day, were road-weary and irritable. Mildly impressed by the minister's bloodline, Holmes wrote home of having encountered the "brother of Margaret."[24] Abbott was far from dazzled, and something in Fuller's demeanor nettled him; in a letter, he re-christened the cleric as the "Rev. Dr. Snob and Toady Fuller."[25] In his eyes, the minister's family and educational pedigree did not compensate for other faults. There was a peerage of the stouthearted to which the priggish Fuller need not apply.

Setting forth on foot across enemy territory, unprotected, was no joke, as Holmes and Abbott promptly learned. Union pickets warned them to keep a sharp eye out for Confederate "guerrillas."[26] Though none presented themselves, a piercing rainstorm did, and the bedraggled pair took shelter in the dilapidated home of a black family, drying themselves by a wood fire. The next day, the two men slogged more than twenty miles along muddy, cut-up roads. From time to time they stopped for rest at secesh houses, where the women, though surprisingly hospitable to the two bluecoats, vowed that the South would "stick it out to the end." Although moved by the sight of hungry young men far from home, one of their reluctant hostesses shared her opinion that Federal soldiers had no business eating her food and filling her beds. Boys like Holmes and Abbott, she said, were better advised to "stay home and get stronger." Abbott later recalled to Holmes with deep fondness "our [march] across the country." He added, "That was, after all, a devilish pleasant journey to look back on. I have felt a sort of brotherhood ever since. However, that sort of talk is spooney."[27]

A nother day, and more miles to walk. Footsore and mud-spattered, the two officers were now an almost comical sight. Passing soldiers, mistaking them for stragglers, sneered at them. At last, on November 19, the days of misery and indignity yielded to elation; on the outskirts of Falmouth, the Twentieth finally came in view. In a letter home, Wendell summed up his feelings by writing, in capital letters, "THE REGIMENT."[28]

Holmes treated himself to a much-needed bath, after which he felt "bully." Abbott washed down a hearty meal with pints of stoutly brewed coffee and tea, which he strongly favored over the weak infusions he had been served at home. The good feelings started to erode as the two men studied the regiment's condition. Abbott learned of how his comrades had wept when McClellan was dismissed. A harder blow was the news of Colonel Lee's breakdown; the damage to his nerves was now consid ered permanent. In his place as acting colonel was Ferdinand Dreher, who had taken the horrible wound to the face at Ball's Bluff. Supporting him was Lieutenant Colonel Allen Shepard. Holmes called Dreher "crack brained" and thought Shepard an "obstinate ignoramus." Between them, he predicted, the Twentieth would go "to H—l as fast as ever it can."[29] With winter coming on, Holmes foresaw a sad outcome for all the army's efforts. The South, he believed, was "a great civilized nation," one that Lincoln's battered, ill-managed armies could never subdue. He sensed that, in effect, the Confederacy had already won its independence. He was almost ready to hope that, in the coming spring, the South would win the war and send everyone home. Austin's doctrine that force is superior to righteousness had taken hold. "Believe me," he told his sister, "we shall never lick 'em."[30]

✶

WHILE MOST OF THE ARMY SEEMED willing to give Burnside a chance, some officers had resigned; they would serve no one other than McClellan. Abbott wrote that many high-ranking men had stayed only because the War Department issued a general order threatening dishonorable discharge to any officer who left the army and gave McClellan's removal as his reason.[31] "Our men care for nothing now," a soldier from the Fifth Corps murmured blankly. "We feel now just like a large family, who has lost its father."[32]

Burnside confronted a twofold difficulty. On the one hand, he needed to convince his troops that he was not so different from McClellan: firm, outwardly confident and inspirational, yet deeply solicitous of his soldiers' well-being. At the same time, he needed to persuade his superiors in Washington that he was anything but an imitation of his predecessor. In his relations with the government, McClellan had been struttingly arrogant; Burnside had to show humility. In the field, where McClellan had been timid, Burnside needed to be bold. Whereas McClellan's love of his men had kept him from risking the bloodshed necessary to defeat the Rebels, Burnside would have to treat his men as an expendable resource, to be risked and used up as the situation demanded. Burnside kept insisting that he did not "feel equal to" the task of leading the army, and some found his self-deprecation refreshing.[33] But the strategic situation he had inherited called for decisiveness. To distinguish himself from his predecessor, to prove himself as a fighter, Burnside had to strike a telling blow against Lee before winter forced the fighting to pause. McClellan had always waited for the perfect moment to take the initiative. That moment had never come. Burnside meant to create his own moment.

In November 1862, the chief dividing line between the Union and Confederate forces in Virginia was the Rappahannock River. If the Federals were to attack Richmond, they would have to cross that river. The question was where. McClellan had initially favored marching down through the heart of Virginia, along the Orange and Alexandria Railroad. Preparing to follow that route, he had massed his forces around

Warrenton. But Lee had effectively blocked his path, and supply lines along that way were vulnerable as well. In his last days of command, McClellan had begun weighing a more elaborate plan: he might march his men about forty miles south by southwest along the Rappahannock and cross at Fredericksburg, a small city situated not only on the river but also astride the Richmond, Fredericksburg, and Potomac Railroad. Just hours before he was relieved of duty, McClellan had ordered a small force to reconnoiter Fredericksburg.

McClellan had not even had time to bid farewell to the army before Secretary of War Stanton began to pressure Burnside; he wanted to know immediately where Burnside meant to march. Burnside promptly wired his reply. After a brief feint along the upper portion of the river, he would swing his entire force down toward Fredericksburg and establish a base across the Rappahannock at Aquia Landing, where his supply lines connected with the Potomac. From there, the army would cross into Fredericksburg and commence its drive south toward Richmond.

Lincoln had misgivings about Burnside's preferred route of attack; it seemed circuitous and overly complicated. The more elaborate the troop movement, the more could go wrong. The president favored a more direct confrontation with Lee, taking, as he had told McClellan, the path "*nearest* the enemy, so as to operate on his communications."[34] Two days after Burnside sent his telegram, Lincoln sent four of the most influential men in the capital to press Burnside to give up his designs on Fredericksburg and to strike, as McClellan had first intended, near Culpeper. The quartet consisted of General-in-Chief Halleck; Secretary Chase; Quartermaster General Montgomery Meigs, responsible for the army's logistical support; and Colonel Herman Haupt. A talented military engineer, Haupt had supervised the construction of military railroads around Washington.[35] With so much authority seated at the table, the meeting seemed certain to yield some answers.

★

MEANWHILE, GEORGE WHITMAN WAS FEELING IMPATIENT. After the fury of South Mountain and Antietam, it was a relief to be away from the sound of cannons, which he had heard almost daily for two or three weeks. But in another sense the lull, caused by McClellan's inaction, annoyed him. If it were not for bad management, cowardice, or treachery on the upper levels of the Union command, George felt certain that Lee could have been beaten by now.[36] The back-and-forth movement of the troops, seeming to accomplish nothing, irked him. "I dont like the idea of fighting the same ground over three or four times," he grumbled, "but I supose it all right."[37] He could see, though, that it was not all right for the farmers who called the contested territory home. The Virginia fields and villages through which the Fifty-First marched had been reduced to wretchedness—"the most God forsaken places I ever saw." The men who tended these lands had all gone into the army, and foragers had picked the landscape clean. It moved him to pity. "How they are going to get through the winter," he wrote, "I dont know."[38]

George had heard continual reports that masses of fresh troops were joining the Union cause. He complained that the men at the front had not seen the proof of it. "Where in thunder does all the troops go," he demanded, "that the papers say are leaving New York, and the other Citys every day[?] Why dont they send em, out to the front, and let us old veterans come home, and see our Mammies[?]"[39] Unable to obtain leave to visit home, he created in his mind's eye a scene from the home he missed so much and sent the description to his mother:

> *I often think that I can imagine just what you are all doing at home and ile bet now, that Mother is makeing pies. I think Mat is putting up shirt bosoms like the deuce so as to get through before dinner. I guess Sis is down stairs helping Mother mix the dough, Walt is up stairs writing, Jeff is down town at the Office, Jess is pealing Potatoes for dinner, and Tobias has gone down cellar for a scuttle of coal.*[40]

Despite all the seeming futility, George was convinced that victory in the war was not far distant. Unlike the Union commanders, he saw no need for subtle strategies. He thought the army had sufficient force "to go right ahead and balsmather the seceshers."[41]

*

ARTHUR FULLER REJOINED THE SIXTEENTH MASSACHUSETTS on October 29, 1862. He found the regiment just south of the Potomac, encamped near the Fairfax Seminary in Alexandria. The reception he was given made all the pain and trouble of his journey worthwhile. Upon hearing that their chaplain had returned, the men "thronged down to the foot of the hill to carry [his] valise and press about [him] with offers of service."[42] Especially jubilant were the men whose sickbeds Fuller had attended at Harrison's Landing. Insisting that they owed their lives to the bespectacled chaplain, they poured out rivers of praise upon him. So many asked for Fuller's portrait that he wrote home to ask for fifty copies of his engraved likeness.[43] Deeply touched, the minister told Lucilla:

> My own family could not be more . . . affectionate. . . . The poor sick men clasped my hands & said. "O we have missed you so much." I went from company to company, shaking hands with the officers & men & came pretty near shedding tears myself.[44]

Many of the hands he wished to grasp were no longer there. Assigned to defend Washington, the Third Army Corps, of which the Sixteenth was a part, had been spared the slaughter at Antietam. However, less than three weeks before Antietam at Second Bull Run, the regiment had seen heavy fighting, and the brigade to which it had been attached saw fifty-five of its men killed and well over 300 wounded.[45] Once a force of over 1,000 men, the Sixteenth was down to about 300 battle-ready soldiers. As Fuller learned of the regiment's losses and suffering, he fought to control his emotions. It seemed to him as if his illness had been the work of providence; he felt certain that, had he remained with the regiment throughout that time, he would surely have died months ago.[46]

If staying with the regiment would have killed him, coming back to it brought him new life. Whatever doubts he had had about rejoining the army vanished. With emphasis, he told Lucilla, *"It was right that I came back.* Sorry as I am to have left you, I should never . . . have known how much they loved me." He wrote with satisfaction, "I shall prosper here I know."[47]

But prosperity demanded health, and anyone could see that the chaplain was not well. Instead of sleeping in a regular tent alongside the officers and men, he spent his nights in a room at the hospital, with his mattress laid atop an iron bed frame that he had had specially delivered from Massachusetts. Two days after his return, the men of the regiment were ordered to cook two days' rations and prepare for a march. Whether Fuller stayed or went was up to the regimental surgeon, a Dartmouth graduate named Charles Jewett. Dr. Jewett tried to imagine the frail minister sleeping on the hard ground with no tent to shelter him and subsisting on salt meat and hardtack. No, the danger was too great. Furthermore, the hospital staff was shorthanded; Fuller could be a great help to Jewett and his assistant in looking after the sick and the suffering. The surgeon's verdict surprised no one; on November 3, when the Sixteenth marched to Centreville, they went without their chaplain.

Fuller reproached himself for the weakness of his body. Still, his work with Jewett pleased him. Dr. Jewett and his aides were responsible for more than 530 patients, housed in five large buildings. Fuller's services were very much in need. Moreover, fifty-two of the sick men belonged to the Sixteenth, so his staying behind was perfectly in keeping with his duty to the regiment. The chaplain had learned much about hospital work at Harrison's Landing, and, while he now had to take more precautions, he did his tasks eagerly and effectively. He liked Jewett a great deal, and they took their meals together. Fuller's room was large and comfortable, warmed by a good wood fire. The camp, perched on a high hill, offered the most pleasing vistas he had seen during the war. The air was as pure as the breath of heaven. Looking out on the trees clad in scarlet, he thought of inviting Lucilla to bring the children for a visit. He was pleased to report, "We live very well."[48]

Still, the guilt of not having marched with the regiment assailed him. Almost every letter to Lucilla repeated some argument about why he had been wise to stay behind; he was trying hard to convince himself that he had done right. On November 5 he told her, "I do not want to throw my life away," and two days later he repeated his wish to stay alive.[49] In the mellow beauty of the Virginia autumn, with important work to do, life just then was sweet and precious.

But life also refused to stand still. Within a few weeks, the government broke up the hospital where Fuller had so happily settled, leaving him at loose ends. On the 12th of November, after a brief stay in Washington, he took a risk; he boarded a southbound train and set out to rejoin the regiment. Not for the first time, he shared his car with distinguished travelers: riding in the same coach were Secretary Chase, General Halleck, Colonel Haupt, and General Meigs, on their way to confront Burnside.[50]

Seeing that they were "much absorbed in their duties of counsel, finance, supply and transportation," Fuller did not disturb them.[51] In any event, his attention was absorbed by the presence of yet another luminary: Major General Joseph Hooker, under whose command the Sixteenth Massachusetts had fought both during the Seven Days Battles and at Second Bull Run. Despite Hooker's reputation as a self-promoting opportunist, Fuller was fond of the general and was honored to converse at length with him. A trifle starstruck, Fuller wrote to his wife that Hooker "impressed me with renewed & even increased respect & confidence in him, both as a patriot & a soldier. He is indeed a noble general."[52]

The trip to visit the regiment made Fuller more feeble. For the first time since he left his sickbed in Massachusetts, he confessed that his future in the army was in doubt. He confided to Lucilla that he was far from well. Indeed, unless the regiment went into winter quarters soon, Fuller fretted that he would have to resign "if I would save my health or even my life." Yet in the same letter, with some degree of contradiction, he asked Lucilla not to worry. "Have no anxiety about me," he told her. "A good God cares for me always."[53]

✵

THE CHAPLAIN MIGHT TRUST IN GOD. The generals and secretaries needed to trust one another. At the meeting between Burnside and the president's delegation in Warrenton, the trust was thin; Halleck and his companions had every reason to worry about Burnside's lack of experience at his new level of command, and Burnside had every reason to chafe under their scrutiny. Most troublingly, Burnside continued to be unnerved by his new responsibilities. He had exclaimed, "I am not fit for [them]. There are many more in the army better fitted than I am; but if you and the President insist, I will take it and do the best I can."[54] One could hear his claims of unworthiness only so often before wondering whether they were true.

When Lincoln's team arrived, Burnside reiterated his plan to march on Fredericksburg. In the end, his wishes carried the day; they did so in large part because of Colonel Haupt's assessment of the logistical situation. Haupt, who knew more about rail support than anyone else in the Union, reminded everyone that supplies for an inland advance would have to travel along the Orange and Alexandria Railroad, a single line of track highly vulnerable to Confederate attack or sabotage. He added that even if the Orange and Alexandria could be adequately protected, it could carry only 700 to 900 tons of supplies *per diem*, a fraction of the 1500 tons that the army consumed each day. From a standpoint of pure feasibility, Haupt concluded, Burnside had the better idea.

Out-argued, Halleck returned to Washington to brief the president. With Lincoln's reluctant approval, Halleck sent Burnside a conditional endorsement: "The President has just assented to your plan. He thinks it will succeed, if you move rapidly, otherwise not." Perhaps afraid that his first caveat was not sufficient, Lincoln paid a personal visit to Burnside's headquarters. Not only must the army make haste, he told the general, but it was also imperative that they cross the river "free from risk."[55]

The army began to move. Holmes and Abbott had failed to catch up with the Twentieth at Warrenton because it had been among the first to march toward Fredericksburg.[56] On November 17, the day the two men handed their valises to Fuller, the first Union divisions reached Falmouth. Burnside had easily outdistanced the Confederates in the race to the Rappahannock. Lee's army was broadly diffused across the countryside, with Jackson's entire corps occupying the Shenandoah Valley, almost 200 miles' march from Fredericksburg. Only a token Confederate force defended the town. Cross the river now, and Burnside's force might make things quite warm for the Rebels. But Burnside stalled. He had proposed to cross the river on temporary pontoon bridges, to be laid by the army's engineers. Without the crude boats on which to lay the bridges, no occupation of the town would be attempted.

But the pontoons did not arrive. The initial requisition had been made on November 6, the day before McClellan was relieved. However, for fear that a telegram might be intercepted, the order had been sent by mail and was received almost a week later. At the time, there were only twelve serviceable pontoon boats in all of Washington—a fraction of the more than one hundred boats that Burnside would need for his crossing. On November 14, thirty-six boats arrived in Washington, with another forty due the following day. But then the process slowed again. Conveying the cargo from Washington to Falmouth was the task of the Fiftieth New York Engineers. No one had explained to Major Ira Spaulding, the unit's commander, that the request for the materials was an urgent matter, and he chose to take his time.[57]

The only way to move the boats and the other equipment for the bridges overland was by horse- and mule-drawn caravans. Acquiring and harnessing the animals took time. Working night and day, the engineers could not get the wagons moving until the 19th of November. Their efforts were greeted by a continuous, pelting rain that turned the dirt roads to clinging, bottomless mud.[58] The men who led the mules soon became almost indistinguishable in function from the mules themselves, as they, too, plunged into the muck, pressed their shoulders to the wagons, and fought with all their strength to keep the heavy vehicles rolling. After crossing Occoquan Creek, the engineers divided the cargo. The boats and whatever else could float were sent down the Potomac, while the horses, mules, and wagons continued to slog overland. The boats made landfall in good order at Belle Plain, a hamlet on the eastern shore of the peninsula formed by the Potomac and the Rappahannock. However, Burnside had provided no means to carry the boats across the peninsula to Falmouth. All the while, more Confederates were joining the force on the high ground behind Fredericksburg. Precious days flew by.[59]

✶

As Burnside fumbled, Fuller tried to readjust to life in the field. As he did so, he sought companionship from many sources, including Confederates who had lately been taken prisoner. One of these was a Louisiana surgeon who jabbed at the chaplain's pride, both as a Northerner and as a minister, by arguing that the Southerners were more religious than the Northerners. The proof, he said, was obvious: "Our rulers appoint more public religious days than yours: we have more days of fasting, humiliation and prayer than you—." Fuller returned fire before the man could finish. "Of course you do," he said, "because you have more sins as a people and [as] an army to pray over and humble yourselves for, especially the sin of rebellion against a noble and good government." As for the South's habit of fasting, Fuller teased, everyone had heard that the Confederacy was short of food. If half the stories of their privations were true, the South was fasting, not out of piety or virtue, but necessity.[60]

Fuller's antagonist laughed pleasantly. "Well," he rejoined, "we also have many thanksgiving days, too, and expect many more before the war ends." Fuller's replies turned scriptural. He reminded the surgeon of a passage from Isaiah: "Your appointed feasts my soul hateth. . . . Your hands are full of blood." No ceremonies, Fuller argued, could call themselves religious if they were not supported by right actions, which included "ceasing from evil, learning to do well [and] letting the oppressed go free." The minister's words carried a sharp edge. Nonetheless, the two men's tone remained civil and respectful. Fuller came away thinking well of the doctor and his friends, wishing only "that they were enlisted in a better cause."[61]

On Sunday, November 16, Fuller had just concluded religious services with his regiment when word came that General Burnside was nearby. Men of the Sixteenth Massachusetts marched spontaneously to the headquarters where their commander had stopped. When Burnside stepped outside to greet them, they erupted into cheers. Pressed by the crowd to speak, the general sputtered enough words to show that he was, as Fuller put it, "neither a fluent or graceful speaker." Yet his very awkwardness seemed to endear him to the men. And, Fuller noted, the general said the one word that, after McClellan's excessive caution, the army was most eager to hear: "Forward."[62]

For Fuller, however, it seemed that there would be no going forward. On the same day that the chaplain heard Burnside's ungainly rallying speech, Dr. Jewett, with regrets, wrote the words that would end Fuller's service to the regiment: "Revd. A. B. Fuller, Chaplain of the 16th Mass. Regt. is compelled on account of his health to give up service in the field, and is desirous to continue in some sphere of usefulness to the soldiers." Attesting to the "unremitting, kind, and judicious" service that Fuller had rendered in the crowded hospitals at Harrison's Landing and Alexandria, Jewett advised that Fuller be reassigned to a hospital chaplaincy.[63]

Fuller accepted Jewett's judgment. But he did not do so happily. The reassignment would take him away from the men of the regiment, whom he loved, and from the experience of being a soldier, which was now essential to how he saw himself in the world. During his last days with the regiment, Fuller wrote, "Better war than dishonor. Better still give up our heart's blood in brave battle, than give up our principles in cowardly compromise."[64] He told Lucilla, "You can hardly realize the pain I felt when I found I *could* not go on the field campaign without throwing away health & life." He set his sights on obtaining a post either in Washington or Baltimore. However, he could not bear to resign his commission with the regiment immediately. Instead, he postponed the inevitable by requesting a medical leave. On November 17, Fuller met Henry Abbott and Wendell Holmes and took charge of their luggage. That same day, the Sixteenth marched toward Falmouth without their chaplain. They would never march with him again.

For the frail minister, it was now a matter of waiting. On the 18th he rode back to Washington and took a room near the offices of the Sanitary Commission. He became a regular customer at a neighborhood restaurant, where he got his meals for a frugal 75 cents a day. The situation was far more comfortable than what he had been enduring, but his idleness tore at him. To shake off the monotony and to make himself useful, he visited a camp of paroled prisoners in Annapolis. He found more than 7000 soldiers, recently freed from enemy prisons. He stayed only a day or two, but during that time another 480 parolees arrived from Richmond. Their stories shocked him. Their captors had stolen their overcoats and had fed them rations that amounted to slow starvation. Yet, they added, the jailors suffered from as much hunger as their captives. As the war's second winter drew near, Lee's army lacked the clothing and provisions to satisfy its own basic wants. Fuller did not preserve many details of the prisoners' recent sufferings. He summed up much of it in a single word: "brutality." Annapolis struck Fuller as dull and forlorn, further evidence of the irresistible power of slavery "to curse and destroy with its blight and mildew."[65]

Back in Washington, Fuller sought the help of a friend, New Hampshire senator Daniel Clark. After some discussion, Clark promised to do what he could to find a hospital chaplaincy for the pastor. As Fuller waited, he took almost his only comfort in his correspondence with Lucilla. She wrote to tell him that the family had missed him at Thanksgiving and that his son Richard, now twenty-one months old, had laughed when he heard a line from one of the minister's letters, in which he had written that "papa wants to see his darling baby." Fuller wrote in reply, "Well, papa & baby will have a good laugh together if papa ever gets home again." He had missed Thanksgiving. Would he miss Christmas, too? As the days shortened, he wondered whether he should even try to continue serving his country. If the appointment fell through, he would be home again, and it seemed to him that even the darkest clouds would vanish if he could be with his wife and children. Yet he knew that, in the past, he had always managed to produce his own foul weather, no matter how hopeful his surroundings. He observed, "God has always given me sunshine, but I have made for myself clouds of anxiety about the future, which have kept me from enjoying the present." [66] The chaplain's life had been suffused with the light of divinity. Nevertheless, thwarted by his physical frailties and unable to free himself from melancholy, he had not yet turned that life into a statement of enduring affirmation.

On December 4 came the much-awaited news. President Lincoln granted Fuller a commission with full powers as chaplain in a hospital or stationary camp, and the minister was to have his choice of locations. If he wished, he could go to New York, and the prospect tempted him. However, Fuller was resolved "not to do what is pleasant but what is right." He inclined instead toward the convalescent camp in Alexandria, the most challenging option available. Eagerly, Fuller described his prospective post to Lucilla:

> *I shall have a good tent . . . & they promise to take good care of me. By railroad I can reach Washington in half an hour. . . . There are to be fifteen thousand men under my care. I never expected so large a parish. Can't you come & bring the funny baby & live with me in my nice house tent this winter?*[67]

Serving this multitude of men, gathered from every loyal state and regiment, Fuller looked forward to being more useful than he had dared to dream.[68] He blessed the divine hand that had guided him so close to satisfaction.

On the last Sunday in November, Fuller had given his final sermon as Chaplain of the Sixteenth Volunteer Infantry, at the same convalescent camp where he now intended to become the hospital chaplain. Some five hundred sick and wounded men came to hear him preach. He spoke to them simply and earnestly. They received his words warmly, and Fuller felt reassured that he would be contented there. The one known account of the sermon he gave that afternoon, though fragmentary, appears to capture the essence of the moment:

"My boys," said he, "you know what a thrill the cry of 'Mail' in camp sends through each one of us; you know [how] eagerly we peruse the dear words from the hand of some cherished one; the letters from home are the manifestations of love from father, wife, or sister. So indeed are the words of Christ. The New Testament is full of letters from home. It speaks to us in the language of human affection. Its words are those of encouragement and good cheer."[69]

Not a single man left his place before the service ended.

A week later, on December 7, Fuller was in Falmouth, across the Rappahannock River from Fredericksburg. He had returned to the regiment, not to sermonize, but to say goodbye. After a dress parade and a brief service, the regiment formed a hollow square to hear the minister's farewell. As they listened, Fuller recalled the perils and privations they had shared, trials of both fire and cold that had, in his eyes, made them into brothers. He assured them that he would never have chosen to leave them if not for his poor health. Wherever their paths might cross in future, they could greet him as a friend. He ended with a fervent prayer, asking Heaven to bless the president; the country; its brave, loyal army; and the gallant, heroic regiment he had been honored to serve.[70] On Monday the 8th he tendered his resignation. The next day he wrote Lucilla. He thought it likely that his service had permanently weakened him and that he would never again know perfect wellness. Nevertheless, the sights he had seen and the work he had done had been worth the price he had paid. He had no regrets.[71] On Wednesday the 10th, Chaplain Fuller received his honorable discharge. In Alexandria, good, redemptive work stood waiting to be done. But the true adventure of Arthur Fuller's life, it seemed, was over.

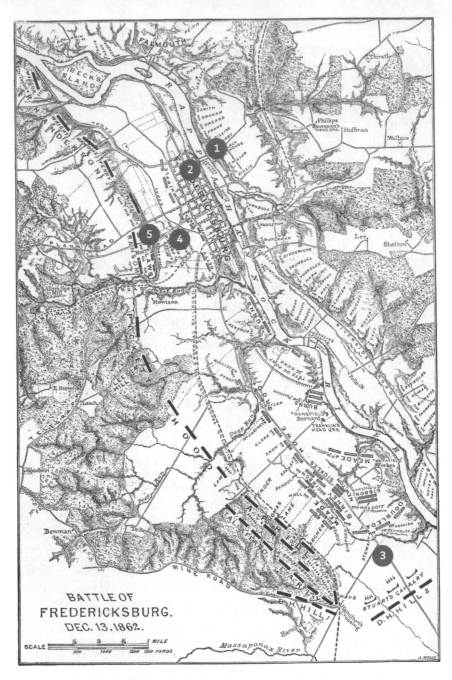

The Battlefield at Fredericksburg, December 11–13, 1862

1.   The northern crossing of the Rappahannock. Here, on December 11, the Nineteenth and Twentieth Massachusetts staged a riverine assault.

2.   The intersection of Caroline and Hawke Streets. Here, Arthur Fuller made good on his vow to "do something for my country."

3.   Hamilton's Crossing. Here, on December 13, John Pelham stymied the advance of the Union Left.

4.   The Brick Kiln. Near this spot, a shell fragment wounded George Whitman.

5.   The Stone Wall. Here, John Suhre of the 133rd Pennsylvania was shot through the lung.

From *Battles and Leaders of the Civil War*

Book 3

~

"A WORSE PLACE THAN HELL"

Chapter Nine

~~~

Caroline Street

At long last, General Burnside had the materials for his pontoons. Spaulding, his engineers, and the building material for the bridges had finally reached Falmouth on November 25, fittingly enough in another rainstorm. But their arrival was too late to do any immediate good. If the pontoon bridges had arrived even on the 19th or 20th, the army could have crossed into Fredericksburg with trifling opposition. But now a large force under Lieutenant General James Longstreet was firmly established on the high ground behind the town. Burnside knew that both the engineers who would try to build the bridges and the troops that would cross on them would come under heavy artillery fire.[1] On the Confederate side, Longstreet's officers were feeling confident. Typical was Major General Lafayette McLaws, the Georgia veteran who led one of Longstreet's divisions. On the 22nd, he wrote, "Our camp fires shine up & light the air so far and wide as those of the enemy, and we no longer care for any attempt they may make to cross the river."[2] Burnside's window of opportunity had been slammed shut.

The mere presence of Burnside's army across the river and the threat that it presented were enough to shred the fabric of the lives of the 5000 inhabitants of Fredericksburg. The town was as pretty a place as one could find in Virginia, though it could hardly be called one of the luckiest. In 1807, a massive fire had half destroyed it, and another blaze fifteen years later had devastated the commercial district. Nevertheless, its residents believed that, thanks to its admirable frontage on the Rappahannock and its ready accessibility from both Washington and Richmond, Fredericksburg would eventually flourish. Carpenters and brick masons flocked to the town, and, as one local historian recorded, "the music of the hammer, the saw and the trowel greeted the ear from early morning until late in the afternoon."[3] Mingled in this rhapsody, though, were voices with tragic stories to tell: according to the 1830 census, more than a third of Fredericksburg's thirty-three hundred residents were enslaved African Americans.[4]

Many of the houses near the river, though fairly modest in size, boasted elegant furnishings. A few blocks back from the river stood more stately homes that might fairly be described as mansions. By 1840, the town was doing a robust business as a center for trade in grain, flour, corn, and tobacco. The absence of a rail line to the rich agricultural valleys farther inland prevented Fredericksburg from experiencing a full-scale boom. Yet the town's slow growth kept prices low, and life for the fortunate was pleasantly languid. Fredericksburg was well known for the polite, refined quality of its social circles, as well as "a quiet and chastened dignity of age and respectability, both attractive and impressive."[5]

In 1860, as secession began to tear the country in two, most of Fredericksburg's influential citizens were loyal to the federal government; when Virginia called a state convention to vote on secession, the town's voters overwhelmingly chose a pro-Union delegate to represent them. But when, on April 15, 1861, President Lincoln called for 75,000 volunteers to quell the Southern rebellion and made it clear that all the loyal states would be expected to turn against the secessionists, opinion swung violently against the Union. Two days later, Virginia seceded, with the vote of the Fredericksburg delegate having switched to the majority.

By mid-1862, almost all the town's white men of military age had joined the army, leaving among the whites only the elderly, the very young, and the women. Now, as Burnside's army massed across the river to the east and Longstreet's men fortified the high ground to the west, most of the remaining residents made plans to flee. On the 21st of November, Burnside demanded that Lee give over the town. Lee declined. Burnside countered with a threat: if Lee did not reconsider, he would shell the town at nine on the morning of the 23rd. The hour came and went without incident, but the population now expected to be bombarded at any moment. On the evening of the 24th, Lee directed residents to abandon their homes without delay. Elderly men and women panted as they tottered through the mud, their breath condensing in the frigid air. With mounting fear, a widow called the names of her three young daughters, who had somehow gotten swallowed up by the crowd. Under the eyes of the Yankee gunners across the river on Stafford Heights, a stream of wives and children, taking only what they could carry in boxes and bundles, filled the roads and the railway cars that would take them south, toward shelter in Richmond.

The passenger trains alone could not handle the swarm; when they were full, mothers guided their children onto cattle cars that were sometimes laden with five hundred other riders. Southern army ambulance drivers did what they could to handle the overflow. General McLaws watched the vehicles going back and forth all day, carrying families to safety.[6] A Union shell—whether fired by accident or with intent was unknown—exploded near a carload of refugees, causing alarm but injuring no one.[7]

As fear and confusion swept the crowd, a more hopeful migration out of the city was starting to take place. Seeing that their chance had come, countless enslaved men, women, and children began an exodus from Fredericksburg. By the time the battle was over, the fugitives from bondage were to number in the thousands. An escapee named John Washington recalled that, as Burnside's army approached the city, "No one could be seen on the street but the colored people, and every one of them seemed to be in the best of humors."[8]

Those unable or unwilling to try their fortunes in Richmond scattered across the countryside. The generous opened their homes to as many as they could accept, spreading pallets on their floors and tucking spare sheets into sofas to accommodate a few more of the dispossessed. Even as they fled, some of the departing citizens were defiant in the face of the Union forces. Word reached the Union lines of embattled women who had pleaded on their knees to General Lee never to surrender the town, even if it meant that their homes would be destroyed. Such stories led one Union staff officer to comment, "Were the ladies of the North to imitate the South, they would make heroes of us all."[9] The few denizens of the town who resolved to stay waited anxiously for the bombing to begin.

But the shelling did not come. Burnside was still hesitant to move directly against the town. Indeed, as he was forced to admit, delays were causing the entire campaign to unravel. On November 22, he advised the War Department, "I deem it my duty to say that I cannot make the promise of probable success with the faith that I [previously] did."[10] Burnside pursued one further alternative to a direct assault on Fredericksburg. Several miles downstream lay a crossing called Skinker's Neck. Receiving word that Skinker's Neck was suitable for a large-scale advance, Burnside arranged for four Yankee gunboats to support the maneuver. The flotilla steamed toward its appointed position, its commander unaware of two holes in Burnside's plan that had doomed it to failure. First, Burnside had underestimated the extraordinary speed with which Stonewall Jackson's corps, summoned by Lee from the Shenandoah Valley, had covered the intervening distance. A force so adept at swift marching that they were known as "the foot cavalry," Jackson's men had begun to move on November 21. Even though many of the soldiers marched barefoot, the last of them arrived in Fredericksburg on December 3, having traveled 175 miles in just twelve days. When the gunboats rolled up the Rappahannock, Jackson's men greeted them with cannon fire.

Burnside also failed to account for Stuart's cavalry and Pelham's ubiquitous Horse Artillery; both the cavalry general and the artillery major had been assessing the terrain for days, ascertaining the best possible placement for their cannons if Union gunboats should come. Always eager to temper his hard work with genteel diversions, Stuart often stopped at a plantation named Gay Mont, the home of the in-law relatives of one of his staff officers. There, as he and Pelham drank tea and conversed with the ladies of the house, the younger man exuded effortless charm. One of the women told her diary, "Major Pelham . . . pleased us extremely, a mere youth apparently, beardless & slender almost to a fault, but quick and energetic in his movements & with an eagle eye that shows his spirit. . . . He . . . looks like a man who would make his mark upon the world."[11]

The now-familiar pattern of Pelham's life—interludes of gentility punctuated by episodes of life-threatening violence—resumed. On December 4, Burnside's detachment of gunboats made their move to clear the way for the crossing at Skinker's Neck, bombarding the town of Port Royal. Despite the damage that the gunboats inflicted on the town, they failed to dislodge the Rebel military presence. Jackson's cannons drove them back down the river, and directly into the close range of Pelham's Horse Artillery.

As in the past, Pelham's daring verged on recklessness. He had wheeled his guns to within 300 yards of where the gunboats would pass. The tactic worked; both the narrowness of the channel and the nearness of Pelham's fire made it almost impossible for the Union sailors to answer back. Nevertheless, a missile from a Yankee cannon succeeded in blowing a leg off one of Pelham's gunners. Pelham was operating at a level of expertise and daredevilry where skill and luck were becoming hard to distinguish. Stuart's praise for his role in the fight was, as had become the cavalryman's custom, without reserve. [12] Von Borcke, enraptured though he was by the young man's performance, was starting to suspect that talent explained only a part of it. He wrote, "Pelham with his horse artillery had met with his usual good fortune."[13]

Can a man have a genius for rolling dice? All agreed that Pelham handled his guns with consummate skill, always, it seemed, placing them perfectly and firing them with unmatched speed and accuracy. They marveled, too, at his capacity to tiptoe on the edge of disaster. Time and again, the force of the Union army had turned upon him, and each time he had prevailed, escaping without a scratch. A similar guardian angel seemed to ride with Stuart. He had circled the opposing army twice. Bullets had passed through his coat. In a skirmish near Amissville, Virginia, a Federal bullet had taken off half his mustache. Yet, he, too, always came through without harm. Stuart and Pelham seemed linked, not only by a strong personal attachment, but also by a knack for good fortune that defied explanation. They were growing bolder, continually more confident, it seems, that they were fated never to fall in battle.

As the gunboats vanished down the river, so, too, did Burnside's hope of crossing at Skinker's Neck. Still, the Union commander was not quite ready to abandon his stratagem. The next day, December 5, in a steady rain that turned the roads to soup, he marched two-thirds of his army toward the crossing. While his forces were en route, the temperature plunged. The rain and mud turned to snow and slush. With their sodden clothes freezing on their backs, the grumbling columns slogged on until, abruptly, their officers cried halt. Burnside's advance scouts had confirmed that Confederate infantry were awaiting the Federals in force, and the general had wisely countermanded the marching order. In their huddled thousands, the bluecoats passed a frigid night by the side of the road that their boots had churned into a quagmire. By morning, at least three inches of snow had fallen on them. In a spirit of futility, they retraced their steps to camp.

Crossing the Rappahannock at Fredericksburg had stopped being a wise option from the moment Longstreet's men had started digging in behind the town. Now, however, if Burnside were to cross at all, it was the only place where he could do it. On December 9, he called a council of his senior generals at Chatham, a handsome mansion with a full view of the Rappahannock and the city beyond. Despite the forces massed on the heights beyond the town, Burnside had convinced himself that the Confederates would not expect a direct attack on Fredericksburg. One of his most respected division commanders, Winfield Scott Hancock, objected; the Rebel position was simply too strong. Burnside fired off a pointed retort. "Your duty," he told Hancock, "is not to throw cold water, but to aid me loyally with your advice and hearty service."[14] The crossing would take place at Fredericksburg.

On the 11th, Burnside was awake by four in the morning. At his headquarters at the Phillips House, a two-story brick home on the east side of the river, he waited as, in the bitter cold, his engineers began to lay the pontoons. The two bridges farthest downstream, which were to carry the army's Left Grand Division, took shape with relatively little incident. The Confederate force was not strong at that point, and although the Southern pickets inflicted a handful of casualties among the engineers, artillery fire from the bluecoats drove them back. By late morning, these two bridges were complete. Upstream, the story was different.

The two northernmost bridges were to lead directly into the town. On the opposite shore, they would connect with a grassy area that sloped upward to Sophia Street, the first road running parallel to the river. Intersecting with Sophia Street, a quiet lane called Hawke Street would lead the soldiers into the town. This part of the river crossing was fraught with hazards. From every door, window, and tree on the opposing shore, Confederate sharpshooters could open fire. If no one challenged them, they could pick off the engineers on the bridges practically at will. The darkness and thick fog that lay across the river were, for a time, the engineers' best friends. As the workmen started their laborious progress across the river, they were shielded from the view of the Confederate forces on the far bank. For the time being, they were also out of firing range. For the moment at least, all was well.

Putting the bridges together would require the army's engineers to perform repetitive work, which had to be done both carefully and quickly. Once the end of the incipient bridge had been secured to the shoreline, a team of six men had to move the first pontoon boat into place and anchor it. Then they had to lay a number of twenty-five-foot-long timbers, known as balks, over the boat in perpendicular fashion and tie them into place. These were then topped with the chesses—wooden boards about fourteen feet long and a foot wide. These were laid parallel to the boats underneath, creating a walkway that was then bordered by a rail along each side. Another thirteen or so feet outward from the shore, another boat was maneuvered into position, and the sequence began again. In all, a bridge at this point needed to be four hundred feet long. During much of the process, the engineers would be plainly visible to the Confederates on the opposite bank—and well within firing range. The Yankee riflemen behind the engineers would be hard pressed to give them adequate cover.

All that night, in defiance of the cold, a dark figure on horseback had been patrolling the Fredericksburg side of the river, carefully noting his impressions. Mississippian William Barksdale had been thirty-nine when the war began. Well fed and slightly dandyish in his chin whiskers and longish hair, he had looked much more like the newspaper editor and politician he was than the military officer he was about to become. But he had a fighting spirit, having served in the Mexican War, and his distaste for both the Union and abolition was profound. A congressman in 1856, he had been present when his South Carolina colleague Preston Brooks took a cane to the abolitionist senator Charles Sumner and beat him senseless on the floor of the Senate chamber. It was variously rumored that Barksdale had either held Brooks's coat during the attack or physically prevented bystanders from interfering as Brooks laid into the senator. In September, Barksdale had commanded the troops that had driven Holmes and the rest of the Twentieth Massachusetts from the West Woods at Antietam. If he was to meet them again, he meant to give them an equally memorable whipping.

Entrusted with guarding the riverfront against a Union crossing, Barksdale had set up his headquarters on Princess Anne Street in the commercial heart of Fredericksburg. He had moved two regiments, the Seventeenth and Eighteenth Mississippi, into town. Around 11 p.m. on

December 10, he directed these regiments to double the number of soldiers on picket duty. Now, he rode up and down along the bank, halting his horse from time to time to take some measure of the situation. In the foggy darkness, Barksdale couldn't see much, but his ears were telling an engrossing story. The low murmur he was picking up from across the river could only mean that the Federals were on the move. Before two o'clock had passed, Barksdale stood convinced that Burnside was preparing to cross the river. He sent word to rouse his men from sleep and dispatched a message to his commanding officer, General McLaws, that a critical moment was coming.

Around 4 a.m., the Confederate forces on Marye's Heights were awakened by the report of a large cannon. A civilian in the camp bounced up as if mounted on a spring: "Wake up! wake up! what's that?"[15] The roar of a second gun followed—the prearranged signal for the artillery to take their positions in the redoubts on Marye's Hill and wait for events to unfold. To the tune of "Boots and Saddles," Longstreet's artillerymen moved to the hill. Finding the breastworks thrown up by the army engineers too low for their liking, the men used picks and shovels to raise the fortifications a little higher. They then bored out embrasures through which they could fire. The engineers protested; they were proud of their handiwork, and the gunners were now ruining it. A cannoneer replied, "We have to fight here, not you; we will arrange them to suit ourselves."[16] The Rebels wheeled their cannons into place, and then—nothing. The fog that hung over the river had extended over the town, and no one could discern what was happening below.

None of this, as it turned out, mattered much to Arthur Fuller's former regiment. In Burnside's reorganization of the army, the Sixteenth had been assigned to Brigadier General Daniel Sickles's division of the Center Grand Division under Major General Hooker. Sickles's division was not involved in the crossing of the river on the 11th. Two day later, while other troops were being mowed down below Marye's Heights, Sickles's men were only lightly engaged. Combined, the five regiments that made up the Sixteenth Massachusetts's brigade reported only eleven men killed at Fredericksburg. In a battle where safety was decidedly relative, the Sixteenth turned out to be one of the safest places to be. (There was a notable absence from Burnside's force, and from all other Union armies up to that time: in this war for freedom, black troops were not authorized to join the armed forces until the signing of the Emancipation Proclamation. Fredericksburg was, therefore, a white man's battle.)

The night when Burnside's engineers started assembling their bridges was the last that Fuller planned to spend with his comrades in uniform. An anonymous memoirist, the only person who wrote an account of Fuller's final dinner with the Sixteenth, described it in terms faintly reminiscent of the Last Supper: "I think I took the last meal with Mr. Fuller. It was dinner (beefsteak and hard bread). He asked *all* to partake with him: the teamsters, sergeants, and myself. I told him I feared he had none too much for himself. 'Oh, yes, he had plenty.' And whatever he had, no matter how little, he always wished to share with those around him." When the meal was over, Fuller turned to his servant-boy and said, enigmatically, "Johnny, you [soon] may cook my supper over on the other side, in Fredericksburg."[17]

After this meal, Fuller's precise movements are hard to trace. The memoirist just quoted seems to have been convinced that the reverend had every intention of taking part in the battle. Yet many of the actions he attributes to the gentle minister seem oddly out of character. The writer avers that, by the morning after his farewell dinner, Fuller had borrowed a revolver, telling a lieutenant that he "had seven shots to deposit somewhere." "Ah, Rev. Fuller," the lieutenant reputedly exclaimed, "are you going, too?" Fuller reportedly answered, "Yes, Lieutenant; I wouldn't miss this fight for a hundred dollars."[18] The memoirist reports, however, that the colonel of the Sixteenth Massachusetts, Thomas Tannatt, got wind of the former chaplain's intentions and ordered him to give the firearm back. Tannatt wanted no part of letting a civilian arm himself and go into the fray.

But Arthur Fuller did not want to be safe. At some point, he put on a captain's coat, slipped away from the Sixteenth, and headed north toward the area where General Sumner's Right Grand Division was readying itself for battle. One account maintains that he had gone there with no grander purpose than to bid farewell to friends in the Nineteenth Massachusetts.[19] But if the anonymous source is correct, the chaplain was already thinking about joining the fight that was about to begin.

As Reverend Fuller ate his farewell dinner, the Third Brigade of Oliver O. Howard's division, which included the Seventh Michigan and the Nineteenth and Twentieth Massachusetts, received an order. The next day, as soon as the bridges leading to Sophia Street were in position, the

Third Brigade was to charge across them and establish a bridgehead on the far shore. But on the morning of the 11th, the bridge-borne assault could not get underway. Barksdale's men had settled into virtually every corner of the opposing shore, some occupying cellars and vacant buildings and others secreting themselves behind stone walls or fences that they had made musket-proof by piling cordwood and other materials against them.[20] As soon as they came within range of Barksdale's sharpshooters, the construction crews barely stood a chance. Men from the Seventh and the Nineteenth were ordered to the bank of the Union side of the river to provide cover for the embattled builders, but with no effect. The fire from the Confederate rifle pits continued to sweep the half-formed bridges. Nine "distinct and desperate times," the builders tried to extend the bridges, but each time the Confederate fire inflicted too many losses for them to continue.[21]

Around 10 a.m., the engineers suspended their efforts. Greater force was needed. For that force, Burnside had already turned to Brigadier General Henry Hunt, commander of the Army of the Potomac's artillery brigades. Realizing that only a heavy bombardment had any hope of dislodging Barksdale's gunmen, Burnside told Hunt, "Bring all your guns to bear upon the city, and batter it down."[22] Burnside's order to Hunt marked a turning point in the conduct of the war. Even if the presence of sharpshooters had transformed them into military targets, and whether or not they had been evacuated, the houses, stores, and churches of Fredericksburg were, by some understandings, civilian structures. For the first time in the war, a general was ordering a massive assault on the homes of noncombatants. At 9 a.m., and again a half-hour later, Hunt intensified his attack on the city. Eventually, some 147 pieces of Union artillery were engaged, firing more than seven thousand rounds of ammunition into Fredericksburg.[23] General McLaws watched helplessly as the cannons tore the town apart:

> [The] iron hail [was] hurled against the small band of defenders and into the devoted city. The roar of the cannon, the bursting shells, the falling of walls and chimneys, and the flying bricks and the other materials dislodged from the houses by the iron balls and shells, added to the fire of the infantry from both sides and the smoke from the guns and the burning houses, made a scene of indescribable confusion, enough to appall the stoutest hearts![24]

Destroying another person's home is a solemn, ugly task. Some of the Federals who observed the bombardment were deeply sobered by the harshness of it all. "There are," a New York soldier lamented regarding the bombardment, "many things connected with this war that seem hard for an enlightened and Christianized nation such as we claim to be."[25] Yet to quite a few of the Union men who had seen comrades killed and maimed on Burnside's miserable pontoons, the shelling of the city brought a surge of joy that, in the moment, felt far from shameful. One soldier was unabashedly gleeful: "It was a great amusement to us to watch a solid shot tear through a building, beat down a wall, topple over a chimney or root out a nest of sharpshooters."[26] An especially rapturous recollection came, understandably, from one of the beleaguered engineers: "Oh! It was terrific! From the time the fire opened until about 11 a.m., it was one continuous roar."[27]

The response from the other side of the line was less cheerful. By choosing to defend the town and by using its structures to conceal his sharpshooters, General Lee had turned Fredericksburg into a battleground like any other, and Burnside was, at least arguably, acting within accepted rules of engagement by firing on the city. However, the Southern commander was disposed to forget that point. From his vantage point above the city, Lee stood, wrapped in his cape and plunged in melancholy. Staring fixedly at the flames rising from the houses near the river, he could see the bombardment only as an act of cowardice and treachery. "These people," said the Virginian after a long silence, "delight to destroy the weak and those who can make no defence; it just suits them."[28]

Hunt's mission to silence Barksdale's riflemen failed. Instead of being driven back, the Mississippians dug in harder. They took to the town's cellars and found deeper ditches from which to pour forth their fire. After the bombardment, the Union engineers tried to resume their work. Once more, the Confederates drove them off.[29] Hours passed, and only one of the bridges into town was progressing to any extent.

Colonel Norman Hall commanded Howard's Third Brigade, which included Wendell Holmes's regiment. As the frustration and the casualties mounted, Hall consulted with Hunt and Brigadier General Daniel Woodbury, the engineer overseeing the construction of the pontoons. The three men agreed on an alternative tactic, proposed, evidently, by Hunt: a detachment of the boats intended to support the bridges would be used as transport vessels, carrying the advance troops across the river ahead of the bridges. The initial crossing was reconceived on the spot as a riverine assault.

Hard pressed for options and inspired by necessity, the three officers probably did not realize just how novel their proposition was: no American military force had ever before established a bridgehead under fire. Whether or not he knew the history, Colonel Hall distinctly perceived the hazards. He later admitted that, as he contemplated the attack, he "felt apprehensions of disaster." The pontoon boats had not been built for maneuverability, and the soldiers' skill in piloting them could hardly be counted on. The small flotilla might easily become knotted and confused in midstream, giving Barksdale's riflemen an even more defenseless target than the engineers had been. Yet it seemed like the only way. Lieutenant Colonel Henry Baxter, commanding the Seventh Michigan, told his men of the new plan, and they volunteered to lead the attack. The Nineteenth Massachusetts agreed to follow.

In another attempt to silence the Rebel sharpshooters, Hunt resumed the cannonade. By now, the destruction that his guns had visited upon Fredericksburg had become, in the words of one Yankee observer, "truly deplorable":

> Walls were breached; roofs crushed in; fronts rent, shattered, tottering; interiors demolished; a dozen homes burning; dwellings and furniture alike left by the frightened inhabitants, most of whom . . . were then encamped in the woods beyond [the city].[30]

As Hunt's shells exploded over the Confederates, the amphibious strike took shape. Engineers carried boats down to the shore. The riverbank was almost flat, and getting the boats into position was a fairly easy task. As they were still being loaded, Hunt's barrage abruptly ceased—the signal for the boats to launch. Colonel Hall suffered an anxious moment; many of the boats intended for the assault still lay empty. Yet it seemed best to push forward with those that were ready. Now that the cannonade had ceased, it would not take long for Barksdale's riflemen to resume their positions. It was time to move.

Led by their lieutenant colonel, Henry Baxter, the Michigan men raced across the mudflat and clambered into the first six boats, about 135 men in all.[31] One small additional passenger, quite uninvited, also made the crossing. A drummer boy of the Seventh Michigan named Robert Henderson turned twelve that day. Intending "to make his birthday memorable," the boy leaped into one of the boats but was ordered out by the captain. Undeterred, Henderson made as if to push one of the boats off from the shore. Instead of releasing his grip after the vessel was afloat, he held onto the stern, and the rowers unwittingly towed him through the frigid waters to the other side. Once there, Henderson snatched a musket from the body of a dead soldier and fought in the ranks for the rest of the day.[32]

Around 3 p.m., the Michigan infantrymen began to cross the Rappahannock. Twenty of the soldiers crowded into each vessel, stooping as low as they could below the gunwales to protect themselves from enemy fire that seemed to come from a hundred points at once.[33] Pushing hard at their poles, pulling hard at their oars, they slid the boats out into the icy current. The vessels were graceless and clumsy, but they were being driven forward with all possible speed. The middle third of the river was the most perilous; it was near enough to be well within the range of the Confederate rifles but not so close that the steep riverbank toward which they were rowing could provide cover. By the time the boats had made it this far, the Confederate sharpshooters were back in action, firing rapidly. Baxter reeled and fell, his lung pierced by a Rebel bullet. Mercifully, moments later, the boats passed the point beyond which the ten-foot-high bank on the Confederate side shielded them from fire. A scraping sound and a sudden halt announced that the boats had reached their goal. In an instant, men in the bows were leaping onto the shore, while those farther aft splashed into the water and waded the few remaining yards to land. "The water was cold," one recalled, "but it was no time for ceremony."[34]

Taking command from the wounded Baxter, Major Thomas Hunt ordered the first sixty to seventy men into formation and urged them forward. The men clambered up the steep embankment and onto Sophia Street, an anxious run of ten to fifteen seconds. From their hiding places, the Rebels started up and tried to scramble away. Several were brought down by Union bullets.[35] At least thirty were taken captive. The bridgehead had been secured.

Moments after the Seventh Michigan had launched, the Nineteenth Massachusetts prepared to follow. Arthur Fuller looked on. Mentally and morally, he found himself at a crossroads. His duty to God counseled the minister not to kill. His duty to the Union urged him to take up arms. Grave practical concerns confronted him as well. If he joined the men in the boats, he would be taking an extraordinary risk. If anything, he had gone out of his way to increase his personal peril; for the occasion, he had put on the coat of a staff officer, despite knowing that officers were the preferred targets of Rebel sharpshooters. Moreover, with his discharge papers literally in his pocket, Fuller was now a civilian.[36] If he were killed, his family would have no right to a government pension. If he were taken prisoner, Fuller would be less protected than the men he walked alongside. Although the Confederate government was obliged to exchange captured soldiers, they were entitled to deal with civilians as they chose. Fuller knew these consequences. He stepped forward.

Four companies of the Nineteenth Massachusetts—B, D, E, and K—hurried into the boats.[37] It was not until after a craft carrying men from Company K pushed off from the shore that the officer in charge of the boat noticed a stranger in staff dress, his coat causing him to stand out among the plainer uniforms of the other passengers. Private George Wentworth heard the officer ask the man what he was doing there. The stranger said that he wanted to do something for his country.[38] Turning the boat around was out of the question, and the interrogation of the unknown passenger stopped there. He was a frail, aristocratic-looking man with only one eye.

After climbing the embankment, the Michigan men who had preceded the Nineteenth had pushed toward the left of their point of landing. The Massachusetts men were ordered to take the ground that lay to the right. They formed themselves by companies, but there was no time to organize into regimental formation. As soon as could be managed, they charged ahead.[39] Their path took them up a slight incline along the north side of Hawke Street, toward Caroline Street. No man could have viewed the prospect with much pleasure. As at the riverfront itself, Barksdale's Mississippians had hidden themselves in and around the buildings that looked onto Caroline. Any window or doorway might conceal a Confederate musket. None of the tactics that had seen the Massachusetts men through previous battles were of any use. The street warfare could only be conducted from yard to yard, from house to house. Some of the buildings were burning. Others contained a remnant of women and children who had resisted the order to evacuate. Their shrieks and moans, coupled with the smoke and blaze, added to the confusion. Barksdale's lead regiment, the Seventeenth Mississippi, had been enraged by the bombardment of the city. They wanted not only to defend the town, but also to exact revenge. Perfectly invisible to their foes, they contested every foot of the Yankees' advance. The advance of the Seventh Michigan ground to a halt. Somehow, the Nineteenth kept moving. Up the street, through backyards and gardens they came, about 110 men in all.

At Caroline Street, a block above Sophia Street, the crossfire became appalling. Two days later, Lieutenant John Hudson of the Thirty-Fifth Massachusetts would join the attack on the stone wall below Marye's Heights, in the same brigade as George Whitman. As horrifying as that action was, Hudson believed that the street fight on the December 11 was immeasurably worse.[40] Company B lost ten men out of its original thirty in less than five minutes, and the other companies were taking similar losses.[41] Captain Moncena Dunn, commander of Company D, deployed his twenty-five men on the street as skirmishers. The exposed position alarmed one of Burnside's aides. He accosted Dunn and asked the captain what he thought he was doing. Dunn replied that he was under orders to hold the position. The aide argued that orders must sometimes give way to common sense: if the rebels pressed too hard, the Nineteenth would have to retreat.

Moments later, the unfamiliar man in an officer's coat appeared at the captain's side, holding a musket. The man saluted and repeated what he had told the officer in the boat: "Captain, I must do something for my country. What shall I do?" Captain Dunn studied the man for an instant. Surely this was no officer. Who are you? Dunn asked. The answer was calm and terse: the chaplain of the Sixteenth Massachusetts. Dunn scanned the minister's demeanor for signs of agitation. For skirmish duty, a soldier needed to be utterly in command of himself, for a single excited man could distract and endanger all the others. This man showed no signs of rash impulse. He was, it seemed, "perfectly cool and collected." Nevertheless, Dunn at first advised the chaplain not to go in; but the man was determined.[42] Well, all right, then. "Never a better time than the present," said Dunn; Fuller could take a place on the left of the company.[43] The preacher did as he was told, finding a space about fifteen feet away from the captain. In front of a grocery store, on the cold December afternoon, the half-blind, malarial minister, who had not fired a shot since his teens, shouldered his gun and began to do what he could.[44] It seemed to Captain Dunn that Chaplain Fuller had time to fire only once or twice. His armed defense of the Union lasted no more than five minutes.

It is possible that, in those brief minutes, Arthur Fuller found something that had always eluded him—that, for an instant, he ceased to be a coddled son, an overshadowed brother, or even the sickly, sometimes peevish chaplain who had too often lacked the health and strength to march with his men. One would hope that Fuller finally became, in his own mind, a victor over frailty and fear. But not even the soldiers with whom he was standing could know what he was thinking, and to the outward view, but for his purloined officer's coat, he looked more or less indistinguishable from the other embattled riflemen of the Nineteenth Massachusetts, holding their ground and fighting for their lives. But to be just like them was the very thing that Fuller had wanted all along.

The two bullets that hit the minister evidently struck in quick succession. Captain Dunn had been in fights where men had been hit without knowing it, so he could not be sure whether the ball that caught Fuller below the arm came a short time before the second, or whether the two shots did their work more or less simultaneously. Another witness said that Fuller was spun partway around by the first shot. In any case, it was the second shot that made the difference. Dunn swore later that he saw the flash of the musket that sent this second bullet on its way. A fraction of a second later, the ball slammed into Fuller's groin, crushing the femoral artery. Fuller called out, "I am hit!"[45] Immediately, he went limp, felled by an impact so violent that Dunn presumed that death was instantaneous. In this, he was likely mistaken. A wound to an artery can kill quickly, but not in an instant. And yet, after Fuller fell, Dunn did not see the minister make a move, and he did not hear him utter a sound. The dying man's inertness looked very much like acceptance. From Reverend Fuller, surrounded by men who did not know his name, there came no struggle, no inspiring last words as his life spilled out onto Caroline Street. To all appearances, death was only death.

But it was not with the thought that death was only death that Arthur Fuller took up his position at the intersection of Hawke and Caroline, and it was almost surely not this belief that occupied the chaplain's mind as he lay dying. His thoughts were likely closer to those he shared in one of the few of his sermons that he ever saw published. There he had declared:

> [A] faith which promotes a good life insures also a good death; . . . he who lives well *always* dies well. Yes; let the lightning's vivid flash; let storm, or poison, the gleaming dagger, the noon-day pestilence—let any of them be the instrument by which the spirit is disrobed of its fleshly clothing; let death come in slowly wasting years, or in but one moment's agony; in calm consciousness or in delirious dream, death is good and welcome, if man has passed existence and proba-tion wisely; for a better life is hid with Christ, and the freed spirit does but go *home* to be with God.[46]

The mourning for Fuller had to wait. The entire regiment was still under heavy fire. A half hour after the clash began, definite orders at last came through: the Nineteenth must pull back. The Bay Staters retreated, leaving Fuller's body where it lay. A wounded man, Private Michael Red-ding, lay near him. When a comrade offered to carry him to the rear on his back, Redding replied, "No, you'll be back again shortly and I'll sit here and wait for you."[47]

On the other side of the river, the Twentieth Massachusetts did not hear of the Michiganders' offer to cross the river in boats until after the attempt was underway. The news provoked a stir in Holmes's regi-ment. "This," Henry Ropes later wrote, "was indeed a desperate thing."[48] Almost as soon as the Seventh Michigan had gained the opposite bank, the Twentieth received the order to march down the bluff to the riv-er's edge and await instructions there. Wounded men from the Seventh Michigan and the Nineteenth Massachusetts were already being ferried back to safety when the next order came: the engineers now had some breathing space in which to complete the bridges, and the Twentieth was to cross as soon as the structures were in place. However, Acting Major George Macy, the officer who had rescued Colonel Lee after Antietam, misunderstood the order; he thought that the regiment was to cross in boats as the others had done. As soon as the returning craft were emptied of their wounded, Holmes's companions climbed in to take their place.

For this first part of their task, the Twentieth was remarkably well adapted. Many of the soldiers of Holmes's regiment hailed from Nantucket and were the sons of whale hunters. Quite unexpectedly, their long-dormant prowess as oarsmen became a most useful skill. One of them, Captain Leander Alley, who had circled the globe in a whaling ship, seemed to have been made for this moment. When the boat he was in began to drift with the current because an enlisted man faltered at his oar, Alley took charge of it. His expertise and strength promptly put the vessel back on course as he shouted instructions to the other boats. Seizing command of the moment, Alley put some steel into the men around him. "*What an example!*" one of the regiment's corporals recollected, "Could I, no matter how much of a Coward I might be, *flinch then?*" A month or so later, the same man's enthusiasm climbed higher at his recollection: "'Twas Glorious—'twas Grand—bullets, shells and death were forgotten. Hurrah for victory and death to the Rebs!"[49]

When they arrived on the other side, however, the Twentieth met with a new perplexity. Although Barksdale's Mississippians had more or less conceded the waterfront, their strong defensive positions in the houses and cellars of the lower part of the town had denied the Seventh Michigan and the Nineteenth Massachusetts any further progress. As those regiments had been driven back and additional troops from the rear continued to land, a worrisome bottleneck was forming near the shore. Although the troops were now crossing in relative safety, they were piling up in a compact, unmanageable mass once they arrived. As the first signs of chaos became visible, Colonel Hall sent urgent requests across the river to stop the flow of men, but his messages were ignored. Instead, an order came back that the force must press ahead.

Hall faced a dreadful prospect; he must send still more men into the shooting gallery where the Seventh and the Nineteenth had already been riddled with casualties. The freshest troops at Hall's disposal were Holmes's regiment. He therefore sent orders to Acting Major Macy: the Twentieth was "to clear the street leading from the bridge at all hazards."[50]

Led by two platoons of thirty men under the command of Holmes's friend Henry Abbott, the Twentieth climbed up the riverbank and fell into a column with rows of four men abreast. When they reached Sophia Street, they came under murderous fire from Barksdale's riflemen. Moving away from the river onto Hawke Street, they found themselves a block below Caroline Street, the place where the Nineteenth had been driven back and where Arthur Fuller's body was still lying. There seemed no reason to believe that the Twentieth would succeed where the Nineteenth had failed. But Macy was determined to drive the rebels from their position, and he knew the man he wanted for the job. "Mr. Abbott," he said, "you will take your first platoon forward." Making no reply, Abbott turned to his men and, taking the lead of the column, said simply, "First Platoon forward—march." The knot of men progressed only a few yards when several of them fell, laid low by enemy fire. Colonel Hall shouted to Abbott to bring up his remaining platoon. Again, Abbott did not hesitate: "Second Platoon forward."[51]

As Abbott's men advanced, another company of the regiment guarded their right flank. Their leader, Captain Charles Cabot, cried out, "Oh, God!" and collapsed, his skull pierced by a Rebel bullet. Men were being cut down "like wheat swaths." But the indomitable Abbott pressed on.[52]

Colonel Hall commented later that the Twentieth Massachusetts, which contained more literary men than any other regiment in Burnside's army, had "no poetry in a fight."[53] Indeed, Abbott's conduct in front of his company had not an ounce of drama, but its very lack of brio made it extraordinary. The diminutive captain's unshakable calm in the face of disaster made an indelible impression on those who witnessed it. More than twenty years later, in a Memorial Day address, Holmes paid tribute to his friend's "sublime" self-mastery:

His few surviving companions will never forget the awful spectacle of his advance alone with his company in the streets of Fredericksburg. In less than sixty seconds, he would become the focus of a hidden and annihilating fire from a semicircle of houses. His first platoon had vanished in an instant, ten men falling dead by his side. He . . . was again moving on, in obedience to superior command, to certain and useless death. . . . The end was distant only a few seconds; but if you had seen him with his indifferent carriage, and sword swinging from his finger like a cane, you never would have suspected that he was doing more than conducting a company drill on a camp parade ground.[54]

Holmes's memory of Abbott's brave stand seems marvelously vivid. But Holmes himself did not bear witness to "the awful spectacle." He did not observe Abbott's stoic demeanor, and he did not see the sword swinging nonchalantly from Abbott's finger. For, when Abbott called his platoons forward, indifferent to death itself, Wendell Holmes was not with them.

Earlier in the day, when the call had come for the regiment to organize itself for the trip across the Rappahannock, Holmes had been in no condition to respond. A few days earlier, nausea and abdominal pain had begun to overtake him. Soon he became almost incapable of controlling his bowels. With each passing day, illness and lack of nourishment had made him weaker. By the morning of December 11, he was unable to march, "stretched out miserably sick with the dysentery."[55]

For a young man of Holmes's pride, the illness meant a painful dose of humiliation, but the indignity was hardly the worst of it. In a Civil War camp, a diagnosis of dysentery was often a death sentence. The disease was responsible for more than one in ten military deaths during the conflict as a whole. What a bullet through Holmes's neck had failed to do, a microbe was now likely to accomplish.

As the regiment went into battle, it was clear that Holmes would have to stay behind. The feelings that washed over him were "worse than the anxiety of danger." Physically exhausted, he gave in to the rage and shame that consumed him in his helplessness, and he wept. The regiment marched away. The only tent left standing was the field hospital. Listless and miserable, Holmes made his way there. As he arrived, the orderlies were just removing a dead soldier. Nearby, another man lay moaning, near death from the same complaint that had incapacitated Holmes. Holmes spent the entire day there, unbearably idle, "with no prospect of being moved or cared for."[56]

From the hospital tent, the cannonade was clearly audible. There could be little doubt that the Twentieth had found its way into a scrap. Convinced that "one of the great battles of the war" was underway, Holmes tried to rally; he had to make it to the field.[57] But he was too weak. He sank back into his bedding, just as helpless as before. With no books at his disposal, he tried to calm himself by drawing. Yet he could not escape his feelings of impotency and self-accusation. The regiment was in a struggle for its survival, and he was not with them. For an earnest soldier, few circumstances could feel more damning. Two decades later, Holmes would still feel the damnation.

Across the river, as they slugged their way up Hawke Street, Holmes's regiment was sustaining frightful losses. By degrees, though, they were moving forward. They were getting practically no help from the Seventh Michigan, whose force and will seemed utterly spent. Macy urged Major Thomas Hunt, whom the various woundings of superiors had left in charge of the Michiganders, to order his men forward. Hunt protested wanly that he had had no orders to push the attack further. Macy replied hotly that he had had no doubts concerning his own orders, which were to follow the Seventh—something he could do only if the Seventh would take the trouble to lead. After a few minutes of Macy's exasperated pleading, it became clear that Hunt would not budge. As Macy ordered his own men up the street, Hunt shouted a warning, which also gave away the real reason for his refusal to advance: he thought that "no man could live round that corner." Macy shot back some heartfelt advice of his own: Hunt could "go to hell with [his] regiment."[58]

Macy was showing no lack of courage. What he needed just as much—and assuredly did not have—was a plan. "I advanced," he later recollected, but "had hardly the least idea of what to do." Daylight had faded, and the gunfire from the houses flashed against the darkness. The bullets came "from front, rear and sides . . . from windows, sheds, corners, brick houses and behind fences."[59] Two cousins from Nantucket fell, one wounded in the head and shoulder, the other gazing at a knee that he would never use again. By some miracle, Macy himself was untouched, although, he later wrote, more than a dozen wounded men literally fell on him. If any of the advancing troops had taken a moment to look down, they would have seen a fresh abomination: Private Redding of the Nineteenth, the wounded man who had told his comrades to come back for him later, was dead—bayoneted in seven places by Rebels as he lay helpless.[60] Nearby was the inert form of Fuller. Although the Confederates had done no mischief to his body, the corpse had been robbed; his watch, his money, and portions of his clothing were gone.[61]

Abbott, like Macy, was untouched. He somehow managed to get his platoon to the west side of the intersection. At that moment, the tide shifted in their favor. Abbott's men made a rush for the houses that had sheltered the enemy, bursting through doors and driving their antagonists out the other side of the dwellings. To the right of the Twentieth, the Nineteenth had also rallied and was turning Barksdale's flank. Finally,

at 7 p.m., fighting stopped. General McLaws ordered Barksdale to withdraw from the town, and the Mississippians retreated up the sloping
ground to the west of the town, taking a defensive position behind a stone
wall on Marye's Heights.

Covering the Rebel retreat was a company of men led by Lane Brandon, a Mississippi lieutenant who, while attending Harvard Law School,
had become friends with Abbott. As his company was falling back
through the town, Brandon learned from some captured soldiers that
the regiment pursuing him was the Twentieth Massachusetts. Far from
horrifying him, the idea of fighting his friend excited Brandon almost to
a frenzy. Disobeying orders to withdraw, he wheeled his men around and
attacked the Twentieth, pushing it partway back to the river. Another
order came to Brandon to pull back, but he ignored it, keeping up the
fight until his fellow Confederates had to arrest him.[62] Friendship took
strange forms in the streets of the battered town. Brandon's resistance
having ceased, the first day's action at Fredericksburg was over. The town
belonged to the Union.

For the men of the Twentieth, the price of winning the town had been
high. They had fought in the streets for two and a half hours. Of Abbott's
sixty men, ten were dead and another twenty-five were wounded.[63]
Although the toll among the regiment's other companies was not as great,
all had suffered considerably. In his official report, Colonel Hall wrote
that the regiment had lost ninety-seven killed or wounded in the space
of approximately fifty yards.[64] To those who had survived the street fight
on Caroline Street, the shock of the unit's losses was partly balanced by a
measure of redemption. At Ball's Bluff, and again at Antietam, they had
been forced to run. Today, the struggle had been equally fearsome, but
there had been no running.

But on the other side of the river, Holmes was none the wiser. All
that night no word came from across the river. On the morning of the
12th, the rumors trickled in—wild and exaggerated at first, then gradually settling into confirmed fact: Captain Cabot was dead; Holmes's
second lieutenant, Tom McKay, had been wounded. Cabot's death had
particular meaning for Holmes. Before the battle, Holmes's Company
A had been consolidated with Company F, under Cabot's command.
Thus, Cabot had marched up Hawke Street in the same position of
leadership that Holmes would have occupied had he been healthy. Now

Cabot was gone, and Holmes, by a stroke of fate or providence, or who knows what, was alive.

Also on the eastern side of the river, John Suhre's regiment, after marching about two miles on the "double quick," had been placed in battle-ready position and told to await further orders. For hours, the men of the 133rd Pennsylvania stood with their knapsacks on their backs, no one knowing when or whether the command would come to cross the pontoons. When night fell, along with most of Burnside's army, they were still waiting. They watched as "the sun set in the smoke of battle," a sight that, for some of them, surpassed anything they had ever imagined. Now and then a shell would explode against the sky, ironically forming "the most beautiful wreaths" of color. As the sound of the artillery rolled on, the heavens darkened, and the blood-red sun went down, Chaplain Hartsock thought "the orb of day" wore "a fitting appearance" as it looked down "upon the crimson tide that flowed from American veins."[65]

Over in the town, here and there, a pale beam from behind a closed casement advertised the presence of some person who had been unwilling or unable to obey the evacuation order. Otherwise, however, the captured town was almost completely dark. Scarcely a building had escaped being struck by cannon fire, and it seemed that not a single window had survived the onslaught.[66] The occupying soldiers broke up fences from nearby houses to fuel their campfires, dispel some of the gloom, and cook their suppers. Some of the men wandered about to take in their surroundings. Others sat on curbstones, smoking and talking. George Anson Bruce of Holmes's regiment spotted a New York infantryman who had made himself particularly at home. He had purloined a jar of jelly from one of the houses and had also dispatched a chicken, which now lay nicely roasted on his plate. A pot of coffee brewed cheerily nearby. After taking a contemplative sip from his cup, the soldier coolly balanced his beverage on the body of a dead Confederate lying conveniently next to him. The grisly shape of his coffee table caused no apparent shock to his sensibilities, nor any loss to his appetite.[67]

The next day, the 12th, there was little fighting to speak of, though some of the fires from the previous day's bombardment burned on. In the streets of Fredericksburg, a new destructive force was gathering momentum. As Union regiments poured over the pontoon bridges into the vanquished city and it became evident that the Confederates had withdrawn, colonels and majors celebrated by rewarding their men with whiskey rations. Some of the Federals went quietly about their business; John G. B. Adams of the Nineteenth Massachusetts remembered simply, "We buried our dead, sent the wounded back to the hospital, and made ready for the battle which we knew must come."[68] But other portions of the army suffered a moral collapse unlike any they had ever known. The alcohol coupled with anger; many of the soldiers saw the houses around them not as cherished homes left behind by frightened refugees, but as the dens from which skulking adversaries had lately tried to kill them. In fury and frustration, they resorted to vandalism.

For some, the merriment was relatively innocent. Across the town, a host of fine pianos were dragged from fashionable parlors and into the streets, where soldiers pounded out tinny versions of "Yankee Doodle" and "The Star-Spangled Banner."[69] But others were less restrained. Men and boys eager to enrich themselves with the spoils capered about, laden with silver pitchers, lamps, and spoons. Alabaster vases and splendid pieces of statuary became projectiles, vengefully hurled at mirrors and windows. Wine cellars, patiently filled over the course of decades, were raided for their riches, and what could not be consumed was added to the general smash. The streets grew littered with "every conceivable article of goods, chattels and apparel."[70] Libraries worth thousands of dollars were thrown into the streets. Tiring of the efforts of their musical comrades, soldiers kicked the insides of the pianos to bits and set the instruments ablaze. "Everything," a major of the 108th New York lamented, "[was] turned upside down."[71]

His statement was both literally and metaphorically true. The men who pillaged Fredericksburg were striking, pulling, and tearing not only against the artifacts of Southern aristocracy, but also against the principles of their own upbringing. Bruce Catton has noted that the soldiers responsible for the worst excesses of the mayhem were not back-country ruffians or, as some later tried to place the blame, untutored immigrants. They were chiefly Easterners, their families long settled in America. Many of them were members of what had been thought the most disciplined units in Mr. Lincoln's army. What they stole, they took not out of need, but from spite. What they wrecked and trampled, they destroyed only because, on the most animal of levels, it felt good. When one recalls the sack of Fredericksburg, one may feel disinclined to mourn the annihilation of family fortunes built on the labor and suffering of enslaved women and men. But one should always regret, and regret deeply, the downfall of decency in every soldier who, in the streets of the Virginia town, raised a hand against the values of mercy, honor, and respect.

The chaos of December 12 erupted mere paces away from the spot where, the day before, Arthur Fuller had bled to death. It is sadly fitting that as Fuller died, his vision of a just war, fought by noble men for lofty aims, was also on the verge of dying. With his hymnals, his sermons, and his example, Fuller had hoped somehow to Christianize the war. But the war would not be Christianized, and if ever it had been capable of such a transformation, it was becoming less and less so now. Incidents like the street fight in Fredericksburg, where every window and cellar had become a potential rifle pit, were blurring the distinction between combatant and civilian. What had begun as a casual disregard for the rights of citizens was hardening, bit by bit, into customary cruelty. More than two years later, as peace flickered on the horizon, President Lincoln would urge the nation to carry on "with malice toward none, with charity for all."[72] But by the time those words were spoken, the smoke and stench of ruin that had stung nostrils at Fredericksburg had been smelled in Atlanta; in Charleston; in Chambersburg, Pennsylvania; in Corydon, Indiana; and in other places large and small. By 1865, America had borne witness to almost as much concentrated malice as a nation could withstand, and seldom would the American capacity for charity and forgiveness be so sorely tested.

Chapter Ten

Pelham Does First Rate

When he looked back on the early morning of December 13, 1862, Heros von Borcke remembered the quiet. The silence had a brooding, portentous feel, the way it always felt to him just before a battle.[1] The stillness then yielded to an indistinct murmur; down by the banks of the Rappahannock, thousands of blue-coated soldiers were preparing themselves for battle. They milled about, trying to muffle their noise but not quite succeeding. Together, they raised a hum that reminded von Borcke of a distant, gigantic swarm of bees.[2]

Uncertain sounds; uncertain sights as well. Just as it had done two days before, a dense fog concealed the river. Not knowing bred tension, and as the morning light spread over the sad, violated town of Fredericksburg, everything was indistinct. In the cold, damp dawn, two armies waited.

On the Confederate right, Jackson and Stuart consulted with General Lee, eager to turn the conditions to their advantage. They urged him to make a quick, aggressive move. The fog, they insisted, would make it impossible for the Federals to use their long-range guns with any kind of accuracy. Deprived of artillery cover and thrown into confusion by the fog, the Union force would be ripe for destruction. General Lee was not persuaded. Jackson had found good ground; he had anchored his corps just west of the Richmond, Fredericksburg, and Potomac Railroad line, along a wooded eminence with a commanding view of the field below.[3] The mist would dissipate as the morning rolled on. Once it did, the Federals would be easy targets, distinctly visible to Jackson's riflemen.[4]

Jackson's preparation, however, was incomplete. Daniel Harvey Hill's infantry division, which had been defending a river crossing at Port Royal, some eighteen miles away, had arrived only around daybreak and had been hustled into position with no chance to dig in.[5] Jackson's position also featured a worrisome flaw: a 600-yard-wide patch of ground, marshy and thickly overgrown, lay between the brigades of another division commander, A. P. Hill. One of the latter Hill's officers pointed out the gap, but the general took no action; he presumed that, for the same reasons that he could not position any regiments there, any advancing Federal units would find the ground impassable. Gap or no gap, however, Lee knew that his right flank was better situated than the men who were getting ready to attack it. He ordered Jackson to let the fight come to him.

At midmorning the sun broke through. Eyes that had struggled in vain to pierce the fog now squinted as the brilliant light fell upon the thin but dazzling snow that covered the ground. The sun also reflected from thousands of polished bayonets as the left flank of Burnside's army—the Left Grand Division under Major General William B. Franklin—made ready for its attack. Whereas the Confederate lines looked worn and tattered, the Union men looked ready for a parade. Officers in their dress uniforms rode from point to point on restless horses. Field-artillery pieces were whisked into position. The well-drilled foot soldiers and cavalry presented so majestic a pageant that one observer called it "the grandest martial scene of the war."[6]

The spectacle impressed von Borcke as well. Franklin's Grand Division looked to him like "a moving forest of steel, their bayonets glistening in the bright sunlight . . . waving their hundreds of regimental flags."[7] Watching the blue lines moving slowly forward, the tall Prussian felt anxious. When he confessed his fear, he happened to be standing near Jackson. The general responded as if von Borcke's jitters were a personal affront. "Major," he replied, "my men have sometimes failed to *take* a position, but to *defend* one, never!"[8]

If the Federals looked resplendent, Lee's lieutenants, too, had their grandeurs. The usually drab and disheveled Jackson had donned a new uniform that he had recently received from Stuart. The outfit reflected the giver's love of frippery. As Jackson rode among his troops that morning, he was a vision of gold braid, and his appearance gave no end of merriment to the soldiers who saw him. One sang out, "Stonewall has drawn his bounty and has bought himself some new clothes," while another observed with mock concern, "Old Jack will be afraid of his clothes and will not get down to work."[9]

In Stuart's camp, John Pelham also put on a special piece of regalia. Captain Lewis Phillips, an English officer traveling with Lee's army as an observer, was accustomed to wearing a narrow red-and-blue-striped necktie, emblematic of his regiment, the Grenadier Guards. He handed the tie to Pelham, asking that he wear it into battle as a good-luck charm. Pelham received it, von Borcke remembered, with a blush of modesty and pride. Instead of looping the cravat around his neck, he tied it around his hat. Thus jauntily adorned, he mounted his horse and galloped off with Stuart's command to take their position on the far right of the Confederate line.[10]

Orders came from Jackson: Pelham was to take his Horse Artillery and open fire immediately on the Union flank.[11] Jackson's goal was simple: his late-arriving units were still getting organized to resist the coming assault, and he needed to buy time. The longer Pelham could disrupt and delay the Federal advance, the better Jackson's chance of holding his position. Pelham had eighteen cannons under his command. For the plan he was evolving on the spot, however, he wanted only one. He begged Stuart to allow him to take one of the lighter, more maneuverable guns—a smooth-bore Napoleon—to an intersection on the stage road that led toward Richmond. He would pepper the Union flank from there.[12]

The crossroads would offer Pelham an enviable angle along which to conduct a bombardment; hurtling obliquely through the Federal units, each shot could tear through a number of men. However, Pelham's proposal was manifestly risky; he would have only a few minutes to fire unopposed before a host of Federal guns would be trained on him. Furthermore, the position from which he meant to fire was well in advance of the main Confederate line. Nolan's treatise on tactics warned that horse artillery should not venture more than two or three hundred yards ahead of their cavalry.[13] As Pelham advanced, only a single brigade of cavalry, under the command of Rooney Lee, would be nearby. Pelham would have little protection from other Southern units if anything went wrong. Stuart weighed the odds for a moment, then approved the hazard. Urged on by the enthusiastic cheers of the cannoneers who stayed behind, Pelham and a small detachment of men took the Napoleon and sped away.[14]

Pelham's choice of terrain was superb. Whereas one's natural tendency in confronting an enemy would be to choose the high ground, Pelham selected a spot at a somewhat lower elevation than his targets, at the bottom of a little swale that hid him from his adversaries. Coming to a hedgerow of cedars at the southwest corner of the intersection, Pelham ordered his men to unlimber the gun. The units on the left flank of the Union army were less than four hundred yards distant—a stone's throw for a Civil War cannon. Pelham's men loaded the gun with solid shot. It was ten o'clock.

The troops at the extreme left of the Federal line were men of John F. Reynolds's First Army Corps. More specifically, they belonged to several brigades of the Pennsylvania Reserves, commanded, as at Antietam, by Major General George Meade. Among these men, in the Tenth Reserves, was Michael Conrad Lowry, the half-brother of John Suhre. The Reserves had been in the war from its early days; Lowry's unit had been mustered in for a three-year hitch on the same day as First Bull Run. They were staunch, battle-tested veterans of the Seven Days Battles, Second Bull Run, and Antietam —men not given to panic. When they heard the first report from Pelham's cannon, they felt no alarm. The shot came from nearby and from a place not known to be occupied by Confederate forces; surely it was just an exuberant or accidental firing from some fellow bluecoats who had indulged in a little too much "commissary." But then more volleys swiftly followed, and a wave of dread swept over the Pennsylvanians. Some of them dived to the ground, their cheeks pressed against the cold mud. Some who were slower to react had no time to regret their indecision, as Pelham's enfilading fire began to cut bloody swaths through the dense formations of the Pennsylvanians.

George Shreve, one of Pelham's gunners, was convinced that their assault was sowing the Federal lines with a confusion that amounted to terror. Although Shreve and the rest of the crew were themselves "fearing annihilation . . . in such close range of their infantry," Meade's bluecoats remained rooted in place. To Shreve's grateful surprise, "Instead of rushing for us and overwhelming us with their numbers, they were evidently afraid of us, judging no doubt that we had a strong force concealed."[15]

While Meade's infantry froze, the Union artillery replied with admirable speed; Pelham managed to get off only three rounds before he felt the shock of return fire. First, the lighter batteries attached to Meade's division were turned against the lone Napoleon. Soon after came a greeting from the longer-range guns across the river on Stafford Heights. Within minutes, the young major had called down upon his detachment the fury of half of Burnside's cannons. The Federals needed to land only one well-placed shot, and Pelham's assault would abruptly end.

But to stop him, the bluecoats had to hit him, and hitting him proved an all but impossible task. Pelham's position in the swale, the lingering traces of morning mist, and the thickness of the cedar boughs made him practically invisible. And it was not merely that; it was also a tricky business for the Union artillery to find the proper range. Ironically, many of the Union guns were too close to Pelham to inflict damage. Likewise, the gunners on Stafford Heights could not depress their barrels far enough to achieve the right trajectory, and their missiles howled harmlessly over the Confederates' heads. Similarly, Meade's cannon repeatedly overshot the mark. Amid all the catapulting iron, Pelham and his men were surprisingly safe, though not entirely so. Just moments into the action, a Federal shell came close to knocking the Napoleon out of commission, striking Private Hammond, one of Pelham's soldiers who was just in the act of sponging the gun's barrel between shots. The tale of Hammond's service to his cause is affectingly brief; not even his first name has been preserved. His only recorded words were his last: "Tell mother I die bravely."[16]

Despite the loss of Hammond and the screams of the Yankees' projectiles above them, Pelham's gunners worked with cool efficiency. They were firing, worming, swabbing, and reloading so fast that more than one Federal officer was convinced that Meade's cannons were dueling not with a single gun, but with a battery of four.[17] In the heat of the moment, one especially rattled Union brigadier sent a dispatch claiming that two batteries, or no fewer than eight cannons, had put a halt to the Union advance. "They must be silenced," urged the general, "before [Reynolds] can advance."[18] It was not as if the Federals weren't trying. In addition to the shelling from the heavy guns across the river, Pelham found himself opposed by at least five Union batteries from closer range. Because Union batteries typically comprised six guns—not the four that were typical in Lee's army—Pelham's men were being outgunned more than thirty to one. But the Napoleon would not be silenced. One of its projectiles struck and disabled a Yankee cannon; another crashed into an ammunition chest, blowing it to pieces.[19] Sometime later, a twelve-pound iron ball from Pelham's gun ripped through the ranks of the 121st Pennsylvania, cutting down seven men. Another shot tore a man in half. What had looked like a dress parade just minutes earlier now more closely resembled a slaughter pen.

As he inflicted these losses, Pelham took care not to expose his gunners to needless risk. He ordered that whenever a crew member was not actively at work, he must lie prone on the ground, minimizing his exposure to incoming fire. However, Pelham did not heed his own advice. With Phillips's necktie flapping from his hat, he remained defiantly in the saddle, contemptuous of the fire that the Federals had turned against him. Pelham's prudent order did not shield his men perfectly; a shot from a Union cannon struck a gunner as he lay on the turf, taking his head off his shoulders.

History has given us ample cause to question whether warfare can ever be beautiful. Nevertheless, those who saw John Pelham and his men working their lone Napoleon had no doubt that they were watching something magnificent. As if the visual spectacle were not enough, the Louisiana Creoles in Pelham's command erupted into song, bellowing the *Marseillaise* as they readied the cannon for every shot. An eyewitness called it "the grandest sight [he had] ever seen."[20] The gunners themselves required no persuasion: a day of glory had indeed arrived.

At the start of his attack, Pelham had benefited from at least some protection, thanks to the presence of Rooney Lee's cavalry brigade. It didn't last. The Union general C. Feger Jackson, in charge of the infantry brigade that contained Michael Lowry, observed Lee's cavalry moving through the hedgerows near Pelham's ground, and he sent two companies from Lowry's regiment to drive them from the area. Union general Abner Doubleday—the man erroneously credited with inventing baseball—sent in men from eight different regiments to support Feger Jackson's push. Overpowered, Lee's horsemen fell back, and Doubleday's men wheeled an artillery battery into position on Pelham's flank.

Jeb Stuart loved the thrill brought on by extreme risk, but the sight of Pelham battling such fearsome odds agonized him. He ordered his staff officer John Esten Cooke to take a second gun crew out toward the crossroads to add some desperately needed firepower to Pelham's stand. Cooke, however, lacked Pelham's eye for ground. Placing his cannon, a British-made rifled Blakely, in an exposed position, he paid almost instantly for his carelessness. His men had fired only once when a Union missile slammed into the Blakely's axle, putting it out of action and killing two members of the crew. Once again, Pelham's Napoleon stood alone. To those who looked on from Jackson's line, it seemed that Pelham's stand could not continue.[21]

With a nonchalance that imperfectly masked his mounting worry, Stuart sent a courier to Pelham with a simple message: "I want to know how he's getting on." The messenger found Pelham still astride his horse, superintending the fire of his cannon. His answer was almost as terse as his commander's query: "Go back and tell General Stuart I am doing first rate."[22]

But his luck was starting to erode. Minutes later, a Union shell detonated near the Napoleon, killing one man and wounding several others. Pelham dismounted and ran to one of the injured men. Jean Bacigalupo, the plucky teenaged Creole, was jerking spasmodically, his chest torn open by a shell fragment. The wound was plainly mortal. Pelham attempted to comfort the boy and ordered two men to carry him to a surgeon. As the crew's casualties began to rise, another rider came forward from the line; it was von Borcke, carrying a second message from Stuart: Pelham should withdraw "if he thought the proper moment had arrived." The blond major bristled: "Tell the general I can hold my ground."[23]

As he fought, Pelham was drawing needed strength from a fellow officer. Captain Mathis Henry, a low-ranking classmate of Pelham's at West Point, had frequently battled illness at the Academy. Since then, he had overcome his frailties and had flourished under Pelham's command. As the odds against hanging on steadily mounted, Pelham was starting to waver. He was on the verge of giving an order to withdraw when Captain Henry pleaded for the major's attention: might they hold out a little longer? Henry swayed his leader's judgment; continuing their bob-and-weave tactic of firing, relocating, and firing again, the crew kept up their defense of the crossroads. A third communiqué arrived from Stuart, now emphatic: "Get back from destruction, you infernal, gallant fool, John Pelham!"[24]

He was disobeying orders now. He heard the fear and love and rage commingled in the general's words, but they could not call him back. Captain Henry's valor had steeled his own, and he could not retreat from the strangely beautiful terror he had summoned up around him—not quite yet. It took eight or nine men to worm, sponge, load, aim, and fire the Napoleon. Pelham had lost so many gunners to death and injury that those who were left could not service the gun without him. As he had done in the past, Pelham dismounted and worked the piece alongside the remnants of his crew, courage verging on madness. At last, word came from Jackson himself: Pelham must retire. Jackson's aide-de-camp James Power Smith, who brought the order, could not forget the scene: "I remember my ride across the field under fire to bear orders to Pelham to retire his guns and how cool and quiet he was . . . in the open field in the center of the converging fire of a hundred cannon."[25]

It was over. The corps commander had spoken, and the ammunition was either gone or nearly so. Pelham ordered his men to limber up and withdraw. Still under fire, begrimed with smoke and mud, the gunners rode back to the safety of Hamilton's Crossing. Almost unaided, Pelham had stopped the advance of a third of Burnside's army for at least an hour. On a distant hill, through field glasses, General Lee had observed the action. Who was it, he asked, that had so defied the Federals? Pelham's name was already well known to the famous commander. Upon hearing it again, he gave a reply that students of the war still know by heart: "It is glorious to see such courage in one so young!"[26]

Pelham had left the crossroads from which he had visited so much damage on Meade's division, but the effect of his action still resonated. Having absorbed such punishment, the Federals could not convince themselves that the attack was over. Fearful that another assault would come from the same direction, General Franklin left Doubleday's division—the largest force in the First Army Corps—to guard the crossroads vacated by Pelham. As the Left Grand Division finally moved forward against Stonewall Jackson's line, it did so without the services of six thousand men who were defending against a thrust that never came.[27]

The Tenth Reserves moved toward the woods that concealed Confederate brigadier general James J. Archer's brigade. The Confederates had orders to hold their fire until Feger Jackson's men set foot on the rail bed of the train line—orders that required tremendous discipline to follow after the Yankee troops began to fire shortly before reaching the appointed landmark. But when the Northerners did reach the rails, the effect was like the tripping of a landmine. At Archer's shout, his line erupted into a blaze of devastation. Rebel memoirists recalled the scene with affecting metaphors. One wrote that the fire from his ranks "caused [the Yankees] to melt away as did the mist of the morning before the sun." Another thought that the blue-coated infantry fell "like hay before the mower's blast."[28]

In the midst of such a firestorm, there is little to distinguish one dead man from another. With luck and patience, some burial crew may later attach a name to the broken remnant of a person. But in the moment of his passing, Michael C. Lowry lay nameless and forgotten. He was denied even the dignity of an anonymous grave: his body was never found.[29] The Tenth Reserves, stung by Archer's fusillade, remained pinned down near the railroad and took no part in the fleeting success enjoyed by the rest of Meade's division. Not long after the deadly first assault from Archer's rifles, Feger Jackson, his horse already shot from under him, was dead as well, killed by a bullet in his skull. A historian would later write, "Of all Meade's brigades, Feger Jackson's would accomplish the least."[30] It is a bitter epitaph for men who fought so hard.

Beyond the tracks of the Richmond, Fredericksburg, and Potomac Railroad lay the wooded, marshy ground that A. P. Hill had deemed impassable and chosen not to defend. But the 600-yard gap in his line proved more penetrable than Hill had calculated. His error afforded the Federals the best chance at victory that they encountered all day. Almost by chance, Meade's Pennsylvania Reserves, along with the 121st and 142nd Pennsylvania, happened upon the weak point and plunged into the breach. From this pouch in the Confederate line, the leading Yankee brigades, urged on by Colonels William Sinclair and Albert Magilton, lashed out fiercely in all directions. On the right, Magilton gave a brigade of North Carolinians under Brigadier General James Lane all they could handle. At the center, regiments from Sinclair's force pushed hard into the brigade of South Carolinians commanded by Brigadier General Maxcy Gregg, penetrating so deeply around his right flank that Gregg was at first convinced that the Pennsylvanians must be a misdirected unit of the Confederate army. Sinclair's troops mortally wounded Gregg and shattered his regiments, sweeping them through the woods. On the left of the pouch, the remainder of Sinclair's command combined with regiments from Feger Jackson's brigade to achieve a near breakthrough, flanking and inflicting heavy punishment on the Nineteenth Georgia and the Fourteenth Tennessee under Archer. Both of these regiments were, in the laconic phrasing of Archer's report, "compelled to retire, leaving about 160 prisoners in the enemy's hands."[31]

The gap in Hill's line cost his division a horrific number of casualties. But Stonewall Jackson's second line behind Hill was strong and deep. After the initial Yankee breakthrough, Stonewall struck back. On the Confederate left, a brigade of Virginia men under Colonel James Walker raced forward "with a yell that would have scared the very devil himself."[32] Walker's regiments slammed into the flank of the First and, subsequently, the Sixth Pennsylvania Reserves, the units that had been tearing into Gregg's South Carolinians. The Federals scattered and fled. At almost the same time, on the Confederate right, a brigade of Georgians under Colonel Edmund Atkinson hit the flanks of the Union troops who had almost devastated Archer's brigade. Jackson's counterattack caused what remained of Meade's division to crumble, and it took back all the hard-won ground west of the railroad and beyond. By the time Meade's force had retreated to the east side of the tracks, at least a third of its men had been killed, wounded, or captured.

Though Pelham's greatest moments on this day were past, he was far from idle during Meade's assault and its repulse. Now directing fifteen cannon instead of one, Pelham laid down a crossfire against Meade's advancing troops that, according to one witness, "perfectly accomplished [its] objective." Eventually some fifty Rebel cannon challenged Meade's advance. The Yankee batteries answered, both from across the river and from Meade's own artillery detachment. Just as noticeable as Pelham's performance was his almost giddy enthusiasm, as the adrenaline from his morning's work continued to surge. He was seen capering among the guns "like a boy playing ball." The action was hotter than many of the gunners had seen before, and one of them nervously asked Pelham's old friend Tom Rosser how long the blond major meant to keep it up. "Oh," came the offhand answer, "at least until *you've* been killed!"[33]

Some ninety minutes later, as Atkinson and Walker drove Meade's Pennsylvanians back across the railroad, Pelham again bedeviled the Union men, pulling his guns forward as the enemy fell back, hitting their lines at an angle calculated to inflict the greatest possible damage. Then, at last, the Union forces stiffened; renewed resistance from the Northern batteries drove back the Confederate artillery, and a belated stand by the

Federal infantry halted the advance of Jackson's gray line. The battle in Pelham's portion of the field was, for the most part, over.[34]

After the First Battle of Bull Run, Pelham had written of how the true horror of the event had come upon him only after it was over—how the battle itself had taken place in a kind of intoxication that had blotted out the agony. At Fredericksburg, that drunkenness of glory had come upon him again. His almost mad tenacity, his refusal to pull back, even under orders, amply showed the power that this feeling exerted over him. It also led him, in the thick of the fight, to pay another Confederate battery one of the strangest compliments ever uttered: "Well, you men stand killing better than any I ever saw."[35]

Not all of Pelham's men stood killing as well as he did. Four days later, one of his enlisted men, William P. Walters, wrote of the bleaker side of Pelham's stand:

> There were 3 Floyd [County] boys wounded. Joseph Phlegar, Samuel Evans and Henderson Boothe. [An]other 5 were all slightly wounded but . . . Phlegar lost his right arm. Evans was struck on the breast. The doctor doesn't think he will ever get well. . . . The shells flew as thick as hail [and] burst all around me, but thank God they never touched me yet. They struck so close to me that several times they threw my face full of dirt. We had 14 horses killed, 2 of them [with]in 3 or 4 feet of me. There isn't any fun in this sort of work, so I won't say any more about it.[36]

Yet there appears to have been fun in it for Pelham. Despite his early misgivings at First Bull Run, warfare seems to have become for him something fulfilling and inspiriting—not just a grim duty that needed to be done. It was at Fredericksburg that Robert E. Lee, watching Carolina troops burst into tears when they were ordered to cease their pursuit of retreating bluecoats, famously remarked, "It is well that war is so terrible—we should grow too fond of it."[37] And at Fredericksburg John Pelham displayed a similar fondness for battle.

The fondness was blunted later that evening. When the tumult and the musketry had died away, Pelham sought out the mortally wounded Jean. The only account of their farewell appears in a novel by Stuart's staff officer John Esten Cooke, and the fiction in the passage is impossible to separate from the fact. Cooke probably invented much of the dialogue. However, his account of how Jean died in his captain's arms, of how Pelham shed tears and wondered how he could possibly tell Jean's mother the news, is now as much a part of the Pelham story as any other. In Cooke's account, Pelham cradled the dying man's head, assuring him that he was among friends who loved him. Just before expiring, in a broken combination of French and English, Jean reportedly replied that Pelham had called him brave. To hear those words from his commander, he said, was comfort enough.[38]

Confederate memoirists and the battle's early historians enshrined Pelham's stand at Fredericksburg as one of the greatest tactical maneuvers and most dazzling acts of courage of the war. However, the best-informed, most recent commentators on the battle, George C. Rable and Francis Augustín O'Reilly, have both questioned the accuracy of this judgment. Rable points out that Jackson's lines were naturally strong enough to have withstood the Union assault with or without Pelham's delaying mission. He further suggests that, through both Franklin's timidity and the slow pace of the Yankee troop movements, the Left Grand Division did more damage to its own cause than Pelham's cannonade inflicted.[39] O'Reilly argues that Pelham's stand would have been shorter and less spectacular if Captain Henry had not pleaded with him to hold the position longer. He cites South Carolina artillerist John Cheves Haskell for the interesting, though decidedly minority, view that it was Henry, not Pelham, who deserved the credit for the day's heroics.[40] Both Rable and O'Reilly note that General Lee thought that Pelham opened his barrage too soon, and that he would have strewn much more mayhem among the Union lines had he given the Federals time to march deeper into the trap he had set.[41] All these observations tend to reduce Pelham's achievement to human proportions.

Yet there can be no gainsaying that Pelham displayed singular valor and that, with a single gun, he unleashed a fire so determined that his enemies believed they were up against several times his actual force. Moreover, legends have their own truth, and the stories that men tell, stretched around the edges as they may be, possess their own power. Of all those who fought on that terrible Saturday, Pelham left a unique impression of purity and grace. Within the din and dread of an appalling moment, he was steady and precise, and he showed that even in the midst of the worst hell that humans can contrive, there is virtue to be found. In being who he was, in doing as he did, he filled a need among those who saw and later heard and told of his triumph. He became, as Rable calls him, "the perfect Confederate hero"—young, blue-eyed, and handsome, striving and succeeding against impossible odds.[42]

Chapter Eleven

———⌣———

The Stone Wall

The wall that now lines the base of Marye's Heights at Fredericksburg is mostly a reconstruction of the barrier that lay there in December 1862. Built as a retaining wall on the Fredericksburg side of a sunken road, the stone wall extends north and south for about an eighth of a mile. When a young officer of General Lee's Washington Artillery first saw the wall and the Sunken Road, he exclaimed, "What a place for infantry!"[1] Walking the ground today, one sees at once that he was right. The barrier stood about four feet high—just the right height for a rifleman to rest his gun barrel, and more than high enough to protect him as he sank down to reload. James Longstreet, the corps commander in that sector of the Confederate line, placed four ranks of infantrymen behind that wall, with ample reinforcements ready to come up if the men in those lines grew tired.

Behind the Sunken Road, the terrain slopes sharply upward; the crest of Marye's Heights is about forty feet higher than the stone wall. It was as ideal a place for artillery as the stone wall was for infantry. Guns on Marye's Heights had almost perfect command of the open stretch of several hundred yards between the stone wall and the western edge of town. In that exposed ground, which slopes more gently upward toward the wall, there is one slight swale in which men might fall on their bellies and be shielded from Confederate fire. Beyond the swale lay no protection at all. E. Porter Alexander, a highly talented artillerist in Lee's army, told Longstreet, "General, we cover that ground now so well that we comb it as with a fine-tooth comb. A chicken could not live in that field when we open on it."[2]

When the fighting on Pelham's end of the line died down, the long day had only begun on the Union right. Still incapacitated by his illness, Wendell Holmes continued to languish in a hospital tent, unable to rejoin his unit. He added another section to the letter he was preparing for his mother, trying to maintain a jaunty tone of voice to mask his melancholy. "This morning," he told her, "there's heavy cannonading and just now there's a very lively musketry practice going on—and many a nice fellow going off, I doubt not. Still the popping keeps up lively but somehow it doesn't settle down to a good steady roll—but it's brisk."[3] Shortly after one in the afternoon, the popping concerned the Twentieth Massachusetts, and the nice fellows going off began once more to include men with whom Holmes had marched, broken bread, and shared stories.

Henry Abbott had just finished a letter to his mother when the Twentieth was ordered to the front. Hall's brigade was on the extreme right of the Union line, which eventually extended far enough that the Massachusetts men did not have to contend with the riflemen behind the stone wall. However, the Confederate formation that awaited them was no more inviting. The heights at that sector of Longstreet's line were reinforced by rifle pits, manned by the Twenty-Fourth and Twenty-Fifth North Carolina—two regiments that had progressively hardened under fire ever since the Seven Days Battles of the early summer. From behind these pits came a thick and deadly blaze of artillery. After the street fight two days earlier, no one could question the valor of the Twentieth Massachusetts, or that of the Nineteenth, which again stood with them. But the carnage on Caroline Street had depleted the two regiments terribly. That struggle, coupled with "the recollection of their awful loss & defeat at Antietam," had also produced a draining psychological effect. Hall's entire brigade was, in Abbott's estimation, "considerably demoralized." No man ever took deeper pride in his fighting unit than Henry Abbott, yet now even he thought that he belonged to "the weakest brigade in the army."[4]

Abbott considered the leader of his division, Brigadier General Oliver Otis Howard, "a most conscientious man, but a very poor general."[5] Howard had proved his courage at the Battle of Fair Oaks, where he had lost his right arm and demonstrated a valor that won him the Medal of

Honor. (Howard had teased another Union general, Philip Kearny, who had lost his left arm in the Mexican War, by saying that they could now shop for gloves together.[6]) On the right at Fredericksburg, Howard did little that would refute the less generous half of Abbott's opinion, though, in fairness to him, no general in blue fared much better that day. The hope was that an advance by Howard's men might take some pressure off the division led by Winfield Scott Hancock, which had already taken frightful losses slightly to the south of Howard's position. If everything went just right, Howard might even be able to turn the Confederate flank and win the day for the Union.

Not much went right, for the terrain seemed almost fashioned to thwart the Union hopes. To outflank the rebels, Howard's division would have to extend to the right and northward, past the end of the Confederate line. But that tactic was rendered difficult by a swampy, nearly impassable area called Gordon's Marsh. Through the marsh ran a millrace, a canal that carried water away from a paper mill some distance north of town, which further slowed any forward progress. Troops advancing toward the marsh had only two options: They could shift to the left and proceed up Hanover Street, but this path only funneled them toward the stone wall where hundreds of bluecoats had fallen, and were falling still. Alternatively, the units could slog ahead, splashing through muck and inevitably falling out of sync with one another. Colonel Hall attempted the latter; he ordered the Twentieth and his other regiments into "as broad a column as the street would allow" and marched them through the bog. On the other side, he fanned them out, placing the Twentieth on the extreme right, the Nineteenth next to them, and three other regiments farther to the left.

The men got through the swamp in only minor disarray, but then confusion swept the line. The Nineteenth, thinking they were supposed to attack, charged ahead. They had no sooner reached the crest of the hill in front of them than the Confederates met them with gunfire. The Nineteenth broke and ran for cover, "tumbl[ing] right back head over heels" into the Twentieth. "Then," Abbott wrote, "came our turn." From the 322 men who had gone into battle two days before, the regiment had been reduced to about 200. By Abbott's reckoning, they advanced ten or fifteen yards "under a murderous fire, without the slightest notion of what was intended to be accomplished."[7] In fact, nothing was, at that moment,

232 + "A Worse Place Than Hell"

intended to be accomplished, for no order to attack had yet been given. The Nineteenth had gone forward by mistake, and the Twentieth had more or less blindly followed. Colonel Hall watched the movement with dismay; he perceived that even if, by some miracle, the rifle pits could be taken, they would be cruelly broadsided by Confederate cannon. He ordered the Twentieth back to the previous line, and the dwindling force obeyed in good order.[8] The brigade re-formed and tried again, this time with better coordination, but, Holmes was later told, "got it with cannister."[9] The three regiments on the left soon gave way, leaving the Nineteenth and Twentieth Massachusetts again to bear the brunt of the resistance. Shortly afterward, the Nineteenth reeled backwards as well, with thirteen officers wounded and no man senior to a captain left to take command. The Twentieth now stood alone, but it stood firm, returning the enemy's fire until Colonel Hall could rally the brigade for yet another advance. Hall was later to praise the Twentieth for its unrivaled courage and discipline, but these virtues were not enough to carry the attack farther forward.[10] Driven back again, they dropped to the ground below the brow of the hill. There they lay pinned down until two the next morning, as the night turned Marye's Heights "into a wall of blackness."[11]

According to Abbott, the Twentieth had been under fire for only a few minutes. In those few minutes, however, sixty-three men were killed or wounded. Captain Dreher, the stalwart German whose face had been partly shot away at Ball's Bluff, was shot through both legs. He would fight for life until the end of April, when his infected wounds finally ended his struggle. Leander Alley, who had urged the Nantucket men across the Rappahannock in the pontoon boat two days earlier, was killed outright, felled by a bullet through the eye.

Abbott, though his scabbard had been smashed by a Confederate minié ball, escaped injury. He gave no great thanks for his deliverance. Instead, he railed against the "blood-stained scoundrels" in Washington. Burnside, he said, was "a high-minded donkey."[12] He grieved especially for Lieutenant Alley, whose loss caused him a pang almost identical to what he had felt at the death of his brother. Abbott thought the Northern leadership had murdered Alley "just as much . . . as if he had been deliberately thrown into the river with a stone tied round his neck."[13] Unable to contain his outrage, Abbott echoed Hall's judgment that "the whole attempt by such a weak, exhausted brigade [was] simply ridiculous," and put his personal feelings succinctly: the Twentieth, like the rest of the army on this day, had gone forward "with the conviction, almost the determination, of getting licked."[14] The enthusiasm of the army, Abbott judged, was utterly spent. They were fighting now "only . . . from discipline & old associations."[15]

East of the river, too anxious to keep still, Holmes summoned enough strength to leave his billet and to see what could be seen of the battle. With a lieutenant from another regiment, he climbed a neighboring hill and gazed at the distant confusion. The two men could see "the smoke of the musketry; the flash of the shell[s] as they burst; & the rest." The vastness of the struggle dwarfed the participants; it was like a surging organism, living out its brief, spasmodic life with none of its individual cells exposed to view. Holmes wrote tersely, "We couldn't see the men but we saw the battle." And then the tide of guilt arose again. The vista from the hilltop was "a terrible sight when your Regt is in it but you are safe—Oh what self-reproaches have I gone through for what I could not help and the doctor, no easy hand, declared necessary."[16]

Holmes heard the following day that half the men in his company had become casualties. The regiment as a whole had lost over thirty percent of its strength in the streets of the town on December 11, and thirty-three percent of those who still remained on the slope below Marye's Heights two days later.[17] Holmes took a mental inventory of the officers with whom he had left home in 1861. Apart from Abbott, scarcely anyone remained unharmed. Holmes deemed the battle "an infamous butchery." It was, he wrote, "one of the most anxious and forlornest weeks of my military experience."[18]

The shooting had taken place on the other side of the river. Death, however, was everywhere. In Holmes's hospital tent, the soldier whose moans had welcomed him to the infirmary gave up his battle. Another was evidently nearing his final throes. Holmes could respond only with a shrug and a grim joke:

> *Poor devils—there's little enough comfort in dying in camp except it be that one gets accustomed to it (as an Irishman might say) and has plenty of company.*[19]

The slap at the Irish was gratuitous. One likes even less to repeat what Holmes wrote next, for it shows how much he relied on his sense of social superiority to deflect the horror that surrounded him: "It's odd how indifferent one gets to the sight of death—perhaps, because one gets aristocratic and don't value much a common life—Then they are apt to be so dirty it seems natural—'Dust to Dust.'" It was not that he did not care. "I would do anything that lay in my power . . ." he added in the next sentence, but did not complete the thought.[20] It was vain to wish for powers he did not have.

The bitterness of the moment was not improved by an additional discovery: as Holmes told his mother, "I heard incidentally that the Revd. Fuller (frère Margaret—who stowed our valises at Wn. for us) had perished."[21] His comment on the minister's passing was as flat and emotionless as his remarks regarding "dust to dust." The dust filled up his thoughts. For now, there was nothing further to express.

✯

ABOUT A THIRD OF A MILE to the south of the Twentieth Massachusetts and less than an hour after that unit had been driven back, George Whitman and the Fifty-First New York were also ordered in. For days before this battle, George had chafed and fretted as the army's inaction thwarted his urge to plunge into battle. On December 8, he had written to his mother that the Rappahannock was shallow and, in places, easy to ford. It was narrow, too—so narrow that he could easily converse with the Rebels posted on the opposing bank. Yet his orders strictly forbade him to let a single shot be fired "unless the Rebs commenced the performance." In fact, he no longer expected any fight at all, since he and his regiment had been told to fix up their tents as though they were not expected to move for some time. The Confederates, it seemed, had a different expectation; George observed that they "seem[ed] to be buisy, building breastworks and preparing for us." If the Rebels were right and a scrap was coming, that was fine with George. Breastworks or no breastworks, he thought it "would not be much trouble for us to drive them out of Fredericksburg if we went about it." Indeed, he wished "we could have one good big square fight that would settle the Rebs, and the war at the same time."[22] But trouble was coming, and the fight that greeted the Fifty-First on December 13, though big, was neither good nor square.

The regiment's action at Fredericksburg began with a pair of false alarms. The day of the first crossing had begun with the most terrible artillery barrage that George had ever heard.[23] Two hours later, the Fifty-First had marched from its camp to the grounds of Ferry Farm—George Washington's boyhood home—where it could make ready to cross into the town. There it had waited throughout the day, watching as the army engineers struggled to assemble the pontoon bridges. As the sun was setting, the soldiers received orders to return to camp. They were on their way when another order came; General Burnside now wanted the Fifty-First to help his engineers, who were still being fired upon, to finish laying the pontoon bridges.[24] The regiment did an about-face and was on its way to the river when yet another command stopped them. The bridges had been finished, and the Fifty-First was again ordered back to camp. Whitman and the regiment crossed into town the following day, bringing with them their mascot, a large, beautiful black dog that was much beloved among the men. Once across the Rappahannock, however, the Fifty-First had little to do beyond stacking their weapons with the rest of the army and waiting. If George took any part in the looting of the town, he made no note of it.

The thirteenth began with more waiting. After falling in around 8 a.m. and marching to the western outskirts of the town, the Fifty-First stood idle. Then, the other regiments of Ferrero's brigade, including the Pennsylvanians who had charged with George at Antietam, were sent to the front. Whitman's New Yorkers were detached from the unit and given a separate mission. Around 11:30 (Whitman put the time nearer to 9:00, but the official reports contradict him), they were ordered to defend an artillery battery under the command of Lieutenant George Dickenson. The battery had unlimbered toward the left flank of the forces that were attacking Marye's Heights, near a brick kiln at the crest of a small hill within firing range of the enemy's works. Whitman put the distance around 500 yards, though the reports called it more than twice as far. The exposed position was a lamentable choice of terrain. Rebel sharpshooters, concealed within a ravine to the front of the battery, began making targets of Dickenson's men before they had even wheeled their first cannon into position. The staccato pop of the Confederate musketry was soon joined by the whistle and roar of artillery from the Heights, as solid shot tore through Dickenson's position. Instead of giving support to the infantry units that were pushing ahead of them, the members of the Yankee battery were, from the outset, fighting for their lives. They returned the fire of the Confederate cannons, but to no effect. They were beginning to train their fire on the sharpshooters in the ravine when the enemy cannoneers changed their ammunition to canister, "which burst just at the point to make them most destructive, and continually their fragments and bullets hailed upon the battery."[25]

The Fifty-First was powerless to stem the carnage. The incoming fire became so fierce that Dickenson's men were briefly forced to abandon their own cannons where they stood. A few minutes later, without having to be ordered, they came back and tried again. Driven away a second time, they returned for a third attempt. But they had been falling fast. In Whitman's words, the cannoneers' position was "in such an exposed position that they could not work the guns."[26] Less than twenty minutes after the battery's work had begun, Dickenson was dead. After ten more minutes of futility and bloodshed, his second in command saw that the prospect was hopeless; holding the position could only result in the battery's being destroyed to the last man. The remnant withdrew, leaving nearly half their men killed or wounded.[27]

Thus far, the Fifty-First had suffered only a few casualties.[28] But their work had barely begun. As the other regiments in Whitman's brigade had prepared to march out of the town and into the line of fire, General Ferrero had spoken to them like an adult coaxing a child in for a swim: "Keep cool: it is good fun once you get in!"[29] Almost immediately, his exhortation was turned into a bitter joke. As the brigade had moved past the brickyard where Dickenson's artillery was soon to be routed, Rebel cannonballs struck a pile of bricks, covering men from the Fifty-First Pennsylvania with reddish dust. Other more harrowing shots had reduced men to "mere bundles of rags and mutilated flesh."[30] In spite of themselves, some of those still standing began to cry.

Lying in their path was a lower portion of the same millrace that had bedeviled the Twentieth Massachusetts. The canal held only about three feet of water, but the ditch was deep, and the banks were high enough to disrupt an organized advance. George Whitman described the race as "a narrow creek, with a steep muddy bank on each side, over which it would be impossible to charge."[31] Beyond the race was a fairground, an ironic setting for the scenes that were unfolding. Miraculously, Ferrero's men had met with some initial success. The general reported that his men had driven their enemies "from their advanced position," by which he surely meant some rifle pits well below the wall.[32] But they were now within easy range of the marksmen behind that wall, and the Rebels were spewing fire with blind fury. The line had wavered, stopped, and shivered "like some great ship that is beaten by a storm," one New Hampshire soldier remembered.[33] Mercifully, the brigade had found the swale in the slope that led toward the wall, and the depression offered some protection from the gunfire. From their bellies, from their knees, the brigade returned fire, but they were low on ammunition and in dire need of reinforcements. General Ferrero realized that his brigade needed all the firepower it could muster. The Fifty-First must now move forward.

Around 3 p.m., Whitman's regiment was ordered to move to the front and to link up with the rest of the brigade. Across the exposed field they went, braving "the most terrific fire of grape, canister, percussion shell, musketry and everything else" that George had ever seen. Though he seldom made aesthetic observations, Whitman was moved by the sight of his men moving forward in perfect order. They "advanced beautifully," he said, though a grimmer beauty can hardly be imagined.[34]

Whatever was pleasing to the eye about the advance soon withered into ugliness. When Ferrero's other regiments had marched toward the inferno, they had at least had one another for protection. Whitman's regiment, by contrast, went in with no support.[35] As they crossed the exposed field, they seemed to draw fire from all directions.[36] Whitman saw a Rebel battery planted directly in front of his company, and the Rebels were "pouring grape and cannister into us like the very devil."[37] The Fifty-First was, as Ferrero set it down in his report, "losing terribly."[38] The adverb hardly did justice to the truth; fully a third of the regiment fell dead or wounded in five minutes. It was, Whitman wrote with typical understatement, "a mighty warm place." Nonetheless, the regiment pressed on and, when close enough to the Rebel force, opened fire. But everyone seemed to know that their attack was in vain. Unconsciously echoing Porter Alexander's boast about the strength of the Rebel position, Whitman wrote, "They could take as deliberate aim as a fellow would at a chicken."[39] Reaching the rest of the brigade, the men who had gotten through discovered that two of the regiments they had been called forward to support, the Eleventh New Hampshire and the Fifty-First Pennsylvania, had both exhausted their ammunition. The New Yorkers scrambled into position in front of the New Hampshire men, their left flank covering the right of the Pennsylvanians'. After reaching the edge of the millrace, they threw themselves to the ground and blazed away.

The regiment's handsome black dog had been with the men during the shelling at the brickyard. It was with them now, a small source of comfort as the world seemed to split apart. Evidently aware of the danger, the dog had crouched close to the ground, beneath the path of the incoming bullets. But dogs and men both grow tired, and the mascot at last found it could no longer stay in the same cramped position. It stood up to shift itself and, in that instant, was hit.[40] Though the dog was in agony, no one could bear to kill it, even in mercy. The poor creature did not breathe its last until sometime near dark.

The men had sixty rounds of ammunition, and they fired them all, keeping up their fusillade until nightfall. But the night did not come soon enough to shield George Whitman from harm. It was on the open field leading to the millrace where the mischief happened. The Confederates had been lobbing percussion shells into the regiment, killing or wounding three or four soldiers with every pop. One moment, George was alongside his companions. The next, a shell burst at his feet. Whitman could not evade a shard of metal, flying up at high speed, directly toward his face.

★

BETWEEN 2 AND 3 P.M., SHORTLY before Whitman's regiment was ordered forward from its position near the brick kiln, orders also came to Colonel Franklin B. Speakman, who commanded the 133rd Pennsylvania, and, among its ranks, Private John Suhre. After an interminable period of anticipation, they and the rest of their division were to cross the river, move up George Street, and ready themselves for their turn at the stone wall. That morning, Louisa May Alcott was in Jersey City, boarding the train that would take her to Georgetown and her duties at the Union Hotel Hospital. She, of course, knew nothing of Suhre, and he knew nothing of her. And, as a New Hampshire soldier gently phrased the matter, "We had something else of importance on our minds just then."[41]

On the previous day, as hastily established field hospitals near the regiment's bivouac tended to the first of the wounded, Chaplain Hartsock had been surprised to find the men largely indifferent to the roar of the distant cannons. "The only feeling," he told his diary, "seems to be a desire to get within sight of the field." But even then, it had felt as if a larger struggle might not happen. Captain John M. Jones of Company F suspected that there would not be much fighting; he was more or less convinced "that the rebels will not stand here."[42]

By midday on December 13, however, no one doubted that the time for the 133rd was coming soon. From their place near the Phillips House, they could hear the volleys of musketry mingling with the sound of artillery. Around 1 p.m., when Suhre's division marched to the hill that overlooked the field of battle, the first of Burnside's assaults on the stone wall had already been shattered. No figures could be discerned amid the smoke, but the fire belching from every Confederate battery was plainly visible. One or two nervous hours passed, and then the order came to the division's commander, Brigadier General Andrew Atkinson Humphreys, to bring his men across the river.

Humphreys was "well-bred, courteous, [and] honorable," a man of courtly manners and romantic sensibilities who had served the army as a capable topographical engineer.[43] A sharp taskmaster, he had taken charge of his newly created division just five days before Antietam. In the months that followed, he had done his best to mold his regiments, mostly comprised of nine-month enlistees, into a battle-ready force. Before Fredericksburg, Humphreys had never led a force into battle. The realization that his day had finally come thrilled him beyond measure. Around 2:30, he was at army headquarters at the Phillips House when Burnside directed General Hooker, who led the Center Grand Division, to throw in all the force he had and drive Longstreet's men from Marye's Heights. When Hooker began to protest, Burnside shot back, "Those heights must be taken." Why should General Hooker question his order at this time? Hooker tried meekly to explain: "I thought that, in view of the terrible losses. . . ."[44] His sentence trailed off into silence. With emphasis and finality, Burnside repeated the order.

The command that frightened Hooker exhilarated Humphreys. As he rode to meet his men, an aide recalled, the general's features bore a look of intense satisfaction. "We *must*," he told the aide, "gain the crest."[45] As his division prepared to cross the pontoons, Humphreys's first attempt at a rallying oration fell flat; he told the men they were the "forlorn hope" of the army—a polite way of saying that the day was already lost and that they were being thrown against the Rebel guns in desperation.[46] The predictable reaction made it evident to Humphreys that something less than complete honesty might get better results. A bit awkwardly, he switched stories, telling them, "Your comrades are before the enemy. They have driven him, and now hold the lines. You are the *reserve* of the army and we go to win the day."[47] A proud and eager shout went up from the ranks. Later, as his columns neared George Street, which would lead them out of town and into the fray, Humphreys rode ahead and had the wounded that lined the avenue spirited away down side streets, for fear that his men "should be depressed by the sight."[48] In short, he did all in his power to convince his regiments that a light task lay before them and that, as Hartsock believed, "we were going to certain victory."[49]

The certainty began to fade even before the first man of the 133rd planted a foot on the soil of Fredericksburg. The division consisted of two brigades, composed entirely of Pennsylvanians. As they had done since leaving their home state, Speakman, Suhre, and the 133rd marched in the brigade commanded by Colonel Peter Allabach. The other brigade took orders from Brigadier General Erastus Tyler, an erstwhile fur merchant. Tyler's men took the lead toward the pontoons. On their way, they passed General Burnside—so close in fact that they bumped against his horse. "You need not crowd, boys," Burnside assured them. He then added breezily, "There is plenty to do over there."[50]

Around 3 p.m., Suhre and his comrades moved across the same bridges that Reverend Fuller had died defending two days earlier. They came under a terrifying barrage. They had been warned that trying to dodge the shells would be futile. Still, as the projectiles shrieked around them, they all instinctively cringed and ducked in such unison that the bridges plunged and rose beneath them. Once he had reached the shoreline, Chaplain Hartsock parted company with the soldiers, going instead with the regimental surgeons to find some safe dwelling in which to set up a hospital. They chose some handsome brick mansions a few blocks up from the river, though Hartsock was already persuaded "that there was no safe retreat on that side of the river." Going from one hospital to another meant "going through a *storm* of *flying iron*," and the chaplain saw "men mangled and torn in every part."[51]

Despite Humphreys's order to clear the wounded soldiers onto side streets, there was no concealing the wreckage. As the men of his division filed through the town, they could see makeshift coffins stacked by the score and awaiting occupants. The effort to hustle the wounded out of view failed pathetically, for the town was now awash in casualties. A soldier from Tyler's brigade reported seeing "hundreds of wounded men from different regiments, on stretchers and on foot, some with ghastly wounds."[52]

Suhre and the 133rd marched south through the town, surely spending no unnecessary time at intersections where the Confederate cannon had a clear shot all the way down to the river. They then turned right onto George Street, which conducted them up toward Marye's Heights, three-quarters of a mile away. Between four and four thirty, Humphreys gave Allabach's brigade the order to advance. Allabach arranged his four regiments two by two. The 123rd and 131st Pennsylvania assumed the two rear positions, while the 155th was assigned the left front and Suhre's 133rd took the lead on the right.[53] Tyler's brigade followed, its four regiments also marching two to the front, two to the rear. As they moved into position, the heavy smoke of gunfire made it virtually impossible to see forward.[54] Had the smoke been absent, however, the situation would have barely improved; the December sun, already low in the sky, glared harshly at that hour through the tree line above Marye's Heights. Suhre and his comrades made their advance half-blind and squinting.

The artillery fire from both armies was shaking the ground. On Allabach's orders, Suhre and his mates were suddenly running, bolting, racing forward to the millrace, as salvos from the Confederate guns tore through them. Observing what had happened to the brigades that had preceded him up the slope, General Humphreys concluded that the Heights could not be taken with firepower. A further inference would have led him to decide that they could not be taken by any means, but his mind was firmly closed to that deduction. Remarking to his aide, "The bayonet is the only thing that will do any good here," he gave the order that his men must unload their muskets.[55] To make sure his command had been obeyed, he further ordered that the weapons should be "rung," that is, to have ramrods dropped into their barrels to assure that they were empty.

As these preparations were being made, the Federals observed with astonishment that the Rebel batteries that had lacerated the advancing Union lines all afternoon appeared to be withdrawing. This movement was detected by General Hancock, who conveyed the information to Major General Darius Couch, his corps commander. Couch, on whose orders Humphreys was waiting to advance, told Humphreys, "Hancock reports the enemy is falling back; now is the time for you to go in!"[56]

Now was emphatically not the time for Humphreys to go in, for Hancock was entirely mistaken. On the Heights, the Rebel gunners known as the Washington Artillery had run low on ammunition. They were pulling their guns back so that fresh cannons under Porter Alexander could move in to replace them. The Rebel position was not weakening, but growing stronger. As Humphreys received Couch's order, his face took on an expression of grim determination that Couch recalled a quarter-century later. Humphreys spurred his horse and rode away. Minutes later, greeting his staff officers, he told them jauntily, "Gentlemen, I shall lead this charge; I presume, of course, you will wish to ride with me?"[57] The grandeur of the moment transported Humphreys. He wrote later of his rising excitement: "As I led the charge and bared my head, raising my right arm to heaven, the setting sun shining full upon my face gave me the aspect of an inspired being."[58] His son, a lieutenant serving as his aide de camp, thought that his father had become at this moment a "thorough impersonat[ion] [of] the God of War."[59]

Their bayonets fixed, Humphreys's men unslung their knapsacks. From horseback, the general urged them on. They moved forward about two hundred fifty yards, where they came upon a line of survivors from a previous assault, pinned down and immobile under enemy fire. As Suhre and his comrades reached this spot, some of these troops reached up from the filthy ground and clutched at the shirts and trousers of the advancing men. "Don't go forward, it is useless, you will be killed!" they pleaded.[60] Speakman's men paused in confusion. Were they supposed to move forward or throw themselves to the ground? In their uncertainty, they ducked down and "covered themselves as well as they could in the rear of this line."[61] Speakman received a second order to press on. Humphreys and Allabach moved among their prone soldiers, urging them to continue the advance, and, with some trouble, got them going again. But as the men struggled against deepening mud, their lines grew disordered. Some soldiers from Suhre's regiment found cover behind a brick house, and then surged around the structure, coming back out into the open. A staff officer galloped into view, shouting at the men to re-form their ranks. As he was shrieking his commands, a blast erupted from behind the wall. Alexander's cannons had now taken the place of the Washington Artillery, and their salvos cut down whole sections of Humphreys's line. "The stone wall," the general recounted, "was a sheet of flame."[62] Miraculously, Humphreys came through unhurt, as did his son—the only member of his staff not to be hit. In the midst of the catastrophe, Humphreys remained impervious, whistling a tune called "Gay and Happy."[63]

At this point, John Suhre was probably still untouched. As yet, the 133rd was still under orders not to load or discharge their weapons; but a letter sent from the hospital where Suhre was later treated says that he had exhausted his ammunition firing at the enemy. With the rest of his still-uninjured comrades, Suhre probably made it to within fifty yards of the wall—the nearest approach of any Union regiment that attempted the feat. "Though many exhibitions of heroism were witnessed that day," wrote George Bruce from Holmes's regiment, "nothing was seen that excited more admiration than the charge of that division."[64] Here, as the Rebel fire became too intense to allow another step forward, the men of the 133rd dived to the earth. Finally loading their weapons, they fired back as ably as they could, until the sky turned black.[65] As evening fell, said Bruce, the battle "assumed such intensity as if passions more than human were urging it on." Bruce chose the same metaphor as Humphreys to describe the gunfire: "Sheets of flame flashed along the lines a mile in length, cleaving the darkness with wedges of light, that leaped forward and sprang back like the flying shuttles of a loom."[66] The 133rd held their position for an hour. Finally, they were ordered to withdraw.

During that hour beneath the wall, his ammunition gone, Private John Suhre felt two bullets pierce him, one lodging in his breast and the other passing through his left lung.[67] At first, there was no way to help him. During the night, his regiment sent out squads to recover its killed and wounded. But Confederate sharpshooters behind the wall slowed the efforts at retrieval. Many of the wounded died where they lay, victims of either their injuries or exposure. The corpses stiffened in the wintry air, and the night was filled with the moans of those who begged for relief and were not to get it soon enough.

Suhre must have passed first back through the town, where churches and meeting halls had been transformed into impromptu hospitals. Amid extractions and amputations, Chaplain Hartsock was experiencing "mental anguish . . . enough almost to dethrone reason."[68] After nightfall had diminished the risk somewhat, he ventured out to the picket line and, from among the hundreds who lay suffering, he called out for soldiers of the 133rd. Erroneously, he told his diary that Suhre had been killed outright.[69] Hartsock found a few men from the regiment, but from every corner his summons was answered by cries of "Take me!" He had come to carry men to safety, but as he walked the street, it seemed that he would soon need someone to carry him.

The surviving men of the 133rd were fated to serve out the remainder of their nine months of duty without seeing any more significant action. Virtually their entire experience of combat was compressed into less than four hours of fighting, but those hours were terrible. Suhre's brigade, a force of 2300 men, reported 562 killed, wounded, or missing: nearly a quarter of its strength. The 133rd had gone into battle about 500 strong. It suffered 184 casualties.[70] Despite their utter lack of experience under fire, their division had fought valiantly. Francis Palfrey, in his respected memoir of the battle, observed, "Some of the very best fighting that was done at Fredericksburg was done by the Third Division of the Fifth Corps. The division was commanded by General Humphreys, who was probably the best officer in the Army of the Potomac that day."[71] Yet knowing that they had done their utmost failed to dull the sense of futility with which the 133rd retired from the field. One soldier in Humphreys's division wrote, "We went out in buoyant spirits, with the mighty array that was to invest the rebel stronghold. . . . We returned tired, forsaken and dispirited—our bands mournfully filling the air with requiems for the dead."[72]

After receiving some brief attention in Fredericksburg, John Suhre became part of the great, undifferentiated mass of wounded that moved in a slow stream toward the hospitals of Washington. The evacuation took place in long, slow stages: back across the Rappahannock, then a train ride across the Northern Neck peninsula to Aquia Creek, followed by a steamboat ride up the Potomac to the hospitals of Washington. One of the bullets that struck Suhre had broken a rib, and every breath he took brought a new jab of pain. Nevertheless, convinced that his wound was not truly serious, he repeatedly gave up his place in the convoy so that more desperate-looking cases might reach a bed before him. Young and strong, Suhre could barely entertain the thought that the dirges of the regimental bands might soon be played for him.

Chapter Twelve

<hr>

Southbound Trains

From her upstairs window at Orchard House, through the cold rains of late autumn, Louisa May Alcott could see the old road that connected Concord with Lexington. It was the road the redcoats had taken toward their defeat at the Old North Bridge in 1775. The red coats had given way to blue; at least five Concord men had been captured at First Bull Run alone.[1] In the room next to Louisa's, sister May had traced images of Greek gods and goddesses on the walls. But she had little time to sit still among them, busy with teaching drawing, going to parties, riding horses, rowing boats, and doing whatever else befitted "a very gay & pretty girl." Downstairs, Abba bustled in the kitchen, "sing[ing] away among her pots & pans," though moving more slowly than in earlier years.[2] In his study, Bronson reread Emerson's essays, observing how the hope and freshness of the early pieces had mellowed into prudence and confidence in the later works. Bronson was writing notes for a series of public conversations he was soon to hold on the great men of New England—and thinking about how small his career had been in comparison with theirs. Having failed to acquire a concise and powerful writing style as a young man, he regretted that his lack of ease in expression had left him "lame at last."[3]

Louisa, by contrast, lacked nothing in her power to express herself. But she was thirty now, and her dreams of literary fame had not come true. She was taking to heart her mother's motto, "Hope and keep busy."[4] When she wasn't doing an ever-increasing share of the housework, she was filling stacks of pages with her stories—vivid and full of plot, just as Frank Leslie and the other penny-press editors liked them.[5] As she wrote her thrillers, she couldn't keep still. For a change of scene, she sometimes left her room and scribbled while sitting on the large sofa in the parlor. To deter her family and visitors from breaking her concentration, she used a bolster pillow somewhat in the fashion of a tollgate. If the pillow stood on its end, interruptions were welcome. If it lay on its side, no one dared disturb her.[6] The stories were selling briskly, but they weren't enough to satisfy her restlessness. If only she were a boy, she wrote her grandmother, "I'd march off tomorrow."[7] With her nursing application in the hands of the government, she waited.

During the days when her enlistment was pending, Alcott affected a military air in her speech and manners, calling her dinner her "rations" and substituting a salute for her usual greeting. She attended to her wardrobe, washing and mending with a will, and still had time to grow "powerfully impatient" before the arrival of her letter.[8] She also picked out a number of books to take with her. She was sure that soldiers' spirits could only be improved as she read to them from Dickens.

Her own literary diet had transformed. She pored over the latest literature on the treatment of knee-joint injuries, and mined Florence Nightingale's *Notes on Nursing*, published three years earlier, for every scrap of information on the care of the sick and wounded.[9] From Nightingale, Alcott learned above all else the necessity of fresh air and cleanliness. Nightingale insisted that the air a patient breathed must be as pure as outdoor air.[10] Still, no degree of ventilation would suffice where the most meticulous cleanliness was not observed.[11] Nightingale also strengthened Alcott's respect for the vocation into which she was preparing to enter. Too often, Nightingale, observed, people made no distinction between a nurse and an unskilled drudge. "A nurse should do nothing but nurse," Nightingale insisted. "If you want a charwoman, have one. Nursing is a specialty."[12] Alcott was stoking herself not only with information, but also with ideals about how nursing should be practiced. She was teaching herself nursing by the book, little dreaming how many of the principles she was acquiring were being flouted daily in the Washington hospitals.

Applying to the nursing service was a bold and unconventional step for a woman of her social position. Julian Hawthorne called her decision to serve almost unheard of. Mingling pride with some quantity of dismay,

Bronson remarked that he was sending his only son to war.[13] Yet, Julian noted, the war had so kindled her that no one ventured to stop her once she had made her intentions known.[14] It would have been difficult to oppose her. In the months before she became eligible for nursing service, Alcott met the writer Rebecca Harding Davis, made newly famous by her extraordinary story, "Life in the Iron-Mills." Even before Alcott first spoke to her, Davis observed in her "that watchful, defiant air with which the woman whose youth is slipping away is apt to face the world which has offered no place to her."[15] If the world were to offer her no place, Alcott was determined to find or seize or create one, and do it at once. Only a fool would have stood in her way.

On the same day that Arthur Fuller bled to death on Caroline Street, Alcott received the notice that her application had been approved: she was to become a nurse in the Army of the Potomac. Her orders commanded that she should "start for Georgetown the following day."[16] The letter also contained the first disappointment of her nursing career. Alcott had hoped to serve at Armory Square, one of the best-run army hospitals.[17] Instead, she had been assigned to a converted hostelry: the Union Hotel Hospital at Bridge and Washington Streets in Georgetown. Considered one of the poorer facilities in the Washington area, it was reserved for enlisted men; sick and wounded officers were thought entitled to better accommodations. Alcott knew already that the Union Hotel was "a hard place."[18] However, help was needed there, and she was in no position to choose, and so the rush to depart began. Sophia Hawthorne came across the woods to write Alcott's name in her clothes in indelible ink. Some agitated relative put salt in Alcott's tea instead of sugar; politely, Alcott choked it down.

The packing was soon done. Then came the hardest part. Alcott knew that in volunteering for the army, she had taken her life in her hands. But now the reality struck her in a new way: she might never see her home again. The family had all been full of courage until the last moment. Then everyone broke down at once. Alcott turned to Abba and hugged her close. "Shall I stay, Mother?" she asked. Mrs. Alcott had not raised her children to be timid. "No, go! and the Lord be with you!" came the staunch reply.[19] In the December twilight, Louisa rode out of sight, escorted by May and Julian. As she began to round the corner, she could still see her mother waving a handkerchief from the doorstep. Some time after nightfall, she was in Boston.

The next day, as Union troops sacked and vandalized the town of Fredericksburg, Alcott received her first dose of army bureaucracy. Somehow managing in the midst of it all to get a tooth filled, she spent much of December 12 on what had seemed like a simple errand: obtaining the free rail pass to which her appointment entitled her. Every official to whom she applied seemed to know nothing—except that he was the wrong person to be asking. She tramped from the State House to Milk Street to Haymarket Square to Temple Place, crossing Boston Common three times before she found the right authority and held the precious pass in her hands. She got the last of the necessary approvals barely in time for a hasty dinner with her sister Anna and her husband. About forty-five minutes after sunset, she boarded her train. "Full of hope and sorrow, courage and plans," she was traveling farther from home than she had ever been in her life.[20]

Alcott eased into her seat with satisfaction. She had embarked on "a most interesting journey into a new world, full of stirring sights and sounds, new adventures, and an ever-growing sense of the great task" she was undertaking.[21] As the fields grew dark outside her window, she munched some gingerbread, fumbled for her ticket, found it, and lost it again. Feeling lonely and wishing to prove that she was not an exemplar of "petrified propriety," she struck up a conversation with the gentleman next to her. They traded thoughts about "the war, weather, music, Carlyle, skating, genius, hoops and the immortality of the soul" as the sky went black and the train steamed through the raw New England night.[22]

No direct rail service existed then between Boston and Washington. One took a train to New London, Connecticut, boarded an overnight boat to Jersey City, and boarded another train to the capital the next morning. In New London, Alcott climbed aboard the *City of Boston* with some trepidation. She could swim a little, but she had once had a premonition of drowning, and her imagination turned lurid. Trying to look like an experienced seafarer, she convinced no one, and, when told to secure her berth, could only follow the motions of her neighbors. Listening to the swash of the waves and wondering whether a steamer's machinery always creaked so lugubriously, she looked about for some improvised lifebuoy that might be her salvation. Finding nothing more promising, her eyes fixed upon a plump, elderly woman, engrossed in reading the cabin Bible. The old dowager looked extremely buoyant. Alcott resolved

at the first sign of an emergency to fasten herself to the dear, plump creature and cling to her "through fire and water."[23] At daybreak on the 13th,
she was mildly shocked to find herself still alive, savoring a sandwich and
some thoroughly crushed gingerbread, and making her way through the
Jersey City depot.

Passing through Philadelphia, Alcott thought the houses, with their
prim outside shutters, looked like tiny jails. She saw fine buildings, too,
but had no idea what they were. As the scenery slid by, she regretted not
having time to seek out her birthplace in Germantown. Baltimore made
a worse impression. Alcott thought it "dirty [and] shiftless," her perceptions no doubt colored by the fact that it was the first slaveholding city
she had ever seen.[24] She also recalled the violent reception that Baltimore
had given the Sixth Massachusetts when it passed through town the week
after Fort Sumter. The memory made her want to throw a stone at someone, hard. After a broken coupling delayed its progress, the train passed a
training school for cavalrymen, and a countryside dotted white with military tents. Alcott said a prayer for the country, "all alive with patriotism,
and already red with blood."[25] By the time she alighted in Washington,
it was dark. In the time it had taken her to travel from Jersey City to her
destination, John Pelham had made his gallant stand, George Whitman
had taken a wound to the face, and John Suhre had charged the stone
wall and felt a bullet tear his lung. More than ten thousand men had been
wounded, and almost two thousand hearts had stopped beating.

Alcott knew none of this as she took her long carriage ride to the
hospital. Tired from her journey, she gazed out at the Capitol and stared
hard at the White House, all lit up with carriages rolling in and out
of its impressive gates. Pennsylvania Avenue, with its bustle, lights, and
music, reminded her of a carnival. As her driver played tour guide, she
dutifully called out "Splendid!" at each new landmark, though she feared
that she was often observing some point of interest other than the one
being shown her. She was adrift in a late-evening daydream when her
carriage arrived at the hospital. Her heart started to pound as she remembered how far she was from home, but she was determined to make a
good show. As she marched to the door with false bravado, the men
there stepped back, the guards touched their caps, and a boy swung the
door open. Hannah Ropes, the hospital's matron, almost never noted the
arrival of a new nurse in her diary, but now she made an exception: "We

are cheered by the arrival of Miss Alcott from Concord—the prospect of a really good nurse, a gentlewoman who can do more than merely keep the patients from falling out of bed."[26]

✹

THE TERSE, HARD-BITTEN UNION GENERAL William Tecumseh Sherman harbored no illusions about the glories of warfare. "I think we understand what military fame is," he wrote: "To be killed on the field of battle and have our names spelled wrong in the newspapers."[27] Sherman might have smiled grimly if he had been present on December 16, 1862, as Walt Whitman scanned the *New York Herald* for news of the battle at Fredericksburg. On the last page of the paper, he found the list of casualties from the Fifty-First New York. The names of the ten dead and fifty-eight wounded filled about a third of a column. Fourth from the bottom, Whitman saw a line that instantly changed his relation to the war and that would, in time, transform his idea of himself, both as a person and as a poet. It read simply, "First Lieutenant G. W. Whitmore, Co. D."[28] The *Herald* was mistaken as to the soldier's rank; the day before the attack on Marye's Heights, he had been promoted to captain, retroactive to November 1. As to the nature and severity of the officer's injury, the paper was silent.

The name, of course, was misspelled, but that error did not deceive Walt. His brother's letters had never mentioned a Whitmore among the officers of the Fifty-First. The wounded man could only be George. Before the battle George had signed his last letter "Good Bye," an unusual closing for him to use. Might he have had a premonition? No matter; in the moment Whitman read the listing of George Whitmore among the wounded, the inertia of his preceding months vanished. Walt Whitman, of Manhattan the son, was no longer adrift. Within hours, he had secured the help of Moses Lane, his brother Jeff's superior at the Brooklyn Water Works, in obtaining a pass that authorized him to go to the front. The next day, Whitman was pounding the streets of Washington, looking for George.

His passage to the capital had not gone without incident. As he was switching trains in Philadelphia, his mind set on other matters, Whitman had failed to notice a deft hand reaching into his pocket. The next time the poet searched for his money, it was gone. He had landed in a pretty situation—in a strange city, without a dime, and wholly ignorant of where to turn in search of his brother. With no money for carfare, with nothing but hope and chance to guide him, he did the only practical thing: he started walking.

For two days and nights he walked from hospital to hospital. He applied as well to officials in the government who he thought might help. His congressman, Moses Odell, would not so much as see him, and no one in the hospitals had any information. His interval of homelessness and worry seemed longer than it was; he called it "about three days of the greatest suffering I ever experienced in my life."[29] He trudged on.

Finally, his luck turned. Evidently by chance, he ran into two of the men who had helped him in Boston with the printing of the 1860 *Leaves of Grass.* William O'Connor, who had taken a job in the Treasury Department, lent him some money. From Charles W. Eldridge, now with the Army Paymaster's office, he secured passage to the encampments of Burnside's army at Falmouth, Virginia, where, heaven willing, he might find George.

Down at the docks, he boarded a government boat that carried him downriver to Aquia Creek. Once there, he settled onto the train that took him to a place that even his broad imagination could never have conceived. He arrived at the perimeter of the battlefield on December 19. The impressions of the place almost overpowered him. One of his first stops was at Chatham, where, a few days earlier, General Burnside had scolded Winfield Scott Hancock for "throw[ing] cold water" on his battle plan. The mansion was now a field hospital, its handsome floors of yellow pine now stained with blood. Outside, no more than ten yards from the door that looked out over the Rappahannock to the town of Fredericksburg beyond, two ancient catalpa trees still stand, their stark shapes weathered and twisted by time. They were there in 1862, and, near the foot of one of them, Whitman happened on an appalling sight. The surgeons inside the house had used the tree as a dumping site for severed limbs. The poet found himself gazing at "a heap of amputated feet, legs, arms [and] hands," not just a few, but "a full load for a one-horse cart."[30] Nearby lay several corpses, each of which had received the small, spare dignity of a brown woolen blanket. The path leading to the house now led past an array of freshly dug graves, most of them belonging to officers, the names hastily scratched onto barrel staves or broken boards that had been jammed into the dirt.[31]

Inside the house, which was crowded with some of the most desperate cases, medical personnel coped with the chaos as best they could. Whitman could observe no order or system—"everything impromptu" was the way he put it—but he could think of no better methods than the makeshift measures he saw.[32] As he wandered among the wounded and the dying, both upstairs and down, Whitman grew acutely conscious of his empty hands. There was need on every side, but he had not a thing to give. Instinctively, he resorted to the one tool that did not fail him: words. At the behest of some of the injured men, he wrote letters to their families. He also talked to three or four for whom he thought talking would do most good.

Chatham was hardly a tranquil scene, yet, strangely, what Whitman remembered about it was its quiet—quiet, at least, when compared with the deafening roar of the previous week. Whitman had missed all that, of course, yet somehow he seemed to hear it. "Probably," he wrote, "the earth never shook by artificial means, nor the air reverberated, more than on that winter daybreak of eight or nine days since."[33]

Surprisingly, despite all the travail and fretfulness that preceded it, Whitman seems never to have noted in writing exactly when or where he discovered George. As to his own thoughts when Walt slouched into view, George was equally silent. Presumably he was surprised, having had no notice that Walt was on his way. But what mattered was that George was alive and well. "O you may imagine," Whitman wrote his mother, "how trifling all my little cares and difficulties seemed—they vanished into nothing."[34]

The shell fragment that had flown at George was, thankfully, tiny, but it had made contact within inches of his eyes. It had passed completely through his cheek and had torn a hole through which "you could stick a splint through into the mouth."[35] George described his wounding to their brother Jeff a few weeks later: "The range was so short, that they threw percussion shels into our ranks, that would drop at our feet and explode, killing and wounding Three or four every pop. It was a peice of one of that kind of varmints that struck me in the jaw. The shell burst right at my feet, so I think that I got off pretty luckey."[36] The hole in his cheek had hurt George a little, and it had scared him a good deal more, but neither the hurt nor the fear had stopped him. He had stayed with the regiment as it picked its way to the front line. In only five minutes, a third of the regiment was cut down.[37] George related that he "had several pretty narrow chances that day, but you know the almynack says, a miss is as good &c."[38] He did not leave the field until after dark, returning with those who could still walk to bivouac by the river. By the time the assault was over, six of the regiment's officers had been wounded. The casualties among the enlisted men had tallied sixty-three.

Fredericksburg did not end for Captain Whitman on December 13. The next day, he was sent out on picket duty to almost the same spot where he had fought to stay alive less than twenty-four hours earlier. That night, George and his men experienced a vision that must have seemed to some of them like a dream. George, ever prosaic, did not mention it in either his letters or his journal. Others never forgot it. Around 6:15, the sky to the north of Fredericksburg weirdly transformed. It started with a glow emanating from below the horizon. At first, some thought that a forage depot had caught fire. But it was not fire. Streaks of pale yellow light filled the heavens. Then they seemed to blend together, producing a spectacle of blood red. Columns of light shot into the air, filling those who saw them with astonishment until at last they faded away. The armies had witnessed a display of the aurora borealis.

George was confident that his wound would heal. Barring an infection, it posed no threat, so he carried quietly on, not missing a day of duty. Without question, he was annoyed with the regiment's colonel, Robert Parker. Knowing that his wound had done no serious damage and not wanting to alarm his family, George had specifically asked not to be named among the wounded, but his superior had included his name against his wishes. George probably objected less when he learned that Parker's report specifically mentioned George's "excellent conduct."[39]

Walt examined the hole in George's cheek. It was already starting to heal. George's spirits were not much the worse for his close call. Although Walt suspected that he was more tired and homesick than he let on, the captain was eating with a lusty appetite and seemed to be "stand[ing] it upon the whole very well."[40]

George welcomed his brother to join him in the tent he was sharing with another captain and two other men. The temporary addition of Walt to the little household, a tent that covered only twelve feet square, made for tight accommodations, but Walt felt that the five of them got on quite well. It is easy to imagine the pride with which George showed Walt the new "half-hut and half-tent" that he was building for his winter quarters and talked about his cook, a disabled soldier named Tom who had proved quite handy with a skillet. Tom's proficiency around the campfire was matched by his extraordinary loyalty. When, on the day of the battle, Tom learned that George was wounded, he had dropped everything, found a way across the Rappahannock, and hunted for the captain "through thick and thin."[41] Finding both the company and the food to his liking, Walt felt his mood pass quickly from anxiety to mild elation. To his welcome surprise, he was having "a tip-top time every way."[42]

Many times during his stay, Whitman indulged his ample curiosity by looking over the rest of the encampment. Through the cold, clear days and nights, he mingled with the men, taking an avid interest in their conversation. The social atmosphere he found among the soldiers could hardly have differed more from what he had known at Pfaff's. It went without saying that the wit was not as sharp and sophisticated. Indeed, what first struck Whitman about the soldiers was not their humor, but their capacity for complaint. Before long, though, he got used to their growling. He observed, "A large proportion of men in the world, even the good fellows, would burst if they couldn't grumble."[43] Once accustomed to their crotchets, Whitman found that he had entered a new world of story and song. In his notebook he mentioned with relish "the bivouac fires at night, the singing and story telling among the crowded, crouching groups."[44] The tales they told were not always for the squeamish. One spoke of having seen a dead soldier sitting on the top rail of a fence, "staring with fixed eyes in the morning," determined not to fall, even in death.[45] Even in such gruesome vignettes, Whitman heard an untutored lyricism. Of George's regiment, Whitman wrote, "Any one of [them] had now an experience, after eighteen months, worth more, and more wonderful, than all the romances ever written—whose story, if written out, would be first class."[46]

Already for Whitman, the problem lay in *how* to write these stories. He was sadly aware that no one would or could ever tell them as they deserved to be told. Never had he felt more intensely the desire to take down the stories all around him, and seldom had he felt so unequal to the task. Much of Whitman's groundbreaking poetry had aspired to an extraordinary largeness. But here in the camp of the Army of the Potomac, he was discovering that the American story was grander than he had imagined, one beside which even a sprawling, soaring work like "Song of Myself" seemed minuscule. It was unclear how he could write another poem that would not be dwarfed by all he had seen and now knew about his country.

If any aspect of Burnside's soldiers impressed him more than the unrhymed poetry of their stories, it was their almost holy simplicity—the way in which they passed through gigantic events, greeted them with a dismissive shrug, and then went about doing what they had to do. The bohemians at Pfaff's had always acted much bigger than they were. In George's regiment, that relation was reversed. He spent time with another soldier from the Fifty-First, John Lowery, whose shattered arm had just been removed by an army surgeon. Finding Lowery lying on the ground and considerably bloodied, Whitman was astonished by the sangfroid with which the young private was taking his misfortunes. "He was very phlegmatic about it," Whitman observed, "munching away at a cracker in the remaining hand, made no fuss."[47] A friend of Lowery's, Amos Vliet, sat nearby, nursing the frostbitten feet he had suffered during the long, frigid night of the 14th. Unfortunate as these two men seemed, they chose not to complain; their miseries were slight when contrasted with what lay around them. As Whitman watched a burial detachment do its work, his reflections turned grim:

> Death is nothing here. As you step out in the morning from your tent to wash your face, you see before you on a stretcher a shapeless, extended object, and over it is thrown a dark grey blanket—it is the corpse of some wounded or sick soldier of the reg't. . . . No one makes an ado. There is a detail of men made to bury them; all useless ceremony is omitted. (The stern realities of the marches and many battles of a long campaign make the old etiquets a cumber and a nuisance.)[48]

The patients Whitman had encountered at Chatham were fortunate when compared with others he saw. The various brigades and divisions whose campgrounds he visited could often manage no hospital better than a simple tent, and often a very poor one. He saw no cots and only an occasional mattress. A wounded man was fortunate if he had some layers of pine or hemlock twigs under his blanket to insulate him from the frigid soil. What Whitman saw deepened his feelings of powerlessness, but at the same moment it also awakened in him a resolute sense of duty. He wrote, "I do not see that I do much good to these wounded and dying; *but I cannot leave them*."[49] In fact, he was doing them immeasurable good, for a gift they greatly needed was the one he was most able to supply: an unassuming, freely given sympathy.

Early one morning, very likely the day after Christmas, Whitman's meanderings took him to a hospital tent. Three corpses lay outside on stretchers, each with a blanket laid over him. Whitman paused over one of the men and raised the cloth. The voice that Whitman uses in his notebook changes at the instant when his eyes fall upon the dead soldier's benign and tender face, shifting from desultory prose to trademark Whitmanesque verse:

[T]hree dead men lying, each with a blanket spread over him—I lift up one [corner of a blanket] and look at the young man's face, calm and yellow, 'tis strange!

(Young man: I think this face of yours the face of my dead Christ!)[50]

The slain Christ on whom Whitman gazed could not be resurrected. But, failing that, he might still possess the power to redeem. It may not be supposing too much to think that Whitman's shift in tone also signaled a small spiritual conversion. At Falmouth, the stubbornly resurgent life that Whitman saw emerging from the desolation called him toward his own rebirth. It was in Falmouth that Whitman jotted down a draft of his poem "Quicksand Years," in which he rued the time and energy he had lost at Pfaff's. And it was in Falmouth that he first felt that empty phase of his life coming to an end.[51]

On December 28, Whitman awoke before dawn. He boarded one of the trains that were evacuating wounded men to Aquia Creek, where they would await a government steamer for Washington. He rode with the men on an open platform car, and, as the sun rose, he could see large cavalry camps not far from the tracks. Soldiers entrusted with guarding the rails emerged from their tents, looking rumpled and half-awake.

The landing at Aquia Creek was crammed with casualties; it would be three hours before they could board a steamboat to the capital. Whitman passed the time walking among the men, offering to write letters for them to parents, wives, and brothers. He was busy on the boat as well; though he did not bother to describe the help he was offering, he later recollected, "I had my hands full."[52] Not everyone lay within his power to save; one of those who had boarded the steamer alive left it as a corpse.

Initially, Whitman intended to spend only a week to ten days in the capital, visiting a handful of soldiers from Brooklyn before returning home.[53] By the next day, however, the poet was formulating a plan: his "New York stagnation," broken up by his wanderings in the camp at Falmouth, was not to be resumed. He would stay in Washington and live in what he called "the wise old way"—pushing his fortunes, getting a job, and earning an income. He was determined to do it, he wrote, at least until he had freed himself once and for all from his "horrible sloughs."[54] He immediately sent a letter to Ralph Waldo Emerson, requesting letters of recommendation to Secretaries Seward and Chase, as well as an introduction to Massachusetts senator Charles Sumner. It seems that he still had some doubts to resolve, for, on January 2, before he had heard back from Emerson, he wrote to his brother Jeff's wife Martha that he would be "especially" satisfied "if only I can be with you again, and have some little steady paying occupation in N.Y. or Brooklyn."[55]

Yet later that same day, even before he had posted the letter to Martha, Whitman paid a visit that, in its eventual consequences, changed everything. He had received a note from John Lowery, the man whose arm had been amputated. Lowery and Amos Vliet were now convalescing at the Campbell Hospital, a compound at the end of a horse-railway track on Seventh Street.[56] The two men, having learned that the poet was in town, hoped that he might come to see them. Whitman promptly obliged.

On a typical day, the ward where Lowery and Vliet lay recovering housed between eighty and a hundred men, more or less equally divided between the sick and the wounded. It was a simple, barracks-like hall, lined with plain, narrow bedsteads. To relieve some of the starkness of the whitewashed wooden walls, someone had hung decorations woven out of evergreen branches, depicting stars, circles, and the like. Having satisfied himself that Lowery's stump was healing pretty well, Whitman looked around him. His compassion for helpless young men in need—

first sparked among the sick and injured wagon drivers of Manhattan, then kindled by his visit to the battlefield at Fredericksburg—burst into full flame. "O my dear sister," he wrote to Martha, "how your heart would ache to go through the rows of wounded young men, as I did."[57]

He noticed in particular the painful groans of a young man with a "thin, pallid-brown young face"—a soldier whom, evidently, even the surgeons and orderlies had failed to notice. The patient's glassy, sunken eyes conveyed a mute despair. Here, Whitman thought, was a case that called "for ministering to the affections first, and other nourishment and medicines afterward."[58] The young man was dying for want of love. Gently, Whitman began to administer his particular brand of therapy—a treatment he was to repeat, with variations, hundreds of times for the rest of the war:

> I sat down by him without any fuss—talked a little—soon saw that it did him good—led him to talk a little himself—got him somewhat interested—wrote a letter for him to his folks in Massachusetts . . . soothed him down as I saw he was getting a little too much agitated, and tears in his eyes—gave him some small gifts, and told him I should come again soon.[59]

By then, Whitman knew the soldier's name: John A. Holmes of the Twenty-Ninth Massachusetts. Stationed at the quiet center of Burnside's line at Fredericksburg, the Twenty-Ninth had come through the battle virtually unscathed; the entire brigade to which it was attached reported only seven wounded and not a single man killed. These statistics omitted Holmes's ordeal. The soldier was evidently no relative of the famous doctor. If he was, the connection had been too remote to buy him any privileges. Despite already suffering from diarrhea, Holmes had stood in wait with his company at Fredericksburg. Consigned to the regimental hospital after the battle, he had received almost no attention. He had lain on the cold ground, getting worse. Once the field doctor determined that nothing could be done for him there, Holmes was sent toward Washington on an open platform car similar to the one Whitman himself had ridden—"such as hogs are transported upon," an aghast Whitman later reported.[60]

At Aquia Creek the train crew dumped Holmes onto the boat that would take him and a mass of other sick and wounded men to the capital.

Holmes had fallen down like a rag, too sick and weak to sit up or help himself in any way. Night fell during the voyage and, with it, a raw December chill. Holmes struggled to unpack the two blankets he had stowed in his knapsack but was too feeble for the task. He sought the assistance of a deckhand, who replied that if he could not get them himself, he might then go without them. He arrived at the Campbell Hospital having had neither food nor water since leaving Falmouth. Hospital regulations demanded that he be given a bath and a change of clothes before being put to bed. The cold water of the bath was too much for him; half-frozen and exhausted, he collapsed unconscious in the arms of the attendants. For days since, he had lain on his cot, sometimes out of his wits. No longer asking for any relief, he was waiting to die. With pardonable melodrama, Whitman wrote, "His heart was broken. He felt the struggle to keep up any longer to be useless. God, the world, humanity—all had abandoned him. It would feel so good to shut his eyes forever on the cruel things around him and toward him."[61] It was then that Walt Whitman strolled into John Holmes's life. Some time later, he told Whitman "that this little visit, at that hour, just saved him—a day more, and it would have been perhaps too late."[62]

Whitman used Holmes's account in a newspaper story he wrote for *The New York Times*. Toward the end of it, he observed, "A benevolent person with the right qualities and tact, cannot perhaps make a better investment of himself, at present, anywhere upon the varied surface of this whole big world, than in these same military hospitals."[63]

Chapter Thirteen

"A Worse Place Than Hell"

As the enormity of his army's defeat burst in upon him, Burnside was overcome by grief and horror. At his headquarters, he exclaimed, "Oh! those men! those men over there! I am thinking of them all the time."[1] As his mind reeled under the shock, his judgment, which had been so poor throughout the battle, began to desert him further still. In a pathetic attempt to conceal the extent of his blunder until he could somehow atone for it, he ordered that all telegraphic communications with the North regarding the battle be halted—a measure that hardly eased concern among the anxious denizens of Washington, who were free to imagine the worst when the lines abruptly went dead. Before daybreak on December 14, before shutting down communications with the capital, Burnside cabled optimistically that his forces held the first ridge outside of town and that he hoped to seize the high ground later that day.[2] But the ensuing silence made Navy Secretary Welles suspicious. Welles had feared that Burnside lacked "sufficient grasp and power" to lead the army.[3] The hope that he might be proved wrong was fading by the hour. "When I get nothing clear and explicit at the War Department," he fretted, "I have my apprehensions. They fear to admit disastrous truths. Adverse tidings are suppressed, with a deal of fuss and mystery, a shuffling over of papers and maps, and a far-reaching vacant gaze at something undefined and indescribable."[4] On the 15th, as the information embargo still held, Welles would write in his diary with terse impatience: "No news from Fredericksburg; and no news at this time, I fear, is not good news."[5]

While the telegraphs sat silent, Burnside searched desperately for a way to salvage the situation. But he was a man of slight imagination, and his thoughts kept returning to the same intermingling of valor and folly that had led him thus far. He began making plans to go down to the field himself and to rally his old corps, the Ninth, which included George Whitman's regiment. His confidence in these men was absolute, and he was convinced that if he could personally lead them up Marye's Heights, in defiance of Longstreet's muskets and three hundred enemy cannon, they would somehow prevail.

But before Burnside could start forming his columns, Major General Sumner came to him, saying, "General, I hope you will desist from this attack. I do not know of any general officer who approves of it, and I think it will prove disastrous to the army."[6] Sumner was the same man who had marched Wendell Holmes and the Twentieth Massachusetts into the catastrophe of the West Woods at Antietam, and his Right Grand Division had borne the worst of the fighting below the wall on the previous day. He was no coward, and Burnside knew it. Checked but not yet dissuaded, Burnside appealed to his corps and division commanders. All of them sided with Sumner. Still unwilling to abandon his fantasy, Burnside crossed the Rappahannock and spoke with officers closer to the scene of Saturday's mayhem. They, too, strongly cautioned against the attack. Astonishingly, Burnside was still not fully convinced; his dismay at having lost so many men, coupled with his dread of dishonor if he failed to make amends, spoke almost as powerfully to him as the massed, well-reasoned counsel of his entire chain of command.

In the end, his indecision settled the issue. He dallied all day on the fourteenth. Finally, on the 15th, choking back tears, he gave the order to withdraw.[7] The pontoon bridges that the Grand Divisions had crossed into battle days earlier now became narrow causeways for a stream of ambulances. Dirt and hay were strewn along the soon-to-be-dismantled spans to muffle the sound. As they made ready to evacuate the town they had fought so hard to occupy four days earlier, Burnside's men received orders not to speak above a whisper and to secure their gear so it would not make noise as they fell back; if Lee knew that the bluecoats were retreating, he might hit them in the rear, turning the retreat into an even worse debacle than the battle itself.[8] That night, as the Army of the Potomac slunk to safety, a driving rain swept across them. Except for a tiny scattering of rearguard actions, the Battle of Fredericksburg was over.

Unable to communicate by wire, a lone journalist had resorted to more ancient means of communication. Henry Villard, covering Burnside's campaign for Horace Greeley's *New-York Tribune*, had seen the battle, and he was determined to file his story. When he observed that his rival correspondents had been stymied by Burnside's news embargo, his resolve intensified; he had a tremendous scoop, or "beat," as he called it, on his hands, if only he could get to Washington.

At 3 a.m. on the 14th, Villard rode alone for the docks of Aquia Creek. He traveled through almost perfect darkness, able to see nothing beyond his horse's head. There was no road worthy of the name—only a broad track of mud, churned by the wheels of countless wagons. For most of the distance, Villard and his mount slogged through mud as much as two feet deep. Four times, the struggling animal fell, once throwing Villard into a pool of muck. As the sun rose, Villard found that, by some miracle, he had not lost his way. Still, a ride that should have taken three hours cost him six.[9]

At Aquia Creek, in the tent of the quartermaster in charge of the supply depot, an exhausted Villard shared news of the battle and was rewarded with a plentiful breakfast. He then learned to his dismay that Burnside's desire for secrecy had arrived before him; the quartermaster was under orders to let no one, and especially no reporter, go north without a special permit from army headquarters.[10] Balked but not yet beaten, Villard paced the dock, trying to devise a way to slip through the embargo. He thought about stowing away on one of the ships at anchor, but none were leaving until the next day. Then came inspiration. He noticed a pair of black men in a small rowboat, preparing to go fishing. After a time he summoned them over, handed each a dollar, and asked if he might join them. When the three were safely out in the stream, Villard promised each of his new companions a five-dollar note if they would wait with him for a larger vessel to pass and put him on board.

A likely looking freighter steamed into view less than an hour later. The captain, too, had heard of Burnside's order, and seemed about to refuse to take him on, but Villard forced the issue. As the fishing boat pulled next to an opening in the guard rail of the larger craft, he leaped aboard, tossed the promised money to the fishermen, and shouted for them to make off as fast as possible, which they did. Showing the outraged captain his credentials, Villard assured him that he could wield enough influence to keep him and his crew out of trouble. By a quarter past eight, Villard was in Washington, his dispatch written and ready to send. Another roadblock now arose: Secretary Stanton had followed Burnside's lead and decreed that no news from Fredericksburg could be sent by telegraph without his personal approval. Compared to the other obstacles Villard had surmounted, however, this one was feeble; he handed his story to a messenger and put him on the night train to New York.

That night, the 14th, Abraham Lincoln spent one of the most dismal evenings of his presidency. At nine, as the paucity of sound intelligence from the front made him more and more anxious, he called for an interview with Herman Haupt, the same officer who had met with Burnside and Halleck in November to plan the Fredericksburg campaign. On the 11th, Haupt, now a brigadier general, had been sent to Fredericksburg with orders to build a rail bridge across the Rappahannock. Haupt had arrived at the battlefield to find the works too badly damaged to build the span, and he spent all of December 13 near a window at Burnside's headquarters, surveying the battlefield and listening to reports as they filtered in.[11] Haupt's account was unsettling. Lincoln's confidence in Burnside abruptly weakened, and he began to fear that a still greater slaughter was soon to come. He asked Haupt to walk with him from the White House to the "Eye" Street office of General Halleck, on the other side of Lafayette Square. The president demanded that Halleck telegraph Burnside to withdraw his army to safety. Halleck paced back and forth for a short time and then firmly threw the president's command back in his face. "I will do no such thing," the general replied heatedly. "If such orders are issued you must issue them yourself. I hold that a general in command of an army in the field is the best judge of existing conditions."[12]

Stung by Halleck's retort but also sensing its prudence, Lincoln fell silent, but his expression showed his agitation. Moved by sympathy, General Haupt sought to calm the anguished president. He told him that the situation was not so dire as Lincoln imagined. He explained that the pontoon bridges could not be enfiladed by enemy fire. He further believed that the Confederates would be loath to cause further damage to the town by shelling it, and that Burnside was likely already pulling back of his own accord. Lincoln sighed. "What you say gives me a great many grains of comfort," he said at last.[13]

But Lincoln's fears were only partly allayed, and it was not long before they welled up again. Later that evening, a fellow Illinoisan, Senator Orville Browning, called on the president and found him deeply worried. Burnside could not advance, nor could he stay where he was. At the same time, however, it would be dangerous to retreat across the river in the face of the enemy. Lincoln candidly confessed that he "was troubled about the army and did not know what was to become of it."[14]

Meanwhile, Henry Villard had run into Henry Wilson, a senator from Massachusetts. Like the rest of Washington, Wilson was desperate for news. Villard gave a grim response. He told Wilson that Burnside had been routed and the army's peril was severe; Wilson could do no greater service to the republic than to go at once to the White House and tell the president, "if he does not know what has happened on the Rappahannock, to make an immediate demand of the truth."[15] Better yet, Lincoln should wait for no further confirmation; he should instantly order the army back across the river. Wilson carried the solemn tidings directly to Lincoln, and a short time later, still in the mud-encrusted clothes he had been wearing since the previous night, Villard was called to the White House.

In a second-floor reception room, Lincoln grasped Villard's hand, thanking him and explaining that the absence of news had put him and his advisors in a very anxious mood.[16] After listening to Villard's outline of how the battle had unfolded, Lincoln peppered the newspaperman with questions for half an hour. They discussed the physical and moral condition of the troops, the feelings among the generals, the extent of the army's losses, and the chances for renewing the attack. On this last point, Villard was emphatic: every general he had seen, both during and after the assault, believed that if the attack were resumed now, the army would suffer the worst disaster it had yet experienced. The president's face darkened. As Villard prepared to leave, the president managed a melancholy smile and remarked, "I hope it is not so bad as all that."[17] Villard walked away feeling that he had discharged a patriotic duty; he had confirmed to the president that his impulse in asking Halleck to order Burnside to withdraw had been absolutely right. No one knows whether Lincoln was now motivated by a desire to stand by Halleck, a lingering faith in Burnside to see the situation clearly, or simple indecision. Whatever the reason, the president gave no order to withdraw, and Burnside was left on his own.

Lincoln's long night of worry was not yet over. After midnight, he received at least one more visitor: Governor Andrew Curtin of Pennsylvania. Curtin, too, had just come from Fredericksburg. If anything, he was even more pessimistic than Villard. "Mr. President," he intoned, "it was not a battle, it was a butchery."[18] As Curtin told his tale, the president appeared heartbroken and "soon reached a state of nervous excitement bordering on insanity."[19] Apologetically, Curtin reached for Lincoln's hand. Surely, the governor said, the individual sufferings he had seen had given him too dark an impression of the overall battle, and matters would look brighter when the official reports came in.

Having nothing else to fall back on, Lincoln then offered up one of his apparently endless reserve of funny stories. The yarn concerned an angry hog that, having gotten loose, had chased one boy up a tree and had run at a second one, who had saved himself only by grabbing the animal's tail. As pig and boy whirled around and the latter felt his strength beginning to fail, he called up to the other boy, "I say, John, come down quick, and help me *let this hog go!*" Now that, Lincoln said, was his condition precisely; he wished someone might come along and "let this hog go."[20] Generations earlier, Thomas Jefferson had compared America's problem with slavery with having a wolf by the ears: one could not hang on but dared not let go. Now Lincoln was in a death grip with his own vicious animal, and no escape seemed possible.

Lincoln put the best public face on the tragedy of Fredericksburg. He issued a public letter of thanks to his defeated army, praising the valor of its men: "Although you were not successful, the attempt was not an error, nor the failure other than an accident. The courage with which you, in an open field, maintained the contest against an entrenched foe, and the consummate skill and success with which you crossed and recrossed the river, in the face of the enemy, show that you possess all the qualities of a great army, which will yet give victory to the cause of the country."[21] Burnside, now that any hope of mitigating the calamity was gone, offered his resignation. Lincoln declined to accept it.[22]

Fredericksburg had also confirmed for Lincoln a terrible truth—one that, though ghastly in its implications, pointed a way toward vanquishing the Confederacy. The Rebels had won convincingly at Fredericksburg, but even so crushing a victory was helping to bleed the Southern cause to death. Lincoln knew that if the same battle were to be fought every day for a week, "with the same relative results, the army under Lee would be wiped out to its last man, [but] the Army of the Potomac would still be a mighty host." Staggering from disaster to disaster, the Federals would prevail if only, when falling, they would perpetually fall forward. Lincoln conceded, "No general yet found can face the arithmetic." Nevertheless, he insisted, when that general was finally found, the end of the war would be at hand.[23] Privately, though, the president was sunk in anguish. "If there is a worse place than hell," he said despairingly, "I am in it."[24]

All at once, Lincoln was confronting one of the deepest crises of his presidency. For months it had been clear to many, from George Whitman and Henry Abbott to the president's cabinet, that the Emancipation Proclamation would be only a sad joke if Lincoln had no power to force the Southern states to comply. His latest attempt to impose his will upon the South had ended in the slaughter on Marye's Heights. His promise of freedom to the enslaved millions within the Confederacy now looked embarrassingly empty. Less than three weeks before he was scheduled to sign the measure, it seemed likely that the president would have to pull his Proclamation off the table.

A more immediate emergency arose, one that threatened the future of the Lincoln administration. On December 17, Frederick Seward, the son of Secretary of State Seward who served as his assistant, came to the White House. A Republican senator from New York, Preston King, came with him. The younger Seward handed the president a letter. It was Secretary Seward's resignation. "What does this mean?"[25] Lincoln asked with blank surprise. Senator King explained: The disaster at Fredericksburg had thrown the Senate Republicans into a near panic. Convinced that unless the administration radically changed course, the country would be ruined and the war lost, the senators had caucused behind closed doors.[26] Their wrath had fallen on Seward.

Over the next few days, the reason became apparent. For months, Treasury Secretary Salmon P. Chase had viewed Seward's close relationship with the president with suspicion. Lately, he had imprudently shared with some Republican senators his conviction that Seward was secretly controlling Lincoln, even leading him to overrule the decisions of the full cabinet. In part because Seward had formerly supported General

McClellan, the more hawkish Republicans in Congress had already questioned Seward's commitment to winning the war. Now, intensified by
the slaughter of Fredericksburg, their simmering distrust of the secretary
had come to a boil.[27] In a divided vote, the Senate Republican caucus
had proposed a no-confidence vote in Seward. The body also drafted a
resolution demanding that, henceforth, "the Cabinet should be exclusively composed of statesmen who are the cordial, resolute, unwavering
supporters" of the war effort.[28]

At first glance, the senators' scapegoating of Seward for Fredericksburg made hardly any sense. The secretary was responsible for none of the
decisions that had led to the rout. Moreover, the Republicans' complaint
had always been that the secretary was too cautious. Yet the blunder at
Fredericksburg had not been one of McClellanesque over-caution, but
of headlong rashness. Moreover, the caucus's action flirted with uncon-
stitutionality. The Senate confirms or rejects cabinet nominees when the
president first proposes them. After that, its only power over a cabinet
secretary is impeachment; votes of no confidence form no part of its
function, and certainly cannot be issued by a partisan faction. As *Harper's
Weekly* put it, the Constitution gave the Senate no more power to demand
the resignation of an obnoxious secretary than to appoint a mayor of New
York.[29] Nevertheless, the caucus was calling for Seward's head, and the
secretary's allies in the Senate found themselves playing for time. With
some difficulty, they persuaded their colleagues to table the resolution
until the following day.

Secretary Seward learned of these events from Senator King, who had
violated an order of secrecy by telling him. As the two men discussed the
caucus's actions in the library of Seward's home, the secretary saw that
the senators were trying to attack the president through him. If Lincoln
defended Seward, he would fuel the argument that the secretary was his
special favorite, perhaps even a manipulative power behind the throne.
If Lincoln dismissed Seward, he would appear to have bowed before
an overreaching Congress and would weaken himself in the eyes of the
nation. Seeing no other way around the dilemma, Seward exclaimed,
"They may do as they please about me, but they shall not put the President in a false position on any account."[30] Then he reached for a pen. A
few minutes later, Fred Seward and King were on their way to the White
House carrying the secretary's letter of resignation.

Lincoln rushed to Seward's house. The secretary explained that he was not offering to quit merely out of duty. Stung by the caucus's resolution, Seward was weary of the petty sniping to which his position exposed him. It would be a relief, he said, "to be freed from official cares." That was all right for Seward, Lincoln rejoined, but it was no solution for him. Ruefully, the president recalled the caged starling from Laurence Sterne's *Sentimental Journey* that could say only four words: "I can't get out."[31]

Later that day, the caucus reconvened and deputized a nine-member committee to meet with the president the following evening, Thursday, the 18th of December, to personally deliver its resolution. Senator Browning, who was not among the nine, came to see Lincoln, whom he found with "more than usual trouble . . . pressing upon him." "They wish to get rid of me," said Lincoln, "and I am sometimes half disposed to gratify them."[32] Browning advised him that the committee's feelings toward the administration were vehemently hostile. The senators believed that their resolution was actually an expression of restraint, being "the gentlest thing that could be done."[33]

The date for signing the Emancipation Proclamation was just two weeks away. If Lincoln lost the fight to keep Seward, other dominoes in the cabinet might also fall. If they did, the Proclamation would look all the more like a meaningless piece of paper, scribbled by a government incapable of giving it the slightest bit of force. No one could be sure that the administration would survive. Lincoln acknowledged as much when he told Browning, "We are now on the brink of destruction." His features were etched with despair. "I can hardly see a ray of hope," he added.[34] The committee arrived at seven. The president, with his usual civility, welcomed them in.[35]

★

AT FREDERICKSBURG, AS THE SUN SET on December 11, Confederate cannons had sounded across the sky as two Massachusetts lieutenants roamed through the town collecting boards, from which they meant to fashion a temporary coffin for Chaplain Fuller. Two other men, aware that a shell might explode near them at any moment, hurried to construct the simple box. One of the lieutenants, John Hudson, helped to cover the body with a white cloth, to lift it from the rude door on which it had been lying, and to lower it into the coffin. Frank Fay, the mayor

of Chelsea, Massachusetts, who had been traveling with the army and
attending to its ailing soldiers, identified the remains and offered to pay
to transport them back across the river. A number of men from other
regiments passed by to gaze upon the pastor's face. Some called him
"their most edifying preacher"; others, "a most valued adviser"; and still
others "a most faithful friend."[36] The minister's corpse was carried first
to Washington for embalming. From there, a series of trains and boats
brought the remains of Chaplain Fuller home to Watertown. His body
arrived on the 18th—precisely one week after his death, the same day
that President Lincoln first met with the Committee of Nine, and a week
before Christmas.

The family gathered at Richard Fuller's house for a private farewell.
Then in Boston, on Christmas Eve, came a more public leave taking,
attended both by the Commonwealth's governor, John Albion Andrew,
and by its chief justice, George Tyler Bigelow. A handsome rosewood casket lay in front of the pulpit, and a party of mourners quietly approached
to cover it with wreaths. On the metal plate affixed to the coffin were
etched Chaplain Fuller's words, almost the last he was heard to speak,
which had been widely reported in the New England press: "I must do
something for my country."[37]

A debate had arisen over the minister's demise: had he set a laudable
example of patriotic courage, or had he died the pointless death of a
deluded, headstrong fool? Unsurprisingly, at the man's funeral, the former view held sway. Nonetheless, his eulogists were uneasily aware of the
contrary opinion. Erastus Haven, himself a clergyman, fretted over the
impression, regarding both the American pulpit and the country itself,
that an act like Fuller's might create. Recalling Fuller's last moments,
"clad in the soldier's garb, with deadly weapons in his hands, in the forefront of terrible strife," he confessed:

> Many are shocked at the thought of such a scene. Distant lands will
> wonder when they hear the report. It will be quoted as an indication
> of the fearful passion for blood which has usurped the American
> mind. There are some, even at home, who will timidly inquire, Why
> this waste of life? Why must the ambassador of the Prince of Peace
> subject himself to the violence of war? . . . Has there not been a mis-
> apprehension of the duties of a Christian minister?[38]

Haven hastened to quell the criticism. It was not folly, but valor that had guided the reverend to take his stand for that fleeting moment on Caroline Street. Fuller had gone into battle not because he thought too little of his own life, but because "to him, life was intensely valuable," because "a little thought makes man a coward, but deeper thought fills him with courage." Haven insisted that such a man at such a time could not be timid, "for God is in him."[39] Another speaker, Edmund Sears, added, "It is better to die for one's country, than to live on with no country to die for."[40]

Crowned with heavy black plumes, four horses pulled the carriage bearing the minister's remains to Mount Auburn Cemetery in Cambridge. The hearse that held the casket was draped in the colors of the flag and trimmed with rosettes of black and white. Through streets decorated for the holiday, the mourners followed to the grave site. Then, having nothing more to do, they departed, each by her or his own path, to their respective homes. It was time to make ready for the next day's celebration of the birth of Christ.

Arthur Fuller had long worried that he had not brought sufficient honor to his family. Thus, his brother Richard had special reasons to cherish a letter from the governor of Massachusetts, calling Arthur's conduct "worthy [of] his State and his blood."[41] But the Fuller family faced another problem. Chaplain Fuller's resignation from the Sixteenth Massachusetts had become official on December 10. Thus, the following day, Reverend Fuller had crossed into Fredericksburg as a civilian. Therefore, his survivors had no right to a military pension. For Lucilla Fuller and her four children, the technicality threatened a cruel deprivation. Possessing some of the fighting spirit of the family into which she had married, she petitioned Congress for a special act conferring on her the pension owed to a military widow. Presented to the Senate by Charles Sumner, Mrs. Fuller's petition promptly led to a bill that was brought before the upper house by Senator Daniel Clark, the man who had procured the hospital chaplaincy that the reverend had died before he could fill. Unanimously approved by both houses, the Act directed the secretary of the interior to confer upon Mrs. Fuller a pension of twenty dollars a month, to continue until she either died or remarried.[42] Clark told his fellow senators, "A more sincere Christian, a more patriotic man, a better man, scarcely ever lived."[43]

ON DECEMBER 18, AS LUCILLA FULLER grieved over her husband's body in Watertown, President Lincoln sat with the nine senators who seemed intent upon upending his cabinet. Stifling his emotions, Lincoln let the senators speak. For an exhausting three hours, the senators peppered him with their grievances. The president, they said, was making improper use of his cabinet. They argued that the secretaries were not intended as mere advisors to the president or as superintendents of their given departments. To the contrary, said the committee, all important public measures and appointments should be the result of their combined wisdom and deliberation.[44] In other words, a president should not be the ultimate arbiter of executive policy; it was to be established instead by the majority rule of his secretaries.

Having claimed that Lincoln had arrogated too much power to himself, they then accused him of giving too much of it away, or at least placing it in the wrong hands. In particular, they accused Lincoln of entrusting the conduct of the war principally to bitter and malignant Democrats, including General McClellan.[45] Yet McClellan had repaid the president's support by blackguarding the administration. The committee saved its harshest condemnation for Seward, who, they claimed, had been too half-hearted in his dedication both to freeing the slaves and to winning the war. It is not known whether the senators repeated the charge, then being whispered in the halls of the Capitol, that Seward was like "a sponge saturated with chloroform" being held constantly beneath "Uncle Abe's nose."[46] The senators held to the conviction that, whatever the president's good intentions, Seward had "contrived to suck them out of him unperceived."[47]

By the time they finally took their leave, the senators had said more than enough to drive the president into a justifiable fury. Nevertheless, he had so successfully masked the anguish he had expressed to Browning only hours earlier that one of the nine even found him "cheerful" and "pleased with the interview."[48] This feat of self-mastery was in itself a victory for Lincoln, though he still faced an uphill fight to keep Seward in the cabinet. From here until the end of the crisis, however, every move the president made would be steady and sure.

Lincoln called a special meeting of the cabinet for 10:30 the following morning, notifying all its members *except* Seward. He was not seeking to isolate the secretary or to conduct business behind his back. To the contrary, he wanted to rally support for Seward in a way that would not be possible if he were present. Lincoln told the cabinet of Seward's pending letter of resignation, and of the demands and accusations he had received from the Committee of Nine. Lincoln stated that the movement against Seward had left him "shocked and grieved."[49] To the evident discomfort of Chase, who had told various members of Congress that the cabinet was in bitter disarray, Lincoln assured the assembled secretaries that he felt that whatever their previous party feelings or associations, the cabinet had been, for the most part, harmonious. Admittedly there had been differences, but the quarrels had never been so serious as some outsiders had been led to suspect.[50] The president insisted that, indeed, the cabinet's loyalty had strengthened him indispensably. Throughout the trials that the nation had undergone, "he had been sustained and consoled by the good feeling and the mutual and unselfish confidence and zeal that pervaded the Cabinet."[51]

Lincoln asked that the cabinet reassemble that evening, at a meeting also to be attended by the Committee. Chase, knowing that the gathering would bring together two audiences to whom he had made very different representations, sputtered his disapproval. He added, almost certainly falsely, that he had known nothing either of the Senate's attacks on Seward or the latter's resignation before he had walked into the room. At first, the cabinet divided over whether the proposed second meeting should take place, with both Chase and Attorney General Bates arguing the negative. However, both Navy Secretary Welles and Postmaster General Montgomery Blair rallied to the president's support, and, finally, all of them agreed.[52]

That evening, eight of the nine senators returned to the White House. The full cabinet, again with the exception of Seward, also took their places. After reading aloud the senators' resolutions, Lincoln assured them of his cabinet's unity. If his advisors did not always think alike, they had always accepted the administration's decisions once they had been reached. He then paused and asked Chase himself: did he think that any of the cabinet disagreed with their chief's assessment of their collegiality? Chase was fuming. Here, in the presence of his peers, he had no choice but to disavow his negative statements. Bitterly, he declared that he would not have come to the meeting had he known that he would be arraigned before a Senate panel. But, yes, he admitted, the cabinet had been consulted on most of the signal issues confronting the nation, though perhaps not as fully as he might have wished.[53] Moreover, he conceded, no member had opposed a measure after it had been adopted. William Fessenden of Maine, speaking for the senators, started to back down. Perceiving that the caucus had overstepped its bounds, he assured everyone that the senators had meant only "to offer friendly advice, and not to dictate to [the president], or interfere with his prerogative."[54]

Against the proposal that the cabinet should govern by majority rule, the postmaster general took the lead. Blair pushed back hard against the theory of a plural executive. The president was and ought to be in charge. He might ask the opinions of the whole cabinet, or some of them, or none. He was free to heed or reject their advice as he chose. Attorney General Bates voiced his agreement. On that issue, the senators were routed.

Moving to the main point, Lincoln defended Seward, noting in particular his earnestness in prosecuting the war. However, despite adopting a carefully conciliatory tone, he made only modest headway. Four of the eight senators, including Charles Sumner, still urged that Seward should go. Of the remaining four, only one, Senator Harris from Seward's home state of New York, wanted Seward to stay. The other three declined to commit themselves. It was almost midnight when the two delegations left the president. Seward's fate remained undecided.

Lincoln had partially mollified the Committee of Nine. However, the upper echelons of his cabinet were in turmoil. The Senate's campaign against Seward had come upon the secretary unawares and had left him mortified. Chase was also reeling from what he regarded as an ambush; Lincoln's calling out of him in front of the Committee felt like a betrayal. For his part, Secretary of War Stanton was disgusted by the cabinet's behavior.[55] As he told one of the senators the following day, every assertion the Committee had made about divisions and petty rancor in the cabinet was true, but Chase, under the pressure of the moment, had lied to protect himself. Stanton said the treasury secretary had made him "ashamed."[56] Attorney General Bates feared the power of gossip to destroy the administration. "The town," he told his diary, "is all in a buzz—all the cabinet to resign."[57] Welles, calmer than most of his brethren, was at the White House the next morning as soon as Lincoln had finished his breakfast, urging him not to yield to the Senate's assault on the independence of the executive branch. The president agreed. If he permitted the Senate to dictate the workings of the cabinet, Welles heard him say, "the whole Government must cave in. It could not stand, it could not hold water."[58] The two also agreed that Lincoln must not accept Seward's resignation. With the president's blessing, Welles went at once to Seward's house to assure the latter that his job was safe and to prevail upon him not to resign.

Welles calmed and persuaded Seward. Having secured Seward's promise to stay on, he rode back to the Executive Mansion, where he found both Chase and Stanton waiting for the president. Lincoln walked in moments later. He first asked Welles if he had "seen the man." Welles, taking care not to mention Seward's name in front of Chase, gave Lincoln to understand that "the man" was still in the government. Chase, still fuming after his embarrassment the previous evening, told the president that he had been so painfully affected by the proceedings that he, too, had prepared a letter of resignation. Lincoln's eyes lit up, like those of a chess player whose opponent has just released his hand from a blundering move. "Where is it?" he demanded. When Chase produced the paper from his pocket, Lincoln extended his arm toward Chase, who, startled by the chief executive's reaction, was suddenly reluctant to hand the paper over. But it was already in the president's hands. He broke the seal of the envelope and scanned the paper's contents. A look of satisfaction suffused his face. Unable to suppress a laugh of triumph, he told Welles, "This cuts the Gordian knot. I can dispose of this subject now without difficulty. I see my way clear."[59] Chase stood by, astonished and uncomprehending. Stanton interjected, "Mr. President, I informed you day before yesterday that I was ready to tender you my resignation. I wish you, sir, to consider my resignation at this time in your possession."[60]

At any other time, Stanton's proffered resignation might have struck like a thunderbolt. Now, Lincoln brushed it aside like a mosquito. "I don't want yours," he said dismissively. "This is all I want . . . I will detain neither of you longer."[61] Chase made his exit, no doubt astonished to discover how keen the president was to eject him from the cabinet. But Lincoln had a subtler stratagem in mind. He wanted Chase's letter so badly, not so that he could accept the secretary's resignation, but so that he could decline it. Here was the beauty of Lincoln's idea: he had meant all along to refuse Seward's offer to resign, but to do so in the absence of any other action would have shown favoritism regarding Seward just when siding with him was most problematic. Indeed, the gesture might have been seen as confirming the Senate's worst suspicions. However, by refusing *both* resignations, Lincoln could present himself as evenhanded, acting to preserve the integrity of the entire cabinet, rather than the interests of one faction or the career of a single politician. Lincoln used an apt but homely metaphor to describe the deliverance that Chase had given him. "Now I can ride," the president announced. "I have a pumpkin in each end of my bag."[62]

Lincoln's maneuver worked to perfection. The day before Christmas, all the cabinet secretaries were back at their posts, Seward telling the president that he had "cheerfully resumed the functions of this Department in obedience to your command."[63] Seward even invited Chase to dine at his house on Christmas Eve, though Chase sent his regrets, claiming illness. The Committee of Nine, its purposes thwarted, was heard from no more. The president had been offered the resignations of his three most powerful cabinet officials, and for a few days the executive branch had seemed on the verge of collapse, yet he had had the calm and wisdom to stand firm. In a moment of self-congratulation, he told his private secretary, John Hay, "I do not see how it could have been done better."[64]

Nevertheless, the other great question of the moment had not yet been resolved: Would the defeat at Fredericksburg compel the president to withdraw the Emancipation Proclamation? Doubts had begun to circulate even before the battle's climax. On the eve of the struggle for Marye's Heights, Harriet Beecher Stowe wrote a fretful letter to Charles Sumner. "Everybody I meet in New England," she told the senator, "says to me with anxious earnestness—*Will* the President stand firm to his Proclamation?"[65] Frederick Douglass pondered a daunting hypothetical: "What if the President fails in this trial hour, what if he now listens to the demon slavery—and rejects the entreaties of the angel of Liberty?"[66] In New York, prominent lawyer and diarist extraordinaire George Templeton Strong asked, "Will Uncle Abe Lincoln stand firm and issue his promised proclamation? . . . Nobody knows."[67] Newspapers sympathetic to the Democratic party, including the *Chicago Times*, confidently predicted that Lincoln would withdraw the Proclamation; the *New York*

Times alluded to a "general air of doubt."[68] Millions wondered whether Lincoln would keep his promise.[69]

No uncertainty, however, seems to have existed in the one place where it would have mattered: the mind of Lincoln himself. Charles Sedgwick, a lame-duck Republican congressman, attested to the president's will: "Every conceivable influence has been brought to bear on him to induce him to withhold or modify [the Proclamation] . . . but he is as firm as a mule."[70] It was not mere stubbornness that held Lincoln to his resolve. He was persuaded that withdrawing the Proclamation now would incite "a rebellion in the north, and . . . a dictator would be placed over his head."[71] The importance of staying firm was also more than practical; the president stood convinced that signing the Proclamation was the right thing to do. On the evening of December 27, Lincoln welcomed Senator Sumner to the Executive Mansion. Sumner handed the president a memorial, signed by a group of clergymen who urged him to stand by the Proclamation. Sumner called the document "an act of justice & humanity which must have the blessings of a benevolent Govt." Lincoln reassured Sumner that he "could not stop the Proclamation if he would, & would not if he could."[72] Still, even though his mind was made up, Lincoln chose not to tip his hand to anyone outside the upper circles of power. On New Year's Eve, he greeted a committee of abolitionist ministers who sought to know whether the signing would take place as scheduled the following day. Lincoln put them off: "Tomorrow at noon, you shall know—and the country shall know—my decision."[73]

On the appointed day, Lincoln was obliged to endure the customary pomp of a new year at the White House before seeing to the real business of the afternoon. The president did not complete the last revisions of the Proclamation until midmorning. One of the last additions was a rhetorical flourish from Secretary Chase: "and upon this act, sincerely believed to be an act of justice, warranted by the constitution, upon military necessity, I invoke the considerate judgment of mankind, and the gracious favor of Almighty God."[74] Lincoln sent the text off to the State Department for a final copy to be made. When Secretary Seward and his son Fred returned with the finished draft, Lincoln perused the document and found an error. He sent the paper back for correction.

At 11 a.m., the president's official guests arrived: diplomats and cabinet secretaries; the justices of the Supreme Court; a select cadre of army officers, led by General Halleck. Around noon most of the cabinet slipped out to avoid the crowd and to preside over their own New Year's receptions. At the same hour, into the White House came a crush of less-credentialed well-wishers. The president stood in the Blue Room with Mrs. Lincoln, who was making her first appearance at a public reception since Willie's death the preceding February. The handshaking that had begun an hour earlier went on until almost 2 p.m. The last of the crowd were ushered away. Fatigued, his right hand swollen, the president mounted the stairs to his office. Secretary Seward and his son Fred joined him, bearing the emended version of the Proclamation.

When the parchment was unrolled, Lincoln dipped his pen in ink and prepared to add his signature. Then he stopped; his hand, still affected by the countless handshakes of the previous three hours, was trembling. "I never, in my life, felt more certain that I was doing right, than I do in signing this paper," he said apologetically.[75] If his name ever went into history, he said, it would be for this act, and he then added, "My whole soul is in it." He paused a trifle longer, preparing his aching hand for the task. "Now, this signature is one that will be closely examined," he explained, "and if they find my hand trembled, they will say, 'he had some compunctions.' But, anyway, it is going to be done!" Then, after hesitating precisely so that his penmanship would show no sign of hesitation, he drew his name "slowly and carefully" across the page, producing a signature, as Fred Seward called it, "unusually bold, clear, and firm, even for him."[76]

Book 4

———

TWO NURSES

Chapter Fourteen

The Prince of Patients

On December 14, the day after the slaughter below Marye's Heights, Louisa May Alcott awoke on a narrow iron bed beside a pair of roommates and commenced her first morning of duty at the Union Hotel Hospital.[1] Even in its former function as a hotel, it had been looked on as a seedy, even "unsavory" accommodation.[2] In the eyes of Mrs. Ropes, it was "a one-horse establishment," and the long-suffering hospital matron suspected that no length of service would ever improve its reputation.[3] Until the Battle of Fredericksburg, the hospital had acted chiefly as a way station, a place for recovering soldiers to rest and be made comfortable for a while before being moved on to facilities farther north.[4] If the structure had a redeeming feature, it was the view from the heights on which it sat. Gazing southward, over what was then a dangerous and disreputable part of town, a visitor looked down upon the Potomac. "Calm, of uncertain color and clearness," the river offered a reassuringly broad line of defense against Confederate attack. Beyond the river lay Virginia, dotted everywhere with Union tents by day and lit by countless campfires by night.[5]

The visual attractions of the spot did little to lift the spirits of the patients, who, according to the matron, were generally demoralized and weary of life. The month before Alcott arrived, Mrs. Ropes had sat by the bed of a man who claimed to have made up his mind to die. She told him firmly that he had no right to an opinion in the matter, that no one could know the boundaries of his life, and that his own existence, however shabby it might currently seem, was still a gift from God.[6] Ropes supplemented her sermon by giving the man a half-tumbler of port wine, and the combined infusion of spirit and spirits seemed to do the trick. Not all cures came so simply.

The start of what Alcott termed her "new life" coincided with the end of another: a patient on her ward who had been wounded in some earlier struggle lost his fight for survival as her first day in Georgetown dawned.[7] Otherwise, the hospital was mostly quiet for the time being. She spent the day in a ward populated by twenty strong faces, seating herself between a boy with pneumonia and a man who had been shot through the lungs. The older man seemed to resist her sympathy. He lay back and stared at her, and the silent gaze of his black eyes made her uneasy. In a strange new place without a friend, she felt painfully how little she knew and how awkward her first efforts were likely to be. The boy, thankfully, was more responsive. When he sat up, fighting for breath, Alcott took the little black shawl that her mother had given her and draped it around the young man's shoulders. Marmee's talisman performed its tiny bit of magic. The boy smiled and said, "You are real motherly, ma'am."[8] In that moment, Alcott felt that she was getting on. As she surveyed the room and looked at her twenty charges, she hoped that the others, too, would come to find her motherly. "My thirty years made me feel old," she wrote, "and the suffering round me made me long to comfort every one."[9]

It turned out to be no small ambition. A day or two after she arrived, one of the other nurses unexpectedly quit, and Alcott found herself in charge of forty beds. Her waking hours evaporated in a constant round of "washing faces, serving rations, giving medicine, and sitting in a very hard chair, with pneumonia on one side, diphtheria on the other, five typhoids, on the opposite, and a dozen dilapidated patriots, hopping, lying, and lounging about."[10] Her unease at being stared at worsened, as scores of eyes seemed to judge her every move. Assuming a matronly air to mask her misgivings, she fumbled through with Spartan firmness. She hoped that the men admired her efforts. She suspected they did not.

It was not what she had imagined. She had sought "a new world of stirring sights and sounds [and] new adventures."[11] So far she had found blank drudgery. "Rheumatism," she conceded, "wasn't heroic, neither was liver complaint, or measles."[12] Even fever, she found, had lost its romantic glow. With a naïve taste for ghastliness and with little thought of what she was asking, she longed for the Fredericksburg wounded to arrive.[13]

Mrs. Ropes had already closed too many glassy eyes and pressed her lips against too many ice-cold foreheads to share Alcott's excitement. The day after the catastrophe at Fredericksburg, before the first of the battle's wounded had arrived, she found time to write in her journal. As she did, she heard a steady background noise, a "mingled sound of active purposes and wailing griefs."[14] More grief, she knew, was coming, but she felt strong in her purpose. In a voice both firm and passionate, she wrote:

> This is God's war, in spite of uncertain generals, in spite of ill success; in spite of our own unworthiness; the cause is that of the human race, and must prevail. Let us work then with a good heart, here and at home. . . . Now is the judgment of the world. . . . No soul now can stand on neutral ground. . . . Let us be loyal and true . . . even though the waves of war's uncertain tide swallow us in the general wreck![15]

As the gray light dawned on Alcott's third day at the hospital, she was jolted into awareness by a loud knock at her door and the terse announcement, "They've come! They've come! hurry up, ladies—you're wanted!"[16] Groggy and disoriented, Alcott thought for a moment that Lee's army had reached the capital. A glance out the window dispelled her confusion. In the street below stood a great clot of vehicles that looked like market carts. Instead, they were some forty ambulances, disgorging their shattered human cargo. Above the din, Alcott heard the voice of a six-year-old boy who had recently escaped slavery by passing through the Union line. They were coming, the boy shouted, heaps of them. He was especially fascinated by one body that had been brought in dead. As the boy darted away, Alcott thought she heard him singing like a bird.[17]

As she descended to the wards, she was greeted by an appalling stench and a stunning influx of ruined humanity, some on stretchers, some in the arms of comrades, some faltering along on crutches. The dead man lay covered, a nurse duly recording his name before sending him to the dead house. Those who could sit lined the walls. Those who could not sit lay on the floor, almost covering it. In the hotel's former ballroom forty beds were hastily made ready. Ragged and pale, a handful of men stood by the large stove, their calves encased in drying mud. Their coats had either been lost or rendered useless, so they pulled blankets around them to keep off the cold. The bandages they had worn for days looked filthy.

Gaunt and bewildered, the dreary little group silently attested to the enormity of Burnside's blunder.[18]

Louisa May Alcott's first weapon in the struggle against slavery had been the needle she had used to sew uniforms for the Concord volunteers. She now was given a new one: a block of coarse brown soap. "Wash as fast as you can," she was told. That seemed all right, but another task appalled her: she had also been told to order her patients to disrobe. The Concord spinster had found words to describe the wounded. However, the job of viewing and scrubbing several dozen naked "lords of creation," as she delicately called them, left her all but speechless. Even months later, she could only sputter that the experience had been "really—really—." Yet she remembered that she had come to do as she was told. No time for nonsense now. She "drowned [her] scruples in [her] wash-bowl, clutched [her] soap manfully," and plunged ahead.[19]

Hours later, she and her fellow nurses had produced a minor miracle of orderliness. The men lay or sat on their beds, each of them "transformed from a dismal ragamuffin into a recumbent hero." Washed and shorn, they dug into the bread, meat, soup, and coffee that had poured forth from the kitchen.[20] Alcott received a small memento of the day: a New Hampshire soldier, wounded by an exploded shell, reached under his pillow and handed her a pair of earrings, which he had harvested from one of the damaged houses of Fredericksburg.[21] Alcott accepted the baubles, hesitating only because she was depriving the soldier of his relics; her recounting voices no misgivings about accepting stolen property.

The hospital was no easy place in which to radiate good cheer. The wards suffered from a stifling lack of ventilation, and Alcott was forever flinging open the windows, though her patients grumbled at the introduction of the fresh but freezing air. Despite the best efforts of the staff, dirt and contagion were everywhere. The matron complained bitterly of the body lice that seemed to find their way into every garment, and she wrote that no amount of money would induce her to invite her daughter to visit.[22] Alcott observed, "a more perfect pestilence-box than this house, I never saw—cold, damp, dirty, full of vile odors from wounds, kitchens, wash rooms, and stables."[23] Her personal affection for Mrs. Ropes did not prevent her from angrily denouncing the facility's disorder, discomfort, and poor management, all of which combined to reduce the Union Hotel to a condition that Alcott lacked the words to describe.[24]

In such a place, routine produces calm, and Alcott noted the rhythms and rituals that helped to make up for the dirt and chaos. She rose in the dark at six and dressed by gaslight, then went to her ward to poke up the fire and distribute blankets. She then proceeded to "open doors & windows as if life depended on it; mine does." She then sat down to her breakfast of "fried beef, salt butter, husky bread & washy coffee"— a dreary meal that the company of her fellow diners did nothing to improve. Instead of leaning on her new comrades for support, Alcott quietly despised them. The eight female nurses with whom she broke bread she dismissed as "silly, stupid, or possessed of but one idea." The male members of the staff sat engrossed in their breakfasts and in themselves to a degree that Alcott found ludicrous and provoking. As they proclaimed their half-formed but firmly held opinions, Alcott choked into her cup and finished her food as fast as she could, trying to keep from laughing at their pompous inanities.[25]

Mornings were a flurry of chores, most of them more befitting a maid of all work than a nurse. Alcott summarized her tasks in breathless fashion: "Cutting up food for helpless 'boys,' washing faces, teaching my attendants how beds are made or floors swept, dressing wounds . . . dusting tables, sewing bandages, keeping my tray tidy, rushing up & down after pillows, bed linen, sponges, books, and directions."[26] At noon a large bell sounded: dinner for the patients had arrived—soup, meat, potatoes, and bread. After the meal was finished, the soldiers slept, read, or asked the nurses to write letters for them. Letter writing was perhaps the best part of Nurse Alcott's day. Though she took care to remain grave and respectful on the surface, she smiled and chuckled inwardly at the odd incidents and comic phrasings she was asked to take down. Yet correspondence, too, had its melancholy side; letters would sometimes come for patients who had not lived to receive them. Answering these, said Alcott, was the saddest and hardest duty she was given to perform. Supper came at five, followed by a slow winding down, enlivened by newspapers, gossip, and last doses of medicine for the night. The night bell rang at nine, the gaslights were turned down, and Alcott, exhausted, sank into her bed.[27]

Among the doctors, one in particular was exempt from Alcott's quiet scorn. Dr. John Winslow was a sentimental man whom Alcott called both plain and odd. Winslow had grown up as a Quaker and was, Alcott felt, as kindhearted as a woman.[28] Friendly to all, painstaking in his work, the doctor was a pleasure to watch as he ambled among his patients. He took Alcott to hear the renowned minister William Henry Channing preach in the Capitol and to dine at an amusingly bad German restaurant. He quoted copiously from Robert Browning's poems, appeared often at her door with books to share, and asked her out for a walk now and then. Charmed, Alcott dropped enough of her reserve to call him "Dr. John." The doctor enjoyed sharing confidences in the twilight and was, Alcott told her journal, "altogether . . . amiably amusing, and exceeding *young*."[29] Alcott underlined the last adjective, and the two teetered on the brink of something more than friendship. But Dr. Winslow's awkward charm and Nurse Alcott's loneliness did not conquer her sense of propriety. He invited her to his room. She did not go.

As the days passed, the stream of wounded from Fredericksburg continued to arrive. Before long, Alcott found herself surrounded by three or four hundred men in every phase of suffering, decline, and recovery.[30] On December 16, Matron Ropes counted seventy-one new patients. Anticipating many more, she wrote a letter referring to Fredericksburg as "murder ground."[31]

John Suhre arrived a day or two after most of the others; his insistence that more desperately wounded men should go before him had slowed his evacuation. Suhre's reputation preceded him. A comrade, also presumably from the 133rd, had arrived earlier. Fretting over Suhre's fate, this man never tired of praising him: his courage, his sobriety, his self-denial, and unfailing kindness of heart. "He's an out an' out fine feller, ma'am," the friend told Alcott. "You see if he aint."[32]

It was probably December 16 but possibly the 17th when she first saw him: gray eyes, fair skin, and hair that the army had recorded as black but she would remember as brown. Suhre's service records state that he stood 5'9". But he was done with standing now. He must have looked old for his twenty-one years, for Alcott described him in her journal as about thirty.[33] In the conversations they would later have, he may have mentioned his family's various ties to Bethany College, which was near his home but lay across the state line in the part of Virginia that was soon to break away from the Confederacy and become the new state of West Virginia. This possibility would explain why Alcott described him, in both her journal and her published writing, as a Virginian instead of a

Pennsylvanian—an error that was to deceive her biographers and conceal Suhre's origins for more than 150 years. She recalled another detail correctly: before joining the army, Suhre had been a blacksmith.[34]

Suhre's bed was not in the ballroom, but alongside a dozen other men in a space that Alcott called "my pathetic room."[35] It was a stony sort of room, wrote Mrs. Ropes, close into the street, without a single attractive quality.[36] The matron saw in Suhre something finer than the common soldier, and she hated that his place of rest was there, in a welter of disorder.[37] She expected him to revolt against his surroundings, but he did not. Quietly, enigmatically, he watched and waited.

Staying up past lights-out, Alcott watched and waited, too; she observed Suhre for a night or two before trying to win his friendship. She did not approach him at once, for she regarded him with a kind of awe. She called his bearing stately. His eyes she considered the serenest she had ever encountered. He had, as well, "a most attractive face . . . comely featured and full of vigor."[38] Mrs. Ropes admired his face, "composed in its manly beauty."[39] But he was not merely manly. Alcott said he had a smile that could make his mouth as sweet as any woman's, and those serene eyes had as well the flicker of a child's, "looking one fairly in the face, with a clear, straightforward glance, which promised well for such as placed their faith in him."[40] Alcott noted Suhre's androgynous charm in both her journal and the published fiction that she closely based on him.[41] In his various aspects, he lay before Alcott as male and female, adult and child, embodying the best traits of all the human family. He was, she soon decided, a "piece of excellence," unparalleled in her experience.[42]

Considerable as his physical beauty was, Suhre attracted her still more powerfully with his almost perfect self-control. Propped high upon his pillows, he rarely spoke, never complained, and demanded no one's pity. He appeared to love his life and his dignity in equal measures, and he was loath to part with either. It seemed to Alcott that he had learned the secret of content. In her journal she pronounced him her "prince of patients."[43]

But beneath the stoic surface, Suhre was beginning to worry. He still expected to recover, but something, perhaps in the way the surgeons looked at him, was starting to gnaw at his confidence. One day, one doctor brought another to examine him. The added attention made the private anxious. He asked the elder of the two physicians, "Do you think I shall pull through, sir?" The reply was only mildly reassuring: "I hope so, my man." As the surgeons retreated, a shadow passed over the soldier's face, though his impassive expression came back moments later. It seemed to Alcott "as if, in that brief eclipse, he had acknowledged the existence of some hard possibility, and, asking nothing but hoping all things, left the issue in God's hands."[44]

Suhre could keep up his perfect façade of pious resignation for only so long. He was in tremendous pain, and slowly his suffering ate away at his resolve. Alcott herself did not guess the misery of his situation until, on Christmas Eve, she happened to ask a surgeon who among her patients was suffering most. To her surprise, the surgeon glanced toward Private Suhre. "Every breath he draws," the doctor said, "is like a stab; for the ball pierced the left lung, broke a rib, and did no end of damage here and there; so the poor lad can find neither forgetfulness nor ease; because he must lie on his wounded back or suffocate."[45] The doctor predicted a hard struggle with only one possible outcome: Private Suhre must die. He had, at best, two days to live. The doctor, however, lacked the courage to tell Suhre that his wounds were fatal. Lamely protesting that a woman was better suited to the task, he told Alcott that she must tell Suhre the news.

Both the doctor's prognosis and his cowardly command moved Alcott to the verge of tears. She felt a sudden, fuming anger with the other patients on the ward who, though broken, were on their way to partial recovery. In her fury, she saw them as mere "worn-out, worthless bodies . . . gathering up the remnants of wasted lives, to linger on for years perhaps, burdens to others, daily reproaches to themselves."[46] The gift of life seemed wasted on such men. She could barely express her loathing for Burnside, whose sheer stupidity had condemned John Suhre to death. But she checked herself; tears and anger were pointless now. Disobeying the surgeon and still daring to hope, she did not tell John at once that his end was coming. Before she could do that, there was a different message that she had to convey.

Their time for talking came after Suhre had had a new dressing placed upon his wound. He sat silently, with his head lowered and his hands folded across his knee. As Alcott drew nearer, she saw tears rolling down his cheeks. It was a new sight for her. Men in the hospital groaned or swore or toughed it out. They never cried. Yet Suhre's tears were just the solvent needed to melt her reluctance to talk with him. She gathered his head into her arms as she would a child's and said, "Let me help you bear it, John." In all her previous writing, Alcott had never found the voice that came to her as she later recounted the scene that followed:

> Never, on any human countenance, have I seen so
>> swift and beautiful a look of gratitude, surprise
>> and comfort, as that which answered me more
>> eloquently than the whispered—
> "Thank you, ma'am, this is right good! this is what
>> I wanted!"
> "Then why not ask for it before?"
> "I didn't like to be a trouble; you seemed so busy,
>> and I could manage to get on alone."
> "You shall not want it any more, John."[47]

From that moment, Alcott treated Suhre as her special charge. She spent as much time with him as her other duties allowed. When it came time to probe, clean, and dress his wounds, she sat beside him as he pressed her hand tightly in his own. When the painful work was done, she washed his face, brushed his hair, and laid a small knot of flowers on his pillow. He took the little bouquet in his hand and smelled it gratefully. As she neatened the table at his bedside, he softly touched her gown to assure himself that she was there.[48]

Gradually, Suhre's wounds reduced his voice to a whisper, and he could talk only a little at a time. Nevertheless, Alcott gleaned from him some small scraps of his private history. Suhre was unmarried; his mother was widowed, and he had a younger brother and sister. He had been slow to enlist because the family needed his income. The John of her fiction says, "I went [to join the army] because I couldn't help it. I didn't want the glory or the pay; I wanted the right thing done. . . . I was in earnest, the Lord knows! but I held off as long as I could, not knowing which was my duty; Mother saw the case, gave me her ring to keep me steady, and said 'Go:' so I went."[49] His story tallied closely with her own. He was a thirty-year-old (as she presumed) whose family depended heavily upon him, but whose sense of duty to country and social justice finally outweighed more personal duties. It seemed to her that the two of them had very much in common.

Though his condition was worsening, Suhre still thought he would survive. Alcott shielded him from the truth until he finally confronted her. With simple frankness, he said, "This [was] my first battle; do they think it's going to be my last?" Alcott could not dodge him now. "I'm afraid they do, John," she replied. Suhre seemed startled for a moment. Then he looked down at his powerful blacksmith's body and said, more in bewilderment than in protest, "I'm not afraid, but it's difficult to believe all at once. I'm so strong it don't seem possible for such a little wound to kill me."[50] He asked Alcott to take down a letter for his brother. Though Alcott had taken dictation from many soldiers, she considered Suhre's the best she ever transcribed. According to *Hospital Sketches*, it imparted excellent advice and said its farewell in words whose naïve inelegance and lack of grammar made their message even sadder. The letter has never been found.

Suhre held on until the day after Christmas. Then, as Alcott and the matron sat beside him and Louisa gave him a swallow of water, he said, "Thank you, madam, I think I must be marching on."[51] The moment reminded Alcott of the passing of her sister Lizzie; once again a spirit entwined with hers was composing itself for its final journey. But unlike Lizzie, who had been so fragile at the end, Suhre was still strong, and so was his instinct for life. There was nothing easy about his passing. The fight went on for hours. Alcott wrote, "His limbs grew cold, his face damp, his lips white, and, again and again, he tore the covering off his breast, as if the lightest weight added to his agony."[52]

In *Hospital Sketches*, Alcott wrote that her fictional alter ego, Trib Periwinkle, had just set down the fan with which she had been cooling him when John rose up in his bed and cried out in agony, "For God's sake, give me air!" An attendant opened a window. "The first red streak of dawn was warming the grey east, a herald of the coming sun; John saw it, and with the love of light which lingers in us to the end, seemed to read in it a sign of hope of help." He breathed a while longer. Then, as the tide went out, he grasped Periwinkle's hand, so hard and tight that she could not withdraw it after death came. The attendant helped peel back the dead man's fingers, saying as he did so that it was unsafe for dead and living flesh to lie so long together. Nurse Periwinkle's own hand felt stiff and cold. She looked down and saw four white marks across its back.[53]

✴

ALCOTT THE STORYTELLER COULD NOT RESTRAIN herself from adding a romantic gloss to the death of Private John Suhre. In *Hospital Sketches*, she scatters the scene with the conventions of Victorian novels. The men of the ward gather in a circle around him, their faces full of awe and pity. The particular friend who first described John to Nurse Periwinkle steps forward and pledges to honor the dying man's last wish: to carry his belongings back home and tell his family that their kinsman had done his best.[54] The two men part with a kiss, as tender as one that might have passed between two women.

It does no harm to accept the account from *Hospital Sketches* as true wherever the factual record does not contradict it. Yet the dutiful Mrs. Ropes, lacking Alcott's artistic motive to idealize the moment, tells a somewhat different story. Unlike Alcott's *Sketches*, which set Suhre's passing at dawn, the matron's journal placed the time of death at "eight o'clock in the evening, the gas burning brightly." It was a full two hours before he died, Ropes recorded, when Suhre "reached his right hand into Miss Alcott's lap and firmly grasped her wrist," able to speak "but a word at a time." When Suhre died, the matron wrote, Nurse Alcott was not there. Ropes claimed for herself the exclusive privilege of watching Suhre depart:

> The matron is left alone when the breath ceases—she, still watching with loving sympathy and a farther reaching consciousness of this process through which he is passing, keeps close by with her hand on his forehead, as though she would cross palms with the angels commissioned to take her work out of her hands.[55]

Impressed with "the wondrous manly beauty of [Suhre's] whole person" even in death, Ropes sent an attendant to call Alcott back to the bedside.[56]

The impulse to idealize episodes in the war was hardly Alcott's alone. It is certainly one reason why Walt Whitman was correct when he wrote, "The real war will never get in the books." The people who knew the war built fictions around what they had known, whether to make it grander, more personal, or simply easier to bear. Alcott was intentionally writing fiction, but crafting some fiction or other was essential to almost everyone. The power to soften the edges, or, if need be, to sharpen them; the ability to recast the pain and the passion, the triumph and the loss in one's own subjective light; and the prerogative, too, to leave it all in shadow by writing nothing at all—these, to every survivor of the war, were necessary things.

Ropes and Alcott let Suhre's body lie in state in the hospital ward for half an hour before it was taken away—an unusual honor in a busy place where beds were scarce. To Alcott, the recumbent Suhre looked like an effigy of some young knight asleep on his tomb. She cut some locks of his hair and took the ring from his finger to send to his mother. She then placed a letter from home, which had arrived just too late for him to see, into his motionless hands. Both Alcott and the matron kissed the hero before he went. Then the business of saving lives went on.

✳

BACK IN CONCORD, AS THE FIRST of January approached, Bronson Alcott prepared to bring his usual New Year's Day gifts—apples from his cellar and bottles of his homemade hard cider—to the Hawthornes and the Emersons. He also made plans to attend a great gathering at the Masonic Temple on Tremont Street in Boston, the same building that had once housed his Temple School. This New Year's party had a significance like no other, for it was the day when President Lincoln would sign the Emancipation Proclamation. Both William Lloyd Garrison, editor of *The Liberator*, and the incomparable Frederick Douglass were expected to attend. Garrison, as it turned out, was absent; he had gone instead to a more fashionable, considerably whiter event at the city's Music Hall, also attended by Emerson, Harriet Beecher Stowe, and the elder Holmes. Bronson, however, wanted to be among the black celebrants. It was their day. With deep interest, he listened not only to Douglass but also to two of his fellow speakers—the journalist and black historian William Cooper Nell and the lecturer and novelist William Wells Brown. Enthralled by what he heard, Bronson told his journal, "The black men have the eloquence and carry the meeting as they ought." Douglass made the deepest impression. Though robbing the great orator of his final "s," Bronson atoned for his error with lavish praise: "I am struck by the sense and bearing of Douglas. One does not often meet a more imposing person. . . . The [Daniel] Webster of his race, he spoke well for it and the country."[57]

At the hospital in Georgetown, Louisa's celebration was less grand, though equally gratifying. She had never looked forward to any New Year's Day with more excitement. One day in the nurses' kitchen, after hearing a colleague speak slightingly of blacks, she made a show of ardently hugging and kissing a black baby. She proudly observed that, in a city where by no means everyone supported abolition, her demonstrations of solidarity with black people were earning her the reputation of "a dangerous fanatic."[58] On New Year's Eve, she stayed awake until midnight, awaiting the start of the day when the Proclamation would be signed. As the hour struck, she danced out of bed, threw open a window, and, with a gentle cheer, waved her handkerchief at a group of black men who were lighting firecrackers and singing "Glory, Hallelujah." Alcott's joy was great, but even as she joined in the celebration, she was disturbed by a nagging cough. At the time, it seemed like nothing important.

Another evening. The bells of the Georgetown Seminary marked the hours as Alcott watched at the bedside of a soldier with wound fever. As she sat, a poem took form in her mind. She wrote it down. The verse told of how after Thoreau's death the previous May, a passing breeze had blown through his flute as it hung near the Concord River, producing a brief, haunting tune. Although Alcott's elegy mourned that "The Genius of the wood" was gone, it also recalled that little wind-song, which had seemed to her to say, "For such as he there is no death." Unable at the time to finish it just as she wanted, Alcott tucked the draft into her belongings and then forgot it.

The cough got worse. Almost since her arrival, the cumulative effects of the bad air, food, water, and constant overwork had gradually pulled her down.[59] The Alcott women had always responded to crises by redoubling their energies, and to that remedy Louisa instinctively resorted. Each morning, she tried to rally herself with a long run, sometimes halfway to the Capitol. Her circumstances were hazardous, yet she found herself yearning for more danger, not less. In the distance she would observe long trains of army wagons on their way to the front. "That way the fighting lies," she wrote, "& I long to follow."[60] Running raised Alcott's spirits, but the energy she expended was no longer there to help her fend off disease. Her body needed that strength more than she knew.

The nurses at the Union Hotel Hospital needed almost as much care as their patients. One of them, a volunteer from Plymouth, Massachusetts named Julia Kendall, was forced to retreat to her bed when one of her knees refused to walk or to bend. Several colleagues warned Alcott that she was on the verge of contracting pneumonia, but she shrugged them off. Mrs. Ropes observed, "the house has been very sick and we nurses have fairly run down."[61] The matron was failing, too. On January 9, she wrote her son, "The tax upon us women . . . is tremendous." She added ominously, "I am doing my last work now." In the same letter, she wrote that she and Alcott, whom she called "a splendid young woman," had struggled together to save four dying men.[62] All but one of the four had recovered. It was less clear that the two women could save themselves.

Letters from Louisa arrived in Concord, bearing vivid descriptions of her hospital work. Bronson read them with deeply mixed emotions. "She seems active, interested, and, if her strength is adequate to the task, could not better serve herself, nor the country." His pride, however, was edged with worry. "But I fear," he continued, "this will end in her breaking down presently."[63] His concerns were well founded. One day, not long after saving the three soldiers, Alcott sank to a sitting position on the stairs, pressing her head against the cold banister and coughing uncontrollably. Her feet seemed to cleave to the floor, and her head felt like a cannonball. The walls bulged and undulated, and the bottles on a shelf seemed to mock her with a derisive dance. Unable to carry out her duties, she retreated to her bed. For a day or two, she appeared only at meals. After that, the exertion of walking down two flights of stairs became too much. On January 11, she was confined to her room on orders from the matron, and a mustard plaster was applied to her chest.

Alcott revised her once-dismissive judgment of her fellow nurses. Her colleagues tended to her "like a flock of friendly ravens," bringing both food and much-needed good cheer to her bedside. In her suddenly dependent state, she found herself comfortably "be-teaed and be-toasted, petted and served."[64] In the wit of her conversation and in the depth of her learning, Alcott had felt greatly superior to these women. Now, she discovered, there were many among them who quietly outdid her in the more important fields of compassion and charity. Divided by class and education, Alcott and her fellow nurses were finally united by purpose and kindness. They were more of a team than she had imagined. It was a humbling but powerful lesson.

But the attentive treatment did not cure her illness, or even keep her from feeling desperately alone. The headache, the fever, the dizziness, and, now, a sharp pain in her side, refused to go away. Her cough still tormented her and made her think uneasy thoughts about her lungs and bones. She read when she could and sewed garments for the soldiers. She tried to talk and stay cheerful, but all the mirth was feigned. Besieged by nightmares, she would awake unrefreshed, think of home, and wonder if she would ever set eyes on it again. "A pleasant prospect," she wrote dolefully, "for a lonely soul five hundred miles from home."[65] The attentions she was receiving now only added to her melancholy. One doctor took her pulse and asked if she was consumptive. Another examined her lungs and looked grim. The faithful John Winslow brought books and firewood, but even his presence felt haunting. Anxiously, the other nurses wondered aloud whether she should go home. But Miss Alcott of Concord had some hard opinions about the performance of duty. She refused to leave.

In Concord, on January 14, Bronson Alcott was preparing to hold a series of public conversations in Boston when a telegram arrived from Mrs. Ropes: someone must come for Louisa, and quickly. Bronson immediately postponed his speaking engagements and caught the noon train from Boston, following the same amphibious route that Louisa had taken a month before. In New York, anxious hours ticked by as a heavy fog prevented him from crossing the Hudson. It was not until six in the evening when, under a darkening sky, Bronson Alcott boarded the train in Jersey City that would carry him to Washington. As he tried to arrange himself comfortably enough to steal a few hours' sleep, he had no clear image of the sobering scene that awaited him, and no assurance that he would arrive in time.

Chapter Fifteen

"Death Itself Has Lost All Its Terrors"

As Gideon Welles closed his diary for 1862, he turned to the metaphors of a worried physician. "The national ailment," he wrote, "seems . . . chronic. The disease is deep-seated. Energetic measures are necessary, and I hope we may have them. None of us appear to do enough, and yet I am surprised that we have done so much."[1] In the cold, short days of the ensuing January, a poet immersed himself in a personal mission of healing.

Whitman settled into a third-floor room at 394 L Street, a few doors up from Fourteenth Street Northwest. His living space was modest, but the fireplace exuded a cheery warmth on evenings when the poet sat beside it and wrote letters.[2] Almost immediately, he started paying regular visits to the hospitals. The best part of the living arrangement was the family upstairs, who insisted that he take all his meals with them: William O'Connor, the same man who had lent Whitman money when he had arrived in the capital a few weeks before; O'Connor's wife Nellie; and their five-year-old daughter Jeannie. William, a devotee of radical politics and humanistic reforms, was "warrior-like for the anti-slavery idea"—so much so that Whitman, who distrusted fanaticism even in a noble cause, was somewhat put off. In his better moods, the Irishman impressed people as "earnest, eager, [and] passionate."[3] He was also a man of athletic grace. Whitman felt he had "the movements of a beautiful deer." His body swung with a strong, light step, and a free, defiant bearing.[4] O'Connor was, however, not devoid of demons. Given to episodes of gloom, he would often eat breakfast and depart for his office at the Treasury without saying a word. Sometimes he did not return until the early hours of the morning, giving no account of where he had been.

Still, the time Whitman spent with the O'Connors was far more peaceful than the bedlam of his family's home in Brooklyn. Moreover, in contrast to the puzzled tolerance that Whitman had endured under his mother's roof, the O'Connors virtually worshipped him, and he warmed to their fond attentions. More than a quarter century later, Whitman wiped away tears as he reminisced, "The O'Connor home was my home. They were beyond all others . . . my understanders, my lovers: they more than any others. . . . A man's family is the people who love him—the people who comprehend him."[5]

Walt was Nellie's companion during her husband's mysterious absences. That winter, he laughed with her over hot toddies as the snow came down outside. His jovial mood and luxuriant whiskers reminded her of the Spirit of Christmas. Their attraction observed polite limits, but Nellie felt a deeper pull. On various occasions, she wrote to Whitman in terms that showed both the depth of her feelings and her failure to accurately interpret his:

> I think I never in my life felt so wholly blue and unhappy about any-
> one's going away as I did, and have since, about your going . . . Ah!
> Walt, I don't believe other people need you as much as we do. I am
> *sure* they don't need you as much as *I* do.[6]

Elsewhere, Nellie accused him of not being able to love her as she did him "Because you are great and strong, and more sufficient unto yourself than any woman can be. Besides, you have the great outflow of your pen, which saves you from the need of personal love."[7]

She misread him, and not only because she misunderstood his sexual orientation. Contrary to Nellie's perception, Whitman required tremendous affection, but his overflowing kindness led people not always to recognize that need. Whitman's poems call out insatiably for human contact. His tireless efforts to promote himself also reveal his deep wish to be accepted and beloved. The work that he was starting to perform in the hospitals was strikingly generous, but he also did it to fill the empty spaces in his own heart, and those spaces were immense. Nellie

O'Connor saw Whitman as the most self-sufficient of men. He was often the loneliest one in the room.

Whitman's quest for steady employment quickly stalled. He brought in some income as a real-life Bartleby, copying documents for pay. Writing articles for the press earned a further scattering of dollars. Eventually he found part-time work in the Army Paymaster's bureau. Though he still aimed for a government clerkship, he pursued that goal with only mild interest. He obscurely professed to be looking for work "on literary grounds, not political," a stance that surely perplexed more than one prospective hirer in the most political of American cities.[8] Emerson obligingly sent the letters of recommendation that Whitman had requested. Emerson commended the poet as "a self-relying, large-hearted man . . . entirely patriotic & benevolent in his theory, tastes, & practice." While acknowledging that Whitman's poems had stirred controversy, Emerson called them "more deeply American, democratic, & in the interest of political liberty than those of any other poet."[9] But Whitman did not use the letters for months. After they arrived, he wrote in an unsent letter intended for Emerson that he was mostly "hanging around"; his "plans, wants [and] ideas" were only gradually taking shape.[10]

By mid-January, Whitman was visiting the hospitals daily: the large, well-managed one at Armory Square as well as small facilities on H Street and Eighth Street. Some of the larger ones seemed like towns in themselves. By now, the first shudder he had felt when wandering among the ailing and the abject had faded. Now, the poet was finding "deep things, unreckoned by current print or speech."[11] To those who saw only surfaces, an army hospital was a repulsive place: a mass of wounds and fevers; a nest of attendants made careless and short-tempered by overwork.[12] But Whitman saw something different. From his "good American boys, of good stock, decent, clean well-raised boys," he felt and absorbed "a sweet, unwonted love."[13] Taken all in all, this vision of "masculine young manhood"—of "America . . . brought to the Hospital in her fair youth"—was offering him "the best expression of American character I have ever seen or conceived." Whereas the patrician Wendell Holmes had found his interactions with ordinary Americans a perpetual disappointment, Whitman seemed to feel his pride grow greater with every meeting. He wrote, "I find the masses fully justified by closest contact, never vulgar, ever calm, without greediness . . . no frivolity, responding electric and without fail to affection, yet no whining."[14]

It was a far brighter picture of the nation than he observed inside the whited walls of the Capitol. "Well-drest, rotten, meagre, nimble and impotent, full of gab, full always of their thrice-accursed *party*," the senators and congressmen repelled Whitman.[15] He felt that the government in Washington was in no way "representative," if being representative meant reflecting the best qualities of the electorate. For Whitman, the country's truest representatives were the "freight of helpless, worn and wounded youth" he saw each day in Armory Square. Calling them the "genuine of the soil," the poet rejoiced in this "first unquestioned and convincing western crop, prophetic of the future," these men who radiated a "perfect beauty, tenderness and pluck" that the world had never rivaled.[16] Everything Whitman could spare, he sacrificed for the aid and comfort of the soldiers. Scarcely two weeks after settling in Washington, he wrote to his brother Jeff that his odd jobs had earned twenty-seven dollars. He had spent ten of them on "little items and purchases and money gifts" for the sick and wounded. He considered it a bargain. "I wouldn't take a thousand dollars," he exclaimed, "for the satisfaction it has been to me."[17] Nor did the poet stop there: he prevailed upon Jeff to start a subscription fund among his business acquaintances to furnish more donations.

Whitman reasoned that the men would respond better to a neat appearance. As his dedication to the wards deepened, he put away his slouch hat and open shirt. With his remaining wages, he acquired a fine pair of boots "with magnificent black morocco tops," which he wore over his trousers.[18] He bought a suit, plain but nice, of a dark wine color, which he set off with respectable-looking shirts and a necktie. All in all, he wrote his mother, "You can imagine I cut quite a swell."[19] As to his beard, however, he refused to compromise. In his first five months away from Brooklyn, he never trimmed it once. Each day, he prepared himself meticulously for his rounds, resting up, eating a good meal and taking a bath, and picking out clean clothes.[20] The self-respect that had wavered during the nights at Pfaff's was returning, and it showed.

As far as can be known, Whitman did not venture as far as the Union Hotel Hospital, and it seems that his path and Nurse Alcott's did not cross. However, his rounds did include some strange infirmaries. Early in the war, as one relief worker noted, any building was considered fit for a hospital; even a portion of the Capitol building had been pressed into service.[21] The army also commandeered a wing of the United States Patent Office, which Whitman called "that noblest of Washington buildings." There, he found three huge rooms of the second story crowded to capacity with rows of sick and badly wounded soldiers. Two of the three immense apartments were lined with tall glass cases, housing miniature models of every conceivable kind of tool, machine, or invention. Along the middle of the hall, the floor was packed with a double row of beds. Additional beds were wedged among the display cases. Still more of the sick and wounded were given space in a gallery running above the hall. Illuminated at night, the improvised ward struck the poet as an especially peculiar sight:

> The glass cases, the beds, the sick, the gallery above and the marble pavement underfoot; the suffering, and the fortitude to bear it in the various degrees; occasionally, from some, the groan that could not be repressed; sometimes a poor fellow dying, with emaciated face and glassy eyes, the nurse by his side, the doctor also there, but no friend, no relative—such were the sights but lately in the Patent Office.[22]

Whitman embraced his role as an angel of mercy with surpassing zeal. In earlier times, he had filled his notebooks with the physical traits of the handsome young men he had seen on Broadway. He was still recording the names of young men, but now it was to remind himself of the little gifts he would bring to make their lives more bearable: preserved peaches for Clinton Minzey; a jar of jelly for Joe Armstrong; some oranges for Jimmy Culver; something to read for Tom Butterworth.[23] The poet gave almost every form of sustenance: blackberries, peaches, lemons, preserves, pickles, milk, wine, brandy, tobacco, tea, underclothing, and handkerchiefs all passed into the hands of his grateful boys.[24] He wrote countless letters and read aloud, both from his own poetry and from whatever material a soldier might fancy. It seemed to Whitman, however, that the most precious gift he gave lay in "the simple matter of physical presence, and emanating ordinary cheer and magnetism."[25]

One July afternoon, he sat at the bedside of Oscar Wilber from the 154th New York, a man doubly afflicted by diarrhea and a bad wound. At

Chancellorsville, a Confederate shell fragment had broken Wilber's femur in two. For ten agonizing days, he had lain on the field unattended before finally being evacuated.[26] Wilber asked Whitman to read him a chapter from the New Testament; which one would be Whitman's choice. The poet opened to a passage describing the last hours of Jesus, leading up to the Crucifixion. Then, very slowly, Whitman read the story of the Resurrection. With tears in his eyes, Wilber asked Whitman if he enjoyed religion. The question called for some diplomacy. The poet replied gently, "Perhaps not, my dear, in the way that you mean, and yet, may-be, it is the same thing." Whitman had few doubts that Wilber was going to die. Having done what he could to reassure him, Whitman left him with a kiss that the private "return'd fourfold."[27]

The poet's little kindnesses could not always compensate for the appalling negligence that plagued some of his patients. Whitman wrote with disgust of the ward master who dosed a Delaware private with an ammonia compound intended to be used in washing the soldier's feet. A Massachusetts private at Campbell Hospital fared tragically worse; an ignorant orderly overdosed him with opium pills, killing him.[28] But in the main, Whitman felt proud and humbled to observe that as long as a patient stood a chance, "the surgeon and nurses work[ed] hard, sometimes with curious tenacity, for his life, doing everything, and keeping somebody by him to execute the doctor's orders, and minister to him every minute night and day."[29]

Yet there was a strict efficiency to the way the staff expended their efforts. One began to know at a glance when a patient was likely to die, and once the decline was beyond reversal, the attitudes of the doctors and nurses swung decisively. When it was useless to do more, no more was done. "There is no fuss made," Whitman remarked. "Not a bit of sentimentalism or whining have I seen about a single death-bed in hospital or on the field, but generally impassive indifference."[30] Life and death were a business in this war, and an investor had to perpetually cut his losses.

Whitman knew why the surgeons and nurses could not afford to linger over lost causes. Refusing to engage emotionally was, for some, the only way to avoid being inwardly torn apart. But it was not a course that Whitman could follow. He wrote, "Can you wonder at my getting so attached to such men, with such love, especially when they show it to me—some of them on their dying beds, & in the very hour of death[?]"[31]

Even in the brutal August heat, Whitman kept up his rounds, never missing a day. He rose early, made himself "a capital cup of tea" to go with his bread and preserved fruit, and then was off to the wards, where he worked until three before heading to a restaurant for his second and usually last meal of the day, normally a twenty-five-cent plate of meat and potatoes.[32] After that, he was back again among the wounded.

If Whitman's recollections are to be trusted, he tried earnestly to maintain, even in his nearest encounters with patients, "an exquisite courtesy—man to man. . . . I could say in the highest sense, *propriety—propriety*, as in the doing of necessary unnameable things, always done with exquisite delicacy."[33] Lover of masculine beauty that he was, he could not help being affected by the sights that surrounded him. At times, he was badly shaken by the human ruins that he both adored and pitied. As the news from Gettysburg was arriving, Whitman wrote to his mother, "One's heart grows sick of war . . . when you see it for what it really is—every once in a while I feel so horrified & disgusted—it seems to me like a great slaughter-house & the men mutually butchering each other."[34] Worst of all, however, was the fear that he would grow accustomed to it and accept it as merely normal. He reflected, "I have seen now so much [of the] horrors that befall men, (so bad & such suffering & mutilations, &c that the poor men can defy their fate to do anything more or any harder or worse agony) that I sometimes think I have grown callous, but no, I don't think it is that, but nothing of ordinary misfortune seems as it used to, & death itself has lost all its terrors."[35] Almost as an exercise to preserve his humanity, he used his imagination to trade places with the poor victims, putting himself "in fancy in the cot, with typhoid, or under the knife."[36] Such a degree of sympathy demanded much of Whitman. However, he would have ceased to be himself had he forbidden himself to feel.

The dying private Wilber was far from being the only wounded man whom Whitman caressed. He viewed the soldiers, he said, as he would regard "my own children or younger brothers. I make no bones of petting them just as if they were—have long given up formalities & reserves in my treatment of them."[37]

Some of the kisses were not, it seems, merely brotherly, and the emotions could spill into riskier territory. Whitman's struggle to determine just how much affection he could safely show is reflected in a poem he was writing at the time, a lyric for *Drum-Taps* that he called "Vigil Strange I Kept on the Field One Night." The poem tells of a soldier keeping watch over a fallen comrade, "passing sweet hours, immortal and mystic." The draft of the poem uses the word "darling" three times. It also features the words "sweetest" and "my love." Whitman deleted these terms from the published poem, though he boldly let stand the line "Vigil for boy of responding kisses, (never again on earth responding)."[38] Quietly, he endured the realization that he could not speak his whole heart.

Whitman's attentions fell particularly upon two wounded men: a country boy from Maryland named Lewy Brown, who had joined Company H of Purnell's Legion at the age of eighteen; and a sergeant of the Eleventh Massachusetts Volunteer Infantry named, ever so improbably in retrospect, Tom Sawyer. Brown had taken a bad leg wound the previous summer.[39] The wound had refused to heal, and Brown had lain at the Armory Square Hospital for months. Sawyer was a soap maker from Cambridge. No record apparently survives of his physical condition when Whitman met him. He was perhaps a patient at the Armory, or he may simply have frequented the facility to bring cheer to suffering friends. Whitman did not know with whom Sawyer was "most intimate" at the hospital, but everything suggests that the sergeant was well known there.[40]

Whitman first encountered Lewy Brown on February 19, 1863, as the poet was distributing paper and envelopes in the wounded man's ward. Whitman stayed late to help serve dinner: "pretty fair grub—beef . . . good soup, pudding, potatoes &c." Stopping to talk with Brown, he found him "a most affectionate fellow, very fond of having me come and sit by him."[41] As if by instinct, Brown engaged Whitman's sympathies. He told the poet affecting stories of the cruel ways that officers imposed discipline in the camps, often for trifling transgressions. He particularly deplored the practice of bucking and gagging. The offending soldier would have "a stick [put] in his mouth (like a horse's bit)." The soldier inflicting the punishment would then "tie it with a knot behind the head—then they tie his hands behind him."[42] Brown had seen men bucked and gagged and left to sit for as long as six hours, and sometimes for no worse offense than refusing to bring water for a "female follower of the camp."[43]

Pity and affection were closely linked in Whitman's heart. He was soon writing letters to Brown, showing great concern for the young man's well-being, cautioning him not to "go around too much, nor eat & drink too promiscuous, but be careful & moderate."[44] But carefulness and moderation were not in Whitman's style when he wrote these letters. He greeted the Maryland private as "my darling" and "my dear son & comrade," calling the sight of his face "welcomer than all."[45] Brown was literate only up to a point, and Whitman worried that his own skill with words might intimidate the young man and discourage him from writing back. He gently prompted, "My darling boy, when you write to me, you must write without ceremony . . . you need never care how you write to me, Lewy, if you will only—I never think about literary perfection in letters either, it is the *man* & the *feeling*."[46]

In April, the feelings found open expression. In the fading light of evening, Whitman sat with Lewy as the latter talked of how he planned to get along despite his disability. The young soldier spoke cheerily of his plans to return to Maryland, learn to write better, and to do a little book-keeping. Whitman was moved; barely more than a boy, Lewy seemed "so good, so affectionate." As Whitman prepared to take his leave, he saw Brown raising his face toward him. Whitman wrote to Tom Sawyer, "I put my arm around him, and we gave each other a long kiss, half a min-ute long."[47] The physical contact became a habit, and over the months Whitman's accustomed level of intimacy with all the men grew deeper. In midsummer 1863, he wrote:

> *I have long discarded all stiff conventions (they & I are too near to each other, there is no time to lose, & death and anguish dissipate ceremony here between my lads & me)—I pet them, some of them it does so much good, they are so faint & lonesome—at parting at night sometimes I kiss them right & left.*[48]

Whitman's conduct did not escape the attention of the regular hos-pital personnel, who were not always appreciative. Harriet Hawley, a member of the Sanitary Commission, viewed the poet's intrusions with undisguised loathing. Whitman happened to pass by as Hawley was writ-ing to her husband, and she interrupted her train of thought to vent her revulsion: "Here comes that odious Walt Whitman to talk evil and unbe-lief to my boys. I think I would rather see the Evil one himself—at least if he had horns and hooves. . . . I shall get him out as soon as possible."[49] It is not clear that Hawley also observed Whitman's casual physical intimacies, but he made her uneasy enough as it was.

Whitman's expressions toward Sawyer were the most forthright of all. Whereas the plights of Lewy Brown and others prompted Whitman to test the limits of propriety as he sat at their bedsides, Sawyer's influence sent the poet reeling into a realm of escapist fantasy. In the same letter that recalled his half-minute kiss with Brown, Whitman offered Sawyer both a deep expression of feeling and an extraordinary proposal. He wrote:

> Dear comrade, you must not forget me, for I never shall you. My love you have in life or death forever. I don't know how you feel about it, but it is the wish of my heart to have your friendship, and also that if you should come safe out of this war, we should come together again in some place where we could make our living, and be true comrades and never be separated while life lasts—and take Lewy Brown too, and never separate from him.[50]

If he could not establish his dreamed-of bachelor's hall in this life, Whitman held out hope that he might find it in heaven. He added:

> Or if things are not so to be—if you get these lines, my dear, darling comrade, and any thing should go wrong, so that we do not meet again, here on earth, it seems to me, (the way I feel now,) that my soul could never be entirely happy, even in the world to come, without you, dear comrade.[51]

Whitman wrote Sawyer at least a half dozen more letters. He asked the sergeant up to his room, promising to give him "a good strong blue shirt, a pair of drawers & socks," if only Sawyer would come in person to accept them.[52] Sawyer responded to Whitman's first overture with a letter expressing polite interest, reciprocating the poet's friendship, and offering his hope that they might meet again. Thereafter, as the poet's entreaties mounted in unsettling fashion, Sawyer fell silent. To Whitman, the reason seemed all too clear. He prayed that God might infuse the sergeant's heart with at least some of the feeling that Whitman bore toward him. If Sawyer were to return even a quarter of his affections, he would be satisfied. However, he acknowledged that his pleas for affection might "sound strange & unusual" to Sawyer's ears, as almost certainly they did.[53] Sawyer declined the invitation to Whitman's room and left Washington.

Whitman's urge to elope with Sawyer and Lewy Brown can be understood as only partly a romantic fantasy, for now there was much in his life from which any man might want to run away. The randomness of events and the suffering they brought oppressed him. In a letter home, he exclaimed, "Mother, it is all a lottery, this war, no one knows what will come up next."[54] His nursing work was feeling more and more essential, and he seemed unable to leave it. In June, he noted that he had not missed a day in more than three weeks. He was working chiefly with cases "that would literally sink & give up, if I did not pass a portion of the time with them."[55] He was spending most of his time at the Armory Square Hospital because, in his estimation, it contained by far the most desperate cases.[56] He stayed in the wards from noon until four, and then again from six until nine: seven hours a day surrounded by the most spiritually crushing sights and sounds. Heartsick, he told his mother, "O the sad, sad things I see, the noble young men with legs & arms taken off—the deaths—the sick weakness, sicker than death, that some endure, after amputations."[57] The stream of broken youth and early manhood, "faint & hungry . . . fagged out with a long rough journey, all dirty & torn . . . pale as ashes . . . all bloody," was, for the poet "the most pitiful sight."[58]

He tried to get used to the carnage and to the slow tragedies of illness and death. He could not. More than nine months after his first walk through the wards, he confessed, "I thought I was cooler & more used to it, but the sight of some of them brought tears into my eyes. . . . I have to bustle round, to keep from crying."[59] By the end of July 1863, after the new torrent of casualties had arrived from Gettysburg, Whitman was mentally near the breaking point. "I see so much of butcher sights," he wrote, "so much sickness & suffering I must get away a while I believe for self-preservation."[60] And yet he stayed. In the wards of Washington, he had found a family. He could not abandon them.

It was not only the sufferings of the sick and wounded that were breaking Whitman's heart. About a week before Gettysburg, he had encountered an older man who was overcome with grief and weeping inconsolably. Bitterly the man told of a horror that had unfolded the previous Friday in Leesburg. His son, a private in his late teens named William Grover, had served honorably in a dozen battles with the Forty-Sixth Pennsylvania Volunteer Infantry but had never been granted a single furlough. Seeing that other men had slipped away from the regiment and returned days later without punishment, he had run off temporarily to visit his mother. Grover had been caught, tried, and shot as a deserter.[61] In the young man's execution, Whitman saw an act of plain murder. Decrying "the horrid . . . sarcasm of this life" and too agitated to register his reaction in strictly grammatical form, the poet scribbled out his rage and pity at the monstrous bureaucracy that had made a blood sacrifice of Willie Grover:

> While all this gaud and tinsel shines in people's eyes, amid the count-less officer straps . . . amid all the wind & puffing & infidelity—amid the swarms of contractors & their endless contracts, & the paper money—amid
> out from all this /
> — stalks like a phantom that boy, not yet nineteen years of age . . . stalks forth I say that single simple boy, out of all this huge composite pageant, silently with a bandage over his eyes &—the volley—the smoke—the limpsing, falling body the blood streaming in stains & splashes down the breast[62]

Writing later that summer, Whitman conceded that the army's problem with desertion had become frightful: "O how the conscripts & substi-tutes are deserting down in front, & on their way there. You don't hear anything about it, but it is incredible—they don't allow it to get in the papers."[63] Yet the arbitrariness of Private Grover's punishment stunned him. Could the fight for freedom really demand such acts of tyranny?

The threats to Whitman's peace of mind were no less powerful than the challenges to his physical well-being. In letters, he typically presented a brave face, bragging of his "first-rate . . . health," calling himself "so large and well—indeed like a great wild buffalo," and insisting that the work was "not so exhausting as one might think."[64] At other times, how-ever, he confessed that the atmosphere of the wards was starting to affect him. "I am told," he wrote, "that I hover too much over the beds of the hospitals, with fever & putrid wounds, etc."[65] In the summer of 1863, while assisting with an amputation, Whitman sustained a cut on his right hand. Infection followed. Both his hand and arm grew inflamed, and the vessels of the swollen limb looked like red snakes as they ran up to his shoulder.[66] For three weeks, he was ill. He was lucky, though; the inflammation died down, and he was well again by mid-August. But now Washington's summer heat was playing havoc. He awoke one morning bathed in sweat, and the sun was continually giving him headaches. Fearful that the heat would addle his wits, he took to moving "pretty cautious" and carried a parasol and a fan everywhere.[67] He looked, he thought, "quite a Japanese."[68]

Coming home one evening after an especially harrowing day in the wards, Whitman thought he had seen about all he could stand. He exclaimed to O'Connor, "This war must stop!" O'Connor countered that it must not stop until the slaves were freed. The poet snapped back with an ugly epithet: "I don't care for the niggers, in comparison with all this suffering and the dismemberment of the Union!"[69] The irritability showed how worn out he was becoming. There were better places for a tired man of forty-four.

Displays of kindness and fellow feeling kept him going. One hot August night at Armory Square Hospital, as he sat with a wounded soldier, he heard voices from an adjacent ward, singing to the accompaniment of a melodeon. He followed the sound into the sickroom, parted some mosquito netting so that another man could have a better view, and sat down to listen. The principal singer was a young female nurse, joined by comrades from the other wards. The women sent their melodies up to the rafters, where they resonated charmingly. A handful of patients were singing along. It was a far cry from the grand opera performances of New York. Nevertheless the quaint songs and hymns, in their humbler fashion, pleased Whitman just as much. The simple eloquence of the music, the grateful attention of the wounded men who silently listened, the white sheets and curtains amid the deep shadows—all of it was "a sight to look around upon again and again."[70] The little concert had no discernible influence on the famous poet's life or writing. But one night in Washington, amid desolate scenes, the sweet songs of nurses made Walt Whitman feel happy and good.

Another more frequent sight also helped to raise his spirits. During the stifling summer nights, President Lincoln did not sleep at the White

House. He rode out regularly to the Soldier's Home, a government-run retirement community for disabled veterans some three miles north of the capital. Whitman got into the habit of watching as, guarded by twenty-five cavalrymen or more, the president, dressed in plain black and a stiff hat, rode a gray horse at a slow trot toward his nightly rest. Sometimes Lincoln's son Tad rode alongside on a pony. On other occasions, the president sat in an open barouche. When his wife Mary rode with him, she was also invariably dressed in black, with a long crepe veil: she was still mourning Willie.

Not always taking care to brush the dust from his suit, the chief executive looked liked "the commonest man" until one saw his face.[71] It was dark brown, with deeply cut lines, and suffused with a profound, unspoken sadness. Once the Lincolns passed very close to Whitman, and the abstracted gaze of the President fell directly on the poet. Lincoln bowed and smiled, and it occurred to Whitman that no painter or photographer had captured the subtle, indirect expression of this face. It was a task for one of the Old Masters. "Who," Whitman wondered, "can see that man without losing all wish to be sharp upon him personally? Who can say he has not a good soul?"[72] It was, he thought, the face of "a Hoosier Michelangelo."[73]

Whitman evidently never spoke to Lincoln. How much Lincoln knew about the poet is unclear. A clerk in Lincoln's law office in Springfield recalled that before he became president, Lincoln had read aloud from *Leaves of Grass* to his office mates.[74] Another story relates that, gazing one day from a White House window, Lincoln caught sight of the poet and remarked, "Well, *he* looks like a man."[75] The truth of both these stories is hard to establish. In any case, Whitman felt a tacit bond with the president. It got so that they saw each other almost every day, "exchang[ing] bows, and very cordial ones." Whitman's bows were reverent. He felt that the prairie politician had exercised "an almost supernatural tact in keeping the ship afloat at all . . . and flag flying in sight of the world."[76] He detected in Lincoln "the invisible foundations and vertebra[e] of his character, more than any man's in history . . . mystical, abstract, moral and spiritual."[77] In sum, Whitman wrote, "I love the President personally."[78]

During this same summer or perhaps the early autumn, Whitman thumbed through Alcott's *Hospital Sketches*. He seems to have considered the book a rather slight affair, one that he could easily outdo if he had the chance. In October, he took the bold step of writing to Alcott's publisher, James Redpath, promising a book that would far outshine the work of the Concord storyteller—"something considerably beyond mere hospital sketches." In it, Whitman would paint verbal pictures of the persons, places, and sights he had seen since the previous December. He also offered to advocate for what he called a "very big & needed truth": to call for a revolutionary reordering of the Union's armed forces. He denounced the feudal spirit that had enthroned the current military aristocracy; the army was being led by little people with illustrious names. "Nearly the entire capacity, keenness & courage," Whitman insisted, "are in the ranks." And it was from the ranks that officers should almost invariably be chosen. The army should be "made to tally with democracy, the people."[79] In order to call prompt attention to the problem—and to capitalize on the holiday market—the poet urged that the proposed volume "should be got out *immediately*."[80] But Redpath never issued Whitman's book, and Whitman's privately published *Memoranda during the War* did not appear until 1876. Although Whitman's allusion to Alcott seems slighting, biographer Jerome Loving has suggested that *Hospital Sketches* inspired Whitman to write his most important publication about the war: the collection of poems he titled *Drum-Taps*.[81]

Whitman's employment prospects brightened briefly toward the end of 1863. An old friend, John Townsend Trowbridge, had come to Washington to write a campaign biography for Salmon P. Chase. Ever ambitious, Chase was thinking of challenging Lincoln for the Republican nomination in 1864. Trowbridge used his contact with the secretary as an opportunity to show him the recommendation letter, now months old, that Emerson had written for Whitman. The stratagem backfired spectacularly. When he learned that he was in a position to do a favor for Emerson, Chase was at first pleased and excited. However, the letter's mention of Whitman's poetry jogged the secretary's memory, and his goodwill faded. "I am placed," he said, "in a very embarrassing position."[82] Even before Whitman had come to Washington, Chase had been repulsed by Whitman's literary improprieties; in June 1862, he had seen a copy of *Leaves of Grass* lying on a table and had demanded of its owner, "How is it possible you can have this nasty book here?"[83] Chase now reaffirmed his stand: *Leaves of Grass* "had made the author notorious," and "he did not know how he could possibly bring its author into the government service, especially if he put him in contact with gentlemen employed in the bureaus."[84] Trowbridge remonstrated: Whitman was as quiet in his manners and conversation as any man who had ever entered Chase's home or office. Chase held firm; he had no place for such a man.[85] The secretary, an amateur collector of autographs, slid the letter into his pocket. "I have nothing of Emerson's in his handwriting, and I shall be glad to keep this," he said.[86] When Trowbridge reported his failure to Whitman, the poet allowed himself a moment of bitterness. Noting "some choice scandals" that were currently roiling the Treasury Department, Whitman murmured, "He is right in preserving his saints from contamination by a man like me."[87]

With his employment problem still unresolved, Whitman kept on with part-time work at the Paymaster's office.[88] Sometimes, his desire was simply to find comfort and share it with others. After his landlord sold the boardinghouse on L Street in the summer of 1863, the poet found new lodgings in a third-story back room on Sixth Street, a stone's throw from Pennsylvania Avenue, though on Sundays he still sought out the O'Connors for good conversation and a plate of roast beef, lima beans, and stewed tomatoes.[89] The stairs that led to the poet's room were dreary and dark. Behind the door, the room itself was sparsely furnished, containing little more than a bed, a table, and a couple of chairs stacked high with newspapers. But when the bearded tenant lit his lamp, cleared a space for his friends, and chatted about Shakespeare and *Leaves of Grass*, the hospitality was as warm as in the city's mansions.

A few days after New Year's, 1864, Lewy Brown's wounded leg was finally amputated, five inches below the knee. As the saw did its work, Brown was unconscious, thanks to a heavy dose of ether. Whitman stood in the doorway, watching over his friend. As the stump was being sewn up, Brown came partly out of his stupor. Horribly, the wound started to bleed again, and the surgeon's assistants had to cut the sutures to see whether an artery had opened. When they sewed it up a second time, they did not dare apply more ether; Brown had already been given as much as was safe. Not fully awake but conscious enough to experience pain, Brown felt every stitch. Still standing at the door, Whitman listened helplessly to the soldier's cries and half-coherent blather. When the surgery was finally over, the poet sat beside his exhausted friend as he fought for breath and groaned at the phantom pain from the leg and foot that were no longer his. Whitman described the night that followed as "very bad." He spent that night, and the next one as well, on the cot next to Brown's.[90]

Whitman's poems make liberal use of the word "perfect." Early in his poetic career, he was all but obsessed both with the beauty of the human form and with its erotic idealization. He wrote of perfect men formed from the bodies of perfect women, demanded "perfect men and women out of [his] love-spendings," and declared, "if a thousand perfect men were to appear it would not amaze me."[91] But the hospitals surrounded Whitman with tens of thousands of imperfections. Every day he spent there, he saw his dreams of physical splendor crushed and mutilated. None of these shocks was more jarring than the surgical maiming of Lewy Brown. Yet, as he noted, the "fearful suffering . . . amputations, & weary sickness" brought people "very, very close."[92] Because of their various woundings, Whitman loved Brown and his fellow patients all the more.

In the emotion that we call love, the ancient Greeks observed not one feeling, but three: *philos*, the love that unites brothers; *eros*, or sexual desire; and *agape*, the selfless, charitable love that Paul described in his letters to the Corinthians. Whitman was never an unkind person. Still, in his prewar writings, *eros* crowded *agape* into the margins. The hospitals had no discernible effect on Whitman's sexual drive. Nevertheless, the fulcrum of his loving shifted. Amid the broken bodies, compassion deepened. The need for perfection receded. He cared for worldly things less than ever.[93] The love of comrades that had once been chiefly fueled by erotic dreams was now equally sustained by a need to care for the helpless and to strengthen the weak. *Agape* had risen to the fore. And the crowning beauty of it was that the shift had begun with an act of *philos*: Whitman's journey to Fredericksburg in search of his wounded brother.

Whitman's dreamed-of retreat with Sawyer and Brown after the war never came to be, but his tie with Brown remained warm for several years. Discharged from the army later in 1864, Brown found a job the following year in the Treasury Department, where he was eventually promoted to chief of the Paymaster's Division. Brown lived well into his eighties and died in 1926.

Lewy was starting to get around on crutches when Whitman sought a new adventure. Both as a writer hungry for material and as a devotee of the Union cause, he was regretting the fact that he had witnessed only the aftermath of warfare—he wanted to witness an actual battle. In February 1864, he seized an opportunity to go to the front, "in the midst of the Army," at Culpeper.[94] Though he had no sympathy for the local politics, Whitman felt a true affection for Virginia's countryside. Blighted by war though it was, its fields and hills continually won his admiration. He was moved as well by the people who clung to the stricken land. He passed a night at the home of "a real secesh woman," whose dead husband was related to the deceased Confederate general Turner Ashby. She gave Whitman a good supper, and she made up for her "very faded" clothes with fine manners and educated talk. But the war had made her melancholic. She had remained here amid the chaos and bloodshed on account of her children, and, though forced to live on "chance and charity," she struggled to keep her spirits high. It was necessary to defeat the men this woman loved. Whitman thought one could hardly do so without pity.[95]

Whitman's hopes of seeing a great battle were disappointed; Fredericksburg and the Mud March that followed had taught the Army of the Potomac not to attempt grand offensives in the winter. Still, he caught enough of the spirit of battle to excite him. Awakened one night by shouts, he arose and beheld the "curious sight [of] shadowy columns moving through the night": the unit he had been visiting had received orders to evacuate. Some of the men took time to talk with him. As they unconsciously impressed him with their abundance of "gayety, endurance, and many fine little outshows," Whitman thought about "the most excellent good manliness of the world." In the darkness, the poet watched a regiment file past, its men carrying their usual burdens of guns, knapsacks, and blankets. Though the mud through which the soldiers marched was deep, the poet heard scattered laughter and snatches of song. In that moment, he felt struck by a powerful truth. "It may have been odd," he later wrote, "but I never before so realized the majesty and reality of the American people *en masse*. It fell upon me like a great awe."[96] He wrote his mother, "You don't know what a feeling a man gets after being in the active sights . . . of the camp. . . . The flag, the tune of Yankee Doodle . . . produce an effect on a fellow never such before."[97] Enraptured, and despite never having traveled outside the country, he proclaimed that young American men made all others seem "pale & puny in comparison."[98] It was not so sudden a revelation as Whitman made it sound;

his poems had been celebrating the collective grace and heroism of the American people since 1855. The sight of these soldiers was not so much a revelation as a confirmation. It was as if a wilderness prophet had been proclaiming the existence of a new god for long, lonely years and finally saw his deity face to face.

But the war still had a long course to run, and so, too, did the poet's labors. Back at the hospitals in March 1864, he found them worse than ever. It was bad enough to be among the wounded, but it was still more sobering to care for the men who were simply "getting broke down after two years, or two & a half," by the exposure, the wretched diet, and the contaminated water.[99] The cases of diarrhea alone were "the most horrible . . . you ever conceived of."[100] To make matters worse, many of the hospital personnel had sunk into stony indifference. The coolness that had once been assumed only toward patients who were beyond recovery seemed now to be adopted regardless of the patient's condition. Some of the personnel, perhaps, had been flinty characters to begin with; the sympathies of others had simply been exhausted. It made Whitman sick to think of nurses and orderlies who were "so cold & ceremonious, afraid to touch" the patients whom a decent quantity of loving touches might have healed.[101] Humbug preachers gave the wounded no rest. Scoundrel attendants stole money from under their pillows. Seeing it all, Whitman grew "almost frightened at the world."[102] The poet had personal worries to contend with as well. He was living "very close by the wind" now, and he was soon to economize further by moving to a third-story bedroom on Pennsylvania Avenue near Third Street—a lodging that was, he would soon admit, "not a very good place."[103]

On May 5, General Grant attacked Lee's army at the Wilderness, commencing the bloodiest campaign of the war. A week later, badly wounded men flooded the hospitals, and Whitman found his hands continually full. In previous campaigns, there had been a sharp increase in the number of new patients a few days after a battle, but then it would subside. Now, as Grant pressed Lee incessantly, the wounded kept coming. Whitman was awash in the monotony of death. He wrote home despairingly, "Mother, it is just the same old story, poor suffering young men, great swarms of them . . . every day. All battered & bloody."[104] Fifteen hundred arrived on the 24th of May; four thousand more came up the next morning. A few weeks before the Wilderness, Whitman had written his mother, "You ought to hear the soldiers talk—they are excited to madness."[105] What had then been a mere metaphor for the thrill of anticipation was now a present horror. Whitman had seen terrible physical wounds, but now he was seeing a new kind of casualty. "One new feature," he told his mother, "is that many of the poor afflicted young men are crazy; every ward has some in it that are wandering—they have suffered too much, & it is perhaps a privilege that they are out of their senses." Whitman himself was nearing his limit. "Mother," he continued, "it is almost too much for a fellow, & I sometimes wish I was out of it."[106]

A doctor who knew him saw the strain. In early June, after the flood of casualties had been surging for a month, he told Whitman bluntly that he had "continued too long in the hospitals . . . & [had] absorbed too much of the virus in [his] system." Whitman protested: a day or two of rest would cure his sickness and fatigue.[107] Four days later, however, the caution became a command: the doctors ordered Whitman not to come back to the hospitals. The poet was forced to agree. He had become subject to fainting spells, and he had a persistent bad feeling in his head, a sensation of "fullness & pain." "It is probable," he wrote, "that the hospital poison has affected my system, & I find it worse than I calculated."[108] He thought seriously of going back to Brooklyn, but one thought still held him to his task: "All I think about," he confessed, "is to be here if anything should happen to George."[109]

George, as it happened, was doing well. Thanks to his excellent service record and the depleted number of officers in his regiment, he had been promoted to acting major—a rank that was to be made permanent the following year. George wrote proudly of a day when he led the regiment out to dig rifle pits but came under harassing fire from Rebel skirmishers. Seeing that he was likely to lose quite a number of men unless they were better shielded from the enemy bullets, George rounded up a number of large, empty wooden cracker boxes. He gave each man two boxes and ordered him to crawl out on the line, lie down, and fill the boxes with earth. The makeshift bulwarks worked splendidly, and the men were soon working away with "first-rate protection."[110] George had just slipped away for a cup of coffee when his break was interrupted by a Rebel yell; the Southerners were charging the regiment's position. George's men flung down their spades and seized their rifles. In a few minutes, the Confederates to their front had been repulsed, but a blue regiment to the right of the Fifty-First gave way. In danger of being taken prisoner, George ordered his men to fall back to the next line of breastworks, where other Northern units lay in line of battle. George's command escaped the tight spot with only minor losses, and headquarters praised the regiment for its resourcefulness and coolness under fire.[111]

As George stood firm against the Rebel infantry, Walt's resistance proved less hearty. On June 22, 1864, he left Washington and traveled home to Brooklyn. It took a while to recover from the "faintness, head-ache & trembling & tossing all night" that had made a misery of his last days in the capital.[112] After arriving home, he needed almost three weeks' rest before he was strong enough to leave the house. Slowly, he regained strength, writing a few letters and husbanding his resources until, toward the end of July, his head grew clear and comfortable again. He eased into a pleasant routine, going on regular carriage rides and fishing trips. His habit of hospital visits proved too ingrained for him to set aside. The Brooklyn City Hospital, which had taken in about two hundred recovering soldiers, stood only a quarter mile from Louisa Whitman's house, and it drew Walt irresistibly. It was, in his opinion, the dullest, most low-spirited hospital of any he had seen. Finding that the staff's efforts to entertain the men were utterly deficient, Whitman filled the gap by spending long summer evenings chatting with and reading to the patients. It felt good to give the men some "sympathetic connection with the outside world."[113] Producing peaches, apples, tobacco, and writing paper from his ample pockets, he was again the St. Nicholas of the wards.

Until the end of September, Whitman fell mostly silent. Most days, he kept what he called "old-fashioned hours," rising early, dining at one, in bed before ten.[114] Then, in the first days of October, his calm was shattered: his brother George had been captured near Petersburg, Virginia, and was now a prisoner of the Confederate States of America.

Chapter Sixteen

"Our Fearful Journey Home"

Confined to her upstairs room and forbidden to interact with patients, Louisa May Alcott had almost nothing to do. She had lost her voice, and her distracted mind had made reading either unattractive or impossible. But she could still sew, and she mended soldiers' shirts to pass the time and to make herself useful. This was the same war work that she had done at home in Concord. It had not been enough to satisfy her then. It felt even less satisfying now. Worse than that, it reminded her too easily of her sister Lizzie. Because it was the one productive task she had still been able to do, Lizzie had sewed constantly before she died.

An excellent way to learn the humane side of hospital work is to be a patient in one. Only now did Alcott fully understand the feelings that had made her patients sigh—the impatient wait for better days, the loneliness, the boredom. More and more, she was grateful for the help and concern of her fellow nurses. Every evening, on tired feet, several of them climbed the stairs to her garret. They poked up her fire, rallied her with their conversation, and did what they could to make her cozy during the night.[1] For the first time, Alcott truly knew "how acts of kindness touch and win; how much or little we are to those about us; and for the first time really see that, in coming there, we have taken our lives in our hands, and may have to pay dearly for a brief experience."[2] Her patients, missing her, sent up little gifts and messages, as well as reports of their progress. Each day the doctors also came, checking her lungs and giving doses of medicines whose purposes they did not explain. For the naturally inquisitive Alcott, the physicians' reticence was maddening. Yet they evidently thought it best to keep from her the diagnosis at which they had arrived: typhoid pneumonia.[3]

It took no special knowledge to see that she was getting worse. Her sense of time became uncertain. People looked strange, and peculiar faces began to haunt her room. Through the nights, she waged a quiet battle with weariness and pain. The chorus of her colleagues' voices, telling her to leave, only made her more stubborn. She had promised the army three months, and she was determined to keep her vow. Like Burnside at the Rappahannock, she refused to admit defeat "before I was fairly routed."[4]

After his all-night train ride from Jersey City, Bronson Alcott reached Georgetown on the morning of January 16, 1863, and made his way to the hospital. Nothing in his life had prepared him for the suffering and squalor he witnessed as he walked through the wards, which no amount of effort could make clean or orderly. "Horrid war," he told his journal, "and one sees its horrors in hospitals if anywhere."[5] Upstairs in Louisa's room, another unnerving scene awaited him. The wind whistled desolately through five broken panes in the two windows, and only a pair of sheets suspended over them kept out the cold. Two rickety chairs and a pair of wobbly tables stood here and there. A tin basin, a blue pitcher, and a pair of yellow mugs comprised the toilet articles. Rats scuttled in the closet, and insects darted in and out of view. On a thin mattress, propped up by a few derelict pillows, lay Louisa.

She stared silently at the gray-headed gentleman who stood beside her hearth, rising like a ghost above her. He spoke only two words that she later recalled: "Come home."[6] He had been summoned without her knowledge, and seeing him unleashed a clash of emotions: anger, for she knew that her father's coming meant the end of her service; but also some of the sweetest relief she had ever known. With her father's simple invitation, a spell was lifted. She wrote in *Hospital Sketches*, "At the sight of him, my resolution melted away, my heart turned traitor to my boys, and . . . I answered, 'Yes, father.'"[7] She had not gone to war to impress him, nor had she insisted so long on staying because she thought he demanded it of her. Nevertheless, she knew no one who was more ethically demanding than her father. If he believed that she had worked and suffered long enough, then truly her duty was complete.

Louisa was in no condition to travel, and Bronson decided to wait until she had more strength to bear the risks of the journey. Yet there was risk in staying as well; Bronson could not see how she could gain either in strength or in spirits by staying where she was. Days passed. On the 20th, the doctors approved her departure. That same day, a tragedy down the hall helped to decide the issue: worn down by the same disease that had ravaged Louisa, Hannah Ropes died. Even as the Alcotts prepared to go, the hospital staff was busy draping the building in black in Ropes's honor. A heavy rainstorm prevented their leaving at once. On the 21st, having received a package of items for Louisa's comfort, assembled by Dorothea Dix herself, and accompanied by two nurses from the hospital, the anxious father and his broken daughter began their trek back to Concord.[8] Bronson referred to it later as "our fearful journey home."[9]

For those who awaited her return, like Julian Hawthorne, the long days of anticipation were, "almost like a funeral, with the pain of uncertainty to boot."[10] On his way home from school, Julian stopped each day at Orchard House in hopes that his figurative older sister had returned. Pale and downcast, Mrs. Alcott would shake her head. Louisa's younger sister May had no smiles to give, and her eyelids had turned red. Julian would walk on, heavy-hearted.

Bronson worried that Louisa might not make it home. The journey, he wrote, "required all her strength and courage to come through."[11] Faint and exhausted, Louisa arrived in Boston with her father on January 24th, just missing the four o'clock train to Concord.[12] The two spent the night with Louisa's cousins, the Sewalls. Then, in the company of Hawthorne's daughter Una, the two returned home to Orchard House the following afternoon. Having temporarily set aside her worries, May had been having a carefree day, skating with her friend Frank Stearns and then coming home to a delicious dinner. The mood changed dramatically when she went with Ellen Emerson to meet Louisa's train. "I was greatly shocked," she wrote, "to find Louy so pale & weak for I had no idea she was so sick."[13] Julian was equally stunned; although he could still detect the glimmer of a smile in Louisa's deep and sunken eyes, she seemed only "a white, tragic mask of what she had been."[14]

The day after her sister's return, May felt almost overcome with worry. Louisa had a burning forehead, and her throat seemed almost entirely blocked.[15] That same evening, Bronson reported to Anna, his eldest daughter, that Louisa was "communicative, and though much spent, seemed far better" than he had feared. Despite her discomfort, she was able to sleep, and when awake was able to speak "in her usual lively way."[16] Two days later, on the 27th, he added reassuringly, "She is out of the dangers of that infected place . . . and so likely to be well again."[17] But Bronson was merely trying to spare the nerves of Anna, who was in the latter phases of her first pregnancy. He did not tell Anna that when Louisa arrived home, she had been "delirious and devoured with fever," not only convinced that her family did not wish to see her but also persuaded that Orchard House had lost its roof.[18] Her delirium was so deep that, just four days later, when Bronson told her the story of their homecoming, she had no recollection of anything he mentioned. Surprised by the twists and turns of his narrative, she laughed over it, "as if it were a tale of her imagining."[19] During a lucid interval, she was permitted to peruse a newspaper account of the death of Mrs. Ropes. It was perhaps not the wisest choice of reading material for the still-struggling patient.

To cool Louisa down, the doctors ordered her head shaved. Her beautiful, carefully tended hair, a yard and a half long, all came off. Her hallucinations, however, only intensified. As Abba gently advised her "Lie still, my dear," Louisa conceived the delusion that she was being addressed by "a stout, handsome Spaniard, dressed in black velvet," who claimed to be her husband and caressed her with his "very soft hands." She developed "an awful fear of the Spanish spouse, who was always coming after me, appearing out of closets, in at windows, or threatening me all night long."[20] Her mother could only look on, astonished and helpless. "Her mind wanders," she told her brother, "and she has whole hours uttering . . . things."[21] Still trying to free herself from the imagined Spaniard, Louisa made desperate appeals to the pope in gibberish that seemed to her like Latin. At other times, she thought she was back at the hospital, tending millions of sick men who could neither die nor get well.[22] Then she would abruptly panic, "flying off the bed in terrible confusion."[23] A variety of fears tormented her: a mob of Baltimore secessionists was trying to get her; she was to be hanged, stoned, or burned to death as a witch; one of the Georgetown doctors and two of the nurses were tempting her to join them in worshipping the Devil. The worst of the fits seemed to come twice every twenty-four hours. For Louisa, the intervals of calm were as bad as the attacks themselves; in between crises, she lay in dread of the feverish dreams that she knew would come again and again.[24]

Having sat with Louisa at the Union Hotel Hospital and having ridden with her on the long journey home, Bronson knew more vividly than anyone else in the family how close she had come to dying. He set aside his preparations for a conversation series to assist at her bedside. His journals became dotted with notations that he hastily scribbled when a moment's respite came: "Wait on L."; "Watch and wait on our patient"; "Sit with Louisa into the night, reading from Gospels and Herder."[25]

By taking turns watching Louisa, Bronson and Abba managed to get some sleep every night. Observing the strain that his friends were undergoing, Emerson hired a woman to handle the Alcott family housework. His intervention, however, did little to soothe Abba's disquiet. Ever protective of her independence, Mrs. Alcott accepted the help only reluctantly. "While I am able to move," she protested, "I will not have a nurse. It would not relieve my anxiety, and might hinder my own action." To her brother Sam, Abba fumed, "I hate Drs. and all their nonsense." She firmly believed that if Louisa were "to be saved from violent death or the slow ravages of chronic ailments," her survival would not be due to physicians and medicines, but to "faithful, vigilant care." Abba's determination to give Louisa the best support she could was matched only by her futile outrage against the cosmos. She meant to help her daughter "if all the rest of the world goes to the dogs, for *we* have been cruelly dealt by in it—and owe it no more sacrifices of flesh and blood. If we have sinned greatly against The Lord, and these are the compensations he takes, he is welcome and I am sure will be satisfied, if the amount of personal suffering and misery caused, is the true test of the penalty."[26]

Charitable and reform-minded to a fault, Abba Alcott had reached her limit. She had toiled and starved at Fruitlands in hopes of bettering the world, and the family had been reduced to poverty. Her daughter Lizzie had brought food and comfort to a wretched family in New Hampshire and had come home with a fever that eventually killed her. Now her most beloved child, who had gone bravely to fight for freedom and the Union, lay in her upstairs room, feverish and raving. Abba had had quite enough of being Christlike. She told her brother, "Divinity has its uses, but humanity has its necessities. . . . Oh my dear Sam, can we not save our dear children—will they fade from us? I tremble in my soul and my heart takes no comfort, for I cannot see God in all this."[27]

Anna sent oranges, a welcome balm for Louisa's sore throat. On January 29, when her patient said she might soon be strong enough to write letters, Abba began to feel hopeful. She started to take time away from the sickroom without feeling guilty, and resumed some of her housework with something like cheerfulness. But the dark days were not over. The next day Louisa was restless and distracted throughout the night. Her conversation grew disconnected, and her fever mounted. On the first of February, she was delirious yet again. Doctor Bartlett remained optimistic, but he had no more remedies to propose. There was nothing to do but wait.

Then, on February 4, the fever finally broke, and Louisa came back to her right mind. She began to sleep comfortably again, and when awake she asked impatiently for food. Bronson wrote to Anna that weeks of careful nursing still lay ahead. However, he affirmed, "We trust the main perils are past, and that her recovery dates from this hour."[28] Someone held up a mirror to Louisa's face. The image she saw there was "queer, thin, [and] big-eyed," and she did not recognize herself. Then came another moment of distress. Trying to walk, she discovered that she could not, and she began to cry at the realization that her legs "wouldn't go." But after several days they finally did, and on the 22nd, she was able to leave her room.[29] May delightedly told her diary, "Louy downstairs & dressed for the first time. She is very feeble but entirely herself. She has on her new flannel dressing gown & it is very pleasant to see her about again."[30] When Louisa had recovered enough to reflect on her ordeal, she looked upon it as "new & very interesting."[31] Now that she was alert enough to notice it, the dreary process of her recovery wore upon her: "Such long long nights—such feeble, idle days, dozing fretting about nothing." The hallucinations had been so vivid that she still thought they were real and "deluded mother & May with the most absurd stories, so soberly that they thought them true."[32]

More days passed, and Louisa was able to be carried out of the house to sit in the sunshine. Julian Hawthorne brightened as Louisa's sociability and good cheer came back to her. Even now, however, he was unsettled by "occasional tones in her voice and expressions of eyes and mouth that indicated depths of which she could not speak."[33] Though her appearance remained somewhat disquieting, she was now capable of some light literary work. She reread the ode to Thoreau she had composed on her night watch at the hospital and added some lines. Then she put the piece aside. It might do for her scrapbook, she thought, but not much else.

On March 28, Bronson went to Boston to attend a meeting of the

Atlantic Club, where he talked awhile with Oliver Wendell Holmes Sr. It is not known whether the two men compared notes on the heroes of their respective families. A snow descended as Bronson made his way homeward. At some point that day, he received joyful news from his son-in-law. Returning home that evening, he strode through the door of Orchard House, snow-covered and beaming. Anna, he announced, had delivered a fine boy. As Abba cried, May laughed, and Louisa crowed over the addition of a boy to "the feminine family," Bronson seemed dreamily apart from the hubbub. A delighted smile adorned his face as he kept repeating, "Anna's boy, yes, yes, Anna's boy."[34]

Week by week, Louisa's strength returned. At the end of the month, when her mother went to help Anna with the baby, Louisa felt strong enough to clean the house. The work felt congenial, she thought, "for an invalid." Her recovery coincided with the delicious moment when spring returned to Concord. The bluets and cinquefoils bloomed, and the white maples resounded with the hum of honeybees, just in time for Louisa to see and hear them as she started to emerge regularly from the house.[35] The world seemed beautiful and new. She, too, felt reborn. "To go very near to death," she told her journal, "teaches one to value life."[36]

Seldom far from her thoughts was the life of the soldier she had treasured but lost. She had known him so briefly that she was already unsure of his last name; in her diary for April, he turns up as "John Sulie."[37] As her father's apple trees budded and blossomed, she had much reason to recollect the stalwart Pennsylvania private. The letters she had sent her family from Washington, which would later be lost, had made the rounds among her parents' friends. They had been seen by Moncure D. Conway, an abolitionist minister who, interestingly enough, had been born and raised in Falmouth, Virginia, the site of the Union army's camp at Fredericksburg. During the same month as Antietam, Conway had joined with Franklin Benjamin Sanborn, a friend from his college days at Harvard, in founding an antislavery newspaper they called the *Boston Commonwealth*. Finding her letters to be full of "every variety of ability," Conway teased and cajoled Alcott: she should really consider revising her letters into a series of sketches for his paper.[38] Conway was now out of the country, having embarked on a lecture tour in the United Kingdom to rally support for the Union cause. But his co-editor now pressed his invitation to Alcott.

Frank Sanborn had been a friend of the Alcott family since 1853, when, at age twenty-one, he had met Bronson at the Harvard Divinity School. Sanborn had achieved notoriety in 1859 as a member of the Secret Six, the band of radical reformers that covertly funded John Brown's raid on Harpers Ferry. Louisa had known Sanborn at least as early as 1856, when she had often gone to the home of Theodore Parker, another member of the Six, to listen to Sanborn, William Lloyd Garrison, and Wendell Phillips debate the politics of freedom.[39] In 1858, Sanborn had been, along with Emerson and Thoreau, a pallbearer at Lizzie Alcott's funeral. In April 1860, when Sanborn was illegally arrested in Concord in connection with his role in John Brown's raid, Louisa had denounced his detention as a kidnapping and grew so indignant that she did not "dare to unbottle [her]self for fear of the explosive consequences."[40]

Like Conway, Sanborn considered Alcott's hospital letters "witty & [sym]pathetic," and, it seemed, just the thing for a public eager for touching accounts of the country at war.[41] Alcott did not find her letters nearly so engaging. Her artistic reservations, however, were overcome by the promise of money. In between sewing shirts and gowns for her new nephew, she settled into the task, calling up memories of her days amid the charitable chaos of the hospital and the long, sleepless nights when she had presided "like a massive cherubim . . . over the slumbering sons of man."[42] Recasting her experiences as a work of fiction, she chose for her alter ego a funny name worthy of Dickens: Tribulation Periwinkle. In the Victorian language of flowers, periwinkles stood for early friendship and the pleasures of memory.[43] Alcott, whose first book was called *Flower Fables* and whose use of floral imagery in *Little Women* was pervasive, surely knew of these associations. Given that *Hospital Sketches* centered on a friendship destined never to have any other phase than "early," and on memories that were only occasionally pleasant, Alcott's decision to call herself Nurse Periwinkle was a piece of calculated irony.[44]

Alcott chose for the centerpiece of her sketches an episode that she titled "A Night." The mildly fictionalized narrative told of a New Jersey boy driven half-mad by the terrors of Fredericksburg, who, in his ravings, counted the invisible men who fell around him and clutched at Alcott's sleeve to pull her away from the path of an imagined artillery shell. It also recalled a Pennsylvania amputee whose wound fever had driven him from his bed and made him hop about like a meditative stork on his remaining leg. But more than half of the sketch and most of its reverence were devoted to John Suhre and his quiet, patient struggle with death. Writing with an ease and eloquence she had never before achieved, Louisa crafted her account of Suhre's last days, honoring his piety, praising his fortitude, bearing witness to the humble life that, but for the harshness and tragedy of its end, would never have known any fame at all. Having paid him all the tribute she could give, she bade him farewell, mistaking one last time the place from which he had come:

> Then I left him, glad to have known so genuine a man, and carrying with me an enduring memory of the brave Virginia blacksmith, as he lay serenely waiting for the dawn of that long day which knows no night.[45]

Alcott was fond of noting that everything about her seemed to "go by contraries."[46] The projects on which she pinned her brightest hopes typically fizzled with the public, whereas the ones in which she placed the least confidence won acclaim. To Alcott's astonishment, the sketches she prepared for the *Commonwealth* "made a great hit, & people bought the papers faster than they could be supplied." Another discovery may have gratified her more than any other: the sketch she had called "A Night" had won particular favor. "I was glad," Alcott wrote, "for my beautiful 'John Sulie' was the hero, & the praise belonged to him."[47]

Months later, to Alcott's surprise and delight, her sketches continued to be noticed and talked about.[48] A letter came from Henry James Sr., the father of the soon-to-be-famous novelist, lauding her "charming pictures of hospital service."[49] In June Alcott received two offers to bring her sketches out in book form. The first of the two suitors was James Redpath, a Scottish-American journalist. Redpath had been an avid apologist for John Brown, whom he had interviewed just days after Brown's notorious massacre of proslavery settlers in Kansas. Also vying for Alcott's attentions was the publishing house of Roberts Brothers, represented by the editor Thomas Niles. Experienced and opportunistic, the thirty-eight-year-old Niles had been an assistant to James T. Fields, reading submissions for his press at the time Fields had told Alcott that she couldn't write. Niles had joined Roberts Brothers earlier in 1863 and was presumably eager to add to the house's stable of authors. Niles offered more money than Redpath. However, the Scotsman understood, as Niles did not, the Alcottian penchant for charity and self-sacrifice. He proposed a novel arrangement: for every clothbound copy sold, Alcott would receive five cents. An additional dime, however, would be set aside in a fund, administered by Redpath, to benefit the widows and orphans of the Union dead. Such generosity, coupled with Redpath's credentials as a backer of Brown, to whom Louisa alluded as "St. John the Just," was beyond her power to resist. Redpath got the contract.

Enthusiastically, Alcott sandwiched her three magazine sketches between two new introductory chapters and a postscript, increasing the length of her text by about two-thirds. On August 25, Alcott received her copies of the book, which she praised as "quite a neat little affair."[50] At year's end, she noted in her journal that she had received 200 dollars for her *Sketches*, a figure suggesting that the edition had sold out. Alcott was not an avid reader of her own press notices, and there is no way of knowing which ones actually came to her attention. She surely would have been pleased, however, that both the *Boston Evening Transcript* and the *National Anti-Slavery Standard* offered particular praise for her portrait of John Suhre.[51] *The Taunton Daily Gazette* also singled out the episode of Suhre's death:

> [H]er characters are all heroes, and were ready to her hand . . . she has not only reached their hearts but taken all restraint from their deepest and tenderest emotions. It is thus that we have her picture of the Virginia blacksmith—for it is beyond the creative power of genius.[52]

Alcott's pride in her achievement eventually mingled with disappointment; Redpath, she later concluded, lacked skill as a publisher, and she firmly believed that *Hospital Sketches* had earned her far less money than it should have.[53] Nevertheless, she had gotten her first real taste of literary fame.

As Louisa had been working on *Hospital Sketches*, her father found another way to nudge her writing reputation upward. Looking among her papers, he found her poem on Thoreau. Proudly, he read it aloud to Hawthorne. Impressed, the novelist asked Louisa for a fair copy. Now came the time for some backdoor diplomacy. Hawthorne enlisted his wife Sophia to show the poem to Annie Fields, the wife of *Atlantic Monthly* editor James T. Fields—the same authority who, barely a year earlier, had told Louisa to stick to her teaching. To his credit, Fields now changed his mind; he wanted the poem for his magazine. While still polishing the last of her sketches for the *Commonwealth*, Louisa meticulously revised "Thoreau's Flute," even asking Fields's wife to critique her revisions. As Alcott punningly explained, "If my little ship is to be launched in the *Atlantic*, I must attend to her build & rigging & see that she does not founder for want of proper ballast."[54] Fields accepted her revision and printed it in the September issue. Soon, Alcott enjoyed three pleasures at once: the gentle revenge of watching Fields eat his words and publish hers; the honor of becoming a new star in the literary firmament of New England; and the delight of a ten-dollar check, which, for a struggling denizen of Apple Slump, meant almost as much as seeing her name in print. And yet, for her literary lessons, her emergent success, and the recovery of her father's love, Alcott had a price to pay.

As her health returned, no one seemed to notice that some of her symptoms had nothing to do with typhoid. She had wanted to eat but found she "had no mouth to do it with, mine being so sore & full of all manner of queer sensations it was nothing but a plague."[55] Abba had also observed that Louisa's throat, teeth, and tongue were "in the most tender and sensitive state," but she had no idea what to make of it.[56] Even after Louisa's recovery was otherwise complete, peculiar, intermittent pains continued to nag her, cropping up in one place, only to vanish altogether before recurring, maddeningly, in another. For years, Louisa had no explanation for the searing headaches and fatigue that continually bedeviled her. Then, on a visit to France in 1870, after enduring two weeks of miserable pains in her leg, she sought the advice of Dr. William Kane, a former army surgeon who was spending time in Dinan. The gray-haired Englishman asked about Louisa's medical history: had she ever been treated with the medicinal compound known as calomel? Alcott remembered: the doctors in Georgetown had given her calomel to treat her fever. Dr. Kane's response was that of both a successful detective and a fellow sufferer. While serving in India, he had contracted jungle fever and received the same medicine. He had "never got the calomel out of him."[57]

Calomel was the popular name for mercurous chloride, a medication that had been highly popular in America for decades. At the Union Hotel Hospital, as at others, the wartime doctors used it liberally. The substance was not as toxic as either pure mercury or its chemical cousin, mercuric chloride. However, when improperly stored, it could break down into these more lethal forms. If unaccompanied by any agent to help flush it from the body, the medicine amounted to a poison. When Alcott had received her treatment, some physicians were already doubting calomel's usefulness and fearing its effects. In 1860, Oliver Wendell Holmes Sr. had denounced the overmedication of American society. "The popular belief is all but universal," he said, "that sick persons should feed on noxious substances." He cited in particular the almost patriotic devotion to mercurous chloride. He lamented, "The American eagle screams with delight to see three drachms of calomel given at a single mouthful."[58]

Later in 1863, the Union army's surgeon general ordered the suspension of treatment with calomel, though the interdiction was largely ignored.[59] The ban came too late for Alcott. As Dr. Kane described it, the drug "lies round in a body and don't do much harm till a weak spot appears when it goes there and makes trouble."[60] The explanation was vague, but it identified the likely cause of Alcott's misery. The toxins ineradicably lodged in her system had permanently compromised her health.

No amount of worldly success and no degree of personal redemption could fully compensate Alcott for the loss of her health. The most beautiful girl runner, and the young woman who had, with mild exaggeration, boasted of never having known a day of illness, was gone forever. Yet in another sense, Alcott knew how lucky she had been. In January 1863, she had barely escaped death. Half a year later, she was one of the most famous women in Massachusetts, marveling at her newly found status as a literary celebrity. Bronson's pride poured out into the pages of his journal that August. He wrote, "I see nothing in the way of a good appreciation of Louisa's merits as a woman and a writer. Nothing could be more surprising to her or agreeable to us."[61]

In September, a company of Concord soldiers, having fought at Gettysburg two months earlier, returned home. In expectation of their arrival, the normally placid town was, as Alcott described it, as wildly excited as it could be "without dying of brain fever." Flags flew everywhere, and it seemed that every available space had been festooned with wreaths and "Welcome Home" banners. The town drum corps, which various enlistments had reduced to eight small boys with eight large drums, practiced for the soldiers' arrival, beating out a ragged but earnest tattoo.[62] May Alcott and Julian Hawthorne, now a recent Harvard admittee, were at work for hours, as they and the other youth of the town mixed enough lemonade "to flavor Walden Pond."[63] Wearing white frocks, the Alcott women and twenty or more young women, "the prettiest in the village," as Julian recalled, laid long boards across sawhorses for tables and covered them with their brimming cups. Louisa wore her nursing uniform for the occasion and supervised the festivities.

Almost sixty years later, Julian Hawthorne recalled the gleam of the gun barrels, the bronzed faces, and the dust-covered uniforms. With no music to herald their approach, the company of sixty young veterans came up along the same road from Lexington that the redcoats had followed in 1775. They passed in front of Orchard House. Julian and the rest of the throng waved flags and shouted; he saw a tear run down Louisa's cheek. But the column of soldiers showed no sign of stopping, and it seemed for a moment as if the welcome had been prepared in vain. Then, all at once, the captain called the men to a halt. He gave a second command: "Parade rest!" Taking this moment as their signal, the maidens of Concord snatched up the cups of lemonade and carried them to their heroes. Louisa went with them. After a cordial but brief greeting to the captain, she mingled with the company, speaking with them in the soldier's language that she knew so well and, for the moment, becoming once again the mother and sister she had been to "her boys" in Georgetown. As she moved among the soldiers, it seemed to Julian that a part of her was far away, again in the hospital among the wounded and the dying. "Deep tremors passed through her," he wrote, and "her smiles had the pathos of remembered pain."[64]

The ranks re-formed. The young ladies stepped back, and the company wheeled to face the Alcotts' venerable house. As one, the men lifted their caps in salute to the nurse who, like them, had risked her life in the nation's service. They raised a hearty, grateful cheer for Nurse Alcott and marched on.

✷

ALCOTT TOLD HERSELF THAT IF SHE had the strength to do it, she would go back to Georgetown the next day and resume nursing. The trials she had undergone had tested and proved her courage. Her sacrifices had, in her view, sweetened her character. Though it had been "a rough school," the hospital had led her to a deeper faith, in both God and herself.[65] These benefits, coupled with the wisdom of experience, made up for all the pain. Both Alcott's innate kindness and her ingrained ferocity against all things Southern had driven her to enlist. Following the war, although her contempt for the Confederate cause was unabated, the lessons of forgiveness predominated. She was kinder now to herself as well. Her old habit of self-accusation diminished, and her despairing evening on the Mill Dam faded to a distant memory.

Alcott's service in the aftermath of Fredericksburg brought her many more benefits than her first popular literary success and a handful of life lessons. The first of these was a crucial shift in one of her most vital personal relationships. Bronson had been moved profoundly by his daughter's work to save the Union and by the ultimate price she had almost paid in serving her country. He wrote of her toil and collapse, "That was our contribution to the war and one we should not have made willingly had we known the danger and the sacrifices."[66] Bronson had lost one daughter. The near-loss of a second stunned him. The courage she had shown opened his eyes to what a remarkable person she was. Whereas he had once seen her as a self-centered rebel, he now regarded her as an emblem of noble self-sacrifice, and he prized nothing more highly than the surrender of oneself for a noble cause. After he rescued her from the Union Hotel, Bronson seems never to have written another negative word about her.

Alcott's sense of herself as a writer also transformed. The *Sketches*, she observed a decade and a half later, "showed me *'my style,'* & taking the hint I went where glory [a]waited me."[67] Before her journey to Georgetown, Alcott's writings had been immersed in fantasy: stories of daggers and damsels; of glow-worms and dew-elves; of rival painters in Renaissance Italy—in short, any subject that had taken her away from cooking, cleaning, and Concord. Her own life, which she had previously considered ordinary and unworthy of literary investigation, now stood revealed to her as possessing simple warmth and human appeal. She had experienced nothing else that matched the drama of the hospital. Nevertheless, since childhood she had been unconsciously acquiring the material for stories of earnest strivings and humble virtues. In time she would tell these stories.

Her discovery of a fresh and distinctive tone mattered just as much. The key, perhaps, was that *Hospital Sketches* had begun as a series of letters to her family. In writing them, Alcott had made no pretense to high literary art. The intimacy of the communication and the knowledge that their recipients would read them in a generous spirit gave her the freedom to be unguarded and confessional. She could cast aside both melodrama and reserve. Writing for her family, she could be herself, and that self was appealing. Reviewers of *Hospital Sketches* expressed surprise at the volume's tone: astonishingly, despite their sad subject matter, Alcott's scenes were, in places, funny. In the infuriating wartime bureaucracy, in an overweight officer trying to squeeze his eminence into a painfully tight uniform, and in the plight of a demure New England nurse obliged to wash a host of naked men, Alcott found a wealth of comic instances. In clumsier hands, the humor might have clashed awkwardly with the hideousness of the war. Alcott, however, played light against dark with marvelous skill, making her readers chuckle and cry at almost the same moment. To her great surprise, she found herself being hailed as a budding master of the tragicomic. "I find," she wrote, "I've done a good thing without knowing it."[68]

Someone who certainly did know it was Thomas Niles. Although he and Roberts Brothers lost the competition to publish *Hospital Sketches*, Niles kept imagining ways to enlist Alcott's talent. In September 1867, he sought her out with a new idea. He foresaw a large, as yet untapped market for books for girls. He wanted Alcott to write one. Alcott demurred. Apart from her sisters, she had not known many girls while she was growing up, and the ones she had known she had not much cared for. Besides, at the same time that Niles extended his offer, she had been invited to edit a children's magazine called *Merry's Museum*. The job would entail some drudgery, but its guarantee of five hundred dollars a year sounded better than the more speculative prospect of Niles's book. After an abortive attempt at writing for Niles, Alcott set the project aside and took the editorship.

Niles, though, did not give up. The following spring, Bronson approached him with a proposal of his own. Now sixty-eight but aiming for a literary comeback, Bronson was writing a set of philosophical pieces he called "Tablets." He thought it would be a fine idea for Roberts Brothers to bring out his book and a "fairy book" by Louisa at the same time. Niles had no interest in a fairy book. However, if Louisa were to submit the girls' book that he had previously suggested, then that volume and *Tablets* might be published more or less simultaneously.

Though her misgivings persisted, Alcott gave in. Without relish, she began work on a novel about four sisters, modeled on herself and her siblings. "I plod away," she wrote, "though I don't enjoy this sort of thing."[69] Recollecting the fun she had shared with her sisters two decades earlier, she added, "Our queer plays and experiences may prove interesting, though I doubt it."[70] By the end of June 1868, she had finished a dozen chapters, which she considered dull. She sent them to Niles, half hoping that their indifferent merits would send him looking for another author who could do better. Niles, too, found the chapters lacking. Then, however, he happened to show them to his niece, who adored them. Sensing a hit, he urged Alcott to press on without delay. She threw herself into the project. Fighting exhaustion and headaches, she submitted over 400 pages of manuscript to Niles on July 15. By early October, *Little Women* was in the bookstores and selling briskly.

The contours of *Little Women* owe much to Alcott's experience of the war. In the novel, as in life, a family is divided when one of its members goes to war on an errand of mercy. Alcott had gone as a nurse; the father of the fictitious March family goes as a chaplain. In both the real story and the invented one, the absent member falls dangerously ill and must be rescued from an army hospital: Alcott by her father and Mr. March by his wife. And, in each instance, the action leads to the second-eldest daughter's loss of her "one beauty": the phrase Alcott used both in her journal after her doctors had ordered her head shaved, and in the novel when Jo March sells her tresses to finance Marmee's journey to save her husband.[71] Moreover, the importance of *Little Women* to its first generation of readers cannot be separated from the war. The March sisters must learn how to carry on in the absence of their loving father. Their struggles spoke directly to girls and their mothers across the country whose fathers and husbands were never coming home. *Little Women* became so cherished in part because it showed that families deprived of their male leadership could still create lives of courage and joy, sacrificing for the Union but deriving strength from one another. For such families, Alcott became, as she was fond of signing her autographs, "Very truly your friend." *Little Women* owed its very existence to the war. Alcott undertook *Little Women* only at the insistence of Thomas Niles, and Niles might hardly have known Alcott was alive without *Hospital Sketches*. In a real and undeniable sense, *Little Women* was born in the Union Hotel Hospital.

Like a handful of other books, *Little Women* has changed the lives even of those who have never read it. For generations, it informed and helped to redefine the acceptable conduct of young women in the culture at large, so much so that girls who never opened the book were still guided by its counsels. Alcott's re-envisioning of young feminine behavior worked in two directions. Of course, *Little Women* argued in favor of moral and emotional self-restraint, encouraging its readers to subdue their vanity, impulsiveness, and anger. At the same time, however, the novel stood for a freeing of restrictions with regard to ambition and creativity. *Little Women* made it seem a little more normal for girls to run and climb trees. It approved of girls who wrote plays and performed them on Christmas, and of women who tried to become successful writers or went to Europe to study art. The March sisters helped to awaken American girls to the possibilities that awaited a young woman with enough pluck and enterprise to grasp them. Reading *Little Women*, Alcott's multitudinous fans saw the selves they wanted to become.

Just as importantly, *Little Women* answered the question of how America might redirect its sentimental inclinations in the wake of a war that had dramatically shown the dangers of romantic thinking. After the Civil War, it seemed evident to some that the catastrophe had been brought on by religious and quasi-religious zeal. The fiery speeches of the abolitionists, the evangelical urgings of *Uncle Tom's Cabin*, the passion shown by Thoreau and others in their defense of John Brown—all of these had overthrown America's capacity for peaceful resolution. The positive result had been the freeing of the millions of enslaved. The cost, however, had been over 750,000 dead. Alcott herself had felt the vengeful ardor of the times, and she wrote with passion for freedom and for Union. Yet, in *Hospital Sketches*, in *Little Women*, and in many of the books that followed, Alcott disconnected sentiment and romanticism from the ferocity of war and reattached it to more positive goals: to mercy, to healing, and to the sweetness of shared struggle. Standing at the very beginning of the American canon of children's literature, *Little Women* infused its nascent genre with values of community and tenderness. They were values that were already ingrained in Alcott before she arrived in Georgetown, but which her nursing experience solidified. If a more militant sentimentality had led the nation into war, the gentler heart of Alcott led it out again.[72]

Remarkably for an author whose pre–Civil War forte was escapist tales of fantasy, *Little Women* maintains a more realistic focus than a great deal of classic children's literature that came after her. Tom Sawyer, Dorothy Gale, and Peter Pan seek or inhabit realms of flight from responsibility and unpleasantness, even away from growing up itself. By contrast, the March sisters, with no Jackson's Island, Oz, or Neverland to run to, stand their ground, facing their problems and preserving a clear line between the real and the fanciful. Having confronted reality in its starkest form, Alcott had no desire to spare her readers from essential truths: that daily life poses moral challenges; that one's character is proven by how one confronts them; and that the most powerful enemies a typical child must face are not monsters or pirates, but rather the flaws in one's own nature.

Also remarkably for a children's story, *Little Women* ends with none of its protagonists having realized their most fondly cherished dreams. Meg's vision of a lovely home with "heaps of money," like Jo's and Amy's yearnings for authorial fortune and artistic fame, goes unfulfilled. Even modest Beth, who hopes for nothing more than to stay at home and care for her parents, is thwarted by her early death. Despite all the broken dreams, however, *Little Women* ends optimistically. Having conquered their inner failings and discovered more modest satisfactions, the three surviving sisters have arrived successfully at adulthood. Surprisingly secular for its time—the sisters, although their father is a minister, never set foot inside a church—the book concludes with a trinity of its own creation: its penultimate sentence ends with the triad of "motherly love, gratitude, and humility."[73] The lessons of the Union Hotel Hospital had been handed forward.

On December 11, 1862, Union troops fought from house to house as they made
their way through Fredericksburg. It was here that Arthur Fuller insisted,
"I must do something for my country." *Library of Congress, LC-USZ62-132748*

That same day, Union artillery devastated the town. This once-handsome street lay largely in ruins.
Library of Congress, LC-DIG-ppmsca-32890

Frail and professorial in this photograph *(left)*, Arthur Fuller became almost unrecognizably robust in a flattering engraving. *Left: Library of Congress, LC-ppmsca-40577. Right: PD-US-expired*

Arthur *(left)* posed in the early 1850s with *(l. to r.)* his brother Eugene, his sister Ellen, his mother Margarett, and his brother Richard. *MS Am 2594, Houghton Library, Harvard University*

Arthur's elder sister Margaret was possibly the most brilliant woman in America in the first half of the nineteenth century. A tragic shipwreck ended her life at forty. *Houghton Library, Harvard University*

Jane Pierce, wife of the future president, looks approvingly at the couple's son Benny. Arthur Fuller sat only a few feet away from the Pierce family as the train they were riding derailed. *Collection of the Pierce Brigade at the Pierce Manse, Concord, NH*

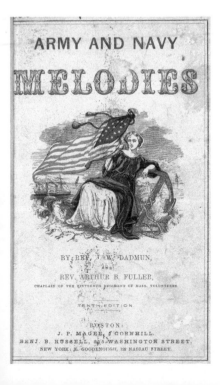

Arthur Fuller was deeply proud of his edited collection of military hymns, *Army and Navy Melodies. Widener Library, Harvard University*

Intelligent but touched by melancholy, Louisa May Alcott sat for this photograph in the 1850s. *Used by permission of Louisa May Alcott's Orchard House*

When Alcott became an army nurse, her father Bronson observed that he was sending his only son to war. *Used by permission of Louisa May Alcott's Orchard House*

Alcott's nursing service nearly killed her. As the young writer hovered between life and death, her mother Abigail, pictured here, lamented, "We have been dealt cruelly by [the world] and owe it no more sacrifices of flesh and blood." *Used by permission of Louisa May Alcott's Orchard House*

Aged prematurely by her struggles with typhoid pneumonia and mercury poisoning, Alcott thought she resembled a relic from the Great Boston Fire. *Used by permission of Louisa May Alcott's Orchard House*

Alcott denounced the Union Hotel Hospital as a "pestilence-box." It lived up to her description.
Library of Congress, LC-DIG-npcc-28306

John Suhre wrote only one surviving letter. Its first and last pages are reproduced here for the first time. *Courtesy of the Historical & Geneaological Society of Somerset County*

Dunker Church, Antietam. Confederate infantry swept past this modest house of worship before driving Holmes's regiment out of the West Woods, seen here in the background. *Library of Congress, LC-DIG-cwpbh-03384*

After Antietam, President Lincoln paid an uneasy visit to General McClellan. The president's stovepipe hat made the two men's difference in height impossible to ignore. *Library of Congress, LC-DIG-cwpb-04352*

Behind the stone wall at Fredericksburg. James Longstreet's infantry defended Marye's Heights. A Confederate artillerist had prophesied that "a chicken could not live on that field" once the graycoats opened fire on it. *Library of Congress, LC-USZ62-134479*

At the mansion known as Chatham, across the river from Fredericksburg, Walt Whitman beheld a pile of severed limbs. *Library of Congress, LC-DIG-ppmsca-35122*

COLUMBIA. "Where are my 15,000 Sons—murdered at Fredericksburg?"
LINCOLN. "This reminds me of a little Joke—"
COLUMBIA. "Go tell your Joke at Springfield!!"

In a blistering political cartoon, Columbia excoriates President Lincoln
for the slaughter at Fredericksburg. *Wallach Division Picture Collection, The New York Public Library*

Lincoln presenting the Emancipation Proclamation to his cabinet. After the calamity at Fredericksburg, the nation wondered whether he would pull the document off the table. He did not.
Library of Congress, LC-DIG-pga-02502

Chapter Seventeen

The Song of the Hermit Thrush

Since bidding farewell to Walt at the end of 1862, George Whitman had done some traveling. In February 1863, with the rest of the Ninth Corps, the Fifty-First was ordered to Newport News. In March, after spending a ten-day furlough with his family in Brooklyn, George returned to discover that his regiment and the rest of the Ninth Corps had been ordered out of Virginia. He and his comrades were sent to Kentucky, where they remained until June. Then they were sent to Mississippi to support General Grant's siege of Vicksburg, which fell on July 4, the day after Pickett's Charge at Gettysburg. Under the command of Sherman, George and the Fifty-First then swung eastward to Jackson, Mississippi, to engage with a Rebel force led by Joseph E. Johnston. They marched through dust and terrible heat, subsisting mostly on green corn and drinking from whatever little ponds lay in their path, no matter how impure the water. Hunger, heat, and disease were now worse enemies than Confederate bullets. When Johnston withdrew, abandoning Jackson to the Union forces, George got a fore-taste of the brand of warfare that Sherman would bring to Georgia and South Carolina the following year. "The western armies," George wrote to his mother, "burn and destroy every thing they come across, and the same number of men, marching through the country, will do three times the damage of the Army of the Potomac."[1]

George's regiment slowly made its way back to Virginia, passing several uneventful months in Kentucky, Tennessee, and Maryland before finally being called on to take part in the Wilderness campaign. Before rejoining the Army of the Potomac, the Fifty-First took part in a grand review of the troops in Washington on April 25, 1864. Knowing that George's regiment would march in the review, Walt picked his way through the large crowd at Fourteenth Street and waited three hours for the Fifty-First to pass. The review was no fancy-dress occasion. The endless ranks of marchers were "worn & sunburnt & sweaty, with well-worn clothes & their bundles & knapsacks, tin cups & some with frying pans, strapt over their backs." As befitted a haggard but proud fighting force, the only items they carried that looked neat and proper were their muskets, which shone as bright as silver.[2]

At last Walt caught sight of his brother, looking tanned and hardy. "George stands it very well," he later told his mother, "& looks & behaves the same good & noble fellow he always was & always will be."[3] Breaching the decorum of the occasion, Walt stepped out of the crowd and fell in alongside George, distracting him so much that George failed to take notice of President Lincoln and General Burnside as his unit passed the reviewing stand and forgot to salute them. George was annoyed at his lapse, and probably with his brother for having caused it, but his irritation faded as Walt walked along, telling him the latest news from home.[4]

The Fifty-First took hard punishment in the new campaign. At the Wilderness, the regiment lost seventy in killed and wounded, and George lost nearly half his company. Only a week later, the Battle of Spotsylvania Court House cost the regiment another twenty casualties. George himself survived a pair of close calls. At the Wilderness, a projectile had smashed into the canteen he carried on his hip, wrenching away half the vessel but leaving George untouched. As the fighting died down at Spotsylvania, George thought that he had come through without incident. Then a comrade pointed to his coat. One side of it had been "riddled & wrinkled & slit in the most curious manner ever seen." It had been shredded by grapeshot. Astonished, George could not recall when or how this latest brush with death had happened. A soldier from the regiment told Walt that George was the luckiest man in the army.[5]

By mid-September 1864, after the siege of Petersburg was well underway, George wrote that he was having easy times. But the regiment was battered. Although it claimed 800 men on paper, the regiment could put only about half that many in the field. It was being sustained solely by vast infusions of new recruits; George reported that 650 new names had been added to the rolls of the Fifty-First since the previous winter. The army as a whole was in similar straits. Between the outset of the Wilderness campaign in May and the middle of September, a jaw-dropping sixty percent of the Union soldiers who had begun it had been killed, wounded, or captured. To General Meade, the grinding, appalling war of attrition brought to mind a nursery rhyme: he told General Grant that the two armies were like the two cats of Kilkenny that had fought until there was nothing left of either of them. Grant did not dispute the grim analogy. Instead, he replied, "Our cat has the longer tail."[6]

The end of the fighting came for George Whitman on September 30, 1864, at the Battle of Peeble's Farm. As the Ninth Army Corps attacked near Poplar Springs Church, the Fifty-First found itself on the front line, at the far edge of the Union left, forming part of a brigade under Colonel John Curtin. A broad swale, poorly defended, separated them from the much stronger remainder of the Union force. Confederate division commander Henry Heth, whose men had been the first Rebels into battle at Gettysburg, saw the weakness. He sent a regiment of North Carolina men charging into the gap. The Federal troops to the right of the swale fell back in disorder. Curtin's brigade was completely cut off, with no means of retreat.

The Fifty-First made a bold attempt to fight its way out, charging into the Fifty-Second North Carolina and momentarily turning the enemy's flank. But the Rebels counterattacked, supported by the Horse Artillery that had once been the pride of John Pelham. The final blow came from dismounted Confederate cavalry, under the command of Rooney Lee. George proudly wrote afterward that the regiment stood and fought until it was entirely surrounded.[7] But then the fight turned hopeless. Colonel Curtin made a break for it, spurring his Kentucky thoroughbred toward safety. Just as the horse was leaping a fence, a Confederate soldier shot the animal dead. Curtin's forward momentum carried him out of his saddle and over the fence. The colonel scrambled to his feet and didn't stop running. His command was not as lucky. Their resistance fell to pieces. Of the three regiments on the far left—roughly a thousand men—only thirty-seven soldiers evaded capture. The Fifty-First surrendered and were taken prisoner to the last man. The official report listed two men killed, ten wounded, and 332 missing or captured. Later that evening, in the darkness, sixteen of the New Yorkers escaped. George was not among them. The Fifty-First New York, the heroes of Burnside's Bridge, had ceased to exist as a fighting force.[8]

In Brooklyn, Walt was feeling tolerably well, though he still had not regained the "unconsciously hearty" state of health he had enjoyed before his illness.[9] At his mother's home in early October, he scanned the papers for news of the battle. When the regiment's fate was confirmed, he commented that the Fifty-First was entitled to a newspaper obituary.[10] He feared that George might soon be in line for a death notice as well. Walt had seen survivors of Confederate prison camps, and their stories haunted him: "hard, ghastly starvation . . . rags, filth, despair, in large, open stockades, no shelter, no cooking, no clothes."[11] Walt had heard that, because there were too few of them to keep order by ordinary means, Confederate prison guards had taken to "shooting the prisoners literally just to keep them under terrorism."[12] The thought of George in such conditions made him almost sick with worry. Mrs. Whitman knew about these atrocities as well; reading accounts in the papers of how the prisoners were being mistreated, she would set her head in her hand and sit silently for an hour afterward.[13]

From his captivity, George tried to allay his family's fears. He managed to send a letter home two days after his capture, assuring his mother that he was "in tip top health and Spirits, and . . . tough as a mule and shall get along first rate."[14] Fearing this letter had been lost, he had sent another one three months later, and then . . . nothing. The silence brought the Whitman family close to despair.[15]

Adding to the Whitmans' torment was the knowledge that no prisoner exchange was in the offing. Earlier in the war, the two sides had freely made such exchanges on a one-to-one basis. But by the time George was captured, General Grant perceived that the South was running out of manpower. Trading prisoners, who could then re-enlist with their respective armies, would improve the ratio of Southern troops to Northern, potentially lengthening the war and costing more lives in the long run. No matter that the prison camps, both North and South, were degenerating into death traps; the Union would not abet the Rebels in replenishing their ranks.[16] Whitman had heard that President Lincoln favored instituting a general exchange of prisoners, but that the War Department was resisting him. To the poet, it seemed as if Secretary Stanton was bent on giving the administration "a name for bad faith which will tell for years to come." Venting his rage on a scribbled scrap of paper, Whitman emphasized the words, *"Their blood is on our own heads."*[17]

The day after Christmas brought a melancholy present to the Whitmans' doorstep: George's trunk of belongings arrived from Virginia. For hours, no one could bear to open it. When they did, Whitman's mother looked over the contents: papers; a book or two; a revolver; a diary; a case of photographs of his wartime comrades, many of them already killed; and the dress uniform George had received and worn with such pride. It was a solemn inventory. By that time the family had not heard from George since October 3. For all they knew, they were piecing through the personal effects of a dead man.

The same day, an anguished Walt dashed off a blistering editorial to the *New York Times*, decrying the "hunger, cold, filth, and despair" of the prisons—conditions that, even when they did not kill, reduced men to "mental imbecility." Denouncing the government's policy as "more cruel than anything done by the Secessionists," Whitman claimed that over a quarter of the "helpless and most wretched men" who had been taken prisoner had already been "exchanged" to the next world by death from starvation. He asked, "Mr. Editor, or you, reader, do you know what a death by starvation actually is?"[18]

Walt imagined what it might be like to write "a perfect poem of the war, comprehending all its phases, its passions, the fierce tug of the secessionist, the interminable fibre of the national union, all the special hues . . . of the actual battles, with colors flying, rifles snapping, cannon thundering . . . and all the profound scenes of individual death, courage, endurance & superbest hardihood."[19] Such a book, he knew, was beyond his power to write; to attempt it, he would have needed to see the army in combat, and all his efforts to observe a battle had failed. Yet, as 1865 began, he had high hopes for a collection of poems that he meant to bring out, dealing principally with the war. By January 6, his manuscript was complete.[20]

Whitman called the new collection "Drum-Taps." In his view, as a work of art it surpassed *Leaves of Grass*. It now seemed to him that his earlier work had erred on the side of exuberance. In its drive to embrace and celebrate the whole of life, *Leaves of Grass* had, he thought, fallen out of balance, evincing a spirit of excessive abandon and "perturbations" from which *Drum-Taps* had entirely gotten free. The new work was "adjusted in all its proportions"; while still a work of passion, its emotions were under control.[21] Whereas the earlier poems had sometimes rambled, *Drum-Taps* did not contain a single word that was not indispensable to its effects and meanings.

What pleased Whitman most was the way in which he had captured the historical moment. He had caught "the pending action of this *Time & Land we swim in*, with all their large fluctuations of despair and hope, the shiftings, masses, & the whirl & deafening din." He had warmly portrayed "the beautiful young men, in wholesale death & agony, everything sometimes as if in blood color, & dripping blood."[22] Whitman was a sadder, more disciplined man than before the war. His work was more restrained and sadder, too, but it was precisely their melancholy consciousness that had enabled these poems to express "an undertone of sweetest comradeship & human love," accented by "clear notes of faith and triumph."[23] The love that Whitman expresses in *Drum-Taps* was richer than before, matured and deepened by the knowledge of pain.

This love animates the most autobiographical and best poem in the collection, "The Wound-Dresser." If it merely offered a description of Whitman's ministrations to the injured and the helpless, the poem would be a valuable document. Its artistry, however, resides in the poet's agile manipulation of perspective and time. Written while Whitman was immersed in his hospital work, the poem imagines a future time when, as an old man, the narrator is asked by children to recall his struggles in the war. The old man's narration commences with a story more proper to George than to Walt. Trying to impress the children, the narrator waxes hyperbolic; his early lines are almost a caricature of courage: "Soldier alert I arrive after a long march cover'd with sweat and dust, / In the nick of time I come, plunge in the fight, loudly shout in the rush of successful charge, / Enter the captur'd works."[24]

But then these martial visions fade and subside, as the persona chooses to "dwell not on soldiers' perils or soldier's joys." The scene abruptly shifts to a hospital, the narrator now seeing himself "bearing the bandages, water and sponge," as he goes straight and swiftly to his wounded compatriots. For the narrator, the transition is from recollection to reverie; the hospital passages begin "in silence, in dreams' projections." The old soldier's fantasy of caring for his wounded comrades is a dream so strong that it displaces and outweighs his heroism in the field. But if "The Wound-Dresser" is really Whitman's own story, the displacement works in reverse: the gentle bard who quietly envies the valor of the foot soldier sets aside his fantasy of glory and embraces the true tale of his humble service in the wards.

The remainder of the poem recounts the quiet courage of loving stead-fastness. The narrator no longer speaks of the quick, adrenaline-fueled charge into the fight, but of enduring constancy: "I am faithful, I do not give out . . . I sit by the restless all the dark night." As the poem ends, the children who asked the old man for a good war story or two—and who have been forgotten since the opening lines of the second stanza—are likely puzzled; the man's reflections do not end with guts and glory, but with a vision of healing, reconciling love, in which dream and memory merge: "Thus in silence in dreams' projections, / Returning, resuming, I thread my way through the hospitals, . . . I recall the experience sweet and sad, / (Many a soldier's loving arms about this neck have cross'd and rested, / Many a soldier's kiss dwells on these bearded lips)." No reader can ignore the erotic tint of these kisses. But these are different feelings from those of the Calamus poems of five years earlier, for during these years Whitman's understanding of love had grown richer in its appreci-ation of loyalty and sacrifice and selflessness. In Whitman's verse as well as in his life, *eros* had yielded at least partly to *agape*.

Shortly before Lincoln's second inauguration, Whitman went walking by the Capitol after sunset. He decided to go in, and no sentry stopped him. Feeling less critical of the building's finery than in former times, he wandered the corridors with "more satisfaction than ever."[25] All lit up, the illuminated rotunda looked very fine. He looked up at the inside of the dome, which had been mere empty space when the war began, and he gazed for a long, long time. The sight filled him with comfort. The building was starting to look complete, and the Union was looking that way, too. In the legislative chambers, both the House and the Senate were holding late, extended sessions. The hard, good business of democracy was flowing on.

At the same time, Whitman and his brother Jeff were redoubling their efforts to locate George and bring him home. Had they known where he was, the truth would have filled them with horror. George and the other captured officers from the Fifty-First had been taken to Danville, Virginia, and incarcerated at a facility fashioned from six erstwhile tobacco ware-houses. As an officer, Whitman was assigned to Building Number One, though the numerical designation scarcely implied better treatment. By the admission of the Rebels' own prison inspector, A. S. Cunningham, the prisoners at Danville were "in very bad condition, dirty, filled with vermin, little or no ventilation." They had almost no clothing, no blan-kets, and a very small supply of fuel. The emissions from the coal stove rendered the air fetid and impure.[26] Major Abner Small of the Sixteenth Maine recounted the inhuman circumstances: "None of us had more space to himself than he actually occupied, usually a strip of the bare hard floor, about six feet by two. We lay in long rows, two rows of men with their heads to the sidewalls and two with their heads together along the center of the room, leaving narrow aisles between the rows of feet."[27] Inspector Cunningham considered it remarkable that the prisoners could even exist in such crowded, toxic conditions.[28] But many of them were not continuing to exist. About five men died each day, mostly from star-vation. A prisoner's daily ration of food was twenty-four ounces of corn bread, into which a good deal of cob had been ground along with the ker-nels. The men supplemented this fare as best they could, using what one officer delicately called "nameless portions of the animal economy"—his euphemism for stewed rat meat. Overall, Cunningham viewed the prison at Danville as deficient in "a sense of common humanity."[29]

As George languished, Walt and Jeff sought to redeem him. They were working in the dark until January 19, when a slip of paper from George, dated November 23, reached their mother by way of an exchanged chap-lain. George wrote that he was at Danville, but hastened to reassure the family that he was "well and hearty."[30] The next day came a longer letter from November 27, in which George again made light of his imprison-ment and emphasized his continued good health. However, the chaplain offered a different view. He told the Whitmans that George, like all the other inmates, was "starved, miserable & naked, to the last degree."[31] Moreover, from November to January is a long time in a prison camp, and the thought of all that George might have suffered during his silence made Walt more eager than ever to seek new information and to secure his brother's release.[32]

Walt returned to Washington before the end of January. Braving the freezing weather, he tracked down a lieutenant colonel who knew the best ways of sending boxes of food through the lines to prisoners. Walt heard from two other officers of the Fifty-First, also at Danville. Having apparently learned from George about Walt's penchant for good works, they urgently requested salt pork and hard tack. Jeff assembled a more ambitious shipment that included ham, smoked beef, coffee, potatoes, and canned peaches. He also threw in some much-needed items of clothing. The brothers sent their gifts, trusting to providence that they would not fall prey to some dishonest courier. Ever the optimist, Walt thought there was a fair chance that the packages would get through to George.[33]

The harder task was having George set free. Jeff had heard that although regular exchanges of prisoners were still suspended, the right pressure in the right place could prompt a "special exchange." Jeff also knew that General Grant had been grateful for the support he had received from John Swinton, the managing editor of the *New York Times*. Swinton, conveniently, was a friend of Walt's. Jeff noted, "Grant is just now in a position where a few words of censure in . . . the *Times* would do him great injury."[34] He was positive that if Swinton could be prevailed upon to send Grant a letter pleading George's case, the general would pull the necessary strings to give George his freedom. On February 3, Walt wrote his letter. Invoking the deep distress of his mother, whose health was being overcome by worry, Whitman begged Swinton to petition Grant to order a special exchange for George and a fellow officer, Lieutenant Sam Pooley, of whom George was especially fond.[35] The next day, Whitman also applied to a paper-pushing major general, Ethan Hitchcock, asking him, too, to engineer an exchange. Despite having made callous public statements that only cowards were taken prisoner, Hitchcock granted the request at once. However, this action meant little by itself, for the official machinery could be expected to move slowly.[36] The wait would go on.

On February 17, "a heavy, sulky night" made more dismal by a "beating snow storm," Whitman opened his window and stared out into the darkness. The silence was broken now and then by the sound of drums and bugles.[37] He had been trying to keep up his work around the hospitals but had been feeling the need to taper off. He still spent most of the day on Sundays with the men, but otherwise he came by for a few hours from time to time, mostly by day but occasionally in the evenings. His health was making it hard to do more: the doctor said that his system had been attacked by malaria—a disease that Whitman called "tenacious, peculiar and somewhat baffling."[38]

Earlier that day, Whitman had heard an encouraging report: General Grant had ordered a special exchange for George and Lieutenant Pooley. However, two other pieces of information that arrived the same day dampened the joy. Whitman received a printed list of Danville's prisoners, dated February 1. George's name was not there. The other news was more ominous. About a week earlier, the Danville prison had caught fire, and much of the facility had been destroyed. "Just now," Walt wrote, "it is all suspense."[39] Suspense was better than despair.

Meanwhile, George had been passing through dark times. Inadequately clothed, he had developed a lung complaint. His fellow prisoners looked concerned as he started to fail. "O, I feel well enough," he would tell them. "There's nothing the matter with me, of any account."[40] But one day George slipped into delirium. For three days, he lay on the bare floor before being transferred to the hospital. Once there, he worsened. He was out of his head much of the time, and, for a week, his strength ebbed. As he lay there one night, a thrill ran through him—a thrill that told him he was dying. In the dark, he called for a male nurse to bring a light, a pencil, and a piece of paper. He wrote to his mother that his last night had come. Ever the businessman, he scribbled out for her the amount of money that the government owed him. Then he told the man to blow out the light. He closed his eyes, expecting not to open them again.[41]

✳

ON THE SAME DAY THAT GRANT had ordered George's special exchange, federal policy shifted, and a general exchange of prisoners was finally authorized. A little more than a week later, Whitman heard to his delight that all the prisoners at Danville had been sent north. But his hopes, briefly raised, were summarily dashed. On the 26th, word came that neither George nor any of the other officers of the Fifty-First were among the released prisoners. Whitman instantly presumed that the Southerners were playing foul—that they had deliberately held these men back and were perhaps even moving them deeper into the interior of the country. Heartsick, Walt fell into a depression. The quick successions of exaltation and despair, so common in the war, made a wearisome pattern.

But these months were not all fretting and misery. One blustery night in the late winter, Whitman said good night to some friends at their house on Capitol Hill, threw a blanket around his shoulders, and caught a horse-drawn omnibus on Pennsylvania Avenue. The conductor was Peter Doyle, a twenty-one-year-old Confederate veteran who had deserted in April 1863 and had sworn allegiance to the Union the following month. Whitman was the only passenger. Something about the poet attracted Doyle, who later recalled what happened next:

> The storm was awful. Walt had his blanket . . . he seemed like an old sea-captain. . . . It was a lonely night, so I thought I would go in and talk with him. Something in me made me do it, and something in him drew me that way. . . . We were familiar at once—I put my hand on his knee—we understood.[42]

Whitman did not get off at his stop. He rode back with Doyle to the vicinity of the Navy Yard, where Doyle kept house. Whitman's own room stayed empty that night.

✳

IN THE PRISON CAMP, GEORGE HAD rallied. The morning after he wrote what he thought would be his final words to his mother, the hospital attendants, presuming that he would be dead, had come to clean out his pockets. To everyone's surprise, he had awoken, Lazarus-like, with his fever declining. The doctor pronounced him well. On February 19, George was released from the wretched warehouse and sent to Libby Prison in Richmond on the first leg of his journey home. By some minor miracle, he found the boxes "filled with Clothing and grub" from his family, which had never made it to Danville, awaiting him there. "The way we went into the eatables while we were in Libby," he wrote, "were a caution." By the 24th, he was in Annapolis, Maryland; "If ever a poor devil was glad to get in a Christian country it was me."[43]

Walt was the last member of the family to learn that George was safe. George's letter from Annapolis went to his mother. On February 28, the *Times* ran a list of about 500 parolees, including George. Mrs. Whitman assumed Walt had seen the notice and gone to Annapolis to meet him.

But Walt still knew nothing. Although the date is unclear, he traveled to Annapolis but somehow missed his brother. What he did not miss, however, was the shock of seeing several hundred men issuing from one of the transport ships. Only three were able to walk. The rest were carried ashore and set down. They lay still, with horrible looks in their eyes, many of them lacking enough flesh on their lips to cover their teeth. "Can those be men?" wrote Whitman in dismay, "those little livid-brown, ash-streak'd, monkey-looking dwarfs?—are they really not mummified, dwindled corpses?" Whitman knew that some crimes could be forgiven. This, however, he could never excuse. Its perpetrators had steeped themselves "in blackest, escapeless damnation."[44] And for all Whitman knew, George had not even made it this far.

Whitman's mother forwarded him the good news about George on March 4, the day of Lincoln's second inauguration. Still not knowing that his brother had been spared, Whitman attended the president's swearing-in. He saw Lincoln riding in his two-horse barouche, his son Tad seated by his side. Four years earlier, Lincoln had ridden this route surrounded by a dense cluster of cavalrymen, eight horses deep, their sabres drawn, and sharpshooters had been stationed at every corner. Now no soldiers guarded the president. Lee's army, dug in at Petersburg, was virtually powerless. Surrender was coming; an air of peace and safety ruled the day. Whitman came close enough to the president to study his countenance. The chief executive looked "very much worn and tired; the lines, indeed, of vast responsibilities, intricate questions, and demands of life and death, cut deeper than ever upon his dark brown face." This surface, though, was just the patina of care and time. Beneath it, Whitman still saw "all the old goodness, tenderness, sadness, and canny shrewdness."[45]

As Lincoln began his second term, Whitman found himself frequently looking up at the night sky. It had been a foggy, leaden winter in the capital, with periods of bitter cold and "some insane storms." But the weather was turning now. Whitman rhapsodized that neither "earth nor sky ever knew spectacles of superber beauty than some of the nights lately here." The "western star," as Whitman called Venus, had never looked so large and clear. As it hung close to the moon, like a child near its mother, the planet seemed to Whitman "as if it told something, as if it held rapport indulgent with humanity, with us Americans." Its shining miracle "suffused the soul." The ancients would have taken this heavenly sign for a portent. With the war almost over and the president preparing for four more years, the omens could only be favorable.

The day after the inaugural, George returned to Brooklyn, to what must have been an extraordinary reunion. Mrs. Whitman, prepared for the worst, had cause for great relief: George was thin and worn down but was at least ambulatory and also in a highly conversational mood.[46] He told his mother of how he had expected to die of his fever and how he had inexplicably recovered. His constitution, George said, had saved him.[47]

In mid-March, Walt secured a two-week leave from his job and came up to Brooklyn, eager to reunite with George and to see about finally getting *Drum-Taps* to press. Although George had pains in his legs that kept him awake at night, he was in fine spirits and, despite all he had endured, was eager to return to service when his furlough expired on April 4.[48] Realizing that his brother was weaker than his pride would allow him to admit, Walt offered to get George's leave extended. Sulkily, George at last admitted that he was too ill to resume his duties.[49] He consented to the extended furlough and stayed in Brooklyn.

Walt had never enjoyed a home visit more richly.[50] The publication of *Drum-Taps*, however, had stalled. The printers complained that production costs had spiked. They advised Whitman to wait ten days or so until the price of paper and typesetting fell.[51] Whitman obtained an extension of his leave; he would not return to Washington until April 17.

Thus, Walt was still in Brooklyn when, on April 1, Union troops under Major General Philip Sheridan smashed a division of Lee's army at Five Forks, forcing the Confederates to abandon their defense of Petersburg and precipitating the fall of Richmond a day later. Walt's intercession to extend George's furlough had deprived Confederate soldiers of their last chance to kill him. On Palm Sunday, April 9, Lee surrendered the broken remnant of the Army of Northern Virginia at Appomattox Court House. By the time George rejoined the army, there was no fighting left to do. He was sent to Alexandria, where he assumed command of the Prince Street Military Prison. The jailed had become the jailer.

Walt's relationship with Peter Doyle had begun to flourish. They were on their way to becoming, as Doyle put it, "the biggest sort of friends."[52] Stuck in Brooklyn, however, the poet was unable to join the young man for an evening out on April 14. For that evening, Doyle purchased a second-gallery ticket at Ford's Theatre to see the Tom Taylor farce *Our*

American Cousin. He had no great interest in the play. However, he remembered, "I heard that the President and his wife would be present and made up my mind to go." The president came late. Presumably, Doyle stood and applauded with the rest of the crowd when the presidential party arrived around 9 p.m. and settled into a box overlooking the stage. The actor Harry Hawk, playing the role of Asa Trenchard, had just ad-libbed a joke, and he thought the ovation was for him. "That line went well!" he whispered to his co-star, Laura Keene.[53]

At 10:15, another of the play's characters, Mrs. Mountchessington, rebuked Trenchard for not knowing the manners of good society. The actress flounced offstage, leaving Hawk alone under the lights. "Don't know the manners of good society, eh?" said Hawk. "Well, I guess I know enough to turn you inside out old gal—you sockdologizing old man-trap!"[54] Then, before Hawk could quite finish his line, everything stopped making sense. "I heard the pistol shot," Doyle recollected. "I had no idea what it was, what it meant—it was sort of muffled. I really knew nothing of what had occurred until Mrs. Lincoln leaned out of the box and cried, 'The President is shot!' "[55]

Through the telegraph wires, news of the catastrophe raced to New York. The following morning, as Louisa Whitman made breakfast for Walt and herself, it was already in the papers. That breakfast went uneaten. With a mechanical attachment to routine, Mrs. Whitman made the other meals that day as well, but all were left untouched. Walt wrote, "We each drank half a cup of coffee; that was all. Little was said. We got every newspaper morning and evening, and the frequent extras of that period, and pass'd them silently to each other."[56]

That afternoon between four and five, Walt left off his somber reading, made his way to Manhattan on the ferry, and walked alone up Broadway.[57] He took out a notebook and jotted his bleak impressions without pausing to structure them into sentences: "Black—business public & private all suspended, & the shops closed—strange mixture of horror, fury, tenderness, & a stirring wonder brewing." In a city where Whitman had been accustomed to seeing color, vibrancy, and "countless gay flags" everywhere, he now saw everything eerily draped in a funereal monochrome, mounting, it seemed, all the way to the heavens: "Black, black, black—as you look toward the sky—long broad black like great serpents slowly undulating in every direction." The weather turned foul, and Whitman's notebook jottings assumed an almost apocalyptic tone, then died in mid-thought: "Drip, drip, & heavy moist black weather . . . the rain sent the women from the street black clothed me only remained . . . Black clouds driving overhead—the horror, fever, uncertainty, alarm in the public—every hour brings a great history event on the wires—at 11 o'clock the new president is sworn—at 4 the murder is. . . ."[58] Whitman let his idea trail off into nothing. All seemed blank and broken, and in the "sulky, leaden" street, the poet was reminded of "continualy [sic] moist tears."[59]

By the thousands, grieving citizens converged on Washington, exceeding the capacity of the city's hotels and boardinghouses to hold them. Still in Brooklyn, Whitman had gone back to revising *Drum-Taps*. He could not bear to see the collection into print without any material responding to Lincoln's death. On April 19, as President Andrew Johnson and assembled dignitaries paid their respects to Lincoln's remains at the White House, Whitman delivered the hastily composed "Hush'd Be the Camps To-Day" to his printer in hopes of filling the gap. Still dissatisfied, however, he ended up postponing the book's release until October. Returning to Washington on April 22, two days before the viewing of Lincoln's body in New York, Whitman missed one final chance to gaze at the president. Lincoln's death had left Whitman, the most communicative of men, almost incommunicably alone.

On scraps of paper, using a black pencil, Whitman began jotting notes for an elaborate poem that would express both the community and the loneliness of loss. On two sheets, he set down a litany of words and phrases that he linked with sorrow and dejection: "melancholy dismal heavy-hearted tears . . . lamenting mute grief eloquent silence bewail." Tentatively, exhaustively, he searched his vocabulary for the right expressions: "obscurity partial or total . . . darkness (as the gloom of a forest— gloom of midnight) . . . Calamity disaster something that strikes down."[60] These preliminary jottings pointed in no obvious direction. But on some other scraps, in irregular writing, as if he were holding the paper in the palm of his hand, Whitman set down some information he had gotten from his friend John Burroughs about a brown-backed bird that most Americans had probably never seen.

Hermit Thrush/ Solitary Thrush/ moderate sized grayish brown bird/ sings oftener after sundown sometimes quite in the night/ is very secluded/ likes shaded, dark, places in swamps—is very shy/ sings in May & June—/ not much after June/ is our best songster/ song clear & deliberate—has a solemn effect—his song is a hymn/ real, serious sweet—in earnest . . .

—it is perhaps all the more precious, because it is only sung in secluded places—he never sings near the farm houses—never in the settlement/ is the bird of the solemn primal woods & of Nature pure & holy—[61]

As a poet, Whitman had never been much of a shy bird. He had been the poet of the "gab" and the "barbaric yawp," shaking his "locks at the runaway sun." But now, as he readied himself to write a poem worthy of the greatness of Lincoln, he chose a small, earnest voice. He would sing his song, not from a rooftop, but from a place of deep seclusion.

To the trope of the hermit thrush, Whitman added two others, creating a trinity of metaphors that were to entwine and gently reinforce each other throughout his poem: his beloved western star, suspended and "droop'd" in the sky; and a bush of lilacs, every one of its heart-shaped leaves a rich, green miracle.[62] Each of the three images relates primarily to a separate sense—the sound of the bird, the sight of the star, the scent of the flowers—and each speaks in its own way of distance and evanescence. The voice of the bird is "reedy" and delicate, trilled by an invisible, civilization-shunning creature. The star, fitfully revealed and obscured by "the black murk" that hides it, is an inconstant light, shining from an insuperable distance. Its light, the poet knows, "will soon depart." As for the lilac, though it blooms perennially, its season is brief, typically lasting only a fortnight before its flowers fade. The poem describes the song of the thrush as "loud and strong." It deems the lilac's odor "mastering." Yet the adjectives do not so much argue the power of the bird and flower as they indicate the enfeebled spirit of the narrator. Heartsick, seeking in his grief whatever comfort he can find, he finds strength in the frailest sensations.

In its relation to historical events, the poem notably focuses neither on Lincoln's murder nor on his burial. It comments instead upon a journey: the long trip back to Springfield of the president's casket. It is a poem of death, yet it chooses to tell a story of movement. The fifth section of the poem is arresting in its syntax; it consists of a single sentence, ingeniously inverted so that its subject comes as the very last word: "coffin." To get to that word, the reader must undertake an expedition, one that winds through both the land and its cities, "amid lanes and through old woods," fields of "yellow-speared wheat," and groves of apple trees blooming "white and pink in the orchards." It is a passage through America. If we are to follow and catch the coffin in its path so that we may pay our due respects, we must also pass and see and pay mute reverence to the land. Just as Lincoln's work brought the country back together, so the journey of his coffin binds the established East with the burgeoning West. Although the fifth section ends, as noted, with "coffin," the journey has not come to a dead end. Rather, it resumes in the ensuing section, which, in chiastic fashion, begins with the word "coffin" and leads back through grief and into life. A section of dirges and mournful voices and dim-lit churches, it nevertheless ends with an emblem of love and springtime renewal: on the slowly passing coffin, the poet places his sprig of lilac.

Whitman divided his poem into sixteen sections, a detail that seems a mere accident of structure until one considers the date of Lincoln's death, April 1865. Lincoln was assassinated on the night of April 14, 1865, marked on the Christian calendar that year as Good Friday, the day of the Crucifixion. It is in its fourteenth section that the poem nears the crescendo of its anguish, and it is here, too, that the only italicized lines in the poem appear. They are an invitation to death, put forth in a passage that sets aside the star, the bird, and the flower, and begins: *"Come lovely and soothing death, / Undulate round the world, serenely arriving, arriving, / In the day, in the night, to all, to each, / Sooner or later delicate death."*[63] The fifteenth section of the elegy is a metaphorical descent into a tomb, recounting Whitman's grisly recollections of the war. Among all the sections of the elegy, it is the only one crowded with dead bodies:

> I saw battle-corpses, myriads of them,
> And the white skeletons of young men, I saw them,
> I saw the debris and debris of all the slain soldiers of the war.[64]

This section marks the moment when grief becomes most hopeless, and when the private woe of the poet becomes universal: "The living remain'd and suffer'd, the mother suffer'd, / And the wife and the child and the musing comrade suffer'd, / And the armies that remained suffer'd."[65] In his fleeting allusion to the suffering mother, Whitman encapsulates the nation's countless episodes of maternal pietà.

The sixteenth and final section of the poem brings catharsis and hope. The once-mournful song of the thrush, resonating with the song of the poet's soul, is now transfigured, moving slowly but confidently from Purgatorio to Paradiso, from keening sorrow to exclamatory joy:

> Victorious song, death's outlet song, yet varying ever-altering song
> As low and wailing, yet clear the notes, rising and falling flooding
>   the night,
> Sadly sinking and fainting, as warning and warning, and yet
>   bursting again with joy,
> Covering the earth and filling the spread of heaven.[66]

Again, the numbering of the sections is filled with meaning. Saturday, April 15, 1865, was Holy Saturday, commemorating the day when Christ lay silent in the crypt, and that April 16, reflective of the stanza of the poem that signals redemption and rebirth, was Easter Sunday.

Using the poem's first line as its title, "When Lilacs Last in the Dooryard Bloom'd," Whitman published his elegy as part of a twenty-four-page sequel to *Drum-Taps* in October 1865. Through the summer and into the fall, the business of the war wound down. Now employed in the attorney general's office, Whitman was entrusted with welcoming "a great stream of Southerners" who came each day in search of pardons for their role in the rebellion.[67] The higher-ups of the erstwhile Confederacy—military officers and the like—were legally denied basic rights of citizenship, including the making and enforcing of contracts, until they had secured the government's amnesty, which President Johnson was typically in no hurry to grant. Whitman talked with the petitioners frequently, listening to their tales and opinions. He knew that storytelling was as necessary to reconciliation as any piece of paper. In "Reconciliation," one of the lesser poems from *Drum-Taps*, he confesses his eagerness to put the heartbreak of the war behind him: "Word over all, beautiful as the sky, / Beautiful that war and all its deeds of carnage must in time be utterly lost, / That the hands of the sisters Death and Night incessantly softly wash again, and ever gain, this soil'd world."[68]

In the poem, Whitman has one more kiss to give, having saved it for a Confederate soldier, white-faced in his coffin.

Whitman decided to remain in Washington; after two and a half years, it felt like home. By midsummer, George was out of the army; the Fifty-First was mustered out of service on July 25, 1865. He had gone into the service as a private. He departed as a brevet lieutenant colonel. During George's stay in Alexandria, Walt had kept him company from time to time, crossing the river twice to enjoy dinner with him. George was going back to Brooklyn to resume his trade. The tough, impassive carpenter would be a carpenter once more.

Two days after the Fifty-First was officially disbanded, in the midst of a heat wave, its veterans marched across Long Bridge and through the capital city to the Baltimore depot. Walt was there to see his brother off. He watched as the train, some twenty cars long, rounded the curve and disappeared on its way to New York. Bearing the men of countless regiments, the train's interior was not large enough to accommodate them all. To Whitman, the troops who swarmed over the roofs of the cars looked like clusters of blue-coated bees. It was, the poet said, "quite a sight."[69]

✶

THE COMING OF PEACE DID NOT end Whitman's hospital visits. Men whose wounds were slow to heal still needed care, and he did not forget them. At last, however, he had more time to see to his pecuniary needs. Early in 1865, with the help of William O'Connor and a well-connected lawyer, J. Hubley Ashton, Whitman had secured a low-level clerkship in the Bureau of Indian Affairs, an arm of the Department of the Interior. The pay, a hundred dollars a month, was not lavish, but it covered the poet's basic wants. The work, consisting mainly of copying documents, was pleasantly undemanding for a man whose preferred vocations were writing poems and comforting the needy. The job also exposed him to a part of America he had never seen before: a steady succession of envoys from western tribes. Some of them wearing face paint and bedecked in bear-claw necklaces, they ventured to Washington in search of help in sustaining their imperiled societies. Whitman was sure that these ambassadors and their cultures, proud and beautiful amid the slow catastrophe of Anglo-American expansion, were soon to pass away. He saw in them "something very remote, very lofty, arousing comparisons with our own civilized ideals," but destined "never [to] be transmitted to the future, even as reminiscence." These "aboriginal Americans," like the war, could never be set down in any book.[70]

Whitman won immediate favor with his work at the Bureau, earning a promotion barely three months after he started. He might have happily remained there if not for the fastidious morals of the Interior Department's new secretary, appointed by President Johnson in May 1865. A devout Iowa Methodist, James Harlan vowed to purge his fiefdom of all employees who, in his judgment, "disregard[ed] in their conduct, habits, and associations, the rules of decorum, [and] propriety proscribed by a Christian civilization."[71] According to the poet, Harlan loitered about the office one evening until Whitman went home. He then went to Whitman's desk and reached into the drawer where the poet kept a copy of *Leaves of Grass.* The next day, he fired Whitman for having written an indecent book.

Initially shamed and stung by his dismissal, Whitman mostly forgave Harlan later. Beyond doubt, the secretary was "ignorant of literature . . . ignorant of life," but his provincialism was at least sincere. Harlan earnestly believed that he was defending the Republic against an enemy of its morals, an action that, the poet decided, "was all right for Harlan and all right for his kind of Iowa."[72] In retrospect, the poet could afford to be magnanimous. The same friend who helped O'Connor find Whitman a job at the Bureau soon came up with a similar opening for him in the Justice Department. For Whitman, one clerkship was about as good as another.

More importantly, Whitman's dismissal led to a remarkable evolution in his public reputation. A handful of Washington's young writers and journalists wrote vehemently in the press to denounce the poet's ill treatment. Their indignation, however, had almost no impact in comparison with the fiery response of Whitman's old friend William O'Connor, who published a pamphlet that eloquently defended not only Whitman, but also freedom of artistic speech in general: an essay titled *The Good Gray Poet: A Vindication.*

Assessing Whitman's poetry, O'Connor spared no hyperbole: all previous American works were, he said, mere "constructions." *Leaves of Grass* was, by contrast, a "creation," thrusting its author into the ranks of Shakespeare, Cervantes, and Dante, "the brothers of the radiant summit."[73] More important than O'Connor's views on Whitman's work, however, was his portrait of the man himself—a depiction that forever changed Whitman's place in the popular imagination. O'Connor pushed aside the image—long cultivated by Whitman himself—of the rough, lusty denizen of lower Broadway. He erected in its place a figure of grandfatherly warmth and genteel compassion, much more the patriarch than the prodigal. O'Connor emphasized Whitman's personal magnetism, the mysterious quality in his character that drew simple, unlettered people toward him "as their natural mate and friend."[74] He also lauded the poet's love of country; no mere intellectual attachment, Whitman's patriotism rose to the level of "a personal passion."[75]

At the core of O'Connor's praise lay his regard for Whitman's work in the hospitals—how he had come to the wards of the wounded and the dying "in the spirit of Christ, soothing, healing, consoling, restoring, night and day . . . never failing . . . doing everything that it is possible for one unaided human being to do."[76] O'Connor called his friend's labors a "sublime ministration." "Immense and divine," they were the supremely loving gifts of a man whose generosity had made him outwardly poor, but whose poverty was illuminated by goodness and genius.[77] O'Connor eagerly stretched the facts, but the myth that he originated took hold. Whitman was to take his place in America's cultural imagination as O'Connor drew him: the gentle stalwart, the sanctified bard.

At the same time, *Drum-Taps* was also reshaping Whitman in the eyes of the public. He might have been happy if he were becoming known for "When Lilacs Last in the Dooryard Bloom'd." Ironically, the poem that captured the greatest enthusiasm was another, much shorter lyric, also included in *Drum-Taps'* sequel. "O Captain! My Captain!," as has often been observed, was one of the least typically Whitmanesque lyrics the poet ever wrote. The poem, also written in memory of Lincoln, elaborates a single, predictable metaphor: the ship of state, having endured a perilous voyage, sails safely into its harbor, its captain lying dead upon the deck. Conventional in its meters, guileless in its emotions, the poem does not fit many critics' ideas of great poetry. Instead, it exudes a naïve purity and patriotism that Whitman's America could not resist. It was to be endlessly anthologized. Thousands of schoolchildren, over several generations, committed it to memory. It became Whitman's most popular poem. Called on to read it publicly more times than he cared to consider, Whitman eventually rebelled against his creation. "Damn My Captain!" he once exclaimed. "I'm almost sorry I ever wrote the poem." The suggestion that it was his best poem exasperated him. "God help me!" he exclaimed. "What can the worst be like?"[78]

In 1871, Whitman published another expanded edition of *Leaves of Grass*. He reprinted the exuberant, sexually assertive poems of the prewar editions: those feelings were still a part of him and were still, therefore, a part of his book. The latest leaves, however, had a more autumnal color; they made readers more conscious that death was a part of life as well. As Whitman put it, the new poems had changed his work into "the expression, more decidedly than before, of that combination in which Death and the Unknown are as essential and important to the author's plan of a complete human personality as Life and the Known, and completes his original design."[79] Whitman remained true throughout his career to his belief that his book should be his second self—that its mission was to express in full "my own physical, emotional, moral, intellectual, and aesthetic Personality."[80]

Critics have typically presumed that Whitman made almost all his signature contributions to literature before the war, with the "Lilacs" elegy standing as a spectacular exception. Whitman, however, thought the critics missed the point. He declared, "No one will get at my verses who insists upon viewing them as a literary performance, or attempt at such performance, or as aiming mainly toward art or aestheticism."[81] He was not seeking to create a perfect image or to produce some critically pleasing thing of beauty. His work, perhaps especially his later poems, raised honesty above beauty, charity above perfection. He was not writing works of clever artifice. What he wrote, he wanted to be real.

So long as Whitman's character kept evolving, *Leaves of Grass*, too, remained a fragment. For years, Whitman had written and rewritten his poem of America, trying to express in verse the exuberance of American life. The Whitman who had descended into Pfaff's at the start of the 1860s was a man who had lost his personal exuberance, one whose faith in both his own creative powers and in the nation's future had reached its lowest ebb. Wonderfully, it was in the hospitals of Washington, places of unspeakable brokenness and sorrow, that he became whole again. Amid the saddest of scenes, he recovered his capacity for joy and generosity, and his vision of America was restored and forever strengthened.

Whitman also learned in the hospitals that both the nation and the poetry were incomplete because neither had passed through the annealing, purifying fire of tragedy. In his great work *The Varieties of Religious Experience*, William James quotes Richard Maurice Bucke, a devoted friend of Whitman's later years, for the judgment that the poet was incapable of "fretfulness, antipathy, complaint, and remonstrance."[82] James himself ascribes to Whitman "an inability to feel evil." These judgments were mistaken. Whitman saw and knew evil in the Civil War as extensively as anyone, and it moved him profoundly. The difference was that he saw the evil as essential to the attainment of a greater good. Before the war, Whitman wrote, the states had "learn'd from joys and prosperity only." Now, "from crises of anguish, advancing, grappling with direst fate and recoiling not," they had taken new and deeper lessons. With iron and blood, the war had brought the country to its consummation. "I know very well," he wrote, "that my 'Leaves' could not possibly have emerged or been fashion'd or completed [from anything other than] the absolute triumph of the National Union arms."[83] In an 1871 poem, he declared, ""My book and the war are one."[84] At Gettysburg, Lincoln proclaimed a new birth of freedom. Now Whitman, too, proclaimed a moment of metamorphosis. The change he observed in *Drum-Taps*—the change that finally made the country—was an agony that balanced and subsumed both birth and death.

All the while, "O Captain! My Captain!" was helping to fuse together in the American mind the legends of Whitman and Lincoln. It was an association that Whitman actively cultivated. In old age, he was to tell his friend Horace Traubel, "I hope to be identified with the man Lincoln, with his crowded, eventful years—with America as shadowed forth into those abysms of circumstances."[85] In his last years, Whitman cemented that connection. Starting in 1879 and periodically until 1890, he marked the anniversary of Lincoln's assassination by delivering a public speech about the president's death, based on Peter Doyle's eyewitness recollections. Whitman gave his memorial address as far north as Boston and as far south as Maryland, always beginning more or less as follows:

How often since that dark and dripping Saturday, that chilly April day now—years ago, my heart has entertained the dream, the wish to give of Abraham Lincoln's death its own special thought and memorial. Yet, now the sought-for opportunity offers, I find my notes incompetent, and the fitting tribute I dreamed of seems as unprepared as ever.[86]

The speech was neither incompetent nor ill prepared. It was, however, misleadingly advertised; promoters led attendees to believe that Whitman had been present at Ford's Theatre. Whitman said nothing to expose the falsehood, narrating the murder as vividly as any eyewitness. Like Holmes recalling the street battle at Fredericksburg, like Alcott recounting the death of John Suhre, he wanted to imagine himself near his hero at the moment of crisis. Mark Twain heard the speech. So, too, did Andrew Carnegie and General Sherman. Whitman's words routinely brought forth a tumultuous response and, when he recited "O Captain! My Captain!" as an encore, the clapping would give way to tears. By the time he finished, Whitman's tears might also be seen covering his cheeks and glistening in his beard. When Whitman concluded his speech at New York's Madison Square Theatre on April 14, 1887, a young girl, wearing a Normandy cap and a suit of Quaker gray, came onstage, carrying a basket overflowing with lilacs. The old poet gratefully accepted them and kissed the child twice before reciting "O Captain! My Captain!" The crowd applauded warmly as the curtain came down.[87]

Book 5

TWO SOLDIERS

Chapter Eighteen

St. Patrick's Day, 1863

Broad, immaculate horse farms now blanket the terrain near Kelly's Ford, Virginia, and the mist lies low and heavy in the early mornings over the Rappahannock, a little less than thirty miles above Fredericksburg. It is a place, even today, of surpassing tranquility; its only notes of restlessness are sounded by a steady drone of crickets and the eager honks of wild geese on the move. There is a piety in quiet places.

On Saint Patrick's Day, 1863, the war came to Kelly's Ford, though not with the sustained, operatic fury with which it had swept through the West Woods or down from Marye's Heights. Its fields became the scene of a brief but bitter skirmish, pitting about eight hundred of Jeb Stuart's cavalrymen, led by Fitzhugh Lee, Robert E. Lee's nephew, against a much larger force under Brigadier General William Woods Averell. The word "skirmish" suggests a sharp but fleeting hornets'-nest affair, quickly arising and quickly ending. A skirmish attracts no great remembrance— no information centers, no park rangers, no detailed markers to tell the visitor "It was here. . . ." One must be satisfied with a numbered sign by the side of a road, on which a dozen lines suffice to tell of the struggles, triumphs, and tragedies of unnamed men. But no place where life has been risked and taken should be considered trivial.

That day, John Pelham also came to Kelly's Ford, though he had very little business being there. Three months had passed since his stand at Fredericksburg had made him a hero. They had been months of relative calm, as the two armies, at rest in their winter camps, repaired themselves and watched the snow fall. In January, Burnside had tried to salvage his reputation with one last assault against Lee, an elaborately planned flanking maneuver that fell victim to miserable weather and ended in a quagmire on the shores of the Rappahannock. Far from rescuing either Burnside's personal honor or the flagging morale of his army, the infamous and abortive Mud March succeeded only in inflicting another humiliation on an army that had already endured too many. Days after the fiasco, Burnside was ousted from the command that he had never wanted. Lincoln replaced him with Joseph Hooker, who at least had the good sense not to pursue any further glories until springtime.

For Stuart's cavalry and Pelham's Horse Artillery, there had also been a last hurrah before the long winter hiatus. On December 26, eighteen hundred of Stuart's troopers, along with four cannons under Pelham's command, crossed the Rappahannock at Kelly's Ford and passed the night some ten miles east in Morrisville. Stuart then boldly divided his force into three more or less equal units, entrusting each with a separate objective. The raid was something of a family affair: in addition to a party led by South Carolinian Wade Hampton, the other two prongs served under General Lee's son Rooney and his nephew Fitzhugh. To the left, Hampton's men were ordered northeast to Occoquan to seize the Telegraph Road north of Dumfries and block the possible arrival of Yankee reinforcements. Fitz Lee was to take control of the highway leading north to Dumfries. He was then to link up with Rooney Lee, whose center prong was to proceed directly to Dumfries.

The raid required some daring, as well as some determined effort by Pelham to get his guns across Selectman's Ford near Occoquan—a river crossing thought to be impassable for wheeled vehicles. The Confederates, despite some early confusion, carried off the operation well. Only one of them was killed, and they lost a mere twenty-six in wounded and missing. In exchange, Stuart's men counted about 200 prisoners, a like number of horses, twenty supply wagons, and at least a hundred firearms. Potentially of much more significance, the raid ended with Stuart in possession of a Union telegraph office only fifteen miles from Washington. His men had seized the office so quickly that the operator, who was transmitting messages by which a Union general was trying to direct maneuvers against Stuart, had no time to send off an alarm. Stuart, who traveled with a telegraph operator of his own, found himself in control of an asset of tremendous potential value, arguably even better than Lee's Lost Order. The Lost Order had supplied McClellan only with a snap-shot of the Confederate army's whereabouts. Undiscovered control of an enemy telegraph transmitter, by contrast, was a gift capable of extended giving. Not only could Stuart intercept the plans of the Union army, but he might even send out disinformation to lure the Army of the Potomac into making a considerable blunder.

But Stuart, being Stuart, could not help himself. He used the enemy telegraph to send a taunting wire to Quartermaster General Meigs, com-plaining that the poor quality of Burnside's army's mules was making it difficult for Stuart to move the Federal wagon trains once he had cap-tured them. Stuart attached his name to the message, burned a railroad bridge, and moved on.

Clever though the joke may have been, it was costly. The message dis-closed Stuart's precise location and, of course, let the Union army know that their communications had been compromised. It was as if McClellan had sent the Lost Order back to Lee with a message disparaging Confed-erate cigars. Stuart's bit of fun also tweaked the nose of the Union cavalry once too often. Stuart had mounted his raid in order to create a "system of irritation," by which he could harass the Union cavalry and his enemy's supply lines.[1] Irritate them it did, but it did little more, and doing so was, in the longer term, a more hazardous game than Stuart seems to have recognized. An opponent will sometimes bear a defeat more patiently than a humiliation, and Stuart's disrespect of his adversaries had passed to a new, intolerable level of insult. When the two armies' cavalries met again in the spring, the bluecoats would be determined to show that they belonged on the same field with Stuart's men. The Union horsemen had always enjoyed superior numbers. They were on the way to acquiring a matching resolve.

But in the camp where John Pelham passed the winter of 1863, little thought was given to the possibility that the Union cavalry might soon approach the level of professional skill that had long been Stuart's calling card. The fame that had come to Pelham after Fredericksburg was no doubt gratifying, but it did little to transform the daily life of an offi-cer in the field. He spent part of January reinforcing and adding a few comforts to the modest shelter that he had erected for winter quarters. He shared the impromptu dwelling with John Esten Cooke, the most literary member of Stuart's entourage. More than almost any other single factor, Pelham's choice of roommate led to establishing his own enduring image: the exemplar of courtly perfection that both charms romanticists and perplexes biographers. Cooke entertained a highly roseate view of the Confederate rebellion, and his sentiments suffused the memoirs, poetry, and fiction that he left behind. Pelham supplied the perfect subject for Cooke's artistry and idolatry. The author was later to recall the sight of the young artillerist on horseback:

> I had reached a lofty hill at some distance from the house, when the last regiments of cavalry appeared falling slowly back, and Pelham's guns were seen bringing up the rear. . . . [T]he red light of the setting sun was streaming splendidly, and in front was seen the slender form of Pelham, with his smooth, girlish face, and his brave, gay smile. The crimson light illuminated his figure, and fell around him like a glory.[2]

But the admiration came not only from Southerners. Somewhere around this time, Pelham received a slip of paper from his old classmate George Armstrong Custer: "After a long silence, I write. God bless you, dear Pelham; I am proud of your success. G. A. C."[3] Though often indifferent to or discomfited by praise, Pelham carried Custer's note with him.

During the winter calm, Pelham passed the time writing letters and catching up on some reading. He and Stuart's adjutant, W. W. Blackford, entertained each other by reading aloud from the Bible and a book on the Napoleonic Wars. Also brought together by their love of fine horses, Pelham and Blackford became close friends. At least once, Pelham stole away to visit Richmond, though whether he did so to demand supplies for his men or to sample the social life of the capital is impossible to determine. In Stuart's company, he would pay his respects to Stonewall Jackson, ensconced for the season at the stately, pillared plantation known as Moss Neck Manor. Even if one's spirits were flagging, so much time in the company of Jackson and Stuart would surely have raised one's faith in the strength of the Confederate arms. But Pelham's confidence needed no bolstering. After Burnside was dismissed and General Hooker replaced him, Pelham sent an ebullient letter to Llewellyn Hoxton, a friend from his West Point days, now serving in the Army of Tennessee. Annoyed that the winter's snow and mud had postponed what he now saw as the swift and obvious conclusion to the war, he wrote, "I hope 'Fighting Joe' Hooker will come over and give us a chance as soon as the weather will permit. *This army is invincible*—whenever you hear of it fighting you may add one more name to our list of victories—for such will certainly be the result."[4]

Pelham's own exploits had supplied some of the factual basis for this prognosis, and his boundless optimism was typical for an officer in Lee's army in the aftermath of Fredericksburg. With a spectacular combination of daring and skill, he had challenged a third of the Army of the Potomac and had brought its parade-perfect advance to an embarrassed halt. Now that he had done this deed, what set of odds could not be overcome? Pelham could only believe that Lee's forces would triumph and that Jefferson Davis would soon preside over a newly established nation.

Pelham also passed much time at the home of Judge Henry Shackelford in Culpeper, where he enjoyed the attentions of the judge's black-haired daughter Bessie. Despite the apparent cultural limitations of her rather small town, Bessie was well versed in the arts. Her knowledge of politics and her willingness to debate them challenged the earnest but somewhat unsophisticated mind of the young artillerist. Bessie appears to have seen more deeply into Pelham than he into her, and she was struck by the peculiar contradiction that lay manifest in the handsome major:

> You couldn't help being drawn to him. He was really fascinating. He had great blue eyes and lovely golden-brown hair and a beautiful face, beautiful manners, too. He spoke gently and he moved quietly. . . . Sometimes I used to sit and just look at him and wonder if it could be true that he was the man they were all talking about, the man who could aim those guns so that they would kill and kill and kill. He didn't look as if he could ever order anybody to be killed. There wasn't a single line of hardness in his face. It was all tenderness and softness, as fresh and delicate as a boy's who liked people and who found the world good.[5]

Pelham's contradictions absorbed and attracted Bessie. But was there not something disquieting about the moral puzzle he presented? As much as they enjoyed each other's company, no deep romantic attachment formed.

Pelham, it seems, was stunningly adept at fitting his outward demeanor to the requirements of the moment: implacable and deadly in combat, courtly and suave when the occasion called for small talk and flirtation. Cooke observed the change that came over Pelham when his soldierly zeal yielded to more affectionate impulses. The soldier would take on "a long, sad, yearning look." The penetrating eyes would turn soft. The laughter on his lips would disappear, and a tender expression would relax his features.[6] But those expressions were only for the parlor. On the battlefield, Cooke observed, the teeth would clench, and the eyes would blaze. Amid thick and daunting fire, Pelham was motionless and cool.[7] His reserves of self-control were so deep as to defy comprehension, and the people who truly tried to comprehend him were distinctly few. Those who could not understand decided instead that they would simply adore, and the adoration that filled the pages that memoirists and early historians lavished on Pelham makes it hard to see him as ordinarily human even to this day.

Yet Pelham did not always relish the attention. He had begun to chafe under Stuart's constant supervision. "General Stuart," Blackford remembered, "loved [Pelham] like a younger brother and could not bear for him to be away from him." On the morning of Sunday, March 15, 1863, encamped with Stuart and his staff near Fredericksburg, Pelham was all duty and decorum. He attended church alongside Stuart, and appeared immersed in the sermon.[8] But inwardly, Pelham was evolving a plan, if only for a day or two, to flee. The inspiration for his escape came from a letter and a package of candy, sent to Stuart by one of the general's eligible cousins, Nannie Price. Quite familiar with the general's love of sweets, Price had sent the box from the town of Orange Court House, where she and her friend Lucinda Brill had been busying themselves in the kitchen. They were not the most skillful confectioners—they had both burned their fingers in their efforts—but Nannie hoped that their sufferings would make the results seem a good deal sweeter. She wrote, "Miss Brill sends some of it for the 'Gallant Pelham,' which you must be sure to give him."[9]

Though Pelham was determined to thank the ladies in person, he feared that Stuart would deny him permission. He therefore invented a story about having to inspect a battery of the Horse Artillery, then stationed at Orange Court House, and he asked the general for an order granting him leave. He evidently found Stuart in a liberal mood: the cavalryman signed the order. But Pelham knew better than to trust too much in his superior's passing sentiments of goodwill; the man who gave the order that evening might also countermand it the next morning, and he must not be given the chance. Thus, before sunrise on the 16th, Pelham rode off, intent on taking breakfast when he passed through a camp along the road.

When Stuart arose for breakfast, he had already forgotten the order he had issued the previous evening. Glancing over his assembled staff with mild bewilderment, he asked, "Where's Pelham?" The answer brought the realization of a tiny betrayal, one that Stuart could not allow. At once, he had a countermanding order drafted and sent a courier to retrieve Pelham with all possible speed. By the time the courier overtook him, Pelham had almost reached Orange Court House, and evening was coming on. Surely, Pelham reasoned, Stuart would not want him to return that night. He meant to savor his having outwitted his clinging commander.

At this point, the chronology of Pelham's movements becomes muddled. Some sources say he stayed in Orange Court House on the 16th, intending to obey Stuart's order belatedly by returning to camp the next day. They are contradicted, however, by the memoirs of a Confederate cavalry captain named Harry Gilmor. On the 16th, Gilmor recalled attending a court-martial where he was first introduced to Pelham.[10] That evening, Gilmor attended "a jovial party" in the rooms of Lieutenant Colonel Welby Carter at Culpeper's Virginia Hotel, attended by Pelham and his old friend Tom Rosser.[11] Eight or so officers were there, exchanging stories and pleasantries well into the evening. Of the convivial group, five would be dead by the following summer.

✱

FITZHUGH LEE HAD BEEN FEELING CONFIDENT, and some of Stuart's habit of tweaking the Yankee cavalry's noses had rubbed off on him. The Yankee commander who opposed him, William Averell, had been a classmate of Fitz Lee's at West Point, and Fitz rarely missed a chance to goad him. Three weeks before the action at Kelly's Ford, Lee had embarrassed Averell with a successful raid at Hartwood Church. He had then sent Averell a message: would the general kindly oblige him by leaving his state, and, if he did not, would he pay Lee a visit across the river, and bring along a sack of coffee, if he could?[12] The incident infuriated General Hooker, and even President Lincoln asked to see Fitz Lee's note. Some of Fitz's jauntiness faded, however, shortly after dawn on the morning of March 17; Union cavalry had crossed the Rappahannock and captured twenty-five of his pickets at Kelly's Ford. Averell's visit had begun.

Stuart and Pelham were already aware that the coming day might grow turbulent. Pelham had been awake only a short time when he dashed off a note to Marcellus Moorman, one of the captains of his Horse Artillery: "Be on the alert. Large force of cavalry between Morrisville and Bealeton Station. If everything is quiet I will be at Rapidan Station tomorrow." Pelham and Stuart were at breakfast when word came that Averell's men had crossed the river and were moving toward the Orange and Alexandria Railroad. Defending that rail link, as Stuart and Pelham both understood, was vital to preserving Lee's communications and supply lines.

Having arrived at Culpeper by train, Pelham needed a horse. He decided to borrow a black mare that belonged to Stuart's banjo maestro, Sam Sweeney. Pelham and Stuart were already astride their mounts when they were approached by Gilmor, who had heard that action was expected and could not resist going into battle under Stuart's and Fitzhugh Lee's command. He humbly asked—might Stuart take him on for the day as a temporary staff officer? Stuart assented. As he readied himself, Gilmor took special note of Pelham's demeanor. To him, the artillerist looked "fresh, and joyous, and rosy as a boy ten years old."[13] Leaving town, the three soldiers passed Judge Shackelford's home. From a balcony, Bessie waved a handkerchief. Gilmor slowed his horse and, with a wave of his hat, acknowledged her goodwill.

Stuart decided that, in the main, the day should belong not to him, but to Fitz Lee. Even though Stuart outranked him, Stuart meant to partake only as a spectator. Lee presumed that Averell had only a few platoons at his disposal, and he considered his own force more than adequate to drive the Federals back. He miscalculated. Against Lee's eight hundred troopers, Averell had about three thousand. Averell also had the leisure to choose the ground he wanted to defend. He established a formidable line, his left flank guarded and concealed by a thick woods and his center anchored behind a stone wall.

Before committing his cavalry, Lee sent a band of unhorsed sharpshooters to test the Federal strength. From their concealed position, Averell's men opened fire, stunning the Confederates and driving them back in frightened disarray. Stuart, incapable of standing by, spurred his horse into the midst of the panicked men, rallying them and directing them to a sheltered position from which they might return fire with relative safety. The fight now grew fiercer, as Fitz Lee began to order his cavalry into the fray. Weapons drawn, the Third Virginia Cavalry spurred their horses toward the wall. Though Union fire cut holes in their line, the riders reached the barrier, hacking with their sabers and firing their pistols at point-blank range. But they could go no farther; they could find no point where the wall could either be breached or leaped over.

The failure of the Third notwithstanding, Fitz Lee remained convinced that he commanded the larger force. He sent in two more units, the First and Fifth Virginia. Leading the Fifth was Tom Rosser. Caught in an enfilading fire and grasping that they were desperately outnumbered, Rosser's men teetered on the verge of panic. As Rosser tried furiously to preserve order, he spotted one of his officers, Major John Puller, motionless on his horse and seemingly indifferent to the rising chaos. Irritably, Rosser called on Puller "in the name of God" to help steady the men. But Puller, his face turning ashen, was doing all he could just to stay mounted. "Colonel," he replied simply, "I'm killed." Struggling to achieve a more erect posture, he pitched headfirst out of his saddle and onto the ground. Soon Rosser was also in trouble; a minié ball had struck him in the foot, and blood was flowing through a hole in his boot.[14] Somehow, he managed to remain in front of his regiment, leading them in stalwart fashion until the end of the day.

Stuart was later to argue that, at Kelly's Ford, Pelham had acted "in the *strict* and *legitimate* discharge of his duty." Stuart underscored the adjectives. Still not feeling that he had made his point strongly enough, he then added that the young major had engaged in "no display of *rashness* and *excessive zeal*, as some have insinuated."[15] Actually, many "have insinuated," and Stuart's protestations have not grown more persuasive over time. Pelham was an artillery officer. His cannons began the day far from Kelly's Ford, and when one of his batteries eventually did arrive, he remained with his gunners only long enough to help them find their range. No one knows the reasons that drove Pelham to join in a cavalry charge against Averell's stone wall, or what he imagined might be gained from his participating. The simplest supposition is as good as any: he saw other men risking their lives at a moment when the day might be won or lost, and he believed he could help them. In the deliberations of the moment, little else mattered.

What does it mean to be prudent in war? Caution in such circumstances can only be relative. One trusts to courage and good fortune, knowing that the latter may fail and hoping that the former will hold firm. It is possible that Pelham felt Stuart had been holding him too close, that the older man's protectiveness was growing intolerable. Days earlier he had shown his independence by slipping away to Orange Court House. Now, again, riding forward under no one's command, he chose for himself.

Pelham looked on as the Third Virginia, re-formed and spirited, gathered for another assault upon the wall. As the last horseman rode past, an impulse arose. Drawing his sword, Pelham rode at full gallop toward the head of the advancing line. This time, the gray riders had finally found a gap in the stone fence and were surging into the breach. Brandishing his saber, Pelham urged the men on, shouting at the top of his lungs for them to hurry. Henry McClellan, an officer with the Third Virginia, recalled the image as one of singular beauty:

> At that moment his appearance was superb. His cheeks were burning; his bright blue eyes darted lightning; and from his lips, wreathed with a smile of joy, rang, "Forward!" as he cheered on the men. He looked the perfect picture of a hero. . . . For an instant he was standing in his stirrups, his sabre flashing in his grasp; for a moment his clarion voice rang like a bugle that sounds the charge.[16]

Seconds later, Pelham's world went silent and dark. A Federal shell exploded overhead, sending metal in all directions. A single fragment, no larger than a man's fingertip, angled and spun almost directly downward. It struck Pelham in the back of the head, just at the hairline. Though it missed the brain, it crashed into the base of the skull, creating a broken mess of nerves, blood, and bone before exiting two inches below its point of entry. Falling from his saddle, Pelham landed on his back amid the churning hooves of the charging horses. By a small but meaningless mercy, he escaped being trampled. He lay with his face toward the bright sky, his lips forming a tranquil smile.

Harry Gilmor saw Sweeney's riderless horse moving slowly away. Glancing earthward, he saw Pelham, whose expression impressed him as "very natural." Gilmor recalled that Pelham's eyes were open; McClellan recollected that they were closed. Both, however, noted that the boyish face was unmarred. Gilmor had not heard the telltale sound of a missile colliding with flesh, which he had never failed to hear when a man nearby to him had been struck. Surely, in another moment, Pelham would rise again, retrieve his mount, and resume his cries of "Forward!" But Pelham did not move.

A captain sitting nearby guessed the truth. "My God," he shouted. "They've killed poor Pelham!"

A single thought seized Gilmor: the Yankees must not capture the body. With the help of two other officers, he lifted Pelham from the ground and slung him across Sweeney's mare. What he remembered most was the blood, which was flowing steadily from the wound. Gilmor's thoughts became confused and contradictory. He felt convinced that Pelham was dead, yet it also seemed imperative to find help for him. Gilmor called out to two dismounted men and gave them an urgent order: they must take Pelham to the nearest ambulance and call a surgeon. Gilmor also knew the person who most needed to be told the news.

Jeb Stuart, after restoring order to the band of sharpshooters earlier in the day, had retired to a less exposed area to observe the action as it unfolded. His thoughts were interrupted when he saw Gilmor riding toward him at a gallop. The captain's appearance alarmed him: Gilmor's hands and uniform were stained with blood. Had he been wounded? Gilmor blurted his report. It was not his own blood, but that of Pelham, killed a few moments before. A wave of distress and horror passed over the general's features. An instant later, shock yielded to self-preservation, as the sudden advance of an enemy regiment threatened to cut Gilmor and Stuart off from their men. And then they were riding through a dense wood, and then they stopped again. Still only partly comprehending, Stuart asked Gilmor to repeat his story. Having heard all, Stuart bowed his head upon his horse's neck and wept. He choked out a few words: "Our loss is irreparable."[17]

Stuart ordered Gilmor to Culpeper to send a telegram to General Lee.

On the way, Gilmor overtook the two men he had entrusted with Pelham's body. The lack of care that they had taken with their cargo dismayed him. Instead of obeying orders and finding the nearest ambulance, the men had decided to take the body to Culpeper, a distance of eight miles. They had covered about half the distance. They had treated Pelham like a piece of meat. His head and arms dangled limply on one side of the horse, his legs on the other. The angelic face and hair were now caked and clotted with blood and mud. In fury, Gilmor upbraided the two simpletons. After ordering them to lay Pelham on the ground, Gilmor examined him. His shock deepened: though gravely wounded, John Pelham was still alive.

At once, Gilmor sent for an ambulance and rode off to send his telegram. Word was sent ahead to the Shackelfords', where Bessie and the other women hurriedly prepared to receive their wounded friend. Three surgeons were summoned. Carried to a bed, Pelham received every attention from a host of hands that bathed him in warm water and swathed his feet and hands in flannel. A quantity of brandy was given, and the doctors started their work. They found the base of the skull badly shattered. To relieve pressure on the brain, they removed some fragments of bone, one of which Gilmor pocketed as a macabre souvenir. The prognosis came quickly: Pelham could not recover. Having done what they could, the doctors withdrew. Friends shuffled in and out as Gilmor and Bessie Shackelford maintained a helpless watch.

At one in the morning, Jeb Stuart rode alone toward the Shackelford house. Around the time the clocks were striking the hour, Pelham opened his eyes. After a moment of vacant, insensate staring, he closed them again, drew a long breath, and died without a struggle. Harry and Bessie had just gotten Pelham into his best uniform and laid him on the bed when the door swung slowly open. His plumed hat trailing from his hand, Stuart stepped to Pelham's bedside. With his frame trembling and tears flowing down his cheeks, the general gazed down at his comrade's perfect face.[18]

*

AFTER THE BATTLE, GENERAL AVERELL REPAID Fitz Lee for his earlier joke. He sent Lee a sack of coffee along with a note: "Dear Fitz: Here's your coffee. Here's your visit. How do you like it?"[19] But no one in Stuart's command was laughing now.

With the death of Pelham, a Stuart biographer wrote, "there passed from the army something youthful and golden."[20] Many among the highest echelons of Lee's army, including Lee himself, still considered their force unconquerable. Yet Pelham's loss could be seen as an early crack in the illusion. A "most profound grief" swept "throughout the army and the country."[21] Until Kelly's Ford, no individual in the Confederate Army had seemed more invincible than Pelham. His risks had never been punished, and his audacity had been continually rewarded. If he could fall, so, too, might the army he left behind.

Stuart's camp fell into a mood "of melancholy sorrow . . . beyond description." Blackford, who had been reading with Pelham about Napoleon, put the book aside and never reopened it. Esten Cooke closed his diary and did not return to it for weeks. Stuart himself wrote openly of "the tears of agony we have shed" over Pelham's loss. A few days after Pelham died, someone mentioned Pelham's name to Stuart, and again the general wept. "Poor boy—he loved me so much," he said.[22] He wrote to a cousin, "To behold that calm sweet face that so quickened at the battle cry . . . now cold in the sleep of death, wrings tears from the most obdurate." To his wife Flora, Stuart wrote of Pelham's passing, "You must know how his death distressed me." He wrote despairingly that he now considered his own survival of the war "extremely improbable." Flora had been born in Missouri. Her husband now told her, as if the worst had already come, "I wish . . . that you will make the land [presumably the state of Virginia] for which I gave my life your home."[23]

In Richmond on March 19, in anticipation of Pelham's arrival, a handsome iron coffin was fitted with a small glass window, through which passing mourners might glimpse the face of the dead major. Expressing great distress, Willis and Newton, the two enslaved brothers who had seen to Pelham's needs throughout the war, begged to be allowed to take charge of his body on its way home. Heros von Borcke, who received their request, was deeply moved by their behavior. However, perhaps suspecting a ruse by which the two might flee to freedom, he felt constrained to reject their petition.[24] Pelham's body arrived in the Confederate capital ingloriously, laid in a wooden crate. When the ordered hearse failed to appear, Pelham's remains were borne away from the train station by a common one-horse wagon. After that, however, his journey was that of an acknowledged hero. Soon transferred to his more impressive casket, bedecked with flags and an evergreen wreath, Pelham lay in state in the capitol building for thirty-six hours. He was the youngest man and the most junior in rank to be accorded that honor. That rank was about to change. Before Kelly's Ford, Stuart had lobbied without success to have Pelham promoted. Now, as Pelham lay in the capitol of the Confederacy, a more influential man took up the effort. Robert E. Lee petitioned Jefferson Davis and the Confederate senate, arguing for 'the promotion he had richly won."[25] Davis and the senators assented. Pelham would go to his rest as a lieutenant colonel.

The great majority of those who filed past Pelham's catafalque were women, many of whom left garlands and bouquets. A number of them put on full mourning dress. The face they saw through the pane of glass was pale and cold, but the embalmers had left intact the sweet, sad smile. Stuart, unable to attend, ordered his staff and all members of the horse artillery to wear black armbands for the following month. Making its way by train to Alabama, the coffin traveled circuitously, so that a number of large cities could pay their respects. The casket passed through Knoxville, Chattanooga, and Atlanta, and finally was met at the Alabama border by a guard of honor that accompanied it the rest of the way. The funeral train stopped in Montgomery, where a large crowd, led by the governor, saluted its arrival, and in Selma, where another throng paid its respects. The final legs of the railway journey slowed to a virtual crawl, as every town along the route demanded some time with the remains of the state's most admired son.

On March 28, four snow-white horses drew Pelham from the little rail station at Blue Mountain to his home in Alexandria. His brothers were all with their regiments, leaving only his sister Betty and his mother and father to receive the body. Betty and Atkinson were too devastated to leave their upstairs rooms when the carriage arrived. Only Pelham's mother came to usher the pallbearers into the parlor. Alone, she directed "where he must be laid where the light would fall on his face when Sunday came." Only a few of her words on the occasion were remembered: gazing on the pallid face of her son, she said that he had been "made white with the blood of the Lamb."[26]

The morning after John Pelham was brought home, Jeb Stuart wrote a letter of condolence to Atkinson Pelham. Grieving for his "friend, all but brother," Stuart called him the nation's "lost hero—so nobler—

so chivalrous—so pure," and then, with emphasis, "*so beloved.*" Stuart added, "He has won a name immortal on earth, and in heaven he will reap the rewards of a pure and guileless heart."[27] Turning delicately to more practical matters, he asked Atkinson how he should dispose of Pelham's property: his trunk, his sword, two horses, and the two slaves Willis and Newton. The blood of the lamb had, perhaps, atoned for the sins of John Pelham. The sins of the system for which he had fought were not so promptly washed away.

Chapter Nineteen

"The Duty of Fighting
Has Ceased for Me"

A day or two after the Twentieth Massachusetts was driven back at Fredericksburg, Colonel William Lee came back to them at Falmouth, trying to take command one last time. It made Captain Abbott's heart ache to see the little man trying to answer duty's call. "A single week of it," said Abbott, "would have killed him outright." It was no use. Two days after his return, broken and sobbing, Lee climbed into an ambulance and rode away. Despite his litany of failures, the men still loved him. Wendell Holmes wrote "a very good address" to the colonel to express his officers' good wishes.[1] Abbott hoped it would comfort the brave but fragile man who had so little to console him.

Holmes did not cross the river into Fredericksburg. Nevertheless, he saw more than enough of the battle's aftermath to convince him that the Army of the Potomac had an almost impossible fight ahead of them. A week after the doomed charges up Marye's Heights, he assured his father that there had been "no wavering in my belief in the right of our cause." But it was now clear to him that righteousness would decide nothing. As to his father's optimism regarding the war, Wendell had lost all patience. Testily, he told his father that the latter did not begin to "realize the unity or the determination of the South. I think you are hopeful because (excuse me) you are ignorant."[2]

If the extant letters create an accurate impression, Holmes wrote home less often than previously during the deepening winter and early spring of 1863. He recovered from his dysentery as well as could be expected and, in early January, went on sick leave to Philadelphia, where the ever-hospitable Hallowells awaited him. While there, he received a visit from his parents, though no details of their meeting are known. Having been confined to a tent during the battle, Holmes had every reason to think that, finally, no one would dream of immortalizing his experience in a published writing. Absurdly, though, the effort to make a hero out of the famous poet's son had not quite run its course. A Philadelphia poet, George H. Boker, somehow got hold of Holmes's story and promptly transformed it into a patriotic ode, "The Crossing at Fredericksburg." In the poem, the bedridden narrator watches and listens from a hospital tent as his regiment marches to the river. Like Holmes, the narrator can hardly bear to be left behind:

"Where go they?" "Across the river."
    O God! And must I lie still,
While that drum and measured trampling
    Move from me far down the hill? . . .

"Oh, to go; but to go with my comrades!
    Tear the curtain away from the hook;
For I'll see them march down to their glory,
    If I perish by the look!" . . . [3]

Boker was a close friend of Dr. Holmes, close enough that, when Ticknor and Fields published Boker's *Poems of the War* in 1864, the author felt comfortable asking the elder Holmes to write a prologue—a request that the doctor declined.[4] Presumably it was the garrulous Holmes Sr. who relayed his son's story to Boker in the first place. At least Boker's poem did not mention Wendell by name. But the poem enjoyed a circulation wide enough that Lincoln's private secretary, John Nicolay, owned a copy of *Poems of the War*, and probably more than a few people guessed the identity of the ailing soldier who heard the call to arms and could not follow.[5] Again, it seems, the Autocrat had thrust his son, unbidden, in the direction of the spotlight.

Though the surviving evidence is indirect as to its causes, friction was mounting between father and son. Near the end of March, Captain Holmes sent a letter to his "Dear Old Dad," apologizing for a "blowoff" in one of his recent letters home and asking to "now let bygones be bygones."[6] The earlier, antagonistic letter was evidently destroyed. Imagining its contents, the highly reliable biographer Mark De Wolfe Howe states, "probably it concerned some preachment of his father's, relating to war objectives and his son's falterings of faith as to their attainment."[7]

Ideologically, the two men had been trading places since the war began. Holmes Jr., who had burned for desperate glory on the battlefield, still took pride in his regiment's performance under fire. Although he had once been an aspiring poet, it pleased him when an old officer from the regular army told him, "The 20th have no poetry in a fight." Wendell agreed; he wrote that when the Twentieth got down to business, there was "about as little excitement & hullabulloo on those occasions as may be."[8] But his satisfaction was no longer in any sense romantic. Wendell now regarded fighting as a repellent task, good only for sending brave, earnest men to the cemetery.

By contrast, Holmes Sr., despite his sobering visit to Antietam and his son's repeated brushes with death, could not put notions of the romance of the struggle out of his head. The war, he insisted, was the grand expression of a supreme moral sentiment; it was a revolution in the name of freedom that was "wav[ing] its flambeaux over a great gulf." The Governor still believed that wars were won not with blood and iron, but with pure hearts. He told an English acquaintance, "If the people are good and sincere enough we shall succeed now. . . . The Devil always makes a good fight . . . [but] we will have his horns off yet."[9] Eager to illuminate his son's service with the proper literary spark, the doctor even prescribed a reading list for him. Holmes Jr. replied, "It's very well to recommend theoretical porings over Bible & Homer—One's time is better spent with Regulations & the like, and any connected study situated as I am is rather impossible."[10]

An officer between campaigns often enjoys some relative quiet. In the spring of 1863, however, Holmes was busier than most. As a reward for its distinguished service at Fredericksburg, the Twentieth was assigned to act as provost guard at army headquarters. Upon returning to Falmouth, Holmes was appointed provost marshal, meaning that, during the town's occupation, he essentially served as sheriff, charged with tracking down deserters, ferreting out spies, confining prisoners, and maintaining civic order among both soldiers and civilians. On occasion, provost courts tried cases against military personnel accused of crimes against the local community. Sadly, no records of Holmes's activities in this line, his first exposure to legal practice, appear to have been preserved. However, his work captured the attention of one of the army's most respected officers, Major General John Sedgwick.

Sedgwick had been in the West Wood at Antietam when Holmes's regiment had been driven back among the trees. Wounded three times in that battle, Sedgwick had missed Fredericksburg but had now returned to active duty, commanding the army's Sixth Corps. A former teacher, Sedgwick savored witty and enlightened conversation. Having already had at least one pleasant meeting with Holmes, the general said to his aide-de-camp, Charles Whittier, "Tell Captain Holmes he must come over again soon. I want to hear him talk."[11] Reflecting further, Sedgwick decided that a conversation here and there would not suffice; he asked Whittier whether Holmes might enjoy a place on the general's staff. As Holmes confessed to his parents, Sedgwick's interest "did tickle me a little."[12] He boasted, "I fancy old John rather likes me & you must know that John Sedgwick is one of the biggest Maj. Genls. now in our army."[13] But, as Whittier predicted, Holmes did not accept. As word of his skill in law enforcement spread, it was also suggested that he become the permanent provost marshal of his entire corps. Again, Holmes declined. "I should like a good staff position," he admitted, "but I wouldn't leave the Regt."[14]

Holmes's feelings about his service—an almost contemptuously low opinion of the army and its prospects, coupled with an adoring loyalty to his regiment—were common in the Army of the Potomac. Certainly they were shared by Captain Abbott. In the bleak January of 1863, when the mention of Lincoln or Burnside brought groans around the Yankee campfires, Abbott remained certain that the Twentieth could be depended on to "fight, if without enthusiasm, as bravely as ever."[15] Abbott told his mother, "Oh, by jove, you don't know how much I would give to be permanent commander of this regt., & I can hardly imagine greater bliss than to be commander of a regt. in which all the companies were as good as my own."[16] Holmes agreed. "I very much doubt, " he told his father, "whether there is any Regt. wh. can compare with ours."[17]

In the first days of May 1863, the valor of the Twentieth was again tested. The Battle of Chancellorsville is remembered as Robert E. Lee's most brilliant tactical triumph and as a crushing embarrassment for the Army of the Potomac's new commander, Joseph Hooker. It was also Stonewall Jackson's last battle. As he rode with his staff reconnoitering Federal positions after sunset on May 2, Jackson was surprised by a regiment of North Carolina infantry, who opened fire. Wounded three times, Jackson died eight days later. On May 3, Jeb Stuart, in his first significant action since Pelham's death, took temporary command of Jackson's corps. Despite never having led infantry before, Stuart deftly coordinated an attack on Hooker's right flank. A high-ranking Confederate artillerist wrote admiringly, "I do not think there was a more brilliant thing done in the war" than Stuart's rallying of Jackson's men.[18]

The day after Jackson's wounding, about ten miles east of the scene of Stuart's triumph, two smaller detachments from the two armies engaged in a small but bitter reenactment of the Battle of Fredericksburg. As in December, Confederate forces stood behind the stone wall on Marye's Heights. As in December, the Union forces were tasked with dislodging them. This time, however, the odds had shifted. Although the rebels had approximately 9000 men in the vicinity, their commander, Jubal Early, had other points of possible assault to defend. Reasoning that the Federals would remember the folly at Marye's Heights five months earlier and would not risk a similar disaster a second time, Early assigned only a brigade and three additional companies of infantry under William Barksdale—the same general who had defended the town from house to house in December—to hold the stone wall. These troops enjoyed strong support from Southern artillery. Against them, however, stood Sedgwick's Sixth Corps, with almost 25,000 men at its disposal. What had been an impossible task in December looked almost easy in May.

Though they were formally part of John Gibbon's division of Darius Couch's Second Corps, the Twentieth Massachusetts moved that morning with Sedgwick's corps. The day began with an eerie experience of déjà vu. Again the regiment marched down from Falmouth. Again pontoon bridges were laid across the Rappahannock. This time, however, no snipers occupied the town, and the bluecoats crossed without incident. Rather than risk another street fight, they turned right along the river road, skirting the town and moving toward Marye's Heights in more circuitous fashion. Bayonets fixed, they started to advance upon the wall. Even when lightly garrisoned, the sunken road below the heights was a defender's dream. The skeleton force of Rebels beat back two assaults before the break finally came, and Union troops bounded over the wall. Reduced to fighting hand to hand, Barksdale's men resisted savagely. Sedgwick's men matched them with a fury so titanic that many of the Southerners concluded that their attackers were drunk.[19] The Yankee bayonets did fearsome work. As midday approached, the Army of the Potomac had its revenge: the Stars and Stripes flew over Marye's Heights.

But, just as Wendell Holmes had been spared the horrors of December, he was denied the glories of May. On their way toward the heights, the regiment had been blocked by a deep canal, more than fifty feet wide. In anticipation of an attack from this quarter, the Confederates had stripped the closest bridge of its planks. As a detachment from the Nineteenth Massachusetts scrambled to strip a nearby house of its siding, to be used as replacement planks, Confederate artillery prepared to fire on the stymied column. Just as Holmes's brigade was crossing the hastily refurbished bridge, Confederate canister shot flew over them. Throwing himself onto his stomach, Holmes could only watch as the enemy steadily improved its aim. Later that day he wrote, "Pleasant to see a d[amne]d gun brought up to an earthwork, deliberately brought to bear on you—to notice that your Co. is exactly in range—1st discharge puff—second puff (as the shell burst) and my knapsack supporter is knocked to pieces." The man in front of Holmes was hit. Wendell had an instant to give thanks for his close call, but the instant passed. A third shot came: "Whang," he wrote, "the iron enter[ed] through garter & shoe into my heel."[20]

Holmes had absorbed enough anatomy lessons from his father to identify his wounded bone as the "os calcis."[21] A shell fragment had driven deep into it. Borne off on a stretcher, Holmes was given chloroform, and pieces of the bone were extracted. He was taken across the river to the same house where Whitman had been stunned to behold a pile of severed limbs. For a while, it looked as if Holmes's lower leg might become part of a similar stack. By the next day, though, the surgeons concluded that the foot would recover; no amputation was performed. Back across the river, when the Twentieth finally made it to the stone wall, the fighting there was all but over. They walked easily across the field where, months earlier, not a single Yankee had been able to step.

At first blush, Holmes's injury seemed a trifle compared to his wounds at Ball's Bluff and Antietam. But the heel was slow to mend, and Holmes returned home for his third convalescence of the war. Two months after his wounding, he missed Gettysburg, where, on the 3rd of July, the Twentieth absorbed the force and fury of Pickett's Charge. From the moment that the charge began, Abbott guessed the outcome. "I knew we should give them Fredericksburg," he wrote. "So did everybody." The Twentieth let the Rebel line come to within a hundred feet and then "bowled them over like nine-pins."[22] The victory came at a cost. Holmes's young cousin, Sumner Paine, had just exclaimed, "Isn't this glorious?" when two bullets struck him in the chest, killing him.[23] Lieutenant Colonel Macy lost a hand. The day before the charge, Major Revere had taken a canister ball through his lungs and abdomen. He lingered two days before dying. Gettysburg shredded the Twentieth Massachusetts. The regiment incurred thirty-one dead and ninety-three wounded. Of the regiment's thirteen officers who rode into the battle, only three—the invincible Abbott and two lieutenants—came through unhurt. Recounting the struggle, Abbott could not help feeling a great weight upon his heart.[24] A month afterward, the regiment counted only 145 men reporting for duty. Though Abbott insisted that he and the other two remaining officers could "run the machine," the unit that Holmes had joined two years earlier was now barely recognizable.[25]

Inwardly, Holmes was not fully recognizable, either. For his parents, he kept up a brave front; the short letters he sent from Fredericksburg after his heel wound were almost jocular. Once he had been brought home, Wendell was, the "Governor" said, "a quite endurable patient," putting up with his father's wretched puns and suppressing his annoyance when, thinking themselves clever and original, visitor after visitor called him "Achilles."[26] But his private thoughts were dark, in a way that only his friend Charles Whittier seems to have guessed. In a letter to Holmes, Whittier casually noted a conversation he had had with Nathan Hayward, the regimental surgeon who first examined Holmes's foot. Hayward had told Whittier, "Holmes seemed to be rather sorry that he wasn't to lose his foot."[27] It was true, though Holmes did not admit the fact until more than seventy years later; to his law clerk Mark De Wolfe Howe, he vividly recalled praying that he might lose his foot, so that duty would not call him back to the front yet another time.[28] Wendell would sooner go back to the line than ever be thought a coward for staying home. But he would rather have been crippled for life than have to go back. He had joined the army to achieve completeness as a man and victory for the cause. Instead, the war had all but shattered him.

The day after Pickett's Charge, Dr. Holmes delivered a Fourth of July oration, which he called "The Inevitable Trial." Although his stated audience was the City Authorities of Boston, the poet really addressed his remarks to a larger contingent: those who, after more than two years of war, had become depleted of their moral force and had lost their taste for further fighting.[29] Holmes declared his intention to approach these wavering souls fairly and generously.[30] Yet his speech was a sustained cry of war fever. The South was to blame for the conflict, said Holmes, and the first cannon that had fired on Fort Sumter had slapped every loyal American full in the face.[31] The Union had been stolen from the lover of freedom, just as if a robber "had laid hands upon him to take from his father's staff and his mother's Bible."[32] Whether or not that theft would be avenged depended above all on whether the North had virtue and manhood enough to see the struggle through to its end.[33] Dr. Holmes gave thanks that the war had not been easily won; it was necessary to reduce the South to utter ruin, depriving it of the means by which it might rebel a second time.[34] Evoking the Crusades, he called the Rebels "the Saracens of the Nineteenth Century: a fierce, intolerant, fanatical people."[35] The doctor was prepared to meet fanaticism with fanaticism. In exchange for total victory, he would gladly sacrifice not only the last man and the final dollar, but "the last woman and the last dime, the last child and the last copper!"[36] The struggle was now "our Holy War," and the "pouring out [of] the most generous blood of our youth and manhood" was the inevitable price of redeeming the nation.[37]

In response to his father's effusions, Wendell seems to have observed a prudent silence. Captain Abbott was less guarded. Exasperated by the doctor's fireside patriotism, he wrote to his father, "Holmes, senior . . . is a miserable little mannekin, dried up morally & physically, & there is certainly nothing more aggravating than to have such a little fool make orations & talk about traitors & the 'man who quarrels with the pilot when the ship is in danger' &c, &c." Abbott was quick to add, however, that Holmes Jr. was "a good fellow & remember is 6 feet high."[38]

Months passed. Wendell's wound refused to heal. Adding to his distress, the War Department issued an order that any officer absent from his command beyond a specified period would be subject to dismissal.

The edict was soon rescinded, but not before it had moved Abbott to fury on Wendell's behalf. Abbott decried "The outrage of refusing a gentleman thrice wounded an extension. . . . They certainly ought to take into consideration the worrying & harassing a fellow [goes through] who has been out & got hit where they don't dare go."[39] If anyone had earned the right to stay at home as long as he liked, Abbott thought Holmes was the man.

Wendell's emotions about going back to war were painfully divided. His love of the regiment pushed him toward returning. However, no one relishes the prospect of being shot a fourth time. Moreover, he feared that his protracted absence had made him look like a malingerer. He considered resigning. Abbott begged him not to. "For God's sake, my dear fellow," he enjoined, "don't think of it, if it can possibly be avoided. . . . I tell you we can't afford to lose you."[40]

As for Holmes's fear of being greeted as a coward for having dragged out his recovery so long, Abbott insisted that that kind of thinking was nonsense. Everyone knew that Holmes had been wounded twice before and had hurried back each time. "Any good officer," Abbott assured him, might have stayed home "twice as long." If anyone gave him trouble about having stayed away, Abbott authorized Holmes to "punch his head." [41] But Abbott did not fully grasp the conflict in Holmes's mind, or the harshness of the accusations that Holmes brought against himself. He did not know how deeply Holmes reproached himself for being absent at Fredericksburg, and again at Gettysburg. Holmes was wrestling with the darkest of angels.

Holmes never did resume service in the Twentieth in any real sense. The reason was not trepidation, but red tape. The death of Colonel Revere and the maiming of Lieutenant Colonel Macy at Gettysburg had shattered the regiment's command structure, and a new lieutenant colonel was required. Holmes, though he was the senior officer in line, wanted to defer to Abbott, whom he deemed both more capable and more deserving. Abbott, however, would not hear of such an irregularity, and Holmes gave notice that he would accept the promotion. He rejoined the Twentieth on January 3, 1864, only to learn that his promised colonelcy had evaporated. Although his new commission was still technically valid, it could not take effect. The position was still officially held by Macy, who was to be elevated to colonel. However, Macy was still recovering from the loss of his hand and could not be mustered in at his new rank until he returned to duty. To make matters worse, new men had been mustered in at Holmes's rank of captain, so there was no vacancy for him at that level, either. As far as the Twentieth was concerned, Holmes was caught in bureaucratic limbo. Before the month was out, Holmes's ally Major General Sedgwick stepped in to cut the knot: he issued a special order assigning Holmes to a staff position with Brigadier General Horatio Wright, who led a division in Sedgwick's corps. Instead of leading men in battle, Holmes was to lubricate the general's administrative machinery: drafting and delivering dispatches, even requisitioning hay for the division's horses. Abruptly, Holmes's time in the Twentieth was over.

He was still exposed to danger. He wrote, "You show your nose anywhere and sizzle come the bullets at it . . . and they shoot pretty well."[42] Nevertheless, he was safer now than if he were still on the line. If his duty now seemed easier on the surface, though, inwardly the months that stood between him and the end of his three-year enlistment were among the hardest of all. Already the emotional strain of his service had weakened him. He privately confessed that a "sufficient reason" for the change in duty was "my honest belief that I cannot now endure the labors & hardships of the line."[43] Holmes had been away for eight months, by far his longest period *hors de combat*. Instead of effecting an emotional healing, the time away had given him too much time to think: about the dangers of returning; about the frailty of his emotional condition; about the absurd, ongoing immolation of his generation that no cause, however just, could fully vindicate. Leaving the Twentieth further undermined his morale. For longer than two years, the regiment had been more than a second family. At the same time that its many tragedies had pulled him down, the pride and companionship he had found there had given him a sustenance that he could not replace. He would never speak of his service to General Wright with the same fervor or devotion.

As the spring campaign drew near, Captain Abbott turned somber. He missed Holmes "exceedingly."[44] He was also extrapolating from recent experience in the field and not liking what he foresaw. The corps had lost forty-five percent of its strength at Gettysburg. Abbott thought it was likely to lose more than fifty percent of what was left this time around. "It makes me sad, " he told his mother, "to look on this gallant regiment which I am instructing and disciplining for slaughter, to think that probably 250 or 300 of the 400 which go in, will get bowled out."[45]

Holmes felt a similar foreboding. Among the few impulses that kept him moving forward was a tattered but stubborn belief in the sanctity of his mission. In April, a few weeks before Ulysses S. Grant, now in command of the army, began his spring campaign, Holmes wrote to thank Charles Eliot Norton for an article the latter had written about a medieval French hero who had been martyred in the Third Crusade. Holmes reaffirmed his "steadfastness in the Christian Crusade of the 19th century." He averred, "If one didn't believe that this war was such a crusade, in the cause of the whole civilized world, it would be hard indeed to keep the hand to the sword." Holmes confessed that he was no longer being "borne along on the flood of some passionate enthusiasm" but was instead "rather compelled unwillingly to the work by abstract conviction."[46] He needed the examples of all the saints and saviors he could find.

The month of May smashed nearly all the remaining steadfastness out of Holmes. The violence of the war, always dreadful, now reached a new pinnacle of savagery. In the past, Lee had always been able to rely on the failure of his opponent's nerve. Except for the disastrously aggressive Burnside, the Union commanders in Virginia had almost invariably been overly tentative. Even when they won a battle, they had lacked the will to follow up on their success. Such was not to be the case with Grant, who intended "to take the initiative whenever the enemy could be drawn from his entrenchments."[47] He pursued this policy with cold determination, only to find that Lee was just as resolute. The ground between the two generals was a dismal woodland, almost more jungle than forest, choked with vines and brambles. On May 5, Lee attacked the Army of the Potomac on this ground, the place called the Wilderness.

At Ball's Bluff, at Antietam, at Fredericksburg, one can quickly find one's bearings. There are broad, open spaces, clear landmarks, and a kind of logic to the terrain. By contrast, the Wilderness, with its dense woods and baffling network of badly maintained roads, was a place seemingly made to produce confusion. The generals could not improvise tactics because they could see neither the enemy nor even their own troops. Standing on this field even today, one can readily fall prey to an inarticulate uneasiness and fear. It was, as Bruce Catton has observed, "the last place on earth for armies to fight."[48]

The shock to Holmes began on the morning of the first day, when a

Confederate shell struck within a yard of where he and some other staff members were sitting on horseback and bounced under their mounts. As a regiment filed past to their right, another missile smashed into it, spattering many of Wright's staff with brains. All day the armies struck at each other, fiercely, blindly. After several hours, portions of the woods caught fire. Unable to escape, wounded men on both sides were burned to death. On the eighth, as the Sixth Corps prepared to position itself for a new round of fighting, Holmes "found woods afire & bodies of Rebs & our men just killed & scorching."[49]

Two days before the onslaught began, Holmes had boasted to his parents of his health and "excellent spirits."[50] By May 7, however, he was finding the struggle "very fatiguing." Though he seems to have succeeded in keeping his mind calm, his body started to rebel; he wrote "my heart beat strangely"—simple words for deep and overpowering feelings.[51] On May 9, Holmes was with Major General Sedgwick when the corps commander was teasing another man for ducking as bullets rang out from a Confederate sharpshooter's rifle. "Why, man," Sedgwick chortled, "they couldn't hit an elephant here at this distance."[52] Moments after Holmes rode away, Sedgwick fell to the ground senseless, his face torn open by a lethal bullet.

A more personal loss had come on the second day of the fighting. Under a determined attack from Longstreet's corps, James Wadsworth, the leader of a division that did not include the Twentieth Massachusetts, nevertheless ordered the regiment forward in a counterattack that Colonel Macy immediately recognized as suicidal. Exclaiming "Great God! That man is out of his mind!" Macy called his officers together. The attack was "certain death," he told them, but orders must be obeyed.[53] In the rush forward, Wadsworth took a fatal bullet to the head. Macy, too, was soon disabled, both of his legs pierced by bullets. Command of the regiment then fell to Henry Abbott. With the same icy calm that he had shown at Fredericksburg, he ordered his men to lie down. In order to direct their fire, however, Abbott remained standing. Impervious to the grave danger, he strolled up and down the line as Rebel bullets nipped at his clothing. A junior officer later wrote, "My God . . . I was proud of him as back and forth he slowly walked before us."[54]

For a seeming eternity that actually slipped by in seconds, Abbott somehow escaped harm. Then came the shock, a searing pain in the abdomen, and the realization among his men that an incredible streak of luck had ended. Abbott was down.

The regiment pulled back. In a desperate effort to save Abbott, three of his men laid him on a blanket and, using it as a stretcher, carried him two miles to a field hospital. Barely able to speak, Abbott directed that all his money should be set aside for the widows and orphans of the regiment's men. He asked someone to tell his parents that his last thoughts were of them. He then asked to be left alone so he could think. About four hours after his last charge, Abbott passed away. For his burial back home in Massachusetts, a metal plate was affixed to his coffin. It read, "Sans peur et sans reproche."[55] Obliged to remain at the front, Holmes could not attend the funeral. The gloom around him grew deeper. Twenty years later, he was to tell an audience of veterans, "His death seemed to end a portion of our life also."[56]

The strain on Holmes grew still worse a week later, when he toured the field at Spotsylvania Court House. The day before, at a sector of the line thereafter known as the "Bloody Angle," thousands of men had gone temporarily mad. At this crossroads, Grant had tried to split Lee's army in half. Both sides knew that the war might hinge on the outcome of this struggle. The Confederates had hastily dug trenches and prepared to defend them at all costs. In a war that did not lack for fierceness, the combat at the Bloody Angle was the most crazed and desperate of all. The two armies met at the edge of a clearing. Their fear turned to frenzy. Order fell away. Brigades and regiments were now meaningless designations. The armies devolved into two unreasoning masses, locked in a killing orgy.

As the fighting became abominable, either side might have broken and run. Neither did. For an appalling and incredible twenty-two hours, men fought hand to hand. Exhausted, some men drifted away a few yards and fell sound asleep amid the mayhem, then awoke and went back to fight some more. Bodies piled up a yard deep, then even deeper. Just behind the Confederate line, an oak tree almost two feet in diameter fell; the incessant gunfire had cut it down. Some of the dead were trampled in the fray, driven completely out of sight beneath the rain-soaked and boot-tossed muck. It was not even murder, for murder calls for rational premeditation. Men killed with cold, unthinking hatred—hatred for the war, for the enemy, for the miserable fate that had led them here, hatred perhaps above all for themselves. Many of the participants who told of it later, even though they had seen the slaughter with their own eyes, could not believe the heartbreaking truths that they were telling.

As Holmes walked the ground, he saw "the dead of both sides . . . piled in the trenches 5 or 6 deep—wounded often writhing under super-incumbent dead. The trees were in slivers from the constant peppering of bullets."[57] The war that Holmes had described as a saintly crusade less than a month before now resembled a crusade only in its sheer fanaticism. There was nothing holy in it, and very little recognizably human.

Holmes was nearing the point where the assaults on his mind and spirit were likely to do deep and permanent damage. Perhaps he had passed that point already. He knew in his core that he had to get out. During the heat of the fighting, he wrote home at every opportunity, but the notes were terse and factual, doing little more than to assure his parents that he was unhurt and, at times, to marvel at the quantity of bloodshed. Three days after he walked along the Bloody Angle, the fields were quiet, and he had time for a more reflective message. Still, he was in no mood to share details; by the time his letter arrived, his family would have seen "the butcher's bill" in the papers, and it would have spoken for itself.[58] What he had seen, he kept largely to himself. What he had felt, he could no longer restrain. He wrote, "These nearly two weeks have contained all of fatigue & horror that war can furnish . . . nearly every Regimental off[icer] I knew or cared about is dead or wounded."[59] What Holmes wrote next dismayed his father:

> I have made up my mind to stay on the staff if possible till the end of the campaign & then if I am alive, I shall resign—I have felt for some time that I didn't any longer believe in this being a duty.[60]

As important as the plans that Holmes announced were his reflections on the nature of duty. At least since Fredericksburg, where he had been able to do nothing more than watch as his regiment marched off to slaughter, the question of duty had been heavy and haunting: how did a man know when he had done enough? The demands of service to country were both pressing and potentially endless. When so much was asked, could a man of conscience ever be justified in saying, "This much, but no more"? Having enlisted in the army, Holmes had given his consent to die for a cause. But in 1861, no one had dreamed of Antietam,

Fredericksburg, or the plain, mad murder of Spotsylvania. Could this consent have a reasonable limit?

Back in Boston, the Governor was in no mood for philosophizing. The letter he sent his son in reply is lost, but if one may judge from his son's response, the elder Holmes was furious with his son's decision. The last three years had transformed the politically diffident doctor into a vociferous patriot. In part, he had undergone the change to protect his son; writing poems and giving speeches had seemed like his most effective means to rally other young men to the Union's cause. The Governor had wanted to bring victory as soon as possible, to bring his son home safe. The previous summer, he had stood before the most powerful men in Boston and pledged his willingness to have the Union defend itself to the last woman and child. But now his own son was leaving the fight that the doctor had urged so many to join. Did the boy wish to make a fool and a hypocrite of him? No, Wendell must stay and fight. This message, or something like it, Dr. Holmes must have sent to Wendell.

The irony was great. Trapped by the rhetoric that he had first adopted in hopes of saving him, the doctor now demanded that his son continue to expose himself to mayhem. Wendell wrote back with indignation. With stunning forthrightness, he called his father "stupid." The doctor had somehow gotten the idea that Wendell meant to resign *before* the campaign was over. He had also apparently imputed cowardice, for Wendell hotly wrote, "I must say I dislike such a misunderstanding, so discreditable to my feeling of soldierly honor, when I don't believe there was a necessity for it." His father had, evidently, further nettled him by trying to debate his motives for wanting to come home. His reasons, Wendell wrote testily, were "satisfactory to myself. . . . If I am satisfied, I don't really see that anyone else has a call to be otherwise." He also hinted at a reason that ought to have felt sufficient to anyone: he was on the verge of mental and physical collapse: "I am convinced from my late experience that if I can stand the wear & tear (body & mind) of regimental duty that it is a greater strain on both than I am called on to endure."[61]

Again that word: "duty." It lay at the very fulcrum of Wendell's thoughts now. The allusion to his mental strain was also telling. He was seeing the same phenomenon that had caught Whitman's notice—the mass of men whom combat was simply driving insane. He was soon to write home, "I tell you many a man has gone crazy since this campaign begun from the terrible pressure on mind & body."[62] Holmes felt the clouds of his own potential madness gathering near. He had to escape them if he could.

A week after the letter in which he had called his father "stupid," he wrote his mother about his decision to leave the service. It had not arisen, he assured her, from a reflex of despair. Rather, it was the fruit of his mature and measured judgment. He told her, "I started in this thing a boy. I am now a man and I have been coming to the conclusion for the last six months that my duty has changed."[63] He elaborated his thought:

I can do a disagreeable thing or face a great danger coolly enough when I know it is a duty—but a doubt demoralizes me as it does any nervous man—and now I honestly think the duty of fighting has ceased for me— ceased because I have laboriously and with much suffering of mind and body earned the right . . . to decide for myself how I can best do my duty to myself, to the country, and, if you choose, to God.[64]

Holmes had reached more than the limit of duty to his country. He had also reached the end of his loyalty to his father. Through all the carnage, one could see now that this war, which had infamously pitted brother against brother, was also a struggle between children and their parents. A generation of young men and women were suffering and sacrificing because their parents had failed to peacefully resolve the questions of slavery and secession. The individual stories often reflected the story of the whole, whether it was Louisa May Alcott going to war to win her father's love, Arthur Fuller seeking a manliness worthy of his father's legacy, or Wendell Holmes trying to live up to an ideal of honor that had less reality in the world than in his father's imagination. If Holmes had fought for America's new birth of freedom, he had also been fighting to free himself from paternal judgments. He had fought, in his own simple words, for the right to choose for himself.

Wendell wrote a sonnet in Henry Abbott's memory. The poem figures his fallen comrade as the captain of a ship who "steered unquestioning nor turning back, / Into the darkness and the unknown sea; / He vanished in the starless night, and we / Saw but the shining of his luminous wake."[65] Holmes wanted no more fame from the war than had already been given him. When the sonnet appeared that fall in the *Boston Evening Transcript*, it was published anonymously.

The poem ends with the sailor passing "into the glory of the perfect day." Holmes was a long way from feelings of glory. He had known loneliness before in this war—as he lay wounded and left for dead at Antietam, as he sat helplessly in his hospital tent at Fredericksburg. Now, with his Harvard comrades slaughtered almost to the last man, with his father impugning his courage and his manhood, the isolation was almost total. In the end, war taught no lesson more thoroughly than the pain of solitude. The starless night into which Abbott had vanished could also envelop the living.

On May 29, General Wright ordered Holmes to carry a dispatch to division headquarters and not to spare his horse. On his way, a young Union scout from Emory Upton's camp came galloping up to him. Holmes must turn back, the boy urged. Confederate cavalry lay ahead; the scout had been shot at and had barely escaped. Holmes, however, resolved to follow orders. He cajoled the youth into joining him, and, after assembling a motley escort—"a straggler . . . an unarmed man on a mule [and] a sick officer"—moved ahead.[66] A bit farther on, he encountered three or four Union cavalrymen. He "got them & sent back [the] rest except Upton's boy." Holmes, the boy, and the handful of horsemen had passed the place where the scout had been fired upon when Holmes heard bullets whiz past them: they had encountered about twenty Rebels. Initially mistaking the men for friendlies, Holmes prepared to halt. Then, seeing their gray jackets, he clapped his spurs to his horse's flank and sped away under fire. A Rebel soldier came into the road and, crying out "Surrender," started to unsling his carbine. No choice now. Holmes put his pistol to the man's breast and pulled the trigger. It misfired. Holmes made a break for it, sliding down on the side of his horse "Comanche fashion" and riding as fast as he could.[67] He escaped, got the message through, and won the praise of his comrades, who called his action "rather a gallant thing." Holmes crowed to his mother about the adventure, calling it "a jewel in the head of this campaign."[68] Finally, a taste of the heroism he had craved since 1861 was his.

The facts surrounding the last significant episode in Holmes's service are hard to determine. In early July Holmes and the rest of General Wright's corps were sent to Fort Stevens, an installation within the borders of Washington that guarded the northern approaches to the city. As the troops arrived on July 11, the fort had come under attack from Confederate infantry under Jubal Early. That same day, President Lincoln rode out to visit the fort and went onto its parapet to view the Confederate position. As he stood there, absentmindedly exposed to enemy fire, a soldier shouted at him "to get down or he would have his head knocked off."[69] In his later years, Holmes got in the habit of telling people that he was the soldier and that he had actually seized the president's arm while yelling, "Get down, you damn fool, before you get shot!"[70] Various people in Holmes's circle, including Felix Frankfurter, Alger Hiss, and Holmes's niece Esther Owen, claimed to have heard him tell the story. Yet neither Holmes's journals nor his surviving letters mention the encounter. The tale is impossible to confirm, as is Lincoln's alleged response: "I am glad you know how to talk to a civilian."[71]

Six days later, Holmes left the army. By this time, the Twentieth Massachusetts, which had continually brought in new recruits, had sustained more casualties than the number of men who had first joined it.[72] On the day of his discharge, Holmes received a humorous note from his friend Charles Whittier, one of the last remaining officers from his days in the Twentieth: "Citizen Holmes will proceed at once to Boston and take drinks accordingly."[73] He arrived home just in time to accept an invitation to a reunion dinner being held by his Harvard class. As class poet, he was asked to honor the occasion with some original verse. Holmes gamely bowed to the request. The stanzas that he hastily scribbled for the evening included the following quatrain:

But, all untuned amid the din of battle,
Not to our lyric the inspiring strains belong;
The cannon's roar, the musket's deadly rattle
Have drowned the music, and have stilled the song.[74]

Chapter Twenty

"To Act with Enthusiasm and Faith"

The music of life never again sounded the same to Wendell Holmes. After the war, he still loved to raise a glass and to trade *bons mots* with clever acquaintances, but his true personal intimacies were few. The memories of battle had made him distant, "even a little hard" as one biographer has phrased it.[1] He seemed to have less use for human warmth, finding no utility "in unproductive emotion that merely detracts from one's working force."[2] Alcott's and Whitman's solution to the pain of war was to love more broadly. Holmes found it more convenient, and possibly safer, to love less.

He returned to civilian life knowing that many soldiers had outshone him on the battlefield. If he had ever truly believed that his intellect and ancestry had set him above the mass of humanity, he no longer thought so. Later in life, he told his friend Harold Laski, "However fine a fellow I thought myself in the usual routine, there were other situations . . . in which I was inferior to men that I might have looked down upon had not experience taught me to look up."[3] His continued need to distinguish himself came, in part, from the war. Referring to himself and his fellow veterans, he later wrote, "If we would be worthy of the past, we must find new fields for action or thought, and make for ourselves new careers."[4] He had barely returned to Massachusetts when the urge came again to be up and doing.

Holmes had formed his intention to attend law school before the war began. The choice had not been completely his then, and it was still not entirely his in the fall of 1864. He was still living at home, and his father "put on the screws to have me go to the Law School—I mean he exerted the coercion of the authority of his judgment."[5] Discussing the episode with Felix Frankfurter, Holmes was blunter: "When I came back from the war, my head was full of thought about philosophy, [but] I was kicked into the law by my Governor."[6] But not all the motivation came from outside. Wendell, who had once believed that the moral universe could be explained by referring to Sir Philip Sidney, now recognized that far more reflection was needed to make sense of the world—if one could make sense of it at all. The Wilderness campaign had revealed the madness that can ensue when the restraints of civilization are stripped away. Yet conversely, Fredericksburg had shown the folly of rigid men like Burnside, who insisted on order and system and could not depart from orthodoxy even when it pointed toward disaster. The war had not shown him any path through life that consistently made sense, and in 1864 Holmes craved reason and purpose, both in his life and in the cosmos. Perhaps he could find some logic in the law.

But Holmes's search for reason yielded few results. "Truth," he wrote, "sifts so slowly from the dust of the law."[7] Dust was an apt metaphor for his legal studies. Harvard's law faculty consisted of only three professors, all of them content to teach their subjects as a pile of established precedents and black letters. They thought neither of how law might be changed to benefit society nor of how its principles might be theorized as a coherent philosophy. In frustration, Holmes wondered "whether the subject was worthy of the interest of an intelligent man." As practiced in Cambridge, the study of law "required blind faith—faith that could not yet find the formula of justification for itself." Having survived the war by mere chance, Holmes found in the law another grand instance of haphazardness. Having evolved almost at random, formed by force instead of philosophy, the law was "a ragbag of details," a patchwork creation.[8]

In the 1860s, a Harvard Law student typically graduated in four semesters. Holmes walked away after three. He thought his time was better spent as an apprentice in a firm. Curiously, the university that had tormented him about graduation requirements in 1861 now abandoned its fussiness; it gave him a degree though he never completed the recommended course of study. Despite the indifferent, haphazard nature of Holmes's law school training, Boston attorney John Ropes, who helped the young man prepare for the bar, wrote that he had never known anyone who studied the subject as hard as Holmes.[9]

The young man set aside less and less time for enjoyment. He became, in the words of a friend, "a powerful battery, formed like a planing machine to gouge a deep, self-beneficial groove through life."[10] It was ambition more than pleasure that drew Holmes onward. He later likened his scholarly odyssey to a voyage on an indifferent, unforgiving ocean:

> There were few of the charts and lights for which one longed. . . . One found oneself plunged in a thick fog of details—in a black and frozen night, in which were no flowers, no spring, no easy joys.[11]

Intellectually, he had set forth on a journey "for the pole," confronting the inescapable "loneliness of original work."[12] It was work for which combat had fitted him. Others plainly saw that Holmes's defining characteristic was now his driving ambition to excel.[13] That urge toward greatness promised one form of rich fulfillment, but it led him perpetually away from the pleasures, friendships, and loves that might have guided his spirit toward healing and peace.

He was seeking more than knowledge. He was looking for honor, comparable to but different from that which had evaded him when he ran through the woods at Antietam, when he sat in the hospital tent at Fredericksburg, when he prayed that he would lose his foot after Chancellorsville. In the library, too, one found great quests to pursue. He wrote:

> No man has earned the right to intellectual ambition until he has learned to lay his course by a star which he has never seen—to dig by divining rod for springs which he may never reach. In saying this, I point to that which will make your study heroic.[14]

To think great thoughts, Holmes decided, one had to have not only the mind of a scholar, but the heart of a voyager.

When Holmes did tear himself from his studies, his circle of preferred acquaintances, though small, was remarkably select. The young women with whom he associated were among the most intellectually engaging in Boston: Clover Hooper, the photographer who later married the historian and biographer Henry Adams; Minny Temple, later immortalized as the doomed heroine of *The Wings of the Dove*; and Fanny Dixwell, whom Holmes would later marry. The friend who likened Holmes to a battery was William James, the future psychologist and author of the brilliant *Varieties of Religious Experience*, who returned in March 1866 from a specimen-collecting expedition to Brazil with the famed naturalist Louis Agassiz. William's younger brother Henry, the aspiring novelist, liked Holmes well enough to invite him for vacations in the White Mountains of New Hampshire. But it was with William that the mental sparks flew. Emotional and intuitive, William thought Holmes could sometimes be too exclusively intellectual. Nevertheless, he wrote to a friend, "The only fellow [in Boston] I care anything about is Holmes, who is on the whole a first-rate article, and one which improves by wear. He . . . sees things so easily and clearly and talks so admirably that it's a treat to be with him."[15] Holmes evidently reciprocated his friend's regard; the two young men met every Saturday evening to discuss philosophy, a standing rendezvous that continued until James voyaged to Germany the following year.[16]

In 1868, after eighteen months abroad, James came back to Boston. He and Holmes co-founded a club—unimaginatively christened "The Club"—that gathered each month at dinner for the purpose, as James put it, of discussing "none but the very tallest and broadest questions."[17] The Club counted among its members not only Henry James but also Henry Adams; the budding author William Dean Howells; and the future founder of the Boston Symphony Orchestra, Henry Lee Higginson. Higginson thought that The Club offered the best conversation in town, and he had no doubts as to the two most scintillating participants. In their contrasting mental habits, Wendell and William James complemented each other admirably. James was a Darwin aficionado and a skilled visual artist who spoke three languages and had dabbled in chemistry, philosophy, and medicine; the very range of his attributes had almost paralyzed his efforts to choose a career. If James's mind was everywhere at once, Holmes's was steadily narrowing toward a tight focus on law and legal philosophy. Holmes, James conceded, had "a far more logical and orderly mode of thinking than I," and the forcefulness of the lawyer's speech often put James on the defensive. But in their exchanges, James, with his "ruder processes," gave as good as he got.[18] Higginson recalled, "It used to be great fun to hear William James and Wendell Holmes . . . spar, or at any rate excite each other to all sorts of ideas and expressions."[19]

The Club was a precursor of the famed but short-lived Metaphysical Club, formed in January 1872. Along with Charles Sanders Peirce,

Holmes and James co-founded that society as well, although, as historian Louis Menand observes, Holmes probably did not participate often in its discussions.[20] The Metaphysical Club began to dissolve in the summer of the same year, and during that time Holmes married Fanny Dixwell. He was also lecturing on law at Harvard, keeping up his legal practice, and immersing himself in his most important legal work to date, preparing an edition of James Kent's *Commentaries on American Law.* Holmes carried his manuscript around in a green bag, which he would not let out of his sight even long enough to visit the bathroom. Regarding Holmes's obsession, James's mother observed, "His pallid face, and this fearful grip on his work, make him a melancholy sight."[21]

Holmes did spend enough time with another Club member to make a difference in his thinking. Chauncey Wright drank too much and was a poor manager of the practical aspects of his life. However, Holmes considered him a philosopher of true merit. Two of Wright's propositions especially attracted him. First, Wright argued, "The questions of philosophy proper are human desires and fears and aspirations—human emotions—taking an intellectual form."[22] That is, people are guided in the first instance by their subjective wants and impulses; rules and principles come later, in service to those urges. Often, what we take as the products of our reasoning really originated in our will.[23] Second, Wright embraced the idea that human knowledge is profoundly limited and, even in its limited state, is surrounded by clusters of primitive beliefs that go far beyond our personal knowledge. Unable to know things directly and perfectly, we instead make choices and predictions based on probability and totemic biases rather than certainty or immutable laws. Holmes wrote in later life that Wright had taught him to be "a *bet*tabilitarian. I believe that we can *bet* on the behavior of the universe in its contact with us."[24] Wright thus joined with Holmes Sr., Emerson, James, and the war as one of Wendell Holmes's essential but conflicting influences. The soldierly scholar now had all he needed to tease out his theories of the law.

✶

CONDITIONED TO CHAOS BY HIS YEARS at war, Holmes also saw much disorder in the law. "The law," he wrote, "did not begin with a theory. It has never worked one out."[25] To him, the standpoint of the "bettabil-

itarian" had more intuitive appeal than that of the logician. Whitman
had come to see the war as a kind of lethal lottery.[26] Holmes, whose life
had been spared at Antietam by a fraction of an inch, would hardly have
argued. The war had taught him that people live amid largely random
forces. Holmes accepted this state of uncertainty. The question for him as
a legal scholar was how the law should respond to it: What kinds of wagers
should it subsidize? What were the features of the bettors that it would
set out to reward? Obviously, the law sought to mitigate randomness by
imposing order. At the same time, though, an excess of order could do
harm. If the law were to become nothing more than a system of precedents, judges would find themselves awkwardly applying centuries-old
rules to new conditions—and conditions had never before changed more
rapidly than in the nineteenth century. In earlier, pre-industrialized times,
the law had generally sought to protect people in the quiet enjoyment of
their property; the chief rule was expressed in the Latin phrase *sic utere tuo
ut alienum non laedas*—one used one's resources so as not to harm or disturb others. In Holmes's time, however, the rise of the factory and the railroad had brought the need for new legal rules; an economy of innovation
and growth demanded a law that could innovate and grow in pace with it.
The money was shifting from safer bets to riskier but possibly more remu-
nerative ones. In turn, how could judges accommodate the shift in values
from quiet enjoyment to economic development? Holmes the philosopher
saw the problem with Darwinian and Emersonian eyes.

Like an evolutionist surveying the natural world, Holmes saw human
affairs as neither perfect nor perfectible. If there was a governing force
behind them, it was not fairness but self-interested desire. After Fredericksburg, Holmes had felt persuaded that moral principles would not
decide the war. It had seemed to him then that the South's pure determination would lead it to victory; he had not foreseen the greater determination of Grant and Sherman, combined with superior masses of men
and material. Now, though peace had come, Holmes still saw people
engaged in warlike struggles, contending against social and economic
forces that would crush those who lacked the ability to fight. He also
saw that a shift in the prevailing forces that benefited one person often
penalized his neighbor. Legislatures and courts could not eliminate the
burdens that oppress people in their daily lives; they could only redistrib-
ute them. Always, there would be a rub somewhere. Later in life, Holmes

wrote to his friend Harold Laski, "Every mitigation of the lot of any body of men has to be paid for by some other . . . body of men."[27] The law of human existence was struggle. That law might be softened somewhat by prudence and sympathy, "but in the last resort a man rightly prefers his own interest to that of his neighbors."[28]

To prefer one's own interest was not merely natural or instinctive. Holmes declared it "right." People were welcome to pursue altruism in their private lives, but the legislature was no house of charity. Its task was to implement "the will of the *de facto* supreme power in the community." The great defense against darkness and chaos was not love, but rules. And yet the rules, being made by those in power, predictably served the interests of power. Inevitably, said Holmes, the group that possessed the greater measure of force would have interests that clashed with those of others who had competed unsuccessfully. Although Holmes hoped that the spread of an educated sympathy would reduce the sacrifices of minorities to a minimum, he thought that society's laws would inevitably reflect the interests of the powerful: the processes of government, "like every other device of man or beast, must tend in the long run to aid the survival of the fittest."[29] "Survival of the fittest," a phrase often ascribed to Darwin, was coined by the British social theorist Herbert Spencer. Holmes did not get around to reading Darwin until 1907.[30] Nevertheless, Holmes knew of Darwin through William James, and his most insightful biographer, Mark De Wolfe Howe, aligns Holmes with Darwin, averring that, to some extent, Holmes's worldview "made tooth and claw more significant than heart and soul."[31] The war had persuaded Holmes of the primacy of force in human relations. Kindness and charity were all right in their place, but Holmes's position never gave them significant standing in the law. More than any person before him other than John Marshall and, perhaps, Joseph Story, Holmes was to alter the face of American law. Yet his confidence in law as a tool for achieving justice was laced with skepticism.

As much as the Darwinians insisted that change and struggle lay at the heart of the natural world, Holmes demanded an equivalent dynamism in the legal sphere. What Emerson tried to accomplish for language, Holmes attempted for the law. Emerson's great challenge was how to keep ideas and language alive; how did one keep one's thoughts from turning stale and cold once the ink was dry on the page? "We live amid surfaces," Emerson wrote in his great essay "Experience," "and the true art of life is to skate well on them."[32] The secret for Emerson was to keep one's thought moving, to keep skating from insight to insight, angling from seeming contradiction to seeming contradiction, lest one should ever come to rest in the center of the frozen pond of one's argument and hear the ice cracking under one's feet. Emerson accomplished this motion through an aphoristic prose style and a refusal to arrive at conclusions: each of his thoughts always seems to open onto another thought, and the ideas ingeniously fuel one another in a virtually endless dialectic. Emerson's philosophic system turns out to be the absence of system, because system implies rigidity, stasis, and rhetorical dead ends.

Holmes knew that the law could not express itself in the same way as Emerson wrote his essays. A legal opinion *must* come to a decision and articulate a rule. Holmes understood and revered the rules, and his book *The Common Law* reveals both his superior knowledge of them and his nimbleness in applying them. But the love that Holmes felt for the law did not reside in the articulation of eloquent syllogisms or in eternally binding precedents. It lay instead in the aspects of the law that evaded finality, those that remained supple and capable of change as societies changed and demanded new rules. The lawyer must seek new understandings and novel applications of the law: attorneys, too, must learn to skate.

Judges, too, had their part to play in this intricate dance—indeed, a greater role than they typically imagined. Judges, said Holmes, "have failed adequately to recognize their duty of weighing considerations of social advantage."[33] They needed to appreciate, not only the claims of the parties before them, but the economic and social forces that had brought them there. While Holmes was writing, conversations about socialism were unsettling the comfortable classes. Inescapably, the courts would be called upon to take sides on questions of economic distribution. Holmes thought judges should more explicitly consider the economic impacts of their holdings and should realize that force, not impartial reasoning, underlay many of their assumptions. Law becomes more rational and more civilized when its rules are overtly and articulately connected to the ends that they serve. The language of the judicial decision, Holmes admitted, was "mainly the language of logic." The judge's logical forms and methods appeased the yearning for stability and repose that Holmes observed "in every human mind." But that language was often a cover-up for underlying turbulence. The needs and urges of the masses, too, were forces to be considered. Said Holmes, "certainty generally is an illusion, and repose is not the destiny of man."[34]

It was an astonishing way for a Boston Brahmin to think about the world. Possibly what had always annoyed Holmes most about his father was that the Governor had always been certain: certain of his opinions, certain of his privilege. But Holmes Jr. lashed out at that complacency when he said, "Most of the things we do, we do for no better reason than that our fathers have done them."[35] Holmes's idea of the law was not about reverence for tradition or a faith in the Harvard elite as the rightful philosopher-kings of American society. The law, as Holmes saw it, should always leave the door open for a new social force that might carry it in a new direction. Law was not a mere set of commands to be obeyed. It was an instrument to be used.

In his early examinations of legal philosophy, Holmes found himself continually returning to the question of the limits of duty. He had, it seems, not fully absolved himself for his flight at Antietam, his illness at Fredericksburg, or his eventual departure from the army. He needed a theory that would explain and justify his conduct. While he was studying at Harvard Law School, virtually the only scholarly commentary on duty Holmes could find came from an English thinker, John Austin, whose work had earlier caught his attention after his wounding at Antietam. Austin, now dissatisfied him profoundly. Austin, like Holmes, had been a military veteran, having served five years in the Napoleonic Wars. His view of duty bore the marks of military service: to Austin, duty meant obeying the commands of a person or body that wielded rightful authority. Strongly implied in Austin's formulation were ideas of moral judgment. His approach was, Holmes thought, "the theory of a criminalist."[36] Austin believed that civil suits existed not just to compensate the injured party but to punish the wrongdoer. He treated civil liability as a penalty, predicated on ideas of personal fault. The stark binary of doing or not doing, as well as imputing moral inadequacy to the person who failed, seemed inappropriate to Holmes. Remarkably, Holmes rejected the whole idea that civil liability was meant to impose ethical standards.

Holmes's thoughts on duty carried him back to the idea of bettability. If life was a gamble, then the law existed largely to advise people as to how they might most successfully wager. The law imposed penalties, but more importantly, it offered predictions: it foretold what would likely happen to someone who pursued a particular kind of conduct. Holmes was adamant that the law of torts—the catch-all category for legal wrongs that are neither criminal nor governed by contract—did not exist to punish bad people. Indeed, most tort law cared nothing at all about "the internal phenomena of conscience. A man may have as bad a heart as he chooses, if his conduct is within the rules."[37] Once one comprehends that law has few moral ambitions, that it really is nothing more than a set of "prophecies" as to "what the courts will do in fact," Holmes wrote, "You see how the vague circumference of the notion of duty shrinks." His task, as he put it, was to "wash [the notion of duty] with cynical acid," leaving behind only the essential functions of law.[38] Those functions were to establish predictability, not to instill ideas of good and evil. For Holmes, cleansing the law of unnecessary judgments of right and wrong felt personally essential.

What, then, was the essential duty of a common person, going about her daily business in society, apart from not committing crimes and honoring her contracts? Holmes's favorite illustration came from a case involving two dog owners in 1850. The two Massachusetts men, George Brown and George Kendall, were walking their pets when the two animals lunged at each other. As their fangs flashed, Kendall grabbed a stick and lashed at the dogs, trying to separate them. As Kendall swung the stick backward, Brown recoiled in pain; Kendall had struck him in the eye, causing serious damage. The ensuing lawsuit ended up in the state Supreme Court, led by Chief Justice Lemuel Shaw.[39] Shaw held that if Kendall was acting lawfully in separating the dogs, he would be liable for damages only if he had failed to exercise "that kind and degree of care, which prudent and cautious men would use . . . to guard against probable danger."[40]

In his lectures on the common law, Holmes emphasized that Shaw's rule, the "reasonable man" standard that came to be embedded in the law of negligence, took no account of Kendall's temperament, intellect, or education; the law "does not attempt to see men as God sees them."[41] Nor did the law care whether Kendall thought he had behaved reasonably. Rather, his liability hinged on whether the jury, referring to its own experience and applying the community's idea of what the average prudent person would do under the circumstances, believed that Kendall had exercised due care. By stressing the importance of juries and their reliance on lived experience, Holmes was nudging the law away from deductive methods and toward inductive ones. He was urging a legal regime founded upon what we observe in the world, rather than syllogistic reasoning. "The *life* of the law," Holmes observed, "has not been logic; it has been experience"; and although the italics do not appear in the line as he wrote it, they need to be inferred: the law must live, and like any living thing, it must evolve.[42] That life and evolution could be found in the constantly shifting opinions and changing reasoning of the community. The critical actors in this drama are jurors, who draw on their common-sense understanding to adapt rules to the way that life must be lived in the moment.

Being based on the common-sense impressions of jurors, the reasonable-person standard was democratic. Referring as it did to the practices of the particular community in the particular moment, the standard was also flexible enough to allow for changes in the social reality. As has long been observed by legal scholars, it also tended to favor economic growth, for, in practice, it reflected the view that the quiet citizen must keep out of the way of the exuberantly active one.[43] Indeed, as the deeply insightful Morton Horwitz has observed, the law of negligence, supported by the reasonable-person standard, "became a leading means by which the dynamic and growing forces in American society were able to challenge and eventually overwhelm the weak and relatively powerless segments of the American economy."[44]

Holmes never explicitly connected his theories of legal duty to his experiences of war. But the connection is there. In war, he had seen how easy it was to fall short of someone else's idea of duty. To trace every broken charge and disordered retreat to a moral failure would be to impose burdens of responsibility and guilt that no man should have to bear. The war had brought Holmes face to face with the practical limits of performing one's duty. At Fredericksburg, he had been unable to join his regiment in the battle that had cost them more casualties than any other. After Spotsylvania, it had seemed to him that he could stay in the army only at the cost of his sanity. There were limits to what a man could do; there existed a point beyond which one might refuse a command without incurring ethical blame. In a sensible world, duty would not be absolute, and reason, not moral fault, would supply its measure.

Nevertheless, Holmes never intended for the standard of the reasonable man to be the measure of duty on a battlefield. If Austin's idea of duty as obedience to command has relevance anywhere, it is in the military, where soldiers have little business substituting their ideas of reasonableness for the commands of their officers. Holmes would never have questioned the right of General Burnside to order the Twentieth Massachusetts into action on Caroline Street, nor would he have challenged the agreement by which he had pledged three years of his life to Mr. Lincoln's army. Holmes's standard of reasonableness was meant for civilians: it applied to average people in the conduct of their ordinary lives. But precisely what Holmes loved and revered about military duty was that it called upon people to be more than ordinary. To act greatly was not to behave prudently; it was "to act with enthusiasm and faith." War taught dreadful lessons. Amid the horror and waste, war taught at least one sublime value: the honor that was won by "go[ing] somewhither as hard as ever you can."[45]

★

BETWEEN HIS PUBLICATION OF *The Common Law* and his appointment to the United States Supreme Court, Holmes served twenty years on the Supreme Judicial Court of Massachusetts. During those years, he gave two remarkable Memorial Day speeches, the first in 1884 to a group of veterans and the second in 1895, to Harvard's graduating class. In these two orations, Holmes addressed two very different audiences: one that had lived the war; the other to whom the war was only a story told by books and fathers and mothers. With the first group, an audience of men from his own generation, Holmes spoke to feelings that he knew were shared more or less throughout the room. Chief among these was a remembered sense of energy and zeal. The call to war, it seemed to Holmes, had been a call to personal transcendence—an opportunity to meet with fear and pain and death and to discover that those seeming destroyers truly destroyed nothing. To serve had been to discover life in its pure essence of "action and passion."[46] To have failed to share in that passion was akin to never having lived at all.

It was in his speech to the veterans that Holmes recalled the image of Captain Abbott in the streets of Fredericksburg, fearlessly swinging his sword from his finger like a cane—the sight that Holmes himself had never seen. It was the moment from the war that he described to the veterans at the greatest length. It was, very likely, the moment that spoke to him most poignantly, precisely because he had been absent from it. And now he created the impression, which he made no effort to correct, that he had gone with the Twentieth as it marched toward Caroline and Hawke, that he had witnessed Henry Abbott's matter-of-fact courage and had been exposed to the same level of fire. Holmes should not have created this ambiguity, yet it seems likely that his motive was not chiefly to deceive. He had wished to be with Abbott that day. Now, two decades after Abbott's death, he wanted to be near him still. Fredericksburg remained suspended in Holmes's mind as a mission never to be accomplished. Holmes told the veterans that, in their youth, all of their hearts had been "touched with fire." He called this searing touch a mark of "great good fortune." Because of it, he and his fellows had seen, "with our own eyes, beyond and above the gold fields, the snowy heights of honor, and it is for us to bear the report to those who come after us."[47]

At Harvard in 1895, Holmes came to bear that report to the children of the generation that had seen those heights. To reminisce with old soldiers about battles past was one thing; to urge the young toward future battles was morally quite another. Yet Holmes hardly moderated his message. His remarks began by deploring the materialism and love of commerce that had descended over America since the war—a headlong pursuit of gain and gaudiness that also offended Alcott and Whitman. The quest for honor, Holmes lamented, had fallen out of fashion. It had been replaced "by a rootless self-seeking search for a place where the most enjoyment may be had at the least cost."[48] In Holmes's view, equally contemptible as society's mania for pleasure seeking was its revolt against pain. Holmes railed against the principle that suffering was an evil to be avoided or prevented. He voiced particular scorn for what he termed the "literature of sympathy": soft-hearted books and poems that complained of how hard it was to be injured in life's struggles and "how terrible, how unjust it is that anyone should fail."[49]

To Holmes, this view of life was only so much sniveling. However much one might dislike the struggle of life, it was vain to try avoiding it or to refuse to admit that the destiny of humankind is battle. The only way to face a fight was to run toward it and to fight hard. Defeat might eventually come. In the meantime, the only honorable thing was "to fix our eyes on the point to be stormed, and to get there if we can."[50] Holmes summed up his rejection of the culture of pity in a single line: "If it is our business to fight, the book for the army is a war-song, not a hospital-sketch."[51]

The rebuke to Alcott's work could not be more explicit. It seems highly likely that Holmes was also nodding to Arthur Fuller, for no book that circulated in the Army of the Potomac was more literally a war-song than the chaplain's *Army Melodies*. Indeed, the frail preacher superbly illustrated Holmes's point. Hemmed in by the effete softness of a New England pastorate, Fuller had gone to war in the only capacity that had suited him, bringing Christian sympathy and care to the battlefront. But the tender ministrations of a chaplain had not been enough to satisfy his aspirations as a patriot. It was only in laying down his Bible and picking up a gun that Fuller could finally feel that he had done something for his country.

But the reference to Alcott is more direct and more telling. In contrasting the songs of war with *Hospital Sketches*, Holmes mapped out in plain language the two paths that a culture can follow when its existence has been challenged. Like Alcott, it can choose the path of sympathy. It can respond to horror with compassion and maternal kindness, discovering in adversity the building materials for community and redemptive love. The path championed by Holmes, the path of stoicism and physical courage, was both fearsome and sublime, and the lengths to which he was willing to pursue it were chilling. In his speech, he sought not only to justify the slaughters at Marye's Heights and the Bloody Angle, but actually to make them sweet and beautiful:

> I do not know what is true. I do not know the meaning of the universe. But in the midst of doubt, in the collapse of creeds, there is one thing I do not doubt, that no man who lives in the same world with most of us can doubt, and that is that the faith is true and adorable which leads a soldier to throw away his life in obedience to a blindly accepted duty, in a cause which he little understands, in a plan of campaign of which he has no notion, under tactics of which he does not see the use.[52]

Holmes must surely have felt the irrationality of what he was saying, but these words were not coming from his rational side. In his legal philosophy, Holmes was subtle and nuanced. In his patriotism, he was raw and elemental. Although on one level his speech appeared to condemn the literature of emotion, Holmes, too, was writing from a standpoint of intense feeling. His embrace of blind adherence to duty came from a desire for a transcendence that could be achieved only by the testing of one's limits and by an open defiance of fear and fate. It came from a credo that, in his words, "the joy of life is [in] living [and in] put[ting] out all one's powers as far as they will go; that the measure of power is obstacles overcome."[53] The experience of glory was greater "than the temptations of wallowing ease."[54] All this gave rise to extraordinary emotion, and it was an emotion that Holmes could claim to know: "We have shared the incommunicable experience of war; we have felt, we still feel, the passion of life at its top."[55]

Observing the experiences of Alcott, Whitman, and Holmes, one may justifiably conclude that the war drove a thinking person in one of two directions. Having taken the two authors to the hospitals—places filled with tragedy but also scenes of recovery and renewal—the war led them toward a redoubled insistence on the necessity of community and compassion. Holmes, who experienced the war as a fight for survival, came to see all of life in terms of power and struggle. For him, the years from 1861 to 1864 were a practical course in Darwinism. And yet Holmes could not fully embrace either nihilism or the cynicism of pure realpolitik. He had never professed deep faith in God. He had looked for logic in the law and had not found it. He had to find transcendence and a firmness of meaning somewhere, and he found them in the courage of men like Henry Abbott. Such persons accepted the emptiness of so-called causes, acknowledging the injustice of the world that made the war and the absurdity of the men who ordered them to fight. Yet, as they also knew, this was the world in which they had to strive and vindicate themselves. Holmes's speech was not titled "The Soldier's Destiny." He called it instead "The Soldier's Faith." It remains as compelling a statement of existential courage as one is likely to find before the days of Sartre and Camus.

Holmes had told his parents in 1864 that the war had brought him to the brink of a mental breakdown. In 1895, he insisted that viewing the heaps of bodies at Spotsylvania had shown him a kind of miracle, by which a man could "lift himself by the might of his own soul."[56] Holmes conceded the inconsistency. "War, when you are at it," he told his listeners, "is horrible. . . . It is only when time has passed that you see that its message was divine."[57] He was stating the inverse of John Pelham's insight at First Bull Run; after reveling in the fury of battle, Pelham had felt in its aftermath a sense of anguish and dismay. For Holmes, it was the sublimity, not the awfulness, that finally endured. Whether his immediate sense of horror or his retrospective feeling of divinity was the truer view is a solemn question.

Holmes argued that the most common interpretation of his speech was in error—that he had not intended "to advise young men to wade in gore, but to illustrate the theme of how we all honor a man who dies in a cause he little understands, and romantically transcends his more common self."[58] That transcendence had come to mean more to Holmes than life or death. In his mind, he wanted to revisit the campfires and relive the days of battle. He also wanted to affirm, in the most public way, that the struggles of his comrades had had substance and meaning, not only in terms of military victory, but in the values of Union and freedom, of faith and courage, that they had defended and proclaimed.

Oliver Wendell Holmes Sr. had died the autumn before his son lectured the Harvard graduates about the soldier's faith. At 84, he had outlived both of his other children, as well as Wendell's mother. What few words Holmes Jr. wrote about his father's passing were emotionally restrained. The Governor's death had come before he had suffered many of the worst effects of old age, and his estate raised his surviving son to independent wealth. These facts were on Wendell's mind when he told a friend, "My father's death although of course a very great event in my life seems to me to have come at a fortunate moment. I was fearing many things for him and he painlessly avoided them."[59] Holmes Jr. had devoted great effort and energy to differentiating himself from his father, and later, to surpassing him in fame and cultural influence. In 1902, he began the thirty years of service on the United States Supreme Court that would establish him as *the* Oliver Wendell Holmes of larger consequence in American history. But in his speech to the Class of 1895, with all its romantic zeal and glorification of combat, the younger Holmes did not separate himself from his father. In this one respect, he had become him.

"Real, Terrible, Beautiful Days"

When General Grant received the surrender of Robert E. Lee at Appomattox, the terms of Lee's capitulation were drawn up by Brevet Brigadier General Ely S. Parker, a member of Grant's staff and a Seneca Indian. As Parker gave him the papers for his signature, Lee extended his hand to the brigadier and said, "I am glad to see one real American here." Parker shook Lee's hand and said, "We are all Americans."[1] After the war ended, as the camps of white tents disappeared one by one, Walt Whitman watched in wonder as they were replaced by cemeteries—"camps of green," he called them in an 1865 poem—where two mystic armies of the dead now came together. "There without hatred," the poet wrote, "we all, all meet."[2]

Whitman considered America "the great test or trial for all the problems and promises and speculations of humanity." Like Holmes, he conceived of the country as a bold experiment, of which the Civil War had been, thus far, the most extraordinary episode. After four years of struggle, leaves of grass grew up from shallow battlefield graves across the country. Despite the tremendous cost, the courage and sacrifice that the war had called forth and the final conquest over slavery had shown that the experiment was abundantly worth pursuing.

Paradoxically, however, the prosperous peace that followed the war almost shredded Whitman's hope that America might realize its potential as a republic of virtue. After the South's surrender, the North experienced a surge of economic growth rarely seen in the history of the world. Whitman hailed the railroads, the ships, the machines, and even the "beating up of the wilderness into fertile farms."[3] But the spirit that had come with the great expansion distressed him. He saw in it the seeds of materialistic nihilism and none of the virtues needed to sustain a human soul.

He had written a poem for *Drum-Taps*, called "Song of the Banner at Daybreak," in which a child is enraptured by the sight of the flag, waving in glory against the sky. The boy is diverted from his patriotic reveries by his father, who wants the child to look at "dazzling things in the houses . . . the money-shops opening . . . the vehicles preparing to crawl along the streets with goods." These, the father implies, are the true worth of America, and he calls his child a fool for thinking otherwise. Another voice in the poem, representing Whitman, scorns the materialistic faith of the father. The true nation, the poet argues, will not be found in machinery or products or revenues. The real value, intangible and transcendent, finds its symbol in the flag, "out of reach, an idea only, yet furiously fought for, risking bloody death, loved by me."

In 1871 Whitman again denounced American avarice in *Democratic Vistas*, a prose work containing some of his darkest prophecies concerning the republic. "The magician's serpent in the fable," he reflected, "ate up all the other serpents; and money-making is our magician's serpent, remaining today sole master of the field." The depravity of the American business class was "infinitely greater" than one might suppose. Genuine belief seemed to have vanished. Whitman lamented, "Never was there, perhaps, more hollowness at heart than at present, and here in the United States."[4] Only yesterday, it seemed, the hospitals had opened to him "a new world . . . showing our humanity" in ways that "burst the petty bonds of art."[5] Now he looked upon the same society and saw it broken in the headlong pursuit of individual gain. "The [country's] lack of a common skeleton," he said, "continually haunts me."[6]

Nevertheless, the faith in America that Whitman had absorbed from his "dead Christ" in the high ground above Fredericksburg was not entirely dimmed. He commented, "So much of a race depends on how it faces death, and how it stands personal anguish and sickness." The outstanding young men who had fought the war raised Whitman's hopes for the future of the country. By his own count, Whitman paid over six hundred visits to the hospitals during the war. By his estimate, the sick and wounded among whom he passed totaled between eighty and a hundred thousand. He called the three years of his self-appointed service "the greatest privilege and satisfaction, (with all their feverish excitements and physical deprivations and lamentable sights,) and . . . the profoundest lesson of my life." The time aroused in him "undream'd-of depths of emotion" and supplied him with his "most fervent views of the true *ensemble* and extent of the States."[7] In his 1882 book *Specimen Days*, an autobiographical scrapbook of scenes that concentrated heavily on the war, Whitman wrote the now-famous line "The real war will never get in the books."[8] As he wrote this sentence, he was not thinking of long marches, deafening cannonades, or desperate charges. Instead, he had in mind an ineffable image of the soldier himself "with all his ways, his incredible dauntlessness, habits, practices, tastes, language, his fierce friendship, his appetite, rankness, his superb strength and animality, lawless gait, and a hundred unnamed lights and shades of camp." Not only would these traits never be captured in language, but, Whitman thought, "perhaps [they] must and should not be."[9]

But Whitman did try to get some of the war into the books. He added the poems from *Drum-Taps* and *Memories of President Lincoln*, which included "O Captain! My Captain!" and the "Lilacs" elegy, to the first postwar edition of *Leaves of Grass*, published in 1867. After that, he kept adding to the collection—and adding—until 1891. A mere dozen pieces had comprised the first edition of 1855. The so-called death-bed edition, released the year before the poet's passing in 1892, had swollen to include more than 380 poems. It mattered little to Whitman that *Leaves of Grass* had already been published in three different iterations before the war. In his late essay "A Backward Glance o'er Travel'd Roads," he stoutly claimed, "Without those three or four years [of war] and the experiences they gave, 'Leaves of Grass' would not now be existing."[10] The fact that the editions of 1855, 1856, and 1860 bore the same title seemed now like mere coincidence; they were the expressions of a different soul, writing in a now-vanished time. They were not what he proudly called "the consummated book."[11] As Whitman well knew, the country that had called itself the United States before 1861 was not and could not become the true United States until the war had rooted out its secessionism and slavery. Similarly, without the defining, concentrating experience of the war to tame his exuberance and deepen his empathy, his work was not the true *Leaves of Grass*.

Generations later, the leading modernist Ezra Pound was to write, "Mentally, I am a Walt Whitman who has learned to wear a collar and a dress shirt. . . . Whitman is to my fatherland . . . what Dante is to Italy."[12] Dante had had to pass through the Inferno. Whitman's necessary inferno had been the Washington hospitals.

Whitman knew that the hospitals had made him a more mature and sensitive thinker. He had always striven to be a poet of both the large and small. Before the war, however, his best poems could at times fall victim to declamatory bombast. But in poems like "When Lilacs Last in the Dooryard Bloom'd," the voice is humble and intimate. Two of his later lyrics, "A Noiseless, Patient Spider" and "The Dalliance of Eagles," typify the poet's willingness to focus on the less grandiose details of the natural world, to adopt a meeker, softer voice and, at the same time, to confess his own romantic vulnerability. The war had reinforced for Whitman the value of small things.

For the rest of his life, Whitman felt the presence of the ghosts of battle. He wrote of how, from both North and South, the forms of the departed came back to him: "Noiseless as mists and vapors, / From their graves in Virginia and Tennessee, . . . In wafted clouds . . . they come, / And silently gather round me." But these apparitions did not come to torture his memory. They arrived instead as old friends who knew and understood things he could not speak of. He wanted them not only to "gather closer yet," but also to "follow me ever—desert me not while I live." Whitman published these lines in 1881. The dust of battle had long settled, but one thing had endured. "Love," the poet wrote, "is not over."[13]

The war had strengthened and personalized Whitman's love of humanity; it had dangerously weakened his health. Whitman suffered from hypertension, and the problems he began to notice during the war were symptoms of the disorder: he complained then of periods of faintness and "a bad humming feeling & deafness, stupor-like at times, in my head which unfits me for continued exertion."[14] In January 1873, at fifty-three, Whitman had a debilitating stroke. Months passed before he could walk a single city block without assistance. From that time on, he had only partial use of his left arm and leg. Whitman blamed his work in the hospitals for permanently compromising his health. As he contemplated his "old machine, the body & brain well shatter'd and gone," he observed, "That secession war experience was a *whack* or series of whacks irrecoverable."[15] In another letter he again rued "the old secession war-time overstrain."[16] "I had to give up my health for it," he reflected. "My body—the vitality of my physical self: oh! so much had to go . . . that no man should give up until there is no longer any help for it." Like Alcott, like Holmes, Whitman had not survived the war without making deep and lasting sacrifices. Yet he consoled himself: in return he had gotten "the boys: thousands of them: they were, they are, they will be mine." Moreover, he had won a unique deliverance whose full value only he could understand. He recollected, "All the wise ones said: 'Walt, you should have saved yourself.' I *did* save myself, though not in the way they meant. I saved myself in the only way salvation was possible to me."[17] The hospitals had pulled him from the quicksand. Whitman was, in his fashion, as much a bettabilitarian as Holmes. Whitman, however, placed all his chips on the square called love, and he let the wager ride.

Having married in 1871, George Whitman settled in Camden, New Jersey, and took up the fairly new profession of inspecting gas pipes. He and his wife Lou bought a three-story house with a bay window. Their home was large enough to accommodate Louisa Whitman in the last year of her life. After she died on May 23, 1873, her room became available for Walt. The poet had had an angry falling out with William O'Connor the previous year, and his relationship with Peter Doyle also was less absorbing now; there was less and less to keep Walt in Washington. Granted a two-month leave of absence from his job at the Justice Department and in need of physical care, Whitman traveled to Camden, initially hoping to stay only long enough to recover his strength before going back to work. But time passed, and the poet did not fully regain his health. Unable to return to his duties, the poet was formally dismissed the following year. By that time, George and Lou had more or less accepted Walt as a permanent guest. It was clear to Walt that George's faith remained "in pipes, not in poems." The idea that Walt was a genius never struck George; long after Walt was famous, his brother still could not accept poetry as a form of employment. Almost forty years after the fact, George was to recall that, in the mid-1850s, when Walt was crafting *Leaves of Grass*: "We were all at work—all except Walt." Still, the two brothers appear to have gotten along cordially.[18] The devotion that Walt had shown in searching for George and helping to deliver him from the prison camp during the war was being more than repaid.

Whitman recalled 1874 and 1875 as years of "prostration." Gradually, however, he improved to a state of "semi-renewal."[19] His thoughts became immersed in the natural world. For weeks at a time, he left the city behind, taking a train about twelve miles southeast to Glendale, New Jersey, where he stayed at the farmhouse of his friends George and Susan Stafford. Here he spent "dear, soothing healthy, restoration-hours," sometimes rising just after sunrise to hear the musical drone of bumblebees and "the noisy, vocal, natural concert" of grass birds, bluebirds, and robins, sometimes staying up late to watch the midnight flights of still more birds.[20] In winter, he would pause in the pale gold light of evening, listening for the first hum of spring.[21] In summer, he strolled haltingly to a nearby creek, feeling the warm air on his face and shedding his clothes to bathe in its delicious waters. It seemed to him that he had never seen the sky before.[22]

In 1879, Whitman's American sky became broader than ever. Taking a sleeper car in Philadelphia, he rode west, crossing the Ohio and the Mississippi, rolling through Missouri and Kansas, and stopping at last in Colorado. He breakfasted on fresh trout and griddle cakes. He saw prairie dogs and herds of prong-horned antelope. He met cowboys, "bright-eyed as hawks . . . apparently always on horseback, with loose arms slightly raised and swinging as they ride."[23] He visited a smelting works in Denver and marveled at the vats filled with pure molten silver. And then he wrote about the mountains, which seemed to him "to afford new lights and shades. Everywhere the aerial gradations and sky-effects inimitable."[24] Observing the dazzling sun and savage power of Platte Canyon, he inwardly exclaimed, "I have found the law of my own poems."[25] The blood and suffering of the war had prepared him for these moments. The sublime human struggle of the war years was now matched with the sublimity of western nature. The country was so much bigger than even he had realized.[26]

George and Lou Whitman moved out of their home in 1884, and Walt was on the move as well, purchasing "a little old shanty of my own" at 328 Mickle Street in Camden.[27] The following year, to help the increasingly infirm poet in his travels around town, a group of literati and other well-wishers pooled their contributions to buy him an attractive carriage and a sorrel horse to pull it. Along with the pretty phaeton came a note from the contributors, among them, Oliver Wendell Holmes Sr.[28] Four years later, the carriage was sold; by that time Whitman's only mode of conveyance was a wheelchair. By the end of his life, Whitman was a virtual museum of diseases: tuberculosis, kidney disease, a collapsed lung, a fatty liver. He went to his rest on March 26, 1892. In his obituary, *The New York Herald* predicted that to the great mass of readers, his poetry would "always remain as a sealed book," but added that almost everyone would continue to cherish "O Captain! My Captain!"[29] Whitman's remains lie in a vault in Camden, directly beneath those of his brother George.

The *Herald* got it wrong. Since Whitman's passing, every American poet of stature has had to contend with him, either incorporating his influence or striving against him. T. S. Eliot called Whitman a "born laureate" and credited him with "making America as it was . . . into something grand and significant. You cannot quite say that [he] was deceived, and you cannot at all say that [he] was insincere."[30] Ezra Pound began his career detesting Whitman's legacy, regarding him as "a pig-headed father," but later made peace with him, acknowledging that he and the Good Gray Poet had "one sap and one root." Walt was the spiritual father whom the modernists had both to acknowledge and fight free of. It was Whitman, Pound averred, "that broke the new wood."[31] At the end of her recent term as America's poet laureate, Tracy K. Smith said that her most spine-tingling moment in office came when she examined a collection of Whitman's belongings at the Library of Congress. "There were his eyeglasses, his cane, a bust of his hands, and some notebooks . . . and that was pretty transcendent."[32]

The poet's companion Horace Traubel, who was with Whitman constantly in his final years and who filled nine volumes with their transcribed conversations, once asked the poet whether, in his mind, he ever went back to his days in the hospitals. Whitman replied, "I do not need to. I have never left them. They are here, now, while we are talking together—real, terrible, beautiful days!"[33]

✳

PERPETUALLY, THE WAR ALSO CAME BACK to Oliver Wendell Holmes Jr. Each spring, "at the height of the symphony of flowers and love and life," he heard, through the silence, "the lonely pipe of death."[34] If a sportsman fired a shot in the distance, Holmes would feel his heart stop for an instant as he said to himself, "The skirmishers are at it," and listened for the long roll of fire from the main line—a roll that no longer came. If he chanced to meet an old comrade in arms, the slow, deliberative mental habits of the lawyer and scholar would vanish, and he would recall "that swift and cunning thinking on which once hung life or freedom."[35] Now and then, the dead seemed to come back and live with him: Willy Putnam, the "beautiful boy" lost at Ball's Bluff; the smiling Nantucketer Leander Alley, shot down at Fredericksburg; and, of course, Henry Abbott, pure in his virtues, sublime in action. Though darkened by "the shadow of approaching fate," the faces were forever young. Remote and proud, they came to Holmes with a kindness that was both sweet and melancholy. They passed before him, he wrote, "wearing their wounds like stars."[36]

The war had been, for both sides, he believed, a cause suffused with an almost religious zeal: the holy causes of freedom and Union against the sanctity of the Southern states and their laws. Holmes understood the sense of holiness on both sides of the line, and he publicly averred, "We equally believed that those who stood against us held just as sacred convictions that were the opposite of ours."[37] Arthur Fuller's brother Richard had aptly observed that the American patriot of 1861 saw "in the loved stars and stripes of the Union the standard of the cross," and it was no accident that Lincoln's Second Inaugural Address, gravely sermonic in tone, had seen the war as affirming that "the judgments of the Lord are true and righteous altogether."[38] It had been a struggle of divine fury, and its fires had consumed the country.

And yet that fury, which had horrified Holmes when he was in the center of it, seemed ever more exhilarating and fitting to him as time passed. In later years, he dated letters with references to anniversaries of battles, and every September 17 he drank a toast in memory of Antietam.[39] But he felt more than a spirit of commemoration. It seemed to him that the strife of the war had raised him to a pinnacle of human experience. Its pain had distinguished him. It had given him both a sense of having known life at its most intense and a kind of knowledge that comes only through privation. He came to believe that the courage expressed in defending a cause mattered almost as much as the cause itself.

Indeed, after the war, Holmes was no longer a man of righteous causes. During the conflict, the Union had been guided by a man whose sense of the national destiny verged upon religiosity; it had mattered intensely to Lincoln that his armies were fighting on God's side, and his belief in the holiness of the country's purpose in rescuing freedom and democracy helped to galvanize the nation. After the smoke had cleared, the faith of the nation changed. It believed in hard results, not lofty purposes. Convinced of the power of randomness and the contingency of values that had once seemed transcendent, Holmes both embodied and reinforced the emergent pragmatism.

Holmes's best-remembered work began after Alcott and Whitman had been dead for more than a decade; in 1902, President Theodore Roosevelt elevated Holmes to an associate justiceship on the United States Supreme Court. The president, America's most ardent proponent of "the strenuous life," cared more about manliness and glory than legal theories; he chose Holmes in part because he had been moved by the judge's salute to patriotism and military virtue in the speech he had given at Harvard, "The Soldier's Faith."[40]

Holmes's work on the Supreme Court, which can only be touched on here, has been endlessly documented and analyzed.[41] It was revolutionary. When Holmes arrived on the high court, he joined the most devoutly conservative institution in the federal government. His brethren were generally men of cautious habits. They proceeded from the assumption that law had been established to favor tradition over innovation. Adherence to precedent seemed to them a sanctified aim. For Holmes's fellow justices, the law supplied a steady source of predictability. As Holmes himself observed, the law might be seen as a mere system of prophecies, foretelling what consequences would likely ensue from a given bit of conduct. As America embarked on a new century, however, the prophecies had become too self-fulfilling, and stability was starting to look like stagnation. As a spirit of reform was sweeping through the country's more progressive state legislatures, the high court, committed to its long-standing formalism, lagged behind. When the states or Congress presumed to establish new rights for the people, the court stood ready to strike their enactments down.

Holmes acknowledged that history was and should be a large part of the study of law. His book on the common law was, at least in appearance, just such a historical study. Yet Holmes found it "revolting to have no better reason for a rule of law than that so it was laid down in the time of Henry IV."[42] In 1905 he announced his intent to discover a different path in the case of *Lochner v. New York*. The state had enacted a law prohibiting owners of bakeries from either requiring or allowing their employees to work more than ten hours a day or sixty hours a week. Citing case law that upheld the freedom of contract, the Supreme Court voided the law as "an unreasonable, unnecessary and arbitrary interference with the right of the individual . . . to enter into those contracts" that she or he deemed appropriate or necessary.[43] In dissent, Holmes bristled at the majority's assumption that the Fourteenth Amendment mandated a laissez-faire approach to social questions. "A constitution," he insisted, "is not intended to embody any particular economic theory. . . . It is made for people of fundamentally differing views."[44] If the people of New York wanted to limit the power of employers to exploit their workers, no supreme law prevented them from doing so, and if the justices found that a law embodied a set of philosophical assumptions that differed from their own, that dissonance did not prove that the law conflicted with the Constitution.

Holmes dissented again in 1908, when the Court struck down a federal law that made it a crime for railroads to require that their employees not belong to unions.[45] He doubted whether unions really provided all the benefits that their supporters claimed. For him, however, the question was simply whether the Commerce Clause of the Constitution authorized Congress to regulate labor relations. Important grounds of public policy, Holmes reasoned, might well be served by such laws, whether or not the nine justices happened to agree with the policy being pursued.[46] Ten years later, he again diverged from the majority, this time when his fellow justices rejected a federal law that banned from interstate commerce any goods produced by child labor. The court held that the choice whether to allow children to be exploited for their work was "a matter purely local in character."[47] Holmes fired back, noting that few reforms had enjoyed more unanimous support in the developed world than the elimination of child labor. The same court that authorized child labor had acknowledged the power of the government to regulate the interstate sale of alcohol. Holmes could not see why a different rule should apply when the objectionable product was not strong drink, but "ruined lives."[48]

Holmes's tenure on the bench fell between the landmark cases of *Plessy v. Ferguson* and *Brown v. Board of Education*. He was never called upon to address a major case pertaining to race and civil rights. On the other hand, his contributions to First Amendment law were indispensable. In the second decade of the twentieth century, America's tranquility was shattered both by the First World War and by the infamous Red Scare. Millions of Americans from President Wilson on down had come to doubt whether free political speech could coexist with national security. Holmes thought it could, and his views on the subject alarmed most of his fellow justices. They were especially troubled by the stand that Holmes intended to take in the case of Jacob Abrams. A Russian Jewish immigrant, Abrams had been convicted under the federal Espionage Act for having circulated several thousand leaflets criticizing America's anti-Bolshevist foreign policy and urging munitions factory workers to refuse to make weapons that would be used to aid the cause of White Russia. Abrams's activism had been strikingly futile: no evidence was offered that any of the leaflets had even reached a munitions worker. Nevertheless, Abrams had been sentenced to serve up to twenty years in prison.

Holmes believed that the Great War had made some lower-court judges "hysterical" in their censorship of unpopular opinions.[49] In chambers, he and his fellow justice Louis Brandeis advised their colleagues that they would vote to strike down Abrams's conviction. Shortly thereafter, Holmes was surprised to find three of his fellow justices at the front door of his house. Ushered in, Justices Pitney, McKenna, and Van Devanter urged him to reconsider. Holmes, they said, was more than one voice among nine. His place in the public admiration was high: if he lent his prestige to a band of unwashed subversives, he might unwittingly undermine faith in the republic and encourage worse acts of disloyalty. The three justices were friendly but firm. They persuaded Holmes's wife, but not Holmes himself.

In one of his most memorable moments as a judge, Holmes read his dissenting opinion from the bench. He observed that persecuting others for their opinions was, from one perspective, "perfectly logical." But he went on to imply that that perspective was the viewpoint of a self-assured bully. "If you have no doubt of your premises or your power, and want a certain result with all your heart," Holmes said, "you naturally express your wishes in law, and sweep away all opposition." But, he continued, time had disproved many who had been sure of their correctness. The ultimate good should not be sought by enshrining this or that ideology, but rather by preserving society as an open forum for all intellectual competitors. The good society was marked "by free trade in ideas . . . [T]he best test of truth is the power of the thought to get itself accepted in the competition of the market."[50]

The marketplace was an apt metaphor for Holmes's ideas of free speech. To convey his understanding of the America's supreme law, he also liked invoking the trope of a laboratory, though he might almost as easily have chosen a roulette wheel. Near the end of his dissent in *Abrams*, Holmes observed that the Constitution "is an experiment, as all life is an experiment. Every year if not every day we have to wager our salvation upon some prophecy based upon imperfect knowledge."[51] Holmes put his money on free speech, a perennial underdog that has shown a miraculous capacity to reward its backers.

It was no coincidence that many of Holmes's finest moments came in his dissents. Majority opinions lay down rules. Choosing a side, they put an end to conversations. Holmes's natural elements were dialogue and synthesis; his genius was in creating intellectual spaces where further conversations could occur, in pushing against the wall, not in building it. Nevertheless he did build: the positions for which he argued unsuccessfully—the legitimacy of wages and hours laws; the right to unionize; the prohibition of child labor; and broad protections for free speech—are accepted features of the American legal landscape, though some of them have lately come under renewed attack. Holmes's insistence that the Constitution need not be read as mandating a laissez-faire economic state supplied much of the intellectual platform from which Franklin D. Roosevelt was able to launch the New Deal.

Holmes succeeded in pointing American law in the direction of reform. What is remarkable is that he did so without the crusading intentions of a partisan ideologue. Holmes had no desire to legislate from the bench or to impose his own social outlook on the country. What drove him was not a confidence in his vision but, to the contrary, a deep consciousness of frailty and fallibility—not only his own, but that of human beings in general. It is a beautiful irony—but one very consistent with his experiences and his love of Emerson—that a willingness to question one's own thought served as the intellectual foundation of Holmes's jurisprudence.

Holmes wrote in *Lochner* that concrete cases were not resolved by general principles. To the contrary, law, as well as life, is forever perched on a fulcrum of uncertainty. From case to case, the law sustains itself by endlessly shifting its balance. Fixed principles might supply confidence and stability up to a point, but beyond that point, the intellectual currency must be permitted to float and to seek its own value. Holmes wrote, "To have doubted one's own first principles is the mark of a civilized man."[52] He was approximately echoing his father, who had once observed, "If to question everything be unlawful and dangerous, we had better undeclare our independence at once; for what the Declaration means is the right to question everything, even the truth of its own fundamental proposition."[53] Few paths through life could have entitled anyone to ask more questions than the road that had led through Ball's Bluff, Fredericksburg, and Spotsylvania, and America has seldom if ever produced a more eloquent poser of questions than Oliver Wendell Holmes Jr.

✴

IN THE SUMMER OF 1865, THREE months after Lee surrendered, Louisa May Alcott signed on as the paid traveling companion of a partial invalid—a young woman whose father, incidentally, later endowed a law professorship that Holmes briefly held at Harvard—and boarded a steamer for Europe. She remained abroad for exactly a year. While pausing at a *pension* in Vevey, Switzerland, for the winter holidays, she met the only young man who was to outweigh John Suhre in his influence on her. He was a tall youth from Poland, not more than twenty but endowed with the grace and manners of a diplomat. He was Władysław Wisniewski, a mouthful of a name that the linguistically limited Alcott soon shortened to Laddie. Conversing over dinner and walking the grounds around the *pension*, she discovered features of his life and situation that moved her much as Private Suhre's had done. Like the Pennsylvania private, he had the aura of a hero: he had taken part in a recent Polish uprising against the ongoing Russian occupation. Imprisoned for his role in the failed revolution, he had lost both friends and fortune. Suffering from tuberculosis, Wisniewski also excited her nursing instincts. Indulging her confessed "weakness for brave boys in blue," she fell for him. A gifted pianist, he filled her days "with his fun, his music, and . . . frank, fresh affection." Six months later, they met again in Paris and shared two weeks of affection, though Alcott insisted that her "twelve years' seniority made [their] adventures quite proper."[54] Though she never expressed her feelings in such terms, it may well have seemed as if John Suhre, resurrected and able-bodied, had been returned to her.

Returning to Orchard House, Alcott received a delightful reception. Anna, who had given birth to a second son less than a month before her sister's departure, happily saluted her from the gate, and May flew excitedly around the lawn. But the homecoming was also a return to financial reality. In her absence, the family debts had mounted, and her parents, now in their mid-sixties, seemed less able than ever to steady the household's finances. Alcott had no choice but to resume the chore of churning out thrilling tales for the popular press. By now, she had mastered the form, and the stories she was writing, like "Behind a Mask" and "The Abbot's Ghost," found eager readers. The surge in her popularity that had come from *Hospital Sketches* had largely subsided. She was back to business as usual, until the writing of *Little Women* changed everything.

The importance of Alcott's book for girls can hardly be exaggerated. More than a book for children, *Little Women* is arguably the most important novel about the Civil War written by someone who actually witnessed it, even though it trains its focus on the home front. The book's success also altered the publishing landscape of its time. Before *Little Women*, an American literature for young readers can hardly be said to have existed. The books for the young that did exist were typically flat, pious stories, more interested in imparting a moral than in understanding a young person's actual feelings and struggles. *Little Women* changed that. In the judgment of Alcott's contemporary Constance Fenimore Woolson, the book helped to persuade America that writers for children could stand at the very pinnacle of the profession.[55] It is impossible to say how many other writers were moved toward writing for children by the éclat of *Little Women*.

Apart from Lewis Carroll's *Alice's Adventures in Wonderland,* which predated it by only three years, *Little Women* is the oldest children's book in English that still enjoys a wide audience. It has been cited as an early inspiration by a diverse array of women, including Ursula K. LeGuin, Patti Smith, Connie Chung, and the current empress of Japan. Alcott also invented one of the most enduring conventions of young women's fiction: the quartet of girls or women who both thwart and support one another as they seek their places in the world. The main characters of *The Sisterhood of the Traveling Pants,* the sitcom *The Facts of Life,* and the cable series *Girls* and *Sex and the City* are all, in a sense, Jo March's children.

Alcott added a sequel to *Little Women*, titled *Little Men*, in 1871. Thereafter came a steady stream of novels for children and young adults: *Eight Cousins, Rose in Bloom, Under the Lilacs, Jack and Jill*. To these Alcott added a respectable output of adult fiction: the realist novel *Work*; a rewriting of her early novel *Moods*; and an anonymous jewel, *A Modern Mephistopheles*. These, as well as a flood of short stories, were eagerly consumed by a large and devoted readership. She became, as has been observed in the *Los Angeles Times*, "as great a celebrity in her day as J. K. Rowling is in ours."[56]

Like Holmes and Whitman, Alcott felt uneasy with the material obsessions of the postwar years, though she was most troubled by what those preoccupations meant for American womanhood. Seduced by surfaces, America around 1870 seemed bent upon reducing its women to ornamental irrelevancies—exquisitely mannered and impeccably dressed, but physically weak and inwardly empty, interested only in the husbands they could attract and the baubles they could acquire. In what may have been her best book that did not deal with the March family, *An Old-Fashioned Girl*, Alcott firmly denounced the material culture whose most noteworthy product seemed to be hordes of girls and young women with "nothing to do but lounge and gossip, read novels, parade the streets and dress," and whose sole idea was to "ape the fashionable follies that they should have been too innocent to understand."[57] Modest, unpretentious, and respectful, Alcott's heroine Polly Milton seems at first a drab also-ran alongside her fashion-plate cousin Fanny Shaw. But as Fanny's love of show and artifice leads her deeper into discontent, Polly finds her place in a sisterhood of "busy, happy, independent girls" who approach their lives with "patience and perseverance, hope and courage." In a group of women among whom energy and character count for everything and money, fashion, and position mean nothing, Polly is confirmed in her faith that "purpose and principle are the best teachers we can have, and the want of them makes half the women of America what they are: restless, aimless, frivolous, and sick."[58]

The passage contains echoes of Alcott's nursing days. The women with whom she served in Georgetown had not been perfect beings. Alcott had initially scorned their lack of knowledge and sophistication. Yet their sense of shared purpose had brought them together to save lives and, in desperate times, to care for one another. The kindness and love they sincerely bestowed on her when she was near death had a lesson to impart, and she learned it well. The ideal of a community of women, working together for a selfless goal, appears not only in *An Old-Fashioned Girl* but also at the end of her underappreciated novel for adults, *Work*. John Suhre had given Alcott a model of stoical courage. Less acknowledged, the nurses at the Union Hotel Hospital gave her an experience of loving womanhood that transformed and transfigured her later work.

The poisons she had absorbed during her nursing service, coupled with her obsessive habits of overwork, exacted a steady toll on Alcott's health. The strain grew even worse in 1880, when she adopted the infant daughter of her sister May, who had died of complications from bearing the child, and again in October 1882 when her father Bronson suffered a stroke that devastated the muscular functions of his right side. Earlier in the same month that her father was paralyzed, Alcott had begun work on *Jo's Boys*, intended to be the last book of the *Little Women* trilogy. Whereas she could once churn out a chapter a day, Alcott's family responsibilities and her own precarious health now slowed her productivity almost to a halt. She did not complete *Jo's Boys* until the summer of 1886. She felt less triumph than relief: on the last page of the novel, alluding to the recent discoverer of the ruins of ancient Troy, she wearily confessed that she was tempted to end the March family saga with a cataclysmic earthquake that would "engulf Plumfield and its environs so deeply in the bowels of the earth that no youthful Schliemann could ever find a vestige of it."[59]

Shortly before his paralysis, in his early eighties, Bronson wrote sonnets for each of his four daughters, the two still living and the two who had passed away. His poem for Louisa alludes only briefly to her work as a writer, even though that work had made her internationally famous. Instead, the poem praises above all else her efforts in the hospital, recalling her "buoyant heart" as she had ridden off "to nurse the wounded soldier [and to] swathe the dead." Recalling her brave devotion, Bronson ended the sonnet, "I press thee to my heart as Duty's faithful child."[60] The reconciliation between father and daughter was complete.

On March 1, 1888, Alcott stood at the bedside of her dying father. She noticed that he was smiling. "Sweet and feeble," the old man gestured upward with his good hand. "I am going up. Come with me."[61] She answered, "Oh, I wish I could." Three days later, at 11 a.m., Bronson

Alcott died. That same day, before news of his death could reach her, Alcott wrote to a friend, "[A]s I don't live for myself I hold on for others, & shall find time to die some day, I hope."[62] Word of her father's passing still had not come when, later that day, she felt a headache and lay down to rest. She slipped out of consciousness and never regained it. Two days later, on the day of Bronson's funeral, Louisa May Alcott did, indeed, "come up."

✯

THE TWO WHO DIED IN THE war, Lieutenant Colonel Pelham and Chaplain Fuller, also left their legacies. Of the five people featured in this book, John Pelham was the only one who never met Emerson. Yet, in the way he conducted himself in the war, he was arguably as Emersonian as any of them. Armies, even ones as idiosyncratic as the Army of Northern Virginia, tend to reward obedience and orthodoxy more than individuality. Yet Pelham did not let order and bureaucracy prevent him from fulfilling his personal genius. He was not only brave, but starkly, theatrically brave. When he disobeyed Stonewall Jackson and moved his guns forward at First Bull Run; when he opened the action with his cannonade at Antietam; and above all when he took effective command of the action at Fredericksburg, he expressed a sublime individualism, a daring self-reliance that crystalized the ideal of forthright independence and made it real. An Ohio cadet who was a year behind Pelham at West Point and who wrote extensively on the war, Morris Schaff, thought it likely that "the dew [would] sparkle brighter on Pelham's memory" than on any of the other young West Pointers who went to war. "Poetry and sentiment," he observed, seemed drawn toward "great displays of courage and sacrifice of life for a principle," no matter how tarnished that principle might be. Most lovingly of all, Schaff wrote, the romantic spirit tends to cherish "the ashes of brilliant youth associated with defeat." The morning glory, he thought, "blooms freshest over ruins."[63] As George C. Rable has observed, Pelham's extraordinary exploits at Fredericksburg were a mixed legacy for Lee's army. Whereas, on the one hand, his heroics raised morale, they also fostered an unrealistic confidence, a belief that Confederate courage would always win out over the Union's superior force of numbers.[64] That belief was painfully refuted before another year had passed.

The image of Pelham also supported longer-lasting illusions. He died when the South still seemed more than capable of winning the war. His passing froze him in time at a moment of hope and promise, both for himself and the Confederacy. Pelham never ascended to the level of fame occupied by Lee, Jackson, and his mentor Stuart. However, at least as much as they, he became a poetic figure, a martyred Adonis ideally suited for the purposes of elegiac romance. No Confederate officer below the rank of general has received more attention from biographers than Pelham, and no Southern soldier has been accorded more uncritically adulatory treatment. The title of the most balanced and reliable Pelham biography to date contains the word "perfect"—a telling indicator of the regard his reputation has perpetually enjoyed.[65]

In all aspects other than the odious politics he fought to uphold, Pelham was extraordinary: a superb soldier and a gracious man. He served the causes of states' rights and slavery as the fictitious heroes of Scott Fitzgerald would later serve the cause of Mammon—with a gleam and grandeur that could distract one powerfully from the mortal sins of the society that bred him. Yet it is not only Pelham's youth, character, and dazzling exploits in the field that have made him so easy to idealize. He kept no journal. During the 1920s, a would-be biographer borrowed Pelham's wartime letters and lost them. The only lengthy piece of personal correspondence that survives from the war years is the Bull Run letter, which was published in an Alabama newspaper. Of Pelham's casual utterances, only a handful were preserved. The paucity of documents in his own hand has thrown a veil over the inner man. Intentionally or not, he was to become a dashing but distant enigma. He lives on chiefly as a radiant exterior, seen through the eyes of compatriots who, having survived the war, fervently hoped to preserve its glories and forget its agonies. Among those who knew him, the two most enthusiastic commentators on Pelham's life were John Esten Cooke and Heros von Borcke. Both had a taste for glamorization, and both played up Pelham's youth and captivating good looks. For Cooke, Pelham was "slender, beardless, modest-looking," with flashing blue eyes, an unconquerable spirit, and, of course, a penchant for "blushing . . . like a girl."[66] Von Borcke's memoir, though somewhat less fawning in its use of adjectives, twice calls him "the boy-hero," hails his "noble spirit," and uses the word "gallant" to describe him at least nine times.[67] Together, Cooke and von Borcke set the tone for a chorus of admiration that echoes through every work on Pelham ever written. As if Pelham had not already been young enough, accounts of his career frequently shave a year or two off his actual age.[68] This adulation predictably blocks attempts to see Pelham in three dimensions. By expunging Pelham's faults, Southern historians robbed him of his complexity. Their hero has, over time, become more of a monument than a human being.

Quintessentially, John Pelham stands for a self-image of which the South has needed to let go but that has proved too beguiling for some of its citizens ever to fully overcome. Precisely because he was destroyed in his youth, the beautiful boy hero proved indestructible. Confederate veterans and their descendants could point to Pelham to convince themselves that the war had not been horrible, but courtly and glorious. They could look at Pelham in his prime—a prime that never faded—and imagine an alternate future, one where Southern independence was achieved and a hierarchy of races remained intact. And the beauty of his gaze and the splendor of his accomplishments could allow them to believe, perversely, that that future, too, would have been for the best. The war ought to have revealed the futility of resisting the march of freedom and equality. But it has been easier for some to live with remembered images of honor and of grace, and, for them, the romance continues to shade reality in a regrettable fashion. Dying young and mythologized for his bravery and that grace, John Pelham passed into legend as the Hyacinth of the Confederacy. But such legends, to the extent that they are inextricable from the heritage of slavery, are not benign. One indicator of Pelham's dubious position in history is that he was chosen by the Sons of Confederate Veterans to receive a distinction that is neither recognized nor sanctioned by any existing government: the "Confederate Medal of Honor." Something regarding the sentiments behind this accolade may possibly be inferred from the fact that it has also been conferred on Henry Wirz, the commandant of the infamous Andersonville Prison; and on Nathan Bedford Forrest, Grand Wizard of the Ku Klux Klan.

After Pelham's death, Stuart fought on. At Chancellorsville, less than two months after Pelham's death, he took temporary command of Jackson's corps after the latter had been mortally wounded. On that occasion,

Stuart performed admirably. Two months later, distinction turned to disgrace. Leading his cavalry away from Lee's main force during the Army of Northern Virginia's invasion of Pennsylvania, Stuart failed to give Lee essential information as to the position of the Union army. At Gettysburg, that lack of knowledge cost the Confederates dearly. In October 1863, Stuart's youngest child was born. He named the baby girl for his two most sacred loves, his state and his fallen comrade: Virginia Pelham Stuart. Unlike Pelham, Stuart lived long enough to see the Confederacy begin to fall. His war ended less than a week after Henry Abbott's. Shot through the stomach on May 11, 1864, at the Battle of Yellow Tavern, Stuart died the next evening, on the same day as the slaughter at the Bloody Angle. Taken from the field in agony, Stuart was heard to say, "I had rather die than be whipped."[69]

After Pelham's death, the Stuart Horse Artillery also fought on, though never with the same élan. The Union, too, used horse artillery, but no such unit on either side achieved the success and fame of Pelham's command. A theoretical improvement over slower-moving cannons, the Horse Artillery seems to have required an exceptional officer to realize all its tactical possibilities. In this capacity, as in more personal ones, Jeb Stuart was correct: Pelham was irreplaceable. However, the concept of highly mobile units with devastating firepower lived on, to be updated and improved upon as horses gave way to motorized transport. The feints and dashes of Pelham's artillery tactics foreshadowed tank warfare.

Long after the war, Pelham's champion John Esten Cooke still imagined that he heard bugles in moonlit nights and, in the summer's thunder, the artillery's roar. In the closing pages of his novel, *Surry of Eagle's-Nest*, Cooke concludes that the glory days of Jackson, Stuart, and Pelham could only have been a dream, And yet, he writes, "The dream was glorious—not even . . . surrender can efface its splendor. Still it moves me, and possesses me; and I live forever in that past."[70]

⋆

THE METEOR THAT WAS ARTHUR FULLER's personal fame quickly lost its luster. His death and burial were followed by a brief outpouring of melancholy poems in the Boston newspapers.[71] Arthur's brother Richard, who had already conceived the idea of publishing a sketch of the minister's life while Arthur was alive, converted his project into a memorial biography that he published in 1863. Thereafter, the story of the minister and his desperate desire to "do something" for his country faded from the public memory; the war had produced too many martyrs for any single one, short of the president himself, to command lasting attention. Absent from all but the most detailed histories of the war, Chaplain Fuller is much less an icon than an emblem: a representative of the countless warriors who gave all that they had for a cause they revered, but whose memories, despite their earnestness and valor, have had scarcely more permanency than initials carved into a block of ice in early spring.

Nevertheless, Arthur B. Fuller passed down a legacy that changed America, though he achieved it not through his actions, but through his DNA. The month before the reverend died at Fredericksburg, his toddler son Richard B. Fuller had laughed excitedly at the hope of seeing his papa again—a reunion that never took place. Some thirty-two years later, Richard fathered a son, whom he also named Richard B. To distinguish himself from his father, Richard B. Fuller Jr. tried using various forms of his name until deciding on the one that he eventually made famous: R. Buckminster Fuller.

Buckminster Fuller grew up knowing next to nothing about his illustrious great-aunt Margaret. "Nobody played up the Fullers' intellectual side," he recalled. "Aunt Margaret was just somebody in the family to me."[72] Whereas the extraordinary Margaret was, for the young Buckminster Fuller, no more than a deceased relative, the story of his grandfather's courage was kept alive—and somewhat embroidered—within the family. In hearing these retellings, Bucky Fuller acquired an exaggerated understanding of Arthur's heroism in the field; he wrote that the chaplain "was killed leading a successful Union attack at Fredericksburg."[73] At least two of Buckminster's biographers embroidered the tale still further, claiming that the chaplain died "while leading a charge."[74] If nothing else, Bucky's misinformed visions of his grandfather's supposed leadership added a few grains to his confidence that a Fuller could act audaciously in the world.

Bucky Fuller displayed his own bravado neither in the pulpit nor on the battlefield, but in the realm of design, applying his original and imaginative talents to problems of transportation and architectural innovation. He happened upon perhaps his greatest revelation as a shipboard radio operator during World War I, as he contemplated the structures of bubbles being churned up in the wake of his vessel. As Fuller observed their shifting shapes and odd trajectories, it occurred to him, as the critic Hugh Kenner later put it, "that nature does not use *pi*."[75] Reprising the transcendentalists whom his grandfather had known, Bucky Fuller set about discovering a concept of the universe in which forms were forever fluid and in which matter was an expression of energy. Kenner calls Fuller's insights Transcendental. Unlike Emerson, however, Fuller looked for this transcendence not in philosophy but in physics. He was trying, he said, "to find nature's geometry."[76] Building on the research of others, working with lines of force instead of points and planes, he perfected and popularized the structure known as the geodesic dome. Among the strongest, lightest, most efficient ways of enclosing space ever created by human beings, the dome has a mathematical formula that applies as well to the structure of the protein shell that surrounds a virus.[77] Fifty years after Fuller's shipboard epiphany, he unveiled a geodesic structure at Expo '67 in Montreal. It stood twenty stories high and, because of its structural principles, weighed only a hundredth of what existing science said that such an edifice must weigh. The ratio between the weight of the dome's materials and the load on its foundations was such that, if it had been a mile wide, it would have floated away.[78]

Arthur Fuller inhabited a world whose vision and principles were also floating away. His death, after he had tried so hard to Christianize the war and to infuse it with the purity of a holy crusade, is a fitting emblem for the passing of a particular way of seeing the war and, perhaps for a larger shift in the culture of America. Chaplain Fuller believed that the war could be fought on ethical terms, separating with surgical precision the violence necessary to win the war from that which served only to gratify one's baser passions. He imagined a war of hymns and temperance, one that would punish evil without harming the innocent, and he was not alone in cherishing this dream. Yet he died just hours before the sack of Fredericksburg took the idea of a civilized war and enthusiastically broke it to pieces, smashing and splintering it like the pianos hauled into the city's streets. The looting of Fredericksburg came at a time when depredations against the civilian population were matters of spontaneity, not military policy. But the event came as a shocking preview of the campaigns of total warfare that were eventually to follow. Coming close on the heels of the chaplain's death, the sack of Fredericksburg gave a foretaste of just how unchristian the war was to become.

A larger change was also at work. Arthur Fuller, with his firm faith in salvation through Christ, represented convictions that were firmly ensconced in the American mind when he was born, but which were increasingly questioned by the time of his death. The assault on the old view had, for Fuller, begun shockingly close to home. His own sister had conspicuously abandoned Christian teachings when she insisted that upward striving and secular self-culture, instead of appeals to God and Christ, were legitimate paths to redemption. Her close friend and some-time employer, Emerson, had preached still more luxuriant blasphemies about the self-determination of the soul. Of the other four major figures in this book, only John Pelham was an orthodox Christian believer, and each of them, Pelham included, pursued a vision of self-perfection that called for values other than Christian rebirth. Alcott and Whitman both despised the self-appointed angels of the gospel who besieged wounded soldiers with tracts and sermons. Instead, the novelist and the poet sought to elevate themselves and others through their acts of human kindness. Pelham considered no man truly fulfilled who did not revere and practice physical courage. And Holmes, turning his back on salvation altogether, embraced the conclusion that life was ruled by randomness and that all human beings are fatally flawed and require a rule of law to protect them from their worst excesses. In its religious disposition, America was to remain a stoutly Christian nation. However, the age of the minister as the intellectual leader of his community had mostly run its course and, with only rare exceptions like Martin Luther King Jr., would not come again.

✷

THIS HAS BEEN A STORY OF courage. It has been a story about children seeking to live up to the ideals of their parents and, in several instances, about parents seeking the understanding of their children. It has been a story of illness and recovery, of death and memory. But it is to redemption that one's thoughts continually return. All five of the heroes of this story confronted war and struggled to redeem themselves within it. Amid the misery and the blood, they tried to find a core of virtue that could balance and justify the evil: Whitman through his sublimated Eros; Alcott through compassion; Pelham through valor; Fuller through a kind of saintly mar-tyrdom; and Holmes through a succession of broken strategies—through chivalry, through logic, and finally through a mythology of sacrifice of which he knew both the passion and the pity. The violence of war itself could not be redeemed—it was too sordid and horrible for that. But if they fell short in their larger quests, all five succeeded in redeeming and vindicating themselves, enough at least that, over a century and a half later, we remember their deeds and find their stories worthy of telling.

✶

HOLMES REMAINED ON THE SUPREME COURT until the age of ninety. As of this printing, he remains the oldest justice ever to serve on the Court. Ironically, the man whose record for longevity he surpassed was Roger Taney, the author of the *Dred Scott* decision. Holmes had no children. He remained lifelong friends with Carolyn Kellogg, the girl he called Buster and with whom he exchanged letters after his woundings at Ball's Bluff and Antietam. If the war was the closest thing in his life to Dante's *Inferno*, Carolyn was his nearest approximation of a desexualized Beatrice, her innocent purity leading him gently toward the light. The last time they met, he was past ninety and she was near eighty. She asked him if he was still improving his mind. He replied, "No, I'm reading Gibbon again."[79]

Having already outlived all the other major figures in this book by nearly forty years, Holmes retired in early 1932. By then, his presence on the bench was iconic. Eager young law students made pilgrimages to the Court just to see him on the bench. As Holmes made ready for his retirement, a group of leading justices and other well-wishers contributed to a book of essays praising him. Chief Justice Charles Evans Hughes presented it to Holmes uttering, "The most beautiful and rarest thing in the world is a complete human life, unmarred, unified by intelligent purpose and uninterrupted accomplishment. . . . Such a rarely beautiful life is that of Mr. Justice Holmes."[80]

As he read his last opinion from the bench on January 11, 1932, an eight-to-one majority holding that addressed a violation of the Prohibition laws, Holmes's voice faltered and became barely audible.[81] Afterward, as an attendant helped him to put on his overcoat, the tired justice said, "I won't be down tomorrow."[82] Union Hotel, where Alcott labored and Suhre died, was demolished the same year.

Three years later, as his ninety-fourth birthday came near and friends made ready for a party, Holmes contracted bronchial pneumonia. On March 5, 1935, three days before his birthday, he was placed in an oxygen tent. James Rowe, Holmes's private secretary, saluted him. "Every soldier to his tent, Captain Holmes," he said with a twinkle. The ancient warrior thumbed his nose.[83]

Hours before dawn on March 6, Brevet Colonel Oliver Wendell Holmes Jr., of the Grand Army of the Republic, passed away. His funeral took place two days later at Arlington National Cemetery. He had chosen to be buried, not in Massachusetts with the Wendells, Jacksons, and Holmeses of his distinguished family tree, but amid the veterans of the war that had scarred and shaped him. For years, two blue uniforms had hung in his closet. As the caisson was drawn to his grave, they were hanging there still. The note pinned to them read, "These uniforms were worn by me in the Civil War and the stains upon them are my blood."[84] In his safe deposit box were two musket balls, extracted from him during the war. At the gravesite, as President Roosevelt paid his respects, silver rain and sleet fell from the cold, dark sky. Someone thought to apologize to Holmes's caretaker, Mary Donellan, for the unpleasant weather. She gave five words in response:

"Soldiers don't mind the rain."[85]

Acknowledgments

All real invocations express love. If one writes a book in the way that it should be written, one takes a journey not only of the mind but also of the heart, opening oneself to express and to receive this highest of emotions in illimitable ways. One learns the meaning of gratitude in its fullest sense.

I owe a tremendous debt of thanks to my extraordinary agent, Chris Calhoun, who offered not only the services of an able negotiator, but also the counsel and reassurance of a wise friend. This book is my fourth undertaking with a remarkable editor, Amy Cherry, who has shaped and informed my career as few persons have done. My gratitude is as deep as the ocean. Amy's assistants, Zarina Patwa and Bee Holekamp, gave steady and unerring support. The book's copyeditor, Jodi Beder, saved me from countless embarrassments. Dassi Zeidel did a splendid job with the finishing touches. In securing the permissions for illustrations, I never had to lose a moment's rest, thanks to the sage and stalwart efforts of Fay Torresyap.

I am always astonished by the generosity of those who, in the libraries, archives, and historic sites of this country, do all they can to assist a scholar. John Hennessy, the chief historian of the Fredericksburg and Spotsylvania National Military Park, has been both welcoming and wise. Frank O'Reilly, a distinguished historian at the park and author of one of the best books on the subject, more than generously shared his time and insights. Walking the field with him was an unforgettable experience. It seems that I cannot write a book without the kind and able assistance of the staff at Orchard House in Concord, Massachusetts. They are in my heart and soul. The superb librarians of Houghton Library at Harvard University were unstintingly helpful, as were those at the public libraries of Anniston-Calhoun County and Jacksonville, Alabama. Jacob A. Miller and his staff at the Historical and Genealogical Society of Somerset County, Pennsylvania, rendered marvelous assistance, as did the Army War College in Carlisle, Pennsylvania.

Joan Grassey-Spinazola gave valuable time and effort to supply research for the story of Arthur Fuller. Well done! Scott Halvorson and Ariel Clark Silver read and reread the manuscript until they knew this project as well as I do. Their insights and contributions have been indispensable.

For more than twenty years, I have had the honor of serving in the English Department of John Jay College of Criminal Justice. Through good times and bad, I have been ever grateful for the kindness of my colleagues. I am thankful for the stalwart leadership of our chair, Jay Gates. I have been blessed by my association with countless kind, caring, and inspirational students, too many to identify by name. I thank you all. Friday afternoons with Jeffrey Heiman and Adam Berlin provided a series of welcome oases on this long journey. Richard Smith's humor and encouragement made a welcome difference. Across an ocean, the friendship of Paweł Jędrzejko has been constant and transformative.

Surely no book has ever been created under the influence of a greater constellation of muses. I gratefully acknowledge the warm and sustaining spirits of Susan Hoyle Bailey, Ula Bednarz, Deborah Brothers, Patricia Christgau, Joy Curry, Lisa Ann Dillon, Adrienne FitzGerald, Monika Grotek, Heidi Kendall, Vanda Krefft, Louise Ledaguenel, Floriane Reviron-Piégay, Kamelia Talebian Sedehi, Corinne Hosfeld Smith, Caroline Stoessinger, Jan Turnquist, Sara Whitestone, Diane Whitley-Grote, and Kristen Witucki.

During the writing of this book, Dr. Robert Salant discovered that I had cancer. Dr. Ash Tewari performed the surgery that saved me. Dr. James Spikes aided in my recovery. A statement of thanks is not sufficient.

Since the publication of my last book, two peerless mentors have faded from the scene. To Dwight Perkins and Robert Ferguson I offer up my everlasting gratitude and respect.

Both life and writing always lead me back to family. To my wife Michelle and daughter Rebecca I owe the world and more.

Notes

Prologue: A Brahmin's Baptism

1 Richard F. Miller, *Harvard's Civil War: A History of the Twentieth Massachusetts Volunteer Infantry*, 175.
2 The two officers were Lieutenants Alois Babo and Reinhold Wesselhoeft. Richard F. Miller writes that Babo was shot while swimming. It is not entirely clear whether he drowned or died of his wound. Ibid., 77.
3 Oliver Wendell Holmes Jr. to Amelia Jackson Holmes, 23 October 1861, in Oliver Wendell Holmes Jr., *Touched with Fire*, 13.
4 "The Lounger," *Harper's Weekly*, 9 November 1861, 706.
5 Oliver Wendell Holmes Jr. to Frederick Pollock, 28 June 1930, in Mark De Wolfe Howe, ed., *Holmes-Pollock Letters: The Correspondence of Mr. Justice Holmes and Sir Frederick Pollock, 1874–1932*, II: 270.

Chapter One: The Poet's Son

1 John T. Morse Jr., *Life and Letters of Oliver Wendell Holmes*, I: 176.
2 Ibid., I: 179.
3 Oliver Wendell Holmes Sr., *Autocrat of the Breakfast-Table*, 107.
4 Ibid., 4.
5 Oliver Wendell Holmes. Sr., *Elsie Venner*, 13.
6 Holmes Sr., *Autocrat of the Breakfast-Table*, 25.
7 O. W. Holmes Sr. to Mrs. Charles W. Upham, 9 March 1841, in Morse, *Life and Letters*, I:322.
8 Holmes Sr., *Elsie Venner*, 13.
9 Mark De Wolfe Howe, *Justice Oliver Wendell Holmes: The Shaping Years, 1841–1870*, 21.
10 G. Edward White, *Justice Oliver Wendell Holmes: Law and the Inner Self*, 11.
11 Oliver Wendell Holmes Sr. "Mechanism in Thought and Morals," in *Pages from an Old Volume of Life*, 312.

12 John L. Motley to Dr. Oliver Wendell Holmes [Sr.], 16 May 1858, in Motley, *The Works of John Lothrop Motley*, XV: 289.
13 Holmes Sr., *Elsie Venner*, 287.
14 Ibid., 242.
15 Ibid.
16 Oliver Wendell Holmes Jr. to Felix Frankfurter, 21 May 1926, in Robert M. Mennel and Christine L. Compston, eds., *Holmes and Frankfurter: Their Correspondence, 1912–1934*, 202.
17 Holmes Sr., *Elsie Venner*, 242.
18 Henry Adams, *The Education of Henry Adams*, 54–55.
19 Howe, *Shaping Years*, 48.
20 Ibid., 69.
21 Ibid., 35.
22 Francis Bowen, *The Principles of Metaphysical and Ethical Science, Applied to the Evidences of Religion*, vii.
23 Liva Baker, *The Justice from Beacon Hill: The Life and Times of Oliver Wendell Holmes*, 80.
24 Ralph Waldo Emerson, "Self-Reliance," in *Essays and Lectures*, 259.
25 [Oliver Wendell Holmes Jr.], "Books," *Harvard Magazine*, IV: 410, 411.
26 Anon., "Harvard Periodicals," *Harvard Magazine*, IV: 7.
27 Stephen Budiansky, *Oliver Wendell Holmes: A Life in War, Law, and Ideas*, 61.
28 Baker, *Justice from Beacon Hill*, 95.
29 Holmes observed in April 1864, "We all need examples of chivalry to help us bind our rebellious desires to steadfastness in the Christian Crusade of the 19th century. If one didn't believe that this war was such a crusade, in the cause of the whole civilized world, it would be hard indeed to keep the hand to the sword." Oliver Wendell Holmes Jr. to Charles Eliot Norton, 17 April 1864, in *Touched with Fire*, 122n.
30 Holmes Sr., "Bread and the Newspaper," in *Pages from an Old Volume of Life*, 3.
31 Oliver Wendell Holmes Sr., "Currents and Counter-Currents in Medical Science," in *Currents and Counter-Currents in Medical Science, with Other Addresses and Essays*, 27.
32 Holmes Sr., *Autocrat of the Breakfast-Table*, 143.
33 O. W. Holmes Sr. to James Russell Lowell, 29 November 1846, in Morse, *Life and Letters*, I: 295–96.
34 Ibid., 300.
35 Ibid., 300–301.
36 Ibid., 302.
37 Holmes Sr., "Bread and the Newspaper," in *Pages from an Old Volume of Life*, 3.
38 Holmes Sr., *Autocrat of the Breakfast-Table*, 304.
39 Holmes Sr., "Mechanism in Thought and Morals," in *Pages from an Old Volume of Life*, 313.
40 Budiansky, *Oliver Wendell Holmes*, 75.
41 Howe, *Shaping Years*, 76.
42 Henry L. Abbott to Caroline Abbott, 25 September 1861, in Henry Livermore Abbott, *Fallen Leaves: The Civil War Letters of Major Henry Livermore Abbott*, 50.
43 Ibid., 51.

44 Robert Gould Shaw, *Blue-Eyed Child of Fortune: The Civil War Letters of Robert Gould Shaw*, 156n.

45 Julian Hawthorne, "Absolute Evil," in *American Fantastic Tales*, 461.

46 Henry Abbott to Josiah Abbott, May 1861, in *Fallen Leaves*, 32.

47 Ibid.; Henry Abbott to Josiah Abbott, 11 July 1861, in *Fallen Leaves*, 34.

48 Oliver Wendell Holmes Jr. to Amelia Jackson Holmes, 8 September 1861, in *Touched with Fire*, 4–5.

49 Oliver Wendell Holmes Jr. to Amelia Jackson Holmes, 11 September 1861, in *Touched with Fire*, 6–8.

50 Oliver Wendell Holmes Jr. to Sir Frederick Pollock, 1 February 1920, in Howe, *Holmes-Pollock Letters*, 36.

51 George B. McClellan to Mary Ellen McClellan, 11 October 1861, in George B. McClellan, *The Civil War Papers of George B. McClellan: Selected Correspondence, 1860–1865*, 106.

52 George B. McClellan to Mary Ellen McClellan, 30 July 1861, in *Civil War Papers*, 71; George B. McClellan to Winfield Scott, 11 September 1861, in *Civil War Papers*, 98.

53 Revised United States Army Regulations of 1861 (Washington, DC: Government Printing Office, 1863), 536–37.

54 Oliver Wendell Holmes Jr. to Amelia Holmes, 23 September 1861, in *Touched with Fire*, 9.

55 Ibid., 12.

56 Henry L. Abbott to Caroline Abbott, 24 October 1861, in *Fallen Leaves*, 67.

57 Miller, *Harvard's Civil War*, 53.

58 Howe, *Shaping Years*, 96.

59 Ibid.

60 Henry L. Abbott to Josiah Abbott, 22 October 1861, in *Fallen Leaves*, 60.

61 Miller, *Harvard's Civil War*, 72.

62 Ibid., 75.

63 Oliver Wendell Holmes Jr. to Oliver Wendell Holmes Sr., in 23 October 1861, *Touched with Fire*, 13. Holmes wrote, "I . . . asked if none would follow me." I am not able to determine Holmes's precise words. The putative quotation in my text is, however, a faithful approximation.

64 Oliver Wendell Holmes, Sr., "To John L. Motley," 29 November 1861, in Motley, *Works*, XVI: 217.

65 Oliver Wendell Holmes Jr., Diary, in *Touched with Fire*, 24.

66 Ibid.

67 Ibid.

68 Holmes might have smiled to know that, when his father's English friend John Motley heard of his wounding at Ball's Bluff, he coincidentally observed to the elder Holmes, "It is a noble and healthy symptom that brilliant, intellectual, poetical spirits like his spring to arms when a noble cause like ours inspires them. The race of Philip Sidneys is not yet extinct." John Lothrop Motley, "To Oliver Wendell Holmes, Sr.," in Motley, *Correspondence of John Lothrop Motley*, II: 42.

69 Oliver Wendell Holmes Jr., Diary, in *Touched with Fire*, 27.

70 Ibid.

71 Ibid.

72 Ibid., 27–28.

73 Ibid., 28.

74 Ibid., 28.

75 Ibid., 28–29.

76 Ibid., 30–31.

77 Holmes, Sr. gives the date of his son's return as November 14. Oliver Wendell Holmes Sr., "To John Lothrop Motley," in Motley, *Correspondence*, II: 44. Mark De Wolfe Howe puts it somewhat more credibly at November 9. Howe, *Shaping Years*, 111.

78 Oliver Wendell Holmes Sr., to John Lothrop Motley, 29 November 1861, in Morse, *Life and Letters*, II: 158.

79 Anthony Trollope, *Autobiography of Anthony Trollope*, 141.

80 Oliver Wendell Holmes Sr. to John Lothrop Motley, 29 November 1861, in Morse, *Life and Letters*, II: 158.

81 Richard F. Fuller, *Chaplain Fuller: Being a Life Sketch of a New England Clergyman and Army Chaplain*, 190.

82 Ibid., I: 159.

83 "The Lounger," *Harper's Weekly*, 9 November 1861, 706.

84 George B. McClellan to William B. Sprague, 27 September 1861, in *Civil War Papers*, 103. Some sources, including the National Park Service, list McClennan's favorite horse as Dan Webster. http://www.nps.gov/articles/more-than-necessary -horses.htm, accessed August 15, 2020.

85 George B. McClellan to Mary Ellen McClellan, 10 May 1862, in *Civil War Papers*, 263.

86 George B. McClellan to Edwin M. Stanton, 10 June 1862, in *Civil War Papers*, 295.

87 Oliver Wendell Holmes Jr. to Mr. and Mrs. Oliver Wendell Holmes Sr., 2 June 1862, in *Touched with Fire*, 49.

88 Ibid.

89 Ibid., 50–51.

90 Ibid.

91 Ibid., 51.

92 Oliver Wendell Homes Jr. to Oliver Wendell Holmes Sr., 13 June 1862, in *Touched with Fire*, 53–54.

93 Oliver Wendell Holmes Jr. to Mr. and Mrs. Oliver Wendell Holmes Sr. 17 September 1862, in *Touched with Fire*, 63.

94 Bruce Catton, *Mr. Lincoln's Army*, 129; George B. McClellan to William B. Franklin, 13 September 1862, in *Civil War Papers*, 455.

95 George B. McClellan to Henry W. Halleck, 13 September 1862, in *Civil War Papers*, 457. McClennan's superiority in numbers was somewhat deceptive in that his force included a huge contingent of new recruits, who were less than combat ready.

96 Frederick L. Hitchcock, *War from the Inside: The Story of the 132nd Regiment Pennsylvania Volunteer Infantry in the War for the Suppression of the Rebellion, 1862–1863* (Philadelphia: J. B. Lippincott, 1904), 56.

97 Oliver Wendell Holmes Jr., "To Oliver Wendell Holmes, Sr.," 17 September 1862, in *Touched with Fire*, 62–64.

98 The troop movements throughout the battle are minutely documented in Ezra A. Carman, *The Maryland Campaign of September 1862*, vol. 2: *Antietam*.

99 Miller, *Harvard's Civil War*, 172.

100 Howe, *Shaping Years*, 126.

101 Oliver Wendell Holmes Jr., "Memorial Day," in *Speeches by Oliver Wendell Holmes*, 7.

102 Catton, *Mr. Lincoln's Army*, 286.

103 Miller, *Harvard's Civil War*, 174.

104 Francis Winthrop Palfrey, *The Antietam and Fredericksburg*, 87.

105 Howe, *Shaping Years*, 126. Holmes noted, however, that the 20th never ran "except by orders of Sumner at Antietam." Ibid.

106 Catherine Drinker Bowen, *Yankee from Olympus: Justice Holmes and His Family*, 168; Miller, *Harvard's Civil War*, 177.

107 White, *Justice Oliver Wendell Holmes*, 58.

CHAPTER TWO: THE BLOND ARTILLERIST

1 Jerry H. Maxwell, *The Perfect Lion: The Life and Death of Confederate Artillerist John Pelham*, 63.

2 William Woods Hassler, *Colonel John Pelham: Lee's Boy Artillerist*, 2.

3 Ibid., 3.

4 Maxwell, *The Perfect Lion*, 7.

5 Thomas Jefferson, *Note on the State of Virginia*, 170.

6 Maxwell, *The Perfect Lion*, 48.

7 Ibid., 7.

8 Currently a handful of other officials may also submit the recommendation. https://westpoint.edu/admissions/prospective-cadets/nomination-information, accessed 24 September 2019.

9 John Todd, *The Student's Manual; Designed, by Specific Directions, to Aid in Forming and Strengthening the Intellectual and Moral Character and Habits of the Student*, 28.

10 Ibid., 45.

11 *The Student's Manual*, John Pelham collection. Anniston-Calhoun Public Library, Anniston, Alabama.

12 Ibid., 207.

13 Morris Schaff, *The Spirit of Old West Point*, 52.

14 Ibid., 53.

15 Fred R. Martin, "Pelham of Alabama," 10.

16 Thomas Rosser, quoted in Charles G. Milham, *Gallant Pelham: American Extraordinary*, 23.

17 Maxwell, *The Perfect Lion*, 21.

18 Schaff, *The Spirit of Old West Point*, 133.

19 Edward Porter Alexander, *Fighting for the Confederacy: The Personal Recollections of General Edward Porter Alexander*, 174.

20 Ralph Kirshner, *The Class of 1861: Custer, Ames, and Their Classmates after West Point*, 160.

21 Stephen E. Ambrose, *Crazy Horse and Custer: The Parallel Lives of Two American Warriors*, 111.

22 Schaff, *The Spirit of Old West Point*, 138.

23 Ibid., 138–39.

24 Stephen E. Ambrose, *Duty, Honor, Country: A History of West Point*, 169.

25 John Pelham to Atkinson Pelham, 11 December 1860, in Maxwell, *The Perfect Lion*, 37.
26 John Pelham to Jefferson Davis, quoted in Maxwell, *The Perfect Lion*, 40.
27 John Pelham to [name unknown], 17 March 1861. Handwritten transcription, Anniston-Calhoun Public Library, Anniston, Alabama.
28 Mary Elizabeth Sergent, "The West Point Pelham Knew," *The Cannoneer*, November 1985, IV: 6.
29 John Pelham to Marianna [Pelham?], 26 March 1861, quoted in *Maxwell*, 42.
30 Sergent, *They Lie Forgotten*, 95.
31 Maxwell, *The Perfect Lion*, 47.
32 Ibid., 48.
33 Ibid., 49.
34 John Pelham to A. J. Walker, 31 March 1861, quoted in Maxwell, *The Perfect Lion*, 43.
35 Charles L. Scott, *Adventures of Charles L. Scott, Esq.*, 153–54.
36 Walt Whitman, *Specimen Days*, in *Complete Poetry and Collected Prose*, 708.
37 Edmund C. Stedman, *The Battle of Bull Run*, 18.
38 Douglas Southall Freeman, *Lee's Lieutenants: A Study in Command*, I: 74, 79.
39 Maxwell, *The Perfect Lion*, 57. Maxwell, in recounting the story of Pelham's battlefield nausea, calls it "possible, but more likely improbable." However, no reason apart from that author's adoration of his subject seems to exist for doubting the tale's veracity.
40 John Pelham to Atkinson Pelham, 23 July 1861, *Jacksonville Republican*, 8 August 1861.
41 Ibid.
42 Ibid.
43 Thomas J. Jackson, "Report," 23 July 1861, in United States War Department, *The War of the Rebellion: A Compilation of the Official Records of the Union and Confederate Armies* (hereafter cited as *Official Records*), ser. I, vol. II: 481.
44 Louis Edward Nolan, *Cavalry: Its History and Tactics*, 245.
45 Maxwell, *The Perfect Lion*, 64.
46 John Esten Cooke, *Surry of Eagle's-Nest, or, The Memoirs of a Staff-Officer Serving in Virginia*, 347.
47 Heros von Borcke, *Memoirs of the Confederate War for Independence*, 235.
48 Maxwell, *The Perfect Lion*, 69.
49 Von Borcke, *Memoirs*, 235–36n.
50 Cooke, *Surry of Eagle's-Nest*, 235.
51 J. E. B. Stuart to Thomas G. Rhett, 10 May 1862, in *Official Records*, ser. I, vol. XI, part I: 572.
52 J. E. B. Stuart to R. H. Chilton, in *Official Records*, 14 July 1862, ser. I, vol. XI, part II: 515.
53 Ibid., 522.
54 Maxwell, *The Perfect Lion*, 141.
55 Von Borcke, *Memoirs*, 135.
56 Ibid., 136.
57 Ibid., 137.
58 Freeman, *Lee's Lieutenants*, II: 179.
59 Maxwell, *The Perfect Lion*, 154.

60 Catton, *Mr. Lincoln's Army*, 269; Rufus Robinson Dawes, *Service with the Sixth Wisconsin Volunteers*, 88.

61 Dawes, *Service*, 88.

62 Ibid., 87.

63 Maxwell, *The Perfect Lion*, 159.

64 Curt Johnson and Richard C. Anderson Jr., *Artillery Hell: The Employment of Artillery at Antietam*, 48–49.

65 Jennings Cropper Wise, *The Long Arm of Lee, or, The History of the Artillery of the Army of Northern Virginia*, 301.

66 Miller, *Harvard's Civil War*, 172.

67 Ibid., 170.

68 William Thomas Poague, *Gunner with Stonewall*, 47.

69 Maxwell, *The Perfect Lion*, 170.

70 Justin Martin, *A Fierce Glory: Antietam—The Desperate Battle That Saved Lincoln and Doomed Slavery*, 228; Mark P. Brugh and Julia Stinson Brugh, *Civil War Ghosts of Sharpsburg*, 55–56.

71 Cooke, *Surry of Eagle's-Nest*, 332.

72 J. E. B. Stuart to R. H. Chilton, 13 February 1864, in *Official Records*, ser. I, vol. XIX, part I: 821. Stuart's allusion to immortality is explained by the fact that he filed his report, very belatedly, after Pelham's death.

CHAPTER THREE: BURNSIDE'S BRIDGE AND A BROADWAY BAR

1 G. W. Whitman, "Civil War Diary," in *Civil War Letters of George Washington Whitman*, 148.

2 While the spelling of the word "lieutenant" plainly baffled Whitman, one may fairly argue that his misspelling of "captain" was only in fun. He got the latter word right almost all the time but wrote to his mother after Fredericksburg, "Remember that your galliant son is a Capting." George Washington Whitman to Louisa Van Velsor Whitman 19 [?] December 1862, in *Civil War Letters*, 77.

3 George Washington Whitman to Louisa Van Velsor Whitman, 28 June 1861, in *Civil War Letters*, 39.

4 George Washington Whitman to Louisa Van Velsor Whitman, 9 February 1862, in *Civil War Letters*, 42–43.

5 George Washington Whitman to Whitman family, 27 April 1862, in *Civil War Letters*, 51.

6 George Washington Whitman to Louisa Van Velsor Whitman, 12 April 1862, in *Civil War Letters*, 50.

7 George Washington Whitman to Louisa Van Velsor Whitman, 1 June 1862, in *Civil War Letters*, 54.

8 George Washington Whitman to Louisa Van Velsor Whitman, 5 September 1862, in *Civil War Letters*, 62.

9 George Washington Whitman to Louisa Van Velsor Whitman, 9 February 1862, in *Civil War Letters*, 44.

10 George Washington Whitman to Louisa Van Velsor Whitman, n.d., in *Civil War Letters*, 64.

11 George Washington Whitman to Louisa Van Velsor Whitman, 30 September 1862, in *Civil War Letters*, 71.

12 Herman Melville, *Moby-Dick*, in *Redburn: His First Voyage; White-Jacket, or The World in a Man-of-War; and Moby-Dick, or, The Whale*, 915.

13 Horace Traubel, ed., *In Re Walt Whitman*, 35.

14 Ibid., 35–36.

15 The order was issued at 9:10 a.m., at which time Holmes's regiment was engaged in the West Woods. It was not delivered, however, until approximately 10:00 a.m. Stephen W. Sears, *Landscape Turned Red: The Battle of Antietam*, 261. General Jacob Cox confirms that the order did not arrive until ten. Jacob D. Cox, "The Battle of Antietam," in Robert Underwood Johnson et al., eds., *Battles and Leaders of the Civil War*, II: 647–48.

16 George Washington Whitman to Louisa Van Velsor Whitman, 11 July 1862, in *Civil War Letters*, 57.

17 Jacob Cox, "The Battle of Antietam," in *Battles and Leaders*, II: 650.

18 Catton, *Mr. Lincoln's Army*, 306. Shelby Foote, Fort Sumter to Perryville, 696. Steven Sears disagrees as to the depth of the creek, putting it between four and five feet and calling it "a daunting prospect to try to wade under fire."

19 Sears, *Landscape Turned Red*, 261.

20 George Washington Whitman to Louisa Van Velsor Whitman, 21 September 1862, in *Civil War Letters*, 67.

21 Cox, "The Battle of Antietam," in *Battles and Leaders*, II: 652.

22 Catton, *Mr. Lincoln's Army*, 309.

23 Ibid.

24 George Washington Whitman to Louisa Van Velsor Whitman, 21 September 1862, in *Civil War Letters*, 67.

25 Sears, *Landscape Turned Red*, 267.

26 George Washington Whitman to Louisa Van Velsor Whitman, 21 September 1861, in *Civil War Letters*, 68.

27 Ibid., 69.

28 Richard Henry Stoddard, "The World of Letters," in Whitman, *Notebooks and Unpublished Prose Manuscripts*, II: 525.

29 Burroughs, *The Writings of John Burroughs*, X: 29.

30 Jay Charlton, "Bohemians in America," in William Shepard, ed., *Pen Pictures of Modern Authors*, 163

31 Burroughs, *Writings*, X: 29–30.

32 Whitman, *Specimen Days*, in *Complete Poetry and Collected Prose*, 692, 694.

33 Whitman, "There Was a Child Went Forth," in *Complete Poetry and Collected Prose*, 138.

34 Ibid., 139.

35 Robert C. Williams, *Horace Greeley: Champion of American Freedom*, 17.

36 Jack S. Blocker, Jr., David M. Fahey, and Ian R. Tyrell, eds., *Alcohol and Temperance in Modern History: An International Encyclopedia*, I: 23.

37 Williams, *Horace Greeley*, 17.

38 Walt Whitman, *Franklin Evans, or The Inebriate: A Tale of the Times*, 7.

39 Whitman, *Notebooks and Unpublished Prose Manuscripts*, I: 28.

40 Ibid., I: 31.

41 Walt Whitman, *Democratic Vistas*, in *Complete Poetry and Collected Prose*, 937.

42 Horace Traubel, *With Walt Whitman in Camden*, II: 113.

43 Ibid., II: 113–14.

44 Ibid., II: 113.

45 Ibid., III: 525.

46 Jesse's instability appears to have arisen from a potent array of causes, some of them plainly not congenital. Robert Roper traces Jesse's erratic behavior to a head injury sustained when he fell from a mast while working as a sailor in 1848 and suggests that he may also have contracted syphilis (Robert Roper, *Now the Drum of War: Walt Whitman and His Brothers in the Civil War*, 67–71).

47 Edwin Havilland Miller, "Introduction," in Walt Whitman, *The Correspondence*, I: 8.

48 Traubel, *With Walt Whitman in Camden*, VII: 525–26.

49 Traubel, *In Re Walt Whitman*, 36.

50 Ibid., 33.

51 Ibid., 35.

52 Traubel, *With Walt Whitman in Camden*, 526.

53 Whitman, "Talk to an Art Union," in *Complete Poetry and Collected Prose*, 1130.

54 Whitman, *Specimen Days*, in ibid., 703.

55 Just Kaplan, *Walt Whitman: A Life*, 266.

56 Ibid., 703.

57 Whitman, *Notebooks and Unpublished Prose Manuscripts*, I: 322.

58 Ibid., I: 323.

59 Anon., "'The Eve of the Conquest and Other Poems' by Henry Taylor [review], *The Edinburgh Review* (April 1849), 180: 378.

60 "Modern Poetry and Poets," *The Edinburgh Review*, October 1849, 219.

61 Titus Carus Lucretius, *On the Nature of Things: A Philosophical Poem in Six Books*, 109.

62 Ibid., 108, 118.

63 Robert D. Richardson, Jr., *Emerson: The Mind on Fire*, 527–28.

64 Whitman, "Mr. Emerson's Lecture," *New York Aurora*, 7 March 1842.

65 Emerson, "The Poet," in *Essays and Lectures*, 447.

66 Ibid., 462.

67 Ibid., 465.

68 Whitman, *Notebooks and Unpublished Prose Manuscripts*, I: 102.

69 Whitman, "A Backward Glance o'er Travel'd Roads," in *Complete Poetry and Collected Prose*, 658.

70 Whitman, "L. of G.'s Purport," in ibid., 652.

71 Whitman, "A Backward Glance o'er Travel'd Roads," in ibid., 658.

72 Whitman, "Song of Myself," in ibid., 203.

73 Whitman, *Notebooks and Unpublished Prose Manuscripts*, I: 57.

74 Whitman, "[Song of Myself]," in *Complete Poetry and Collected Prose*, 31.

75 Ibid., 32.

76 Ibid., 88.

77 Henry David Thoreau to H. G. O. Blake, 7 December 1856, in *Familiar Letters*, 345–46.

78 Franklin Benjamin Sanborn, "Emerson in His Home," *The Arena* 15: 20. Emerson, Bronson Alcott, and Thoreau wanted to bring Whitman out to Concord as well. The idea, however, was vetoed by Lidian Emerson, Abba Alcott, and Thoreau's sister Sophia. Ibid.; W. H. Trimble, *Walt Whitman and Leaves of Grass: An Introduction*, 74–75.

79 Whitman, "From Pent-up Aching Rivers," in *Complete Poetry and Collected Prose*, 248–49.

80 Ted Genoways, *Walt Whitman and the Civil War: America's Poet during the Lost Years of 1860–1862*, 63.

81 Ibid., 51.

82 Ibid., 49.

83 Significant gaps have lately been filled by Genoways's engaging volume *Walt Whitman and the Civil War*.

84 Whitman, "[Preface to 1855 *Leaves of Grass*]," in *Complete Poetry and Collected Prose*, 5.

85 "A Visit to Walt Whitman," *Brooklyn Daily Eagle*, 11 July 1886, 10.

86 Karen Karbiener, "Whitman at Pfaff's: Personal Space, A Public Place, and the Boundary-Breaking Poems of *Leaves of Grass* (1860)," in *Literature of New York*, ed. Sabrina Fuchs-Abrams, 15; Justin Martin, *Rebel Souls: Walt Whitman and America's First Bohemians*, 17.

87 Richard Henry Stoddard, "The World of Letters," in Whitman, *Notebooks and Unpublished Prose Manuscripts*, II: 528.

88 Richard Henry Stoddard, *Recollections Personal and Literary*, 266.

89 Traubel, *With Walt Whitman in Camden*, IV: 195.

90 "A Visit to Walt Whitman," *Brooklyn Daily Eagle*, 11 July 1886, 10; Albert Parry, *Garrets and Pretenders: A History of Bohemianism in America*, 45. The *Nation* was founded in 1865. Thus, this particular jest of Clapp's postdates Whitman's timer at Pfaff's.

91 John Swinton, quoted in Traubel, *With Walt Whitman in Camden*, I: 416.

92 Whitman, *Notebooks and Unpublished Prose Manuscripts*, I: 216.

93 Ibid., I: 167.

94 Traubel, *With Walt Whitman in Camden*, I: 417.

95 Ibid., VIII: 312.

96 Whitman, *Notebooks and Unpublished Prose Manuscripts*, I: 454–55.

97 Whitman, "Quicksand Years," in *Complete Poetry and Collected Prose*, 563.

98 Genoways, *Walt Whitman and the Civil War*, 116.

99 Ibid., 116–17.

100 William Sloane Kennedy, *Reminiscences of Walt Whitman*, 69–70.

101 Gay Wilson Allen, *The Solitary Singer: A Critical Biography of Walt Whitman*, 273.

102 George Washington Whitman to Louisa V. Whitman, 8 December 1862, in *Civil War Letters*, 74.

CHAPTER FOUR: AN ARMY IN CRISIS

1 George Freeman Noyes, *The Bivouac and the Battlefield; or, Campaign Sketches in Virginia and Maryland*, 203.

2 Catton, *Mr. Lincoln's Army*, 318.

3 Henry L. Abbott to Josiah Abbott, 20 November 1862, in *Fallen Leaves*, 143.

4 Miller, *Harvard's Civil War*, 182–83.

5 Oliver Wendell Holmes, Sr., "My Hunt after the Captain," in *My Hunt after the Captain and Other Papers*, 9.

6 Ibid.

7 Ibid.

8 Holmes Sr., *My Hunt*, 17; Wilder Dwight, *Life and Letters of Wilder Dwight*, 15. The nephew, Charles Wentworth Upham Jr., helped to nurse Dwight back to health when the latter nearly succumbed to typhoid in Brienz.

9 Holmes Sr., *My Hunt*, 18.

10 Ibid., 16.

11 Ibid., 18.

12 Ibid., 29.

13 Ibid., 20.

14 Ibid., 22–23.

15 Ibid., 30.

16 Ibid., 54.

17 Ibid., 54–55.

18 Ibid., 34.

19 Ibid., 45.

20 Oliver Wendell Holmes Jr. to Harold J. Laski, in Mark De Wolfe Howe (ed.), *Holmes-Laski Letters*, I: 112. One Holmes biographer has suggested that Holmes's Antietam wound interfered with his sexual potency. Baker, *Justice from Beacon Hill*, 228–29.

21 Oliver Wendell Holmes Jr. to Oliver Wendell Holmes Sr. and Amelia Jackson Holmes, 18 September 1862, in *Touched with Fire*, 64.

22 Holmes Sr., *My Hunt*, 61–62.

23 Oliver Wendell Holmes Jr. to ?, 22 September 1862, in *Touched with Fire*, 67.

24 Alexander Woollcott, *The Indispensable Woollcott*, 468.

25 George B. McClellan to Mary Ellen McClellan, 18 September 1862, in *The Civil War Papers*, 469.

26 John Quincy Adams, *Speech of John Quincy Adams on the Joint Resolution for Distributing Rations to the Distressed Fugitives from Indian Hostilities in the States of Alabama and Georgia*, 25 May 1836, 5.

27 David Herbert Donald, *Charles Sumner and the Coming of the Civil War*, 323.

28 Doris Kearns Goodwin, *Team of Rivals: The Political Genius of Abraham Lincoln*, 448–49.

29 David Von Drehle, *Rise to Greatness: Abraham Lincoln and America's Most Perilous Year*, 218.

30 Gideon Welles, *The Diary of Gideon Welles, Secretary of the Navy under Lincoln and Johnson*, I: 70.

31 Gideon Welles, "The History of Emancipation," *The Galaxy: A Magazine of Entertaining Reading* 14 (December 1872): 842.

32 Ibid., 843.

33 Welles, *Diary*, I: 71.

34 Welles, "The History of Emancipation," 838.

35 Lincoln, "First Inaugural Address," in *Speeches and Writings, 1859–1865*, 215.

36 Julia Taft Bayne, *Tad Lincoln's Father*, 3.

37 W. A. Evans, *Mrs. Abraham Lincoln: A Study of Her Personality and Her Influence on Lincoln*, 55.

38 Bayne, *Tad Lincoln's Father*, 3.

39 Edward Bates, *The Diary of Edward Bates, 1859–1866*, 235.

40 E.g., Doug Wead, *All the Presidents' Children: Triumph and Tragedy in the Lives of America's First Families*, 91; Jennifer B. Fleischner, *Mastering Slavery: Memory, Family, and Identity in Women's Slave Narratives*, 113.

41 Kenneth J. Winkle, *Lincoln's Citadel: The Civil War in Washington, DC.*, 123.

42 John Nicolay, *With Lincoln in the White House: Letters, Memoranda, and Other Writings of John G. Nicolay, 1860–1865*, 71.

43 Anna L. Boyden, *Echoes from Hospital and White House: A Record of Mrs. Rebecca R. Pomeroy's Experience in War-Times*, 56.

44 Allen C. Guelzo, *Lincoln's Emancipation Proclamation: The End of Slavery in America*, 118.

45 F. B. Carpenter, *The Inner Life of Abraham Lincoln: Six Months at the White House*, 22.

46 Welles, "The History of Emancipation," 845.

47 Henry Abbott to Elizabeth Livermore, 10 January 1863, in *Fallen Leaves*, 161.

48 George B. McClellan to Abraham Lincoln, 7 July 1862, in *Civil War Papers*, 344.

49 Salmon P. Chase, *The Salmon P. Chase Papers: Journals 1829–1872*, I: 394.

50 Goodwin, *Team of Rivals*, 467.

51 Guelzo, *Lincoln's Emancipation Proclamation*, 160.

52 William O. Stoddard, *Inside the White House in War Times: Memoirs and Reports of Lincoln's Secretary*, 97.

53 Abraham Lincoln, "Response to Serenade, Washington, D.C.," 24 September 1862, in *Speeches and Writings*, 372.

54 George B. McClellan to Mary Ellen McClellan, 25 September 1862, in *Civil War Papers*, 481.

55 George B. McClellan to Henry W. Halleck, 22 September 1862, in *Civil War Papers*, 478.

56 Arthur B. Fuller, "To Lucilla Fuller," 17 July 1862, Margaret Fuller Family Papers, Houghton Library, Harvard University, MS Am 1086.

57 William H. Powell, quoted in John Pope, "The Second Battle of Bull Run," in *Battles and Leaders*, II: 490.

58 Goodwin, *Team of Rivals*, 484.

59 George B. McClellan to Mary Ellen McClellan, 5 October 1862, in *Civil War Papers*, 490.

60 Henry W. Halleck to George B. McClellan, 6 October 1862, in *Official Records*, ser. I, vol. XIX, part I: 10.

61 Régis de Trobriand, *Four Years with the Army of the Potomac*, 340.

62 Abraham Lincoln to George B. McClellan, in *Speeches and Writings*, 342.

63 De Trobriand, *Four Years with the Army of the Potomac*, 347.

64 George B. McClellan to Mary Ellen McClellan, 7 November 1862, in *Civil War Papers*, 520.

65 Guelzo, *Lincoln's Emancipation Proclamation*, 168.

66 Richard B. Irwin, "The Removal of McClellan," in *Battles and Leaders*, III: 104.

67 George B. McClellan to Mary Ellen McClellan, 7 November 1862, in *Civil War Papers*, 520.

68 George C. Rable, *Fredericksburg! Fredericksburg!*, 44.

69 Catton, *Mr. Lincoln's Army*, 328.

70 David Wright Judd, *The Story of the Thirty-Third N.Y.S. Volunteers*, 215.

CHAPTER FIVE: A MAN OF GOD

1 Revised United States Army Regulations of 1861, 524.

2 Arthur B. Fuller to Lucilla Fuller, 27 October 1862, Fuller Family Papers, Harvard University.

3 Thomas Wentworth Higginson, *Margaret Fuller Ossoli*, 11.

4 Arthur B. Fuller to Richard F. Fuller, 15 February 1850, Fuller Family Papers, Harvard University.

5 Fuller, *Chaplain Fuller*, 11.

6 William O. Blake, *The History of Slavery and the Slave Trade, Ancient and Modern*, 453.

7 Richard F. Fuller, *Recollections*, 55.

8 Richard F. Fuller, *Chaplain Fuller*.

9 S. Margaret Fuller to Eliza R. Farrar, 25 April 1833, Sarah Margaret Fuller, *Letters of Margaret Fuller*, 1: 180.

10 Arthur B. Fuller to Richard F. Fuller, 17 March 1851, Fuller Family Papers, Harvard University.

11 Richard F. Fuller, *Chaplain Fuller*, 41–42. Richard's omission of his brother's accident is made all the more curious by the fact that he gives a highly detailed and somewhat humorous description of the man who caused it.

12 S. M. Fuller to Eliza R. Farrar, 25 April 1833, *Letters of Margaret Fuller*, I: 180.

13 Ibid., 180–81. See also John Matteson, *The Lives of Margaret Fuller*, 90.

14 Margarett Crane Fuller to Timothy Fuller, 15 April 1833, Fuller Family Papers, Harvard University.

15 Margarett Crane Fuller to Timothy Fuller, 18 April 1833, Fuller Family Papers, Harvard University.

16 Richard F. Fuller, *Chaplain Fuller*, 26.

17 Ibid., 24.

18 Ibid., 28.

19 Ibid., 29.

20 Richard F. Fuller, *Recollections*, 12–14.

21 Ibid., 25.

22 S. Margaret Fuller to [?], 3 November 1835, *Letters of Margaret Fuller*, I: 237.

23 Richard F. Fuller, *Recollections*, 27.

24 Arthur B. Fuller to Richard F. Fuller, 10 August 1848, Fuller Family Papers, Harvard University.

25 Richard B. Fuller, *Recollections*, 30.

26 Joel Myerson, ed., *Fuller in Her Own Time: A Biographical Chronicle of Her Life, Drawn from Recollections, Interviews, and Memoirs by Family, Friends, and Associates*, 188.

27 S. Margaret Fuller to Richard F. Fuller, 1 January 1848, *Letters of Margaret Fuller*, V: 40.

28 S. Margaret Fuller to Richard F. Fuller, 17 March 1848, *Letters of Margaret Fuller*, V: 57.

29 Arthur B. Fuller to Richard F. Fuller, 10 August 1848, Fuller Family Papers, Harvard University.

30 Richard F. Fuller, *Chaplain Fuller*, 88.
31 Margarett Crane Fuller to Richard F. Fuller, 21 January 1849, Fuller Family Papers, Harvard University.
32 Margarett Crane Fuller to Richard F. Fuller, 2 July 1848, Fuller Family Papers, Harvard University.
33 Arthur B. Fuller to Richard F. Fuller, 10 August 1848, Fuller Family Papers, Harvard University.
34 Arthur B. Fuller to Richard F. Fuller, 9 August 1848, Fuller Family Papers, Harvard University.
35 Arthur Fuller, quoted in Richard F. Fuller, *Chaplain Fuller*, 87.
36 Frederick Douglass, "Love of God, Love of Man, Love of Country: An Address Delivered in Syracuse, New York, on 24 September 1847," in *Frederick Douglass Papers*, ser. I, vol. II: 96.
37 Arthur B. Fuller, "[To the Editor]," *The North Star*, 4 February 1848, 1.
38 Sophia P. Hawthorne to Elizabeth Palmer Peabody, 1 August 1850, quoted in Megan Marshall, *Margaret Fuller: A New American Life*, 386.
39 Richard F. Fuller, *Chaplain Fuller*, 102.
40 Arthur B. Fuller to Richard F. Fuller, 25 September 1851, Fuller Family Papers, Harvard University.
41 Arthur B. Fuller, quoted in Richard F. Fuller, *Chaplain Fuller*, 109.
42 Ibid., 110.
43 Arthur B. Fuller to Richard F. Fuller, 7 January 1853, Fuller Family Papers, Harvard University.
44 Arthur B. Fuller, quoted in Richard F. Fuller, *Chaplain Fuller*, 111.
45 Arthur B. Fuller to Richard F. Fuller, 7 January 1853, Fuller Family Papers, Harvard University.
46 Arthur B. Fuller, quoted in Richard F. Fuller, *Chaplain Fuller*, 142.
47 Holmes Sr., *Elsie Venner*, 95–96.
48 Arthur B. Fuller, "Our Dangers as a Republic, and Duties as Citizens," quoted in Fuller, *Chaplain Fuller*, 126.
49 Ibid., 126–27.
50 Ibid., 131–32.
51 Arthur B. Fuller to Richard F. Fuller, 4 January 1850, Fuller Family Papers, Harvard University.
52 Arthur B. Fuller to Richard F. Fuller, 24 July 1851, Fuller Family Papers, Harvard University.
53 Arthur B. Fuller to Richard F. Fuller, 13 November 1851, Fuller Family Papers, Harvard University.
54 Arthur B. Fuller, *Historical Notices*, 12.
55 Arthur B. Fuller to Emma Lucilla Reeves, 21 September 1859, Fuller Family Papers, Harvard University.
56 Arthur B. Fuller, quoted in Richard F. Fuller, *Chaplain Fuller*, 151.
57 Arthur B. Fuller, quoted in ibid., 149.
58 Richard F. Fuller, *Chaplain Fuller*, 157.
59 Ibid., 158.
60 Ibid., 157–58.
61 Ibid., 159–60.
62 Ibid.

63 Ibid., 165.

64 Ibid., 167.

65 Ibid., 171.

66 Arthur B. Fuller to Lucilla Fuller, 20 August 1861, Fuller Family Papers, Harvard University; Richad F. Fuller, *Chaplain Fuller*, 173.

67 Arthur B. Fuller to Lucilla Fuller, 20 August 1861, Fuller Family Papers, Harvard University.

68 William R. Eastman, "The Army Chaplain of 1863," in A. Noel Blakeman, ed., *Personal Recollections of the War of the Rebellion*, 349.

69 Steven E. Woodworth, *While God Is Marching On: The Religious World of Civil War Soldiers*, 150.

70 George Whitfield Pepper, *Personal Recollections of Sherman's Campaigns in Georgia and the Carolinas*, 197–98.

71 Gerald F. Linderman, *Embattled Courage*, 253–54.

72 Richard F. Fuller, *Chaplain Fuller*, 181.

73 Ibid., 175–76.

74 J. W. Dadmun and Arthur B. Fuller, *Army and Navy Melodies: A Collection of Hymns and Tunes, Religious and Patriotic*, 2.

75 Ibid., 15.

76 Holmes's verse reads: "When our land is illumined with Liberty's smile, / If a foe from within strike a blow at her glory, / Down, down with the traitor who dares to defile / The flag of her stars and the page of her story! /By the millions unchained who our birthright have gained, / We will keep our bright blazon forever unstained! / And the Star-Spangled Banner in triumph shall wave / While the land of the free is the home of the brave."

77 Arthur B. Fuller to Lucilla Fuller, 3 September 1861, Fuller Family Papers, Harvard University.

78 Arthur B. Fuller to Lucilla Fuller, 25 April 1862, Fuller Family Papers, Harvard University.

79 Arthur B. Fuller to Lucilla Fuller, 5 January 1862, Fuller Family Papers, Harvard University; Richard F. Fuller, *Chaplain Fuller*, 196.

80 Arthur B. Fuller to Lucilla Fuller, 25 April 1862, Fuller Family Papers, Harvard University.

81 Arthur B. Fuller to Lucilla Fuller, 23 August 1861, Fuller Family Papers, Harvard University.

82 Arthur B. Fuller, quoted in Richard F. Fuller, *Chaplain Fuller*, 194.

83 Ibid., 187–88.

84 Ibid., 186.

85 Arthur B. Fuller, quoted in ibid., 199.

86 Ibid., 199–200.

87 Ibid., 201.

88 Ibid., 198.

89 Arthur B. Fuller, quoted in ibid., 224.

90 Ibid., 210–11.

91 Ibid., 228.

92 Ibid., 234–35.

93 Ibid., 235.

94 Ibid., 238–39.

95 Ibid., 240.

96 Arthur Fuller to Lucilla Fuller, 3 April 1862, Fuller Family Papers, Harvard University.

97 Arthur Fuller to Lucilla Fuller, April 1862 (day not legible), Fuller Family Papers, Harvard University.

98 Arthur Fuller, quoted in Richard F. Fuller, *Chaplain Fuller*, 256.

99 Ibid., 326.

100 Arthur Fuller to Lucilla Fuller, 23 June 1862, Fuller Family Papers, Harvard University.

101 Ibid.

102 Bruce Catton, *Terrible Swift Sword*, 336.

103 Richard F. Fuller, *Chaplain Fuller*, 271.

104 Ibid., 275.

105 Ibid., 276.

106 Arthur Fuller to Lucilla Fuller, 17 July 1862, Fuller Family Papers, Harvard University.

107 Ibid.

108 Ibid.

CHAPTER SIX: "THE MOST BEAUTIFUL GIRL RUNNER"

1 "History and Results of the Back Bay Improvement," 95.

2 Louisa May Alcott, *Work: A Story of Experience*, 157.

3 Louisa May Alcott to the Alcott family, [?] October 1858, in *Selected Letters of Louisa May Alcott*, 34.

4 Louisa encountered the elder Holmes while visiting the publisher James T. Fields in the spring of 1862. She read his work and appreciated "the springs of mirth that bubble up so freshly in the heart of our dear & honored Autocrat." Louisa May Alcott to Alf Whitman, 6 April 1862, in *Selected Letters*, 73; Louisa May Alcott to Richard Watson Gilder, 15 August 1884, in *Selected Letters*, 283. However, if she crossed paths with Wendell, neither seems to have found their meeting worth writing about.

5 Louisa May Alcott, *Louisa May Alcott: Her Life, Letters, and Journals*, 57.

6 Sarah Elbert, *A Hunger for Home: Louisa May Alcott's Place in American Culture*, 40.

7 L. M. Alcott, *Life, Letters, and Journals*, 30.

8 Frederick L. H. Willis, *Alcott Memoirs*, 35.

9 Louisa May Alcott, *Little Women* (W. W. Norton, 2004), 13.

10 Louisa May Alcott, *Moods* (Loring, 1864), 63.

11 Anne Brown Adams, "[Louisa May Alcott in the Early 1860s]," in Daniel Shealy, ed., *Alcott in Her Own Time*, 8.

12 [Elizabeth Palmer Peabody], *Record of a School*, 2.

13 A. Bronson Alcott, *The Journals of A. Bronson Alcott*, 28.

14 Louisa May Alcott, *The Journals of Louisa May Alcott*, 55.

15 Ralph Waldo Emerson to Frederick Henry Hedge, 20 July 1836, in *The Letters of Ralph Waldo Emerson*, II: 29.

16 A. Bronson Alcott, *Conversations with Children on the Gospels*, 200.

17 Abigail May Alcott, *My Heart Is Boundless*, 179.

18 Ibid., 160.

19 L. M. Alcott, *Journals*, 59.

20 Ibid., 55.

21 Alcott, *Conversations with Children*, 232.

22 Edward Waldo Emerson, *Emerson in Concord: A Memoir*, 204.

23 L. M. Alcott, *Journals*, 47.

24 Willis, *Alcott Memoirs*, 38.

25 Franklin B. Sanborn, "A Concord Notebook: The Women of Concord—III. Louisa Alcott and Her Circle," in Daniel Shealy, ed., *Alcott in Her Own Time*, 126.

26 L. M. Alcott, *Journals*, 158.

27 Ibid., 65.

28 L. M. Alcott, *Journals*, 92.

29 A. Bronson Alcott, "Love's Morrow," in *Sonnets and Canzonets*, 79.

30 L. M. Alcott, *Journals*, 80.

31 L. M. Alcott, *Life, Letters, and Journals*, 68.

32 Louisa May Alcott, "Reflections of my Childhood," in Daniel Shealy, ed., *Alcott in Her Own Time*, 36.

33 Ibid., 36, 33.

34 L. M. Alcott, *Journals*, 65

35 Ibid., 81.

36 A. Bronson Alcott to Anna Alcott, 28 August 1857, in *The Letters of A. Bronson Alcott*, 251.

37 L. M. Alcott, *Journals*, 85.

38 Ibid., 86.

39 Ibid., 88.

40 Louisa May Alcott, *Hospital Sketches*, 91.

41 L. M. Alcott, *Journals*, 88.

42 Ibid.

43 Ibid., 89.

44 Ibid., 88–89.

45 Ibid.

46 Louisa May Alcott, "To Ellen Conway," 9 February 1869, in *Selected Letters*, 123.

47 Ibid., 90.

48 Ibid.

49 Ibid., 90–91.

50 Louisa May Alcott, "To the Alcott Family," October 1858, in *Selected Letters*, 34–35.

51 Ibid., 35.

52 L. M. Alcott, *Journals*, 91.

53 Ibid., 91, 92.

54 A. Bronson Alcott, *Journals*, 315–16.

55 L. M. Alcott, *Journals*, 95.

56 Louisa May Alcott, "Preface," *Moods* (Roberts Brothers, 1881), v.

57 Ibid., 46.

58 Ibid., 22, 25.

59 L. M. Alcott, *Moods*, 36.

60 Louisa May Alcott, *Hospital Sketches and Camp and Fireside Stories*, 3.

61 Louisa May Alcott to Alfred Whitman, 19 May 1861, in *Selected Letters*, 64.

62 Ibid.

63 Anne Brown Adams, "[Louisa May Alcott in the Early 1860s]," in Daniel Shealy, ed., *Alcott in Her Own Time*, 9.

64 Louisa May Alcott to Alfred Whitman, 19 May 1861, in *Selected Letters*, 64.

65 L. M. Alcott, *Life, Letters, and Journals*, 105.

66 Louisa May Alcott to Alfred Whitman, 19 May 1861, in *Life, Letters, and Journals*, 65.

67 Efforts to establish the precise date of Sarah and Joseph's wedding have not succeeded.

68 "Loss by Fire," *The Somerset Herald and Farmers' and Mechanics' Register*, 6 April 1847.

69 Alcott, *Hospital Sketches and Camp and Fireside Stories*, 54.

70 Rable, *Fredericksburg*, 29; Bruce Catton, *Glory Road*, 13.

71 John Matteson, "Finding Private Suhre: On the Trail of Louisa May Alcott's Prince of Patients," *New England Quarterly* 88: 115.

72 Andrew J. Hartsock, *Soldier of the Cross: The Civil War Diary and Correspondence of Rev. Andrew Jackson Hartsock*, 17.

73 Ibid., 15.

74 Ibid., 18.

75 Ibid., 21.

76 Ibid., 25.

77 Rable, *Fredericksburg*, 71.

78 L. M. Alcott, *Journals*, 109.

79 Ibid., 110.

CHAPTER SEVEN: "BEAUTY" AND "SALLIE"

1 Cooke, *Surry of Eagle's-Nest*, 339.

2 Freeman, *Lee's Lieutenants*, II: 452.

3 Nolan, *Cavalry*, 243.

4 H. B. McClellan, *I Rode with Jeb Stuart: The Life and Campaigns of Major General J. E. B. Stuart*, 173.

5 Nolan, *Cavalry*, 244.

6 Edward Porter Alexander, *Military Memoirs of a Confederate: A Critical Narrative*, 169.

7 John Esten Cooke, *Wearing of the Gray*, 20.

8 John W. Thomason, *Jeb Stuart*, 2.

9 Cooke, *Wearing of the Gray*, 19.

10 Thomason, *Jeb Stuart*, 1.

11 Henry Kyd Douglas, *I Rode with Stonewall*, 196.

12 W. W. Blackford, *War Years with Jeb Stuart*, 89.

13 Emory M. Thomas, *Bold Dragoon: The Life of J. E. B. Stuart*, 261.

14 Ibid., 90. Esten Cooke hints that Stuart may once have spared the life of a young deserter partly because of the soldier's physical attractiveness. Cooke, *Wearing of the Gray*, 224–25.

15 Freeman, *Lee's Lieutenants*, II: 453.

16 Blackford, *War Years with Jeb Stuart*, 90.

17 Ibid., 308.

18 David P. Bridges, *Fighting with Jeb Stuart: Major James Breathed and the Confederate Horse Artillery*, 81.

19 Cooke, *Wearing of the Gray*, 131.

20 Douglas, *I Rode with Stonewall*, 196.

21 Cooke, *Wearing of the Gray*, 139.

22 Blackford, *War Years with Jeb Stuart*, 79.

23 Von Borcke, *Memoirs*, 267.

24 Ibid., 268.

25 Ibid., 269.

26 McClellan, *I Rode with Jeb Stuart*, 136.

27 Blackford, *War Years with Jeb Stuart*, 155.

28 Heros von Borcke remembered Sweeney's first name as Bob. Von Borcke, *Memoirs*, 189.

29 Von Borcke, *Memoirs*, 271.

30 Blackford, *War Years with Jeb Stuart*, 156.

31 Ibid., 90.

32 Cooke, *Wearing of the Gray*, 132.

33 Thomason, *Jeb Stuart*, 295–96.

34 Blackford, *War Years with Jeb Stuart*, 155.

35 Ibid.

36 Victoria Ann Thomas, "Confederate Atrocities: The Northern Perception of the Confederacy's Conduct of the War," 24.

37 Diary of William Heyser, quoted in William A. Harron III, "Wars and Rumors of Wars: Three Northern Communities during Lee's Gettysburg Invasion," 22.

38 Steven E. Woodworth, *Beneath a Northern Sky: A Short History of the Gettysburg Campaign*, 27.

39 Henry W. Halleck to George B. McClellan, 10 October 1862, in *Reports of Committees of the Senate*, II: 520.

40 Blackford, *War Years with Jeb Stuart*, 169.

41 Freeman, *Lee's Lieutenants*, II: 289.

42 Maxwell, *The Perfect Lion*, 199.

43 Ibid., 201.

44 G. B. McClellan to Lorenzo Thomas, 4 August 1863, in *Official Records*, ser. I, vol. XIX, part I: 73.

45 Freeman, *Lee's Lieutenants*, II: 300.

46 Blackford, *War Years with Jeb Stuart*, 176.

47 Ibid., 178.

48 Ibid., 177–78.

49 Robert J. Trout, *With Pen and Saber: The Letters and Diaries of J. E. B. Stuart's Staff Officers*, 117; Thomason, *Jeb Stuart*, 317. Reportedly, Bob returned voluntarily to Stuart's camp on December 1, 1862.

50 Maxwell, *The Perfect Lion*, 219.

51 Ibid., 221.

52 Freeman, *Lee's Lieutenants*, II: 311.

53 Maxwell, *The Perfect Lion*. 222.

54 J. E. B. Stuart, "Report," in *Official Records*, ser. I, vol. XIX, part II: 145.

55 Ibid., 142.

56 Maxwell, *The Perfect Lion*, 233.

CHAPTER EIGHT: "BELIEVE ME, WE SHALL NEVER LICK 'EM"

1 Oliver Wendell Holmes Jr. to Oliver and Amelia Holmes, 22 September 1862, in *Touched with Fire*, 67.

2 Herman Melville, "Shiloh," in *Battle-Pieces and Aspects of the War*, 63.

3 Oliver Wendell Holmes Sr., "The Sweet Little Man," in *The Complete Poetical Works of Oliver Wendell Holmes*, 157.

4 Oliver Wendell Holmes Sr., *The Autocrat's Miscellanies*, 342.

5 Holmes Sr., "My Hunt after the Captain," 72.

6 Howe, *Shaping Years*, 155.

7 Carolyn Kellogg Cushing, "The Gallant Captain and the Little Girl," *Atlantic Monthly* 155 (1935): 545–46.

8 John Austin, *The Province of Jurisprudence Determined*, vii.

9 Ibid., 7.

10 Ibid., 6.

11 Ibid., vii.

12 Oliver Wendell Holmes Jr, to Oliver and Amelia Holmes, 16 November 1862, in *Touched with Fire*, 69.

13 Thomas Wentworth Higginson, *Harvard Memorial Biographies*, II: 107.

14 Charles Francis Adams, *Richard Henry Dana*, II: 273.

15 Oliver Wendell Holmes Jr, "Memorial Day," in *Speeches*, 8.

16 Henry Abbott to Elizabeth Livermore, 10 January 1863, in *Fallen Leaves*, 161.

17 Henry Abbott to Josiah Abbott, 3 September 1862, in *Fallen Leaves*, 140.

18 Henry Abbott to Josiah Abbott, 24 August [?] 1862, in *Fallen Leaves*, 136.

19 Henry Abbott to Josiah Abbott, 3 September 1862, in *Fallen Leaves*, 140.

20 Oliver Wendell Holmes Jr. to Amelia Holmes, 16 November 1862, in *Touched with Fire*, 71.

21 Ibid.

22 Oliver Wendell Holmes Jr. to Oliver and Amelia Holmes, 16 November 1862, in *Touched with Fire*, 70.

23 Ibid., 69.

24 Oliver Wendell Holmes Jr. to Amelia Holmes, 16 November 1862, in *Touched with Fire*, 71.

25 Henry Abbott to Josiah Abbott, 20 November 1862, in *Fallen Leaves*, 142.

26 Oliver Wendell Holmes Jr. to Amelia Holmes, 16 November 1862, in *Touched with Fire*, 71.

27 Henry L. Abbott to Oliver W. Holmes Jr., 5 September 1863, in *Fallen Leaves*, 211.

28 Oliver Wendell Holmes Jr. to Amelia Holmes, 16 November 1862, in *Touched with Fire*, 72.

29 Ibid., 72–73.

30 Oliver Wendell Holmes Jr. "To Amelia Holmes," 16 November [?] 1862, in *Touched with Fire*, 73.

31 Henry Abbott to Josiah Abbott, 20 November 1862, in *Fallen Leaves*, 142–43.

32 Francis Augustín O'Reilly, *The Fredericksburg Campaign: Winter War on the Rappahannock*, 19.

33 Orlando B. Willcox, *Forgotten Valor: The Memoirs, Journals, and Civil War Letters of Orlando B. Willcox*, 383.

34 O'Reilly, *Fredericksburg Campaign*, 22.

35 Meigs, coincidentally, was the son of the Philadelphia obstetrician who had resentfully criticized Dr. Holmes's pleas for better sanitation in childbirth procedures.

36 George W. Whitman to Louisa Van Velsor Whitman, 30 September 1862, in *Civil War Letters*, 70.

37 George W. Whitman to Louisa Van Velsor Whitman, 20 October 1862, in *Civil War Letters*, 72.

38 George W. Whitman to Louisa Van Velsor Whitman, 10 November 1862, in *Civil War Letters*, 73.

39 George W. Whitman to Louisa Van Velsor Whitman, 20 October 1862, in *Civil War Letters*, 72.

40 George W. Whitman to Louisa Van Velsor Whitman, 30 September 1862, in *Civil War Letters*, 71.

41 George W. Whitman to Louisa Van Velsor Whitman, 20 October 1862, in *Civil War Letters*, 72.

42 Arthur Fuller to Lucilla Fuller, 29 October 1862, Fuller Family Papers, Harvard University,.

43 Arthur B. Fuller to Lucilla Fuller, 29 October 1862, Fuller Family Papers, Harvard University.

44 Ibid.

45 "The Opposing Forces at the Second Bull Run," *Battles and Leaders of the Civil War*, II: 498.

46 Richard F. Fuller, *Chaplain Fuller*, 284–85.

47 Arthur B. Fuller to Lucilla Fuller, 29 October 1862, Fuller Family Papers, Harvard University.

48 Arthur Fuller to Lucilla Fuller, 3 November 1862, Fuller Family Papers, Harvard University.

49 Arthur Fuller to Lucilla Fuller, 5 November 1862, Fuller Family Papers, Harvard University; Arthur Fuller to Lucilla Fuller, 7 November 1862, Fuller Family Papers, Harvard University.

50 Arthur Fuller to Richard Fuller, 14 November 1862, Fuller Family Papers, Harvard University.

51 Arthur Fuller, "Letter from the Army of the Potomac," *Boston Journal*, 25 November 1862, 4.

52 Arthur Fuller to Lucilla Fuller, 12 November 1862, Fuller Family Papers, Harvard University.

53 Ibid.

54 Herman Haupt, *Reminiscences of General Herman Haupt*, 158.

55 Ronald C. White, *A. Lincoln: A Biography*, 524.

56 Arthur Fuller, "Letter from the Army of the Potomac," *Boston Journal*, 25 November 1862, 4.

57 Bruce Catton, *Glory Road*, 27; Rable, *Fredericksburg*, 87.

58 Catton, *Glory Road*, 26–27.

59 The agonizing tale of the missing pontoons is ably recounted in Catton, *Glory Road*, 21–28, and more summarily in Rable, *Fredericksburg*, 86–88.

60 Arthur B. Fuller, "Letter from the Army of the Potomac," 4.

61 Ibid.

62 Ibid.

63 C. C. Jewett to Edward A. Whiston, 16 November 1862, Fuller Family Papers, Harvard University.

64 Richard F. Fuller, *Chaplain Fuller*, 286.

65 Ibid., 289.

66 Arthur Fuller to Lucilla Fuller, 2 December 1862, Fuller Family Papers, Harvard University.

67 Arthur Fuller to Lucilla Fuller, 4 December 1862, Fuller Family Papers, Harvard University.

68 Ibid.

69 Helen L. Gilson to Richard Fuller, 26 March 1863, Fuller Family Papers, Harvard University.

70 Richard F. Fuller, *Chaplain Fuller*, 292.

71 Ibid., 293.

CHAPTER NINE: CAROLINE STREET

1 Ambrose E. Burnside to George W. Cullum, 22 November 1862, in *Report of the Joint Committee on the Conduct of the War*, 646.

2 Lafayette McLaws, quoted in O'Reilly, *Fredericksburg Campaign*, 37.

3 S. J. Quinn, *The History of the City of Fredericksburg*, 65.

4 Ibid., 66.

5 Ibid., 71.

6 O'Reilly, *Fredericksburg Campaign*, 37.

7 [Judith White McGuire], *Diary of a Southern Refugee during the War*, 172.

8 William Grimes, "Freedom Just Ahead: The War Within the Civil War," *New York Times*, 5 December, 2007.

9 Rable, *Fredericksburg*, 85.

10 Ambrose Burnside to G. W. Cullum, 22 November 1862, in *Report of the Joint Committee on the Conduct of the War*, 646.

11 Helen Bernard, "Diary," quoted in Maxwell, *The Perfect Lion*, 237.

12 J. E. B. Stuart, "[Endorsement to the Report of Brigadier-General W. H. F. Lee]," in *Official Records*, ser. I, vol. V: 187.

13 Von Borcke, *Memoirs*, 284.

14 Oliver Otis Howard, *Autobiography of Oliver Otis Howard, Major General, United States Army*, I: 321.

15 William Miller Owen, "A Hot Day on Marye's Heights," in *Battles and Leaders*, III: 97.

16 Ibid.

17 Anonymous to Richard F. Fuller, n.d., Fuller Family Papers, Harvard University.

18 Ibid.

19 John Hudson of the 35th Massachusetts, who wrote to Richard Fuller after the battle, said that he had heard that Chaplain Fuller had come to say goodbye to a lieutenant in the 19th Massachusetts and that, before the crossing, "he was most with Lt. Claffy [*sic*]." John Hudson to Richard Fuller, 10 January 1863, Fuller Family Papers, Harvard University. Second Lieutenant Thomas Claffey of the 19th Massachusetts was killed in action two days later. James L. Bowen, *Massachusetts in the War, 1861–1865*, 299.

20 Warren H. Cudworth, *History of the First Regiment (Massachusetts Infantry)*,

317; H. G. O. Weymouth, "The Crossing of the Rappahannock by the Nineteenth Massachusetts," in *Battles and Leaders*, III: 121.

21 Lafayette McLaws, "The Confederate Left at Fredericksburg," in *Battles and Leaders*, III: 86–87.

22 Charles Carleton Coffin, *The Boys of '61, or Four Years of Fighting: Personal Observations with the Army and Navy*, 144.

23 Cooke, *A Life of Gen. Robert E. Lee*, 176.

24 McLaws, "The Confederate Left at Fredericksburg," in *Battles and Leaders*, III: 87.

25 Rable, *Fredericksburg*, 164.

26 O'Reilly, *Fredericksburg Campaign*, 68.

27 Ibid.

28 Cooke, *A Life of Gen. Robert E. Lee*, 177.

29 Freeman, *Lee's Lieutenants*, II: 336–37.

30 Cudworth, *History of the First Regiment*, 316.

31 O'Reilly, 82.

32 George Anson Bruce, *The Twentieth Regiment of Massachusetts Volunteer Infantry, 1861–1865*, 199.

33 Ernest Linden Waitt, *History of the Nineteenth Massachusetts Volunteer Infantry, 1861–1865*, 167.

34 O'Reilly, *Fredericksburg Campaign*, 83.

35 Cudworth, *History of the First Regiment*, 317.

36 William R. Eastman, "The Army Chaplain of 1863," in Blakeman, ed., *Personal Recollections of the War of the Rebellion*, 345.

37 Weymouth, "The Crossing of the Rappahannock by the Nineteenth Massachusetts," in *Battles and Leaders*, III: 121.

38 John Hudson to Richard Fuller, 10 January 1863, Fuller Family Papers, Harvard University.

39 John G. B. Adams, *Reminiscences of the Nineteenth Massachusetts Regiment*, 50.

40 John Hudson to Richard Fuller, 10 January 1863, Fuller Family Papers, Harvard University.

41 Adams, *Reminiscences*, 50.

42 John Hudson to Richard F. Fuller, 10 January 1863, Fuller Family Papers, Harvard University.

43 Moncena Dunn to Richard Fuller, 8 January 1863, Fuller Family Papers, Harvard University; Thomas Wentworth Higginson, "Arthur Buckminster Fuller," *Harvard Memorial Biographies*, I: 91–92. Fuller appears to have crossed the river with Company K but ended up in the ranks of Company D. Given the confusion of the moment, such a shift seems hardly surprising.

44 One source, Lieutenant John Hudson of the 35th Massachusetts, says that Fuller "fell & died in [a] garden." Hudson also writes that Captain Dunn told Fuller to take a place near the right of his company. John Hudson to Richard Fuller, 10 January 1863, Fuller Family Papers, Harvard University.

45 Moncena Dunn to Richard Fuller, 8 January 1863, Fuller Family Papers, Harvard University. The source that says Fuller was struck by the second ball after turning partly around is John Hudson to Richard Fuller, 10 January 1863, Fuller Family Papers, Harvard University.

46 Arthur B. Fuller, *A Discourse in Vindication of Unitarianism*, 16. Emphasis in original.

47 Waitt, *History of the Nineteenth Massachusetts*, 171.
48 Miller, *Harvard's Civil War*, 197.
49 John Summerhayes, quoted in ibid., 199.
50 N. J. Hall to E. Whittlesey, 17 December 1862, in *Official Records*, ser. I, vol. XXI: 283.
51 Miller, *Harvard's Civil War*, 201.
52 Ibid., 202.
53 Ibid., 189.
54 Oliver Wendell Holmes Jr. "Memorial Day," in *Speeches*, 8.
55 Oliver Wendell Holmes Jr. to Amelia Holmes, 12 December 1862, in *Touched with Fire*, 74.
56 Ibid.
57 Ibid., 75
58 Miller, *Harvard's Civil War*, 201.
59 Ibid., 202.
60 Adams, *Reminiscences*, 50.
61 Cudworth, *History of the First Regiment*, 316.
62 Freeman, *Lee's Lieutenants*, II: 338.
63 Miller, *Harvard's Civil War*, 206.
64 N. J. Hall to E. Whittlesey, 17 December 1862, in *Official Records*, ser. I, vol. XXI: 283.
65 Hartsock, *Soldier of the Cross*, 37.
66 Bruce, *The Twentieth Regiment of Massachusetts*, 208.
67 Ibid., 206.
68 Adams, *Reminiscences*, 52.
69 Bruce, *The Twentieth Regiment of Massachusetts*, 210.
70 Survivors' Association, *History of the Corn Exchange Regiment*, 122.
71 F. E. Pierce, quoted in Freeman, *Lee's Lieutenants*, II: 344.
72 Abraham Lincoln, "Second Inaugural Address," in *Speeches and Writings*, 687.

CHAPTER TEN: PELHAM DOES FIRST RATE

1 Von Borcke, *Memoirs*, 307.
2 Ibid., 306.
3 Freeman, *Lee's Lieutenants*, II: 347.
4 J. H. Moore, "With Jackson at Hamilton's Crossing," in *Battles and Leaders*, III: 141.
5 Ibid.
6 Ibid., 139.
7 Von Borcke, *Memoirs*, 308.
8 Ibid., 309.
9 Freeman, *Lee's Lieutenants*, II: 346.
10 Von Borcke, *Memoirs*, 305–6.
11 Freeman, *Lee's Lieutenants*, II: 349.
12 Maxwell, *The Perfect Lion*, 249.
13 Nolan, *Cavalry*, 244.
14 Von Borcke, *Memoirs*, 309. Some accounts of Pelham's exploits state that he began

his sortie with two cannons—the smooth-bore Napoleon and a rifled Blakely—but that the Blakely was promptly disabled.

15 Maxwell, *The Perfect Lion*, 250.

16 Robert J. Trout, *Galloping Thunder: The Stuart Horse Artillery Battalion*, 146.

17 Maxwell, *The Perfect Lion*, 251. In his official report, General Meade wrote of encountering "a brisk fire from a battery posted on the Bowling Green road." *Official Records*, ser. I, vol. XXI: 511. Lieutenant John G. Simpson of the First Pennsylvania Light Infantry stated that he was opposed by "a battery, which was enfilading our troops as they were advancing to the front." *Official Records*, ser. I, vol. XXI: 514. Even one of the Confederate leaders, Brigadier General James Archer, believed that the Union advance was being stalled "by some of our batteries." *Official Records*, ser. I, vol. XXI: 656.

18 James A. Hardie, "Dispatch," 9:40 a.m., 13 December 1862, in *Official Records*, ser. I, vol. XXI: 91.

19 Maxwell, *The Perfect Lion*, 251.

20 Ibid., 253.

21 Douglas Southall Freeman, *R. E. Lee: A Biography*, II: 456.

22 O'Reilly, *Fredericksburg Campaign*, 147.

23 Freeman, *Lee's Lieutenants*, II: 350.

24 Philip Mercer, *The Life of the Gallant Pelham*, 138.

25 James Power Smith, "With Stonewall Jackson," *Southern Historical Society Papers* 43: 30.

26 Freeman, *R. E. Lee*, II: 457.

27 O'Reilly, *Fredericksburg Campaign*, 154.

28 Ibid., 168.

29 Dennis W. Brandt, *Pathway to Hell: A Tragedy of the American Civil War*, 189.

30 Rable, *Fredericksburg*, 209.

31 J. J. Archer to R. C. Morgan, 20 December 1862, in *Official Records*, ser. I, vol. XXI: 657.

32 O'Reilly, *Fredericksburg Campaign*, 206.

33 Maxwell, *The Perfect Lion*, 259.

34 As night began to fall, Jackson commenced an attack that was soon called off. It is recounted in Maxwell, *The Perfect Lion*, 264–66.

35 Shelby Foote, *The Civil War: A Narrative: Fredericksburg to Meridian*, 37.

36 William P. Walters to his wife, 17 December 1862, quoted in Trout, *Galloping Thunder*, 147.

37 Alexander, *Military Memoirs*, 302.

38 Cooke, *Surry of Eagle's-Nest*, 370–72.

39 Rable, *Fredericksburg*, 197.

40 O'Reilly calls attention to the fact that Pelham himself " 'freely gave credit to Henry' if anyone bothered to ask." O'Reilly, *Fredericksburg Campaign*, 148. However, Pelham was always singularly self-effacing when it came to discussing his accomplishments, and his willingness to credit Henry may have had as much to do with his own habitual modesty as with Henry's actual merit.

41 Rable, *Fredericksburg*, 197; O'Reilly, *Fredericksburg Campaign*, 148.

42 Rable, *Fredericksburg*, 198.

CHAPTER ELEVEN: THE STONE WALL

1 Rable, *Fredericksburg*, 219.

2 Freeman, *Lee's Lieutenants*, II: 346.

3 Oliver Wendell Holmes Jr. to Amelia Jackson Holmes, 13 December 1862, in *Touched with Fire*, 75.

4 Henry L. Abbott to Josiah Abbott, 14 December 1862, in *Fallen Leaves*, 149.

5 Ibid.

6 Catton, *Mr. Lincoln's Army*, 32.

7 Henry Abbott to Josiah Abbott, 14 December 1862, in *Fallen Leaves*, 148.

8 Ibid.

9 Oliver Wendell Holmes Jr. to Amelia Holmes, 14 December 1862, in *Touched with Fire*, 76.

10 Bruce, *The Twentieth Regiment of Massachusetts*, 216.

11 Ibid., 219.

12 Henry L. Abbott to Carr[ie] Abbott, 21 December 1862, in *Fallen Leaves*, 155; Henry L. Abbott to Caroline Abbott, 28 December 1862, in *Fallen Leaves*, 156.

13 Henry L. Abbott to Carr[ie] Abbott, 21 December 1862, in *Fallen Leaves*, 155.

14 Henry L. Abbott to Josiah Abbott, 14 December 1862, in *Fallen Leaves*, 149; Henry L. Abbott to George Perry, 17 December 1862, in *Fallen Leaves*, 152.

15 Henry L. Abbott to Josiah Abbott, 14 December 1862, in *Fallen Leaves*, 149.

16 Oliver Wendell Holmes Jr. to Amelia Holmes, 14 December 1862, in *Touched with Fire*, 76.

17 Bruce, *The Twentieth Regiment of Massachusetts*, 221.

18 Oliver Wendell Holmes Jr. to Oliver Wendell Holmes, Sr., 20 December 1862, in *Touched with Fire*, 79; Oliver Wendell Holmes Jr. to Amelia Holmes, 14 December 1862, in *Touched with Fire*, 77.

19 Oliver Wendell Holmes Jr. to Amelia Holmes, 14 December 1862, in *Touched with* Fire, 78.

20 Ibid.

21 Ibid., 76.

22 George W. Whitman to Louisa Whitman, 8 December 1862, in *Civil War Letters*, 72.

23 George W. Whitman, "Civil War Diary," 11 December 1862, in *Civil War Letters*, 151.

24 Ibid.

25 John Egan to W. C. Rawolle, 19 December 1862, in *Official Records*, ser. I, vol. XXI: 318.

26 George W. Whitman to Louisa V. Whitman, 16 December 1862, in *Civil War Letters*, 76.

27 John Egan to W. C. Rawolle, 19 December 1862, in *Official Records*, ser. I, vol. XXI: 318–19.

28 The brigade's colonel called the 51st's losses up to this point "trifling." Robert B. Potter to G. H. McKibbin, 16 December 1862, *Official Records*, ser. I, vol. XXI: 330.

29 O'Reilly, *Fredericksburg Campaign*, 337.

30 Ibid., 338.

31 George W. Whitman to Louisa V. Whitman, 16 December 1862, in *Civil War Letters*, 76.

32 Edward Ferrero to W. C. Rawolle, 16 December 1862, in *Official Records*, ser. I, vol. XXI: 325.

33 O'Reilly, *Fredericksburg Campaign*, 340.

34 George W. Whitman, "Civil War Diary," in *Civil War Letters*, 151; George W. Whitman to Louisa V. Whitman, 16 December 1862, in *Civil War Letters*, 76.

35 Edward Ferrero to W. C. Rawolle, 16 December 1862, in *Official Records*, ser. I, vol. XXI: 325.

36 Ibid., 326.

37 George W. Whitman to Thomas Jefferson Whitman, 8 January 1863, in *Civil War Letters*, 78.

38 Edward Ferrero to W. C. Rawolle, 16 December 1862, in *Official Records*, ser. I, vol. XXI: 326.

39 George W. Whitman to Thomas Jefferson Whitman, 8 January 1863, in *Civil War Letters*, 78.

40 Thomas H. Parker, *History of the 51st Regiment of P.V. and V.V. . .* , 273.

41 O'Reilly, *Fredericksburg Campaign*, 339.

42 Hartsock, *Soldier of the Cross*, 37.

43 Charles Francis Adams, *Richard Henry Dana*, II: 273.

44 O'Reilly, *Fredericksburg Campaign*, 390.

45 Carswell McClellan, *General Andrew A. Humphreys at Malvern Hill Va. July 1, 1862 and at Fredericksburg Va, December 13 1862: A Memoir*, 12.

46 O'Reilly, *Fredericksburg Campaign*, 391.

47 Hartsock, *Soldier of the Cross*, 38. Carswell McClellan, Humphreys's assistant adjutant, writes that Humphreys had been misled. According to that source, Humphreys had received a report that General Couch's men had "gained the heights." By this, Couch meant a slight rise of ground well below the stone wall. Humphreys inferred that Couch's corps had taken the wall. Carswell McClellan, *General Andrew A. Humphreys*, 13.

48 O'Reilly, *Fredericksburg Campaign*, 392.

49 Hartsock, *Soldier of the Cross*, 38.

50 O'Reilly, *Fredericksburg Campaign*, 391.

51 Hartsock, *Soldier of the Cross*, 39.

52 O'Reilly, *Fredericksburg Campaign*, 392.

53 Carol Reardon, "The Forlorn Hope: Brig. Gen. Andrew A. Humphreys's Pennsylvania Division at Fredericksburg," 89.

54 O'Reilly, *Fredericksburg Campaign*, 393.

55 McClellan, *General Andrew A. Humphreys*, 14.

56 Darius N. Couch, "Sumner's 'Right Grand Division,'" in *Battles and Leaders*, III: 115.

57 Rable, *Fredericksburg*, 261.

58 Henry Hollingsworth Humphreys, *Andrew Atkinson Humphreys: A Biography*, 179.

59 O'Reilly, *Fredericksburg Campaign*, 401.

60 Henry Hollingsworth Humphreys, *Major General Andrew Atkinson Humphreys*, 12.

61 F. B. Speakman to P. H. Allabach, 20 December 1862, in *Official Records*, ser. I, vol. XXI: 446.

62 A. A. Humphreys to Daniel Butterfield, 19 December 1862, in *Official Records*, ser. I, vol. XXI: 432.

63 McClellan, *General Andrew A. Humphreys*, 16.

64 Bruce, *The Twentieth Regiment of Massachusetts*, 218.

65 F. B. Speakman to P. H. Allabach, 20 December 1862, in *Official Records*, ser. I, vol. XXI: 446.

66 Bruce, *The Twentieth Regiment of Massachusetts*, 219.

67 Hannah Ropes, the matron at the Union Hotel hospital, counted "three wounds under [Suhre's] shoulders." Ropes, *Civil War Nurse: The Diary and Letters of Hannah Ropes*, 117. However, the letter written to Suhre's mother by Captain E. M. Schrock of Suhre's company states that Suhre received "2 wounds," and that the bullet that caused one of them was lodged in his breast. E. M. Schrock, "To Sarah Suhre," 25 December 1862, quoted in Matteson, "Finding Private Suhre," 121. It is possible that one of the wounds counted by Mrs. Ropes was an exit wound.

68 Hartsock, *Soldier of the Cross*, 42.

69 Ibid., 40.

70 O'Reilly, *Fredericksburg Campaign*, 412.

71 Palfrey, *The Antietam and Fredericksburg*, 170.

72 Reardon, "The Forlorn Hope," 80.

CHAPTER TWELVE: SOUTHBOUND TRAINS

1 L. M. Alcott, *Life, Letters, and Journals*, 68, n. 4.

2 Louisa May Alcott to Mrs. Joseph Chatfield Alcox, December 1862, in *Life, Letters, and Journals*, 80.

3 A. Bronson Alcott, *Journals*, 349.

4 Belle Moses, *Louisa May Alcott, Dreamer and Worker: A Story of Achievement*, 52.

5 L. M. Alcott, *Journals*, 109.

6 John Matteson, *Eden's Outcasts: The Story of Louisa May Alcott and Her Father*, 334.

7 Louisa May Alcott to Mrs. Joseph Chatfield Alcox, December 1862, in *Selected Letters*, 80.

8 Alcott, *Hospital Sketches*, 55.

9 Madeleine B. Stern, *Louisa May Alcott: A Biography*, 112.

10 Florence Nightingale, *Notes on Nursing: What It Is, and What It Is Not*, 8.

11 Ibid., 124.

12 Ibid., 62.

13 Martha Saxton, *Louisa May: A Modern Biography*, 251; Stern, *Louisa May Alcott*, 112.

14 Julian Hawthorne, "The Woman Who Wrote *Little Women*," in Daniel Shealy, ed., *Alcott in Her Own Time*, 194.

15 Rebecca Harding Davis, "Bits of Gossip," in Daniel Shealy, ed., *Alcott In Her Own Time*, 124.

16 L. M. Alcott, *Journals*, 110.

17 Ida M. Tarbell, "Lincoln and the Soldiers," *McClure's Magazine*, June 1899: 164.

18 L. M. Alcott, *Journals*, 110.

19 Ibid.

20 Ibid.

21 Ibid.

22 Alcott, *Hospital Sketches*, 62.

23 Ibid., 64.

24 Ibid., 66.

25 L. M. Alcott, *Journals*, 110.

26 Ropes, *Civil War Nurse*, 112.

27 Lloyd Lewis, *Sherman: Fighting Prophet*, 635.

28 *New-York Herald*, 16 December 1862, 4.

29 Walt Whitman to Louisa Van Velsor Whitman, 29 December 1862, in *Correspondence*, I: 58.

30 Whitman, *Specimen Days*, in *Complete Poetry and Collected Prose*, 712.

31 Ibid.

32 Ibid.

33 Walt Whitman, *Memoranda during the War*, 9.

34 Walt Whitman to Louisa Van Velsor Whitman, 29 December 1862, in *Correspondence*, I: 59.

35 Ibid., 60.

36 George W. Whitman to Thomas Jefferson Whitman, 8 January 1863, in *Civil War Letters*, 78–79.

37 Rable, *Fredericksburg*, 242.

38 George W. Whitman to Thomas Jefferson Whitman, 8 January 1863, in *Civil War Letters*, 79.

39 Robert B. Potter to G. H. McKibben, in *Official Records*, ser. I, vol. XXI: 330.

40 Walt Whitman to Louisa Van Velsor Whitman, 29 December 1862, in *Correspondence*, I: 59.

41 Walt Whitman to Louisa Van Velsor Whitman, 29 December 1862, in *Correspondence*, I: 60.

42 Whitman, *Notebooks and Unpublished Prose Manuscripts*, II: 502. In Whitman's terse description, the food was "good," a somewhat surprising judgment given that it consisted mainly of "salt pork and hard tack." Whitman, *Memoranda*, 10.

43 Whitman, *Notebooks and Unpublished Prose Manuscripts*, II: 509.

44 Ibid., II: 502.

45 Ibid., II: 500.

46 Ibid., II: 504.

47 Whitman, *Specimen Days*, in *Complete Poetry and Collected Prose*, 720.

48 Whitman, *Notebooks and Unpublished Prose Manuscripts*, II: 508–9.

49 Whitman, *Specimen Days*, in *Complete Poetry and Collected Prose*, 713. Emphasis added.

50 Whitman, *Notebooks and Unpublished Prose Manuscripts*, II: 513.

51 Ibid., II: 517–18.

52 Whitman, *Specimen Days*, in *Complete Poetry and Collected Prose*, 713.

53 Allen, *Solitary Singer*, 286.

54 Walt Whitman to Ralph Waldo Emerson, 29 December 1862, in *Correspondence*, I: 61.

55 Walt Whitman to Martha Whitman, 2 January 1863, in *Correspondence*, I: 62.

56 Daniel Mark Epstein, *Lincoln and Whitman: Parallel Lives in Civil War Washington*, 125.

57 Walt Whitman to Martha Whitman, 3 January 1862, in *Correspondence*, I: 63.

58 Whitman, "The Great Army of the Wounded," in *The Complete Prose Works of Walt Whitman*, IV: 88.
59 Ibid.
60 Ibid., 85–86.
61 Ibid., 87.
62 Ibid., 88.
63 Ibid., 89. The *New York Times* piece is "The Great Army of the Wounded," 26 February 1863.

CHAPTER THIRTEEN: "A WORSE PLACE THAN HELL"

1 William Farrar Smith, "Franklin's 'Left Grand Division,'" in *Battles and Leaders*, III: 138.
2 Rable, *Fredericksburg*, 324.
3 Welles, *Diary*, I: 192.
4 Ibid.
5 Ibid., I: 193.
6 John Nicolay and John Hay, *Abraham Lincoln: A History*, VI: 209.
7 Ibid.
8 Rable, *Fredericksburg*, 282.
9 Henry Villard, *Memoirs of Henry Villard, Journalist and Financier*, 385.
10 Frederic Lauriston Bullard, *Famous War Correspondents*, 396.
11 Haupt, *Reminiscences*, 176–77.
12 Ibid., 177.
13 Ibid.
14 Carl Sandburg, *Abraham Lincoln: The War Years*, I: 630.
15 Villard, *Memoirs*, 389.
16 Ibid., 390.
17 Ibid., 391.
18 Allen Thorndike Rice, ed., *Reminiscences of Abraham Lincoln by Distinguished Men of His Time*, xxv.
19 Ibid.
20 Ibid., xxvi.
21 Lincoln, "Message to the Army of the Potomac," 22 December 1862, in *Speeches and Writings*, 419.
22 J. A. Spencer, *History of the United States, from the Earliest Period to the Administration of President Johnson*, IV: 244.
23 Rable, *Fredericksburg*, 549.
24 William O. Stoddard, *Inside the White House in War Times*, 214n. Lincoln's thoughts at this time turned more than once to hell. Five days after the battle, he exclaimed, "if there was any worse Hell than he had been in . . . he would like to know it." Ibid. Mary A. Livermore recollected, "After the dreadful repulse of our forces at Fredericksburg . . . the agony of the President wrung from the bitter cry, 'Of, if there is a man out of hell that suffers more than I do, I pity him!'" Mary A. Livermore, *My Story of the War: A Woman's Narrative*, 561.
25 Goodwin, *Team of Rivals*, 488.
26 White, *A. Lincoln*, 525.

27 Francis Fessenden, *Life and Public Services of William Pitt Fessenden*, I: 253.

28 Fessenden, *Life and Public Services*, I: 239.

29 "The Cabinet Imbroglio," *Harper's Weekly*, 3 January 1862, 2.

30 Frederick William Seward, *Seward at Washington as Senator and Secretary of State: A Memoir of His Life, with Selections from His Letters, 1861–1872*, 146.

31 Todd Brewster, *Lincoln's Gamble: The Tumultuous Six Months That Gave America the Emancipation Proclamation and Changed the Course of the Civil War*, 223.

32 Chester G. Hearn, *Lincoln, the Cabinet, and the Generals*, 140.

33 Theodore Calvin Pease and James Garfield Russell, eds., *The Diary of Orville Hickman Browning*, I: 600.

34 Ibid.

35 Goodwin, *Team of Rivals*, 490.

36 Richard F. Fuller, *Chaplain Fuller*, 305.

37 Ibid., 303.

38 Rev. Erastus Otis Haven, quoted in ibid., 312.

39 Ibid., 313.

40 Edmund Hamilton Sears, quoted in ibid., 316. Sears is best remembered for writing the Christmas carol, "It Came Upon the Midnight Clear."

41 John A. Andrew to Richard F. Fuller, 15 December 1862, quoted in Richard F. Fuller, *Chaplain Fuller*, 323.

42 *The Congressional Globe: Containing the Debates and Proceeding of the Third Session of the Thirty-Seventh Congress*, 242.

43 Ibid., 1090.

44 Fessenden, *Life and Public Services*, I: 239.

45 James Ford Rhodes, *History of the Civil War 1861–1865*, 189.

46 Frederic Bancroft, *The Life of William H. Seward*, 364.

47 Rhodes, *History of the Civil War*, 189.

48 Fessenden, *Life and Public Services*, I: 243.

49 Welles, *Diary*, 195.

50 Ibid.

51 Ibid.

52 Ibid., 196.

53 Fessenden, *Life and Public Services*, I: 244.

54 Ibid.

55 Ibid., 249.

56 Ibid.

57 Hearn, *Lincoln, the Cabinet, and the Generals*, 140.

58 Welles, *Diary*, 200.

59 Ibid., 202.

60 Ibid.

61 Rhodes, *History of the Civil War*, 191.

62 Ibid. Secretary Chase, it should be noted, did not tender his resignation merely in a fit of pique. Chase was concerned that, if Seward left, it might well appear that Chase had maneuvered to get him out—a perception that might be so damaging to Chase "that he could not get along with the Treasury." Fessenden, *Life and Public Services*, I: 249.

63 Seward, *Seward at Washington*, 148.

64 Nicolay and Hay, *Abraham Lincoln: A History*, VI: 271.

65 Sandburg, *Abraham Lincoln*, IV: 10.

66 White, *A. Lincoln*, 532.

67 George Templeton Strong, *Diary of the Civil War, 1860–1865*, III: 282.

68 White, *A. Lincoln*, 532; Goodwin, *Team of Rivals*, 497.

69 Von Drehle, *Rise to Greatness*, 365.

70 John Murray Forbes, *Letters and Recollections of John Murray Forbes*, I: 345.

71 Sandburg, *Abraham Lincoln*, II: 14.

72 White, *A. Lincoln*, 532.

73 Ibid., 533.

74 Josiah Gilbert Holland, *The Life of Abraham Lincoln*, 401.

75 Seward, *Seward at Washington*, 151.

76 Goodwin, *Team of Rivals*, 499.

CHAPTER FOURTEEN: THE PRINCE OF PATIENTS

1 L. M. Alcott, *Journals*, 110.

2 Margaret Leech, *Reveille in Washington, 1860–1865*, 222.

3 Ropes, *Civil War Nurse*, 102.

4 Ibid., 112.

5 Ibid., 103.

6 Ibid., 104.

7 L. M. Alcott, *Journals*, 110.

8 Ibid., 111.

9 Ibid.

10 Alcott, *Hospital Sketches*, 69.

11 L. M. Alcott, *Journals*, 110.

12 Ibid.

13 Ibid.

14 Ropes, *Civil War Nurse*, 112.

15 Ibid., 113.

16 Alcott, *Hospital Sketches*, 68.

17 Ibid., 69–70.

18 Ibid., 71.

19 Ibid., 71–72.

20 Ibid., 75.

21 Ibid., 76.

22 Ropes, *Civil War Nurse*, 115–16.

23 L. M. Alcott, *Journals*, 114.

24 Alcott, *Hospital Sketches*, 97.

25 L. M. Alcott, *Journals*, 114.

26 Ibid.

27 Ibid.

28 Ibid., 115.

29 Ibid. Emphasis in original.

30 Ibid., 113.

31 Ropes, *Civil War Nurse*, 114.

32 Alcott, *Hospital Sketches*, 86.

33 L. M. Alcott, *Journals*, 113.

34 Suhre's forge was in Shanksville, Pennsylvania, the town made sadly famous on September 11, 2001, when United Airlines Flight 93 crashed into a nearby field.

35 Alcott, *Hospital Sketches*, 86.

36 Ropes, *Civil War Nurse*, 118.

37 Ibid.

38 Alcott, *Hospital Sketches*, 86.

39 Ropes, *Civil War Nurse*, 117.

40 Alcott, *Hospital Sketches*, 87.

41 In her journal, Alcott wrote, "Under his plain speech & unpolished manner I seem to see a noble character, a heart as warm & tender as a woman's, a nature fresh & frank as any child's." L. M. Alcott, *Journals*, 113.

42 Alcott, *Hospital Sketches*, 86.

43 L. M. Alcott, *Journals*, 113.

44 Alcott, *Hospital Sketches*, 87.

45 Ibid.

46 Ibid.

47 Ibid., 88.

48 Ibid., 88–89.

49 Ibid., 89–90.

50 Alcott, *Hospital Sketches*, 90.

51 Ropes, *Civil War Nurse*, 117.

52 Alcott, *Hospital Sketches*, 91.

53 Ibid.

54 Alcott, *Hospital Sketches*, 92.

55 Ropes, *Civil War Nurse*, 118.

56 Ibid.

57 A. Bronson Alcott, Journal for 1863, 1 January, Harvard University.

58 Alcott, *Hospital Sketches*, 105–6.

59 L. M. Alcott, *Journals*, 115.

60 Ibid.

61 Ropes, *Civil War Nurse*, 121.

62 Ibid.

63 A. Bronson Alcott, 8 January 1863, *Journals*, 352.

64 Alcott, *Hospital Sketches*, 101.

65 L. M. Alcott, *Journals*, 115.

CHAPTER FIFTEEN: "DEATH ITSELF HAS LOST ALL ITS TERRORS"

1 Welles, *Diary*, I: 211.

2 Walt Whitman to Martha Whitman, 3 January 1863, in *Correspondence*, I: 63.

3 Traubel, *With Walt Whitman in Camden*, III: 75.

4 Ibid., III: 76.

5 Ibid., III: 525.

6 Roy Morris Jr., *The Better Angel: Walt Whitman in the Civil War*, 166.

7 Justin Kaplan, *Walt Whitman: A Life*, 288.

8 Walt Whitman to Ralph Waldo Emerson, 29 December 1862, in Whitman, *Correspondence*, I: 61.

9 Ralph Waldo Emerson to Salmon P. Chase, 10 January 1863, in Whitman, *Correspondence*, I: 65.

10 Walt Whitman to Ralph Waldo Emerson, 17 January 1863, in Whitman, *Correspondence*, I: 68.

11 Ibid.

12 Ibid., 68–69.

13 Walt Whitman to James Redpath [?], 6 August 1863, in Whitman, *Correspondence*, I: 120.

14 Walt Whitman to Ralph Waldo Emerson, 17 January 1863, in Whitman, *Correspondence*, I: 70.

15 Ibid.

16 Ibid., 69–70.

17 Walt Whitman to Thomas Jefferson Whitman, 16 January 1863, in *Correspondence*, I: 67.

18 Walt Whitman to Nathaniel Bloom and John F. S. Gray, 19–20 March 1863, in *Correspondence*, I: 83.

19 Walt Whitman to Louisa Van Velsor Whitman, 19 May 1863, in *Correspondence*, I: 103.

20 Whitman, *Specimen Days*, in *Complete Poetry and Collected Prose*, 727.

21 Nina Silber, *Landmarks of the Civil War*, 57.

22 Whitman, *Specimen Days*, in *Complete Poetry and Collected Prose*, 717–18.

23 Whitman, *Notebooks and Unpublished Prose Manuscripts*, II: 519; 521; 530; 624; Whitman, *Specimen Days*, in *Complete Poetry and Collected Prose*, 726.

24 Walt Whitman to James Redpath, 6 August 1863, in *Correspondence*, I: 122.

25 Whitman, *Specimen Days*, in *Complete Poetry and Collected Prose*, 727.

26 Morris, *The Better Angel*, 116.

27 Whitman, *Specimen Days*, in *Complete Poetry and Collected Prose*, 731.

28 Whitman, *Notebooks and Unpublished Prose Manuscripts*, II: 519.

29 Whitman, *Specimen Days*, in *Complete Poetry and Collected Prose*, 736.

30 Ibid.

31 Walt Whitman to Louisa Van Velsor Whitman, 15 September 1863, in *Correspondence*, I: 148.

32 Walt Whitman to Louisa Van Velsor Whitman, 11 August 1863, in *Correspondence*, I: 131.

33 Traubel, *With Walt Whitman in Camden*, VI: 194.

34 Walt Whitman to Louisa Van Velsor Whitman, 7 July 1863, in *Correspondence*, I: 114.

35 Walt Whitman to Louisa Van Velsor Whitman, 25 August 1863, in *Correspondence*, I: 138.

36 Walt Whitman to Nathaniel Bloom and John F. S. Gray, 19 March 1863, in *Correspondence*, I: 81–82.

37 Walt Whitman to Hugo Fritsch, 7 August 1863, in *Correspondence*, I: 125.

38 Whitman, "Vigil Strange I Kept on the Field One Night," in *Complete Poetry and Collected Prose*, 438–39; Walt Whitman, *Notebooks and Unpublished Prose Manuscripts*, II: 613.

39 Allen, *Solitary Singer*, 297; Kaplan, *Whitman*, 284. The time and place of Brown's

wounding remain uncertain. Gay Wilson Allen calls him a casualty of Cedar Mountain, the same battle where Henry Abbott's brother Ned died. Justin Kaplan says Brown was wounded at Rappahannock Station.

40 Walt Whitman to Thomas P. Sawyer, 21 April 1863, in *Correspondence*, I: 91.

41 Whitman, *Notebooks and Unpublished Prose Manuscripts*, II: 562–63.

42 Ibid., 606. Whitman's description of the punishment is a bit misleading. A soldier who was "bucked" was "placed on the ground in a sitting position, his stretched out arms tightly bound over his lower legs, with a wooden stick or rod placed directly under the knees and above the arms." The procedure is described in Mark Will-Weber, *Muskets and Applejack: Spirits, Soldiers, and the Civil War.*

43 Whitman, *Notebooks and Unpublished Prose Manuscripts*, II: 606.

44 Walt Whitman to Lewis K. Brown, 1 August 1863, in *Correspondence*, I: 120.

45 Ibid., 119–21.

46 Walt Whitman to Lewis K. Brown, 15 August 1863, in *Correspondence*, I: 134.

47 Walt Whitman to Thomas P. Sawyer, 21 April 1863, in *Correspondence*, I: 91.

48 Walt Whitman to James Redpath, 6 August 1863, in *Correspondence*, I: 122.

49 Morris, *The Better Angel*, 110.

50 Walt Whitman to Thomas P. Sawyer, 21 April 1863, in *Correspondence*, I: 93.

51 Ibid.

52 Walt Whitman to Thomas P. Sawyer, 26 April 1863, in *Correspondence*, I: 93.

53 Walt Whitman to Thomas P. Sawyer, 27 May 1863, in *Correspondence*, I: 107.

54 Walt Whitman to Louisa Van Velsor Whitman, 13 May 1863, in *Correspondence*, I: 100.

55 Walt Whitman to Louisa Van Velsor Whitman, 22 June 1863, in *Correspondence*, I: 110.

56 Walt Whitman to Louisa Van Velsor Whitman, 30 June 1863, in *Correspondence*, I: 112.

57 Walt Whitman to Louisa Van Velsor Whitman, 26 May 1863, in *Correspondence*, I: 105.

58 Walt Whitman to Louisa Van Velsor Whitman, 13 October 1863, in *Correspondence*, I: 165–66.

59 Ibid., 156.

60 Walt Whitman to Louisa Van Velsor Whitman, 15 July 1863, in *Correspondence*, I: 118.

61 Whitman, *Notebooks and Unpublished Prose Manuscripts*, II: 572.

62 Ibid., 650.

63 Walt Whitman to Louisa Van Velsor Whitman, 8 September 1863, in *Correspondence*, I: 145.

64 Ibid., 145; Walt Whitman to Louisa Van Velsor Whitman, 15 April 1863, in *Correspondence*, I: 89; Walt Whitman to Moses Lane, 11 May 1863, in *Correspondence*, I: 98.

65 Walt Whitman to Louisa Van Velsor Whitman, 30 June 1863, in *Correspondence*, I: 111.

66 Kennedy, *Reminiscences of Walt Whitman*, 42.

67 Walt Whitman to Louisa Van Velsor Whitman, 18 August 1863, in *Correspondence*, I: 136.

68 Walt Whitman to Louisa Van Velsor Whitman, 26 May 1863, in *Correspondence*, I: 105.

69 Kennedy, *Reminiscences of Walt Whitman*, 35–36.

70 Whitman, *Specimen Days*, in *Complete Poetry and Collected Prose*, 732.

71 Ibid., 733.

72 Walt Whitman to Louisa Van Velsor Whitman, 30 June 1863, in *Correspondence*, I: 113.

73 Walt Whitman to Nathaniel Bloom and John F. S. Gray, 19–20 March 1863, in *Correspondence*, I: 82.

74 Henry B. Rankin, *Personal Recollections of Abraham Lincoln*, 125–26.

75 Donaldson, *Charles Sumner*, 58.

76 Walt Whitman to Nathaniel Bloom and John F. S. Gray, 19–20 March 1863, in *Correspondence*, I: 83.

77 Whitman, *November Boughs*, in *Complete Poetry and Collected Prose*, 1198.

78 Whitman, *Notebooks and Unpublished Prose Manuscripts*, II: 539.

79 Walt Whitman to James Redpath, 21 October 1863, in *Correspondence*, I: 171.

80 Ibid., 172.

81 Jerome Loving, *Walt Whitman: The Song of Himself*, 285.

82 Walt Whitman, *Correspondence*, I: 65, n. 6.

83 John Townsend Trowbridge, *My Own Story, with Recollections of Noted Persons*, 387; Walt Whitman, *Correspondence*, I: 65, n. 6.

84 Trowbridge, *My Own Story*, 387; Walt Whitman, *Correspondence*, l: 65, n. 6.

85 Trowbridge, 388.

86 Ibid.

87 Ibid., 388–89.

88 Morris, *The Better Angel*, 149.

89 Kaplan, *Whitman*, 290.

90 Whitman, *Notebooks and Unpublished Prose Manuscripts*, II: 669.

91 Whitman, "A Woman Waits for Me"; "Song of the Open Road," *Complete Poetry and Collected Prose*, 260, 300.

92 Whitman to Dr. Le Baron Russell, [?] February 1864, in *Correspondence*, I: 200.

93 Whitman to Louisa Van Velsor Whitman, 31 March 1864, in *Correspondence*, I: 206.

94 Walt Whitman to Louisa Van Velsor Whitman, 5 February 1864, in *Correspondence*, I: 195.

95 Walt Whitman to John Townsend Trowbridge, 8 February 1864, in *Correspondence*, I: 196.

96 Whitman, *Specimen Days*, in *Complete Poetry and Collected Prose*, 740.

97 Walt Whitman to Louisa Van Velsor Whitman, 10 April 1864, in *Correspondence*, I: 209.

98 Walt Whitman to Dr. Le Baron Russell, [?] February 1864, in *Correspondence*, I: 199.

99 Walt Whitman to Louisa Van Velsor Whitman, 5 April 1864, in *Correspondence*, I: 208.

100 Walt Whitman to Louisa Van Velsor Whitman, 15 March 1864, in *Correspondence*, I: 203.

101 Ibid.

102 Walt Whitman to Louisa Van Velsor Whitman, 29 March 1864, in *Correspondence*, I: 205.

103 Walt Whitman to Louisa Van Velsor Whitman, 31 March 1864, in *Correspondence*, I: 206; Walt Whitman to Louisa Van Velsor Whitman, 7 June 1864, in *Correspondence*, I: 232.

104 Walt Whitman to Louisa Van Velsor Whitman, 25 May 1864, in *Correspondence*, I: 227.

105 Walt Whitman to Louisa Van Velsor Whitman, 12 April 1864, in Correspondence, I: 210.

106 Walt Whitman to Louisa Van Velsor Whitman, 7 June 1864, in *Correspondence*, I: 231.

107 Walt Whitman to Louisa Van Velsor Whitman, 10 June 1864, in *Correspondence*, I: 233.

108 Walt Whitman to Louisa van Velsor Whitman, 14 June 1864, in *Correspondence*, I: 233.

109 Walt Whitman to Louisa Van Velsor Whitman, 17 June 1864, in *Correspondence*, I: 234.

110 George Whitman to Louisa Van Velsor Whitman, 18 June 1864, in *Civil War Letters*, 121.

111 Ibid.

112 Walt Whitman to Lewis K. Brown, 11 July 1864, in *Correspondence*, I: 238.

113 Whitman, *Notebooks and Unpublished Prose Manuscripts*, II: 717.

114 Walt Whitman to William D. O'Connor, 24 July 1864, in *Correspondence*, I: 238.

Chapter Sixteen: "Our Fearful Journey Home"

1 Alcott, *Hospital Sketches*, 106.

2 Ibid.

3 L. M. Alcott, *Journals*, 116.

4 Alcott, *Hospital Sketches*, 107.

5 A. Bronson Alcott, 18 January 1863, *Journals*, 353.

6 Alcott, *Hospital Sketches*, 107.

7 Ibid.

8 A. Bronson Alcott, *Journals*, 354.

9 A. Bronson Alcott to Anna Alcott Pratt, 29 January 1863, in *Letters of A. Bronson Alcott*, 334.

10 Julian Hawthorne, "Memories of the Alcott Family," in Daniel Shealy, ed., *Alcott in Her Own Time*, 195.

11 A. Bronson Alcott to Anna Alcott Pratt, 27 January 1863, in *Letters*, 333.

12 A. Bronson Alcott to Anna Alcott Pratt, 25 January 1863, in *Letters*, 332–33.

13 May Alcott, Journal, 24 January 1863, Louisa May Alcott Additional Papers, Houghton Library, Harvard University, MS Am 1817.

14 Hawthorne, "Memories of the Alcott Family," in *Alcott in Her Own Time*, 195.

15 May Alcott, Journal, 25 January 1863, Louisa May Alcott Additional Papers, Harvard University.

16 A. Bronson Alcott to Anna Alcott Pratt, 25 January 1863, in *Letters*, 332–33.

17 A. Bronson Alcott to Anna Alcott Pratt, 27 January 1863, in *Letters*, 333.

18 Abigail May Alcott to Samuel J. May, n.d. (1863), Louisa May Alcott Family Papers, Houghton Library, Harvard University, MS Am 1130.9; L. M. Alcott, *Journals*, 116.

19 A. Bronson Alcott to Anna Alcott Pratt, 29 January 1863, in *Letters*, 334.

20 L. M. Alcott, *Journals*, 116.

21 Abigail May Alcott to Samuel J. May, n.d. (1863), Alcott Family Papers, Harvard University.

22 L. M. Alcott, *Journals*, 117.

23 Abigail May Alcott to Samuel J. May, n.d. (1863), Alcott Family Papers, Harvard University.

24 A. Bronson Alcott to Anna Alcott Pratt, 29 January 1863, in *Letters*, 334.

25 A. Bronson Alcott, Journal, 11 February 1863, A. Bronson Alcott Journals, Houghton Library, Harvard University, MS Am 1130.12.

26 Abigail May Alcott to Samuel J. May, (?) February 1863, Alcott Family Papers, Harvard University.

27 Ibid.

28 A. Bronson Alcott to Anna Alcott Pratt, 4 February 1863, in *Letters*, 335.

29 Stern, *Louisa May Alcott*, 129.

30 May Alcott, Journal, 22 February 1863, Louisa May Alcott Additional Papers, Harvard University.

31 Hawthorne's wife Sophia gave credit to a "magnetic healer" named Mrs. Bliss, whom the Alcotts brought in to help with Louisa's cure. Astonished, Hawthorne wrote to James Fields's wife that after Mrs. Bliss had finished her treatment, "Louisa rose out of bed and walked across the room alone. . . . Hitherto she could not stand one moment, and had to be lifted to her easy chair. . . . Mrs. Bliss took all the pain from her back." Sophia Hawthorne to Annie Adams Fields, 20 February 1863, quoted in Taylor Stoehr, *Hawthorne's Mad Scientists*, 46.

32 L. M. Alcott, *Journals*, 117.

33 Julian Hawthorne, "The Woman Who Wrote *Little Women*," in Daniel Shealy, ed., *Alcott in Her Own* Time, 195.

34 Matteson, *Eden's Outcasts*, 289.

35 In his journals from earlier years, Henry Thoreau recorded sights and sounds such as these in the first weeks of April in and around Concord. One may safely assume that the same plants were in flower in April 1863, when Louisa wrote of taking "some pleasant walks and drives." L. M. Alcott, *Journals*, 118.

36 Louisa May Alcott, April 1863, *Journals*, 118.

37 Ibid.

38 Moncure D. Conway, *Autobiography, Memories and Experiences of Moncure Daniel Conway*, I: 328.

39 Louisa May Alcott to A. Bronson Alcott, 29 November 1856, *Selected Letters*, 26.

40 Louisa May Alcott to Alf Whitman, 5 April 1860, *Selected Letters*, 53. Massachusetts Chief Justice Lemuel Shaw declared Sanborn's arrest unlawful, following a hearing attended by Walt Whitman. Sanborn, *Recollections of Seventy Years*, I: 212.

41 Louisa May Alcott, *Journals*, 118.

42 Alcott, *Hospital Sketches*, 81–82.

43 Mrs. L. Burke, *The Illustrated Language of Flowers*, 46.

44 I am indebted to Musarrat Lamia for pointing out this association to me.

45 Alcott, *Hospital Sketches*, 93.

46 Louisa May Alcott to James Redpath, July (?) 1863, *Selected Letters*, 87.

47 Louisa May Alcott, May 1863, *Journals*, 118.

48 Louisa May Alcott, June 1863, *Journals*, 119.

49 Henry James Sr. to Louisa May Alcott, quoted in L. M. Alcott, *Journals*, 123, n. 23.

50 Louisa May Alcott, August 1863, *Journals*, 120.

51 *The Boston Evening Transcript* called "The Death of John" "a noble and touching picture." 4 June 1863. *The National Anti-Slavery Standard* observed, "The touching story of the brave John's struggle and triumph cannot soon be forgotten by those who read it." 18 September 1869. Quoted in Beverly Lyon Clark, *Louisa May Alcott: The Contemporary Reviews*, 9, 17.

52 Clark, *Louisa May Alcott*, 13.

53 L. M. Alcott, *Journals*, 124, n. 24.

54 Louisa May Alcott to Annie Adams Fields, 24 June 1863, *Selected Letters*, 84.

55 Louisa May Alcott, February 1863, *Journals*, 117.

56 Abigail May Alcott to Samuel J. May, n.d. [1863], Alcott Family Papers, Harvard University.

57 Louisa May Alcott to the Alcott family, 30 May 1870, *Selected Letters*, 137.

58 Holmes Sr., *Currents and Counter-Currents*, 193.

59 Harriet Reisen, *Louisa May Alcott: The Woman behind "Little Women,"* 286.

60 Louisa May Alcott to the Alcott family, 30 May 1870, *Selected Letters*, 137.

61 A. Bronson Alcott, *Journals*, 357.

62 Louisa May Alcott to Alfred Whitman, September 1863, *Selected Letters*, 92–93.

63 Julian Hawthorne, "The Woman Who Wrote *Little Women*," in Daniel Shealy, ed., *Alcott in Her Own Time*, 196.

64 Ibid., 197.

65 Alcott, *Hospital Sketches*, 107.

66 A. Bronson Alcott to Anna Alcott, 25 March 1863, *Letters*, 336.

67 L. M. Alcott, *Journals*, 124, n. 24.

68 Ibid., 122.

69 Ibid., May 1868, 165.

70 Ibid., 166.

71 Ibid., 117; Alcott, *Little Women*, 132.

72 Conversation with Ariel Clark Silver, 25 April 2019.

73 Alcott, *Little Women*, 380.

CHAPTER SEVENTEEN: THE SONG OF THE HERMIT THRUSH

1 George Whitman to Louisa Van Velsor Whitman, 23 July 1863, in *Civil War Letters*, 99.

2 Ibid.

3 Ibid.

4 Walt Whitman to Louisa Van Velsor Whitman, 26 April 1864, in *Correspondence*, I: 211.

5 Walt Whitman, Diary, 9 May 1865, Manuscripts of Walt Whitman in the collection of American Literature, Beinecke Rare Book and Manuscript Library, Yale University.

6 W. George FitzGerald, "President Wilson's Dream—and His Dilemma," *Nineteenth Century and After* 81: 30.

7 George Whitman to Louisa Van Velsor Whitman, 23 October 1864, in *Civil War Letters*, 133.

8 Richard J. Sommers, *Richmond Redeemed: The Siege at Petersburg*, 285–89.

9 Walt Whitman to Charles W. Eldridge, 8 October 1864, in *Correspondence*, I: 243.

10 Whitman, *Notebooks and Unpublished Prose Manuscripts*, II: 691.

11 Ibid., II: 745.

12 Ibid.

13 Roper, *Now the Drum of War*, 316.

14 George Whitman to Louisa Van Velsor Whitman, 2 October 1864, in *Civil War Letters*, 132.

15 Walt Whitman to Charles W. Eldridge, 8 October 1864, in *Correspondence*, I: 243.

16 Bruce Catton, "The Politics of War," in *The American Heritage Picture History of the Civil War*, 486–87.

17 Whitman, *Notebooks and Unpublished Prose Manuscripts*, II: 721.

18 Whitman, "The Prisoners," *New York Times*, 27 December 1864, 2.

19 Whitman, *Notebooks and Unpublished Prose Manuscripts*, II: 746.

20 Walt Whitman to William D. O'Connor, 6 January 1865, in *Correspondence*, I: 246.

21 Ibid.

22 Ibid., 246–47.

23 Ibid., 247.

24 Whitman, "The Wound-Dresser," in *Complete Poetry and Collected Prose*, 443.

25 Whitman, *Specimen Days*, in *Complete Poetry and Collected Prose*, 757.

26 A. S. Cunningham to R. H. Chilton, in *Official Records*, ser. I, vol. XLVI, part II: 1151.

27 Abner Small, *The Road to Richmond: The Civil War Memoirs of Major Abner R. Small*, 171.

28 A. S. Cunningham to R. H. Chilton, in *Official Records*, ser. I, vol. XLVI, part II: 1151.

29 Ibid.

30 Martin G. Murray, "Walt Whitman on Brother George and His Fifty-First New York Volunteers: An Uncollected *New York Times* Article." *Walt Whitman Quarterly Review* 18, no. 1: 65.

31 Walt Whitman to William D. O'Connor, 20 January 1864, in *Correspondence*, I: 249.

32 Allen, *Solitary Singer*, 321.

33 Walt Whitman to Louisa Van Velsor Whitman, 1 February 1865, in *Correspondence*, I: 251.

34 Thomas Jefferson Whitman to Walt Whitman, 31 January 1865, in *Dear Brother Walt: The Letters of Thomas Jefferson Whitman*, 101.

35 Walt Whitman to John Swinton, 3 February 1865, in *Correspondence*, I: 252.

36 Roper, *Now the Drum of War*, 308.

37 Whitman, *Notebooks and Unpublished Prose Manuscripts*, II: 749.

38 Walt Whitman to John Townsend Trowbridge, 6 February 1865, in *Correspondence*, I: 254.

39 Whitman, *Notebooks and Unpublished Prose Manuscripts*, II: 750.

40 George Whitman, *Civil War Letters*, 133, n. 5.

41 Louisa Van Velsor Whitman to Walt Whitman, 5 March 1865, Trent Collection of Whitmaniana, Duke University Rare Book, Manuscript, and Special Collections Library.

42 "Interview with Peter Doyle," Whitman, *Complete Prose Works*, V: 5.

43 George Whitman to Louisa Van Velsor Whitman, 24 February 1865, in *Civil War Letters*, 134.

44 Walt Whitman, *Specimen Days*, in *Complete Poetry and Collected Prose*, 765.

45 Ibid., 758.

46 Louisa Van Velsor Whitman to Walt Whitman, 5 March 1865, Trent Collection of Whitmaniana, Duke University Rare Book, Manuscript, and Special Collections Library.

47 Ibid.

48 Walt Whitman to William D. and Ellen M. O'Connor, 26 March 1865, in *Correspondence*, I: 256–57.

49 Walt Whitman to William D. O'Connor, 7 April 1865, in *Correspondence*, I: 258.

50 Walt Whitman to William D. and Ellen O'Connor, 26 March 1865, in *Correspondence*, I: 257.

51 Allen, *Solitary Singer*, 331.

52 "Interview with Peter Doyle," Whitman, *Complete Prose Works*, V: 5.

53 E. Lawrence Abel, *A Finger in Lincoln's Brain: What Modern Science Reveals about Lincoln, His Assassination, and Its Aftermath*, 57.

54 Tom Taylor, *Our American Cousin*, 37.

55 "Interview with Peter Doyle," Whitman, *Complete Prose Works*, V: 8.

56 Whitman, *Specimen Days*, in *Complete Poetry and Collected Prose*, 712.

57 Whitman, *Notebooks and Unpublished Prose Manuscripts*, II: 764.

58 Ibid., 762–63.

59 Ibid., 764.

60 Ibid., 767.

61 Ibid., 766.

62 Whitman, "When Lilacs Last in the Dooryard Bloom'd," in *Complete Poetry and Collected Prose*, 459–67.

63 Ibid., 464.

64 Ibid., 466.

65 Ibid.

66 Ibid.

67 Walt Whitman to Byron Sutherland, 26 August 1865, in *Correspondence*, I: 266.

68 Whitman, "Reconciliation," in *Collected Writings of Walt Whitman*, II: 555–56.

69 Whitman, *Notebooks and Unpublished Prose Manuscripts*, II: 756.

70 Walt Whitman, *November Boughs*, in *Complete Poetry and Collected Prose*, 1172.

71 James Harlan to Bureau Chief, 29 May 1865, National Archives, RG 48, Entry 14.

72 Traubel, *With Walt Whitman in Camden*, I: 3–4.

73 William Douglas O'Connor, *The Good Gray Poet: A Vindication*, 54, 55.

74 Ibid., 10.

75 Ibid., 12.

76 Ibid., 64.

77 Ibid., 63, 68.

78 Traubel, *With Walt Whitman in Camden*, II: 304.

79 Whitman, *Notebooks and Unpublished Prose Manuscripts*, II: 874.

80 Whitman, "A Backward Glance," *Complete Poetry and Collected Prose*, 657.

81 Traubel, *With Walt Whitman in Camden*, II: 460.

82 William James, *The Varieties of Religious Experience: A Study in Human Nature*, 83.

83 Traubel, *With Walt Whitman in Camden*, II: 661.

84 Whitman, "To Thee Old Cause," in *Complete Poetry and Collected Prose*, 167.

85 Traubel, *With Walt Whitman in Camden*, VI: 353.

86 Epstein, *Lincoln and Whitman*, 330.

87 Kennedy, *Reminiscences of Walt Whitman*, 28.

CHAPTER EIGHTEEN: ST. PATRICK'S DAY, 1863

1 O'Reilly, *Fredericksburg Campaign*, 464.

2 Cooke, *Surry of Eagle's-Nest*, 347.

3 Thom Hatch, *Glorious War: The Civil War Adventures of George Armstrong Custer*, 92.

4 Maxwell, *The Perfect Lion*, 188. Emphasis added.

5 Milham, *Gallant Pelham*, 225.

6 Cooke, *Surry of Eagle's-Nest*, 336.

7 Ibid., 349.

8 J. E. B. Stuart to Atkinson Pelham, 29 March 1863, quoted in Maxwell, *The Perfect Lion*, 324.

9 Maxwell, *The Perfect Lion*, 295.

10 Harry Gilmor, *Four Years in the Saddle*, 64.

11 Ibid., 65.

12 Catton, *Glory Road*, 154.

13 Gilmor, *Four Years in the Saddle*, 65.

14 Maxwell, *The Perfect Lion*, 303.

15 J. E. B. Stuart to Atkinson Pelham, 29 March 1863, quoted in Maxwell, *The Perfect Lion*, 324. Emphasis in original.

16 H. B. McClellan, quoted in H. H. Matthews, "Major John Pelham, Confederate Hero," *Southern Historical Society Papers* 36: 382.

17 Freeman, *Lee's Lieutenants*, II: 465.

18 John M. Ward, "The Gallant Pelham," *The Alabama Bible Society Quarterly*, 16: 34.

19 Catton, *Glory Road*, 155.

20 Thomason, *Jeb Stuart*, 361.

21 Maxwell, *The Perfect Lion*, 313.

22 Ward, "The Gallant Pelham," 34.

23 Maxwell, *The Perfect Lion*, 317.

24 Von Borcke, *Memoirs*, 359–60.

25 Robert E. Lee to Jefferson Davis, 19 March 1863, in *Official Records*, ser. I, vol. XXV: 675.

26 Freeman, *Lee's Lieutenants*, II: 466.

27 J. E. B. in to Atkinson Pelham, 29 March 1863, quoted in Maxwell, *The Perfect Lion*, 323.

CHAPTER NINETEEN: "THE DUTY OF FIGHTING HAS CEASED FOR ME"

1 Henry L. Abbott to George Abbott, 21 December 1862, in *Fallen Leaves*, 154.

2 Oliver Wendell Holmes Jr. to Oliver Wendell Holmes Sr., 20 December 1862, in *Touched with Fire*, 79–80.

3 George H. Boker, "The Crossing at Fredericksburg: December 11, 1862," in *Poems of the War*, 82–87.

4 Sculley Bradley, *George Henry Boker: Poet and Patriot*, 215–16.

5 A copy of *Poems of the War*, inscribed by Nicolay, is in the possession of the Gilder Lehrman Institute of American History in New York City.

6 Oliver Wendell Holmes, Jr. to Oliver Wendell Holmes Sr., 29 March 1863, in *Touched with Fire*, 86.

7 Howe, *Shaping Years*, 151.

8 Oliver Wendell Holmes Jr. to Oliver Wendell Holmes Sr., 29 March 1863, in *Touched with Fire*, 90.

9 Augustine Birrell, *Frederick Locker-Lampson: A Character Sketch*, 94.

10 Oliver Wendell Holmes Jr. to Oliver Wendell Holmes Sr., 29 March 1863, in *Touched with Fire*, 91.

11 Oliver Wendell Holmes Jr. to Oliver Wendell Holmes Sr., 18 March 1863, in *Touched with Fire*, 85.

12 Ibid., 86.

13 Ibid., 85.

14 Ibid., 86.

15 Henry L. Abbott to Josiah Abbott, 19 January 1863, in *Fallen Leaves*, 162.

16 Henry L. Abbott to Caroline Abbott, 8 February 1863, in *Fallen Leaves*, 168.

17 Oliver Wendell Holmes Jr. to Oliver Wendell Holmes Sr., 29 March 1863, in *Touched with Fire*, 90–91.

18 E. Porter Alexander, quoted in Jeffry D. Wert, *Cavalryman of the Lost Cause: A Biography of J. E. B. Stuart*, 230.

19 Philip W. Parsons, *The Union Sixth Corps in the Chancellorsville Campaign*, 78.

20 Oliver Wendell Holmes Jr. to Amelia Holmes, 3 May 1863, in *Touched with Fire*, 92.

21 Oliver Wendell Holmes Jr. to Oliver Wendell Holmes Sr., 4 May 1863, in *Touched with Fire*, 93.

22 Henry L. Abbott to Josiah Abbott, 6 July 1863, in *Fallen Leaves*, 188.

23 Miller, *Harvard's Civil War*, 272.

24 Henry L. Abbott to Josiah Abbott, 6 July 1863, in *Fallen Leaves*, 184.

25 Ibid., 186.

26 Oliver Wendell Holmes Sr. to Dr. William Hunt, 25 May 1863, in Morse, *Life and Letters*, II: 25. A specimen of his father's humor survives. Thinking it best to keep the wound open for a time, Holmes's doctor fashioned a little plug out of a carrot and placed it in the aperture. Holmes Senior walked up to where his son was resting. Pinching him on the heel, he asked his son what vegetable he had turned the carrot into. Holmes Junior knew better than to respond. Senior then delivered his punch line: "Why, into a Pa's nip!" Ibid. As to the dreary stream of Homeric allusions he was forced to endure, the captain wrote, "I would see man after man approach with self-gratulatory smile as he made a reference to Achilles. Each had the feeling of personal achievement while he really was moving along the path of least resistance." Howe, *Shaping Years*, 156.

27 Budiansky, *Oliver Wendell Holmes*, 108.

28 Howe, *Shaping Years*, 155.

29 Holmes Sr., "The Inevitable Trial," *Pages from an Old Volume of Life*, 78.

30 Ibid., 79.

31 Ibid., 95.

32 Ibid.

33 Ibid., 100.

34 Ibid., 101.

35 Ibid., 106.

36 Ibid., 108.

37 Ibid., 111, 117.

38 Henry Abbott to Josiah Abbott, 17 August 1863, in *Fallen Leaves*, 201.

39 Henry L. Abbott to Oliver Wendell Holmes Jr., 5 September 1863, in *Fallen Leaves*, 210.

40 Henry L. Abbott to Oliver Wendell Holmes Jr., 22 September 1863, in *Fallen Leaves*, 218–19.

41 Ibid., 219.

42 Oliver Wendell Holmes Jr. to Amelia Holmes, 7 June 1864, in *Touched with Fire*, 142.

43 Ibid., 143.

44 Henry Abbott to George B. Perry, 4 April 1864, in *Fallen Leaves*, 244.

45 Henry L. Abbott to Caroline Abbott, 27 March 1864, in *Fallen Leaves*, 241.

46 Oliver Wendell Holmes Jr. to Charles Eliot Norton, 17 April 1864, in *Touched with Fire*, 122n.

47 Jean Edward Smith, *Grant*, 319.

48 Bruce Catton, *A Stillness at Appomattox*, 57.

49 Oliver Wendell Holmes Jr., Diary, 8 May 1864, in *Touched with Fire*, 109.

50 Oliver Wendell Holmes Jr. to Oliver and Amelia Holmes, 3 May 1864, in *Touched with Fire*, 103.

51 Oliver Wendell Holmes Jr., Diary, 7 May 1864, in *Touched with Fire*, 108.

52 Oliver Wendell Holmes Jr., Diary, 9 May 1864, in *Touched with Fire*, 109.

53 Miller, *Harvard's Civil War*, 338.

54 Robert Garth Scott, *Into the Wilderness with the Army of the Potomac*, 155.

55 Abbott, *Fallen Leaves*, 254. The inscription means "Without fear and without reproach."

56 Oliver Wendell Holmes Jr., "Memorial Day," in *Speeches*, 8.

57 Oliver Wendell Holmes Jr., Diary, 13 May 1864, in *Touched with Fire*, 117.

58 Oliver Wendell Holmes Jr. to Oliver and Amelia Holmes, 16 May 1864, in *Touched with Fire*, 121.

59 Ibid., 122. Emphasis added.

60 Ibid.

61 Oliver Wendell Holmes Jr. to Oliver and Amelia Holmes, 30 May 1864, in *Touched with Fire*, 135.

62 Oliver Wendell Holmes Jr. to Oliver and Amelia Holmes, 24 June 1864, in *Touched with Fire*, 149–50.

63 Oliver Wendell Holmes Jr. to Amelia Holmes, 7 June 1864, in *Touched with Fire*, 142–43.

64 Ibid., 143.

65 Oliver Wendell Holmes Jr., "H. L. A. Twentieth Massachusetts Volunteers," in Miller, *Harvard's Civil War*, 340.

66 Oliver Wendell Holmes Jr., Diary, 29 May 1864, in *Touched with Fire*, 134.

67 Oliver Wendell Holmes Jr., Diary, in *Touched with Fire*, 134. Two members of Holmes's escort also escaped capture.

68 Oliver Wendell Holmes Jr. to Amelia Holmes, 7 June 1864, in *Touched with Fire*, 142.

69 Howe, *Shaping Years*, 167.

70 Baker, *Justice from Beacon Hill*, 151.

71 Ibid.

72 Louis Menand, *The Metaphysical Club: A Story of Ideas in America*, 51.

73 Howe, *Shaping Years*, 175.

74 Ibid.

CHAPTER TWENTY: "TO ACT WITH ENTHUSIASM AND FAITH"

1 Baker, *Justice from Beacon Hill*, 157.

2 Oliver Wendell Holmes Jr. to Lewis Einstein, 10 March 1918, in *Holmes-Einstein Letters*, 163.

3 Oliver Wendell Holmes Jr. to Harold J. Laski, 15 December 1926, in Howe, *Holmes-Laski Letters*, II: 905.

4 Oliver Wendell Holmes Jr., "Memorial Day," in *Speeches*, 11.

5 Howe, *Shaping Years*, 176.

6 Budiansky, *Oliver Wendell Holmes*, 134.

7 White, *Justice Oliver Wendell Holmes*, 87.

8 Oliver Wendell Holmes Jr., "Introduction to the General Survey," in *Collected Legal Papers*, 301, 302.

9 Budiansky, *Oliver Wendell Holmes*, 135.

10 Ralph Barton Perry, *The Thought and Character of William James*, 99.

11 Holmes Jr., "The Path of the Law," *Collected Legal Papers*, 164.

12 Ibid., 165.

13 White, *Justice Oliver Wendell Holmes*, 476.

14 Holmes Jr., "The Profession of the Law," *Collected Legal Papers*, 31–32.

15 William James to Thomas W. Ward, 27 March 1866, in James, *The Letters of William James*, I: 76.

16 Menand, *The Metaphysical Club*, 204.

17 William James to Oliver Wendell Holmes Jr., 3 January 1868, quoted in Baker, *Justice from Beacon Hill*, 214–15.

18 Howard M. Feinstein, *Becoming William James*, 212–13.

19 Menand, *The Metaphysical Club*, 216.

20 Ibid.

21 Mary James to Henry James Jr., quoted in White, *Justice Oliver Wendell Holmes*, 90.

22 Chauncey Wright, "The Philosophy of Herbert Spencer," in *Philosophical Discussions*, 50.

23 Wright, "McCosh on Intuitions," in *Philosophical Discussions*, 338. "Will" can be read here as "wants and impulses."

24 Oliver Wendell Holmes Jr. to Frederick Pollock, 30 August 1929, in *The Essential Holmes*, 108.

25 Oliver Wendell Holmes Jr. *The Common Law*, 77.

26 Walt Whitman to Louisa Van Velsor Whitman, 13 May 1863, in *Correspondence*, I: 100.

27 Oliver Wendell Holmes Jr. to Harold Laski, 24 May 1919, in Howe, *Holmes-Laski Letters*, I: 207.

28 Mark De Wolfe Howe, *Justice Oliver Wendell Holmes: The Proving Years, 1870– 1882*, 48.

29 Oliver Wendell Holmes Jr., "Summary of Events: The Gas Stokers' Strike," *American Law Review* 7 (1873), 583.

30 Budiansky, *Oliver Wendell Holmes*, 170.

31 Howe, *Proving Years*, 46.

32 Emerson, "Experience," *Essays and Lectures*, 478.

33 Holmes Jr., "The Path of the Law," in David Kennedy and William W. Fisher III, eds., *The Canon of American Legal Thought*, 35.

34 Ibid., 34.

35 Ibid., 36.

36 Holmes Jr., *The Common Law*, 81.

37 Ibid., 110.

38 Holmes Jr., "The Path of the Law," in Kennedy and Fisher, *The Canon of American Legal Thought*, 31–32.

39 *Brown v. Kendall*, 60 Mass. 292 (1850). One of the leading American judges during the pre–Civil War era, Shaw became notorious the following year for upholding the new Fugitive Slave Law. He was also the father-in-law of Herman Melville.

40 Ibid., 296. Shaw remanded the case for a second trial.

41 Holmes Jr., *The Common Law*, 108.

42 Ibid., 1.

43 Morton J. Horwitz, *The Transformation of American Law, 1780–1860*, 99. Horwitz notes that Holmes celebrated Shaw's opinion in *Brown v. Kendall* "as a bold and unprecedented" articulation of modern negligence doctrine—an assessment that Horwitz considers overstated. Horwitz, *Transformation of American Law*, 90.

44 Ibid.

45 Oliver Wendell Holmes Jr., "Memorial Day," in *Speeches*, 3.

46 Ibid.

47 Ibid., 11.

48 Oliver Wendell Holmes Jr., "The Soldier's Faith," in *Speeches*, 57.

49 Ibid.

50 Ibid., 58.

51 Ibid.

52 Ibid., 59.

53 Ibid., 63–64.

54 Ibid., 64.

55 Ibid.

56 Ibid., 60.

57 Ibid., 62.

58 Oliver Wendell Holmes Jr. to Margaret Bevan, 19 July 1885, quoted in Baker, *Justice from Beacon Hill*, 310.

59 Budiansky, *Oliver Wendell Holmes*, 227.

EPILOGUE: "REAL, TERRIBLE, BEAUTIFUL DAYS"

1 Arthur C. Parker, *The Life of General Ely S. Parker*, 133.

2 Whitman, "Camps of Green," in *Complete Poetry and Collected Prose*, 607.

3 Whitman, *Democratic Vistas*, in ibid., 936.

4 Ibid., 937.

5 Walt Whitman to Nathaniel Bloom and John F. S. Gray, 19 March 1863, in *Correspondence*, I: 82.

6 Whitman, *Democratic Vistas*, in *Complete Poetry and Collected Prose*, 935.

7 Whitman, *Specimen Days*, in *Complete Poetry and Collected Prose*, 776.

8 Ibid., 778.

9 Ibid., 779.

10 Whitman, "A Backward Glance o'er Travel'd Roads," in *Complete Poetry and Collected Prose*, 666.

11 Traubel, *With Walt Whitman in Camden*, III: 582.

12 Ezra Pound, "What I Feel about Walt Whitman," *American Literature* 27: 145–46.

13 Whitman, "Ashes of Soldiers," in *Complete Poetry and Collected Prose*, 599–600.

14 Walt Whitman to Thomas Jefferson Whitman, 18 March 1863, in *Correspondence*, I: 79.

15 Whitman to William Sloane Kennedy, 27 January 1890, in *Correspondence*, V: 23.

16 Walt Whitman to William T. Stead, 6 January 1891, in *Correspondence*, V: 146.

17 Traubel, *With Walt Whitman in Camden*, III: 581–82. Emphasis added.

18 Ibid., I: 227.

19 Walt Whitman, *Specimen Days*, in *Complete Poetry and Collected Prose*, 780.

20 Ibid., 781, 783.

21 Ibid., 800.

22 Ibid., 793.

23 Ibid., 863.

24 Ibid., 859.

25 Ibid., 855.

26 Conversation with Scott Halvorson, 11 August 2019.

27 Walt Whitman to Annie Gilchrist, 20 April 1884, in *Correspondence*, III: 368.

28 Kennedy, *Reminiscences of Walt Whitman*, 17.

29 Quoted in Allen, *Solitary Singer*, 542.

30 T. S. Eliot, "Whitman and Tennyson," *The Nation and Athenaeum* 40 (18 December 1926): 426.

31 Ezra Pound, "A Pact," in *New Selected Poems and Translations*, 39.

32 Anne Holmes, "Tracy K. Smith Bids Farewell as U.S. Poet Laureate," *From the Catbird Seat* (blog), Library of Congress, 19 April 2019, https://blogs.loc.gov/catbird/2019/04/tracy-k-smith-bids-farewell-as-u-s-poet-laureate/, accessed 5 June 2020.

33 Traubel, *With Walt Whitman in Camden*, I: 115. See also David W. Blight, *Race and Reunion: The Civil War in American Memory*, 19–20.

34 Oliver Wendell Holmes Jr., "Memorial Day," in *Speeches*, 11.

35 Ibid., 4–5.

36 Ibid., 9.

37 Ibid., 2.

38 Richard F. Fuller, *Chaplain Fuller*, 158; Abraham Lincoln, *Second Inaugural Address*, in *Selected Speeches and Writings*, 687.

39 Menand, *The Metaphysical Club*, 3.

40 Budiansky, *Oliver Wendell Holmes*, 254.

41 Excellent introductions to this subject are Henry Steele Commager, *The American Mind: An Interpretation of American Thought and Character since the 1880's* (New Haven: Yale University Press, 1950); and Menand, *The Metaphysical Club*. For a harsher reading of the Holmesian legacy, see Grant Gilmore, *The Ages of American Law* (New Haven: Yale University Press, 1977).

42 Holmes Jr., "The Path of the Law," in Kennedy and Fisher, *The Canon of American Legal Thought*, 37.

43 *Lochner v. New York*, 198 U.S. 45, 56 (1905).

44 Ibid., 75–76.

45 *Adair v. United States*, 208 U.S. 161 (1908).

46 Ibid., 191.

47 *Hammer v. Dagenhart*, 247 U.S. 251, 276 (1918).

48 Ibid., 280.

49 Oliver Wendell Holmes to Frederick Pollock, 26 October 1919, quoted in Baker, *Justice from Beacon Hill*, 536.

50 *Abrams v. United States*, 250 U.S. 616, 630 (1919).

51 Ibid.

52 Holmes Jr., "Ideals and Doubts," in *Collected Legal Papers*, 307.

53 Oliver Wendell Holmes Sr., *The Professor at the Breakfast-Table*, 295.

54 Louisa May Alcott, "My Boys," in *Aunt Jo's Scrap-Bag*, 27.

55 Anne Boyd Rioux, *Meg, Jo, Beth, and Amy: The Story of* Little Women *and Why It Still Matters*, 63.

56 Mary McNamara, "Louisa May Alcott: The Woman Behind Little Women," *Los Angeles Times*, 28 December 2009.

57 Louisa May Alcott, *An Old-Fashioned Girl*, 38.

58 Ibid., 228.

59 Louisa May Alcott, *Jo's Boys*, in *Little Women, Little Men, Jo's Boys* (Library of America, 2005), 1063.

60 A. Bronson Alcott, *Sonnets and Canzonets*, 73.

61 Louisa May Alcott, 1 March 1888, *Journals*, 333.

62 Louisa May Alcott to Maria S. Porter, 4 March 1888, *Selected Letters*, 337.

63 Schaff, *The Spirit of Old West Point*, 131–32.

64 Rable, *Fredericksburg*, 198.

65 Jerry H. Maxwell, *The Perfect Lion: The Life and Death of Confederate Artillerist John Pelham* (Tuscaloosa: University of Alabama Press, 2011).

66 Cooke, *Surry of Eagle's-Nest*, 235.

67 Von Borcke, *Memoirs*, 231, 298; 350; 38, 102, 210, 234, 302 (2x), 350, 351 (2x).

68 Two examples of many are offered here. In his "Address to the Association of the Virginia Division of the Army of Northern Virginia," 1 November 1883, General Alfred M. Scales put Pelham's age at the time of his death at 22. *Southern Historical Society Papers*, XL: 209. Major Harry Gilmor, who retrieved Pelham's body from

the field at Kelly's Ford, writes that Pelham died at "just twenty-one years old." Gilmor, *Four Years in the Saddle*, 74.

69 Thomason, *Jeb Stuart*, 499.

70 Cooke, *Surry of Eagle's-Nest*, 482.

71 More than a half-dozen of these lyrics are collected in Richard F. Fuller, *Chaplain Fuller*, 335–42.

72 R. Buckminster Fuller, *Autobiographical Monologue/Scenario*, 11.

73 Ibid., 10.

74 Hugh Kenner, *Bucky: A Guided Tour of Buckminster Fuller*, 73; Lloyd Steven Sieder, *Buckminster Fuller's Universe: An Appreciation*, 2.

75 Hugh Kenner, *The Pound Era*, 161.

76 Calvin Tomkins, "In the Outlaw Area," *The New Yorker*, 31 December 1965.

77 Ibid.

78 Kenner, *The Pound Era*, 162.

79 Cushing, "The Gallant Captain," 550.

80 Charles Evans Hughes, "Oliver Wendell Holmes at His Ninetieth Birthday," *The Phi Beta Kappa Key* 7, no. 12 (May 1931): 781.

81 *Dunn v. United States*, 284 U.S. 390 (1932).

82 Baker, *Justice from Beacon Hill*, 629.

83 Ibid., 642.

84 White, *Justice Oliver Wendell Holmes*, 488.

85 John S. Monagan, *The Grand Panjandrum: Mellow Years of Justice Holmes*, 147.

Bibliography

Abbott, Henry Livermore. *Fallen Leaves: The Civil War Letters of Major Henry Livermore Abbott*. Kent, OH: Kent State University Press, 1991.

Abel, E. Lawrence. *A Finger in Lincoln's Brain: What Modern Science Reveals about Lincoln, His Assassination, and Its Aftermath*. Santa Barbara, CA: Praeger, 2015.

Adams, Charles Francis. *Richard Henry Dana: A Biography*. 2 vols. Boston: Houghton Mifflin, 1891.

Adams, Henry. *The Education of Henry Adams*. Boston: Houghton Mifflin, 1918.

Adams, John G. B. *Reminiscences of the Nineteenth Massachusetts Regiment*. Boston: Wright & Potter, 1899.

Adams, John Quincy. *Speech of John Quincy Adams on the Joint Resolution for Distributing Rations to the Distressed Fugitives from Indian Hostilities in the States of Alabama and Georgia, May 25, 1836*. Washington, DC: National Intelligence Office, 1836.

Alcott, Abigail May. *My Heart Is Boundless: Writings of Abigail May Alcott, Louisa's Mother*. Ed. Eve LaPlante. New York: Free Press, 2012.

Alcott, Amos Bronson. *Conversations with Children on the Gospels*. Boston: James Munroe, 1836.

———. *The Journals of Bronson Alcott*. Ed. Odell Shepard. Boston: Little, Brown, 1938.

———. *The Letters of A. Bronson Alcott*. Ed. Richard L. Herrnstadt. Ames: Iowa State University Press, 1969.

———. *Sonnets and Canzonets*. Boston: Roberts Brothers, 1882.

Alcott, Louisa May. *Aunt Jo's Scrap-Bag*. Boston: Roberts Brothers, 1872.

———. *Louisa May Alcott: Her Life, Letters, and Journals*. Ed. Ednah D. Cheney. Boston: Roberts Brothers, 1890.

———. *Hospital Sketches*. Ed. Alice Fahs. Boston: Bedford/St. Martin's, 2004.

———. *Hospital Sketches and Camp and Fireside Stories*. Boston: Little, Brown, 1922.

———. *The Journals of Louisa May Alcott*. Ed. Joel Myerson and Daniel Shealy. Athens: University of Georgia Press, 1997.

———. *Little Women; or, Meg, Jo, Beth and Amy*. Ed. Anne K. Phillips and Gregory Eiselein. New York: W. W. Norton, 2004.

————. *Little Women, Little Men, Jo's Boys*. New York: Library of America, 2005.

————. *Moods*. Boston: A. K. Loring, 1864.

————. *Moods*. Boston: Roberts Brothers, 1881.

————. *An Old-Fashioned Girl*. Boston: Roberts Brothers, 1870.

————. *The Selected Letters of Louisa May Alcott*. Ed. Joel Myerson and Daniel Shealy. Athens: University of Georgia Press, 1995.

————. *Work: A Story of Experience*. Boston: Little, Brown, 1873.

Alexander, Edward Porter. *Fighting for the Confederacy: The Personal Recollections of General Edward Porter Alexander*. Ed. Gary W. Gallagher. Chapel Hill: University of North Carolina Press, 1989.

————. *Military Memoirs of a Confederate: A Critical Narrative*. New York: Charles Scribner's Sons, 1907.

Allen, Gay Wilson. *The Solitary Singer: A Critical Biography of Walt Whitman*. New York: New York University Press, 1967.

Ambrose, Stephen E. *Crazy Horse and Custer: The Parallel Lives of Two American Warriors*. New York: Random House, 1996.

————. *Duty, Honor, Country: A History of West Point*. Baltimore: Johns Hopkins University Press, 1966.

Asselineau, Roger. *The Evolution of Walt Whitman*. Iowa City: University of Iowa Press, 1999.

Austin, John. *The Province of Jurisprudence Determined*. London: John Murray, 1832.

Bancroft, Frederic. *The Life of William H. Seward*. 2 vols. New York: Harper and Brothers, 1900.

Baker, Liva. *The Justice from Beacon Hill: The Life and Times of Oliver Wendell Holmes*. New York: HarperCollins, 1991.

Bates, Edward. *The Diary of Edward Bates, 1859–1866*. Washington, DC: U.S. Government Printing Office, 1933.

Bayne, Julia Taft. *Tad Lincoln's Father*. Lincoln: University of Nebraska Press, 2001.

Birrell, Augustine. *Frederick Locker-Lampson: A Character Sketch*. London: N.p., 1920.

Blackford, W[illiam] W[illis]. *War Years with Jeb Stuart*. Baton Rouge: Louisiana State University Press, 1993.

Blake, William O. *The History of Slavery and the Slave Trade, Ancient and Modern*. Columbus, OH: J. & H. Miller, 1857.

Blight, David W. *Race and Reunion: The Civil War in American Memory*. Cambridge, MA: Harvard University Press, 2001.

Blocker, Jack S., Jr., David M. Fahey, and Ian R. Tyrell, eds. *Alcohol and Temperance in Modern History: An International Encyclopedia*. 2 vols. Santa Barbara, CA: ABC-CLIO, 2003.

Boker, George H. *Poems of the War*. Boston: Ticknor and Fields, 1864.

Bowen, Catherine Drinker. *Yankee from Olympus: Justice Holmes and His Family*. Boston: Little, Brown, 1944.

Bowen, Francis. *The Principles of Metaphysical and Ethical Science, Applied to the Evidences of Religion*. Cambridge, MA: Allen and Farnham, 1855.

Bowen, James L. *Massachusetts in the War, 1861–1865*. Springfield, MA: Clark W. Bryan, 1889.

Boyden, Anna L. *Echoes from Hospital and White House: A Record of Mrs. Rebecca R. Pomeroy's Experience in War-Times*. Boston: D. Lothrop, 1884.

Bradley, Sculley. *George Henry Boker: Poet and Patriot.* Philadelphia: University of Pennsylvania Press, 1927.

Brandt, Dennis W. *Pathway to Hell: A Tragedy of the American Civil War.* Bethlehem, PA: Lehigh University Press, 2008.

Brewster, Todd. *Lincoln's Gamble: The Tumultuous Six Months That Gave America the Emancipation Proclamation and Changed the Course of the Civil War.* New York: Scribner, 2014.

Bridges, David P. *Fighting with Jeb Stuart: Major James Breathed and the Confederate Horse Artillery.* Arlington, VA: Breathed Bridges Best, 2006.

Bruce, George Anson. *The Twentieth Regiment of Massachusetts Volunteer Infantry, 1861–1865.* Boston: Houghton Mifflin, 1906.

Brugh, Mark P., and Julia Stinson Brugh. *Civil War Ghosts of Sharpsburg.* Charleston, SC: History Press, 2015.

Budiansky, Stephen. *Oliver Wendell Holmes: A Life in War, Law, and Ideas.* New York: W. W. Norton, 2019.

Bullard, Frederic Lauriston. *Famous War Correspondents.* New York: Little, Brown, 1914.

Burke, Mrs. L. *The Illustrated Language of Flowers.* London: G. Routledge, 1856.

Burroughs, John. *The Writings of John Burroughs.* 10 vols. Boston: Houghton Mifflin, 1896.

Carman, Ezra A. *The Maryland Campaign of September 1862,* vol. 2: *Antietam.* Ed. Thomas G. Clemens. El Dorado Hills, CA: Savas Beatie, 2012.

Carpenter, F. B. *The Inner Life of Abraham Lincoln: Six Months at the White House.* New York: Hurd and Houghton, 1868.

Catton, Bruce. *The American Heritage Picture History of the Civil War.* New York: American Heritage, 1960.

———. *Glory Road.* Garden City, NY: Doubleday, 1952.

———. *Mr. Lincoln's Army.* Garden City, NY: Doubleday, 1962.

———. *A Stillness at Appomattox.* Garden City, NY: Doubleday, 1953.

———. *Terrible Swift Sword.* Garden City, NY: Doubleday, 1963.

Chase, Salmon P. *The Salmon P. Chase Papers: Journals 1829–1872.* 5 vols. Ed. John Niven. Kent, OH: Kent State University Press, 1993.

Clark, Beverly Lyon. *Louisa May Alcott: The Contemporary Reviews.* Cambridge: Cambridge University Press, 2004.

Coffin, Charles Carleton. *The Boys of '61, or Four Years of Fighting: Personal Observations with the Army and Navy.* Boston: Dana, Estes, 1896.

Commager, Henry Steele. *The American Mind: An Interpretation of American Thought and Character since the 1880's.* New Haven: Yale University Press, 1950.

Congressional Globe: Containing the Debates and Proceeding of the Third Session of the Thirty-Seventh Congress. Washington, DC: John C. Rives, 1863.

Conroy, James B. *Lincoln's White House: The People's House in Wartime.* Lanham, MD: Rowman & Littlefield, 2017.

Conway, Moncure D. *Autobiography, Memories and Experiences of Moncure Daniel Conway.* London: Cassell, 1904.

Cooke, John Esten. *A Life of Gen. Robert E. Lee.* New York: D. Appleton, 1871.

———. *Surry of Eagle's-Nest, or, The Memoirs of a Staff-Officer Serving in Virginia.* New York: F. J. Huntington, 1866.

———. *Wearing of the Gray; Being Personal Portraits, Scenes and Adventures of the War.* New York: E. B. Treat, 1867.

Cudworth, Warren H. *History of the First Regiment (Massachusetts Infantry)*. Boston: Walker, Fuller, 1866.

Cushing, Carolyn Kellogg. "The Gallant Captain and the Little Girl." *Atlantic Monthly* 155 (May 1935): 545–50.

Dadmun, J. W., and Arthur B. Fuller. *Army and Navy Melodies: A Collection of Hymns and Tunes, Religious and Patriotic, Original and Selected*. Boston: J. P. Magee, 1862.

Dawes, Rufus Robinson. *Service with the Sixth Wisconsin Volunteers*. Marietta, OH: E. R. Alderman and Sons, 1890.

Donald, David Herbert. *Charles Sumner and the Coming of the Civil War*. New York: Alfred A. Knopf, 1960.

Donaldson, Thomas. *Walt Whitman the Man*. New York: Francis P. Harper, 1896.

Douglas, Henry Kyd. *I Rode with Stonewall*. Chapel Hill: University of North Carolina Press, 1940.

Douglass, Frederick. *The Frederick Douglass Papers. Series One: Speeches, Debates and Interviews*. Ed. John W. Blassingame. New Haven: Yale University Press, 1979–92.

Dwight, Wilder. *Life and Letters of Wilder Dwight*. Boston: Ticknor and Fields, 1868.

Eastman, William R. "The Army Chaplain of 1863." In A. Noel Blakeman, *Personal Recollections of the War of the Rebellion: Addresses Delivered before the Commandery of the State of New York, Military Order of the Loyal Legion of the United States*. New York: G. P. Putnam's Sons, 1912.

Elbert, Sarah. *A Hunger for Home: Louisa May Alcott's Place in American Culture*. New Brunswick, NJ: Rutgers University Press, 1987.

Eliot, T. S. "Whitman and Tennyson." *Nation and Athenaeum* 40 (18 December 1926): 426.

Emerson, Edward Waldo. *Emerson in Concord: A Memoir*. Boston: Houghton Mifflin, 1889.

Emerson, Ralph Waldo. *Essays and Lectures*. New York: Library of America, 1983.

———. *Journals and Miscellaneous Notebooks*. 16 vols. Cambridge, MA: Harvard University Press, 1960–82.

———. *The Letters of Ralph Waldo Emerson*. 6 vols. New York: Columbia University Press, 1939.

Epstein, Daniel Mark. *Lincoln and Whitman: Parallel Lives in Civil War Washington*. New York: Random House, 2004.

Evans, W. A. *Mrs. Abraham Lincoln: A Study of Her Personality and Her Influence on Lincoln*. Carbondale: Southern Illinois University Press, 2010.

Feinstein, Howard M. *Becoming William James*. Ithaca: Cornell University Press, 1984.

Fessenden, Francis. *Life and Public Services of William Pitt Fessenden*. 2 vols. Boston: Houghton Mifflin, 1907.

FitzGerald, W. George. "President Wilson's Dream—and His Dilemma." *Nineteenth Century and After* 81 (1917): 30.

Fleischner, Jennifer B. *Mastering Slavery: Memory, Family, and Identity in Women's Slave Narratives*. New York: New York University Press, 1996.

Foote, Shelby. *The Civil War: A Narrative: Fort Sumter to Perryville*. New York: Random House, 1986.

———. *The Civil War: A Narrative: Fredericksburg to Meridian*. New York: Random House, 1974.

Forbes, John Murray. *Letters and Recollections of John Murray Forbes*. Ed. Sarah Forbes Hughes. 2 vols. Boston: Houghton Mifflin, 1899.

Freeman, Douglas Southall. *Lee's Lieutenants: A Study in Command.* 3 vols. New York: Charles Scribner's Sons, 1943.

———. *R. E. Lee: A Biography.* 4 vols. New York: Charles Scribner's Sons, 1934.

Fuller, Arthur Buckminster. *A Discourse in Vindication of Unitarianism from Popular Charges against It.* Manchester, NH: L. & A. Jackson, 1848.

———. *Historical Notices of Thomas Fuller and His Descendants, with a Genealogy of the Fuller Family, 1638–1902.* Cambridge, MA, 1902.

———. "Letter from the Army of the Potomac," *Boston Journal,* 25 November 1862, 4.

Fuller, R. Buckminster. *Autobiographical Monologue/Scenario.* New York: St. Martin's Press, 1980.

Fuller, Richard Frederick. *Chaplain Fuller: Being a Life Sketch of a New England Clergyman and Army Chaplain.* Boston: Walker, Wise, 1863.

———. *Recollections of Richard F. Fuller.* Boston: N.p., 1936.

Fuller, Sarah Margaret. *Letters of Margaret Fuller.* Ed. Robert N. Hudspeth. 6 vols. Ithaca: Cornell University Press, 1983–94.

Genoways, Ted. *Walt Whitman and the Civil War: America's Poet during the Lost Years of 1860–1862.* Berkeley: University of California Press, 2009.

Gilmor, Harry. *Four Years in the Saddle.* New York: Harper & Brothers, 1866.

Gilmore, Grant. *The Ages of American Law.* New Haven: Yale University Press, 1977.

Goodwin, Doris Kearns. *Team of Rivals: The Political Genius of Abraham Lincoln.* New York: Simon and Schuster, 2005.

Grimes, William. "Freedom Just Ahead: The War Within the Civil War." *New York Times,* 5 December, 2007.

Guelzo, Allen C. *Lincoln's Emancipation Proclamation: The End of Slavery in America.* New York: Simon and Schuster, 2004.

Harron, William A, III. "Wars and Rumors of Wars: Three Northern Communities during Lee's Gettysburg Invasion." Undergraduate thesis, Williams College, 2011.

Hartsock, Andrew J. *Soldier of the Cross: The Civil War Diary and Correspondence of Rev. Andrew Jackson Hartsock.* Ed. James C. Duram and Eleanor A. Duram. Manhattan, KS: MA/AH Publishing for the American Military Institute, 1979.

Hassler, William Woods. *Colonel John Pelham: Lee's Boy Artillerist.* Richmond, VA: Garrett & Massie, 1960.

Hatch, Thom. *Glorious War: The Civil War Adventures of George Armstrong Custer.* New York: St. Martin's Press, 2013.

Haupt, Herman. *Reminiscences of General Herman Haupt.* Milwaukee: Wright and Joys, 1901.

Hawthorne, Julian. "Absolute Evil." In *American Fantastic Tales: Terror and the Uncanny from Poe to the Pulps,* ed. Peter Straub. New York: Library of America, 2009.

Hearn, Chester G. *Lincoln, the Cabinet, and the Generals.* Baton Rouge: Louisiana State University Press, 2010.

Higginson, Thomas Wentworth. *Harvard Memorial Biographies.* 2 vols. Cambridge, MA: Sever and Francis, 1866.

———. *Margaret Fuller Ossoli.* Boston: Houghton Mifflin, 1890.

Hinsdale, Mary Louise. *A History of the President's Cabinet.* Ann Arbor, MI: G. Wahr, 1911.

"History and Results of the Back Bay Improvement." In *Report of the Committee*

Appointed under Chapter 93 of the Resolves of 1867, in Relation to the Commonwealth Flats Near South Boston. Boston: Wright & Potter, 1868.

Holland, Josiah Gilbert. *The Life of Abraham Lincoln.* New York: Dodd, Mead, 1887.

Holmes, Oliver Wendell, Jr. *The Essential Holmes.* Chicago: University of Chicago Press, 1992.

———. *Collected Legal Papers.* New York: Harcourt Brace, 1920.

———. *The Common Law.* Boston: Little, Brown, 1951.

———. "The Path of the Law." In David Kennedy and William W. Fisher III, eds., *The Canon of American Legal Thought.* Princeton: Princeton University Press, 2006.

———. *Speeches by Oliver Wendell Holmes.* Boston: Little, Brown, 1896.

———. *Touched with Fire: Civil War Letters and Diary of Oliver Wendell Holmes, Jr.* Ed. Mark De Wolfe Howe. New York: Fordham University Press, 2000.

Holmes, Oliver Wendell, Sr. *The Autocrat of the Breakfast-Table: Every Man His Own Boswell.* Boston: Houghton Mifflin, 1892.

———. *The Autocrat's Miscellanies.* New York: Twayne, 1959.

———. *The Complete Poetical Works of Oliver Wendell Holmes.* Boston: Houghton Mifflin, 1910.

———. *Currents and Counter-Currents in Medical Science, with Other Addresses and Essays.* Boston: Osgood, 1878.

———. *Elsie Venner: A Romance of Destiny.* London: Routledge, Warne, and Routledge, 1861.

———. *Medical Essays: 1842–1882.* Cambridge, MA: Riverside Press, 1891.

———. *My Hunt after the Captain and Other Papers.* Boston: Houghton, Mifflin, 1891.

———. *Pages from an Old Volume of Life: A Collection of Essays.* Boston: Houghton Mifflin, 1891.

———. *The Professor at the Breakfast-Table.* Boston: Houghton Mifflin, 1892.

Horwitz, Morton J. *The Transformation of American Law, 1780–1860.* Cambridge, MA: Harvard University Press, 1977.

Howard, Oliver Otis. *Autobiography of Oliver Otis Howard, Major General, United States Army.* 2 vols. New York: Baker & Taylor, 1907.

Howe, Mark De Wolfe. *Justice Oliver Wendell Holmes: The Proving Years, 1870–1882.* Cambridge, MA: Harvard University Press, 1963.

———. *Justice Oliver Wendell Holmes: The Shaping Years, 1841–1870.* Cambridge, MA: Harvard University Press, 1957.

Howe, Mark De Wolfe, ed. *Holmes-Laski Letters: The Correspondence of Mr. Justice Holmes and Harold J. Laski.* 2 vols. Cambridge, MA: Harvard University Press, 1953.

———*Holmes-Pollock Letters: The Correspondence of Mr. Justice Holmes and Sir Frederick Pollock, 1874–1932.* 2 vols. Cambridge, MA: Harvard University Press, 1961.

Howells, W[illiam] D[ean]. *Literary Friends and Acquaintance.* New York: Harper & Brothers, 1901.

Humphreys, Henry Hollingsworth. *Andrew Atkinson Humphreys: A Biography.* Philadelphia: John C. Winston, 1924.

———. *Major General Andrew Atkinson Humphreys, United States Volunteers, at Fredericksburg Va., December 13th, 1862 and Farmville, Va. April 7th, 1865.* Chicago: R. R. McCabe, 1896.

James, William. *The Letters of William James.* 2 vols. Boston: Atlantic Monthly Press, 1920.

———. *The Varieties of Religious Experience: A Study in Human Nature.* New York: Modern Library, 1902.

Jefferson, Thomas. *Notes on the State of Virginia.* Boston: Wells and Lilly, 1829.

Johnson, Curt, and Richard C. Anderson Jr. *Artillery Hell: The Employment of Artillery at Antietam.* College Station: Texas A&M University Press, 1995.

Johnson, Robert Underwood, and Clarence Clough Buel, eds. *Battles and Leaders of the Civil War,* 4 vols. New York: Century, 1887–88.

Judd, David Wright. *The Story of the Thirty-Third N.Y.S. Volunteers.* Rochester, NY: Benton & Andrews, 1864.

Kaplan, Justin. *Walt Whitman: A Life.* New York: Simon and Schuster, 1980.

Karbiener, Karen. "Whitman at Pfaff's: Personal Space, a Public Place, and the Boundary-Breaking Poems of *Leaves of Grass* (1860)." In *Literature of New York,* ed. Sabrina Fuchs-Abrams. Newcastle-upon-Tyne: Cambridge Scholars Publishing, 2009.

Kennedy, William Sloane. *Reminiscences of Walt Whitman.* London: Alexander Gardner, 1896.

Kenner, Hugh. *Bucky: A Guided Tour of Buckminster Fuller.* New York: William Morrow, 1973.

———. *The Pound Era.* Berkeley: University of California Press, 1971.

Kirshner, Ralph. *The Class of 1861: Custer, Ames, and Their Classmates after West Point.* Carbondale: Southern Illinois University Press, 1999.

Leech, Margaret. *Reveille in Washington, 1860–1865.* New York: Grosset & Dunlap, 1941.

Lewis, Lloyd. *Sherman: Fighting Prophet.* Lincoln: University of Nebraska Press, 1932.

Lincoln, Abraham. *Speeches and Writings, 1859–1865.* New York: Library of America, 1989.

Linderman, Gerald F. *Embattled Courage.* New York: Free Press, 1987.

Livermore, Mary A. *My Story of the War: A Woman's Narrative.* Hartford, CT: A. D. Worthington, 1892.

Loving, Jerome. *Walt Whitman: The Song of Himself.* Berkeley: University of California Press, 2000.

Lucretius, Titus Carus. *On the Nature of Things: A Philosophical Poem in Six Books.* Transl. John Selby Watson. London: Henry G. Bohn, 1851.

Marshall, Megan. *Margaret Fuller: A New American Life.* Boston: Houghton Mifflin, 2013.

Martin, Fred R. "Pelham of Alabama." *Confederate Veteran* 29, 1 (January 1921): 9–10.

Martin, Justin. *A Fierce Glory: Antietam—The Desperate Battle That Saved Lincoln and Doomed Slavery.* New York: Da Capo, 2018.

———. *Rebel Souls: Walt Whitman and America's First Bohemians.* Boston: Da Capo, 2014.

Matteson, John. *Eden's Outcasts: The Story of Louisa May Alcott and Her Father.* New York: W. W. Norton, 2007.

———. "Finding Private Suhre: On the Trail of Louisa May Alcott's Prince of Patients." *New England Quarterly* 88, 1 (March 2015): 115.

———. *The Lives of Margaret Fuller: A Biography.* New York: W. W. Norton, 2012.

Matthews, H. H. "Major John Pelham, Confederate Hero." *Southern Historical Society Papers* 36 (1909): 379–84.

Maxwell, Jerry H. *The Perfect Lion: The Life and Death of Confederate Artillerist John Pelham.* Tuscaloosa: University of Alabama Press, 2011.

McClellan, Carswell. *General Andrew A. Humphreys at Malvern Hill Va. July 1, 1862 and at Fredericksburg Va, December 13 1862: A Memoir.* St. Paul, MN, 1888.

McClellan, George B. *The Civil War Papers of George B. McClellan: Selected Correspondence, 1860–1865.* Ed. Stephen W. Sears. New York: Da Capo, 1992.

McClellan, H[enry]. B[rainerd]. *I Rode with Jeb Stuart: The Life and Campaigns of Major General J.E.B. Stuart.* Bloomington: Indiana University Press, 1958.

[McGuire, Judith White.] *Diary of a Southern Refugee during the War.* New York: E. J. Hale & Son, 1868.

Melville, Herman. *Battle-Pieces and Aspects of the War.* New York: Harper & Brothers, 1866.

————. *Redburn: His First Voyage; White-Jacket, or The World in a Man-of-War; and Moby-Dick, or, The Whale.* New York: Library of America, 1983.

Menand, Louis. *The Metaphysical Club: A Story of Ideas in America.* New York: Farrar, Straus and Giroux, 2002.

Mennel, Robert M., and Christine L. Compston, eds. *Holmes and Frankfurter: Their Correspondence, 1912–1934.* Hanover, NH: University Press of New England, 1996.

Mercer, Philip. *The Life of the Gallant Pelham.* Macon, GA: J. W. Burke, 1958.

Milham, Charles G. *Gallant Pelham: American Extraordinary.* Washington, DC: Public Affairs Press, 1959.

Miller, Richard F. *Harvard's Civil War: A History of the Twentieth Massachusetts Volunteer Infantry.* Hanover, NH: University Press of New England, 2005.

Monagan, John S. *The Grand Panjandrum: Mellow Years of Justice Holmes.* Lanham, MD: University Press of America, 1988.

Morris, Roy, Jr. *The Better Angel: Walt Whitman in the Civil War.* Oxford: Oxford University Press, 2000.

Morse, John T., Jr. *Life and Letters of Oliver Wendell Holmes.* 2 vols. Boston: Houghton Mifflin, 1896.

Moses, Belle. *Louisa May Alcott, Dreamer and Worker: A Story of Achievement.* New York: Appleton-Century, 1936.

Motley, John Lothrop. *The Correspondence of John Lothrop Motley.* 3 vols. London: John Murray, 1889.

————. *The Works of John Lothrop Motley.* 17 vols. New York: Harper and Brothers, 1900.

Myerson, Joel, ed. *Fuller in Her Own Time: A Biographical Chronicle of Her Life, Drawn from Recollections, Interviews, and Memoirs by Family, Friends, and Associates.* Iowa City: University of Iowa Press, 2008.

Nicolay, John. *With Lincoln in the White House: Letters, Memoranda, and Other Writings of John G. Nicolay, 1860–1865.* Ed. Michael Burlingame. Carbondale: Southern Illinois University Press, 2000.

Nicolay, John, and John Hay. *Abraham Lincoln: A History.* 10 vols. New York: Century, 1890.

Nightingale, Florence. *Notes on Nursing: What It Is, and What It Is Not.* London: Harrison and Sons, 1860.

Nolan, L[ouis]. E[dward]. *Cavalry: Its History and Tactics.* London: Bosworth & Harrison, 1860.

Noyes, George Freeman. *The Bivouac and the Battlefield; or, Campaign Sketches in Virginia and Maryland.* New York: Harper and Brothers, 1864.

O'Connor, William Douglas. *The Good Gray Poet: A Vindication.* Toronto: Henry S. Saunders, 1927.

O'Reilly, Francis Augustín. *The Fredericksburg Campaign: Winter War on the Rappahannock*. Baton Rouge: Louisiana State University Press, 2006.

Palfrey, Francis Winthrop. *The Antietam and Fredericksburg*. New York: Charles Scribner's Sons, 1882.

Parker, Arthur C. *The Life of General Ely S. Parker: Last Grand Sachem of the Iroquois and General Grant's Military Secretary*. Buffalo: Buffalo Historical Society, 1919.

Parker, Thomas H. *History of the 51st Regiment of P.V. and V.V., from Its Organization at Camp Curtin, Harrisburg, Pa., in 1861, to Its Being Mustered out of the United States Service at Alexandria, Va., July 27th, 1865*. Philadelphia: King and Baird, 1869.

Parry, Albert. *Garrets and Pretenders: A History of Bohemianism in America*. New York: Covici-Friede, 1933.

Parsons, Philip W. *The Union Sixth Corps in the Chancellorsville Campaign: A Study of the Engagements of Second Fredericksburg, Salem Church and Bank's Ford, May 3–4, 1863*. Jefferson, NC: McFarland, 2006.

[Peabody, Elizabeth Palmer.] *Record of a School: Exemplifying the General Principles of Spiritual Culture*. Boston: James Munroe, 1835.

Pease, Theodore Calvin, and James Garfield Russell, eds. *The Diary of Orville Hickman Browning*. 2 vols. Springfield: Trustees of the Illinois State Historical Library, 1925.

Perry, Ralph Barton. *The Thought and Character of William James*. Nashville: Vanderbilt University Press, 1996.

Pepper, George Whitfield. *Personal Recollections of Sherman's Campaigns in Georgia and the Carolinas*. Zanesville, OH: Hugh Dunne, 1866.

Poague, William Thomas. *Gunner with Stonewall*. Ed. Monroe F. Cockerell. Lincoln: University of Nebraska Press, 1957.

Pound, Ezra. *New Selected Poems and Translations*. New York: New Directions Books, 2010.

———. "What I Feel about Walt Whitman." *American Literature* 27, 1 (March 1955): 56–61.

Quinn, S. J. *The History of the City of Fredericksburg*. Richmond, VA: Heritage Press, 1908.

Rable, George C. *Fredericksburg! Fredericksburg!* Chapel Hill: University of North Carolina Press, 2009.

Rankin, Henry B. *Personal Recollections of Abraham Lincoln*. New York: Putnam, 1916.

Reardon, Carol. "The Forlorn Hope: Brig. Gen. Andrew A. Humphreys's Pennsylvania Division at Fredericksburg." In *The Fredericksburg Campaign: Decision on the Rappahannock*, ed. Gary W. Gallagher. Chapel Hill: University of North Carolina Press, 1995.

Reisen, Harriet. *Louisa May Alcott: The Woman behind "Little Women."* New York: Henry Holt, 2009.

Report of the Joint Committee on the Conduct of the War. Washington, DC: Government Printing Office, 1863.

Reports of Committees of the Senate of the United States for the Third Session of the Thirty-Seventh Congress. Washington, DC: Government Printing Office, 1863.

Revised United States Army Regulations of 1861. Washington, DC: Government Printing Office, 1863.

Rhodes, James Ford. *History of the Civil War 1861–1865*. New York: Macmillan, 1917.

Rice, Allen Thorndike, ed. *Reminiscences of Abraham Lincoln by Distinguished Men of His Time*. New York: North American Review, 1888.

Richardson, Robert D., Jr. *Emerson: The Mind on Fire*. Berkeley: University of California Press, 1995.

Rioux, Anne Boyd. *Meg, Jo, Beth, and Amy: The Story of* Little Women *and Why It Still Matters*. New York: W. W. Norton, 2018.

Roper, Robert. *Now the Drum of War: Walt Whitman and His Brothers in the Civil War*. New York: Walker & Company, 2008.

Ropes, Hannah. *Civil War Nurse: The Diary and Letters of Hannah Ropes*. Ed. John R. Brumgardt. Knoxville: University of Tennessee Press, 1980.

Sanborn, Franklin Benjamin. "Emerson in His Home." *The Arena* 15 (December 1895): 16–21.

———. *Recollections of Seventy Years*, 2 vols. Boston: Richard G. Badger, 1909.

Sandburg, Carl. *Abraham Lincoln: The War Years*. 2 vols. New York: C. Scribner's Sons, 1940.

Saxton, Martha. *Louisa May: A Modern Biography*. New York: Farrar, Straus and Giroux, 1995.

Schaff, Morris. *The Spirit of Old West Point*. Boston: Houghton Mifflin, 1907.

Scott, Charles L. *Adventures of Charles L. Scott, Esq*. Ed. Kathy McCoy. Monroeville, AL: Monroe County Heritage Museums, 1996.

Scott, Robert Garth. *Into the Wilderness with the Army of the Potomac*. Bloomington: Indiana University Press, 1988.

Sears, Stephen W. *Landscape Turned Red: The Battle of Antietam*. Boston: Houghton Mifflin, 1983.

Sergent, Mary Elizabeth. *Growing Up in Alabama*. Middletown, NY: Prior King, 1988.

———. *They Lie Forgotten: The United States Military Academy, 1856–1861, Together with a Class Album for the Class of May 1861*. Middletown, NY: Prior King, 1986.

Seward, Frederick William. *Seward at Washington as Senator and Secretary of State: A Memoir of His Life, with Selections from His Letters, 1861–1872*. New York: Derby and Miller, 1891.

Shaw, Robert Gould. *Blue-Eyed Child of Fortune: The Civil War Letters of Robert Gould Shaw*. Ed. Russell Duncan. Athens: University of Georgia Press, 1992.

Shealy, Daniel, ed. *Alcott in Her Own Time*. Iowa City: University of Iowa Press, 2005.

Shepard, William, ed. *Pen Pictures of Modern Authors*. New York: G. P. Putnam's Sons, 1882.

Sherman, William Tecumseh. *Memoirs of General W. T. Sherman*. Ed. Michael Fellman. New York: Penguin, 2000.

Sherrill, Lee W., Jr. *The 21st North Carolina Infantry: A Civil War History, with a Roster of Officers*. Jefferson, NC: McFarland, 2015.

Silber, Nina. *Landmarks of the Civil War*. Oxford: Oxford University Press, 2003.

Sieder, Lloyd Steven. *Buckminster Fuller's Universe: An Appreciation*. New York: Plenum, 1989.

Small, Abner. *The Road to Richmond: The Civil War Memoirs of Major Abner R. Small*. New York: Fordham University Press, 2000.

Smith, James Power. "With Stonewall Jackson." *Southern Historical Society* 43 (September 1920): 1–110.

Smith, Jean Edward. *Grant*. New York: Simon & Schuster, 2001.

Smith, William Farrar. "Franklin's 'Left Grand Division.'" In *Battles and Leaders*, III: 138.

Sommers, Richard J. *Richmond Redeemed: The Siege at Petersburg*. Garden City, NY: Doubleday, 1981.

Spencer, J. A. *History of the United States, from the Earliest Period to the Administration of President Johnson.* 4 vols. New York: Johnson, Fry, 1866.

Stedman, Edmund C. *The Battle of Bull Run.* New York: Rudd & Carleton, 1861.

Stern, Madeleine B. *Louisa May Alcott: A Biography.* Boston: Northeastern University Press, 1999.

Stoddard, Richard Henry. *Recollections Personal and Literary.* New York: A. S. Barnes, 1893.

Stoddard, William O. *Inside the White House in War Times: Memoirs and Reports of Lincoln's Secretary.* Lincoln: University of Nebraska Press, 2000.

Stoehr, Taylor. *Hawthorne's Mad Scientists.* Hamden, CT: Archon, 1978.

Strong, George Templeton. *Diary of the Civil War, 1860–1865.* Ed. Allan Nevins. New York: Macmillan, 1962.

Survivors' Association. *History of the Corn Exchange Regiment: 118th Pennsylvania Volunteers.* Philadelphia: J. L. Smith, 1888.

Tarbell, Ida M. "Lincoln and the Soldiers." *McClure's Magazine,* June 1899, 164.

Taylor, Tom. *Our American Cousin.* Bedford, MA: Applewood, n.d.

Thomas, Benjamin P., and Harold M. Hyman. *Stanton: The Life and Times of Lincoln's Secretary of War.* New York: Alfred A. Knopf, 1962.

Thomas, Emory M. *Bold Dragoon: The Life of Jeb Stuart.* Norman: University of Oklahoma Press, 1999.

Thomas, Victoria Ann. "Confederate Atrocities: The Northern Perception of the Confederacy's Conduct of the War." Undergraduate thesis, Pennsylvania State University, 2014.

Thomason, John W., Jr. *Jeb Stuart.* New York: Charles Scribner's Sons, 1934.

Todd, John. *The Student's Manual; Designed, by Specific Directions, to Aid in Forming and Strengthening the Intellectual and Moral Character and Habits of the Student.* Thirteenth edition. Northampton, MA: J. H. Butler, 1845.

Traubel, Horace. *In Re Walt Whitman.* Philadelphia: David McKay, 1893.

———. *With Walt Whitman in Camden.* 5 vols. New York: Mitchell Kennerley, 1915.

Trial of Andrew Johnson, President of the United States, Before the Senate of the United States. 3 vols. Washington, DC: U.S. Government Printing Office, 1868.

Trimble, W. H. *Walt Whitman and Leaves of Grass: An Introduction.* London: Watts, 1905.

de Trobriand, Régis. *Four Years with the Army of the Potomac.* Trans. George K. Dauchy. Boston: Ticknor, 1889.

Trollope, Anthony. *Autobiography of Anthony Trollope.* New York: Dodd, Mead, 1912.

Trout, Robert J. *Galloping Thunder: The Stuart Horse Artillery Battalion.* Mechanicsburg, PA: Stackpole, 2002.

———. *With Pen and Saber: The Letters and Diaries of J. E. B. Stuart's Staff Officers.* Mechanicsburg, PA: Stackpole, 1995.

Trowbridge, John Townsend. *My Own Story, with Recollections of Noted Persons.* Boston: Houghton Mifflin, 1903.

United States War Department. *The War of the Rebellion: A Compilation of the Official Records of the Union and Confederate Armies.* 128 vols. Washington, DC: Government Printing Office, 1880–1901.

Villard, Henry. *Memoirs of Henry Villard, Journalist and Financier.* New York: Houghton, Mifflin, 1904.

Von Borcke, Heros. *Memoirs of the Confederate War for Independence.* Nashville: J. S. Sanders, 1999.

Von Drehle, David. *Rise to Greatness: Abraham Lincoln and America's Most Perilous Year.* New York: Macmillan, 2012.

Waitt, Ernest Linden. *History of the Nineteenth Massachusetts Volunteer Infantry, 1861–1865.* Salem, MA: Salem Press, 1906.

Ward, John M. "The Gallant Pelham." *Alabama Bible Society Quarterly* 16 (April 1960): 34.

Wead, Doug. *All the Presidents' Children: Triumph and Tragedy in the Lives of America's First Families.* New York: Atria, 2003.

Welles, Gideon. *The Diary of Gideon Welles, Secretary of the Navy under Lincoln and Johnson.* 3 vols. New York: Houghton Mifflin, 1911.

———. "The History of Emancipation." *The Galaxy: A Magazine of Entertaining Reading* 14 (1872): 838–51.

Wert, Jeffry D. *Cavalryman of the Lost Cause: A Biography of J. E. B. Stuart.* New York: Simon and Schuster, 2008.

White, G. Edward. *Justice Oliver Wendell Holmes: Law and the Inner Self.* Oxford: Oxford University Press, 1993.

White, Ronald C. *A. Lincoln: A Biography.* New York: Random House, 2009.

Whitman, George W. *Civil War Letters of George Washington Whitman.* Ed. Jerome Loving. Durham, NC: Duke University Press, 1975.

Whitman, Thomas Jefferson. *Dear Brother Walt: The Letters of Thomas Jefferson Whitman.* Ed. Dennis Berthold and Kenneth Price. Kent, OH: Kent State University Press, 1984.

Whitman, Walt. *Complete Poetry and Collected Prose.* Ed. Justin Kaplan. New York: Library of America, 1982.

———. *The Complete Prose Works of Walt Whitman.* Ed. Richard Maurice Bucke. 7 vols. New York: G. P. Putnam's Sons, 1902.

———. *The Correspondence.* Vol. 1: *1842–1867.* Ed. Edwin Havilland Miller. New York: New York University Press, 1961.

———. *Franklin Evans, or The Inebriate: A Tale of the Times.* Ed. Christopher Castiglia and Glenn Hendler. Durham, NC: Duke University Press, 2007.

———. *Memoranda during the War.* Camden, NJ: Author's publication, 1875–76.

———. *Notebooks and Unpublished Prose Manuscripts.* 6 vols. Ed. Edward F. Grier. New York: New York University Press, 1984.

Will-Weber, Mark. *Muskets and Applejack: Spirits, Soldiers, and the Civil War.* Washington, DC: Regnery History, 2017.

Willcox, Orlando B. *Forgotten Valor: The Memoirs, Journals, and Civil War Letters of Orlando B. Willcox.* Ed. Robert Garth Scott. Kent, OH: Kent State University Press, 1999.

Williams, Robert C. *Horace Greeley: Champion of American Freedom.* New York: New York University Press, 2006.

Willis, Frederick L. H. *Alcott Memoirs.* Boston: Richard G. Badger, 1915.

Winkle, Kenneth J. *Lincoln's Citadel: The Civil War in Washington, DC.* New York: W. W. Norton, 2013.

Wise, Jennings Cropper. *The Long Arm of Lee, or, The History of the Artillery of the Army of Northern Virginia.* Lynchburg, VA: J. P. Bell, 1915.

Woodworth, Steven E. *Beneath a Northern Sky: A Short History of the Gettysburg Campaign.* Lanham, MD: Rowman & Littlefield, 2008.
———. *While God Is Marching On: The Religious World of Civil War Soldiers.* Lawrence: University Press of Kansas, 2001.
Woollcott, Alexander. *The Indispensable Woollcott.* New York: Book Society, 1951.
Wright, Chauncey. *Philosophical Discussions.* New York: Henry Holt, 1878.

Legal Opinions

Abrams v. United States, 250 U.S. 616, 40 S. Ct. 17, 63 L. Ed. 1173 (1919).
Adair v. United States, 208 U.S. 161, 28 S. Ct. 277, 52 L. Ed. 436 (1908).
Brown v. Kendall, 60 Mass. 292 (1850).
Dunn v. United States, 284 U.S. 390, 52 S. Ct. 189, 76 L. Ed. 356 (1932).
Hammer v. Dagenhart, 247 U.S. 251, 38 S. Ct. 529, 62 L. Ed. 1101 (1918).
Lochner v. New York, 198 U.S. 45, 25 S. Ct. 539, 49 L. Ed. 937 (1905).

Library Collections

A. Bronson Alcott Journals. Houghton Library, Harvard University, Cambridge, Massachusetts. MS Am 1130.12.
Louisa May Alcott Additional Papers. Houghton Library, Harvard University, Cambridge, Massachusetts. MS Am 1817.
Louisa May Alcott Family Papers. Houghton Library, Harvard University, Cambridge, Massachusetts, MS Am 1130.9.
Anniston-Calhoun County Public Library, Anniston, Alabama.
Margaret Fuller Family Papers. Houghton Library, Harvard University, Cambridge, Massachusetts. MS Am 1086.
Jacksonville Public Library, John Pelham Collection, Jacksonville, Alabama.
National Archives, Washington, DC.
John Pelham Collection, Jacksonville Public Library, Jacksonville, Alabama.
Trent Collection of Whitmaniana, Duke University Rare Book, Manuscript, and Special Collections Library.

Index

Page numbers after 434 refer to notes.

DATE DUE

APR 2 0 2021			
JUN 1 0 2021			
AUG 5 2021			
SEP 2 3 2021			
			PRINTED IN U.S.A.